Artificial Intelligence Valuation

Roberto Moro-Visconti

Artificial Intelligence Valuation

The Impact on Automation, BioTech, ChatBots, FinTech, B2B2C, and Other Industries

palgrave
macmillan

Roberto Moro-Visconti
Università Cattolica del Sacro Cuore
Milano, Italy

ISBN 978-3-031-53621-2 ISBN 978-3-031-53622-9 (eBook)
https://doi.org/10.1007/978-3-031-53622-9

This Palgrave Macmillan imprint is published by the registered company Springer Nature Switzerland AG
The registered company address is: Gewerbestrasse 11, 6330 Cham, Switzerland

Paper in this product is recyclable.

Contents

List of Figures

List of Tables

CHAPTER 1

Introduction

1.1 The Historical Background

The origins of AI can be traced back to ancient myths and stories of mechanical beings with human-like capabilities. However, the modern development of AI is rooted in the mid-twentieth century:

a. **Early Concepts (Antiquity to Nineteenth Century)**: The concept of creating artificial beings with human-like intelligence dates back to ancient civilizations. For instance, in Greek mythology, there are stories of automatons like Talos and Pandora. In the Middle Ages, alchemists and inventors attempted to create mechanical beings. However, these were more in the realm of myth and folklore than actual technology.
b. **Early Computational Devices (Nineteenth Century)**: The nineteenth century saw the invention of early computational devices like Charles Babbage's Analytical Engine, which was a mechanical general-purpose computer. These devices laid the theoretical foundation for the idea of automating computation.
c. **Alan Turing and his Test (1930s–1950s)**: Alan Turing, a gifted British mathematician and computer scientist, is often considered one of the founding figures of AI. In his 1936 paper, he introduced the concept of a "universal machine" (now known as a Turing machine) that could simulate any other machine.

R. Moro-Visconti, *Artificial Intelligence Valuation*,
https://doi.org/10.1007/978-3-031-53622-9_1

d. **Early AI Research (1950s–1960s)**: The term "artificial intelligence" was coined in 1956 at the Dartmouth Workshop, which marked the beginning of AI as a formal field of study. Early AI researchers like John McCarthy and Marvin Minsky developed the first AI programs and explored symbolic logic and problem-solving techniques.
e. **AI Winter (1970s–1980s)**: AI research faced significant challenges and funding cuts during the AI winter periods. Expectations had outpaced the capabilities of the technology at that time, leading to disappointment.
f. **Resurgence and Machine Learning (1990s–Present)**: AI experienced a resurgence in the 1990s, driven in part by advancements in machine learning and neural networks. The development of powerful computers and the availability of large datasets enabled breakthroughs in areas like computer vision, natural language processing, and reinforcement learning.
g. **Contemporary AI (Twenty-First Century)**: The twenty-first century has seen remarkable progress in AI, with applications in self-driving cars, virtual assistants, recommendation systems, healthcare, chatbots, generative artificial intelligence, and more. Deep learning, a subfield of machine learning, has played a crucial role in these advancements.

AI boasts a longstanding historical background. The progression of AI has undergone a series of transformations, shifting from rule-based approaches to statistical methods and eventually to data-centric techniques within domains such as computer vision, natural language processing, and machine learning. The interdisciplinary character of AI has resulted in its widespread implementation across various sectors, including economics, manufacturing, healthcare, and defense technologies, thereby influencing contemporary business environments and decision-making processes. The sustainable trajectory of AI development underscores the significance of human–machine collaboration and a technological trajectory focused on computational capabilities, exerting a substantial impact on society. The historical track record of AI has influenced future expectations in several ways, as shown in Table 1.1:

The historical origins of AI have shaped the way people approach and perceive the field. While there have been setbacks and disappointments,

Table 1.1 History of artificial intelligence

Cycles of Hype and Disillusionment	The history of AI has shown cycles of hype followed by periods of disappointment, often referred to as "AI winters". These cycles have made people cautious about overestimating AI's capabilities
Realistic Expectations	Modern AI researchers and practitioners have a more realistic understanding of AI's current capabilities and limitations. They focus on solving specific, practical problems rather than aiming for general human-level intelligence
Ethical and Societal Concerns	The historical development of AI has raised concerns about job displacement, bias in algorithms. These concerns shape the way AI is developed and regulated today
Continuous Progress	Despite past challenges, AI has made significant progress, and this historical track record of innovation fuels optimism about its future potential. It encourages ongoing research and investment in AI technologies

the steady progress and recent advancements in AI continue to influence expectations and drive further exploration of its possibilities and challenges.

The historical evolution of AI considers different stages:

1. **Artificial Narrow Intelligence (ANI)**: ANI, or Weak AI, encompasses the current state of AI technologies. These systems are highly specialized, designed to operate within a specific context or perform particular tasks with remarkable efficiency and accuracy. The ubiquity of ANI in everyday life is evident through various applications, such as virtual assistants (Siri, Alexa), recommendation systems (Netflix, Amazon), and image recognition software. Despite their sophistication, ANI systems do not possess consciousness or the ability to reason beyond their programmed capabilities. Their intelligence is "narrow" because it is confined to specific tasks, lacking the adaptability and general reasoning power of the human mind.

2. **Artificial General Intelligence (AGI)**: AGI represents a future milestone in AI research where systems would exhibit human-like cognitive abilities. This means an AGI system could understand, learn, and apply knowledge across a broad spectrum of tasks, mirroring human adaptability and reasoning. Achieving AGI involves surmounting immense technical and philosophical challenges, as it requires not just advanced computational power but also breakthroughs in understanding human intelligence itself. AGI is seen as a transformative goal that could revolutionize every aspect of society, from science and medicine to art and culture. However, its development raises profound ethical considerations about autonomy, identity, and the potential for AI systems to surpass human capabilities in decision-making and creativity.
3. **Artificial Superintelligence (ASI)**: ASI takes the concept of AI to its theoretical zenith, positing a form of intelligence that far exceeds the brightest human minds in every conceivable domain, including creativity, general wisdom, and problem-solving. The speculation around ASI encompasses not just enhanced cognitive capabilities but also the possibility of AI developing autonomous goals and motivations. The prospect of ASI raises existential questions about humanity's role and control over technology that could potentially possess desires and objectives independent of human input. Ethical debates surrounding ASI are especially complex, touching on issues of control, safety, and the moral obligations of creating an intelligence that could reshape our world fundamentally (Fig. 1.1).

Fig. 1.1 Artificial intelligence types

While this conceptual framework provides a roadmap for AI development, the timeline and achievement of each stage are uncertain. Currently, we are in the ANI stage, with AGI remaining a challenging goal for the future. The transition from AGI to ASI, if it is possible, is even more uncertain and comes with significant ethical and existential considerations.

The evolution of AI is a complex and ongoing process, and the development of AGI and ASI is not guaranteed. Researchers and organizations around the world are working on advancing AI technologies, but the timeline for achieving AGI or ASI remains uncertain and depends on various scientific, technical, ethical, and societal factors (Fig. 1.2).

The history of AI may relate to another aspect that concerns how AI affects historical research.

The digital revolution, particularly with AI and machine learning, has indeed brought transformative changes to historical research. These technological advancements are reshaping how historical data is analyzed, accessed, and understood in several keyways:

a. **Data Analysis and Processing**: AI algorithms can process large volumes of historical data quickly and efficiently. This includes not only textual data but also visual and auditory materials. For example, machine learning models can analyze historical texts, identify patterns, and even predict trends based on historical precedents.
b. **Deciphering Historical Texts**: One of the more specific applications of AI in historical research is in the field of paleography, the study of ancient handwriting. AI can be trained to read and interpret handwritten texts, which are often difficult for modern readers to decipher. This capability significantly accelerates the process of transcribing and interpreting historical documents.
c. **Cross-Referencing and Correlating Data**: AI systems can cross-reference information from various sources, helping historians to correlate data from different texts, archives, or artifacts. This can lead to new insights and connections that might not be apparent through traditional research methods.
d. **Digital Archiving and Accessibility**: AI and digital technologies facilitate the digital archiving of historical documents, making them more accessible to researchers around the world. This not only helps

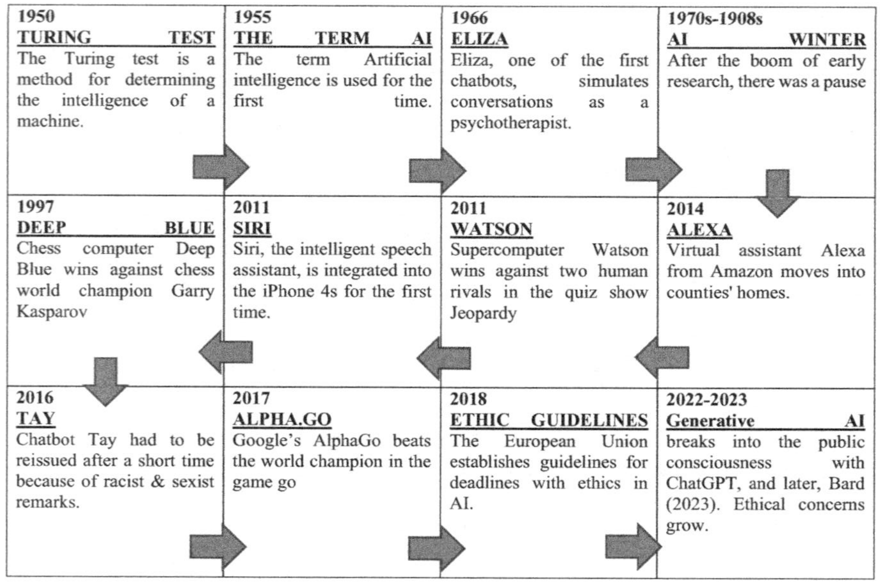

Fig. 1.2 History of artificial intelligence

in preservation but also democratizes access to historical information, allowing researchers from various parts of the world to access documents without the need to physically travel to archives.

e. **Language Translation and Interpretation**: AI-powered tools can translate historical documents written in now-obsolete languages or dialects, making them understandable to contemporary researchers. This broadens the scope of research and allows for a more inclusive understanding of history.
f. **Enhancing Historical Education and Engagement**: AI can also be used to create interactive and immersive historical experiences, such as virtual reality tours of historical sites or interactive timelines. This not only aids in education but also helps in engaging a broader audience with historical content.
g. **Predictive Analysis and Modeling**: In some cases, AI can be used to create predictive models based on historical data. This can be particularly useful in fields like archeology, where predictive modeling can help identify potential sites of historical significance.
h. **Ethical and Bias Considerations**: With the rise of AI in historical research, there are also important ethical considerations, particularly concerning biases in the data or algorithms. Historians and technologists need to work together to ensure that AI tools are used responsibly and that they do not perpetuate historical inaccuracies or biases.

The integration of AI and machine learning into historical research is revolutionizing the field. However, it is also important to approach these technologies with an awareness of their limitations and potential ethical implications.

The history of AI has had a significant impact on its economic, financial, and market valuation in several ways:

a. **Technology Development and Investment**: The evolution of AI, from its conceptual beginnings in the mid-twentieth century to the sophisticated algorithms of today, has drawn considerable investment from both public and private sectors. This investment has fueled further technological advancements, creating a cycle of growth and innovation. As AI technology has matured, it has attracted even more investment, significantly impacting its market valuation.

b. **Industry Transformation**: AI has transformed various industries, from manufacturing and healthcare to finance and retail. By automating tasks, optimizing operations, and enabling new services, AI has created economic value and efficiencies. This transformation has led to increased productivity and new business models, influencing the financial performance of companies and sectors that adopt AI.
c. **Job Market and Employment**: The impact of AI on employment is complex. While it has the potential to displace certain jobs, particularly those involving repetitive tasks, it also creates new job opportunities in AI development, data analysis, and related fields. This shift affects the labor market and can influence economic policies and education systems.
d. **Global Competition and Geopolitical Influence**: AI is a key area of technological competition among nations. Countries investing heavily in AI research and development, such as the United States, China, and members of the European Union, view it as crucial. This competition can affect global market dynamics and trade policies.
e. **Startup Ecosystem and Innovation**: The AI field has seen a proliferation of startups, each aiming to develop unique applications or improve existing algorithms. This vibrant ecosystem fosters innovation and attracts significant venture capital, influencing market valuations and the financial landscape of the tech industry.
f. **Regulatory and Ethical Considerations**: As AI becomes more integral to economic and social systems, regulatory frameworks are evolving to address concerns about privacy, bias, and ethical use. These regulations can impact the development and deployment of AI technologies, affecting market dynamics and company valuations.
g. **Consumer Behavior and Market Demand**: AI-driven products and services, such as personal assistants, recommendation systems, and autonomous vehicles, are changing consumer behavior. This shift influences market demand and opens new revenue streams, impacting the economic and financial valuation of companies in the AI space.
h. **Data as a Key Asset**: The growth of AI has highlighted the value of data as a strategic asset. Companies that can effectively collect,

analyze, and leverage data using AI have a competitive advantage, which is increasingly reflected in their market valuation.

The history of AI has not only propelled technological advancements but has also fundamentally reshaped economic landscapes, influenced financial markets, and altered the competitive dynamics across various sectors.

1.2 Artificial Intelligence Surveys: Pattern Recognition, Machine Learning, Computer Vision, and Other Research Fields

AI has acquired notorious relevance in modern computing as it effectively solves complex tasks traditionally done by humans. AI provides methods to represent and infer knowledge, efficiently manipulate texts, and learn from vast amounts of data. These characteristics are applicable in many activities that humans find laborious or repetitive, as is the case of the analysis of scientific literature (de la Torre-López et al., 2023).

AI technologies include machine learning, deep learning, neural networks, robotics, and others. AI is used in several applications, from smartphone apps and virtual assistants to self-driving cars.

According to Jaber, 2022, AI systems analyze vast amounts of data, recognize patterns, and make predictions or decisions based on that information.

AI (Minh et al., 2022; Saghiri et al., 2022) is a future-oriented technology, as it extrapolates past trends, typically in the form of big data (Acciarini et al., 2023; Duan et al., 2019), to estimate trendy scenarios, enhanced by self-learning processes that add value to the business models that become more sustainable and resilient.

According to Enholm et al. (2022), there is still a lack of the main value-generating mechanisms and there is a missed understanding of the use and adoption of AI in organizations.

Data-Centric Artificial Intelligence

Data-centric AI has become a crucial aspect of big data collection and interpretation, for several reasons such as:

1. **Shift from Model-Centric to Data-Centric Approach**: Historically, much of the emphasis in AI research and development was on designing and improving machine learning models. The quality and quantity of big data have become paramount.
2. **Data-Centric AI**: This emerging concept recognizes the critical importance of high-quality data in achieving AI success. This includes not only the data used for training models but also data used during inference and data maintenance.
3. **Three General Data-Centric Goals**: There are three overarching goals within the realm of data-centric AI:

    a. **Training Data Development**: Ensuring the availability of high-quality data for training machine learning models.
    b. **Inference Data Development**: Focusing on data used during the model's operational phase (inference) to maintain its performance.
    c. **Data Maintenance**: Strategies for continuously improving and maintaining the quality of the data over time.

4. **Representative Methods**: There are various methods and approaches that researchers and practitioners use to achieve these data-centric goals. These methods could include data collection, data augmentation, data cleaning, and data governance techniques.
5. **Automation and Collaboration**: Automation can help in tasks like data labeling, while collaboration can involve various stakeholders working together to curate and manage data effectively.
6. **Challenges**: The challenges associated with data-centric AI include data quality, privacy, bias, scalability, and the cost large datasets.
7. **Benchmarks**: To evaluate progress and performance, benchmarks are often established for various AI tasks. These benchmarks serve as standards for measuring the effectiveness of data-centric AI methods across different applications and domains.
8. **Comprehensive Survey**: a comprehensive overview of data-centric AI, covers various aspects of the data lifecycle, from collection and preparation to ongoing maintenance.

Data-centric AI recognizes that effective AI models rely on high-quality data throughout their lifecycle. This impacts the economic, financial, and market valuation patterns.

1.3 Artificial Intelligence's Definitions and Trends

The term AI (Saghiri et al., 2022) refers to the implementation of human intelligence in machines that are capable of thinking and learning like humans. Specifically, it uses computer systems and algorithms to perform human tasks, such as visual perception, speech recognition, decision-making, problem-solving, and language translation. AI involves computer systems that, thanks to their self-learning behavior, can perform tasks that usually need natural human intelligence (Mikalef and Gupta, 2021).

The term can also be applied to any machine that exhibits traits associated with a human mind, such as learning and problem-solving.

The primary goals of AI (see also https://www.hawaiitelegraph.com/news/273836014/artificial-intelligence-the-future-of-technology) include reasoning, knowledge representation, planning, learning, natural language processing, perception, and the ability to move and manipulate objects. AI is a multidisciplinary field, combining computer science, psychology, linguistics, philosophy, and other areas.

Here are some further definitions of AI:

- The study of intelligent agents: Intelligent agents are systems that can reason, learn, and act autonomously. AI research has resulted in the development of many effective techniques for solving a wide range of problems, from game playing to medical diagnosis.
- The ability to simulate human intelligence: This emphasizes the ability of AI systems to perform tasks typically associated with human intelligence, as language understanding, learning, and problem-solving.
- The branch of computer science that deals with the creation of intelligent agents: This definition is more technical and emphasizes the role of AI in computer science. AI research has had a profound impact on the development of many computer applications, including search engines, virtual assistants, and self-driving cars.
- The study of the mind: This definition is the broadest and most philosophical of the definitions. AI researchers are interested in understanding the principles that underlie human intelligence and using these principles to create artificial intelligence systems.

Several surveys define AI and its boundaries (Batarseh et al., 2021; Došilović et al., 2018; Enholm et al., 2022; Jaber, 2022; Mikalef & Gupta, 2021; Minh et al., 2022; Saghiri et al., 2022).

The categorization of AI into four primary types—reactive, limited memory, theory of mind, and self-aware—provides a clear framework for understanding the evolution and capabilities of artificial intelligence:

1. **Reactive AI**:
   - **Characteristics**: This is the most basic form of AI, which responds predictably to specific inputs. It doesn't have the ability to learn or consider past or future contexts.
2. **Limited Memory AI**:
   - **Characteristics**: This AI learns from past data and experiences. It combines observational data with pre-programmed information to make predictions and perform tasks.
3. **Theory of Mind AI**:
   - **Characteristics**: This emerging AI aims to understand and respond to human emotions, thereby facilitating more natural interactions.
4. **Self-aware AI**:
   - **Characteristics**: Self-awareness and the ability to understand its own emotions and those of others.
   - **Current Status**: This type of AI is still in the conceptual stage, with no existing models or the necessary hardware and algorithms.

The emergence of generative AI indeed holds the potential for significant impacts on the labor market and the broader economy:

1. **Task Automation and Labor Cost Savings**: Generative AI has the potential to automate a substantial portion of tasks across various industries. This automation could lead to labor cost savings for businesses, as AI systems can work around the clock without breaks and require minimal maintenance.

2. **Productivity Gains**: The automation of tasks through generative AI can raise productivity levels in the workforce. Employees can focus on higher-value tasks that require creativity, problem-solving, and human interaction, while AI handles repetitive and routine tasks.
3. **Job Disruption**: As generative AI becomes more capable, it may replace human workers in certain roles. The study suggests that up to one-fourth of current work could be automated using generative AI. This could potentially disrupt the labor market and impact a significant portion of the workforce.
4. **Global Impact**: Not limited to a specific region. Extrapolating the estimates globally, it is suggested that the technology could expose the equivalent of 300 million full-time jobs to automation.
5. **Historical Perspective**: Historically, automation has led to the displacement of workers in certain roles. However, it has also been accompanied by the creation of new jobs in emerging industries and occupations. This process of creative destruction has been a hallmark of technological innovation throughout history.
6. **Potential for a Productivity Boom**: The combination of labor cost savings, job creation in new sectors, and increased productivity for non-displaced workers could potentially lead to a productivity boom. However, the exact timing and magnitude of such a productivity boom are uncertain.

Additionally, policymakers and businesses will need to consider strategies for workforce reskilling and adapting to the changing job landscape to mitigate the potential negative consequences of automation.

The effects of generative AI on the economy will depend on how well society manages the transition, invests in education and training, and creates an environment that fosters innovation and the creation of new job opportunities in emerging fields.

The impact of AI on organizations and the global business landscape is undergoing rapid development and its transformative potential, as shown in Table 1.2:

AI systems are becoming more flexible and capable of handling broader tasks, spanning multiple domains such as vision and language. This represents a notable shift from traditional narrow AI systems to more general and versatile AI models:

Table 1.2 Impact of artificial intelligence on organizations and the global business landscape

Accelerated AI Development	AI research and development have indeed been progressing at an unprecedented pace. Innovations in machine learning models, natural language processing, computer vision, and other AI technologies have paved the way for groundbreaking applications and solutions
Strategic Importance	Data and AI strategy have become essential components of business discussions across industries. Organizations recognize that data-driven insights and AI-driven automation can provide a competitive advantage, enhance decision-making, and drive operational efficiencies
Product and Software Innovation	AI is already reshaping product and software innovation. AI-powered features and capabilities are being integrated into a wide range of products and services, from virtual assistants in smartphones to predictive maintenance in manufacturing
Competitive Landscape	As AI becomes more accessible, the next generation of successful companies and leaders will be those who can effectively harness AI's potential. AI can enable businesses to create innovative solutions, personalize customer experiences, optimize operations, and gain a deeper understanding of their markets
Education and Skill Development	To leverage AI effectively, organizations and professionals need to invest in education and skill development. Understanding AI principles, data management, and the ethical considerations surrounding AI is crucial for success in this AI-driven era
Ethical Considerations	As AI becomes more prevalent, ethical considerations around data privacy, bias mitigation, and responsible AI development gain prominence. Companies and executives must address these issues to build trust with customers and stakeholders

(continued)

Table 1.2 (continued)

Collaboration and Ecosystems	Many AI advancements are driven by collaboration between academia, industry, and startups. Building partnerships and ecosystems can be instrumental in staying at the forefront of AI innovation
Regulatory Landscape	Governments and regulatory bodies are also adapting to the AI revolution by implementing rules and guidelines to ensure ethical AI use. Staying compliant with evolving regulations is critical for businesses

a. **BEiT-3 (Bridging Language and Vision with Pre trained Transformers 3)**: BEiT-3 is an example of a model that excels in both vision and language tasks. It leverages pre-trained transformers to bridge the gap between these modalities, enabling it to understand and generate content that combines visual and textual information. This type of model can be valuable in tasks like image captioning, visual question answering, and more.
b. **PaLI (Pattern-based Language Image Pre-training)**: PaLI is another model designed to handle both language and vision tasks. It learns to represent images and text in a shared embedding space, facilitating seamless interaction between the two modalities. PaLI can be used for various applications, including cross-modal retrieval and multimodal data analysis.
c. **Gato (Generalized Autoregressive Model for Multiple Modalities)**: Gato is a model designed to handle multiple modalities. It can be applied to tasks that involve combining information from different sources to make predictions or generate insights. This kind of model can be valuable in fields like e-commerce, healthcare, and recommendation systems.

The impact of these flexible AI systems on various domains is significant and it is performed through:

a. **Improved User Experience**: Flexible AI models can enhance user experiences by enabling more natural and context-aware interactions with AI-powered applications. For example, chatbots and virtual assistants can better understand and respond to user queries that involve both text and images.

b. **Cross-Domain Insights**: In fields like healthcare and scientific research, flexible AI models can help researchers analyze and draw insights from data that spans multiple modalities, such as medical images and clinical notes. This can lead to more comprehensive diagnoses and discoveries.
c. **Efficiency and Automation**: Businesses can benefit from AI systems that can seamlessly process both structured and unstructured data. This can streamline decision-making processes and automate tasks that involve diverse data sources.
d. **Personalization**: E-commerce and recommendation systems can leverage flexible AI models to provide more personalized recommendations by considering a user's preferences expressed in both text and visual form.
e. **Multimodal Content Generation**: Content creators can use these models to generate diverse and engaging multimedia content, including articles with embedded images, video descriptions, and more.

Overall, the development of flexible AI systems that excel across multiple tasks and modalities represents a significant advancement in the AI field.

AI-driven language models have made significant advancements in terms of generative capabilities and natural language understanding, they still face challenges if we consider complex reasoning and planning tasks, as shown in Table 1.3.

While language models may not yet be on par with human reasoning, they have found valuable applications in various fields, including natural language understanding, text generation, and content summarization. As research progresses, there is optimism that AI-driven language models will continue to improve their reasoning capabilities, making them even more versatile and useful tools for a wide range of applications. However, their current limitations and use them judiciously in contexts where deep reasoning and critical thinking are essential.

Trends in data science and machine learning (DS/ML), related to natural language processing (NLP), data integration, and data warehousing are represented by:

Table 1.3 Artificial intelligence-driven language models

Lack of True Understanding	Language models, including state-of-the-art models like GPT-3 and its successors, are primarily based on statistical patterns in data and do not possess true understanding or reasoning abilities. They generate responses by predicting the most likely next word based on the input data. While this works well for generating coherent and contextually relevant text, it does not necessarily imply deep comprehension or reasoning
Shallow vs. Deep Reasoning	Language models excel at shallow reasoning tasks where the answer can be inferred directly from the information present in the text. However, they struggle with tasks that require deeper reasoning, logical deduction, or long term planning. These models cannot often perform multi-step reasoning or consider complex dependencies
Context and Ambiguity	Language models can be sensitive to the phrasing of questions and may not handle ambiguity well. They may provide seemingly reasonable answers based on the input context, but these answers may lack the depth of reasoning that a human would apply to the same question
Data Limitations	Language models are trained on vast amounts of text data, but this data may not necessarily include examples of complex reasoning or planning tasks. As a result, they may not have learned to perform such tasks effectively
Ethical and Bias Concerns	Language models' responses can sometimes reflect biases present in their training data, which can further complicate reasoning tasks that involve sensitive or nuanced topics To address these limitations, ongoing research is focused on improving language models' reasoning abilities. This includes efforts to incorporate external knowledge sources, develop models that explicitly perform symbolic reasoning, and fine-tune models on specific reasoning tasks

1. **Rapid Adoption of Machine Learning and LLMs**: Many companies are embracing machine learning and large language models (LLMs) at a rapid pace. They are being used in various applications, including chatbots, content generation, and text analysis.
2. **Dominance of NLP**: Natural language processing (NLP) is a dominant use case for machine learning and LLMs. NLP applications

include sentiment analysis, language translation, text summarization, and chatbot development. NLP technologies have proven valuable in understanding and processing human language.
3. **Data Integration Prioritization**: Organizations are investing in data integration products to facilitate their DS/ML initiatives. Data integration is crucial for gathering, cleaning, and preparing data for analysis. As organizations collect and generate vast amounts of data, the need for effective data integration tools has grown.
4. **Lakehouse for Data Warehousing**: The adoption of the "Lakehouse" approach for data warehousing is on the rise. The Lakehouse architecture combines the best features of data lakes and traditional data warehouses, allowing organizations to store and analyze data in a flexible and scalable manner. Innovative tools support data integration and transformation within the Lakehouse architecture.
5. **Databricks SQL**: Databricks SQL is gaining traction as an analytics tool within the Databricks platform. Databricks foster data engineering, data science, and machine learning, making it easier for organizations to work with big data and build data-driven solutions.

These trends, also evidenced by Maslej et al., 2023, reflect the importance of data and machine learning in modern organizations. Companies are recognizing the value of data integration, NLP, and the Lakehouse architecture as they strive to harness the power of data for insights, decision-making, and innovation. These developments also underline the need for robust tools and platforms to support these initiatives effectively.

The rapid growth of the data integration market in AI applications underscores the pivotal role data integration plays in the success of modern organizations, as shown in Table 1.4.

The growth of the data integration market in AI applications highlights the central role of data integration in enabling organizations to harness the full potential of AI. These tools provide the means to manage, prepare, and deliver data for BI, DS/ML, and other AI-driven initiatives, ensuring that AI models are built on a solid foundation of accurate, complete, and timely data.

Data science and machine learning (DS/ML) have become integral to the operations of companies across various industries. These technologies offer numerous benefits, including accelerated growth, improved predictability, and enhanced customer experiences. Large language models (LLMs), such as GPT-3 and its successors, have been

Table 1.4 Data integration market in artificial intelligence applications

Integration of Vast Amounts of Data	AI applications often require access to extensive and diverse data sources. Data integration tools enable organizations to seamlessly bring together data from various upstream and downstream sources, whether they are structured or unstructured, into a single consolidated view. This consolidated view is crucial for providing comprehensive insights and input to AI models
Unified Data Foundation	Data integration products serve as the foundation upon which business intelligence (BI) and data science/machine learning (DS/ML) initiatives are built. Without effective data integration, these initiatives may lack the necessary data completeness, accuracy, and consistency required for meaningful analysis and modeling
Efficiency and Scalability	Data integration tools automate the process of collecting, transforming, and loading (ETL) data, making the process more efficient and scalable. As AI projects often involve large volumes of data, automation becomes critical to keep pace with data demands
Data Quality Assurance	Data integration tools can include features for data quality assurance, which involves cleaning, validating, and standardizing data. High-quality data is essential for AI applications, as errors or inconsistencies in data can lead to inaccurate AI predictions and models
Timeliness of Data	AI models often require real-time or near-real-time data. Data integration solutions help to ensure that data is delivered promptly to AI systems, allowing for timely decision-making and responsiveness to changing conditions
Data Governance and Compliance	As organizations collect and use data for AI, data governance and compliance with data protection regulations (e.g., GDPR, CCPA) become critical. Data integration tools can support compliance efforts by providing data lineage, auditing capabilities, and access controls

(continued)

Table 1.4 (continued)

Flexibility and Adaptability	In dynamic business environments, data sources and requirements may change over time. Data integration solutions need to be flexible and adaptable to accommodate new data sources and evolving business needs
Cost Efficiency	Effective data integration can lead to cost savings by reducing the complexity and redundancy of data processes. This efficiency is particularly important as AI initiatives can be resource-intensive

especially transformative and are leading companies to reevaluate their AI and data strategies in the following ways:

a. **Accelerated Growth**: DS/ML enables companies to analyze vast datasets and extract valuable insights. These insights can inform strategic decisions, optimize operations, and identify growth opportunities. LLMs have opened up new possibilities for natural language understanding and generation, allowing businesses to create innovative products and services.
b. **Improved Predictability**: Predictive analytics and machine learning models are used to forecast trends, customer behavior, and market dynamics. By leveraging historical data and advanced algorithms, companies can make more informed decisions, minimize risks, and adapt quickly to changing circumstances.
c. **Enhanced Customer Experiences**: Personalization is a key driver of enhanced customer experiences. DS/ML enables companies to tailor their products, services, and marketing efforts to individual customer preferences. LLMs can generate human-like text, facilitating more natural and engaging interactions in chatbots, virtual assistants, and customer support.
d. **Data Strategy Reevaluation**: The emergence of LLMs has prompted companies to rethink their AI and data strategies. These models excel in natural language understanding and generation, making them valuable for tasks like content generation, sentiment analysis, and language translation. Companies are integrating LLMs into their workflows to automate and improve various processes.

e. **Efficiency and Automation**: DS/ML can automate repetitive tasks and processes, freeing up human resources for more strategic activities. LLMs are being used to automate content creation, answer customer queries, and analyze unstructured text data, leading to operational efficiency gains.
f. **Competitive Advantage**: Companies that effectively harness DS/ML, including LLMs, gain a competitive edge. They can innovate more quickly, adapt to changing market conditions, and provide superior customer experiences. This can translate into increased market share and revenue growth.
g. **Ethical Considerations**: Alongside these advancements, companies are also grappling with ethical considerations related to data usage and AI. Ensuring responsible and ethical AI deployment is crucial to maintain trust among customers and stakeholders.

DS/ML and the advancements in LLMs are transforming how companies operate and compete across industries. By incorporating these technologies into their data strategies, organizations can unlock new opportunities, gain insights, and create more personalized and efficient experiences for their customers, ultimately driving growth and success.

As it will be shown in paragraph 9.1.1., AI has the potential to both help and harm the environment, and there is growing awareness of the environmental impacts associated with AI systems:

Positive Environmental Contributions of AI:

1. **Efficiency Improvements**: AI can optimize energy consumption and resource allocation in various sectors. For example, in agriculture, AI-powered precision farming can reduce water and fertilizer use, minimizing environmental impact.
2. **Climate Modeling**: AI is used in climate modeling and analysis to better understand climate change patterns and develop mitigation strategies. AI can help identify trends and predict extreme weather events, which is critical for environmental planning.
3. **Energy Efficiency**: AI can be applied to improve the energy efficiency of buildings, transportation systems, and industrial processes. Smart grids, for instance, use AI to manage and distribute electricity more efficiently, reducing energy waste.

4. **Environmental Monitoring**: AI-driven technologies like remote sensing and satellite imagery analysis are used for monitoring environmental changes, deforestation, wildlife conservation, and tracking air and water quality.

Negative Environmental Impacts of AI:

1. **Energy Consumption**: Many AI models, especially deep learning models, require extensive computational power. Training large AI models in data centers can contribute to carbon emissions if not powered by renewable energy sources.
2. **Electronic Waste**: The rapid advancement of AI hardware and devices can lead to electronic waste, contributing to environmental problems if not properly managed and recycled.
3. **Resource Consumption**: The production of AI hardware components, such as semiconductors and GPUs, relies on the extraction of minerals and metals, which can have environmental consequences.
4. **Bias in Environmental Data**: AI models can perpetuate environmental biases present in their training data, potentially leading to unfair or harmful decisions in areas like environmental justice.

To mitigate the negative environmental impacts of AI and harness its positive potential, several strategies can be considered (Table 1.5):

AI's environmental impact is a complex issue that requires a balanced approach. While AI can offer innovative solutions to environmental challenges, it is essential to address its environmental footprint and ensure that its deployment aligns.

Some important challenges arise during the development of intelligent systems, and they will continue to evolve as we move towards more advanced forms of AI, as shown in Table 1.6:

The development of intelligent systems is an ongoing process, and new challenges will continue to emerge as AI technologies advance. Addressing these challenges requires a multidisciplinary approach concerning not only computer science and engineering but also ethics, law, and policy. Responsible AI development involves considering the broader societal impact and ethical implications of these technologies.

Data science (DS), machine learning (ML), and artificial intelligence (AI) interactions are shown in Fig. 1.3. AI encompasses a broader range

Table 1.5 Environmental impacts of artificial intelligence

Energy Efficiency	Develop and promote energy-efficient AI algorithms and hardware. Explore techniques like model quantization, model distillation, and edge computing to reduce energy consumption
Green Data Centers	Encourage the use of renewable energy sources for data centers and AI infrastructure. Improve data center cooling systems to reduce energy use
Responsible AI Development	Implement ethical AI practices, including addressing biases in training data and promoting fairness in AI applications related to the environment
Regulation and Policy	Governments and organizations can establish regulations and standards for AI systems to ensure they are developed and used in environmentally responsible ways
Recycling and Circular Economy	Promote the recycling and responsible disposal of AI hardware to reduce electronic waste

of techniques and approaches to creating intelligent systems, such as reasoning, learning, and problem-solving.

Debate about AI tends to focus on its potential dangers: algorithmic bias and discrimination, the mass destruction of jobs and even, some say, the apocalyptic extinction of humanity. As some observers fret about these dystopian scenarios, however, others are focusing on the potential rewards. AI could, they claim, help humanity solve some of its biggest and thorniest problems. And, they say, AI will do this in a very specific way: by radically accelerating the pace of scientific discovery, especially in areas such as medicine, climate science, and green technology.

This perspective on AI emphasizes its potential as a tool for positive change. By accelerating scientific discovery and innovation, AI can contribute to solving some of the world's most pressing problems, including those related to healthcare, climate change, and sustainable technology. While there are certainly challenges.

Table 1.6 Development of intelligent systems

Security	Ensuring the security of intelligent systems is crucial. As AI becomes more integrated into various aspects of society, the potential for security breaches and malicious use of AI also increases. The challenge is to develop robust security measures to protect AI systems from attacks and misuse
Safety	AI systems must operate safely to prevent harm to humans and the environment. This is especially critical in fields like autonomous vehicles and healthcare, where AI decisions can have life-or-death consequences. Developing AI systems with built-in safety mechanisms is a top priority
Fairness	Bias and discrimination can be unintentionally embedded in AI systems, leading to unfair outcomes. Addressing fairness challenges involves designing algorithms that are less biased and implementing processes to audit and mitigate bias in AI applications
Robustness	AI systems should perform reliably under various conditions, including those they were not explicitly trained for. Adversarial attacks and unexpected data inputs can lead to system failures. Ensuring robustness involves testing AI models thoroughly and improving their ability to handle unforeseen scenarios
Energy Consumption	AI models, particularly large deep learning models, can be computationally intensive and energy-hungry. Reducing the energy consumption of AI systems is not only cost-effective but also environmentally responsible. Researchers are working on more energy-efficient algorithms and hardware

(continued)

Table 1.6 (continued)

Transition to Artificial Superintelligence	As we progress towards artificial superintelligence, the challenges will become even more profound. Ensuring the ethical and responsible development of superintelligent AI is paramount, as it will have the potential to surpass human capabilities in various domains
Transition to Artificial Superintelligence	It involves not only improving the technical aspects of AI but also addressing ethical, societal, and philosophical questions about the implications of creating machines with human-like cognitive abilities

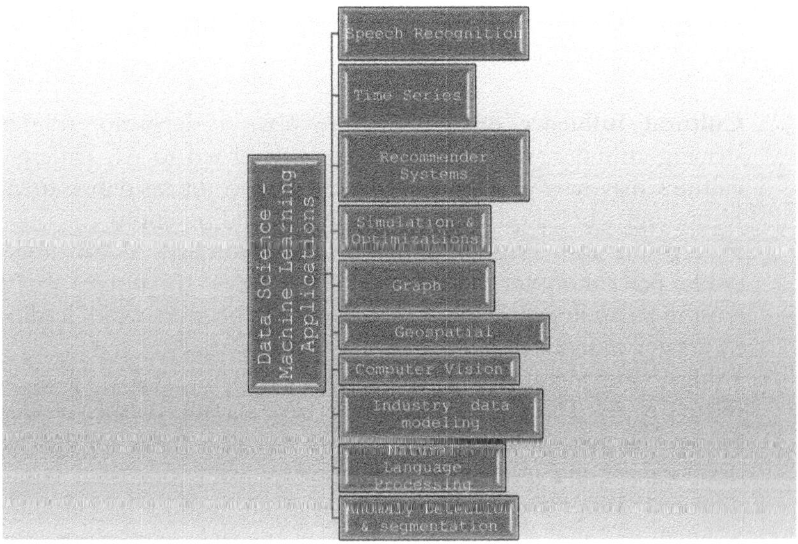

Fig. 1.3 Data science and machine learning applications

1.4 Cultural Aspects and Dystopian Perspectives

The intertwining of cultural aspects and dystopian perspectives of AI is evident in various narratives and analyses. The evolving relationship between human beings and machines, as evidenced in Russian cultural perspectives on AI, has transitioned through utopian aspirations, dystopian apprehensions, and the pursuit of human–technology fusion. These cultural portrayals underscore the deep-seated worries and considerations regarding AI's societal impact and the potential ramifications of advanced technological integration. The narrative examination of AI demonstrates how cultural constructions via storytelling and genre influence the perception of AI, vacillating between utopian fascination and dystopian disillusionment. These diverse cultural standpoints emphasize the intricate interplay among societal values, technological progress, and the portrayal of AI across different cultural milieus. The cultural aspects of AI can have significant impacts on the economic, financial, and market valuation of AI applications:

a. **Cultural Influence on AI**: Culture plays a significant role in shaping attitudes, values, and perceptions related to AI. Different cultures may have varying levels of acceptance or resistance to AI technologies based on their cultural beliefs and traditions.
b. **Perception and Trust**: Cultural attitudes towards AI can affect public perception and trust in AI technologies. In cultures where trust in technology is high, AI adoption may be more rapid, leading to greater economic opportunities for AI businesses.
c. **Ethical Considerations**: Cultural values influence ethical concerns related to AI. Different cultures may have varying perspectives on privacy, fairness, and accountability in AI, which can impact the development and acceptance of AI applications.
d. **Cultural Adaptation**: AI applications often need to be culturally adapted to cater to diverse markets. Language, symbolism, and cultural references must be considered in AI interfaces and content to ensure they resonate with local audiences.
e. **Cultural Representation**: The lack of diversity and cultural biases in AI algorithms can lead to issues of fairness and representation. Cultural awareness is essential to avoid reinforcing stereotypes or excluding certain groups.

f. **Regulatory Frameworks**: Cultural attitudes towards regulation can shape the legal and regulatory environment for AI. Some cultures may favor strict regulation to address ethical concerns, while others may prefer a more permissive approach, impacting the ease of market entry for AI companies.
g. **Labor and Employment**: The cultural view of work and employment can affect the acceptance of AI automation. In cultures that prioritize job security and traditional employment models, there may be resistance to AI-driven workforce changes.
h. **Education, Skill Development, and Awareness**: Cultural differences in education and awareness can affect the adoption and understanding of AI technologies. Cultures that prioritize technology education may have a more informed and tech-savvy population. Cultural attitudes towards education and skills development can influence the readiness of a workforce to adapt to AI technologies. Cultures that prioritize lifelong learning and technology education (Kamalov et al., 2023) may have a competitive advantage in AI-related industries.
i. **Globalization and Cultural Exchange**: The globalization of AI brings cultures into closer contact, leading to cultural exchange and potential conflicts. AI platforms, content, and services need to navigate these cultural dynamics.
j. **Demographic Shifts**: Demographic trends, such as population growth or urbanization, can drive cultural change and influence the demand for AI applications and services in different regions.
k. **Cultural Resistance**: Some cultures may resist certain AI applications, especially if they challenge deeply ingrained cultural practices or beliefs. Overcoming such resistance may require careful consideration of cultural sensitivities.
l. **Cultural Evolution**: Culture itself is not static; it evolves. AI can both shape and be shaped by cultural evolution as societies adapt to technological advancements.

Culture has a deep impact on AI's Economic, Financial, and Market Valuation, as shown in Table 1.7:

In the context of development and growth, culture plays a vital role in determining how AI is adopted, integrated, and utilized within different societies. It can influence the pace of AI adoption, the regulatory environment, and the ethical considerations surrounding AI.

Table 1.7 Culture and artificial intelligence

Market Demand	Cultural factors play a role in determining market demand for AI applications. Companies that consider cultural preferences and values when designing AI products may have a competitive advantage
Global Expansion	Companies expanding globally with AI offerings must navigate cultural differences. Understanding cultural nuances is critical for successful market entry and sustaining growth
Risk Management	Cultural variations can introduce risks related to regulatory compliance and ethical concerns. Firms that address these issues proactively are better positioned to avoid legal and reputational risks that can impact valuation
Investor Sentiment	Cultural factors can influence investor sentiment towards AI companies. Companies that align with cultural values related to ethics and sustainability may attract more socially responsible investors
Consumer Adoption	Consumer willingness to adopt AI products and services can vary across cultures. Companies that can adapt their offerings to align with cultural preferences are more likely to succeed in gaining market share
Talent Acquisition	Companies looking to hire AI talent often consider cultural fit. A diverse and culturally aware workforce can contribute to innovation and success in different markets
Supply Chain Considerations	Cultural aspects impact supply chains for AI components and technologies. Companies must consider cultural differences in sourcing, manufacturing, and distribution
Long-Term Viability	Companies that prioritize ethical AI practices and consider cultural implications in their strategies are more likely to achieve long-term sustainability and maintain or increase their market valuation

Understanding and respecting cultural diversity is essential for AI developers, policymakers, and businesses seeking to navigate the global landscape of AI technology. Cultural aspects of AI are intertwined with economic, financial, and market dynamics. Companies that recognize and adapt to cultural nuances can enhance their competitiveness, market valuation, and long-term success in the AI industry. Understanding and respecting cultural diversity is a key factor in building trust and gaining acceptance for AI applications in a global context.

Enhancing creativity (a value-generating cultural byproduct) with AI involves using AI tools and techniques to stimulate and support creative thinking and problem-solving:

a. Idea generation and brainstorming:
    i. AI-powered idea-generation tools can provide novel suggestions or combinations of ideas based on existing data and trends.
    ii. Natural language processing (NLP) models can assist in generating creative prompts or questions to inspire brainstorming sessions.
b. Content creation:
    i. AI-driven content generation tools can help writers, designers, and artists by providing automated content suggestions or even generating entire pieces of content, such as articles, poems, or art.
    ii. Tools like chatbots can simulate conversations, allowing creators to bounce ideas off AI and receive feedback.
c. Data analysis and insights:
    i. AI can analyze large datasets to uncover hidden patterns, trends, or correlations that can spark creative insights and ideas.
    ii. Machine learning algorithms can help identify user preferences, allowing businesses to tailor their products or services creatively.
d. Personalized recommendations:
    i. AI algorithms can recommend books, movies, music, and other creative works based on individual preferences, helping people discover new sources of inspiration.
    ii. Recommender systems can also suggest creative courses, workshops, or resources.
e. Creative assistance:
    i. AI-powered tools can assist in the creative process by offering suggestions, correcting errors, and providing feedback.
    ii. AI can help automate repetitive tasks, allowing creators more time for innovative work.
f. Virtual collaborators:

   i. Virtual assistants and chatbots can serve as creative collaborators, engaging in conversations, sharing ideas, and assisting in the development of creative projects.

g. Art and music generation:

   i. AI can generate visual art, music, and other creative content autonomously or in collaboration with human artists.
   ii. Generative adversarial networks (GANs) and neural style transfer can be used to create unique and imaginative pieces of art.

h. Gamification:

   i. AI-driven gamification techniques can make the creative process more engaging and fun, encouraging individuals or teams to think creatively and solve problems in a playful way.

i. Knowledge and inspiration databases:

   i. AI can curate databases of creative works, trends, and inspiration sources, making it easier for creators to access relevant information.

j. Learning and training:

   i. AI can offer personalized training and learning experiences to develop creative skills and enhance problem-solving abilities.

k. Collaboration and co-creation platforms:

   i. AI-powered platforms can facilitate collaboration among creative teams by providing tools for idea sharing, feedback, and project management.

While AI can be a valuable tool for enhancing creativity, it should complement and support human creativity rather than replace it entirely. The best results often come from a harmonious partnership between AI and human creativity, where AI aids and augments human creative processes.

AI has a significant impact on culture and creativity, as well as on the economic, financial, and market value of AI-driven firms, as shown in Table 1.8.

AI has had a multifaceted impact on culture and creativity, while also significantly affecting the economic, financial, and market value of firms

Table 1.8 Artificial intelligence's impact on culture and creativity

Impact on Culture and Creativity	a. Creative Assistance: AI tools like generative models can assist artists, writers, and musicians in generating new ideas, content, and designs. They can act as creative collaborators, providing inspiration and even generating original works of art b. Cultural Content: AI can be used to analyze and recommend cultural content to individuals, enhancing their cultural experiences. Streaming platforms use AI to recommend movies, music, and books based on users' preferences, contributing to the spread of diverse cultural content c. Cultural Preservation: AI can play a role in preserving cultural heritage by digitizing and restoring historical artifacts, documents, and artworks. It can also assist in language translation and transcription, making cultural resources more accessible
Economic Impact	a. Automation: AI-driven automation can lead to efficiency improvements in various industries, reducing labor costs and increasing productivity. This can have both positive and negative effects on employment, depending on how it is implemented b. New Business Models: AI enables the development of new business models and revenue streams. For example, companies can offer AI-based products and services, such as chatbots, recommendation engines, and personalization features, which can generate additional income c. Competitive Advantage: Firms that effectively implement AI can gain a competitive edge, which can translate into increased market share and profitability

(continued)

Table 1.8 (continued)

Financial Impact	a. Investment and Valuation: AI-driven firms often attract significant investment due to their growth potential. Investors are willing to allocate capital to companies that are at the forefront of AI innovation, which can increase the financial valuation of these firms b. Stock Market Performance: AI-driven firms may experience volatility in their stock prices as they are subject to market sentiment, regulatory changes, and technological advancements. Their performance can be influenced by factors like quarterly earnings reports and news related to AI breakthroughs c. Mergers and Acquisitions: The AI sector has seen numerous mergers and acquisitions as larger companies acquire AI startups to incorporate their technology and talent. These transactions can have a significant financial impact on both acquiring and acquired firms
Market Value	a. AI Adoption: As more industries adopt AI technologies, the market value of AI-driven firms continues to rise. Companies in sectors like healthcare, finance, e-commerce, and autonomous vehicles rely on AI for innovation and competitiveness b. Sector-Specific Impact: The impact of AI on market value varies by sector. For example, in healthcare, AI can improve diagnostics and drug discovery, leading to increased market value for companies in this field

operating in the AI space. Its influence is likely to continue to grow as AI technologies advance and become more integrated into various aspects of society and the economy.

Dystopian Perspectives

AI holds immense promise for advancing technology and improving various aspects of human life, but it also raises significant dystopian concerns that stem from the potential negative impacts it could have if it is not developed and managed responsibly:

a. **Job Displacement**: One of the most immediate fears is that AI and automation will lead to widespread job losses. As AI systems become more capable, they can take over tasks traditionally done by humans, potentially leading to unemployment in various sectors.
b. **Privacy Invasion**: AI systems can track individual behaviors, preferences, and even predict future actions, which raises concerns about surveillance and data misuse.
c. **Bias and Discrimination**: AI systems can perpetuate and amplify biases present in their training data. This can lead to unfair or discriminatory outcomes in areas like job recruitment, law enforcement, and loan approval processes.
d. **Loss of Human Autonomy**: There is a fear that as AI systems become more integrated into our lives, human autonomy could be undermined. Decisions might increasingly be made by algorithms, reducing human control, and choice.
e. **AI Warfare**: The militarization of AI, including autonomous weapons, raises the specter of new forms of warfare. These technologies could lead to conflicts that are faster, more unpredictable, and more devastating.
f. **Existential Risks**: In the long term, there is the concern that super-intelligent AI could pose existential risks. If AI surpasses human intelligence and operates without effective controls, it could make decisions detrimental to humanity.

Promise and Controversy may be summarized as follows:

1. **Promising Aspects**:

   - **Efficiency and Productivity**: AI can process and analyze data much faster than humans, leading to increased efficiency and productivity in various industries.
   - **Medical Advances**: In healthcare, AI can help in diagnosing diseases, personalizing treatment, and even in drug discovery.
   - **Environmental Benefits**: AI can optimize resource use, improve energy efficiency, and help in monitoring and combating climate change.
   - **Enhancing Human Capabilities**: AI can augment human abilities, making complex tasks easier and enabling new forms of creativity and exploration.

2. **Controversial Aspects**:

   - **Ethical Concerns**: Questions about privacy, surveillance, consent, and the ethical use of AI are central to the debate.
   - **Regulation and Governance**: Determining how to regulate AI and ensure it's used responsibly is a major challenge, especially given its rapid development and global impact.
   - **Economic Impact**: AI's effect on the job market and economy is uncertain, creating anxiety about inequality and social disruption.
   - **Control and Safety**: Ensuring AI systems do what they are intended to do, without malfunctioning or being exploited, is a significant technical and moral challenge.

AI's disruptive potential is both promising and controversial because it holds the capacity to fundamentally reshape aspects of society, economy, and daily life. While it offers solutions to some of our most pressing challenges, it also poses new risks and ethical dilemmas that society must carefully navigate. The future of AI will largely depend on how well we can balance these benefits and risks, ensuring responsible development and deployment of AI technologies.

1.5 Outline of the Book

This book is articulated into 9 further chapters that follow this introduction.

Some contents are readapted from Moro-Visconti (2022a), Moro-Visconti (2022b), or Moro-Visconti (2021), extending digital intangible, startup, or business planning applications to specific AI valuation patterns.

The abstract of each chapter is recalled here.

Chapter 2—The Valuation of Intangible Assets: An Introduction

An intangible is a non-monetary asset that manifests itself by its economic properties. It does not have physical substance but grants rights and economic benefits to its owner. The examination of the general approaches to the valuation of companies is preliminary to the estimation of assets such as intangibles. Intangibles are more specific than other assets and incorporate higher information asymmetries, linked to higher risk profiles and lower collateral value. Their accounting is controversial, privileging prudence over substance. The most widely used approaches to assessing AI-driven intangibles are based on market, income, or cost-related metrics.

Chapter 3—Artificial Intelligence-Driven Digital Scalability and Growth Options

Scalability indicates the ability of a process, network, or system to handle a growing amount of work. Scalability fosters economic marginality, especially in intangible-driven businesses where variable costs are typically negligible. Massive volumes may offset low margins, producing economic gains. Digitalization is defined as the concept of "going paperless", the technical process of transforming analog information or physical products into digital form. Digital scalability operates in a web context, where networked agents interact to generate co-created value.

Economic and financial margins that represent a primary parameter for valuation are boosted by cost savings and scalable increases in expected revenues. Digitalized intangibles synergistically interact through networked platforms that reshape traditional supply chains.

Chapter 4—The Valuation of Artificial Intelligence-Driven Know-How and Patents

The know-how (to do it) and trade (industrial) secrets are proprietary information or knowledge that assists or improves a commercial activity, but that is not registered for protection in the manner of a patent or trademark.

The sharing and transferability of know-how is the basis of its economic appraisal, which is based on complementary methodologies projecting the future usefulness of the costs incurred, the relief-from-royalties by the license, or the differential income from internal exploitation. Unlike patents, the know-how is not independently negotiable and is more difficult to enforce against third parties, but at the same time, it retains some characteristics of confidentiality that with the patenting in part must be disclosed. Patents can create scalable value, levered by debt, and serviced by intangible-driven incremental EBITDA and cash flows.

Chapter 5—The Valuation of Artificial Intelligence-Driven Startups

Innovative AI startups are newly formed companies with no operating profits and history, and with high growth potential, which usually absorb a lot of liquidity in the early years of life, to finance development, against minimal collateralizable assets. This is unattractive for traditional banking intermediaries, usually replaced by other specialized intermediaries such as venture capital or private equity funds, which diversify their portfolio basing their strategies on a multi-year exit with substantial expected increases in value from investments that survive a Darwinian selection. The evaluation of the target companies follows traditional methodologies, accompanied by specific features deriving from varied probabilistic scenarios and multiple exit methods. The technological footprint implies evaluation analogies with patents, know-how, and intangibles linked to AI-driven specific sectors.

Chapter 6—The Valuation of Software as a Prerequisite for Artificial Intelligence

Software, generally understood as a sequence of computer instructions for performing functions on devices such as hardware, falls within the category of intangible assets and, due to its pervasiveness in people's daily lives, represents an essential tool for any user. As a result, some complex legal issues, as well as sophisticated economic evaluation approaches come out, to estimate the damage caused by counterfeiting, in an evolutionary scenario characterized by sharp technological discontinuities. The database indicates a set of data, homogeneous in content and format; these data are stored in a computer and interrogated via a computer-implemented system by using the provided access keys.

The estimation follows the general evaluation criteria of the other intangible assets—the income, cost, or market approach—to be adapted to the specific characteristics of the software or database.

Chapter 7—The Valuation of Artificial Intelligence

AI allows us to think and act humanely and rationally through hardware systems and software programs capable of providing performances that, to an ordinary observer, would seem to be the exclusive domain of natural (human) intelligence. The applications are more and more extensive, thanks also to the big data available today and the ability of self-learning (machine learning) or instead to the synergies with natural intelligence, which for vision and flexibility remains irreplaceable. The examination of the business models of the companies that base their strategies on AI or, more extensively, of the traditional companies using specific applications, is preliminary to a framework of the legal problems (still pioneering) and of the profiles of economic evaluation.

Chapter 8—Chatbots and Generative Artificial Intelligence: From Business Planning to Economic Valuation

Chatbots are generative AI systems that can maintain a conversation with a user in natural language and simulate the way a human would behave as a conversational partner. Such technologies often utilize aspects of deep learning and natural language processing. Business models and subsequent planning represent a prerequisite for economic valuation approaches that consider cost-benefits, ROI, customer value or satisfaction, revenue, and cash flow generation or comparables. The valuation concerns either the market value of chatbot platforms or the benefits for its users.

Chapter 9—Sustainable Artificial Intelligence Issues: From ESG Valuation to Ethical Concerns

Artificial Intelligence presents a range of sustainability issues that span from ESG considerations to ethical concerns. Addressing these sustainability issues requires collaboration among governments, businesses, researchers, and civil society. It involves developing and adhering to ethical guidelines, improving transparency, investing in AI that benefits society, and considering the long-term impact of AI on people, the planet, and governance structures. It's essential to strike a balance between technological advancement and responsible, sustainable AI development.

Chapter 10—Artificial Intelligence-Driven Industry Applications

Artificial Intelligence (AI) has a wide range of industry applications across various sectors, ranging from healthcare to finance, retail (B2B2C), manufacturing, autonomous vehicles, energy, agriculture, education, and other sectors. AI's versatility make it a valuable tool for improving efficiency, decision-making, and customer experiences. As AI continues to advance, its impact on various industries is likely to expand even further.

Chapter 11—Artificial Intelligence Valuation: Empirical Cases and Templates

Two empirical cases of Artificial Intelligence valuation are contained in this chapter, representing a template (sourced by valutico.com AI database) that summarizes the main findings of the other sections. The template is based on the theoretical findings already described, especially in Chapter 2.

The first case is represented by a listed company, C3.AI, which specializes in proprietary, model-driven AI architecture that enhances data science and application development.

A second case is represented by the business model and the consequential valuation of another AI firm focused on a tool designed to facilitate and streamline the user interface (UI) design process.

* * *

This book is dedicated to my beloved grandson Pietro, born in 2022, and representing a remarkable example of natural intelligence. Any digital comment may be sent to roberto.moro@unicatt.it (or by visiting www.morovisconti.com/en).

Milan, Italy, Università Cattolica del Sacro Cuore, July 2024

References

Acciarini, C., Cappa, F., Boccardelli, P., & Oriani, R. (2023). How can organizations leverage big data to innovate their business models? A systematic literature review. *Technovation, 123*, 102713.

Batarseh, F. A., Freeman, L., & Huang, C. H. (2021). A survey on artificial intelligence assurance. *Journal of Big Data, 8*, 60.

de la Torre-López, J., Ramírez, A., & Romero, J. R. (2023). Artificial intelligence to automate the systematic review of scientific literature. *Computing, 105*, 2171–2194.

Došilović, F. K., Brčić, M., & Hlupić, M. (2018). Explainable artificial intelligence: A survey. *2018 41st International Convention on Information and Communication Technology, Electronics and Microelectronics (MIPRO), Opatija, Croatia*, pp. 210–215.

Duan, Y., Edwards, J. S., Yogesh, K., & Dwivedi, Y. K. (2019). Artificial intelligence for decision making in the era of Big Data—Evolution, challenges and research agenda. *International Journal of Information Management, 48*, 63–71.

Enholm, I. M., Papagiannidis, E., Mikalef, P., & Krogstie, J. (2022). Artificial intelligence and business value: A literature review. *Information Systems Frontiers, 24*, 1709–1734.

Jaber, T. A. (2022). Artificial intelligence in computer networks. *Periodicals of Engineering and Natural Sciences, 10*(1), 309–322.

Kamalov, F., Santandreu Calonge, D., & Gurrib, I. (2023). New era of artificial intelligence in education: Towards a sustainable multifaceted revolution. *Sustainability, 15*(16), 12451.

Maslej, N., et al. (2023, April). *The AI index 2023 annual report*. AI Index Steering Committee, Institute for Human-Centered AI, Stanford University.

Mikalef, P., & Gupta, M. (2021). Artificial intelligence capability: Conceptualization, measurement calibration, and empirical study on its impact on organizational creativity and firm performance. *Information & Management, 58*(3), 103434.

Minh, D., Wang, H. X., & Li, Y. F. (2022). Explainable artificial intelligence: A comprehensive review. *Artificial Intelligence Review, 55*, 3503–3568.

Moro-Visconti, R. (2021). *Startup valuation. From strategic business planning to digital networking*. Palgrave MacMillan.
Moro-Visconti, R. (2022a). *The valuation of digital intangibles. Technology, marketing, and the metaverse*. Palgrave MacMillan.
Moro-Visconti, R. (2022b). *Augmented corporate valuation. From digital networking to ESG compliance*. Palgrave MacMillan.
Saghiri, A. M., Vahidipour, S. M., Jabbarpour, M. R., Sookhak, M., & Forestiero, A. (2022). A survey of artificial intelligence challenges: Analyzing the definitions, relationships, and evolutions. *Applied Sciences, 12*(8), 4054.

CHAPTER 2

The Valuation of Intangible Assets: An Introduction

2.1 Purpose of the Firm Evaluation

The evaluation of firms is multifaceted, especially within the emerging AI-driven paradigms. Within the legal domain, AI models are being designed to forecast the performance rankings of lawyers, thereby supporting talent management and aligning it with organizational strategy. The concept of Industry 5.0 underscores the importance of employing AI-based Digital Intelligent Assistants for sustainable and human-centric industrial transformations, necessitating evaluation frameworks that emphasize trustworthiness, usability, cognitive workload, and business advantages. The incorporation of AI into firm evaluation processes is crucial for enhancing performance, anticipating outcomes, and promoting innovation in various industries. There are several important purposes for the practice of business valuation, each serving different needs and contexts:

1. **Objectified Business Value**:
    - **Purpose**: Determine a standardized and objective value for a business.
    - **Approach**: Utilizes an income approach that standardizes assumptions.
    - **Assumptions**: Assumes that the business will continue to be managed based on the existing strategy.

R. Moro-Visconti, *Artificial Intelligence Valuation*,
https://doi.org/10.1007/978-3-031-53622-9_2

- **Considerations**: Takes into account realistic future expectations regarding market opportunities, risks, financial options, and other relevant elements.
- **Legal Requirement**: This may be required by legal provisions, and the valuation approach and extent of standardization are influenced by these requirements.
- **Plausibility Assessment**: The plausibility of the business value determined through an income approach is assessed. Multiple methods or market-based data analysis (stock prices or transaction prices) may be used for this assessment.
- **Small Companies**: For very small companies, multiples based on experience can be used if they are well-established, commonly accepted, and considered reliable by the valuation specialist.

2. **Subjective Business Value**:

- **Purpose**: Determine a value based on subjective ideas, personal circumstances, and other considerations of the investor.
- **Approach**: Utilizes an income approach.
- **Considerations**: Incorporates the investor's subjective views, personal circumstances, and any additional factors like synergy effects.
- **Use**: Typically used by potential buyers or sellers to define upper or lower price limits based on their perspectives and circumstances.

3. **Arbitration Values**:

- **Purpose**: Establish or suggest values in conflict situations, considering different expectations of the parties involved.
- **Approach**: Based solely on factual considerations.
- **Considerations**: Takes into account the differing expectations of parties and aims to find a fair and balanced value that considers alternative investments and personal circumstances.
- **Conflict Resolution**: Often used in dispute resolution and legal proceedings to provide a fair and unbiased valuation that considers the interests of all parties involved.

These different valuation purposes highlight the flexibility and adaptability of valuation methods and approaches to meet specific needs and contexts.

Valuation experts must carefully consider the purpose of the valuation and the relevant factors when determining the appropriate approach and methodology to use. Additionally, the plausibility and reliability of the valuation results should be assessed and, in some cases, corroborated with market-based data or alternative methods to ensure a well-informed and defensible valuation.

Within this general framework, intangible assets are non-monetary assets that lack physical substance but hold economic value for their owner. The valuation of intangibles, such as AI, is typically embedded in the appraisal of firms that either include intangibles or are built around their exploitation. These companies may refer to either AI-driven business models or "brick-and-mortar" firms that buy AI products and services to improve their traditional business.

The valuation of intangible assets can have a significant impact on AI's economic, financial, and market appraisal metrics and patterns. Intangible assets are non-physical assets that are often critical to the success and value of AI companies. These assets can include intellectual property, patents, copyrights, trademarks, brand reputation, and proprietary algorithms, all of which are central to AI development and deployment:

1. **Financial Valuation**:
   - **Balance Sheet**: Valuing intangible assets can significantly impact a company's balance sheet. A higher valuation of these assets produces a stronger balance sheet, which can improve a company's overall financial health.
   - **Income Statement**: Intangible asset valuation can affect the income statement through amortization and impairment charges. High valuations may result in higher amortization expenses, which can impact profitability metrics.
2. **Market Appraisal Metrics**:
   - **Market Capitalization**: A significant portion of AI companies' market capitalization often stems from the value of intangible assets. Accurate valuation of these assets is essential for estimating the company's true market worth.
   - **Price-to-Earnings (P/E) Ratio**: High intangible asset valuations can impact the P/E ratio, potentially making a company appear overvalued if not properly considered in the analysis.

- **Price-to-Book Value (P/BV) Ratio**: The P/B ratio compares a company's market capitalization to its book (accounting) value, which includes intangible assets. High intangible asset valuations can inflate the book value, affecting this ratio.

3. **Economic Impact**:

- **Innovation and Investment**: Accurate valuation of intangible assets can influence a company's ability to attract investment and engage in research and development activities. High valuations may attract more investment, fueling AI innovation.
- **Taxation and Regulation**: The valuation of intangible assets can have tax implications, affecting a company's tax liability. It can also influence regulatory compliance and reporting requirements.

4. **Risk Assessment**:

- **Risk Management**: A proper understanding of intangible asset valuation can help investors and stakeholders assess the risks associated with an AI company. Overvaluation of intangibles produces unrealistic expectations.

5. **Market Patterns**:

- **Investor Behavior**: The valuation of intangible assets can influence investor behavior. If investors perceive that intangibles are overvalued, they may react by adjusting their portfolios or trading patterns.
- **Mergers and Acquisitions**: High valuations of intangible assets can impact merger and acquisition activity in the AI sector. Companies may be acquired or merged based on their intangible asset portfolios.

The valuation of intangible assets is a critical consideration for AI companies and their stakeholders. It affects financial metrics, market appraisal, economic decisions, risk assessment, and even market behavior. Accurate valuation is essential for making informed investment and strategic decisions.

Some contents are readapted from Moro-Visconti (2022a) Chapter 2, Moro-Visconti (2022b), Moro-Visconti (2021) or Moro-Visconti and

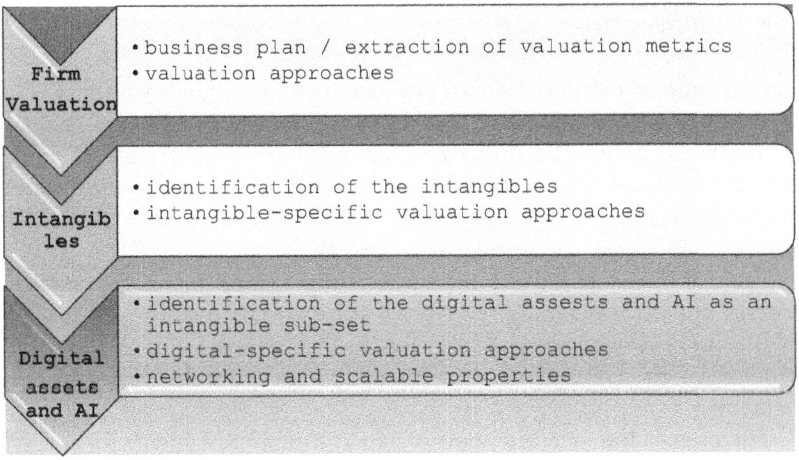

Fig. 2.1 From the valuation of the firm to the estimate of the intangibles and digital assets

Cesaretti (2023), extending digital intangible, startup, cryptocurrency, or business planning applications to specific AI valuation patterns.

Additionally, as AI continues to evolve, the importance of intangible assets in determining the value of AI companies is likely to grow.

The firm evaluation (Fazzini, 2018; Koller & Goedhart, 2015) represents a preliminary step for the assessment of the intangibles that it incorporates. The intangibles, consequently, incorporate digital assets and AI, as shown in Fig. 2.1.

Valuing intangible and digital assets (including AI) is essential in understanding a firm's true worth in today's increasingly digital and knowledge-driven economy. It requires a combination of financial analysis, industry knowledge, and specialized valuation techniques to provide an accurate assessment.

The value of a company is primarily the result of a series of elements, including:

- Net assets, i.e., all the funds contributed by the partners to finance the business activity;
- Ability to generate income, i.e., the ability to produce positive income flows;

- Financial capacity.

The attitude of the net assets to produce income depends on the quality of the means of production and the entrepreneurial capacity. This last circumstance allows an understanding of the presence of profoundly different profit margins between companies operating in the same sector. Under ideal conditions, the subjective "value" must tend to coincide with an objective "price" at the negotiation stage.

Value is estimated from the application of one or more valuation criteria, chosen concerning the type of corporate transaction, the identity of the parties involved, and the activity of the firm. It is ideally independent of the contractual strength of the parties and other subjective elements.

The price is the meeting point of expectations and benefits formulated by the supply and demand involved in the negotiation of the company. A firm can be evaluated, among other things:

1. To trade (transaction purposes);
    - Purchases/sales of shareholdings (the underlying company is valued), companies, or business units;
    - Extraordinary financial transactions (relating to the company/branch of business), M&A, demergers, contributions, disposals, transformations, securitization, ...;
2. For litigation (e.g., compute damage awards in an infringement lawsuit);
3. For arbitration or similar proceedings;
4. For bankruptcy (valuation is required by the Court to dispose of the assets properly and pay back creditors);
5. Because of changes in the equity:
    - Issue of shares (excluding pre-emptive rights; with share premium; ...);
    - Issue of convertible bonds;
    - Issue of warrants;
    - Linked to extraordinary operations (transfers, transformations, mergers, contributions, demergers, etc.);
6. With a view to the purchase of assets by the founding partners;

7. To provide guarantees;
8. For listing on the Stock Exchange (IPO);
9. For "internal" cognitive purposes (financial reporting, etc.);
10. For the evaluation of the withdrawal of the shareholder.

With or without considerations, as shown later (see also paragraph 7.9) identify the additional contribution of AI in the valuation process.

The main approaches for estimating the market value of companies are different and can be divided into empirical and analytical approaches:

- Empirical approaches are based on the practical observation of market prices of assets that are sufficiently similar and, as such, comparable.
- Analytical approaches, on the other hand, have a more solid scientific basis and a more significant tradition in the professional sphere and are based on a revenue-financial approach, to estimate what an asset is worth today based on expected future returns or an estimate of the costs incurred for its reproduction/replacement.

The main approaches to evaluating companies commonly used in practice are:

- The balance sheet-based approach, either simple or complex;
- The income approach;
- The mixed capital-income approach;
- The financial approach;
- Market approaches and valuation through multiples.

The central element in determining the value of a firm is the estimate of its future ability to generate an income or financial flow capable of adequately rewarding its shareholders after debt service.

Among the approaches used by operators to identify the market value of the firm, the financial and income approaches are the most appropriate to represent the expected fair remuneration of shareholders.

Both approaches are widely used because they provide different perspectives on a company's value:

- The financial approach (DCF) focuses on the intrinsic value of a company based on its projected cash flows and the risk associated with those cash flows. It is often used for companies with complex financial structures and unique characteristics.
- The market approach relies on market-derived data and is useful for benchmarking a company's value against its peers or market trends. It can provide insights into market sentiment and pricing.

These approaches can be used in combination or separately, depending on the circumstances and the availability of relevant data. Valuation professionals often consider multiple methods to arrive at a comprehensive perspective of a firm's value.

While the balance sheet-based approach values tangible and intangible resources summing up the values of individual assets, the income and the financial approaches consider them as comprehensive elements able to participate in the context of the entire set of elements for the creation of value. The firm's market value is the result of the interaction of internal variables relating to its tangible and intangible assets and external variables relating to the market. The combined consideration of both makes it possible to estimate the Firm's future results and to assess its risk.

Recent valuation trends have led to the use of two approaches:

- the financial approach based on the estimate of discounted operating cash flows at the weighted average cost of capital (WACC);
- the market approach based on the EBITDA multipliers of comparable companies.

In both cases, the enterprise value (value of the firm, including debt) is estimated, which is then added algebraically to the net financial position to arrive at the residual equity value.

In the evaluation of the intangibles, "*distinctions are sometimes made between trade intangibles and marketing intangibles, between "soft" intangibles and "hard" intangibles, between routine and non-routine intangibles, and between other classes and categories of intangibles*" (OECD, 2022).

The choice of the correct approach and parameters depends on a bottom-up analysis of the business plan of the target firm (Moro Visconti, 2019). This helps in the estimate of trendy parameters (operating and net cash flows; economic margins, etc.) and in the functional analysis that

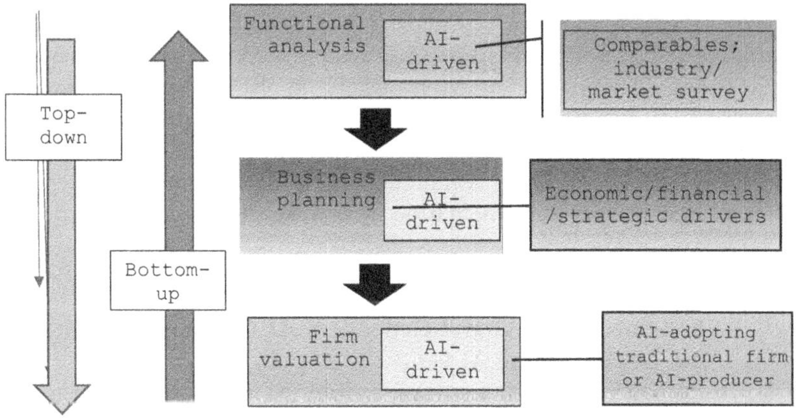

Fig. 2.2 Functional analysis, business planning, and firm valuation

eases the selection of comparable firms (see also: https://fastercapital.com/keyword/similar-companies.html).

The functional analysis is traditionally used for transfer pricing purposes (OECD, 2022). It analyzes the functions performed (considering assets used and risks assumed) by associated firms in a transaction, providing an overview of value creation within the supply chain (Fig. 2.2).

2.2 Artificial Intelligence Business Modeling and Planning as a Prerequisite for Valuation

AI plays a noteworthy role in assessing intangible assets, particularly within companies focused on innovation. The emergence of digitalization and AI has underscored the significance of intangible capital in establishing a company's worth. AI-powered intangibles, such as innovative software and intellectual property rights, hold pivotal positions in the evaluation process, especially amidst economic uncertainty and global instability. Utilizing machine learning techniques, including neural networks and decision trees, has improved the evaluation of the relevance of intangible asset value, addressing the constraints of traditional econometric models. AI aids in enhancing the measurement of intangible assets by capturing complex, non-numeric data and increasing the credibility of model training. This technological progress assists in gaining a deeper insight into the economic advantages and risks linked with intangible assets, ultimately impacting their valuation criteria. Generative AI Learning Planning for decision-makers involves structuring training content in a way that gradually builds from foundational knowledge to advanced concepts. This plan should cater to both business and technical decision-makers, ensuring a comprehensive understanding of generative AI's potential and its implementation, following these patterns:

a. **Foundational Stage**

   1. **Introduction to AI and Generative AI Concepts**
      - Understanding AI basics.
      - Differentiating between various AI types, with a focus on generative AI.
      - Real-world applications and case studies of generative AI.
   2. **Importance of Generative AI in Business**
      - How generative AI is transforming industries.
      - The business value and ROI of investing in generative AI.
      - Ethical considerations and social implications.
   3. **Basic Technical Overview**
      - Basic technical aspects of generative AI (e.g., data requirements, model types).
      - Overview of platforms and tools commonly used.

b. **Intermediate Stage**

   1. **Planning Generative AI Projects**
      - Steps for initiating a generative AI project.
      - Identifying opportunities for generative AI in your organization.
      - Building a business case and securing stakeholder buy-in.
   2. **Data Management and Model Training**
      - Understanding data needs and management for generative AI.
      - An introduction to training generative AI models.
      - Addressing data privacy and security concerns.
   3. **Collaboration between Technical and Business Teams**
      - Fostering collaboration between IT and business units.

- Communicating technical aspects effectively to non-technical stakeholders.

c. **Advanced Stage**

1. **Implementing Generative AI Solutions**
    - Deep dive into technology stack and advanced model training.
    - Integration of generative AI into existing systems.
    - Scaling generative AI projects.
2. **Advanced Case Studies and Industry Applications**
    - Analyzing complex case studies.
    - Exploring cutting-edge generative AI applications in various industries.
3. **Future Trends and Continuous Learning**
    - Keeping up with the latest developments in generative AI.
    - Building a culture of continuous learning and innovation.

Digital business modeling and planning, including AI features, are essential prerequisites for the valuation of digital businesses or businesses with significant digital and AI components:

1. Understanding the Business Model:
    - Before valuing a digital and AI-driven business, it is essential to understand its business model thoroughly. Digital and AI-driven business models can vary widely, from e-commerce and subscription services to online advertising and Software as a Service (SaaS). Each model has unique revenue streams, cost structures, and growth strategies.
    - A comprehensive understanding of the business model is essential for accurately projecting future cash flows, which are a key component of valuation.
2. Revenue and Cost Analysis:
    - Digital businesses often have different revenue streams and cost drivers than traditional businesses. Revenue may come from online sales, digital advertising, data monetization, or other digital sources. Costs may include technology infrastructure, digital marketing, and data analytics.

- Detailed analysis of revenue sources and cost structures is necessary to make accurate financial projections.

3. Market Dynamics and Trends:

   - The digital and AI landscape is highly dynamic, with rapid technological advancements, changing consumer behavior, and evolving market trends. Understanding the current market dynamics and anticipating future shifts is critical for valuation.
   - Market research and trend analysis can help in making informed assumptions about growth rates and market positioning.

4. User and Customer Metrics:

   - Many digital and AI businesses rely on user engagement and customer acquisition and retention. Metrics such as user growth, customer churn rates, and customer lifetime value are essential to understand the health of the business.
   - These metrics can impact revenue projections and, consequently, the valuation.

5. Technology and Intellectual Property:

   - Digital and AI businesses often have valuable technology assets and intellectual property, such as software, patents, or proprietary algorithms. Evaluating the uniqueness and competitive advantage of these assets is important for valuation.
   - Intellectual property valuation can be a complex process, and it plays a role in the overall assessment of intangible assets.

6. Scalability and Growth Strategies:

   - Many digital and AI businesses are designed for rapid scalability, as shown in Chapter 3. Understanding the company's growth strategies, including geographic expansion, product diversification, or partnerships, is essential for estimating future revenue growth.

7. Risk Assessment:

   - Digital and AI businesses may face unique risks, including cybersecurity threats, regulatory changes, and competition from tech giants. Assessing these risks and their potential impact on cash flows is essential for risk-adjusted valuation.

8. Digital Assets and Data:

    - Digital assets, such as websites, mobile apps, and digital content, may have significant value. Additionally, data assets, including customer data and user behavior data, can be valuable for certain digital businesses. AI adds new intangible features.
    - Valuing these digital and AI assets accurately is an important part of the overall valuation.

Digital and AI-driven business modeling and planning provide the foundation for conducting a meaningful valuation of a digital business. They help in creating realistic financial projections, estimating risks, and understanding the unique value drivers and challenges associated with the digital landscape. A well-prepared business model and plan are essential tools for valuation professionals and investors when estimating the worth of digital enterprises.

Business planning follows a typical managerial top-down approach where management-prepared forecasts and projections are conceived within the firm and occasionally compared with market returns. The increasing availability of timely big data, sometimes fueled by the Internet of Things (IoT) devices, allows for receiving continuous feedback that can be conveniently used to refresh assumptions and forecasts, using a complementary bottom-up approach. Top-down and bottom-up are both strategies of information processing and knowledge ordering. They typically follow the patterns shown in Table 2.1.

Many AI-driven organizations find value in combining both top-down and bottom-up approaches. The top-down approach provides strategic direction and alignment, while the bottom-up approach ensures that the plans are rooted in operational realities and can adapt to changing circumstances and updated feedback. The incorporation of big data and IoT data in AI-driven interpretation models further enhances the planning process by providing real-time insights and the ability to validate assumptions with empirical evidence.

This dynamic and adaptive approach produces more effective and resilient business planning.

Optimal business planning using the firm's data is part of business intelligence strategies—a procedural and technical infrastructure that collects, stores, and analyzes the data produced by a company's activities, encompassing data mining, process analysis, performance benchmarking, and descriptive analytics.

Table 2.1 Top-down and bottom-up approaches

Top-Down Approach	**Managerial Perspective**: In the top-down approach, business planning typically begins with the senior management team or executives. They develop forecasts, projections, and strategic plans based on their insights, experience, and understanding of the business environment **Macro-Level View**: This approach often takes a macro-level view, where high-level decisions and strategies are formulated and cascaded down throughout the organization **Market Comparisons**: Management-prepared forecasts are occasionally compared with market data and returns to validate assumptions and ensure alignment with market trends
Bottom-Up Approach	**Grassroots Input**: The bottom-up approach involves collecting input and insights from employees, teams, and departments at various levels of the organization. It starts at the operational level and works its way up **Micro-Level Detail**: This approach focuses on detailed data and insights from the front lines of the business. Employees and teams provide input based on their daily experiences **Agility and Responsiveness**: Bottom-up planning can be more agile and responsive to changing market conditions because it incorporates real-time feedback and insights from those directly involved in business operations

(continued)

Table 2.1 (continued)

Integration of Big Data and IoT	**Continuous Feedback**: The availability of big data, often generated by IoT devices, enables organizations to get back continuous and real-time feedback about customer behavior, production efficiency, and supply chain performance **Refreshed Assumptions**: This data can be used to refresh and validate assumptions and forecasts. **Complementary Approach**: The integration of big data and IoT can complement both top-down and bottom-up approaches. It enriches the planning process with timely and granular information
Information Processing and Knowledge Ordering	**Top-Down**: Top-down planning is a strategy of information processing and knowledge ordering that starts with high-level strategic thinking and aims to align the entire organization with a common vision and set of goals **Bottom-Up**: Bottom-up planning, on the other hand, is a strategy that leverages decentralized knowledge and insights to create a more inclusive and agile planning process

Forecasting accuracy can be substantially improved by incorporating timely empirical evidence, with a consequent reduction of both information asymmetries and the risk of facing unexpected events, concerning the magnitude of their impact. Since risk is represented by the difference between expected and real events, if occurrences are timely incorporated into expectations, this differential is minimized. This intuitive concept is well-known, but its practical implications are amplified by the unprecedented presence of big data.

Valuation criteria of the project or investment are typically linked to business planning metrics, especially if they are based on Discounted Cash Flows (DCF). DCF forecasting can be greatly improved by timely big data feedback that positively affects the numerator, represented by growing cash flows (that incorporate real option flexibility), and decreasing discount rates (cost of capital) that reflect reduced risk. Value-adding strategies can conveniently reshape supply and value chains that embed information-driven resilience.

Network theory may constitute a further interpretation tool, considering the interaction of nodes represented by IoT and big data, mastering digital platforms, and physical stakeholders (shareholders, managers, clients, suppliers, lenders, etc.). AI, database interoperability, and blockchain applications are consistent with the networking interpretation of the interaction of physical and virtual nodes.

The interaction of big data with traditional budgeting patterns creates flexible (real) options nurtured by a networked digital ecosystem, eventually bringing augmented business planning.

The interaction of big data with traditional budgeting patterns has the potential to transform the way businesses plan and make decisions, leading to more flexible and dynamic approaches. This interaction can contribute to augmented business planning, as shown in Table 2.2.

The interaction of big data with traditional budgeting patterns, coupled with a networked digital ecosystem, empowers businesses to embrace flexible options and augmented planning. This approach enables organizations to adapt to changing conditions, make data-driven decisions, and ultimately improve their competitiveness in a fast-paced and interconnected business environment.

Augmented reality (AR) is the real-time use of information concerning text, graphics, audio, etc. It is this "real-world" element that differentiates AR from virtual reality. AR integrates and adds value to the user's interaction with the real world, versus a simulation.

The flow chart of the sequential passages that start from bottom-up data and then impact business planning, making it "augmented", is composed of these consequential steps:

1. The empirical evidence that provides massive information is represented by the ecosystem—a network of interconnecting and interacting parts—where the firm is located. This networked ecosystem is levered by digitalization that transforms into IT data any useful information, fostering its use; the ecosystem is also consistent with personalization, for instance, concerning ESG sustainability goals;

Table 2.2 Interaction of big data with traditional budgeting patterns

Flexible (Real) Options	Traditional budgeting often relies on fixed plans and forecasts that are set for a specific time, such as a fiscal year. However, big data allows for the continuous collection of real-time information and insights By integrating big data into the planning process, businesses can create flexible (real) options. These options enable them to make decisions based on current data and market conditions rather than being locked into rigid budgetary constraints
Data-Driven Decision-Making	Big data provides a wealth of information, including customer behavior, market trends, and operational performance. This data is leveraged for decision making of the organization Instead of relying solely on historical data or predefined budget targets, businesses can use real-time data to make informed decisions, adjust strategies, and seize opportunities as they arise
Networked Digital Ecosystem	The digital ecosystem encompasses a network of interconnected devices, platforms, and data sources. It includes IoT devices, online platforms, social media, and more Businesses can tap into this ecosystem to gather data from various sources, creating a more comprehensive understanding of their operating environment. For example, retail businesses can use data from online sales, customer reviews, and social media sentiment analysis to inform inventory management and marketing strategies
Augmented Business Planning	Augmented business planning refers to the enhancement of traditional planning processes with advanced technologies and data-driven insights. It leverages AI, machine learning, predictive analytics, and big data to provide real-time updates and scenario analyses With augmented business planning, companies can continuously monitor their performance against budgeted targets, identify deviations, and make adjustments as needed. This proactive approach enhances agility and adaptability

(continued)

Table 2.2 (continued)

Scenario Analysis	Big data and real-time data streams enable businesses to conduct scenario analysis more effectively. They can model various "what-if" scenarios to assess the potential impact of different decisions and external elements This capability is particularly valuable in uncertain and rapidly changing environments, allowing businesses to evaluate risks and opportunities more dynamically
Continuous Improvement	The integration of big data into budgeting and planning fosters a culture of continuous improvement. Businesses can learn from data-driven insights and use them to optimize operations, enhance customer experiences, and innovate in response to market dynamics

2. "Small" data, fueled by IoT or any other physical or digital source, are collected in the ecosystem, and their massive gathering makes them "big";
3. Data mastered by digital platforms and their networking properties are then stored in the cloud and fuel interoperable databases. Information is then interpreted with AI (machine learning) algorithms and, if necessary, is validated through tailor-made blockchains. This process brings to "augmented information";
4. Augmented data are then timely incorporated in (traditional) business planning procedures (here exemplified by DCF metrics) bringing flexible readjustments (real-time refreshing). This constant updating ideally produces incremental cash flows that can be interpreted with real option patterns that proxy flexibility;
5. The resilience and potential increase of the cash flows are also reflected in the discount factor represented in the denominator of the DCF formula; the risk is reduced as a consequence of the shrinking difference between expected and real outcomes, due to the continuous refreshing of expectations that makes them closer to the ongoing ecosystem's evidence;
6. Timely reformulation of DCF metrics (current cash flows and their discount factors) impacts prospects within the time-to-maturity interval, bringing to a continuous updating of deterministic expectations;

7. The abovementioned updating may well fuel a stochastic scenario that adds further explanatory power to the standard deterministic outlook.

The model is graphically described in Fig. 2.3.

The methodology shows that business planning can become more valuable—augmented—if it incorporates big data's informative contents, validated by blockchains, and interpreted through AI predictive patterns. The transformation from traditional to augmented business planning through the utilization of AI indicates a movement towards more sophisticated analytics methodologies. This shift has an impact on value co-creation within service systems by empowering decision-making capabilities through Intelligence Augmentation (IA). The utilization of AI and Big Data Analytics assists in the creation of business opportunities by examining extensive datasets, forecasting values, and suggesting strategic business maneuvers. Although AI-powered analytics can automate procedures and offer valuable insights, human decision-making remains essential in interpreting and implementing discoveries.

Figure 2.3 can be further developed, as shown in Fig. 2.4, to express the added value incorporated in augmented business planning.

The interaction of top-down and bottom-up strategies can be synthesized in Fig. 2.5.

2.3 The Balance-Sheet-Based Approach

The valuation of the market value according to the balance-sheet approach (Fernandez, 2001) is based on the current value of the equity contained in the last available balance sheet.

There are three approaches:

- Simple balance sheet-based approach;
- Complex balance sheet-based approach grade I;
- Complex balance sheet-based approach grade II;

This approach is extensively used in continental Europe and less in Anglo-Saxon countries.

The starting point for the use of the balance sheet-based approach, both simple and complex, is represented by the shareholders' equity in the

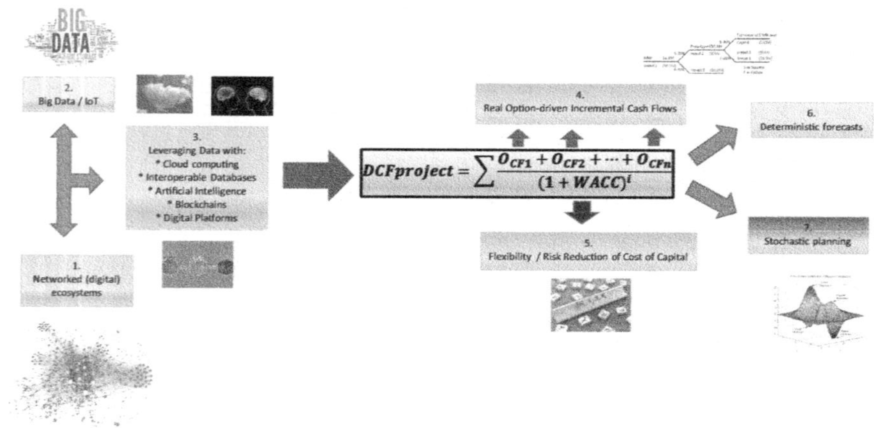

Fig. 2.3 From big data-driven forecasting to augmented business planning

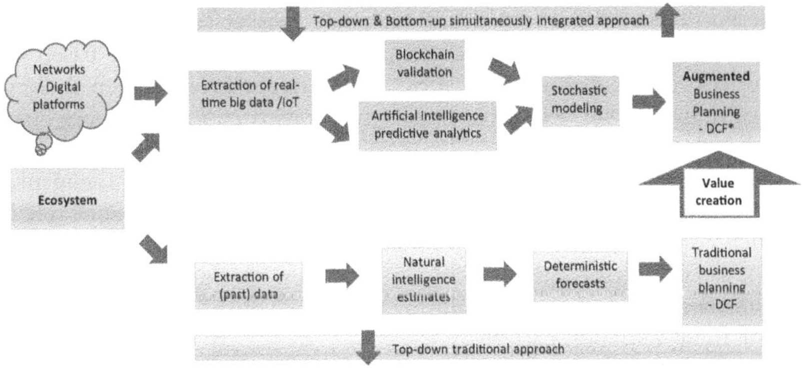

Fig. 2.4 Value creation, from traditional to augmented business planning

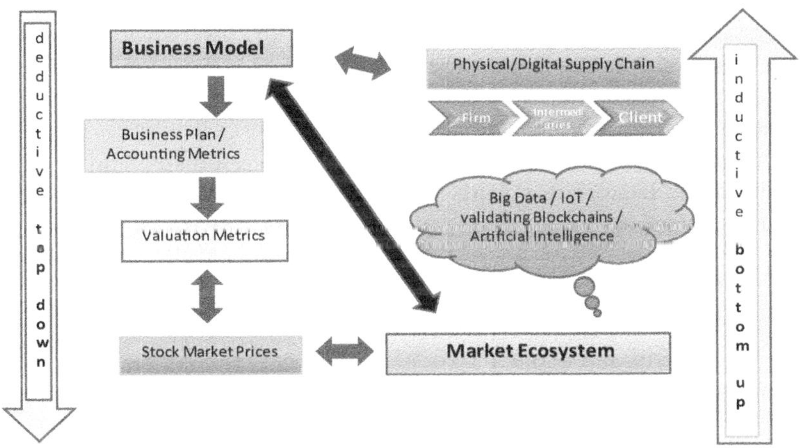

Fig. 2.5 Interaction of top-down and bottom-up strategies

financial statements including the profit for the year net of the amounts approved for distribution.

Based on the values shown in the financial statements, an analysis of assets and liabilities must be carried out, representing non-monetary assets (technical fixed assets, inventories of goods, securities, and, depending on the approach used, intangible fixed assets) in terms of current values, to highlight implicit capital gains or losses compared to the accounting data. For assets with a significant exchange market (e.g., real estate or traded securities), the calculation of present values is generally based on the prices recorded during the most recent negotiations. When there is no reference market, estimates based on reconstruction or training costs may be alternatively used.

The simple balance sheet-based is significant in the case of companies with high equity content (real estate companies, holding companies, etc.). In such companies, the overall profitability/risk profile may represent the synthesis of the patterns implicitly or explicitly considered in the valuation of the individual assets. Traditional firms where AI is introduced may follow these valuation patterns.

This methodology makes the value of the capital coincide with the difference between the current value of the assets and the value of the liabilities that contribute to determining the company's assets.

The asset value corresponds with the net investment that would be necessary to start a new company with the same asset structure as the one being valued. The simple asset value is, therefore, not the liquidation value of the assets, but the value of their reconstruction from a business operating perspective.

Accounting of liabilities should never be underestimated and so their value should be consistent with their bookkeeping or lower.

The formula is:

$$\begin{aligned}\text{Market Value of Equity}\\ &= \text{book equity} + \text{asset adjustments} - \text{liability adjustments}\\ &= \text{adjusted equity}\\ &= K_1\\ &= W_1 \qquad (2.1)\end{aligned}$$

where asset and liability adjustments are defined as capital gains and losses net of the tax impact.

The simple valuation considers, to estimate equity stocks, only tangible assets in addition to loans and liquidity.

The valuation provides for a detailed estimate of the assets at current replacement values, in particular:

- Assets at current repurchase value;
- Assets and liabilities based on settlement values.

The "first-grade complex balance sheet-based approach" also considers intangible assets that are not accounted for but have a market value (for instance, AI solutions). In formula:

$$K_1 + \text{intangible assets not accounted for but with market value} = K_2 - W_2 \quad (2.2)$$

(e.g., bank deposits, insurance premium portfolio, shop licenses, and large-scale distribution)where K_1 is the value of assets determined according to the principles of the simple balance sheet-based approach.

Finally, the complex Tier II balance sheet-based approach also refers to intangible assets that are not accounted for and do not have a specific market value, bringing to the "second-grade complex balance sheet-based approach".

$$K_2 + \text{unrecognized intangible assets without market value} = K_3 = W_3 \quad (2.3)$$

(e.g., product portfolio, patents, industrial concessions, know-how or further AI solutions, market shares and corporate image sales network, management, the value of human capital)where K_2 is the value of assets determined according to the complex-grade I balance sheet-based approach.

Intangible assets that are not accounted for and do not have a market value are:

- Strategy, concerning products and life cycle, customers, markets, market positioning, and market share achieved, orientation towards growth and partnership policies;
- Clients and market;
- Processes and innovation;
- The organization, which includes all the elements related to corporate governance;
- Human resources.

2.4 The Income Approach

Profitability valuation can be particularly appropriate when the company has a sufficiently defined profitability trend, or the approach is deemed reliable for company projections. Or even if the degree of capitalization is not high and there is a significant intangible component.

The income approach makes it possible to estimate the market value based on profits, which the company is deemed to be able to produce in future years.

This methodology is suitable for the evaluation of cyclical companies, which have very volatile incomes, but with a tendency to compensate for overtime. In the presence of cyclical companies, normalization is a process that can identify a stable trend line, underlying the volatile trend of income flows that occur in the various periods of management.

The fundamental elements in an evaluation of an income approach are:

- The estimate of normalized income (incorporating AI),
- The choice of the capitalization rate,
- The choice of the capitalization formula is based on the valuation time horizon that is adopted.

Estimated Normalized Income

As regards the determination of the income to be used as a basis for the valuation, reference is made to the average normalized value of income that the company is expected to produce permanently in future years, even considering the impact of AI. The influence of AI on companies' Estimated Normalized Income is subject to variability depending on various determinants. Although the integration of AI can improve a firm's value and robustness, shareholders' responses to announcements of AI investments might initially result in fluctuations in market value.

Therefore, it is not considered as a series of future incomes, but rather as the expected average normalized value able to reflect the company's average long-term income capacity, in a time horizon consistent with the business model.

Normalized income can be derived from:

- Study of the income statement (historical and perspective);

- Analysis of the financial structure (leverage);
- Consistency between the normalized operating result and the equity evaluation process;
- Normalized income, i.e., average perspective income;
- Alternatively, the evaluator may consider operating result/EBIT, pre-tax result, net income, and operating or net cash flow (if referring to a complementary financial approach).

It is essential to transform the net profit (income) into a "normalized and integrated value" capable of expressing the company's ability to generate income, through three corrective processes:

1. Normalization: this is an articulated process aimed primarily at:
    - Redistribute "extraordinary" income and expenses over time;
    - Eliminate "non-operating" income and expenses;
    - Neutralization of the effects caused by budgetary policies;
2. The integration of changes in the stock of intangible assets;
3. Neutralization of the distorting impacts of inflation, to avoid fictitious losses or profits that could affect the valuation process.

The longer the extension of the evaluation scenario, the likelier the distortions.

The normalization process aims to subtract a series of income components from randomness, to bring them back to a relationship of adequate competence (accrual) with the reference period.

Extraordinary income and expenses are significant and sometimes non-recurring, components of operating income. Extraordinary income may, for example, include the realization of substantial assets on the assets side, such as real estate.

Costs include the economic consequences of exceptional events, such as restructuring costs, costs arising from the effects of natural disasters, and plant removals.

These elements must be redistributed over time to express a measure of normalized income, not burdened by components that do not present the usual manifestation. The objective of the redistribution is to replace a random size with an average value to avoid some businesses being particularly underweighted and others overestimated.

The elimination of income and costs unrelated to ordinary operations must be carried out by bringing the values in the income statement to size in line with the market or practice.

As regards the neutralization of budgetary policies, reference is made to the fundamental estimates (amortization and depreciation, inventories, provisions for risks in industrial and commercial firms, fiscal policies).

The integration process is based on the observation of the dynamics of some values regarding intangible assets (adequately recorded or not in the accounts).

The neutralization of the distortive effects of inflation makes it possible to separate real outcomes from apparent and illusory results since they derive from the sum of values that are not uniform in monetary terms. The most commonly used corrections are as follows:

- The adjustment of the depreciation rates of fixed technical assets at reconstruction costs, i.e., to the updated values of recent estimates;
- Adoption of the LIFO procedure in the valuation of inventories of products, semi-finished products, and raw materials;
- Determination of economic results.

Choice of the Capitalization Rate

The capitalization rate of normalized income represents the opportunity cost of capital employed.

This rate depends on the expected return on the risk-free securities and the risk premium that the market is expected to require for the type of investment being valued. The expected return on risk-free securities is generally identified with that on government bonds. The market return refers to all risky investments available on the market. This is consistent with the Capital Asset Pricing Model.

An alternative criterion for determining the capitalization rate may be to base it on the cost of invested capital from the perspective of the purchaser.

In this case, the value of the company is understood as a series of future incomes that must be discounted based on the average cost of money for the purchaser. Its value, therefore, no longer depends on the degree of risk of the company.

The first approach of determining the rate of capitalization presents a theoretical–practical structure of greater importance but presupposes efficient financial markets since the entire evaluation is based on indicators that can be traced back to them.

Choice of the Capitalization Formula

The determination of the market value, through the discounting of income flows, occurs in many cases using the perpetual annuity formula since the company is an institution destined to last over time.

The attribution, instead, of limited duration to the production of income (from 3–5 to 8–10 years) is an assumption not verified in the business reality and tends to be arbitrary, considering the determination of the time boundary.

It is, therefore, possible to proceed with the calculation of the value of the firm, based on the average normalized value of the income flows, estimated synthetically, generated in protracted-time horizons.

Using the chosen capitalization period, one of these two formulas can be utilized:

- The limited capitalization:

$$W_2 = R\, a_{n\neg i} \tag{2.4}$$

- The unlimited capitalization:

$$W_1 = R/i \tag{2.5}$$

where:

- W is the market value of the company;
- R is the integrated normalized income;
- i is the income capitalization rate;
- n is the period (years) of limited capitalization.

Capitalized Earnings Method

The Capitalized Earnings Method relies on the assumption that the current normalized benefit stream (such as earnings or free cash flow) can be maintained into perpetuity and then capitalizes this stream using a capitalization rate, which can be either the weighted average cost of capital (WACC) or the cost of equity minus the perpetual growth rate:

1. **Normalization of Benefit Stream**:
   - Before applying the Capitalized Earnings Method, it is common to normalize or adjust the historical benefit stream to account for any irregularities, one-time events, or non-recurring items that may distort the true earnings or cash flow of the business.
2. **Assumption of Perpetual Growth**:
   - The method assumes that the current benefit stream can be sustained indefinitely into the future. This assumption implies that the business will continue to generate earnings or cash flows at the same level without significant changes.
3. **Capitalization Rate**:
   - The capitalization rate used in this method is a critical component. It reflects the rate of return expected by investors or the discount rate, depending on whether the WACC or cost of equity is used.
   - The perpetual growth rate (also known as the terminal growth rate) is typically subtracted from the capitalization rate to account for the assumed constant growth beyond the forecast period.
4. **Equivalent to DCF Analysis**:
   - The Capitalized Earnings Method is theoretically equivalent to performing a discounted cash flow (DCF) analysis with specific assumptions.
   - In essence, it simplifies the DCF analysis by assuming that the forecasted growth rate matches the perpetual growth rate and that profit margins remain constant.
5. **Limitations**:

- The method assumes that the business can maintain its current earnings or cash flow indefinitely, which may not be realistic in practice.
- The accuracy of the valuation heavily depends on the selection of the capitalization rate and the perpetuity growth rate, and small changes in these assumptions can significantly impact the valuation.

The Capitalized Earnings Method is a straightforward approach to valuing a business based on the assumption of perpetual growth in the current benefit stream. While it simplifies the complexity of a full DCF analysis, it should be used with caution, and careful consideration of the assumptions made is essential to ensure the reliability of the valuation results.

2.5 The Mixed Capital-Income Approach

The mixed approach (Fernandez, 2019b) is based on the belief that in the long term, the company's asset value is reflected in its earnings and is, therefore, based on the assumption that the use of assets, in the long run, generates an average normalized return.

For example, the mixed approach is suitable in the case of companies with significant equity holdings, which temporarily do not have a regular income capacity. In these cases, the mixed criterion can capture the value linked to the temporary ability for differential income, concerning the norm, under the hypothesis that the remuneration of the assets then returns to normal.

The market value of the company is estimated by referring to the adjusted equity, calculated based on the simple or complex balance sheet-based approach, and the value of the excess revenue (goodwill) that the company can produce compared to the average of the companies in the sector to which it belongs.

The mixed approach "may incorporate different analytical values, including net book value, liabilities, goodwill, and even some specific intangibles (e.g., brands, technologies, customer lists, etc.)".

The components of goodwill can include a variety of non-physical assets, such as a strong brand name, customer loyalty, positive customer relations, robust employee relations, and any patents or proprietary technology the company owns. An impairment loss indicates that the expected future economic benefits from the acquisition are lower than expected.

Goodwill reflects expectations about future profitability and other economic benefits that the acquiring company expects to achieve from the acquisition that is not otherwise reflected in the identifiable tangible and intangible assets. Because it is based on future expectations, measuring and valuing goodwill can be quite subjective and requires significant judgment. See also IVS 210, § 20.6.

This methodology allows combining the requirements of objectivity and verifiability, typical of the equity component, with those of rationality expressed by the estimate of expectations regarding the future income capacity of the company.

The integration of the equity estimate with the value of the goodwill (positive/goodwill or negative/badwill) can be particularly convenient when the profitability of the company shows deviations (positive or negative) concerning the level considered normal by the investors, expressed by the rate of remuneration.

The market value is, therefore, composed of both an equity component and an income component.

In this way, the value of the company is always included in an interval that has as its lower limit the net assets at liquidation value and as its upper limit the value of the company that can be determined by the income approach.

The mixed-income approach has two different formulations:

a. Average value;
b. Independent (autonomous) goodwill estimate.

The Average Value

The market value is determined as the average of the adjusted assets and the value obtained for the capitalization of income, using the perpetual capitalization formula.

$$W = \tfrac{1}{2}(K + R/i) = K + \tfrac{1}{2}(R/i - K) \tag{2.6}$$

where:

- K is the equity expressed at replacement cost according to the balance sheet-based approach. It is an adjusted capital measure, including intangible assets and capital gains, and considering any higher market values compared to the accounting data.
- R is the normalized income expected for the future.
- i is the normalized rate of return for equity, concerning both the level of operational risk borne by the company and the level of risk deriving from the financial structure chosen.

Autonomous Goodwill Estimate

The mixed balance sheet-based approach with an independent estimate of goodwill provides various alternatives, formulated concerning the different assumptions made for the projection and discounting of the over-returns to estimate the goodwill.

Limited Capitalization of Average Profit
It considers the market value as the adjusted equity plus the limited capitalization of the average profit (the difference between the expected income and the return on equity = goodwill):

$$W = K + a_{n\neg i*} (R - iK) \tag{2.7}$$

where:

- i = normalized rate about the type of investment. It expresses the measure of the return considered normal, considering the levels of risk incurred by the company.
- i^* = discount rate of the over-income.
- n = number of years, defined and limited.

Unlimited Capitalization of Average Profit
The market value is the sum of the adjusted net asset value plus goodwill calculated as the perpetual annuity of the surplus profits. It assumes that the company can generate extra profits for an indefinite period, to be taken with caution considering the intrinsically ephemeral nature of

goodwill, which over time inevitably tends to erode:

$$W = K + [(R - iK)/i*] \tag{2.8}$$

and provides for the replacement of $a_{n\neg i^*}$ with $1/i^*$.

2.6 Cash Is king: The Superiority of the Financial Approach

According to Peter Bernstein (Introduction to Rappaport & Mauboussin, 2021), "assets producing cash flows will ultimately return the owner's investment without depending on the whims of other investors. Even if those cash flows are some distance in the future, their prospects endow them with a present value. Financial markets are nothing more than arenas where investors who need cash today can obtain it by selling the present value of future cash flows to other investors willing to wait for the cash payoffs from their capital. The payment medium in this transaction is money. The crucial point: If you invest without expecting future cash flows, then you might as well collect art or play the slot machines".

The financial approach is based on the principle that the market value of the firm corresponds to the discounted value of the cash flows ("cash is king"). The determination of the cash flows is of primary importance in the application of the approach, as is the consistency of the discount rates adopted.

The doctrine (especially the Anglo-Saxon one) believes that the financial approach is the "ideal" solution for estimating the market value for limited periods. It is not possible to make reliable estimates of cash flows for longer periods. "The conceptually correct methods are those based on cash flow discounting" (Fernandez, 2019b); and "nowadays, the cash flow discounting method is generally used because it is the only conceptually correct valuation method".

There are two criteria for determining cash flows, respectively bringing (if appropriately discounted) to the estimate of the equity value or the enterprise value, as shown in Fig. 2.6. In the evaluation of CAPEX investments where the Net Present Value (NPV) is to be estimated, the two criteria can be assimilated, respectively, to the NPV_{equity} or $NPV_{project}$, where the former expresses the residual net return for the investing shareholders (as remuneration of the Equity Value), whereas the latter estimate

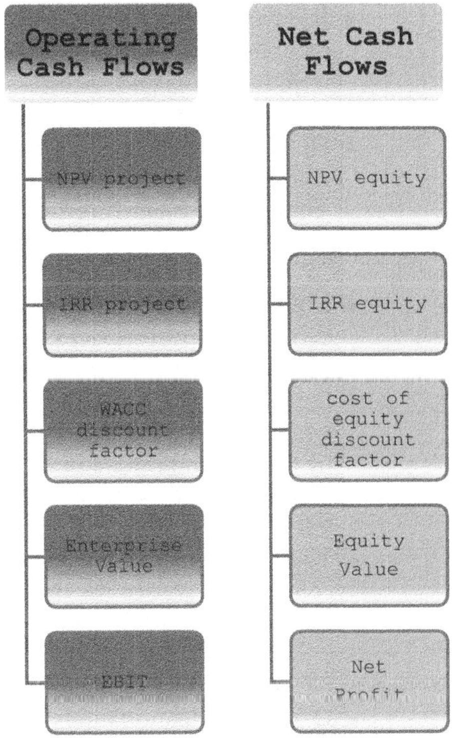

Fig. 2.6 Operating and net cash flows

the return for all the raised capital underwriters (shareholders + financial creditors). The Internal Rate of Return (IRR) is, mathematically, the break-even financial rate that makes the NPV = 0. In the income statement structure, operating cash flows can be compared to operating profit (= EBIT), and net cash flows to net profits.

Discounted Cash Flow (DCF), Leveraged Buyout (LBO), and Dividend Discount Model (DDM) are all cash flow-based approaches to estimate the value using:

1. Discounted Cash Flow (DCF):
   - DCF estimates the present value of a company's future cash flows.

- It involves forecasting the future cash flows generated by the business, including operating cash flows and sometimes terminal value, and then discounting those cash flows back to their present value using a discount rate.
- DCF analysis provides an intrinsic value for the company, to be compared to its current market price to determine whether the stock is undervalued or overvalued.

2. Leveraged Buyout (LBO):

- LBO is often used in acquisitions, where a private equity firm or investor acquires a company using a significant amount of debt financing.
- In an LBO, the purchaser models the future cash flows of the target company and indicates how much debt can be supported by those cash flows.
- The goal is to maximize the returns for the investors by using leverage to increase the potential equity returns.
- The valuation in an LBO depends on the ability of the target company to service the debt and generate cash flows to payoff the debt.

3. Dividend Discount Model (DDM):

- DDM is a valuation method used specifically for companies that pay dividends.
- It estimates the value using the present value of future dividend payments.
- The model considers that dividends will continue to scale up (the dividend growth rate) during an ideally infinite horizon.
- The discount rate used in DDM proxies the required rate of return that corresponds to the cost of equity.
- DDM is most appropriate for mature companies with stable and predictable dividend payments.

These methodologies allow analysts and investors to assess a firm's value company depending on its expected cash flows and its risk factors (embedded in the denominator of Discounted Cash Flows).

I. **The Cash Flow Available to Shareholders (Free Cash Flow to Equity—FCFE)**

It is a measure of cash flow that considers the financial structure of the firm (levered cash flow). It is the ultimate cash flow that remains after the payment of interest and the repayment of equity shares and after the coverage of equity expenditures necessary to maintain existing assets and to create the conditions for business growth. That is why it is also called "free" (= residually available) liquidity for the equity holders.

In M&A operations, the Free Cash Flow to the Firm (FCFF) (operating cash flow) is normally calculated, to estimate the Enterprise Value (comprehensive of financial debt). The residual Equity Value is then derived by subtracting the Net Financial Position.

The residual cash flow for the shareholders can be determined, starting from the net profit (Table 2.3):

Alternatively to this bottom-up calculation, the net cash flow can be calculated with top-down steps, starting from the sales (monetary revenues) in the income statement, arriving at the operating cash flow—see II. below) and eventually the net cash flow (see Table 2.4).

The discounting of the free cash flow for the shareholders takes place at a rate equal to the cost of the shareholders' equity, consistent with the representation of Fig. 2.7. This flow identifies the theoretical measure of the firm's ability to distribute dividends, even if it may not coincide with the dividend paid. The dividend policy of the firm influences the Dividend Discount Model, used as a proxy for calculating the cost of equity.

Table 2.3 Free cash flow to equity

Net profit (loss)
+ amortization/depreciation and provisions
+ divestments (− investments) in technical equipment
+ divestments (− investments) in other assets
+ decrease (− increase) in net operating working capital
+ increases (− decreases) in loans
+ equity increases (− decreases)
= Cash flows available to shareholders (net cash flow or free cash flow to equity—FCFE)

Table 2.4 Free cash flow to the firm

Net operating income (EBIT)
− taxes on operating income
+ amortization/depreciation and provisions (non-monetary operating costs)
+ technical divestments (− investments)
+ divestments (− investments) in other assets
+ decrease (− increase) in operating net working capital
= Cash flow available to shareholders and lenders (operating cash flow or free cash flow to the firm—FCFF)

II. The Cash Flow Available to the Firm (Free Cash Flow to the Firm—FCFF)

The second configuration of flows is used in the practice of Enterprise Value estimate.

It is a measure of cash flows independent of the financial structure of the firm (unlevered cash flows) that is particularly suitable to evaluate companies with high levels of indebtedness, or that do not have a debt plan (as happens in most debt-free startups). If the firm is debt-free, then FCFF ≈ FCFE, cost of debt ≈ cost of equity ≈ WACC, operating profit ≈ net profit, raised capital ≈ equity, ROE ≈ ROI, etc.

This methodology is based on the operating flows generated by the management of the firm, based on the operating income available for the remuneration of own and third-party means net of the relative tax effect. Unlevered cash flows are typically determined with a bottom-up procedure starting from the income statement by using operating income before taxes and financial charges:

The cash flow available to the firm is, therefore, determined as the cash flow available to shareholders, plus financial charges after tax, plus loan repayments and equity repayments, minus new borrowings and flows arising from equity increases. An example is given in Fig. 2.7.

The difference between the two approaches is, therefore, given by the different meanings of cash flows associated with debt and equity repayments. Debt service comes first unless the firm is debt-free: in this case, as anticipated above, FCFF = FCFE.

Cash flows from operating activities are discounted to present value at the weighted average cost of capital (WACC), analyzed in formula (2.12).

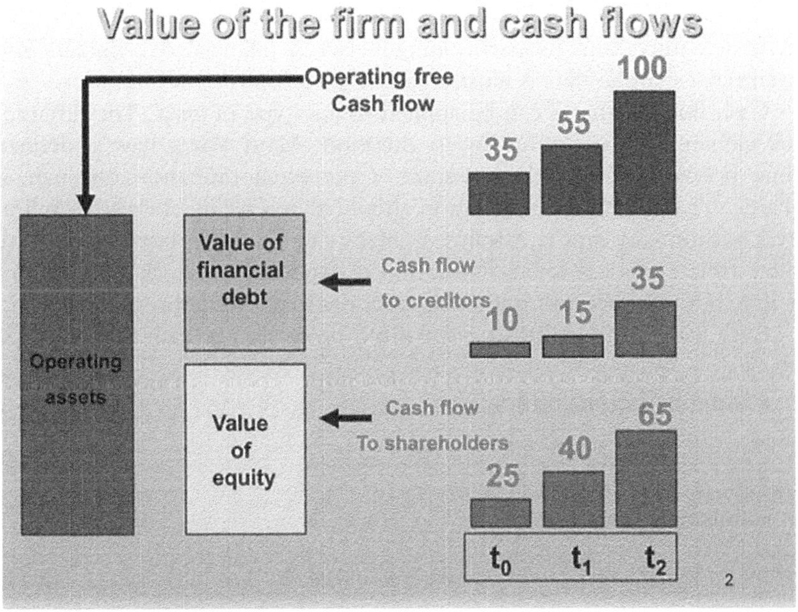

Fig. 2.7 Value of the firm and cash flows

This DCF metrics offers an evaluation of the whole firm, independently from its financial structure (whose impact is considered later, both in the income and cash flow statement). The value of the debt must be subtracted from the value of the firm to rejoin the market value of equity, obtained by discounting the residual cash flows available for the shareholders (FCFE).

The relationship between the two concepts of cash flow is consistent with Tables 2.3 and 2.4 and is as follows:

$$\begin{aligned}
&\text{cash flow available to the firm (FCFF)}\\
&\quad = \text{cash flow available to shareholders (FCFE)}\\
&\quad + \text{financial charges (net of taxes)}\\
&\quad + \text{loan repayments}\\
&\quad - \text{new loans}
\end{aligned} \tag{2.9}$$

An example of the Enterprise Value of the firm (value of financial debt + equity) and its partitioning between financial debtholders and eventually shareholders is illustrated in Fig. 2.7.

Cash flow estimates can be applied to any type of asset. The differential element is represented by its duration. Many assets have a defined time horizon, while others assume a perpetual time horizon such as shares. That is why firm valuation should theoretically always be unlimited, without any time constraint. In many cases, as it has been shown with the estimate of a limited capitalization of expected revenues (par. 2.5.), it is not, but only because unlimited forecasts may prove too subjective.

Cash flows (CF) utilizes a normalized projection of cash flows:

- unlimited capitalization:

$$W_1 = \mathrm{CF}/i \tag{2.10}$$

- limited capitalization:

$$W_2 = \mathrm{CF}\ a\ n\neg i \tag{2.11}$$

where W_1 and W_2 represent the present value of future cash flows. Depending on the numerator of the formula, W_1 or W_2 measures either the Enterprise Value or the Equity Value.

This formulation is like that of expected revenues (see formulae [2.4] and [2.5]), simply replacing expected revenues for forecast cash flows. Theoretical accountants claim that, in the long run, the projection of cash flows should converge to that of comparable revenue returns (and so, operating cash flow ≈ EBIT; net cash flow ≈ net profit). If so, income and financial methodologies should be converging to common estimates.

The discount rate to be applied to expected cash flows is determined as the sum of the cost of equity and the cost of debt, appropriately weighted according to the leverage of the firm (the ratio between financial debt and equity). This produces the Weighted Average Cost of Capital (WACC):

$$\mathrm{WACC} = k_i(1-t)\frac{D}{D+E} + k_e\frac{E}{D+E} \tag{2.12}$$

where:

k_i = cost of debt;

t = corporate tax rate;
D = market value of debt;
E = market value of equity;
$D + E$ = raised capital;
k_e = cost of equity.

The impact of AI on the determination of the WACC is primarily centered on enhancing the efficiency, accuracy, and depth of financial analysis. WACC, which represents a firm's cost of capital where each category of capital is proportionately weighted, is a crucial metric in corporate finance and investment:

1. **Improved Data Analysis and Forecasting**: AI and machine learning algorithms can process large amounts of data more efficiently than traditional methods. This capability allows for a better and comprehensive analysis of the elements influencing a firm's cost of equity and cost of debt, which are critical components of WACC.
2. **Enhanced Risk Assessment**: AI can provide more nuanced risk assessments by analyzing market trends, economic indicators, and firm-specific risk factors. This produces a better determination of the beta coefficient used in the Capital Asset Pricing Model (CAPM), which is often used to calculate the cost of equity.
3. **Automation of Repetitive Tasks**: The process of calculating WACC involves gathering and processing financial data, which can be repetitive and time-consuming. AI can automate these tasks, reducing the potential for human error and freeing up analysts to focus on more complex aspects of financial analysis.
4. **Dynamic Adjustment and Real-Time Analysis**: AI systems can continuously monitor market conditions and automatically adjust the WACC to reflect current economic and financial environments. This real-time analysis can be particularly useful for dynamic investment decision-making.
5. **Scenario Analysis and Predictive Modeling**: AI can enhance the ability to perform scenario analysis and predictive modeling, helping companies and investors understand how different market conditions or firm decisions might impact the WACC.
6. **Integration with Other Financial Models**: AI can integrate data relevant to WACC with other financial models and analyses,

providing a more holistic view of a firm's financial health and prospects.

7. **Customization and Precision**: AI algorithms can be trained to factor in industry-specific or firm-specific variables, leading to a more tailored and precise calculation of WACC.

The consistency between the numerator and the denominator in the discounted FCFF is evident since both parameters represent a mix of financial debt and equity.

The cost of debt capital is easy to determine, as it can be inferred from the financial statements of the firm, representing the ratio between negative interests and financial debt. The cost of equity or share capital, which represents the minimum rate of return required by investors for equity investments, is instead more complex and may use the Capital Asset Pricing Model or the Dividend Discount Model (see paragraph 2.7.1.). Equity is traditionally riskier than financial debt (whose periodical remuneration and payback are contractually predetermined), and so the cost of equity > cost of debt, and also the cost of equity > WACC.

Once the present value of the cash flows has been estimated, the market value (W) of the firm is:

a. the unlevered cash flow approach (to estimate the Enterprise Value):

$$W = \sum \frac{\mathrm{CF}_0}{\mathrm{WACC}} + \mathrm{TV} - D \tag{2.13}$$

b. the levered cash flow approach (to estimate the Equity Value):

$$W = \sum \frac{\mathrm{CF}_n}{K_e} + \mathrm{TV} \tag{2.14}$$

where:

$\sum \mathrm{CF}_0/\mathrm{WACC}$ = present value of operating cash flows (FCFF)
$\sum \mathrm{CF}_n/K_e$ = present value of net cash flows (FCFE)
TV = terminal (residual) value
D = initial net financial position (financial debt—liquidity)
WACC = average after-tax cost of a firm's various capital sources (cost of collecting external capital), including common

stock, preferred stock, bonds, and any other long-term financial debt.

What matters in formulae (2.13) and (2.14) is, once again, the consistency between the numerator and the denominator. Operating cash flows are unlevered since they are considered before debt service, and they so need to be discounted using an "operating" (unlevered) cost of capital that considers both the cost of debt and the residual cost of equity. Net cash flows are consistently discounted at the cost of equity since both the numerator and the denominator refer to the residual claims of the equity holders. Preferred equity is slightly safer than ordinary equity, as it commands a (small) premium and a priority in dividends—that is why a different cost of equity is used.

The utilization of AI technologies within companies has demonstrated a favorable influence on firm performance, encompassing firm value and productivity. The implementation of AI has been identified to yield notable and advantageous impacts on a firm's cost framework, specifically through AI-driven automation. Moreover, adopting AI has been associated with heightened total factor productivity. Integration of AI can optimize a firm's comprehensive efficacy and value, potentially shaping the WACC by enhancing profitability and productivity, thereby potentially decreasing the WACC of a firm that adopts AI. The WACC is the weighted average of the following cost of capital sources (Fig. 2.8):

The residual (terminal) value, more comprehensively described in paragraph 2.13., is the result of discounting the value at the time n (before which the cash flows are estimated analytically). It is often the greatest component of the global value W (above all in intangible-intensive companies) and tends to zero if the time horizon of the capitalization is infinite ($VR/\infty = 0$).

The two variants (levered versus unlevered) give the same result if the overall DCF value of the firm, determined through the cash flows available to the lenders (FCFF), is deducted from the value of the net financial debts. In this case: equity value = enterprise value ± net financial position.

Operating cash flows (unlevered—FCFF) and net cash flows for shareholders (levered—FCFE) are determined by comparing the last two balance sheets (to consider changes in operating Net Working Capital, fixed assets/CAPEX, financial liabilities, and shareholders' equity) with the income statement of the last year, as shown in Table 2.5. which illustrates the accounting scheme of the cash flow statement.

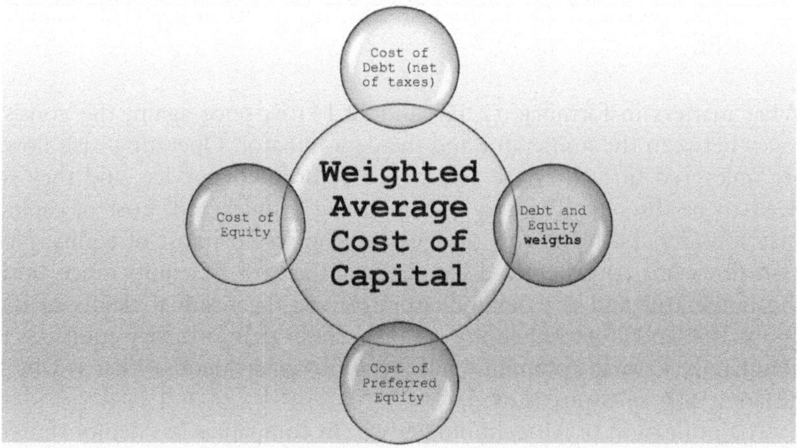

Fig. 2.8 WACC determinants

This cash flow statement is different from the scheme proposed by the international accounting principles (see, for instance, IAS 7) since it considers both the EBITDA and the Operating Cash Flows, whose importance for firm valuation emerges from this chapter. Even if both statements—the one proposed here and the IAS 7-compliant scheme—arrive at the same net result (FCFE), they show important differences "on the road".

The net cash flow for the shareholders coincides with the free cash flow to equity (FCFE) and, therefore, with the dividends that can be paid out, once it has been verified that enough internal liquidity resources remain in the firm to back its going concern perspectives. This feature, associated with the ability to raise equity from third parties and shareholders, allows the firm to find adequate financial coverage for the investments deemed necessary to maintain the firm's business continuity and remain on the market in economic conditions (minimum objectives). They should allow for the creation of incremental value in favor of the shareholders, who are the residual claimants (being, as subscribers of risky capital, the only beneficiaries of the variable net returns, which, as such, are residual and subordinate to the fixed remuneration of the other stakeholders).

The estimate of cash flows can be ideally applied to any activity.

Table 2.5 Cash flow statement and link with the cost of capital

Cash flow statement
EBIT (Operating Profit) + Depreciation and amortization
= EBITDA (A)
± Operating Net Working Capital ± Fixed assets (CAPEX)
= Operating cash flow (unlevered cash flow to the firm - FCFF) (B)
− Financial charges ± Net financial liabilities ± Extraordinary income and charges − Taxes ± Equity
= Net (free) cash flow to the shareholders (levered cash flow - FCFE) (C)
Reconciliation statement:
Closing cash and cash equivalents − Opening cash and cash equivalents
= Change in net cash flow = liquidity (D) = (C)

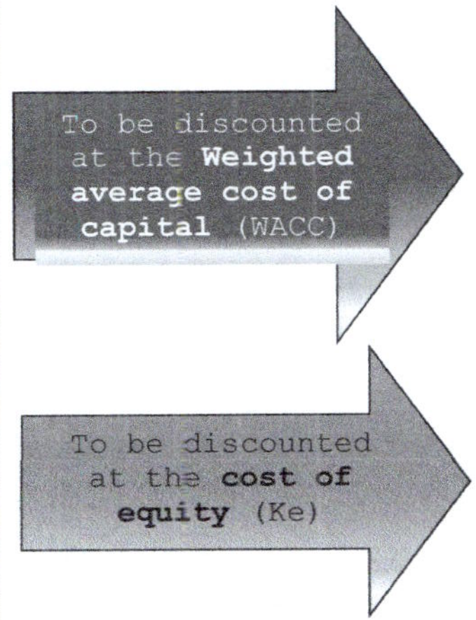

A core differential element is service life. Many activities have a defined time horizon, while others assume a perpetual time horizon such as firm shares, as anticipated.

The discounted cash flow (DCF) approach can be complemented with real options that incorporate intangible-driven flexibility in the forecasts. Real options improve the flexibility of capital budgeting estimates, fostering the NPV (higher resilience decreases the risk that is a major component of the discount factor in the denominator of DCF).

DCF is a foundational tool in the valuation of both tangible and intangible assets, reflecting its versatility and depth in handling complex valuation scenarios. This method's underlying principle involves estimating the present value of an asset based on the cash flows it is expected to generate in the future, adjusted for risk and the time value of money. Its widespread acceptance and use across different valuation contexts stem from its ability to integrate detailed financial forecasting with a systematic approach to risk assessment. (see also Singh, 2013).

The robustness of the model makes it suited to a multitude of valuations. Accounting standards across the globe recognize the efficacy of this model and advocate its use, wherever practicable. FAS 141 and 142 of the United States and IAS 39 which relate to the accounting of intangible assets recommend the use of DCF methodology for attributing a value to such assets.

The Capital Asset Pricing Model and the Dividend Discount Model

The Capital Asset Pricing Model (CAPM) is possibly the most celebrated corporate finance theorem, independently elaborated in 1964–1966 by William Sharpe (a Nobel laureate in Economics), John Lintner, and Jan Mossin, and based on the portfolio diversification insight (1952–1959) of Harry Markowitz, another Nobel Prize laureate.

The model is used to determine a theoretically appropriate required expected rate of return of a security that can be conveniently added to a well-diversified portfolio.

The model considers the asset's sensitivity to non-diversifiable risk (also known as systematic risk or market–idiosyncratic), often represented by the beta (β) coefficient, as well as the expected return of the market and the expected return of a theoretical risk-free asset:

$$\mathrm{ER}_i = R_f + \beta_i(\mathrm{ER}_m - R_f) \tag{2.15}$$

where:

ER_i = expected return on investment
R_f = risk-free rate of long-term Government bonds
β_i = beta coefficient of the investment (i) compared to the market return (m) = cov (i, m)/ s^2m
($ER_m - R_f$) = market risk premium (excess return of the stock market index over the risk-free Government bond)

The CAPM shows that the cost of equity capital is determined only by the beta coefficient. Despite its failing numerous empirical tests, and the existence of more modern approaches to asset pricing and portfolio selection (such as arbitrage pricing theory), the CAPM remains popular due to its simplicity and utility in a variety of situations. In practice, the CAPM sends an important message to firm valuators, considering the trade-off between risk and return: rational investors tend to maximize returns, minimizing risk.

Whenever a firm issues capital, it bears a cost of equity that corresponds to the return on equity for the shareholders (if transaction costs are not considered; otherwise, there is a small differential: e.g., cost of equity 10%, transaction cost 0.1%, return on equity 9.9%). Investors (potential shareholders) look for the market (and not book value) returns, comparing different investment opportunities—hence the concept of "opportunity" cost of capital.

Even if CAPM assumptions rarely hold in the real world (where the rigid assumptions of the original model are inapplicable, should tax, transaction costs, risky bonds, etc. be introduced), the model still holds most of its utility, remembering that the risk-return trade-off remains valid. In corporate appraisal, extensive use of beta coefficients and the basic CAPM formulation represents a common practice to estimate the cost of capital.

Fernandez (2019a) claims that "The CAPM is an absurd model because its assumptions and its predictions/conclusions have no basis in the real world. The use of CAPM is also a source of litigation: many professors, and lawyers ... get nice fees because many professionals use CAPM instead of common sense to calculate the required return to equity. Users of the CAPM make many illogical errors valuing companies, accepting/rejecting investment projects, evaluating fund performance, pricing goods, and services in regulated markets, calculating value creation…".

The Dividend Discount Model is an alternative method of valuing a firm's stock price considering the sum of all its future dividend payments, discounted back to their present value. It is used to value stocks based on the net present value of the future dividend streams, discounted back to their present value, as shown in formula (2.16).

The multi-stage dividend discount model estimates the intrinsic value of a stock by identifying different growth phases of a stock; projecting dividends per share for each period in the high growth phase and discounting them to the valuation date, finding terminal value at the start of the stable growth phase using the Gordon growth model, discounting it back to the valuation date and adding it to the present value of the high-growth phase dividends.

The Multi-Stage Dividend Discount Model (DDM) refines the Constant-Growth Dividend Discount Model (also known as the Gordon Growth Model) by accommodating variations in the dividend growth rate over time, instead of assuming a single, constant growth rate indefinitely. This adjustment allows for a more nuanced and realistic estimation of a stock's intrinsic value, especially for companies whose dividend growth rate is expected to change due to factors like business maturity, market conditions, or company-specific events.

The cost of equity (a part of the denominator of the DCF formula) should ideally be decreasing across time, as initial high growth rates coincide with the startup phase where equity risk is higher (also due to the lower level of leverage that normally characterizes this phase).

The Dividend Discount Model (DDM), (see Damodaran, 1996), is indeed a foundational approach in finance for valuing a company's stock. The model assumes that a stock's intrinsic value is equal to the sum of its future dividends, discounted back to its present value. The Gordon Growth Model, a variant of the DDM, simplifies the valuation by assuming that dividends grow at a constant rate indefinitely. This model is particularly useful for companies that are in a stable growth phase and have a history of paying dividends. The formula is:

$$P = D_1 / (R - g) \tag{2.16}$$

where P is the stock price, D_1 is the dividend per share for the next year, R is the required rate of return, and g is the dividend growth rate.

This model embeds constant growth which is a theoretical oversimplification of the real world.

In synthesis, it may be remembered that the CAPM is often used to extrapolate a market proxy of the opportunity cost of equity, whereas the DDM is less diffused (albeit frequently used in some industries, for instance in the banking sector). Some practitioners consider as a further proxy the Return on Equity (based on the ratio between the net profit over the equity of the firm), a ratio that is much easier to figure out, even if it relies on book values that misinterpret the investor's preference for market returns.

Free Cash Flow Planning

Free cash flow planning is a comprehensive and structured approach used in business valuation and financial analysis:

1. **Information Gathering**:
    - Collect all relevant information, both internal and external, for cash flow planning.
    - Internal information includes firm-specific data and strengths/weaknesses analysis.
    - External information covers industry trends, market conditions, and macroeconomic forecasts.
    - Past and deadline-related data serve as a basis for future projections.
2. **Analysis of Past Performance**:
    - Analyze historical financial statements, cash flow statements, and income statements.
    - Normalize historical data by adjusting for one-time or extraordinary items.
    - Assess factors contributing to past earnings and their potential impact on future earnings.
    - Analyze the operating environment, including market dynamics and external factors.
3. **Planning (Phase Method)**:

- Project future cash flows, typically in nominal terms.
- Develop an integrated business plan that summarizes projected financials.
- Use a phased approach for planning, which may include detailed and simplified phases.
- The detailed planning phase often spans 3–5 years, while simplified phases consider longer-term factors.
- Consider terminal value for periods beyond detailed planning, assuming constant cash flows or growth.

4. **Terminal Year and Assumptions**:

   - Terminal year plays a significant role in valuation; ensure assumptions are critical and consistent.
   - Assess long-term profitability and the ability to generate returns that meet or exceed the cost of capital.
   - Explain reasons for assumptions that imply returns exceeding the cost of capital.
   - Assumptions regarding returns, growth rates, and reinvestment should align with each other.

5. **Plausibility Assessment**:

   - Evaluate formal plausibility by analyzing the documentation and process of preparing the plan.
   - Check for computational accuracy and consistency among sub-plans.
   - Assess material plausibility by critically evaluating underlying assumptions.
   - Identify and scrutinize key value-influencing assumptions.
   - Ensure that planning is derived logically from assumptions and takes all consequences into account.
   - Compare assumptions to past analyses and previous forecasts for reliability.

6. **Insolvency Risk Consideration**:

   - Assess insolvency risk by considering insolvency probabilities, which may be obtained from ratings or other sources.
   - Evaluate how insolvency risk might impact cash flow projections.

This structured approach to financial projections and plausibility assessment is essential for estimating a firm's value accurately. It helps ensure that assumptions are well-founded, calculations are accurate, and the overall projection aligns with historical performance and market conditions.

Adjusted Present Value

The Adjusted Present Value (APV) method accounts for the impact of financial leverage and taxes on the value of a business. It estimates the total value of a business by combining the value of its unlevered operations (assuming it is entirely financed by equity) and the tax shield savings resulting from debt financing:

1. **Calculate the Unlevered Business Value**:
    - Estimate the market value of the business if it were entirely financed by equity. This is done by discounting the free cash flows generated by the unlevered business at the cost of equity for that business.
    - The cost of equity for the unlevered business typically incorporates the risk associated with its core operations and is not influenced by the firm's capital structure.
2. **Calculate the Tax Shield**:
    - Determine the tax savings (tax shield) resulting from the tax deductibility of interest payments on debt in each period.
    - Discount tax shields to assess their present value by applying a risk-adjusted discount factor.
    - The tax shields represent the value created by using debt financing, as interest expenses are tax-deductible.
3. **Calculate the Total Capital Value**:
    - Sum the market value of the unlevered business and the present value of the tax shields. This represents the total value of the business's capital, considering both equity and debt financing.
4. **Determine the Equity Value**:

- Subtract the market value of debt from the total capital value to arrive at the market value of the equity capital (equity value).
- This is the value of the firm's equity that would be available to shareholders after accounting for the impact of debt financing and tax shields.

Some key points to note are the following:

- The APV method allows for a more flexible and detailed analysis of the effect of leverage and taxes on a firm's value compared to conventional valuation methods like the DCF method.
- Unlike the DCF method, which uses the WACC to discount cash flows, the APV method uses a specific cost of equity for the unlevered business.
- The cost of equity may need to be derived or adjusted from the cost of equity for the leveraged business, which can be obtained from the market.
- The APV method is useful when a firm's capital structure significantly changes.

The APV method estimates the value of a business under changing capital structures.

The APV approach and the DCF method that incorporates the WACC are conceptually similar in that both are used to value a firm's future cash flows. However, the key distinction lies in how they treat the impact of debt and taxes:

1. **DCF with WACC**:
    - In the DCF WACC method, the firm's cash flows are discounted using a single discount rate represented by the WACC.
    - The WACC incorporates the cost of equity and the cost of debt, reflecting the firm's current financial leverage.
    - The tax benefits of debt are indirectly considered within the WACC calculation because the cost of debt is reduced by the tax shield that derives from deductible interest expense.
2. **APV Method**:

- In the APV method, the firm is hypothetically treated as unleveraged or "all-equity financed" initially.
- The value of the firm's debt-free operations is determined by discounting cash flows at the cost of equity for the unleveraged business.
- The tax savings value resulting from debt financing (the "tax shield") is estimated separately.
- The tax shield represents the present value of the tax benefits from interest expense deductions and is added to the unleveraged value to determine the total firm value.

The key advantage of the APV method is that it explicitly separates the impact of debt and taxes from the core business operations. This separation allows for a more detailed and flexible analysis of the value drivers related to capital structure decisions.

While both the DCF WACC and APV methods are used for business valuation, the APV method is more specific in the granular assessment of the impact of debt and tax shields by considering them separately from the core business value.

CAPEX, Net Working Capital, and the Firm's Profitability

Both Capital Expenditure (CAPEX) and (operating) net working capital are considered before the free cash flow to the firm (FCFF):

EBITDA
$\pm \Delta$ CAPEX
$\pm \Delta$ Operating Net Working Capital ($NWC_{operating}$)
= Free Cash Flow to the Firm (FCFF) (unlevered cash flow/ operating cash flow)

They may so be considered the same in the assessment of the FCFF, as any increase in their value is an invested capital activity that absorbs liquidity and needs appropriate backing from the raised capital, in the form of equity + financial debt.

They are complementary as they have different properties: the real engine behind long-term growth is represented by the CAPEX, whereas the Operating Net Working Capital is only complementary, as it accompanies short-term growth, with its liquidity impact that is ancillary to sales (with the accounts receivable and stock) and purchases (accounts payable).

The invested capital, backed by the raised capital, is the productivity input that fuels the output, represented by the revenues and costs accounted for in the income statement. The matching of the balance sheet differential with the income statement produces the cash flow statement, whose milestones are represented by the EBITDA, the FCFF, and the FCFE (free cash flow to equity). The cash flow indicates the financial remuneration of the raised capital (financial debt, and, residually, the equity). The overall picture is shown in Fig. 2.5.

The firm raises funds (capital and debt) from investors (debtholders and shareholders); funds raised are invested in fixed assets and net working capital, which generates an operating result and then the cash flows for investors (Fig. 2.9).

CAPEX and Operating Net Working Capital are both essential elements in the financial management of a firm, impacting its future growth and profitability, but they serve different purposes and have distinct impacts.

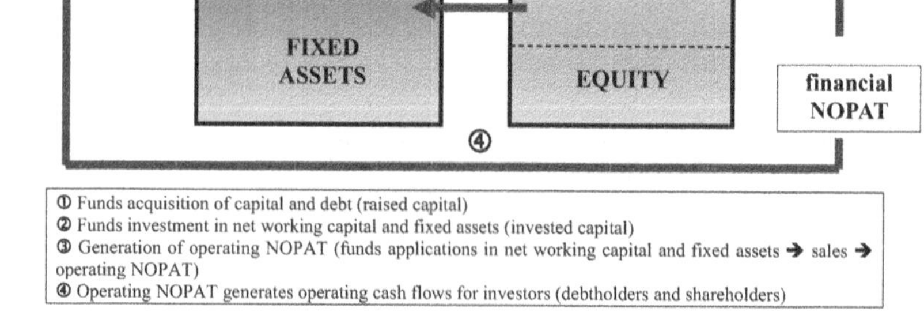

Fig. 2.9 The financial-economic cycle

1. **Impact of CAPEX on Future Growth and Profitability**:
   - **CAPEX**: This refers to funds used by a firm to acquire, upgrade, and maintain physical assets such as property, industrial buildings, or equipment. It is often used to undertake new projects or investments.
   - **Future Growth**: By investing in CAPEX, a firm can expand its operational capacity, or improve its efficiency.
   - **Profitability**: While CAPEX produces higher future profits, it also involves significant upfront costs.
2. **Operating Net Working Capital and Its Role**:
   - **Operating Net Working Capital**: This consists of current assets (like inventory and accounts receivable) minus current liabilities (like accounts payable). It is essential for the daily operations of a business.
   - **Liquidity and Operations**: Effective management of working capital ensures that a firm has sufficient liquidity to meet its current obligations and operational needs.
3. **Comparison and Complementarity**:
   - **Different Objectives**: CAPEX focuses on long-term growth and expansion whereas working capital management is about efficiently running daily operations.
   - **Complementary Nature**: In practice, these two aspects are complementary. Efficient working capital management can free up cash flows that can be invested in CAPEX. Conversely, wise investments in CAPEX can improve operational efficiency, potentially reducing the need for large working capital.
   - **Risk and Return Balance**: Firms need to balance the higher risks and potential long term returns of CAPEX with the immediate necessity and lower risk of managing working capital. This balance is essential for sustainable growth and profitability.

While CAPEX and operating net working capital serve different functions within a firm, they are interconnected. Strategic investment in CAPEX can drive future growth and profitability, but this needs to be balanced with effective management of working capital to ensure ongoing operational efficiency and financial stability.

The impact of AI on CAPEX productivity growth compared to net working capital increase can vary depending on how AI is implemented and utilized within a specific business context. Here are some potential ways in which AI can affect these two aspects:

1. CAPEX Productivity Growth with AI:
    - Improved Decision-Making: AI can enhance decision-making processes related to capital expenditure by analyzing large amounts of data, predicting market trends, and identifying investment opportunities with higher potential returns. This produces a more informed and efficient allocation of capital resources.
    - Predictive Maintenance: AI-powered predictive maintenance systems can optimize the maintenance of physical assets, reducing downtime and extending the lifespan of equipment. This produces cost savings and increased productivity.
    - Automation: AI-driven automation in manufacturing and production processes can improve efficiency and reduce the need for additional capital investments in expanding production capacity. This produces higher productivity without significant CAPEX spending.
2. Net Working Capital Increase with AI:
    - Inventory Management: AI can optimize inventory management by forecasting demand, reducing excess inventory, and minimizing carrying costs. This unlocks cash incorporated in inventory and improves working capital turnover.
    - Accounts Receivable and Payable Automation: AI can automate invoicing, credits, and debt processes, reducing the necessary time to cash in payments and manage vendor relationships.
    - Fraud Detection: AI is useful in the detection of fraudulent activities in financial transactions, preventing losses and preserving working capital.
3. Comparison and Balance:

- Complementarity: AI can enhance the efficiency of both CAPEX decision-making and working capital management. For example, if AI helps identify cost-saving opportunities in CAPEX projects, the funds saved can be used to strengthen working capital. Similarly, improved working capital management can free up funds for strategic CAPEX investments.
- Risk Management: While AI can assist in risk assessment and mitigation, it is important to recognize that AI technologies may also introduce new risks, such as data security and privacy concerns. Therefore, businesses must carefully balance the risks and rewards of AI adoption in both CAPEX and working capital management.

AI has the potential to positively impact both CAPEX productivity growth and net working capital increase by enhancing decision-making, optimizing processes, and improving overall financial efficiency. However, the specific impact will depend on the industry, business model, and how effectively AI technologies are integrated into the organization's operations and financial management strategies. It is essential to assess the potential benefits and risks of AI adoption in these areas and develop a holistic strategy that considers both CAPEX and working capital needs.

2.7 Empirical Approaches (Transaction Multiples and Market Comparables)

Transaction multiples valuation, also known as market-based valuation or comparable firm analysis (CCA), is an appraisal approach that assesses the value of a business by comparing it to similar firms that have recently been sold or are publicly traded:

1. **Comparative Analysis**:
   - Transaction multiples valuation compares the financial metrics (multiples) of the target firm to those of comparable firms in the same sector.
   - Frequent multiples include Price to Sales (P/S), Price-to-EBITDA (P/EBITDA), Price-to-Earnings (P/E), and Price-to-Book Value (P/B), among others.
2. **Plausibility and Validation**:

- Transaction multiples are often used for plausibility checks and validation together with other valuation methods, such as DCF or industry-specific trade multiples.
- Whencomplementary valuation methods converge or are consistent with the transaction multiples, it can increase confidence in the valuation.

3. **Factors Affecting Multiples**:

- Transaction multiples are influenced by various elements, including:
  - Industry: Some industries command higher or lower multiples due to their growth prospects, competitive dynamics, and risk profiles.
  - Company Size: Smaller companies might have different valuation multiples if confronted to larger ones.
  - Market Conditions: Economic conditions and market sentiment can impact multiples.
  - Company-Specific Factors: Differences in growth rates, profitability, and risk profiles among comparable companies produce variations in multiples.

4. **Growth Industries and Multiples**:

- Fast-growing industries often command higher multiples because investors may pay a premium for firms with strong growth potential.
- Mature or slow-growth industries may have lower multiples.

5. **Limitations**:

- While transaction multiples can provide valuable insights, they have limitations. Comparable transactions may be scarce, especially for private companies.
- Multiples are backward-looking and may not fully account for future growth prospects and specific firm attributes.

6. **Valuation Process**:

- It typically identifies a set of comparable companies, calculating their multiples, and then applying those multiples to the financial ratios of the target firm.

- Careful selection of comparable companies is essential, and adjustments could be needed to consider differences between the target and comparables.

Transaction multiples valuation is a valuable tool for estimating the business value by benchmarking it against similar firms in the market. It can provide a quick and useful indication of a firm's worth, but it should be compared with complementary valuation methods and always with a critical eye towards the specific circumstances and comparables chosen. Transaction multiples play a pivotal role in influencing the valuation of firms that adopt AI. Various factors, such as the perception of increased value, cost reduction, and improvements in market structure, can facilitate data transactions between buyers and providers, consequently affecting the valuation of firms that adopt AI. As a result, a comprehensive understanding and strategic utilization of transaction multiples are imperative for AI-adopting firms to evaluate and improve their valuation within the market effectively.

The market value represents:

a. The value attributable to a share of the equity, expressed at stock exchange prices;
b. The price of the controlling interest or the entire share equity;
c. The traded value for the controlling equity of comparable undertakings.

The impact of AI in assessing market value, particularly in the contexts mentioned (a through d), is significant and multifaceted. AI can enhance the process of determining market value in several ways, especially when comparing companies within the same sector with similar financial characteristics:

1. **Enhanced Data Processing and Analysis (a and d)**: AI can efficiently process and analyze large amounts of stock exchange data, including historical prices, trading volumes, and market trends. This capability allows for a better understanding of the equity value (as per option a) and the value derived from stock exchange quotations of comparable undertakings (as per option d).

2. **Improved Valuation Models (b and c)**: For determining the price of controlling interests (b) and the traded value for the controlling equity of comparable undertakings (c), AI can refine valuation models by incorporating a broader range of variables and data points. This produces more precise estimations of a firm's worth in a control transaction.
3. **Predictive Analytics for Market Trends**: AI foresees future market trends and stock performance by analyzing current and historical data. This predictive capability is valuable in estimating the potential future value of a firm.
4. **Sector-Specific Analysis**: When comparing companies within the same sector, AI can be particularly effective in identifying and analyzing key sector-specific indicators and benchmarks. This includes analyzing cash flows, sales, costs, and other relevant financial metrics.
5. **Risk Assessment**: AI can provide a more detailed and sophisticated analysis of risk factors associated with different market scenarios or specific business models. This helps in better understanding the potential volatility in market values.
6. **Real-time Market Monitoring**: AI tools can monitor market conditions in real-time, providing up-to-date information that can impact the valuation of a firm's equity.
7. **Customization and Scalability**: AI models can be customized to account for the unique aspects of different industries and companies, making them more applicable and accurate for sector-specific comparisons.
8. **Automation and Efficiency**: By automating the data collection and analysis process, AI significantly reduces the time and effort required to conduct comprehensive market analyses, thereby increasing efficiency.

Sometimes comparable trades of companies belonging to the same product sector with similar characteristics (in terms of cash flows, sales, costs, etc.) are used.

In practice, an examination of the prices used in negotiations with companies in the same sector leads to quantifying average parameters:

- *Price/EBIT*

- *Price/cash-flow*
- *Price/book value*
- *Price/earnings*
- *Price/dividend*

These ratios seek to estimate the average rate to be applied to the firm being assessed. However, there may be distorting effects of prices based on special interest rates, on a historical context, on difficulties of comparison, etc.

In financial market practice, the multiples methodology is frequently applied. Based on multiples, the firm's value is derived from the market price profit referring to comparable listed companies, such as net profit, before tax or operating profit, cash flow, equity, or turnover.

The attractiveness of the multiples approach stems from its ease of use: multiples can be used to obtain quick but dirty estimates of the firm's value and are useful when there are many comparable companies listed on the financial markets and the market sets correct prices for them on average.

Because of the simplicity of the calculation, these indicators are easily manipulated and susceptible to misuse, especially if they refer to companies that are not entirely similar. Since there are no identical companies in terms of entrepreneurial risk and growth rate, the assumption of multiples for the processing of the valuation can be misleading, bringing "fake multipliers".

The use of multiples can be implemented through:

A. Use of fundamentals;
B. Use of comparable data:

    B.1. Comparable companies;
    B.2. Comparable transactions.

The first approach links multiples to the fundamentals of the firm being assessed: profit growth and cash flow, dividend distribution ratio, and risk. It is equivalent to the use of cash flow discounting approaches.

In some industries, products protected by intangibles can become obsolete or uncompetitive in a relatively short period in the absence of continuing development and enhancement of the intangibles. As a result, having access to updates and enhancements can be the difference between deriving a short-term advantage from the intangibles and deriving a longer-term advantage.

When evaluating and accounting for intangible assets, it is crucial to assess various risks that can impact their value. These risks reflect the uncertainties surrounding the future benefits that these assets are expected to generate. Understanding and mitigating these risks are essential for accurate valuation and effective management of intangibles. By carefully considering these risks, organizations can more accurately value their intangible assets and develop strategies to mitigate potential adverse impacts, thereby safeguarding their value and ensuring sustained competitive advantage.

For the second approach, it is necessary to distinguish whether it is a valuation of comparable companies or comparable transactions.

The comparability concerns different firms but is also related to their contents. Intangible assets are however often hard to compare.

In the case of comparable companies, the approach estimates multiples by observing similar companies. The problem is to determine what is meant by similar companies. In theory, the analyst should check all the variables that influence the multiple.

In practice, companies should estimate the most likely price for a non-listed firm, taking as a reference some listed companies, operating in the same sector and considered homogeneous. Two companies can be defined as homogeneous when they present the same risk, similar characteristics, and expectations.

The calculation is:

- A firm whose price is known (P_1),
- A variable closely related to its value (X_1)

the ratio $(P_1)/(X_1)$ is assumed to apply to the firm to be valued, for which the size of the reference variable (X_2) is known.

Therefore:

$$(P_1)/(X_1) = (P_2)/(X_2) \tag{2.17}$$

so that the desired value P_2 will be:

$$P_2 = X_2\,[(P_1)/(X_1)] \tag{2.18}$$

The main factors to establish whether a firm is comparable are:

- Size;
- Belonging to the same sector—See for instance the Statistical Classification of Economic Activities in the European Community, commonly referred to as NACE;
- Financial risks (leverage);
- Historical trends and prospects for the development of results and markets;
- Geographical diversification;
- Degree of reputation and credibility;
- Management skills;
- Ability to pay dividends.

Founded on comparable transactions, the basis of valuation is information about actual negotiations (or mergers) of similar—i.e., comparable—companies.

The use of profitability parameters is usually considered to be the most representative of firm dynamics.

Among the empirical criteria, the approach of the multiplier of the EBITDA (Earnings Before Interest, Taxes, Depreciation, and Amortization) is widely diffused, to which the net financial position must be added algebraically, to pass from the estimate of the enterprise value (total value of the firm) to that of the equity value (value of the net assets). The formulation is as follows:

$$\begin{aligned} W &= \text{average perspective EBITDA} * \text{Enterprise Value/sector EBITDA} \\ &= \text{Enterprise Value of the Firm} \end{aligned} \tag{2.19}$$

And then:

$$\text{Equity Value} = \text{Enterprise Value} \pm \text{Net Financial Position} \tag{2.20}$$

2.8 The Control Approach

Once the most suitable evaluation approach has been defined, it might be appropriate to use another evaluation approach, to double-check the evaluation carried out with the main approach.

The use of a control approach is applied in all cases where it is possible to estimate the market value of the firm from complementary angles to arrive at a range of values, within which the market value must be positioned.

The comparison between the "main approach" and the "control" approach produces significant differences in absolute terms, especially if the reference values are high. It is, however, to be considered appropriate if, from a relative point of view, the deviations between the two approaches do not exceed an indicative percentage in the order of 20–25%.

2.9 The Accounting Value of Intangible Assets

Intangibles represent a constant challenge for accountants, due to the tension between reliability and relevance, especially in the context of financial reporting and valuation. Intangible assets, such as intellectual property, brand value, and customer relationships, play an increasingly critical role in the value and competitiveness of businesses. However, accounting for these assets remains fraught with challenges due to their inherent characteristics. Addressing the challenges posed by intangible assets requires a balanced approach that enhances the relevance of financial statements without sacrificing reliability (see also Singh, 2013).

As the intangibles are non-monetary assets with no physical form, it is difficult to find evidence for their existence. Intangible assets may be recorded as an asset in the balance sheet if future economic benefits can be expected.

The criteria for an intangible asset to be identifiable and thus recognized in the financial statements are critical for both accounting and reporting purposes. These criteria help ensure that only assets that can likely provide future economic benefits to the company are included on the balance sheet. These criteria ensure that intangible assets are recognized consistently and reliably across entities, providing stakeholders with clearer insights into a company's value and operations (see IAS 38.12).

The requirement for an intangible asset to be "identifiable" is included to distinguish the asset from the (internally generated) goodwill that cannot be recorded.

Many intangibles will not be recognized in the financial statements as they fail to meet the definition of an asset or the recognition criteria. Examples include staff training, brand building through advertising, and the development of new business processes. As no asset is recognized because of expenditure on such activities, it will be reported as an expense, even though it is undertaken to enhance the financial returns in subsequent accounting periods (Lennard, 2018; Lev and Gu, 2016).

Financial statements can only deal with those intangibles that meet the definition of assets and satisfy the recognition criteria, as set out in the IASB's Conceptual Framework.

Intangibles can be acquired by:

a. Separate purchase;
b. Being part of a business combination;
c. Government grant;
d. Exchange of assets, and
e. Self-creation (internal generation).

IAS 38 permits intangible assets to be recognized at fair value, measured by reference to an active market. While acknowledging that such markets may exist for assets such as "freely transferable taxi licenses, fishing licenses or production quotas", it states that "it is uncommon for an active market to exist for an intangible asset".

The observations by Lev (2016) highlight critical issues in the accounting and valuation of intangible assets, reflecting broader challenges in financial reporting. These challenges stem from the accounting principles and practices that govern how intangible assets are recognized, measured, and disclosed in financial statements.

These inconsistencies severely impair the capacity to rely on the accounting data to infer the market value of the intangibles.

The accounting treatment is nevertheless a prerequisite for valuation. The issue is very complex, given that intangible assets are often not directly accounted for in the balance sheet or, in some cases, only appear in the income statement, within the operating expenses (OPEX).

In the attribution of value to intangible assets, it is necessary to consider the income capacity they generate, without which it is difficult to assign a specific value to the "intangible".

The accounting treatment and the consequent under-representation in the balance sheet of the real value of the intangibles often implies the necessity to appraise the growth opportunities that are naturally embedded in the intangibles.

Another accounting issue concerns the net present value of growth opportunities (NPVGO) which calculates the net present value of all future cash flows involved with the growth opportunities of the firm. The NPVGO is not recorded in the balance sheet and is used to determine the intrinsic value of these opportunities to determine how much of the firm's current per-share value is determined by them. The estimation of NPVGO is consistent with the appraisal of the intrinsic value of the real options linked to the intangible assets.

According to Damodaran (2018), the firms with intangible assets have the following characteristics:

a. Inconsistent accounting rules that prudentially prevent capitalization of most operating expenses (OPEX);
b. Conservative financing since intangibles lack any physical collateral;
c. Extensive use of stock options to remunerate the management;
d. The compressed life cycle of tech firms grows faster and stays mature for shorter periods (Damodaran, 2018).

2.10 Valuation Drivers, Overcoming the Accounting Puzzle

The increasing significance of intangible assets represents a complex challenge for accounting practices, standard-setters, and businesses alike. As the economic landscape evolves, with technology, branding, and intellectual property playing central roles in the creation of value, the traditional accounting framework, which heavily favors tangible assets, increasingly misrepresents the true value and financial health of companies. This misalignment has profound implications for investors, managers, and policymakers, as it impacts decision-making, business valuation, and even the broader economy (see also Lev, 2018).

The two biggest challenges in accounting principles are probably represented by the valuation of intangible assets and derivatives. Concerning the former, the international accounting standards (IAS, IFRS) have long adopted a strict view, and the capitalization of intangibles is admitted in very limited cases (such as development costs if they show an expected useful life). This approach privileges prudence over representativeness and may underestimate the real value of the intangibles.

Capitalized intangibles are part of the Capital Expenditure (CAPEX), whereas intangible costs recorded in the income statement are part of the monetary OPEX. Amortization is a non-monetary operating cost that reduces the balance value of the intangible CAPEX.

The two most common valuation approaches for the estimate of the enterprise value are based on the operating cash flows discounted at the WACC or on the EBITDA times a multiple of comparable firms.

The following formulation recalls the two methodologies (for simplicity, DCF does not consider any terminal value):

$$\begin{aligned}
&\text{Enterprise Value} \\
&= \sum_{i=1}^{n} \frac{\text{sales} - \text{monetary OPEX} \pm \Delta\ \text{Net Working Capital} \pm \Delta\ \text{CAPEX}}{(1+\text{WACC})^{n}} \\
&= \frac{\text{Operating Cash Flow}}{(1+\text{WACC})^{n}} \\
&\cong \left(\text{basic EBITDA} + \text{intangible} - \text{driven EBITDA}\right) * \text{market multiplier}
\end{aligned} \tag{2.23}$$

Intangibles impact sales (due to the scalability effect), monetary OPEX (cost of not-capitalized intangibles, net of the savings from synergies), and the CAPEX (capitalized intangibles less the yearly amortization).

The DCF formulation estimates the Enterprise Value of the firm discounting its Operating Cash Flow at the WACC. Since the Operating Cash flow includes both the monetary OPEX represented by the intangibles (intangible costs net of the synergies) and the intangible part of the CAPEX (incremental CAPEX due to the intangible capitalized investments net of the yearly amortization), the numerator of the DCF formula is not affected by the accounting policies of the firm.

The book value of the intangible assets is expressed by the information available from the balance sheet, income statement, and cash flow statement, following the format shown in Fig. 2.10, which comprehensively represents the different valuation approaches.

2.11 Intangible Assets Valuation According to IVS 210

According to IVS 210 § 20.1. "*an intangible asset is a non-monetary asset that manifests itself by its economic properties. It does not have physical substance but grants rights and economic benefits to its owner*".

§ 20.3. indicates that there are many intangible assets, but they are often considered to fall into one of the following five categories (or goodwill):

a. *Marketing-related: marketing-related intangible assets are used primarily in the marketing or promotion of products or services. Examples include trademarks, trade names, unique trade designs, and internet domain names,*
b. *Customer-related: customer-related intangible assets include customer lists, backlog, customer contracts, and contractual and non-contractual customer relationships,*
c. *Artistic-related: artistic-related intangible assets arising from the right to benefits such as royalties from artistic works such as plays, books, films, and music, and from non-contractual copyright protection,*
d. *Contract-related: contract-related intangible assets represent the value of rights that arise from contractual agreements. Examples include licensing and royalty agreements, service or supply contracts, lease agreements, permits, broadcast rights, servicing contracts, non-competition agreements, and natural resource rights, and*
e. *Technology-based: technology-related intangible assets arise from contractual or non-contractual rights to use patented technology, unpatented technology, databases, formulae, designs, software, processes, or recipes.*

OECD (2022) distinguishes between:

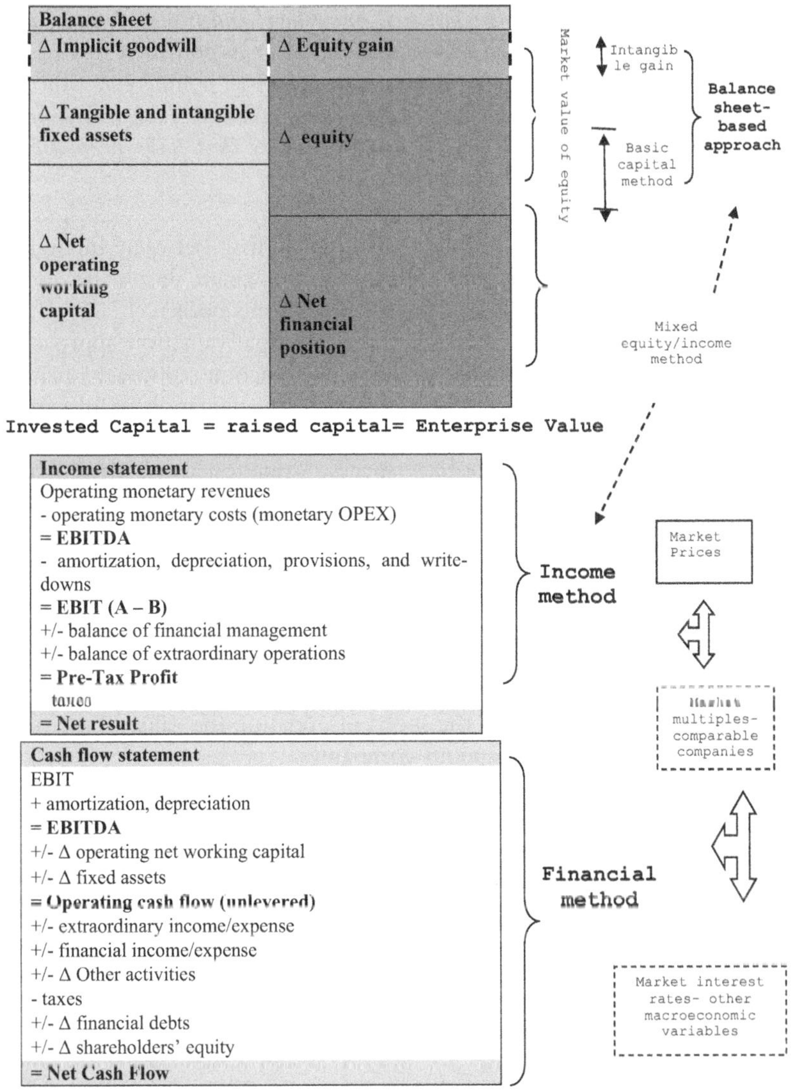

Fig. 2.10 The integrated equity–economic–financial–empirical and market valuation

a. *Commercial intangibles: patents, know-how, industrial designs, and ornamental models used to produce a good or to provide a service;*
b. *Marketing intangibles, as a special category of commercial intangibles, including trademarks, trade names, customer lists, distribution channels, symbols or logos, or unique names that have promotional value.*

Other, more precise classifications distinguish first between intangible goods linked to marketing and technology, to which should be added the world of the internet (hence the subtitle of this book).

IVS 210 § 30.1. recalls that the three principal valuation approaches described in IVS 105 Valuation Approaches (income approach; market approach; cost approach) can all be applied to the valuation of intangible assets.

In terms of intangible resources, specific valuation issues arise, which derive from the nature of these assets. The reproducibility of such goods, the absence of rivalry in consumption (the use of a branded product by a consumer does not prejudice a simultaneous use by others) and scalability can be noticed (examined below in par. 2.14.).

The empirical approaches are based on the practical observation of the market prices of the intangible goods, identical in characteristics, from which formulas and parameters of evaluation can be derived. The use of practical criteria is dictated by the speed of updating the value of the fixed assets in similar and homogeneous companies.

Analytical approaches, on the contrary, are more reliable because they are accepted by theory and consolidated by practice, even if they are often less intuitive.

The three principal valuation approaches described in IVS 105 Valuation Approaches (consistent with IFRS 13—Fair Value Measurement) used—individually or in a complementary way—by professional practice for the economic estimation of the value of intangible assets are (see Fig. 2.11):

1. The market approach;
2. The cost approach (reconstruction or replacement capital);
3. The (incremental) income approach.

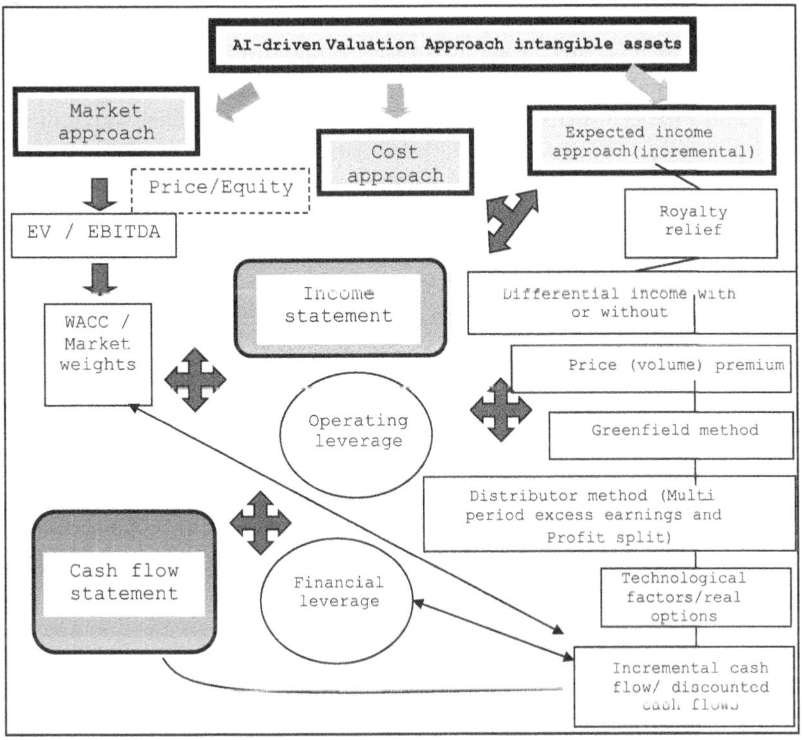

Fig. 2.11 Approaches of valuation of intangible assets

According to the valuation practice, the appraisal of an intangible asset can be made by reference to each of the three known valuation approaches. In selecting the most appropriate approach, the expert should consider the characteristics of the intangible asset and its reproducibility, the nature of the benefits it can generate for the owner (current or potential) and the user, and the existence or otherwise of a reference market.

Valuation issues are even more complex for other intangibles, such as know-how, industrial secrets, unpatented research and development costs, goodwill, etc. ..., which are characterized by limited or absent negotiability, greater information asymmetries, and less defined legal boundaries, particularly in specific sectors.

The valuation of intangible assets not registered or specifically protected, such as know-how, is subject to high inter-temporal variability, being anchored to provisions aimed at drawing up the strategic, industrial, and financial plans applicable to joint-stock companies. Variability is incorporated in the risk, and the information contained in the report on operations can provide valuable insights.

The breadth of the valuation interval is demarcated by upper and lower limits, in the case of (full) going concern (full business continuity) or in break-up (liquidation) scenarios, in which intangible resources traditionally lose most of their value. This happens especially if they are not independently negotiable or can be synergistically linked to other assets. In the case of discontinuity, the "organized complex of assets" that keeps together the firm is eliminated.

The choice of the approaches to be used depends on the type of intangible resource and the purpose and context of the evaluation, but also on the ease with which reliable information can be found.

Of the different approaches, the complementarity in identifying—from different angles—the multifaceted aspects of the intangible object of evaluation, suitable to allow an integrated assessment, must be grasped. For example, the relief-from-royalties is in the function of the incomes or incremental cash flows that derive from the exploitation of the intangible resource and that interact with the market surplus value or the multipliers of comparable companies. Incremental equity derives from an accumulation of differential income. The cost of reproduction estimates the future benefits and differential goodwill. The different approaches should theoretically lead to similar results, although the relief from the royalty and reproduction cost approach sometimes tends to provide lower valuations than the differential income approach or the market comparisons.

The following sub-paragraphs contain a detailed description of the different valuation approaches (cost, income, and market) mentioned above.

Cost Approach

The cost of tangible assets is typically known or can be estimated when the asset is acquired. The economic benefits and their occurrence may be reasonably estimated. In contrast, the cost of many intangibles is unclear, as they are not the result of a project that can be separated from the business activities.

The economic benefits that will be derived from the investment in intangibles (including AI) are typically hard to estimate. Due to the intrinsic risky nature of innovation, many projects will fail and be abandoned and provide little or no benefit to the firm.

The cost approach, particularly in the context of IFRS 13 (Fair Value Measurement), provides a framework for estimating the value of assets and liabilities based on the cost to replace them. This approach is grounded in the principle that a market participant would not pay more for an asset or liability than it would cost to replace it with a comparable one. When it comes to intangible assets, the cost approach is nuanced and requires careful consideration (see also Lennard, 2018). In practice, the cost approach is often used alongside other valuation methods, such as the income approach or the market approach, to triangulate the value of intangible assets. This multifaceted approach helps address the complexities and uncertainties inherent in valuing intangibles. The selection and application of the appropriate valuation method depend on the nature of the asset, the availability of data, and the purpose of the valuation.

Within this framework and provided that these limitations are clear, reference to the cost may still give some useful insights for valuation.

According to the cost approach, the value of an intangible asset is determined by the sum of the capitalized costs, incurred for the realization of the intangible or to be incurred to reproduce it (restoration of rights and brand accreditation represented, in general, by advertising, promotional and distribution network investments ...).

The limitation of this approach lies in the fact that it does not consider maintenance costs and the opportunity cost of time and that it does not apply to assets capable of generating income.

The main difficulties in applying this approach relate to the difficulty in finding costs incurred in the past, especially if the costs have been incurred over several years and have not been capitalized.

There are broadly two main approaches that fall under the cost approach: the replacement cost and the reproduction cost. However, most intangible assets do not have a physical form that can be reproduced, and assets such as software that can be reproduced generally derive value from their function/utility rather than their exact lines of code. As such, the replacement cost is most applied to the valuation of intangible assets.

The Replacement Cost Approach for valuing intangible assets is a pragmatic method that focuses on the cost perspective rather than the future economic benefits that such assets may generate. This approach is grounded in the economic principle of substitution, which asserts that a rational investor would not pay more for an asset than the cost to obtain an asset of equivalent utility or functionality (see also Reilly & Schweihs, 2016). While the Replacement Cost Approach offers a useful perspective, especially for assets that are more utility-oriented, it's often used in conjunction with other valuation approaches like the reproduction cost to provide a more comprehensive assessment of an intangible asset's value. This multifaceted approach helps to ensure that the valuation captures both the cost to replace the asset and its potential to generate future economic benefits.

Income/Financial Approach

It is based on past and future economic benefits that can be linked to an intangible, both in terms of license revenues (royalties) and incremental revenues.

The income approach to valuing intangible assets is a forward-looking valuation method that estimates the present value of an asset based on the income it is expected to generate in the future. This approach is particularly well-suited for intangible assets, whose primary value often lies in their ability to produce future economic benefits, such as revenue from a patent or savings from a proprietary process. The method reflects the principle that the value of an asset is inherently tied to its ability to generate cash flows or save costs in the future (see also Lennard, 2018). With its focus on future economic benefits, this approach offers a robust framework for valuing intangible assets by reflecting their potential to generate income or save costs from a market participant's viewpoint. However, the application of this method demands a deep understanding of the asset in question, the market in which it operates, and sophisticated financial modeling techniques.

In the context of income approaches, intangible assets have value to the extent that they can incorporate a competitive advantage in the form of multi-period excess earnings. This is a pure income estimate, in which intangible assets act as Primary Income Generating Assets. Income approaches are based on estimates of future economic benefits, for example through discounted cash flows.

The income approaches include the financial ones: so the estimate of incremental cash flows or the criterion of discounted cash flows, is functionally linked to the market approaches from which it derives some parameters (in fact, market) for the estimate of the value of shareholders' equity and financial debts.

The linking parameter may be represented by the EBITDA which is simultaneously an economic and financial margin, representing the difference between monetary operating revenues and costs.

The main variants are:

1. **The Relief-from-Royalty Approach:** this allows estimating the income of the intangible asset by deducting from the notional royalties that would be paid to a third party for the use of the intangible under license any direct and indirect costs of maintenance/development of the asset itself not already deducted from the notional royalty;
2. **The Premium Profit Approach or With-and-Without Approach**: indirect approach of determining the economic advantage (premium price), which consists of comparing the performance of the firm that disposes of the intangible asset in question with that of a similar firm without such an asset;
3. **The Excess Earnings Approach**: to be used to estimate the value of an asset that plays a significant or primary role, based on which the notional income is obtained by calculating the income that the firm would record if it was disposed of the ownership of all the other assets to regain the right to use them through licensing or rental or rental contracts. This approach provides a structured way to isolate and value the contribution of intangible assets to a business's overall earnings, making it a valuable tool in the appraisal of businesses with significant goodwill or intangible assets. It is especially relevant when assessing the value of goodwill or specific intangible assets that significantly contribute to the earnings capacity of a business.
4. **The Greenfield Approach**: this methodology isolates the value that a specific intangible asset brings to a business, separate from the contributions of other assets. Given its speculative nature, the results should be considered carefully, often alongside other valuation methods, to gain a comprehensive understanding of an intangible asset's value, used to assess the value of specific intangible assets. It is particularly relevant for valuing intangible assets in a scenario where those assets are deemed to be the primary contributors to the future cash flows of a business. This approach simulates a scenario as if the business were starting anew ("Greenfield") with only the intangible

asset in question, requiring the company to acquire, build, or rent all other necessary tangible and intangible assets to operationalize the business. (see also IVS 210, § 90);

5. **The Distributor Approach**: an innovative method for valuing customer-related intangible assets, especially relevant in scenarios where the primary value of a business lies in its distribution network or customer relationships rather than in the development of intellectual property or manufacturing capabilities. This approach considers the unique role that distributors play in the value chain, focusing on the profit margins earned through distribution activities to estimate the excess earnings that can be attributed to customer-related intangibles. The approach is particularly useful in industries where distribution plays a critical role in business success and where customer relationships are a primary source of value. It offers a nuanced method to isolate and value these relationships, providing a basis for financial reporting, taxation, and transaction-related decision-making.
6. **Real Options** are used to evaluate flexible investment projects with uncertain outcomes (typically patents). Real options are a fundamental characteristic of scalable investments, described in Chapter 3.
7. **Discounting of Differential (Incremental) Income or Cash Flows**: This is based on quantifying and discounting the specific benefits and advantages of the intangible asset compared to "normal" situations, i.e., products, for example, not marked or covered by a patent. Incremental income is obtained by the difference between revenues and costs relating to the intangible asset, with discounting of the differential flows and with the exclusion of extraneous or immaterial income components;

Market Approach

The market approach considers the prices and other relevant information generated by market transactions involving identical or comparable assets.

Many intangible assets, however, are not traded: Lev attributes this to "contracting difficulties, negligible marginal costs, and fuzzy property rights" (Lev, 2001).

As IAS 38 notes: "*An active market cannot exist for brands, newspaper mastheads, music and film publishing rights, patents or trademarks, because each such asset is unique*" (IAS 38, par. 78).

Unicity is a factor of strength but also a weakness: whereas unique intangibles (e.g., a patent) command a premium over other external assets, they are hardly comparable, making valuation more difficult.

Many intangible assets are "context-specific" so they may have little or no value to a purchaser (Haskel & Westlake, 2017).

When applicable, this approach is based on a comparison with similar assets, in terms of income or incremental assets, or on the analysis of comparable transactions and market multipliers.

The main limitation of this approach concerns the information asymmetries structurally connected with the secrecy of intangible assets (including AI), which makes the information necessary for comparisons challenging to find.

Package transactions involving multiple assets or intangibles make the valuation of stand-alone intangibles based on an empirical approach more complicated. These difficulties are even more evident considering that, as anticipated in paragraph 2.10., from an accounting point of view, according to IAS 38, there is no active market for intangible assets, which tend to be not accounted for, and their fair value seems difficult to estimate.

The main approaches are:

1. ***Empirical Approach***: the income attributable to the exploitation of a given intangible asset is multiplied by an expressive coefficient of the strategic strength of the asset, which depends on factors such as leadership, loyalty, market positioning, trends, marketing investments, internationality, legal protection ...;
2. ***Valuation of the Differential (Incremental) Assets***: through indicators of the market surplus value, such as the **Q of Tobin**, which relates the market value of the activities of a firm to their replacement value; if the index is higher than the unit, this is due to the presence of an implicit goodwill which can depend, among other things, on the value (not accounted for) of the intangible.
3. ***Price/Book Value Index***: which compares the stock market price (of a branded or other intangible listed firm) to the book net assets, bringing out a surplus value (if the index is greater than 1) partly attributable to intangible assets.

2.12 Hard-to-Value Intangibles

AI significantly impacts Hard-to-Value Intangibles, such as IT intangible capital, by making additional investments in firm-specific human and organizational capital. The emergence and utilization of AI give rise to concerns related to accessibility in terms of socio-cultural, economic, and ethical dimensions, underscoring the importance of policies tailored to specific nations to address disparities. Deep learning, categorized as a type of AI, has transformed numerous sectors, like asset management, by improving decision-making processes and capabilities, potentially resulting in substantial disruptions. The ongoing enhancement and implementation of AI technologies are projected to wield a profound technological influence on various social and economic domains, pointing towards a transformative impact on human endeavors. "Hard-to-value intangibles" are intangible assets that pose challenges in their determining their fair market value estimate. These assets may lack readily available market-based pricing or require complex methodologies for valuation:

1. **Definition**: Hard-to-value intangibles are non-physical assets whose market value is unclear and uneasy to determine. They often involve subjective estimates and specialized valuation techniques.
2. **Examples**: Common examples of hard-to-value intangibles include:
    - **Brand Reputation**: The value of a firm's brand reputation is challenging to quantify precisely, as it depends on consumer perceptions and market dynamics.
    - **Customer Relationships**: its estimate, especially in long-term contracts or subscriptions, can be complex.
    - **Trade Secrets and Proprietary Technology**: Valuing proprietary technology or trade secrets that are not publicly disclosed can be challenging due to limited information.
    - **Goodwill**: Goodwill on a firm's balance sheet represents the premium paid over the fair value during an acquisition, only considering tangible and identifiable intangible assets. Assigning a specific value to goodwill can be subjective.

3. **Valuation Challenges**:
    - **Lack of Comparable Transactions**: Hard-to-value intangibles often lack comparable transactions in the market, making it difficult to determine their value based on similar sales or transfers.
    - **Subjectivity**: Valuation of these intangibles often relies on subjective judgments and assumptions, which can vary among appraisers.
    - **Complexity**: Some hard to value intangibles, like complex financial derivatives or unique intellectual property, require specialized expertise and methodologies for valuation.
4. **Valuation Methods**:
    - Various valuation approaches can be employed to estimate hard-to-value intangibles, consistently with IVS 210, and so including the income approach (e.g., discounted cash flow analysis), the market approach (using comparable transactions where available), and the cost approach (e.g., figuring out the cost to recreate the intangible asset).
5. **Disclosure and Reporting**:
    - Companies are required to disclose the existence of hard-to-value intangibles in their financial statements, along with any associated risks and uncertainties in their valuation.
6. **Regulatory and Accounting Standards**:
    - Regulatory bodies and accounting standards (e.g., IFRS and GAAP) provide guidelines for the recognition and measurement of intangible assets, including hard-to-value intangibles. Companies must adhere to these standards when reporting their financials.

7. **Auditor Scrutiny**: Auditors and regulators pay close attention to the valuation of hard-to-value intangibles, as their proper assessment impacts a firm's financial health and compliance with accounting standards.

Hard-to-value intangibles present challenges due to their unique characteristics and limited market comparables. Accurate valuation often requires specialized expertise and a thorough understanding of the specific intangible asset's nature and economic significance. Transparency, disclosure, and adherence to accounting standards are essential when dealing with these assets to ensure accurate financial reporting.

Intangibles are so peculiar and difficult to define that in many cases they become hard-to-value, especially if they are unpatented or unbranded. Comparability concerns exacerbate the issue, together with the difficulty of getting input data for the appraisal.

According to OECD (2022):

- "*The term hard-to-value intangibles covers intangibles or rights in intangibles for which, at the time of their transfer between associated firms, (i) no reliable comparables exist, and (ii) at the time the transactions were entered into, the projections of future cash flows or income expected to be derived from the transferred intangible, or the assumptions used in valuing the intangible are highly uncertain, making it difficult to predict the level of ultimate success of the intangible at the time of the transfer*" (par. 6.189).
- "*Transactions involving the transfer, or the use of Hard-to-value intangibles may exhibit one or more of the following features:*

    The intangible is only partially developed at the time of the transfer.
    The intangible is not expected to be exploited commercially until several years following the transaction.
    The intangible is expected to be exploited in a manner that is novel at the time of the transfer and the absence of a track record of development or exploitation of similar intangibles makes projections highly uncertain" (par. 6.190).

Hard-to-value intangibles (HTVI) and AI are closely related in the context of accounting, valuation, and intellectual property management.

HTVI refers to intangible assets that are difficult to quantify or assign a specific value to, often because they lack a readily available market price or comparable transactions. AI plays a significant role in both identifying and managing these hard-to-value intangibles:

1. **Identification of HTVI**:
   - **AI Algorithms and Data Analysis**: AI can be used to analyze large datasets and identify potential hard-to-value intangibles within a firm. For example, it can detect patterns related to customer goodwill, proprietary algorithms, or unique user data that may not have a clear market value.
2. **Valuation of HTVI**:
   - **Machine Learning Models**: AI and machine learning models can be employed to develop better valuation models for hard-to-value intangibles. These models can consider a wide range of elements, including historical performance, industry benchmarks, and market sentiment, to estimate the value of such assets.
   - **Scenario Analysis**: AI can simulate various scenarios to estimate the potential value of HTVI under different conditions, helping stakeholders make more informed decisions regarding their recognition and financial reporting.
3. **Risk Assessment**:
   - **Predictive Analytics**: AI can assess the risks associated with hard-to-value intangibles. Considering historical data and expected market trends, AI identifies potential risks that may affect the value of these assets, helping companies make better risk management decisions.
4. **Intellectual Property Management**:
   - **Patent and Copyright Analysis**: AI tools can be used to analyze patent and copyright portfolios. This analysis can help identify valuable IP assets that might be considered hard to value, such as unique software algorithms or proprietary technologies.

- **Brand Reputation Monitoring**: AI can monitor social media and online content to assess the impact of trademark reputation on the value of intangibles like goodwill and trademarks.

5. **Compliance and Reporting**:

- **Regulatory Compliance**: AI can assist companies in ensuring that their financial reporting complies with accounting standards and regulations, especially when dealing with hard-to-value intangibles.

6. **Market Transactions**:

- **Mergers and Acquisitions (M&A)**: AI can analyze M&A data to identify trends in the valuation of HTVI in similar transactions. This information can be valuable when negotiating deals that involve these assets.

7. **Innovation and R&D**:

- **AI-Powered R&D**: Companies engaged in AI research and development may produce hard-to-value intangibles, such as proprietary algorithms or datasets. AI can aid in estimating the potential value and market applicability of these innovations.

AI data analysis capabilities, machine learning models, and predictive analytics can provide a better and informed assessment of the value and risks associated with intangible assets that do not have easily ascertainable market prices. This relationship between AI and HTVI is particularly relevant in today's technology-driven and data-rich business environment.

2.13 The Intangible Roadmap: From Patents and Trademarks to Blockchains, Big Data, and Artificial Intelligence

The "Intangible Roadmap" refers to the evolving landscape of intangible assets in the modern business world, ranging from traditional forms like patents and trademarks to newer technologies like blockchains, big data, and AI. This roadmap reflects the growing importance of intangible assets in the global economy and how they have evolved.

Due to their immaterial nature and lack of "physicality", intangible assets are often characterized by undefined boundaries and plasticity that make them easily interchangeable, adaptable, and flexible. These properties are typically exalted if the intangible has a digital dimension, as it can be used, and exchanged in real-time within the web.

Intangibles often overlap, as shown in Fig. 2.12. An example is given by know-how that eventually may evolve to protected patenting (implicit) goodwill that expresses the non-recorded potential of trademarks, or even the information value chain recalled in Fig. 2.13. Software is ubiquitous, as it interacts with most intangibles, and algorithms are at the base of AI (machine learning) patterns.

The interrelations between AI and blockchain technology are multifaceted and growing, offering various innovative applications and solutions:

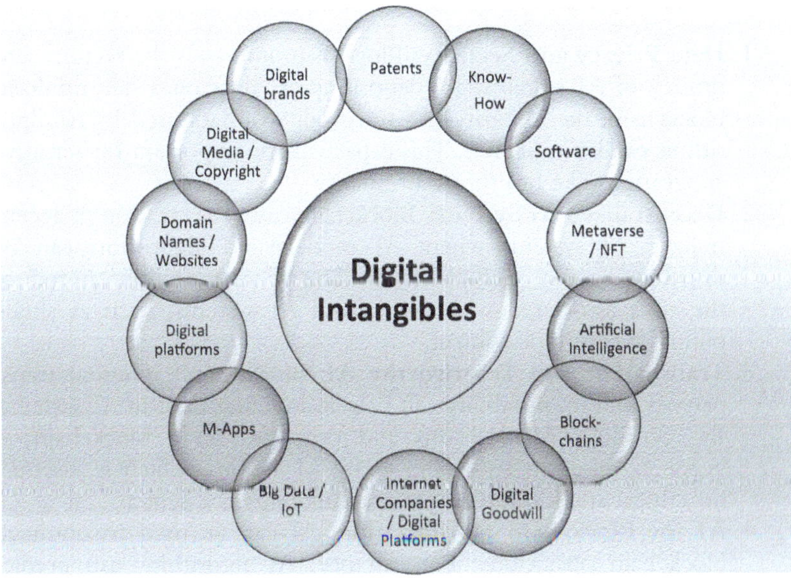

Fig. 2.12 Intangible interaction

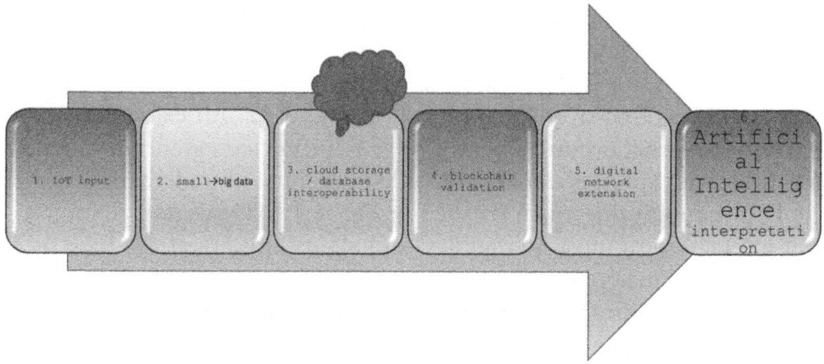

Fig. 2.13 Information value chain

1. **Data Privacy and Security**: Blockchain improves the security and privacy of AI systems. By depositing AI data on a decentralized blockchain, the integrity and traceability of data used by AI algorithms can be improved. This is particularly important for sensitive applications like healthcare or finance.
2. **Decentralized AI Systems**: Blockchain eases the creation of decentralized AI systems where AI models and algorithms can be distributed across multiple nodes. This decentralization can reduce the risks associated with centralized AI systems, such as single points of failure or control.
3. **Transparent and Trustworthy AI**: Blockchain's inherent transparency and immutability can help in building trust in AI systems. By recording AI decisions and processes on a blockchain, it becomes easier to audit and verify AI actions, which is essential for critical applications where accountability is essential.
4. **AI for Blockchain Optimization**: AI can be used to optimize blockchain operations. For instance, AI algorithms can predict the best times to execute transactions to minimize fees, optimize mining processes, or enhance security protocols.
5. **Smart Contracts and AI Integration**: AI can foster smart contracts (self-executing agreements whose terms are directly

written into code). AI can facilitate more complex decision-making within smart contracts, allowing them to execute actions based on external data and more sophisticated criteria.

6. **Tokenization and Incentivization in AI**: Blockchain can facilitate the tokenization of AI models and datasets, creating new economic models for AI development. For instance, contributors to a decentralized AI project could be rewarded with tokens, incentivizing the sharing of data and algorithms.
7. **Data Marketplaces**: Blockchain facilitates the creation of decentralized data marketplaces, where data can be securely and anonymously bought and sold. AI companies can use these marketplaces to access large amounts of training data, while individuals can monetize their data.
8. **Enhanced Data Provenance**: Blockchain can provide robust data provenance mechanisms, which are essential for AI. Knowing the origin and history of data helps in understanding and improving AI models, especially in fields like research where data authenticity is crucial.
9. **Interoperability and Collaboration**: Blockchain can facilitate better interoperability and collaboration in the AI field. By using standardized protocols and decentralized networks, different AI systems can communicate and collaborate more efficiently.
10. **Regulatory Compliance**: Both AI and blockchain must navigate complex regulatory landscapes. Blockchain's transparency and auditability can help AI systems comply with regulations, especially those concerning data privacy (like GDPR) and ethical AI.

Blockchain can enhance the security, transparency, and trustworthiness of AI systems, while AI can optimize and expand the capabilities of blockchain technology.

2.14 Intangible-Driven EBITDA

"Intangible-driven Earnings Before Interest, Taxes, Depreciation, and Amortization" is a financial metric that incorporates the influence of intangible assets on a firm's EBITDA. The influence of AI on Intangible-Driven EBITDA holds considerable significance. Intangible assets encompassing AI have progressively emerged as crucial elements of a firm's comprehensive assets. Moreover, a growing necessity exists for supplementary investments in intangible assets to harness the advantages offered by AI and ICT investments effectively. AI-infused IT Service Operations have brought about transformative changes, enabling enterprises to generate value, enhance sustainability, and optimize processes. This amalgamation of AI within intangible-driven operations reshapes business frameworks and propels economic advancement. When intangible assets, such as intellectual property, brand value, proprietary technology, and big data, contribute to a firm's revenue generation and profitability, estimators consider their impact on EBITDA. This is particularly relevant in industries where intangibles like AI are central to a firm's operations, operating through:

1. **Enhanced EBITDA**:
    - Intangible-driven EBITDA can be higher than traditional EBITDA because it accounts for the value created by intangible assets. For AI companies, this might include the value generated by AI algorithms, proprietary datasets, or AI-driven customer insights.
2. **Valuation Multiples**:
    - Companies with significant intangible-driven EBITDA may command higher valuation multiples. Investors may pay a premium for businesses that have strong intangible assets, especially if those assets are expected to drive future revenue growth.
3. **Risk Assessment**:
    - Intangible-driven EBITDA can also be adopted to determine the risk associated with AI companies. Companies heavily reliant on intangibles may face risks related to changes in technology, data security, or regulatory changes. Understanding the contribution of intangibles to EBITDA helps evaluate these risks.
4. **Comparative Analysis**:

- When comparing AI companies for investment or acquisition, intangible-driven EBITDA provides a better basis for comparison. It explains the role of intangibles in each firm's financial performance.

5. **Mergers and Acquisitions (M&A)**:
   - In M&A transactions involving AI companies, intangible-driven EBITDA can influence deal negotiations. Buyers may pay a higher price for a target firm with valuable intangible assets, leading to a premium on the purchase price.

6. **Strategic Decision-Making**:
   - For AI companies, intangible-driven EBITDA can inform strategic decisions related to investment in research and development, marketing, and IP protection. It highlights the importance of nurturing and protecting intangible assets.

7. **Investor Perception**:
   - Intangible-driven EBITDA can influence the investors' perception of a firm's value and growth. Investors focused on the AI sector may be more inclined to invest in companies with a strong intangible asset base.

8. **Financial Reporting**:
   - Accurate reporting of intangible-driven EBITDA is essential for transparent financial reporting and regulatory compliance. Companies need to adhere to accounting standards when recognizing and amortizing intangible assets.

Intangible-driven EBITDA is a valuable metric for AI companies and industries where intangible assets are significant drivers of revenue and profitability.

Understanding the impact on AI valuation metrics of intangible-driven EBITDA is essential for investors, analysts, and stakeholders when estimating the true value of AI-driven businesses.

More generally, intangible investments impact EBITDA in various complementary ways, often leading to improvements in a firm's financial performance:

1. **Revenue Increases**:
    - Investments in intangibles such as brand development, marketing, and client relationships produce increased sales. Strong brand recognition, for example, can drive customer loyalty and demand for products or services, resulting in higher sales figures.
2. **Product and Service Innovation**:
    - Investment in R&D, which is often considered an intangible asset, can result in the creation of innovative products or services. These innovations produce revenue growth as clients are attracted to new offerings.
3. **Efficiency Improvements**:
    - Intangible investments in process improvements, technology, and intellectual property can enhance operational efficiency. For instance, implementing a new software system that streamlines operations can reduce labor costs and other operating expenses, positively impacting EBITDA.
4. **Cost Reduction**:
    - Intangible assets related to cost-saving initiatives, such as proprietary software or patented processes, can directly reduce fixed or variable costs. This can result in higher EBITDA margins as a percentage of revenue.
5. **Customer Retention**:
    - Investments in customer relationship management (CRM) systems and customer service training can improve client retention rates. Retaining existing clients appears often more

cost-effective than acquiring new ones and can contribute to sustained revenue streams.

6. **Market Expansion**:
   - Investments in intangibles like market research and market development can help a firm expand its client base or enter innovative markets. This expansion produces revenue growth and, consequently, higher EBITDA.
7. **Risk Mitigation**:
   - Intangible assets related to intellectual property protection, compliance efforts, or crisis management planning can soften legal or operational issues that may harm profitability. Lower risk can contribute to a more stable EBITDA.
8. **Brand Value**:
   - The brand is a significant intangible asset that can contribute to pricing power. A strong brand can enable a firm to charge premium prices for its products or services, leading to increased revenue and potentially higher EBITDA margins.
9. **Employee Productivity**:
   - Investments in employee training and development, often considered intangible assets, produce increased productivity, reducing labor costs per unit of output and positively impacting EBITDA.

The impact of intangible investments on EBITDA may, however, not be immediate. Some intangible investments may take time to generate returns, especially those related to R&D or brand building.

Intangible investments impact the EBITDA in many complementary ways, ranging from revenue increases to (fixed and/or variable) cost reduction. EBITDA is the key parameter behind economic and financial marginality, directly influencing profitability indicators and market multipliers:

$$\textbf{Intangible Investments} \rightarrow +\Delta_{\text{EBITDA}} \rightarrow +\Delta_{\text{profitability ratios/market multipliers}} \tag{2.24}$$

Intangibles impact the EBITDA mainly in two (often complementary) ways:

1. Increasing the revenues (e.g., branded products with higher attractiveness and selling capacity);
2. Lowering the operating expenses (OPEX), thanks to production savings (e.g., a patent that makes production quicker and cheaper).

The EBITDA's consideration is consistent with the cost and the income approach, reflecting a parameter that is an income-based economic (and financial) margin, expressed by the difference between monetary operating revenues and monetary OPEX. The link with a complementary methodology—the market approach—is given by EBITDA-driven market multipliers of comparable firms, empirically examined in Paragraph 11.2.

References

Damodaran, A. (1996). *The stable growth DDM: Gordon growth model.* http://people.stern.nyu.edu/adamodar/pdfiles/ddm.pdf

Damodaran, A. (2018). *The dark side of valuation.* Pearson FT Press PTG.

Fazzini, M. (2018). *Business valuation: Theory and practice.* Palgrave McMillan.

Fernandez, P. (2001). *Valuation using multiples. How do analysts reach their conclusions?* IESE Business School. https://www.researchgate.net/publication/4803035_Valuation_Using_Multiples_How_Do_Analysts_Reach_their_Conclusions

Fernandez, P. (2019a). *CAPM: An absurd model.* SSRN. https://ssrn.com/abstract=2505597

Fernandez, P. (2019b). *Valuation and common sense.* https://web.iese.edu/PabloFernandez/Book_VaCS/ContentsValuation.pdf

Haskel, J., & Westlake, S. (2017). *Capitalism without capital: The Rise of the intangible economy.* Princeton University Press.

Koller, T., & Goedhart, M. (2015). *Valuation: Measuring and managing the value of companies.* McKinsey & Company.

IVS 210. (2016, April 7). Intangible assets exposure draft. https://www.ivsc.org/wp-content/uploads/2021/10/IVS210IntangibleAssets.pdf

Lennard, A. (2018). *Intangibles: First thoughts.* Paper presented at IFASS meeting, Mumbai. https://www.efrag.org/Assets/Download?assetUrl=%2Fsites%2Fwebpublishing%2FMeeting%20Documents%2F1709060811163678%2F05-02%20FRC%20presentation%20on%20Intangibles%20TEG%2018-04-06.pdf&AspxAutoDetectCookieSupport=1

Lev, B. (2001). *Intangibles: Management, measurement and reporting*. Brookings institute press.

Lev, B. (2018). *Intangibles*. New York University- Stern school of Business. https://ssrn.com/abstract=3218586

Lev, B., & Gu, F. (2016). *The End of accounting and the path forward for investors and managers*. John Wiley & Sons.

Moro Visconti, R. (2019). *How to prepare a business plan with excel*. https://ssrn.com/abstract=2039748

Moro-Visconti, R. (2021). *Startup valuation. From strategic business planning to digital networking*. Palgrave MacMillan.

Moro-Visconti, R. (2022a). *The valuation of digital intangibles. Technology, marketing, and the metaverse*. Palgrave MacMillan.

Moro-Visconti, R. (2022b). *Augmented corporate valuation. From digital networking to ESG compliance*. Palgrave MacMillan.

Moro-Visconti, R., & Cesaretti, A. (2023). *Digital token valuation. Cryptocurrencies, NFTs, decentralized finance, and blockchains*. Palgrave MacMillan.

OECD. (2022). Transfer pricing guidelines for multinational enterprises and tax administrations. https://www.oecd.org/tax/transfer-pricing/oecd-transfer-pricing-guidelines-for-multinational-enterprises-and-tax-administrations-20769717.htm

Rappaport, A., & Mauboussin, M. J. (2021). *Expectations investing*. Harvard Business School Press.

Reilly, R. F., & Schweihs, R. P. (2016). *Guide to intangible asset valuation*. Wiley Finance.

Singh, J. P. (2013). On the intricacies of cash flow corporate valuation. *Advances in Management, 6*(3), 15–22.

CHAPTER 3

Artificial Intelligence-Driven Digital Scalability and Growth Options

3.1 Introduction

This chapter describes heterogeneous issues that represent the basic background of digital intangibles and their AI-driven digital scalability. A comprehensive understanding of these composite concepts is preliminary to any valuation approach since it helps in the identification of the main value drivers and business model competitive forces. AI has a significant impact on the patterns of value co-creation in scalable digital contexts. The optimization of processes and enhancement of system performance by AI contribute to its ability to scale effectively. Within digitalization, AI plays a critical role in converting analog data into digital format, facilitating efficient interactions among connected agents to create value collectively. The incorporation of AI into scalable systems brings about cost reductions, increases in anticipated revenues, and a transformation of traditional supply chains through the synergistic interactions of digitalized intangible assets on interconnected platforms. Consequently, this leads to higher economic and financial margins, ultimately boosting the economic benefits derived from scalable digital operations.

Most contents of this Chapter are readapted from Moro-Visconti (2022a), or, occasionally, Moro-Visconti (2022b), Moro-Visconti (2021), Moro-Visconti and Cesaretti (2023), extending digital intangible, startup, crypto or business planning applications to specific AI valuation patterns, starting from their value-creating scalable properties. Crypto

R. Moro-Visconti, *Artificial Intelligence Valuation*,
https://doi.org/10.1007/978-3-031-53622-9_3

issues, referring to scalable blockchain properties that can be interpreted even with AI, are examined in Moro-Visconti and Cesaretti (2023).

AI-driven scalability has the potential to significantly impact the economic, financial, and market value of traditional firms:

a. **Economic Impact**
   AI-driven scalability can help traditional firms to improve their economic output in several ways. For instance, AI can automate tasks, improve efficiency, and reduce costs. AI can also be used to develop innovative devices, products and services and to enter new markets. For example, AI-powered chatbots can automate customer service tasks, allowing employees to focus on more complex tasks. AI can also improve the efficiency of manufacturing and logistics operations. Additionally, AI can be used to develop innovative products that are more personalized.
b. **Financial Impact**
   AI-driven scalability can have a significant impact on the financial performance of traditional firms. AI can help to increase revenues, reduce operating costs, and improve profitability. For instance, AI can improve sales prevision accuracy, which can help increase revenues. AI can also reduce costs by automating tasks, improving efficiency, and reducing waste. Additionally, AI can help to improve profitability by optimizing pricing and stock levels.
c. **Market Value Impact**
   The economic and financial benefits of AI-driven scalability can lead to a significant increase in the market value of firms. Investors are willing to pay a premium for firms that are successfully leveraging AI to improve their performance.

AI is pivotal in augmenting scalability, yielding significant consequences on conventional enterprises' economic, financial, and market value. Moreover, AI-driven IT Service Operations engender business value and streamline procedures, freeing employees from repetitive duties and conventional methodologies. The integration of AI technologies by enterprises has been associated with enhanced firm value and cost frameworks, primarily through automation AI, demonstrating favorable outcomes. Furthermore, the increased availability of cutting-edge AI technology has empowered small to medium-sized enterprises to utilize AI for heightened effectiveness and competitiveness across diverse sectors. Here are some examples of how traditional firms are using AI-driven scalability to improve their economic, financial, and market performance:

- Amazon uses AI to automate tasks in its fulfillment centers, improve the accuracy of its product recommendations, and develop innovative products and services.
- Netflix is using AI to personalize its recommendations to users and to improve its content acquisition strategy.
- Walmart uses AI to automate its stores, improve its supply chain efficiency, and develop new products and services.
- JPMorgan Chase is using AI to automate tasks in its back office, improve the accuracy of its fraud detection systems, and develop new financial products and services.

In broader terms, AI-driven digital scalability refers to the ability of organizations to leverage AI technologies and techniques to expand and grow their digital operations, services, and capabilities. This concept encompasses the use of AI to automate, maximize, and improve various aspects of digital business, allowing organizations to achieve greater efficiency, reach, and impact. Here are key aspects of AI-driven digital scalability:

a. **Automation and Efficiency**:

   - AI technologies, including machine learning, natural language processing, and robotic process automation, can automate repetitive tasks and processes. This automation leads to increased efficiency, reduced manual labor, and lower operational costs.

b. **Scalable Infrastructure**:

   - AI-driven systems can dynamically allocate resources based on demand, ensuring that digital services can scale up or down efficiently to handle varying workloads. This flexibility is crucial for handling spikes in user activity or data processing needs.

c. **Personalization and Customer Engagement**:

- AI-powered recommendation engines and personalization algorithms enable organizations to offer tailored experiences to individual users. This improves customer engagement and can lead to higher user retention and conversion rates.

d. **Data Analysis and Understandings**:

- AI-driven analytics tools can process large volumes of data to derive valuable understandings. These insights can inform strategic decision-making, improve product development, and identify growth opportunities.

e. **Predictive Maintenance**:

- In industrial contexts, AI-driven predictive maintenance can maximize the use of machinery and equipment. By predicting when maintenance is needed, organizations can avoid costly downtime and reduce maintenance costs.

f. **Chatbots and Virtual Assistants**:

- AI-powered chatbots and virtual assistants manage customer inquiries and ease requests at scale, providing 24/7 assistance and freeing up human agents for more complex tasks.

g. **Natural Language Processing (NLP)**:

- NLP technology enables organizations to assess and understand large amounts of textual data, such as client reviews, social media posts, and help tickets. This information can be used to improve products, services, and customer experiences.

h. **Fraud Detection and Security**:

- AI algorithms can detect fraudulent anomalies and biases, enhancing cybersecurity and fraud prevention measures.

i. **Content Generation and Curation**:

- AI can assist in content generation, such as automated article writing, and content curation, helping organizations maintain a consistent online presence and engage with audiences across various digital platforms.

j. **Continuous Learning and Improvement**:

- AI systems can learn from data and user interactions, allowing them to continuously improve their performance and adapt to changing conditions. This adaptability is crucial for staying competitive in rapidly evolving digital environments.

k. **Marketplace Expansion**:

- AI-driven recommendations and data-driven understandings can help organizations identify new markets, client segments, and business opportunities for expansion.

AI-driven digital scalability (see also https://fastercapital.com/startup-topic/Intelligence-in-Content.html) empowers organizations to manage their existing digital operations efficiently but also explore new avenues for growth and innovation. As AI technologies continue to advance, their role in driving digital scalability will become increasingly significant in a wide range of industries.

AI-driven digital scalability and growth options represent a range of strategies and approaches that leverage AI technologies to expand and improve businesses (Table 3.1).

To successfully implement AI-driven digital scalability and growth options, businesses need to invest in AI technologies, data infrastructure, and talent. They must also address ethical and regulatory considerations while ensuring that AI aligns with their strategic objectives and client needs.

3.2 Vertical and Horizontal Scalability

Scalability indicates the ability of a process, network, or system to handle a growing amount of work. Scalability refers to the ability of a device to adapt to the changes in the environment and meet the changing needs of clients.

Scalability is also defined as the capacity to handle more work as the size of the IT devices grows. Scalability or scaling is widely used to indicate the ability of hardware and software to deliver greater computational power.

So, in broader terms, scalability means flexibility, which allows us to better address and achieve the specific needs of clients, which are

Table 3.1 Artificial Intelligence-driven digital scalability and growth options

Personalization and customer engagement	AI can analyze large amounts of client data to create highly personalized experiences. By tailoring products, services, and marketing messages to individual preferences, businesses can boost customer engagement and loyalty, leading to growth
Predictive analytics	AI-powered predictive analytics can help businesses forecast demand, maximize inventory management, and make data-driven decisions. This can lead to cost savings and improved resource allocation
Recommendation systems	Recommendation engines, powered by AI, can suggest products or content to users considering their preferences and past behavior. This can drive additional sales and user engagement
Process automation	AI automates repetitive and rule-based tasks across various business functions, such as client help, HR, and finance. This unlocks human resources for more strategic tasks and can result in operational scalability
Market research and competitive analysis	AI-driven tools can analyze market trends and competitive landscapes in real time, helping businesses identify growth opportunities and potential threats
Chatbots and virtual assistants	Implementing AI-driven chatbots and virtual assistants can improve client help and streamline interactions, leading to improved customer satisfaction and scalability in handling customer inquiries
Supply chain optimization	AI maximizes supply chain operations by predicting demand, managing inventory levels, and improving logistics, with consequent cost reductions and scalability improvements
Content creation and curation	AI can generate and curate content, such as articles, videos, and music playlists, at scale. This can be beneficial for content-driven businesses, enabling them to sort out and distribute content more rapidly

(continued)

Table 3.1 (continued)

Fraud detection and ecurity	AI can improve cybersecurity by detecting and mitigating threats in real time. This safeguards business operations and customer trust, allowing for sustained growth
Healthcare diagnostics and personalized medicine	In the healthcare sector, AI-driven diagnostics and treatment recommendations can lead to better patient outcomes and business growth, as healthcare providers can serve more patients effectively
Financial services and risk assessment	AI can be used for credit scoring, fraud detection, and risk assessment in the financial industry, enabling the expansion of lending and investment services
Energy and resource management	AI can maximize energy consumption and resource allocation in industries like utilities and manufacturing, leading to cost savings and sustainable growth
E-commerce and dynamic pricing	E-commerce businesses use AI to dynamically adjust pricing based on demand and market conditions, optimizing sales, and scalability
Remote monitoring and IoT	AI can assess data from IoT devices to predict maintenance needs, monitor equipment performance, and maximize operations, particularly in industries like manufacturing and utilities

never static. People's interests and tastes, as well as environmental conditions, change continuously over time. Scalability is therefore vital as it contributes to competitiveness, efficiency, and quality. Scalability helps the system to work gracefully without any undue delay and unproductive resource consumption while making good use of the available resources (Gupta et al., 2017).

Since scalability depends on the capability of a business to profit from the addition of (internal and/or external) resources, these latter can fall either into the "vertical" or "horizontal" category and generate two different scalability types.

Vertical scalability and horizontal scalability increase the capacity and performance of a digital and IT-driven system:

1. **Vertical Scalability (Scaling Up)**:

   - **Definition**: Vertical scalability increases the resources (such as CPU, memory, or storage) to a single server to improve capacity and performance. Organizations that employ AI observe a surge in leads, a decrease in call durations, and a reduction in sales operation expenses. AI facilitates the generation of profound customer insights, resulting in enhanced conversion rates and decreased workloads for teams. AI streamlines mundane tasks, enhances precision, and reveals latent patterns, thereby revolutionizing internal procedures and augmenting scalability. Moreover, AI assists in the identification of target audiences, delivery of personalized content, and alleviation of workloads through task automation, consequently further advancing vertical scalability in enterprises. The incorporation of AI in recruitment procedures, cybersecurity measures, and maintenance of infrastructure also contributes to the enhancement of scalability and operational effectiveness. AI so plays a pivotal role in driving vertical scalability by optimizing various business functions and processes.
   - **Characteristics**:
     - **Single Machine**: In vertical scale upa single, improved machine is working.
     - **Costlier**: This approach may need costlier hardware components.
     - **Limited Ceiling**: There is a limit to how much a single machine can be scaled up, and once that limit is reached, diminishing returns may come up.
   - **Use Cases**:
     - Vertical scaling is useful when there is a small or predictable increase in workload.
     - It is frequent in one-shot applications.
   - **Advantages**:
     - Simplified Management: Managing a single machine is often easier than dealing with a large cluster of machines.

  - Immediate Impact: Adding resources can provide an immediate boost in output.
- **Disadvantages**:
  - Limited Scalability: There's a finite limit to how much you can scale vertically before one can hit hardware limits.
  - Costly: Acquiring high-end hardware can be expensive, especially for significant scaling needs.
  - Downtime Risk: Scaling up may require downtime or delays during hardware upgrades.

2. **Horizontal Scalability (Scaling Out)**:

- **Definition**: Horizontal scalability increases the number of machines (nodes) to a distributed network system to accomodate for increased workload. It reinforces distributing the load across multiple machines. AI enhance horizontal scalability in systems through the enablement of platforms that have the capacity to provide AI solutions across diverse domains, including but not limited to video games and real-time video processing. These implementations have had a significant impact on aspects like engagement, revenue generation, and resource allocation within the organization. Through the utilization of AI methodologies, these systems are able to manage growing workloads by distributing tasks across multiple resources, thereby enhancing horizontal scalability.
- **Characteristics**:
  - **Distributed Architecture**: There is a cluster of machines working together to share the load.
  - **Cost-Effective**: It can be more cost-effective because you can use commodity hardware and add more nodes as needed.
  - **Higher Ceiling**: There is a higher potential for scalability, as more machines may be added to meet growing demands.
- **Use Cases**:
  - Horizontal scaling is well-suited for web applications, cloud services, and microservices architectures where workloads can be distributed across multiple instances.

  - It seems ideal for handling increasing workloads, exploiting economies of scale.
- **Advantages**:
  - High Scalability: Adding nodes can be introduced to scale horizontally almost indefinitely, accommodating massive growth.
  - Cost Efficiency: Using standard hardware is often more budget-friendly, and you can scale as needed, avoiding over-provisioning.
- **Disadvantages**:
  - Complex Management: Dealing with a cluster of machines can be more complex than managing a single server.
  - Latency: In some cases, distributed systems may introduce network latency compared to a single, local machine.

Initially, vertical scaling may handle a moderate level of traffic, and as demand continues to grow, horizontal scaling can be adopted to ensure cost-effective and highly scalable infrastructure. This approach, known as "scaling up" and "scaling out", allows organizations to balance performance, cost, and flexibility.

Vertical scalability (scaling up) corresponds to the ability to increase the capacity of existing hardware or software by adding more resources to the single system node. For instance, we can add processing power to a server to increase its speed. In the same way, we can scale a system vertically and expand it by providing more shared resources such as processing, main memory, storage, and network interfaces to the main node to be able to satisfy a greater number of requests per system (Gupta et al., 2017).

By contrast, horizontal scalability (scaling out) refers to adding more nodes to the same system, thus impacting, and modifying the supply chain. A real case could be adding computer workstations to a network, meaning connecting multiple computers to accomplish more work in less time. This method allows the system to work as a single logical unit, increasing overall efficiency (Fig. 3.1).

Westlake and Haskel (2017) identify four fundamental properties of intangible assets:

1. *Scalability*: It enables a growth in revenues accompanied by a less than proportional increase in variable costs. This has a positive

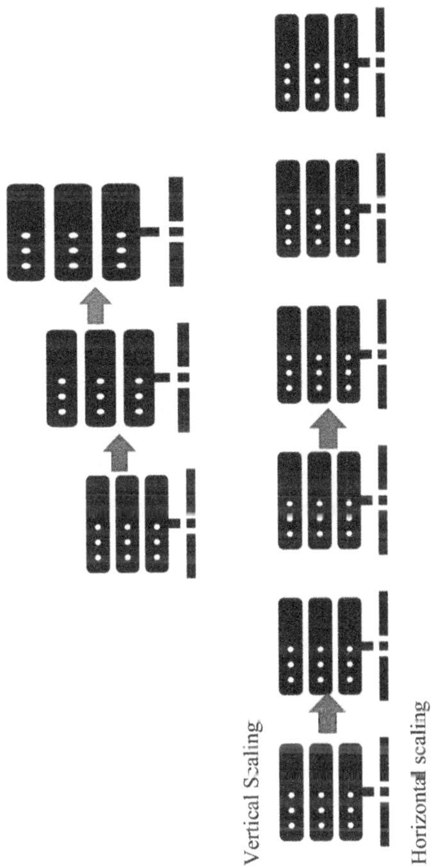

Fig. 3.1 Vertical and horizontal scalability

impact on economic and financial margins, generating a driving force that improves the rating and bankability of intangible-intensive companies. A scalable intangible asset can be used without limits. For instance, oranges (a tangible rival good) can be used to make marmalade, but only for a certain amount. In contrast, a recipe (intangible non-rival good) can be used to make marmalade without limits. Intangible assets such as a brand or an algorithm are considered the easiest to scale up due to network effects affecting them as well as their ability to reap incumbency advantages (e.g., Uber), as compared to tangible assets such as taxi companies.

2. *Sunk Costs*: Intangibles represent sunk costs in a few ways. First, businesses with a lot of intangibles, such as brands or process innovation, often prove worthless if the firm fails. The riskiness of intangible assets stems from the non-transferability of the asset. Tangible assets like land and factories can, in theory, be sold or recycled.
3. *Spillovers*: A business that invests in a tangible asset like a new factory can usually be confident that it will get most of whatever benefits the asset produces. But intangible assets are more slippery, and value is likelier to be diverted.
4. *Synergies*: Intangible assets can be particularly valuable when combined with other assets in a synergistic portfolio (Westlake & Haskel, 2017).

Scalability is intrinsically linked to the characteristics of intangible assets. Intangibles are non-rivalrous goods, i.e., non-excludable public goods that are consumed but whose supply is not depleted by consumption. When a consumer uses that good, the supply left for other people remains unchanged.

Therefore, non-rivalrous goods can be consumed repeatedly without the fear of depletion of supply. The scarcity effect that impacts demand and supply is not present in these cases, and non-rivalrous goods or services are scalable.

Public goods are services and products that are given to consumers by the government. Public goods are non-excludable and non-rivalrous. Whereas food is rivalrous, intangibles are not, and this characteristic allows for their multiple and scalable consumption.

There is a capacity limit for sharing a bottle of beer, but consumers can endlessly enjoy its brand.

3.3 Digital Scalability

AI improves the digital scalability of businesses by transforming operations through innovative business models driven by data. It enables websites to become interactive, secure, and user-friendly, enhancing digital marketing performance. By utilizing AI, firms can redesign their structure around a digital nucleus, improving scalability and logistics management. Using AI applications is pivotal in molding business models, offering entrepreneurs tangible instances to follow in their AI journey. Within digital marketing, AI enhances customer interaction by employing techniques such as SEO, PPC, and Chatbots, thereby collecting valuable customer data to facilitate personalized engagements and increased sales figures. In essence, the influence of AI on businesses extends from enriching website interactivity and security to restructuring organizational frameworks and marketing approaches, ultimately propelling digital scalability and expansion. Digital scalability is influenced by a range of factors, and AI can play a significant role in enhancing it:

1. **Automated Resource Allocation**:
   - AI systems, particularly machine learning algorithms, can assess data patterns in real time and make decisions about resource allocation. For instance, in cloud computing environments, AI can automatically provision additional computing resources (scaling out) or allocate more CPU and memory to specific tasks (scaling up) based on demand.
2. **Predictive Scaling**:
   - AI allows systems to scale proactively, making resources available when they are likely to be needed. This can help avoid performance bottlenecks during sudden spikes in demand.
3. **Load Balancing**:
   - Incoming requests and traffic can be distributed with the help of AI across multiple servers or instances to maximize performance and prevent overloading of any single component. This helps in achieving horizontal scalability and fault tolerance.

4. **Content Delivery Optimization**:
    - AI can maximize content delivery networks (CDNs) by intelligently caching suitable content from geographically distributed servers. This reduces latency and ensures faster content access for users.
5. **Anomaly Detection and Fault Tolerance**:
    - AI-driven anomaly detection can identify unusual patterns or errors in system behavior, such as security breaches or hardware failures. By detecting and mitigating issues early, AI contributes to system reliability and uptime.
6. **Personalization and Recommendation Engines**:
    - AI-powered recommendation engines can provide personalized content or product recommendations to users, increasing user engagement and conversion rates. As user bases grow, these systems can continue to deliver personalized experiences efficiently.
7. **Natural Language Processing (NLP) and Chatbots**:
    - AI-driven chatbots and virtual assistants can handle a high volume of client interactions simultaneously, providing help without additional human resources.
8. **Data Processing and Analytics**:
    - AI fosters data processing and analytics tasks. Scalable AI algorithms assess data at scale.

AI is crucial in enhancing digital scalability by providing automation, and real-time optimization to ensure that systems can grow to meet higher demands while ensuring an improved level of performance and efficiency.

Digital businesses, as defined by Weill and Woerner (2013), leverage the power of digital technology to mediate transactions and deliver products or services. The essence of these businesses lies in their digital core, enabling them to operate with unique characteristics that traditional brick-and-mortar businesses might not possess. So, the term "Digital Scalability" basically refers to the application of the scalability concept by digital companies and devices, to maximize as much as possible digital circuits and operations.

Digital business models are usually designed for rapid growth, and the recent advances in digital technologies continue to sort out new possibilities to scale up and reach a global scale. As described by Gander (2015) the drivers by which digital business models may attempt to gain scale are analyzed in Table 3.2.

3.4 Artificial Intelligence-Driven Scalability as a Real Option

Applying the real options approach allows for the strategic postponement of AI investments. When integrated with scalable learning frameworks and universal algorithms, this strategic viewpoint presents a viable and effective method for overseeing AI implementations in different sectors, guaranteeing flexibility, cost-efficiency, and enhanced decision-making. The increasing technical capabilities of AI systems have led to greater rates of AI deployment in various sectors, and this has significant implications for the scalability of AI and its impact on economic, financial, and market valuation:

1. **AI-Driven Scalability**:
    - **Efficiency**: Advanced AI systems execute tasks more efficiently, reducing manual labor and human intervention. This scalability enables organizations to process more data and tasks at a much faster pace than traditional methods.
    - **Customization**: Scalable AI systems can be tailored to specific business needs and requirements. This adaptability allows organizations to address a wide range of use cases and industries, further enhancing their scalability.
    - **Automation**: AI's scalability automates routine and repetitive tasks, freeing up human resources for more strategic and value-added activities. This can lead to increased productivity and cost savings.
2. **Economic Impact**:
    - **Cost Savings**: Scalable AI systems reduce costs by automating tasks and processes. This cost efficiency can positively impact a firm's economic performance.

Table 3.2 Scalability drivers

Scalability driver	*Features*	*Criticalities*
Learning by using	The greater the scale of a technology (or "the wider the adoption of technology"), the more its users learn about its features, strengths, and weaknesses (also using SWOT analysis)	Disseminating learning between users may be costly and may require managerial attention and resources
Networking (Network externalities)	"Scalability becomes supercharged with network effects" (Haskel & Westlake, 2018). A network is scalable if it can cope with the existing demand placed upon it but also can be flexibly expanded to meet future demand. Network externalities occur when the value obtained by using products or services increases with its greater diffusion among populations of users	Risk of contagion through the network. Examples may derive from epidemic occurrences
Scale economies	Supply-side effects of scale include economies of production and distribution. With large output quantities, the unit cost of each product or service encounter falls due to the spreading of fixed costs, advertising budgets, and research and design costs across a larger quantity of products	Conceive and maintain a generic platform; resources are required to hold non-scalable features away from the ecosystem
Information returns	Reduction in user perception of the risk of adopting a product or service following its use by others. The more widely a technology is adopted, the more it is understood	Conformity to general preferences for products and services does not necessarily imply wider adoption, as individual preferences can be different

(continued)

Table 3.2 (continued)

Scalability driver	*Features*	*Criticalities*
Technological interrelatedness	The wider the adoption of technology, the greater the number of helping technologies that are developed and become part of its infrastructure	Costly and complex to support as the number of product configurations grows with each client
Distributed sourcing	The way resources are decentralized across value chains and ecosystems. The distributed design enables the rapid adoption of a product or service without sacrificing performance or causing bottlenecks in the system which degrades the customer experience	Congestion and consequent bottleneck due to overloading of capacity following a rapid, unanticipated, and sizeable increase in user numbers, which may result in service failure
Economies of experience	Economies in which products or services are sold by emphasizing their effects on people's lives and actions to sort out "memorable customers' experiences"	Additional costs and new know-how are required to switch from product to service/experience orientation. Change of customers' expectations and managers' strategies
Real options	Options available to managers range from business investment opportunities to tangible assets or financial instruments	Difficulties in estimating the exact value of real options
Blitzscaling	Specific techniques allow companies to achieve massive scale at high speed	Disrupting startups can exploit network externalities to sort out digital monopolies. Sharp increases in the volumes of sales are not automatically followed by economic margin improvements

- **New Revenue Streams**. AI-driven products and services can sort out new revenue streams for businesses. Scalable AI allows organizations to reach larger client bases and offer more personalized experiences, potentially leading to increased revenue.

3. **Financial Impact**:
    - **Investor Confidence**: The ability to scale AI effectively can improve investor confidence in a firm's growth potential. Investors may be more inclined to help organizations with scalable AI strategies.
    - **Competitive Advantage**: Scalable AI can provide a competitive advantage in industries where speed, efficiency, and automation are critical. Companies with such advantages are better positioned for financial success.
4. **Market Valuation Impact**:
    - **Market Share**: Companies that scale their AI capabilities successfully improve the market share. This growth potential can positively influence their market valuation.
    - **Innovation**: Scalable AI systems can drive innovation and foster the development of new products and services. Innovators often receive favorable market valuations due to their potential for disruptive growth.
    - **Mergers and Acquisitions (M&A)**: Scalable AI assets are attractive to potential acquirers. M&A activity can have a direct impact on market valuation, as acquisitions or partnerships can lead to increased market capitalization.

The scalability of AI-driven by technical advancements can result in economic benefits such as cost savings and revenue generation. This, in turn, can have a positive financial impact, attracting investor confidence and providing a competitive edge. Successful scaling of AI can also lead to increased market share, innovation, and M&A activity, all of which can contribute to higher market valuations for organizations that effectively harness the power of AI.

AI-driven scalability can be viewed as a real option in the context of business and strategic decision-making. A real option refers to the flexibility or opportunity to make decisions in the future that can potentially improve the value or mitigate risks of an investment or business venture. AI-driven scalability can be considered a real option, as shown in Table 3.3.

AI-driven scalability can be considered a real option because it provides organizations with the flexibility, timing, and risk mitigation capabilities to make dynamic decisions that improve the value and strategic position of

Table 3.3 AI as a real option

Flexibility to scale	AI-driven systems and technologies provide organizations with the flexibility to scale their operations, services, or products in response to changing market conditions, client demands, or technological advancements This scalability can be viewed as a real option because it allows a firm to expand its operations or pivot its business model as opportunities or challenges arise
Timing of investment	Real options often involve the timing of investments. In the context of AI, organizations can choose when and how to invest in AI-driven scalability They may decide to scale up their AI infrastructure and capabilities when market conditions are favorable or when they have a better understanding of the technology's potential impact
Risk mitigation	AI-driven scalability can help mitigate risks associated with uncertainty. For instance, by using AI for predictive analytics, organizations can better anticipate market trends and make informed decisions about scaling their operations This risk mitigation aspect aligns with the real option concept, as it allows organizations to make decisions that reduce downside risks and enhance upside potential
Exploration and expansion	Real options often involve exploration and expansion into new markets or opportunities. AI-driven scalability enables organizations to explore new avenues and expand their business without committing all their resources upfront They can experiment with new AI-driven products or services and scale them up if they prove successful
Dynamic decision-making	Real options are characterized by dynamic decision-making. Organizations can continuously assess the value of their AI investments and adjust their scalability plans accordingly AI-driven systems provide real-time data and understandings, allowing for agile decision-making and adjustments based on changing circumstances
Strategic value creation	Just as real options can sort out strategic value in financial investments, AI-driven scalability can create strategic value for organizations. It allows them to stay competitive, innovate, and respond effectively to market dynamics The strategic value generated by AI can be seen as an option to seize valuable opportunities as they arise

their business. Organizations that leverage AI-driven scalability effectively are better equipped to adapt to a rapidly changing business landscape and capitalize on emerging opportunities.

Flexibility (resilience) represents a key characteristic of scalability and can be improved using real options, concerned with the right—but

Table 3.4 Real options

Real option	*Main features*
Option to expand	To undertake a project to expand the business operations (e.g., a sushi chain considering opening new restaurants)
Option to defer or wait	Option of deferring the business decision to the future (e.g., a sushi chain considering opening new restaurants this year or in the next year)
Option to abandon	Option to cease a project to realize its scrap value (e.g., a manufacturing firm decides to sell old equipment)

not the obligation—to undertake certain business initiatives. In particular, the options available can concern the expansion, the deferral, or the abandonment of a capital investment project, such as described in Table 3.4.

Real options create the right, but not the obligation, to purchase the underlying asset at a defined exercise price. A case of real options application is the use of patents; in fact, patents allow their owners to choose between exclusively commercializing the patented invention sometimes during the patent term, or foregoing commercialization altogether.

So, real options affect the valuation of potential investments and may be incorporated in discount models as the Net Present Value (in the sense that when investments or assets, like patents, are evaluated through NPV techniques, real options can be used to make forecasts more flexible (Iazzolino & Migliano, 2015).

NPV represents the difference between the present value of cash inflows and the present value of cash outflows over a period. NPV is used in capital budgeting and investment planning to assess the profitability of a projected investment or project. Projects with a positive NPV should always be accepted.

For these reasons, real options describe the key tensions that managers face between commitment versus flexibility or between competition and cooperation (Trigeorgis & Reuer, 2017).

The ability to predict and model future and uncertain events connected with the actual economic and financial returns can be usefully codified in earn-out contractual clauses which, in purchases and sales, guarantee the seller an additional price, if certain situations occur, that are particularly uncertain at the time of the stipulation of the contract.

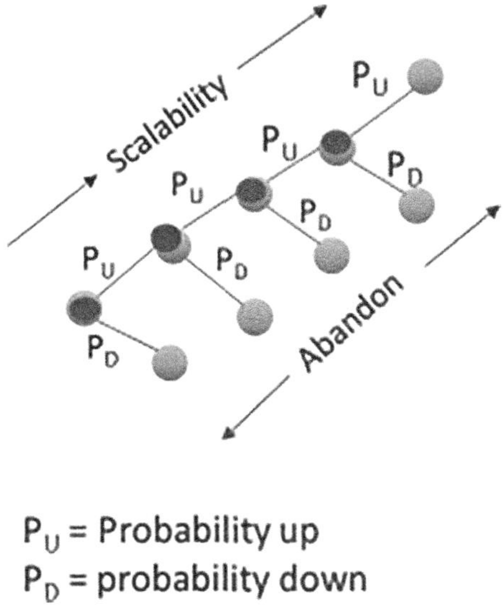

Fig. 3.2 Investment tree and real options

The real options have long been used both in the valuation of patents and in the estimation of internet companies and social networks. Using real options, investment projects should be the source of a series of opportunities that management can seize when certain scenario conditions occur. Opportunities for expansion, contraction, abandonment, or postponement of the launch of an investment project give the decision-maker flexibility, the value of which must be carefully considered for the overall assessment of the project.

Figure 3.2 shows the interaction between a typical investment tree and real options.

Incorporating real options, business models become more resilient, and they improve their DCF or NPV, decreasing the risky factors in the discount rate (cost of capital), and improving the cash flows.

3.5 The Impact of Scalable Intangibles on CAPEX and OPEX

Scalable intangibles are of paramount importance in influencing the capital expenditures (CAPEX) and operational expenditures (OPEX) of investments driven by artificial intelligence (AI). These intangibles, encompassing AI-related assets, significantly contribute to an organization's overall assets, with a disproportionate concentration in certain leading firms. Additionally, exposure to AI skills positively impacts firms' market value, underscoring the significance of technical abilities in enhancing corporate value. Despite the potential advantages, initial reactions from the market to AI investments can be unfavorable, particularly for organizations lacking IT expertise or robust credit ratings. In summary, effectively utilizing scalable intangibles is crucial for optimizing CAPEX and OPEX in AI-driven investments, thus highlighting the complex interplay between intangible assets and financial performance. Scalable intangibles can have a significant impact on both Capital Expenditures (CAPEX) and Operating Expenditures (OPEX) in an organization. Here's how scalable intangibles can influence these financial aspects:

1. **CAPEX (Capital Expenditures)**:
   CAPEX represents the investments an organization makes in long-term assets, infrastructure, or projects. Scalable intangibles can affect CAPEX in the following ways:

   a. **Reduced Capital Investment**:
      - Scalable intangibles often involve digital assets, software, and intellectual property that can be scaled up without the need for significant additional capital investment.
      - This can lead to lower CAPEX requirements because the organization can leverage existing intangible assets to expand its operations or offerings.

   b. **Efficient Resource Utilization**:
      - Scalable intangibles, such as AI algorithms or cloud-based solutions, can maximize resource utilization. For instance, cloud computing allows organizations to pay for computing resources on a scalable, as-needed basis, reducing the need for upfront capital investments in hardware and data centers.

   c. **Faster Time to Market**:

- Scalable intangibles often enable faster product development and deployment. This can result in reduced CAPEX as organizations can bring new products or services to market more quickly, potentially requiring fewer upfront investments.

d. **Asset Optimization**:
- Organizations can maximize their existing intangible assets through scalability, extracting more value from the same investments. For instance, by enhancing and scaling up AI models, they can improve decision-making and operational efficiency without significant additional CAPEX.

2. **OPEX (Operating Expenditures)**:
OPEX represents the ongoing operational costs incurred by an organization. Scalable intangibles can influence OPEX in various ways:

a. **Cost Reduction**:
- Scalable intangibles, such as automation and AI-driven processes, can reduce labor and operational costs. For instance, AI-powered chatbots can handle client inquiries, reducing the need for customer support staff.

b. **Efficiency Gains**:
- Scalable intangibles can improve operational efficiency. Streamlined processes, enhanced analytics, and real-time insights can lead to more efficient resource allocation, inventory management, and supply chain operations.

c. **Predictive Maintenance**:
- Scalable intangibles like predictive maintenance systems can reduce maintenance costs by identifying and addressing equipment issues before they become costly failures. This lowers repair and replacement expenses.

d. **Cloud Services**:
- Scalable intangibles that rely on cloud services often have variable OPEX. Organizations pay for cloud resources based on usage, which can lead to cost savings during periods of lower demand.

e. **Scalable Licensing**:

- Organizations can often scale up or down software and technology licenses as needed. This allows them to align software costs with actual usage and avoid over-provisioning.

f. **Data Management**:
- Scalable intangible assets related to data management reduce data storage and processing costs. Scalable data storage solutions, and data compression can lead to OPEX savings.

Scalable intangibles can lead to reduced operating expenditures by enhancing efficiency, automating processes, and offering flexible cost structures. However, the specific impact on CAPEX and OPEX depends on the nature of the intangible assets, their scalability potential, and how effectively they are leveraged within the organization's operations and strategic planning.

CAPEX and OPEX represent two complementary categories of business expenses, deriving from the capital and operating budgets that are created by companies to help grow and adjust resources.

Capital budgets cover capital expenses, which are capitalized and appear as long-term assets on the balance sheet. CAPEX corresponds to the amounts that companies use to purchase long-term assets as major physical goods or services that will be used for more than one year. These assets may be physical (plant, equipment, property, vehicles, etc.) or represented by intangibles that are not directly expensed in the income statement. As these long-term assets depreciate over their useful lives, the depreciation for a given year shows up on the income statement as a non-monetary expense in that year. Therefore, CAPEX is subject to depreciation (with a linear methodology in constant installments over the useful life or with an impairment test, whenever applicable).

OPEX refers instead to the ordinary costs for a firm to run its daily business operations (purchases; salaries; rents; sales, general, & administrative expenses; property taxes, etc.). OPEX can be divided into monetary OPEX + depreciation/amortization.

Intangibles impact directly on monetary OPEX and CAPEX (when intangible investments are capitalized, and their annual quota is amortized). Amortization is, therefore, a part of non-monetary OPEX. Only monetary OPEX affects the EBITDA.

Scalability is an intangible characteristic of the business that can quickly boost volumes of sales, up to blitzscaling.

Intangibles can, however, have a complementary impact on the business model (and consequent value creation), and they can have a joint impact on both, OPEX and CAPEX.

For what concerns OPEX, intangibles can ignite productivity gains where input costs to reach a target output are minimized. If OPEX is reduced, economic margins such as EBITDA, EBIT, pre-tax profit, or net profit improve.

Capitalization of intangible assets (into CAPEX) instead of accounting within monetary OPEX does not change Operating Cash Flows (O_{CF}) that include these items anyway since:

$$\begin{aligned}\text{Enterprise Value} &= \sum \frac{(\text{sales} - \text{monetary OPEX}) = \text{EBITDA} \mp \Delta\text{NWC} \mp \Delta\text{CAPEX}}{(1+\text{WACC})^i} \\ &= \sum \frac{\text{Operating Cash Flow}}{(1+\text{WACC})^i} \end{aligned} \tag{3.1}$$

where ΔNWC indicates the differential Net Working Capital (concerning the previous year).

While DCF (expressed by $\sum O_{CF}/\text{WACC}$) is invariant to the accounting treatment of intangibles (i.e., to the fact that they are capitalized or not), this is not true in the other valuation method.

EBITDA does not consider non-monetary intangible OPEX, and CAPEX is expressed net of amortization.

Should the Enterprise Value be proxied by the average EBITDA times a market multiplier of a comparable firm, then the EBITDA is influenced by the capitalization of intangibles. More precisely, capitalized intangibles (as development expenses) that become part of the CAPEX (and are never part of monetary OPEX) increase the EBITDA, and so the Enterprise Value that is estimated with market comparables.

Operating costs are divided into variable and fixed costs, to better understand the impact of scalability on operating leverage (EBIT increase due to an increase in sales).

Scalability directly boosts sales but has an impact also on the EBIT that is given not only by increased revenues but also by the presence of fixed costs in the OPEX mix. Since fixed costs are—by definition—invariant to sales, the higher their proportion within the OPEX, the better the impact on the EBIT increase due to growing scalable sales. The opposite happens when sales decrease: in that case, fixed costs are a burden.

Intangibles may have a positive impact even on CAPEX, should they contribute to improving productivity, so decreasing the amount of CAPEX needed to run the business and to generate economic and financial positive margins (EBITDA; EBIT; operating and net cash flows, etc.).

There is a positive impact attributable to scalable intangibles improving the market value of the firm, due to the higher economic and financial marginality.

Higher operating cash flows improve the discounted cash flows (O_{CF}/WACC) and a better EBITDA boosts the economic value complemented by market multipliers.

Accounting distortions may impact the dichotomy between OPEX and CAPEX, due to the slippery qualification of the intangibles and the caution that often prevents their capitalization. There may be, in practice, some difficulty in discriminating about the impact of intangibles on either OPEX or CAPEX, where the impact on CAPEX may be underestimated due to accounting prudentialism.

Scalable intangibles impact on the composition of raised capital (equity + financial debt):

- Any profitability gain improves, ceteris paribus, the net profit and so the equity; if dividends are paid out, then the benefit eventually accrues to the shareholders;
- Improvements in the EBITDA (that represents the contribution of the income statement to the generation of liquidity) may be used to pay back debt (so decreasing the financial leverage, expressed by the debt over equity ratio), or to fuel new investments without increasing outstanding debt or asking additional money to the shareholders. This may have a positive impact on the Weighted Average Cost of Capital (WACC) that is used to discount the Operating Cash Flow in the DCF formulation; any decrease in the WACC improves the market value of the firm, being value $\approx$ O_{CF}/WACC).

Any improvement in the EBITDA backs the pecking order theory, according to which internally generated liquidity (proxied by the EBITDA) precedes the issue of risky debt and then equity.

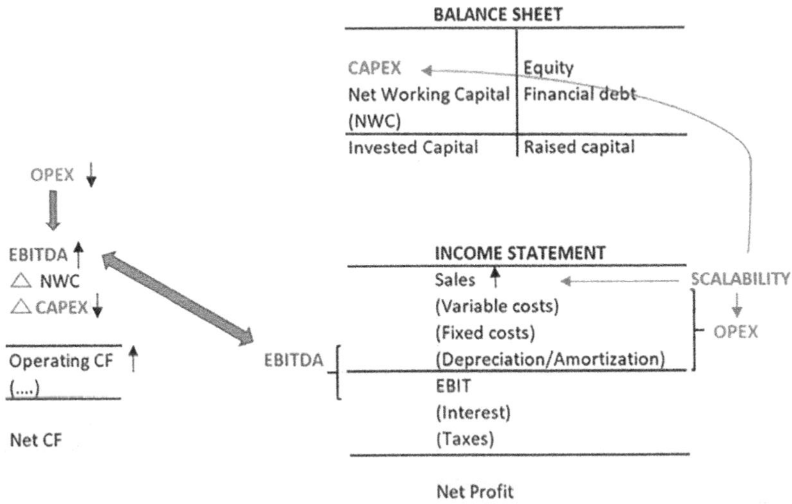

Fig. 3.3 Impact of scalable intangibles on OPEX and CAPEX

These considerations are valid not only for digital-native firms but also for traditional corporations that increasingly use new intangibles, becoming tech-enabled.

Should intangibles improve the flexibility of the supply chain where the firm is strategically positioned, then the business model may become more resilient to downturns and volatile market conditions. This reduces the difference between dreamy expectations and hard reality, decreasing risk and the cost of collecting capital (WACC) and contributes to the reduction of the DCF formula denominator.

Figure 3.3 depicts the impact of scalable intangibles on OPEX, CAPEX, and the economic and financial margins.

3.6 The Accounting Background: Operating Leverage

Operating leverage is a measure of how revenue growth translates into growth in operating income. It is a measure of how risky, or volatile, a firm's operating income is.

Operating leverage is the degree to which a firm or project can increase operating income by increasing its revenues. Essentially, while scalability is about volumes, operating leverage concerns economic margins (volumes * margins).

Operating leverage is a measure of how revenue growth translates into growth in operating income. It is an indication of how a company's fixed costs compare to its variable costs. If a business has high operating leverage, it means that a large portion of its costs are fixed, rather than variable. This structure can significantly amplify profits as sales increase because the fixed costs remain constant while revenue grows. However, this also introduces a higher degree of risk, especially related to forecasting.

When a firm reaches its break-even point (where the operating revenues equal the costs), then it can translate most of its incremental revenues into the EBIT if variable costs are negligible and fixed costs relevant. The opposite, however, occurs when revenues shrink: in this case, the presence of fixed costs is a burden that increases the operating losses. There is a boomerang effect and companies with higher fixed costs are more volatile and riskier, with an impact on valuation (increasing the discount factor—the cost of capital—in the denominator of the DCF formula).

The formula is the following:

$$\text{operating leverage} = \frac{\Delta \text{EBIT}/\text{EBIT}}{\Delta \text{sales}/\text{sales}} \tag{3.2}$$

Operating leverage expresses the ratio between the percentage variation in the operating income (Earnings Before Interests and Taxes, EBIT) and the percentage variation of sales.

Since the EBIT is given by sales—monetary OPEX—depreciation/amortization, operating leverage can consequently be linked to the OPEX/CAPEX classification reported in paragraph 3.5.

The elements influencing the operating leverage are:

- Sale prices;
- The volume of sales;
- Variable costs;
- Fixed costs.

We can consider a profit & loss account (income statement) where fixed and variable costs are represented separately.

1 **Revenues (sales)**
2 (variable costs)
3 **= Contribution margin** (1–2)
4 (fixed costs)
5 **= Operating Profit** = EBIT (3–4)

The contribution margin is the selling price per unit minus the variable cost per unit. It represents the portion of sales revenue that is not consumed by variable costs and so contributes to the coverage of fixed costs. This concept is one of the critical building blocks of break-even analysis.

The contribution margin analysis is a measure of operating leverage; it expresses how growth in sales translates to an increase in operating profits (EBIT).

The contribution margin is computed by using a management accounting version of the income statement that has been reformatted to analytically represent fixed and variable costs.

On-demand intangibles as Software as a Service (SaaS) or Platforms as a Service produce variable costs and reduce fixed costs

The overall contribution margin is given by the product of the unitary contribution margin and the sold quantities (or the services provided). The unitary contribution margin (that expresses an economic differential, influencing the valuation formulae) is mainly determined by the relationship between the "prices and revenues" of the sold products and the "prices and costs" of the variable input factors of production.

Companies with a higher structure of fixed costs (that do not follow the variation of sold quantities, remaining unchanged—fixed) experiment with higher operating levels. If a firm has only variable costs, then the operating leverage has a unitary level, and its contribution margin will coincide with the EBIT; to double the EBIT, sales will have to double, as they grow at the same pace as the variable costs and the contribution margin.

A classic dilemma is represented by the difference between a firm with only fixed costs and another one with just variable costs: which one is better?

Both corner solutions have pros and cons: the former companies find it more difficult to reach a break-even point, but when they do, the marginal growth of revenues is fully translated into higher EBIT, with a scalable impact on economic marginality. Companies with higher variable costs are on the contrary, safer but less profitable when the outlook is positive, compensating for lower risk with smaller trendy returns.

The contribution margin can be increased:

a. With a higher profit margin, expressed by the difference between "price/revenue" vs. "price/cost";
b. Improving the efficiency of variable factors of production;
c. Increasing the volume of sales.

Fixed costs are the second determinant of EBIT. Costs are "fixed" if they do not vary when production changes. The cost structure and the mix of fixed vs. variable costs are a strategic option of any firm but it also depends on the industry. For instance, retail companies can choose from shops that are fully owned or in franchising; staff can be represented by employees or freelance workers, etc. Some sectors, however, have strategic constraints that limit the possibility of the firm selecting its cost structure.

For instance, in the automotive industry, fixed costs and investments are typically high, and they are difficult to reduce below certain thresholds.

Fixed costs are typically significant in the banking sector, where staff costs and IT investments matter, even if FinTech improves flexibility.

Labor cost is just partially fixed, and it has extraordinary components that are linked to performance (stock options, etc.).

The degree of operating leverage (DOL) is a synthetic indicator of the operating risk, estimated by comparing the contribution margin (total revenues – total variable costs) to the EBIT (EBIT = total revenues – total variable costs – fixed costs):

$$\text{DOL} = (\text{TR}-\text{VC})/(\text{TR}-\text{VC}-\text{FC}) = \text{CM}/\text{EBIT} \quad (3.3)$$

where:

DOL degree of operating leverage
TR total revenues
VC variable costs

FC fixed costs
CM contribution margin.

The higher the weight of fixed costs over total costs, the higher the degree of operating leverage.

The cost structure has a remarkable impact on the (operating) net working capital (NWC), which is given by the difference between accounts receivable, stock, and accounts payable.

Fixed costs impact the working capital, producing accounts receivable that are independent of the trend of sales. Variable costs, on the contrary, follow the dynamics of sales, with a double impact on the working capital: sales produce receivables whereas variable costs generate payables. The working capital balance depends on the rotation of the credits and debts (average days of collection and payment).

An EBITDA increase is generated by monetary revenues that grow more than monetary OPEX. This typically produces a working capital increase that absorbs liquidity. Operating cash flows are positively affected by the EBITDA increase, less the increase in the working capital (and in CAPEX, which may grow to sustain higher revenues, contributing to liquidity absorption).

3.7 Break-Even Analysis

The influence of AI on break-even analysis holds significant importance across a variety of sectors. Utilization of AI algorithms has been observed in the automation of the identification of breakdown pressure indicators within hydraulic fracturing activities, optimization of generation schedule allocations within power grids, and development of intelligent break-even analysis frameworks for alternative manufacturing options. These AI applications serve to enhance the decision-making processes by offering precise and effective solutions. Within the realm of break-even analysis, AI plays a role in enhancing cost evaluation, strategic planning, and support systems for decision-making. The break-even point (BEP) analysis is a fundamental tool in financial management, offering a clear, mathematical assessment of when a business or project will become profitable. It demarcates the precise moment at which revenues equal expenses, beyond which the company begins to generate profit.

Break-even analysis gives a dynamic view of the business's financial health. By showing the relationship between fixed and variable costs, businesses can mimimize expenses and improve sales targets. Additionally, it offers insights into how operational changes, market conditions, or strategic decisions may impact the break-even point and overall profitability.

The break-even point is a crucial metric for businesses of all sizes and sectors, as it provides a clear, quantifiable goal for achieving profitability and serves as a foundation for strategic financial planning and operational adjustments.

Return on Sales (ROS) is the ratio EBIT/sales and describes the operating leverage from a complementary side, as shown in paragraph 3.9.

Break-even analysis extends beyond merely pinpointing the moment at which a business recovers its costs. It acts as a versatile tool, informing various strategic and operational decisions across departments, including marketing and operations. Break-even analysis (depicted in Fig. 3.4) serves as a foundational tool not only for financial planning but also for informing strategies across marketing and operational functions. By providing a clear understanding of the relationship between sales, costs, and profitability, it enables businesses to make informed decisions, manage risks, and set targeted goals that support sustainable growth and profitability.

AI-driven operating leverage, in the context of financial analysis, refers to the impact of AI technologies on a firm's ability to achieve operational efficiency and profitability as it experiences changes in revenue or sales. It is closely related to the concept of operating leverage, which measures the sensitivity of a firm's operating income (earnings before interest and taxes, EBIT) to changes in its sales or revenue. Here's how AI-driven operating leverage can be understood:

1. **Traditional Operating Leverage**:

   - In traditional financial analysis, operating leverage measures how fixed costs and variable costs in a firm's cost structure affect its operating income.
   - When sales increase, the contribution margin (sales minus variable costs) increases, resulting in a proportionally higher increase in operating income.

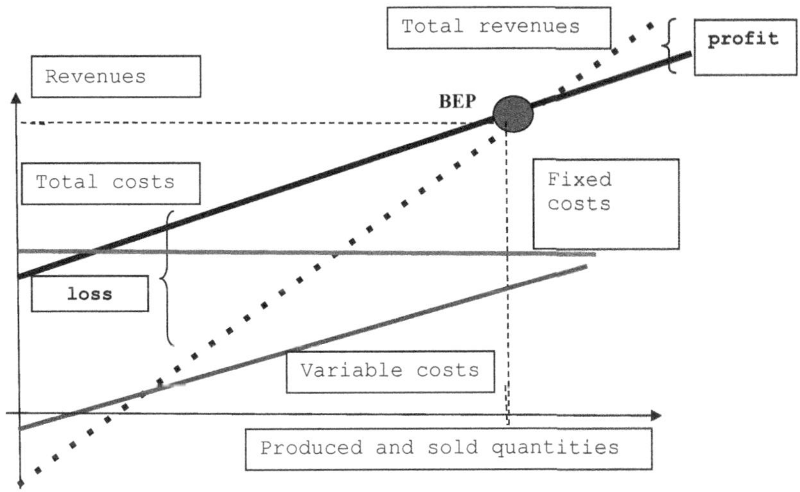

Fig. 3.4 Break-even analysis

2. **AI-Driven Operating Leverage**:
   - AI technologies modify a firm's cost structure, efficiency, and operations. AI-driven operating leverage considers how AI implementations impact a firm's ability to control costs.
   - With AI, a company can optimize supply chains, and make data-driven decisions in real time.
   - As revenue grows or declines, AI can help the firm adapt quickly to changing market conditions, reducing the impact of fixed costs.
3. **Impact on Risk and Volatility**:
   - AI-driven operating leverage can influence how risky or volatile a firm's operating income is when sales change.
   - If AI enables a firm to control costs effectively and adapt to market shifts, it may experience less volatility in its operating income when compared to companies with higher fixed costs and less operational flexibility.

4. **Examples of AI-Driven Leverage**:
   - For instance, a retail firm using AI-powered demand forecasting can maximize inventory levels, reducing carrying costs and waste, and fostering product availability. This can lead to improved operating income stability as sales fluctuate.
   - In the financial sector, AI-driven risk assessment and fraud detection can reduce losses, improving the stability of operating income.

AI-driven operating leverage considers how the adoption of AI technologies can impact a firm's ability to manage costs, maximize operations, and respond to changes in revenue. It can influence the degree of risk or volatility associated with a firm's operating income, as effective AI implementations can improve operational flexibility and efficiency. Companies that effectively leverage AI may experience more stable operating income growth, especially in dynamic and competitive markets.

3.8 The Impact of Scalability on the Enterprise Valuation

AI-driven scalability can have a significant impact on enterprise valuation. Scalability refers to an organization's ability to grow and adapt efficiently, and when AI is integrated into this process, it can improve several key factors that influence enterprise valuation:

1. **Revenue Growth Potential**:
   - AI-driven scalability can enable a firm to expand its customer base, introduce new products or services, and penetrate new markets more effectively. This increased revenue potential is a key driver of enterprise valuation.
2. **Cost Efficiency**:
   - Scalability often involves optimizing operations, automating processes, and reducing costs. AI technologies improve cost efficiency by streamlining workflows, reducing labor costs, and minimizing waste, all of which contribute positively to valuation.

3. **Competitive Advantage**:
    - AI improves customer experiences, improve product quality, and provide data-driven understandings, making it harder for competitors to catch up. This can result in a stronger market position.
4. **Customer Retention and Lifetime Value**:
    - Scalability with AI improves customer retention through personalization, and more accurate targeting. Higher customer retention rates lead to increased customer lifetime value (CLTV), which positively impacts valuation.
5. **Data-Driven Decision-Making**:
    - AI-driven scalability allows organizations to collect, assess, and leverage large amounts of data.
6. **Risk Mitigation**:
    - Scalable AI provides more stability to investors, potentially leading to a higher valuation.
7. **Innovation and Intellectual Property**:
    - AI-driven innovation creates valuable intellectual property (IP) such as proprietary algorithms, datasets, and software. These intangible assets improve enterprise valuation.
8. **Market Position and Growth Potential**:
    - A strong market position and growth potential are factors that investors consider when valuing a company.
9. **Predictive Analytics**:
    - AI fosters predictive analytics, allowing organizations to foresee future trends. This helps investors make informed decisions about a firm's growth.
10. **Mergers and Acquisitions (M&A)**:
    - Scalability with AI can make a firm an attractive target for acquisition by larger organizations looking to leverage its technology and customer base. This can result in premium valuations during M&A transactions.

The scalability driven by AI so has a significant impact on the valuation of enterprises. Using AI in IT Service Operations is critical in establishing business value and long-term viability. Organizations that employ AI technologies demonstrate attributes such as heightened profitability, rapid expansion, and substantial intangible assets, all contributing to their overall valuation. Despite the favorable consequences of AI Service Operations in improving service provision, reducing response times, and enhancing customer satisfaction, the announcement of AI investments may result in a decline in the market value of companies, particularly those in non-manufacturing sectors with limited IT capabilities. Consequently, although the scalability facilitated by AI can optimize operational effectiveness and profitability, its influence on enterprise valuation is intricate and subject to various factors, such as market perceptions and prevailing business frameworks. The impact of AI-driven scalability on enterprise valuation can vary depending on the industry, the quality of AI implementations, the competitive landscape, and the overall market conditions.

The link between scalability and liquidity is a fundamental concept to understand the cash flows that may be generated by incremental economic margins. The key margin is represented by EBITDA which is the only parameter that simultaneously expresses both an economic and a financial marginality. EBITDA is close to EBIT—the target parameter of operating leverage—since it can be calculated from EBIT just by summing up non-monetary operating costs like depreciation and amortization.

Whereas EBITDA already includes operating expenses (monetary OPEX), capital expenses (CAPEX) are reported in the cash flow statement (see the graph below) after the EBITDA and before the operating cash flow.

CAPEX (Capital Expenditures) and OPEX (Operating Expenses) are two critical components of business financial management, each playing a unique role in the company's budgeting, financial reporting, and strategic planning processes. Understanding the distinction between the two is crucial for effective financial management and long-term strategic planning. Understanding the differences between CAPEX and OPEX is vital for making informed financial decisions, planning for the future, and effectively managing a company's resources.

Operating leverage is a measure of how revenue growth translates into growth in operating income (EBIT). If we add up depreciation and amortization to EBIT, we get EBITDA, which is simultaneously an economic and a liquidity margin. There is an important link between operating leverage and liquidity.

Any change in the operating leverage has an impact on liquidity (as shown in Fig. 3.5) because operating leverage is linked to EBITDA which is the first parameter of the cash flow statement.

Any sales increase has an impact on the EBITDA and the EBIT. The fixed vs. variable mix may change, influencing the operating net working capital. Normally, an increase in sales produces an increase in both receivables and stock; higher sales are typically driven by higher purchases, with a consequent increase in payables. If the economic marginality of the sales increase remains positive, then the net working capital is likely to grow, since the increase in receivables and stock exceeds the growth of payables. A higher net working capital absorbs cash and so, part of the liquidity that is generated by a higher EBIT/EBITDA is used for financing this growth. Higher sales are often fueled by an increase in CAPEX that absorbs cash.

The impact of a sales change on the net working capital can be better detected by considering the aging of receivables, stock, and payables:

$$\text{receivables/sales} * 365 \tag{3.4}$$

$$\text{stock/production costs} * 365 \tag{3.5}$$

$$\text{payables/purchases} * 365 \tag{3.6}$$

The balance (EBITDA ± Net Working Capital ± CAPEX) is represented by the Operating Cash Flow which is also known as unlevered (or debt-free) cash flow (FCFF), as it is calculated before the debt service (debt-free companies have an operating cash flow that corresponds to the net cash flow and a raised capital equal to the equity).

3.9 Corporate Profitability and Scalability

Scalability has a marginal (incremental) impact not only on cash flows (starting from the EBITDA) but also on economic margins that are the core component of corporate profitability.

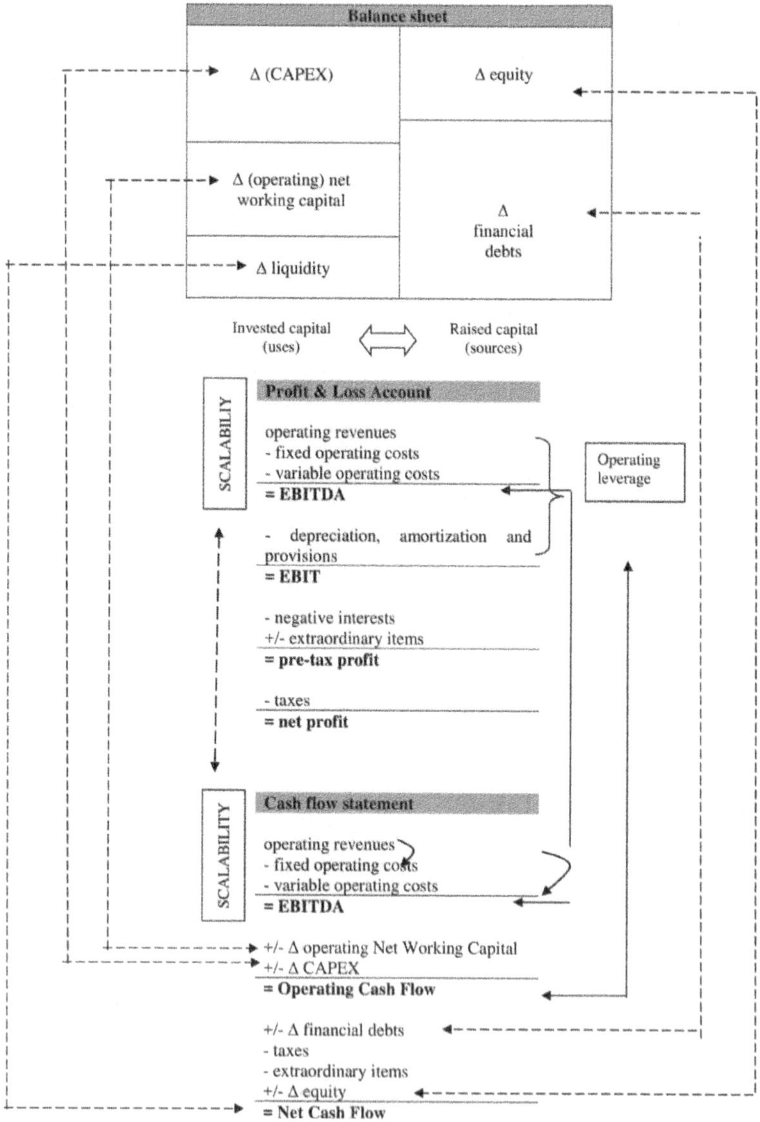

Fig. 3.5 Operating leverage and cash flows

Corporate profitability is a core issue of financial statement analysis and corporate finance. Economic profitability derives from positive marginality where revenues exceed costs.

The return on equity (ROE) is a measure of the profitability of a business concerning the book value of shareholder equity, also known as net assets or assets minus liabilities. ROE is a measure of how well a firm uses investments to generate earnings growth.

ROE is equal to net income (Rn), divided by total equity (E), expressed as a percentage:

$$\text{ROE} = \frac{\text{Net Profit}}{\text{Equity}} \tag{3.7}$$

The return on invested capital (ROIC) is the ratio between the operating profit (EBIT) and the resources that back it (raised = invested capital). A high ROIC means the investment's gains compare favorably to its cost. As a performance measure, ROIC is used to evaluate the efficiency of an investment or to compare the efficiencies of several different investments. In purely economic terms, it is one way of relating profits to capital invested. The formula is the following:

$$\text{ROIC} = \frac{\text{EBIT}}{\text{Invested Capital}} \tag{3.8}$$

Return on sales (ROS) is a ratio used to evaluate a firm's operational efficiency; ROS is also known as a firm's operating profit margin. This measure provides an understanding into how much profit is being produced per € of sales. An increasing ROS indicates that a firm is growing more efficiently, while a decreasing ROS could signal a looming outlook.

ROS measures the performance of a firm by analyzing the percentage of total revenue that is converted into operating profits. It expresses the profitability of sales:

$$\text{ROS} = \frac{\text{EBIT}}{\text{sales}} \tag{3.9}$$

ROE can be decomposed into four ratios that include both ROIC and ROS:

$$\text{ROE} = \frac{\text{sales}}{\text{invested capital}} \frac{\text{EBIT}}{\text{sales}} \frac{\text{invested capital}}{\text{Equity}} \frac{\text{net profit}}{\text{EBIT}} = \frac{\text{net profit}}{\text{equity}} \tag{3.10}$$

A further formulation of ROE is given by Modigliani and Miller's proposition II (Ross, 1988; Modigliani & Miller, 1958).

3.10 Metcalfe's Law

Metcalfe's Law concerns one of the scalability factors recalled in Table 3.1 and highlights the fundamental principle of network effects in telecommunications and digital networks, asserting that the value of a network grows as the square of the number of its users. This concept has broad implications for economics, business management, and the strategic considerations of companies in the tech and telecommunications sectors, especially regarding mergers, market penetration, and platform development strategies.

Metcalfe's Law provides a foundational understanding of how network effects drive the value of telecommunications and digital networks, influencing business strategies and economic outcomes in the connected world. However, its application must be nuanced, considering practical constraints and the quality of connections, not just their quantity.

If a network is composed of n people and each of them assigns to the network a value that is proportional to the number of other participants, then the value that all the n people assign to the network is the following:

$$n * (n - 1) = n^2 - n \tag{3.11}$$

The law has often been illustrated using the example of now old-fashioned fax machines: a single fax is useless, but the value of every fax machine increases with the total number of fax machines in the network because of the total number of people with whom each user may send and receive documents increases. Likewise, in social networks, the greater the number of users with the service, the more valuable the service becomes to the community.

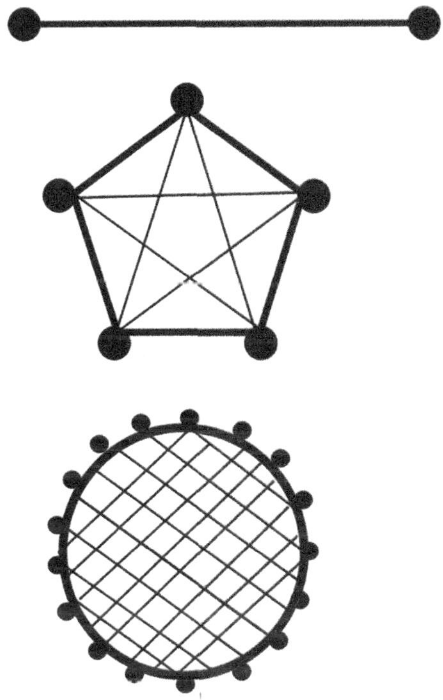

Fig. 3.6 Different types of communication networks

As exemplified in Fig. 3.6, if we take two telephones, they can make only one connection, five can make 10 connections, and twelve can make 66 connections. The formula describes exponential growth.

Figure 3.7 shows the exponential growth of a network following Metcalfe's law.

The Break-even point is in Fig. 3.8.

3.11 Moore's Law and Other Scalability Patterns

Moore's law refers to the computation of the number of transistors in a dense and integrated circuit. Specifically, the computation (i.e., the price) will double about every 18 months.

Recent advancements in digital electronics are strongly linked to Moore's law: quality-adjusted microprocessors, memory capacity, sensors,

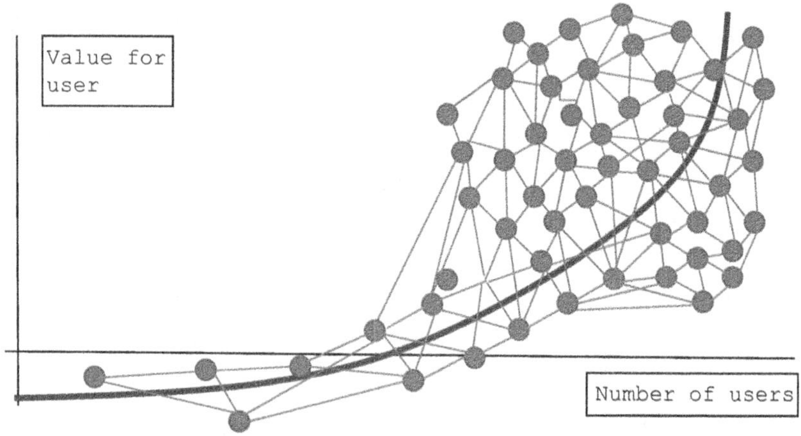

Fig. 3.7 Value for the networked user according to Metcalfe's law

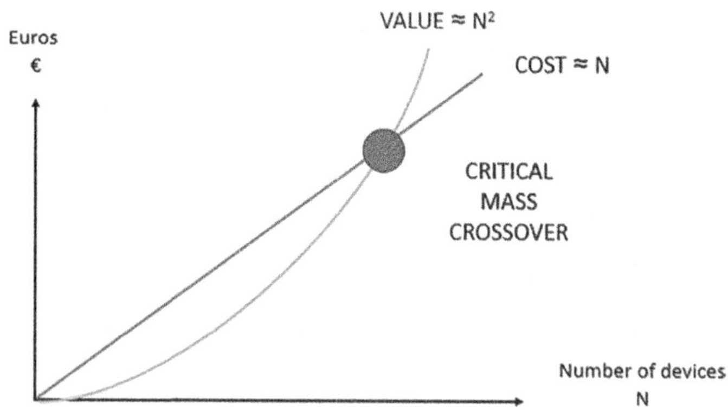

Fig. 3.8 Break-even point with Metcalfe's law

and even the number and size of pixels in digital cameras are affected by it.

Essentially, Moore's law describes an exponential growth pattern in the complexity of integrated semiconductor circuits. This concept was later revised and extended by some computer scientists and researchers to include future forms of technology.

In broader terms, Moore's law describes a driving force of technological and social change, productivity, and economic growth. This is consistent with digital scalability.

Hyoung et al. (2020) summarize the three main Laws of Network Effect that are intrinsically consistent with the scalability properties.

Table 3.3 synthesizes the main properties of some of the most known network laws. Many of these laws are empirical, with a weak scientific background and controversial evidence. Technological evolution is intrinsically difficult to forecast and so differs from its expected patterns. Most of the scalability laws recalled in the following table may look outdated or imprecise. They are, however, useful since they recall some basic principles and retain an orientation predictive power, giving a rough idea of how scalability patterns may evolve. A common denominator is represented by statistical "power laws" (according to which one quantity varies as a power of another) that are intrinsically consistent with the scalability patterns (Table 3.5).

Examples of Reed's law underscore its essence, which posits that the utility of large networks, especially those enabling users to form groups, grows exponentially with the number of users. This law highlights the importance of network structures that support the creation of subgroups, communities, and shared interests, significantly enhancing the network's value beyond just the sum of its individual connections. Here's a closer look at how Reed's Law manifests in each example:

- Social Media Platforms (Facebook, TikTok, etc.)
- Messaging Applications
- Open-Source Software
- Wikipedia
- Online Games with Social Features

Reed's Law highlights the significant strategic advantage internet platforms can gain through network effects driven by subgroup formation and collaboration. By understanding and leveraging these dynamics, platforms can achieve dominant positions in their markets, though they must also navigate the challenges associated with managing large and diverse networks.

Odlyzko and Tilly (2005) challenge the optimistic assumptions underpinning both Reed's and Metcalfe's Laws. While Reed's Law suggests

Table 3.5 Network scalability laws

Scalability law	*Formula*	*Features/Properties*
Sarnoff's law	Network Value = n	The value of a broadcast network is directly proportional to the number of viewers or users. In simpler terms, Sarnoff's Law suggests that the value of a network increases linearly with its audience size. This is because the content is broadcasted to many viewers at the same time, but the value creation is one way and does not benefit from the interactions among those users
Metcalfe's law	Network Value = n^2	Network value increases exponentially with an increasing number of devices on the network. The value of a telecommunications network is proportional to the square of the number of connected users of the system
Reed's law	Network Value = 2^n	The value of a network grows exponentially with the number of its subgroups, rather than just with the number of individual users or connections

Scalability law	*Formula*	*Features/Properties*
Moore's law	$n_O = n_{02}(y_i - y_0)/T2$, where $n_0 n_0$ is the number of transistors in some reference year, $y_0 y_0$, and $T2 = 2T2 = 2$ is the number of years taken to double this number	Moore observed that the number of transistors on a microchip double approximately every two years, though the cost of computers is halved. This observation has broadly been interpreted to mean that computing power and efficiency would significantly increase at an exponential rate over time, while the relative cost decreases. The law's impact extends beyond just processing power, affecting developments in storage capacity, network speed, and even battery life, reflecting the broad influence of this principle on technological progress
Henderson law		Henderson's Law, often associated with the experience curve or the learning curve, is a concept that Bruce Henderson of the Boston Consulting Group introduced in 1968. It posits that with each doubling of cumulative production, the cost of manufacturing (or unit cost) tends to decrease at a predictable rate. This decrease in unit costs is attributed to increased efficiency, learning, and technological advancements as production volume grows. Henderson's Law is a specific manifestation of the broader category of "Power laws", which describe relationships where a relative change in one quantity results in a proportional relative change in another quantity, regardless of the initial size of those quantities

(continued)

Table 3.5 (continued)

Scalability law	*Formula*	*Features/Properties*
Wright's law	$C_n = C_{1n-a}$ where: C_1 is the cost of the first unit of production C_n is the cost of the nth unit of production n is the cumulative volume of production a is the elasticity of cost regarding output	Wright's Law, also known as the experience curve effect, is a foundational concept in the analysis of cost behavior and efficiency improvements in manufacturing and other industries. This principle posits that with each doubling of cumulative production, there is a predictable, constant percentage reduction in the required labor time per unit, or more broadly, in the value-added costs per unit. This reduction reflects efficiency gains from learning and process improvements. The concept has broad implications for strategic planning, cost management, pricing, and competitive analysis
Kryder's law		Kryder's Law suggests that the storage capacity of hard drives would double approximately every 18 months, leading to a rapid decrease in the cost per gigabyte of storage. This exponential increase in data storage density has been crucial for the development and expansion of digital technologies, allowing for the storage of ever-larger amounts of data in smaller physical spaces at lower costs

Scalability law	*Formula*	*Features/Properties*
Butters' law		The cost of transmitting a bit over an optical network decreases by half every nine months. While less well-known than Moore's Law, which predicts the doubling of transistors on integrated circuits approximately every two years, Butters' Law has significant implications for telecommunications and the broader field of data transmission
Nielsen's law		Wired bandwidth growth
Gilder's law		The total bandwidth of communication systems triples every twelve months
Cooper's law		Cooper's Law, named after Martin Cooper, who is credited with inventing the cellular phone, outlines the dramatic growth in the capability to transmit information over the electromagnetic spectrum without interference. Cooper observed that the total capacity of radio spectrum to carry information has doubled approximately every 30 months since Guglielmo Marconi's first wireless transmission in 1895. This exponential increase is attributed to advances in technology, such as improvements in signal processing, the development of more efficient coding schemes, the use of higher frequencies, and more sophisticated network topologies

(continued)

Table 3.5 (continued)

Scalability law	*Formula*	*Features/Properties*
Poor's law		Network address density growth
Beckström's law		The value of a network equals the net value added to each user's transactions conducted through that network, summed over all users
Radoff's law	[qualitative proposition]	The mere size of a network is not the only determinant of its value; rather, how well the network enables and supports interconnections among its participants plays a crucial role
Metaverse extension (Moro-Visconti, 2022c)		The Metaverse is a supercharged network that not only embodies but also extends traditional network properties. Its development will likely continue to evolve the ways in which value and utility are understood and measured in digital spaces, challenging and expanding existing network theories

that the value of a network grows exponentially with the number of users, due to the potential for subgroup formation, and Metcalfe's Law posits that the value of a network grows proportionally to the square of the number of connected users, both perspectives might overlook key practical limitations.

An important trend in modern AI research consists of a shift from the "bigger is better" approach to a focus on making AI models more efficient:

1. Model Size and Gigantism: AI models have been growing in size at an astonishing rate. For example, GPT-4, a recent model, is estimated to have approximately 1 trillion parameters, which is nearly six times more than its predecessor. This trend is sometimes referred to as "gigantism".
2. Increasing Costs: Larger models require more computational resources to train and operate. This leads to increased costs in terms of both hardware and energy consumption. As models become larger, the resource requirements become more significant.
3. Need for Efficiency: To continue improving AI models and addressing real-world challenges, researchers are realizing the need to make models more efficient. This means achieving better performance with fewer resources.
4. Trade-Offs: One approach to efficiency is to make trade-offs, such as reducing the number of parameters in a model while compensating by training the model with more data. This can help maintain or improve performance while reducing computational requirements.
5. Fuzzy Math: Another approach is to use less precision in mathematical computations within the model. By rounding off numbers and using fewer decimal places, the hardware requirements for training and inference can be significantly reduced. This approach is often referred to as quantization.

Efforts to make AI models more efficient are driven by practical considerations, including cost, environmental impact, and the limitations of available hardware. While larger models have achieved impressive results, there is a recognition that such models may not be sustainable in the long term without significant advances in efficiency. Researchers are exploring various techniques to balance model size and computational efficiency to permit AI technology to remain practical and accessible for a wide range of applications.

3.12 Exponential Growth

Exponential Technology can be defined as a type of technology that can double its capability or performance in each period or, conversely, halve its costs in each period.

Examples of exponential technologies include computers, networks, 3D printing, drones, robotics, and AI. According to Ismail (2014), each exponential technology is characterized by the so-called "6 Ds" that are:

1. Digitized: the technology has a digital form;
2. Deceptive: the initial growth may seem slow and not influential;
3. Disruptive: the growth becomes incredibly rapid after a certain threshold;
4. Dematerialized: the technology loses its materiality. GPS or video cameras became smartphone apps, so they no longer need to be carried as separate entities. Location and time do not matter: there are no physical and time constraints (value of ubiquity and "any time").
5. Demonetized: the technology replaces other products/services previously adopted (usually more expensive), for example, Uber rapidly became a remarkable competitor of the traditional taxi industry;
6. Democratic: the technology becomes accessible (and affordable) to most of the population (Ismail, 2014) (Fig. 3.9).

The world of exponential organizations does not ensure a secure position and stable profitability in the market (as happened for *Kodak*, forced to exit the market).

Only scalable, fast-moving, and smart organizations can survive in this dynamic environment and gain exponential success.

"*An exponential organization is one whose impact (or output) is disproportionally large compared to its peers because of the use of new organizational techniques that leverage accelerating technologies*" (Ismail, 2014). This definition implies that both, a large workforce, and large physical plants, are no longer essential for a firm to grow. A dematerialization is

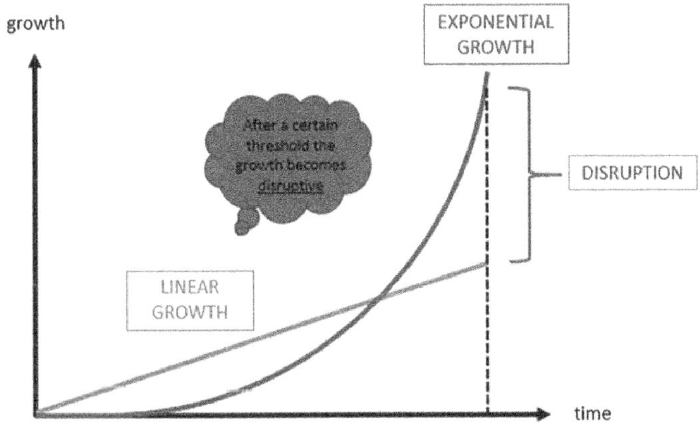

Fig. 3.9 Linear vs Exponential Growth

taking place, and the on-demand market is fast rising: exponential organizations base their activities primarily on information technologies and digital transformation.

Disruptive changes tend to occur every time that fields, which have no elements in common, do connect (as the waterpower and textile loom, whose combination can be considered as the premonitory factor of the Industrial Revolution). Today, due to the massive and detailed quantity of information easily accessible and supported by the strength of technology, cross-connecting innovative fields become easier, so that the most disparate connections arise, such as art and biology, economics, and chemistry. Interdisciplinary approaches add value.

A firm is traditionally characterized by linear, sequential thinking: linear operations, measures of performance, and success make the firm look at the environment from a linear perspective. Nowadays, this approach is overcome by top-down and bottom-up convergence and cross-pollination, and the firm has a multifaceted vision of the competitive environment in which it operates. This increases its flexibility and favors the exploitation of real options.

Communication and interaction among people and companies have been profoundly affected by the advent of the internet which not only reduces traditional costs but also opens completely new advertising sources with still infinite unexplored possibilities for companies. The result of this is that the costs of distributing a product or a service have dropped almost to zero.

According to Ismail (2014), traditional companies can only achieve arithmetic output per input, whereas "an exponential organization achieves geometric outputs per input by riding the doubling-exponential pattern of information-based technologies".

Each exponential organization sets its *Massive Transformative Purpose* (MTP), which is the aspirational purpose of the firm that differs from the simple organization's mission since an MTP should be both, global and transformative. Not only is MTP a strong source of competitive advantage for the "first movers" in the industry since it is hard for competitors to replicate an aim that implies a global vision, but it also attracts new talents and retains them. An effective MTP creates a robust ecosystem around the firm formed by customers, suppliers, partners, developers, and governments.

Exponential organizations tend to choose an external, updated, temporary, and highly specialized workforce: staff on demand is, in fact, a necessary characteristic that improves speed, functionality, and flexibility in a fast-changing world within a growing internet-driven marketplace where expertise gaps need to be filled exogenously (outsourcing).

As already mentioned, Airbnb does not own the property it rents. Similarly, Uber is not the owner of any of the cars' drivers: "Non-ownership, then, is the key to owning the future". These examples show that if an asset is information-based or commoditized, accessing it is better than possessing it. Leveraged assets are consistent with a non-ownership pattern that allows scalable products, lowers the marginal cost of supply, removes asset management, and increases agility and resilience. This process needs an abundance of easily available assets and digital interfaces. However, if an asset is rare, ownership becomes the best solution: Amazon owns its warehouses and Tesla its factories.

In the last few years, the word "engagement" assumed an increasing value for any type of firm: coupons, loyalty cards, and quizzes are just some of the strategies adopted to improve the interaction with customers and, social media, supported by a large and easily accessible amount of data, play the key role in this process. Engagement not only increases customers' loyalty but also amplifies ideation, transforms an unidentified crowd into a real community, leverages marketing, enables play and learning, and provides a digital feedback loop with users.

3.13 Geo-localization and Traceability

Digital ubiquity often needs to be appropriately "grounded" in physical places where consumers live. Hence the importance of geo-localization.

Geo-localization is the attachment of geolocation to an object. Geo-localization involves pinpointing the geographic location of an object or individual using various technologies, ranging from GPS (Global Positioning System) satellites to IP address tracking on internet-connected devices. This capability is both dynamic, reflecting the movement of mobile objects, and static, denoting fixed positions. Geo-localization can relate to network theory since the exact positioning of different nodes represents the starting point for a more comprehensive analysis of their value-adding interactions.

Traceability is a concept that identifies the quality of having an origin or course of development that may be found or followed. Whereas the source is geolocated, its patterns follow a dynamic path that in many cases, can be located—traced—by digital devices (sensors, satellites, etc.). Geo-localized data fuel IoT and big data, populating interoperable databases typically stored in the cloud. Traceability is consistent with digital supply chains where each step needs constant monitoring.

Consequent analysis can be carried on with dedicated software, fueled by IoT and big data, and interpreted with AI. Validation and traceability may be conducted via blockchains (see Harshini & Kumar, 2022). These concepts are consistent with a comprehensive valuation of digital intangibles.

AI has a profound impact on geo-localization and traceability, enhancing these technologies in several key ways:

a. **Improved Accuracy in Geo-Concerns One of the Localization**: AI algorithms can assess data from various sources, such as GPS, Wi-Fi, cell towers, and IoT devices, to improve the accuracy of geolocation services. Machine learning models can learn from large datasets to refine location accuracy, even in challenging environments like urban canyons or indoors.

b. **Real-Time Data Processing and Analysis**: AI enables the processing of large volumes of real-time data from multiple sources.

This capability is crucial for applications requiring up-to-the-minute tracking, such as fleet management, logistics, and emergency response.

c. **Improved Traceability**: In supply chain management, AI can significantly improve the traceability of products. By analyzing data from various points along the supply chain, AI can provide detailed understanding into the journey of a product, from manufacturing to delivery. This enhanced traceability is crucial for quality control, inventory management, and ensuring the authenticity of products.
d. **Predictive Analytics**: AI utilizes historical geolocation data to forecast future patterns and trends. This is particularly useful in logistics and transportation, where predicting traffic patterns, delivery times, and potential delays can maximize routes and improve efficiency.
e. **Customized Location-Based Services**: AI enables the creation of personalized location-based services for users. For instance, retailers can use AI to assess a customer's location data (with consent) to provide targeted advertisements or offers when the customer is near their store.
f. **Anomaly Detection and Security**: AI can detect anomalies in the movement patterns of tracked objects or individuals, which is vital for security and fraud detection. In logistics, for instance, AI can alert if a shipment deviates from its planned route, indicating potential theft or loss.
g. **Integration with Other Technologies**: AI improves the synergy between geolocation and other technologies like IoT, big data, and blockchain. This integration allows for more comprehensive solutions, such as ensuring the integrity of data in traceability systems.
h. **Environmental Monitoring and Management**: AI aids in tracking environmental changes and wildlife movements. By analyzing location data, AI can help in monitoring endangered species, tracking deforestation, or observing climate change impacts.
i. **Automated Decision-Making**: In scenarios like autonomous vehicles or drone navigation, AI's role in geo-localization is critical. It enables these systems to make real-time navigational decisions based on accurate location data.

3.14 From Digital Scalability to Blitzscaling

As already stated, scalability indicates the ability of a business model to generate incremental demand (additional revenues) economically, i.e., without significantly increasing costs.

The concept can be interpreted, in terms of operational leverage, minimizing variable costs, typical of many technological startups: in this case, the increase in revenues creates a virtuous circle and reflects almost entirely on the EBIT.

The scalability of intangible assets allows seeing a growth in revenues accompanied by a less than proportional increase in variable costs. This has a positive impact on economic and financial margins, generating a driving force that improves the rating and bankability of intangible-intensive companies.

The sometimes-explosive effect of this phenomenon can be observed in highly successful companies (such as Amazon, Alphabet/Google, Meta/Facebook, etc.) based on digital business models, where, thanks to the scalability effect, after reaching economic break-even, the higher revenues are almost entirely transferred to operating margins (Gross Operating margin/EBITDA and EBIT).

The bankability of intangible assets is based on a paradox that although they have a lower collateral value than real estate (or even tend to zero, if they are considered intangible such as know-how or goodwill in the absence of business continuity) they have a high capacity to produce incremental economic-income flows, to be used primarily to service debt.

In this context, an application is the "Scalability of contacts" (potential customers) which allows firms to enlarge their user bases with technological devices, leveraging the growth with a synergistic combination of:

- Cloud computing and IT outsourced to remote providers;
- Smartphones and other ICT end-user devices;
- (Viral) Social media;
- M-apps as a bridging gate between the digital firm and its potential customers;
- Limited physical plant and staff with consequent minimization of tangible CAPEX and OPEX;
- Blitzscaling, i.e., adopting a specific set of practices for igniting and managing dizzying growth prioritizing speed over efficiency, and

allowing firms to go from "startup" to "scaleup" (Hoffman & Yeh, 2018);

- Strong revenue growth levered by the factors above;
- Deregulation or "far-West style" lack of regulation, since new business models often precede legal prescriptions aimed at preventing abuses detrimental to consumers and competitors.

Blitzscaling is a strategy that prioritizes rapid growth, often at the expense of short-term profitability, to achieve a dominant market position. When powered by AI, it involves leveraging AI technologies to accelerate growth and innovation.

AI-driven blitzscaling combines the principles of blitzscaling (rapid growth) with AI capabilities. It emphasizes speed, innovation, and market disruption, often prioritizing market share over short-term profitability.

The primary goal of AI-driven blitzscaling is to capture and dominate markets quickly by using AI to sort out innovative products, automate processes, and scale operations at an unprecedented pace.

AI-driven blitzscaling involves leveraging AI technologies such as machine learning, natural language processing, and data analytics to automate tasks, tailorizes user experiences, easing data-driven decisions.

Key Differences and Considerations May Be Summarized as Follows:

- **Speed vs. Stability**: Digital scalability aims for stable and efficient growth, whereas AI-driven blitzscaling prioritizes speed and market disruption, often accepting higher risks.
- **Innovation Focus**: AI-driven blitzscaling places a strong emphasis on AI-powered innovation to sort out disruptive products or services, while digital scalability may focus more on optimizing existing processes.
- **Resource Allocation**: Blitzscaling may require substantial investments in AI research, development, and talent acquisition, which can impact financial metrics in the short term.
- **Market Dominance**: AI-driven blitzscaling seeks to rapidly establish market dominance, while digital scalability may aim for steady, sustainable growth.

- **Challenges**: AI-driven blitzscaling can face challenges related to talent acquisition, regulatory compliance, and managing the risks associated with rapid growth.

The transition from digital scalability to AI-driven blitzscaling represents a shift in strategic focus, where the integration of AI technologies enables organizations to pursue rapid and disruptive growth in a highly competitive landscape. While it offers the potential for market dominance and innovation, it also comes with unique challenges and risks that organizations must carefully manage.

3.15 Scalable and Digital Supply and Value Chains

A supply chain is a network between a firm and its suppliers to produce and distribute a specific product to the final buyer.

Network theory is consistent with the architectural framework of the supply chain, which has gradually been modified by the widespread use of intangibles in the digital society.

Intangibles can strongly contribute to the flexibility of supply chains. What makes supply chains resilient is:

- A synergistic mix of complementary intangibles (e.g., big data and IoT that fuel patented processes and AI applications);
- A scalable network of expanding nodes and linking edges, incorporating growth real options, and B2B or B2C relationships;
- Digital platforms as a service (PaaS) refers to cloud computing services that offer a platform for customers to develop, run, and manage applications without the need to build and maintain the underlying infrastructure. This model provides a comprehensive set of tools, libraries, and frameworks that enable developers to focus on application development and deployment, rather than worrying about the complexities of infrastructure management (Butler, 2013).

Network theory is mostly related to digital platforms, which in turn represent the linchpin of intangibles and scalability. The most powerful active platforms nowadays are Amazon, Apple, Google, and Facebook. They share some common characteristics and are all rooted in equally powerful technologies not predicated on physical assets. They benefit from innovative ecosystems, which emphasize core interactions between platform participants, including consumers, producers, and third-party actors (Jacobides et al., 2018).

Korpela et al. (2017) examine the digital supply chain integration and highlight the evolving landscape of how businesses manage and synchronize their operations across the supply chain. The study underscores the importance of dynamic integration in meeting customer demands more effectively, enhancing product and service delivery visibility, and ensuring comprehensive integration of product data (Figs. 3.10 and 3.11).

As shown in Fig. 3.12, the key value drivers of digital supply chains include:

- Fast (just-in-time) end-to-end integration through digital enablers;
- Traceability and visibility of deliveries through smart logistics partners;
- Cost-effective cloud solutions provided by ICT partners;
- Sharing of timely information stored in the cloud;

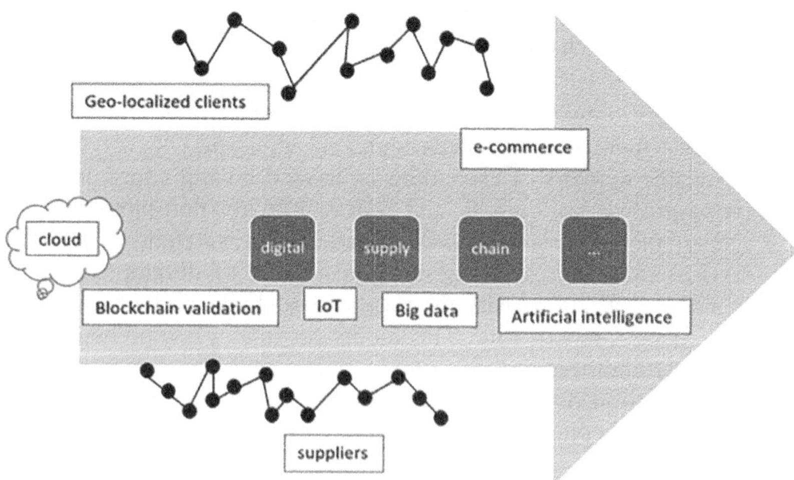

Fig. 3.10 Key-value drivers of digital supply chains

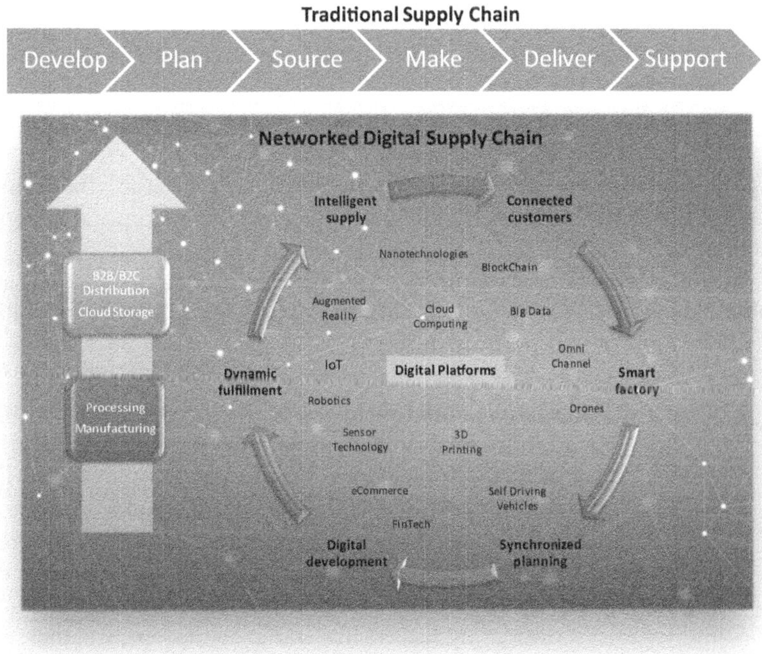

Fig. 3.11 Traditional versus digital supply chain

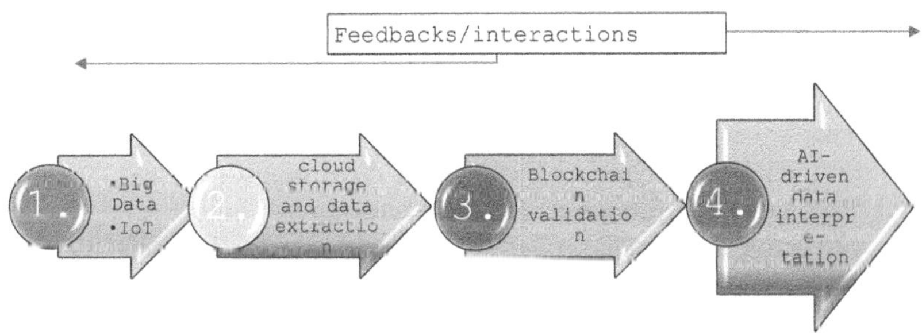

Fig. 3.12 Sequential value chain

- Standardized integration of business transactions and collaboration processes through digital platforms accessed by consortium members;
- Networking with geo-localized e-commerce customers;

Figure 3.11 shows the main differences between a basic (traditional) supply chain and a networked digital supply chain that incorporates trendy intangibles.

AI has a transformative impact on scalable and digital supply and value chains in several ways, significantly enhancing efficiency, visibility, flexibility, and overall performance:

a. **Demand Forecasting and Inventory Management**: AI algorithms predict demand more accurately by examining patterns from market trends, consumer behavior, historical data, and outside factors like weather or economic conditions. This leads to maximized inventory levels, reducing both shortages and excess stock, and thus lowering costs.
b. **Supply Chain Optimization**: AI can optimize supply chain routes and logistics, considering factors like traffic conditions, weather, and fuel costs. This optimization can lead to significant cost savings and efficiency improvements, especially in global supply chains with complex logistics networks.
c. **Improved Visibility and Tracking**: AI provides real-time evidence into the supply chain, tracking the movement of goods and monitoring conditions like temperature or humidity where necessary. This enhanced tracking is crucial for sensitive products and helps in quickly identifying and addressing disruptions.
d. **Predictive Maintenance**: In manufacturing and logistics, AI enables predictive maintenance of equipment and vehicles. By analyzing data from sensors and historical maintenance records, AI can predict when a machine is likely to fail and schedule maintenance before it happens, thus reducing downtime.
e. **Automated Decision-Making**: AI systems can make automated decisions based on real-time data, such as rerouting shipments in response to delays or disruptions. This automation increases the supply chain's responsiveness and agility.

f. **Personalization and Customer Experience**: AI can tailor product offerings and customer experiences by analyzing consumer data and preferences. This personalization leads to higher client satisfaction and loyalty.
g. **Risk Management and Mitigation**: AI can identify and assess risks in the supply chain, from geopolitical issues to potential supplier bankruptcies. By predicting these risks, companies can take proactive measures to mitigate them.
h. **Quality Control**: AI-powered visual inspection systems can improve quality control in manufacturing. These systems can detect defects or irregularities more accurately and consistently than human inspectors.
i. **Integration with IoT and Blockchain**: AI works synergistically with other technologies like the Internet of Things (IoT) and blockchain. IoT provides a wealth of data from connected devices, while blockchain ensures the integrity and traceability of transactions. AI leverages this data and technology to sort out more efficient, transparent, and secure supply chains.
j. **Sustainability and Environmental Impact**: AI can maximize supply chain operations to reduce waste, energy usage, and carbon footprint, contributing to more sustainable business practices.

AI significantly improves the scalability and digitalization of supply and value chains, driving improvements in efficiency, cost-effectiveness, responsiveness, and customer satisfaction. AI has the ability to bolster risk management through the examination of data for the identification of potential risks. Subsequently, AI contributes to the detection of fraud by scrutinizing substantial amounts of data in real time to pinpoint anomalies that could signify fraudulent activities. Furthermore, AI plays a crucial role in optimizing working capital management by scrutinizing inventory levels, order volumes, and payment terms to enhance cash flow.

The economic, financial, and market evaluation metrics are based on a consequential value chain that starts from big data (or the Internet of Things), passes through cloud storage in interoperable databases, and is then validated through blockchain and ultimately interpreted with AI, as illustrated in Fig. 3.12.

3.16 Digital Transformation

Digitalization is defined as the concept of "going paperless", namely as the technical process of transforming analog information or physical products into digital form. The term "digital transformation" refers, therefore, to the application of digital technology as an alternative to solve traditional problems. As a result of digital solutions, new forms of innovation and creativity are conceived, while traditional methods are revised and improved.

Digitally born startups or similar tech businesses are not the only ones interested in adopting digital processes. Traditional businesses may be digitalized as well (e.g., a simple farmer willing to increase exponentially his/her production of tomatoes may digitalize the production activities through new systems or machines). In practice, with digitalization, traditional firms improve their key economic and financial parameters, as the EBITDA, increases, while the WACC reduces, so improving the DCF and the overall enterprise value (EV):

$$\frac{O_{CF} \uparrow}{\text{WACC} \downarrow} \cong \text{Enterprise Value} \uparrow\uparrow \tag{3.12}$$

In synthesis, digitalization brings speed and quality at a low cost, thus representing a key driver for scalability itself. Digitalization enables a business process reengineering of traditional firms which may presuppose incremental production growth.

Figure 3.13 shows the link between digital transformation and scalability.

3.17 Networking Digital Platforms

Digital scalability is increasingly dependent on IT platforms. Spagnoletti et al. (2015, p. 364) define a digital platform as "a building block that provides an essential function to a technological system and serves as a foundation upon which complementary products, technologies, or services can be developed".

Digital platforms and supply chains are naturally linked with the networked firm and improve a scalability multiplier, benefitting also from Metcalfe's effect. An example is represented in Fig. 3.14.

Platforms are facilitators of exchange (of goods, services, and information) between different types of stakeholders that could not otherwise

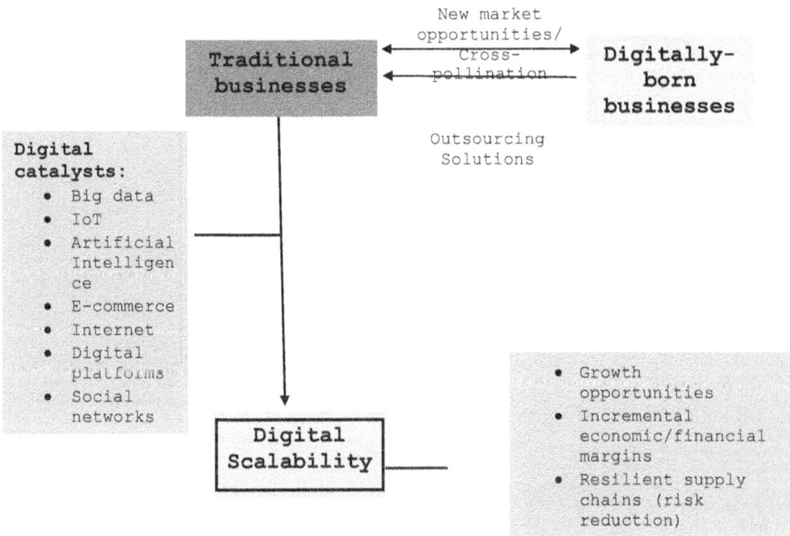

Fig. 3.13 The link between digital transformation and scalability

interact with each other. Transactions are mediated through complementary players that share a network ecosystem (Rochet & Tirole, 2003).

Digital platforms are multisided digital frameworks that shape the terms on which participants interact with one another. Digital platforms are also complicated mixtures of software, hardware, operations, and networks (De Reuven et al., 2018; Gawer, 2014). They provide a set of shared techniques, technologies, and interfaces to a broad set of users; social and economic interactions are mediated online, often by apps (Kenney & Zysman, 2016).

Digital platforms are complementarily defined as "software-based external platforms consisting of the extensible codebase of a software-based system that provides core functionality shared by the modules that interoperate with it and the interfaces through which they interoperate" (Tiwana et al., 2010).

Software platforms represent a technological meeting ground where application developers and end-users converge (Evans et al., 2006).

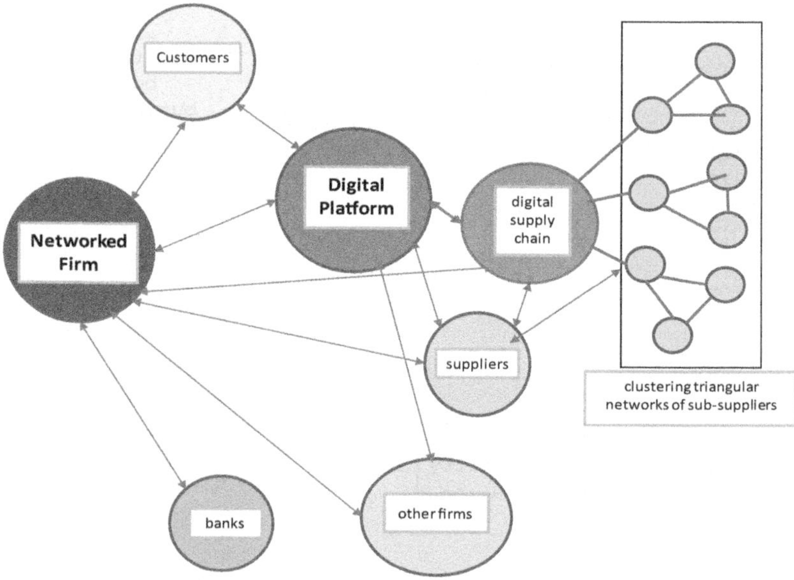

Fig. 3.14 Networked digital platforms

Digital technologies imply homogenization of data, editability, reprogrammability, distributedness, and self-referentiality (Kallinikos et al., 2013; Yoo et al., 2010). Such characteristics of digitality can lead to multiple inheritances in distributed settings, meaning there is no single owner who owns the platform core and dictates its design hierarchy (Henfridsson et al., 2014).

Multi-sided platforms continue to disrupt long-established industries and have governance structures ranging from a very centralistic and autocratic organization to a more split approach with empowerment on the user side (the patient). Also, the accessibility varies from a high degree of openness to detailed background checks users need to pass to participate in the platform (Schreieck et al., 2018). These characteristics may strongly impact healthcare digital platforms.

Digital platforms have transformed the landscape of human activities across various domains. By leveraging the power of the internet and digital technology, these platforms have facilitated new forms of economic transactions, social interactions, and political engagement (e.g., Kane et al., 2014). Platforms, by leveraging networked technologies, have fundamentally transformed the way economic exchanges are conducted, information is transferred, and how people connect. The transformation brought about by digital platforms is profound, reshaping not just individual behaviors but entire market structures and societal norms. While the impact of digital platforms is largely positive, challenges related to privacy, data security, misinformation, and market concentration remain. The future of digital platforms will likely involve navigating these challenges while continuing to harness the benefits of networked technologies for economic exchange, information transfer, and social connectivity. As platforms evolve, so too will their role in shaping the digital economy and society, underscoring the need for ongoing research, regulation, and dialogue among all stakeholders (see Ceccagnoli et al., 2012; Ghazawneh & Henfridsson, 2015; Tiwana et al., 2010).

Due to their plasticity, platforms represent an ideal bridging node between complementary intangibles (e.g., big data vehiculated through mobile apps, stored in the cloud, and interpreted with AI patterns), enhancing value co-creating patterns.

3.18 Sustainable Business Planning

Business planning is a core pillar of dynamic sustainability, as it represents a formal document that envisages long-term economic and financial perspectives. Appropriate business planning, with continuous fine-tuning, backs sustainability strategies and fosters ESG compliance. ESG targets may well be embodied in business planning key factors, for instance, envisaging:

a. A periodical check-up of the business continuity (capacity for the firm to keep a going concern for at least the next 6–12 months);
b. A consequential consideration of the prospective economic and financial equilibrium (capacity of the firm to generate positive economic and financial margins, respectively, represented by EBITDA, EBIT, pre-tax/net profit, or operating and net cash flows).
c. A sensitivity analysis, conducted with a deterministic or stochastic approach that embodies stress tests, to assess the break-even point, with appropriate strategies to avoid or bypass a disaster case;

d. A continuous reengineering and reformulation of the business plan hypotheses, exploiting bottom-up evidence from the external market and customers;
e. A prompt reaction to equity or cashflow burnouts, should these criticalities occur.

Business planning is a well-known tool for strategic formulation and execution (Lasher, 2010; Sahlman, 1997).

The value of planning lies in its ability to assess various courses of action and enhance strategies. This is particularly crucial before entering a market, where the primary objective is to discern viable opportunities from less promising ones. By thoroughly evaluating alternative actions, businesses can identify potential risks, opportunities, and challenges associated with each option. This enables them to make informed decisions based on a comprehensive understanding of the market landscape and potential outcomes (Chwolka & Raith, 2012). Planning is beneficial for performance (Brinckmann et al., 2010). Decision-making, however, remains a challenging task in the current age of forecasting (Asaduzzaman et al., 2015). As Razgaitis (2003) shows, prognosticators apply Monte Carlo simulations to detect future outcomes. This includes Real Options Analysis.

The forecasting effectiveness of traditional financial risk measures can be improved by integrating financial risk with an ESG risk measure that considers the ESG entropy (Ielasi et al., 2021).

Designing and creating a business model is crucial for a successful firm's operation in today's market.

A business model is a factor that differentiates one firm from another—it defines the distinctions of the firm, how the firm deals with the competition, the firm's partnerships, and customer relations (Koprivnjak & Oberman Peterka, 2020). Business modeling is increasingly focused on sustainability orientation, extended value creation, systemic thinking, and stakeholder integration (Breuer et al., 2018).

Business planning follows a typical managerial top-down approach where management-prepared forecasts and projections are conceived within the firm and occasionally compared with market returns. The increasing availability of timely big data, sometimes fueled by the Internet of Things (IoT) devices, allows for receiving continuous feedback that can be conveniently used to refresh assumptions and forecasts, using a complementary bottom-up approach. Top-down and bottom-up are both strategies for information processing and knowledge ordering.

Forecasting accuracy can be substantially improved by incorporating timely empirical evidence, with a consequent reduction of both information asymmetries and the risk of facing unexpected events, concerning the magnitude of their impact. Since risk is represented by the difference between expected and real events, if occurrences are timely incorporated into expectations, this differential is minimized. This intuitive concept is well-known, but its practical implications are amplified by the unprecedented presence of big data.

Valuation criteria of the project or investment are typically linked to business planning metrics, especially if they are based on Discounted Cash Flows (DCF). DCF forecasting can be greatly improved by timely big data feedback that positively affects the numerator, represented by growing cash flows (that incorporate real option flexibility), and decreasing discount rates (cost of capital) that reflect reduced risk. Value-adding strategies can conveniently reshape supply and value chains that embed information-driven resilience.

Network theory may constitute a further interpretation tool, considering the interaction of nodes represented by IoT and big data, mastering digital platforms, and physical stakeholders (shareholders, managers, clients, suppliers, lenders, etc.). AI, database interoperability, and blockchain applications are consistent with the networking interpretation of the interaction of physical and virtual nodes.

3.19 Artificial Intelligence, Scalable Leveraging, and the Pecking Order Theory

AI may play a pivotal role in the examination of financial factors that impact decisions on capital structure, in accordance with the Pecking Order Theory. While the Pecking Order Theory proposes a ranking of financing sources, the integration of AI can assist in streamlining this process through the analysis of data from diverse origins to identify the most appropriate capital structure for companies, particularly those that are small or medium in size. Nevertheless, studies conducted on European companies have yielded varying outcomes with respect to the relevance of the Pecking Order Theory, underscoring the necessity for additional research and examination in alternative scenarios. The amalgamation of AI with the fundamental principles of the Pecking Order Theory has the potential to enhance decisions related to capital structure by capitalizing on insights derived from data and refining financial strategies. Scalable financial leveraging derives from the ability of a firm to raise enough capital to back its investments, with an appropriate financial debt to equity ratio.

The Pecking Order Theory in corporate finance, complementary to the formation and composition of the raised capital (financial debt + equity) suggests that companies prioritize their sources of financing according to the principle of least effort, or, from the least risky to the riskiest. Typically, firms prefer to finance themselves first through internal funds (retained earnings or the cash and revenue-generating EBITDA), then by unsecured and after-secured debt, and finally by issuing new equity. The rationale of this hierarchy considers that income statement liquidity, proxied by the EBITDA, is immediately available with no transaction costs and that the cost of debt is less expensive than the cost of (riskier) equity. The integration of AI into financial management and decision-making processes can impact the Pecking Order Theory in several ways:

a. **Improved Financial Forecasting and Planning**: AI can improve a firm's ability to forecast future cash flows and earnings with greater accuracy. Better forecasting helps in more effective internal capital allocation, potentially reducing the need to seek external financing.
b. **Maximized Capital Structure Decision-Making**: AI algorithms can analyze large datasets to determine the optimal capital structure for a firm, including the ideal mix of debt and equity. This can lead to more informed decisions about financing and investment, in line with the pecking order preferences.
c. **Risk Assessment and Management**: AI can provide more sophisticated tools for risk assessment, including credit risk for debt financing and market risk for equity financing. Improved risk management may allow companies to access external financing more confidently when internal funds are insufficient.
d. **Improved Market Analysis**: AI-driven market analysis can provide an understanding of the optimal timing for equity financing, helping companies avoid diluting their stock when market conditions are unfavorable. This aligns with the Pecking Order Theory's preference for debt over new equity issuance.

e. **Cost of Capital Analysis**: By analyzing various factors that influence the cost of capital, such as market conditions, interest rates, and the firm's risk profile, AI can help in determining the most cost-effective source of finance at any given time.

f. **Debt Management**: AI tools can maximize debt management strategies, including refinancing decisions, interest rate risk management, and debt maturity structure, making debt a more attractive option consistent with the Pecking Order Theory.

g. **Investor Relations and Equity Financing**: In scenarios where equity financing is necessary, AI can help in targeting and communicating with potential investors, making the process more efficient and potentially more successful.

h. **Automation of Finance Operations**: AI can automate many routine finance operations, reducing costs and freeing up resources. This might reduce the immediate need for external financing, allowing companies to rely more on internal funds.

AI impacts the Pecking Order Theory primarily by enhancing a firm's capacity to manage its finances more efficiently and make more informed decisions about financing. This could lead to a more strategic approach to financing that still aligns with the theory's principles but is enhanced through sophisticated data analysis and risk management capabilities. AI does not necessarily change the fundamental preferences of the Pecking Order Theory but can significantly refine how companies apply these preferences in their financing strategies. Further considerations concerning network theory, digitalization, and other impacts on valuation can be found in Baldi and Trigeorgis (2009), Barabàsi (2016), Bezes (2009), Caldarelli and Catanzaro (2012), Cotropia (2009), Costantinides et al. (2018), Delia (2008), Denicolai et al. (2014), Estrada and Knight (2015), Garçia et al. (2008), Gartner (2013), Ghandour et al. (2008), Ipsmiller et al. (2019), Koller et al. (2010), Lennard (2018), López et al. (2017), Maia Ferreire (2018), Miller (1988), Morgan et al. (2009), Moro Visconti (2015), Ross (1988), Simon (2011), Williams and Smith (2004), Zhang et al. (2015).

References

Asaduzzaman, M., Shahjahan, M., & Murase, K. (2015). Real-time decision-making forecasting using data mining and decision tree. *International Journal on Information, 18*(7), 3027–3047.

Baldi, F., & Trigeorgis, L. (2009, Fall). Assessing the value of growth option synergies from business combinations and testing for goodwill impairment: A real options perspective. *The Journal of Applied Corporate Finance, 21*(4), 115–124.

Barabàsi, A. (2016). *Network science*. Cambridge University Press. http://networksciencebook.com/

Bezes, C. (2009, June - n. 2). *E-commerce website evaluation: A critical review* (Working Paper Largepa). https://www.researchgate.net/publication/254419157_e-commerce_website_evaluation_a_critical_review

Breuer, H., Fichter, K., Lüdeke-Freund, F., & Tiemann, I. (2018). Sustainability-oriented business model development: Principles, criteria and tools. *International Journal of Entrepreneurial Venturing, 10*(2), 256–286.

Brinckmann, J., Grichnik, D., & Kapsa, D. (2010). Should entrepreneurs plan or just storm the castle? A meta-analysis on contextual factors impacting the business planning–performance relationship in small firms. *Journal of Business Venturing, 25*(1), 24–40.

Butler, B. (2013, February 11). *PaaS primer: What is platform as a service and why does it matter?* Network World. https://www.networkworld.com/article/2163430/paas-primer-what-is-platform-as-a-service-and-why-does-itmatter-.html

Caldarelli, G., & Catanzaro, M. (2012). *Networks: A very short introduction*. Oxford University Press.

Ceccagnoli, M., Forman, C., Huang, P., & Wu, D. J. (2012). Co-creation of value in a platform ecosystem: The case of enterprise software. *MIS Quarterly, 36*(1), 263–290.

Chwolka, A., & Raith, M. A. (2012). The value of business planning before start-up—A decision-theoretical perspective. *Journal of Business Venturing, 27*(3), 385–399.

Costantinides, P., Parker, G., & Henfridsson, O. (2018). *Platforms and infrastructures in the digital age*. Information Systems Research. Articles in advance pp. 1–20.

Cotropia, C. A. (2009). Describing patents as real options. *Journal of Corporation Law, 34*, 1127.

de Reuven, M., Sørensen, C., & Basole, R. C. (2018). The digital platform: A research agenda. *Journal of Information Technology, 33*, 124–135.

Delia, M. (2008). Impact of E-commerce in supply chain management. *The Amfiteatru Economic Journal, 10*(24), 236–253.

Denicolai, S., Cotta Ramusino, E., & Sotti, F. (2014). The impact of intangibles on firm growth. *Technology Analysis & Strategic Management Online Journal, 27*(2), 219–236.

Estrada, E., & Knight, P. A. (2015). *A first course in network theory*. Oxford University Press.

Evans, D. S., Hagiu, A., & Schmalensee, R. (2006, January). *Invisible engines: How software platforms drive innovation and transform industries*.

Gander, J. (2015). *Designing digital business models*. Kingston University.

Garcia, D. F., Garcia, R., Entrialgo, J., Garcia, J., & Garcia, M. (2008, August 20–22). *Experimental evaluation of horizontal and vertical scalability of cluster-based application servers for transactional workloads*. Paper presented at 8th WSEAS International Conference on applied informatics and communications (AIC'08).

Gartner, M. D. O. T. (2013). *Aligning entrepreneurs, venture capitalists and growth opportunities in entrepreneurial financing decisions: A real options approach* [Doctoral thesis in Business and Management Studies]. Universidade do Porto.

Gawer, A. (2014). Bridging differing perspectives on technological platforms: Toward an integrative framework. *Research Policy, 43*(7), 1239–1249.

Ghandour, A., Deans, K., Benwell, G., & Pillai, P. (2008). *Measuring eCommerce Website success*. ACIS 2008 Proceedings, Paper 24.

Ghazawneh, A., & Henfridsson, O. (2015). A paradigmatic analysis of digital application marketplaces. *Journal of Information Technology, 30*(3), 198–208.

Gupta, A., Christie, R., & Manjula, R. (2017). Scalability in internet of things: Features, techniques and research challenges. *International Journal of Computational Intelligence Research, 13*(7), 1617–1627. http://www.ripublication.com/ijcir17/ijcirv13n7_06.pdf

Harshini Poojaa, K., & Ganesh Kumar, S. (2022). Scalability Challenges and solutions in blockchain technology. In S. Smys, V. E. Balas, & R. Palanisamy (Eds.), *Inventive computation and information technologies*. Lecture Notes in Networks and Systems, 336.

Haskel, S., & Westlake, S. (2018). *Capitalism without capital*. Princeton University Press.

Henfridsson, O., Mathiassen, L., & Svahn, F. (2014). Managing technological change in the digital age: The role of architectural frames. *Journal of Information Technology, 29*, 27–43.

Hoffman, R., & Yeh, C. (2018). *Blitzscaling*. Crown Publishing Group.

Hyoung, Y. J., Park, A., & Lee, K. J. (2020). Why are the largest social networking services sometimes unable to sustain themselves? *Sustainability, 12*(2), 502.

Iazzolino, G., & Migliano, G. (2015). The valuation of a patent through the real options approach: A tutorial. *Journal of Business Valuation and Economic Loss Analysis, 10*(1), 99–116.

Ielasi, F., Capelli, P., & Russo, A. (2021). Forecasting volatility by integrating financial risk with environmental, social, and governance risk. *Corporate Social Responsibility and Environmental Management, 28*(5), 1483–1495.

Ipsmiller, E., Brouthers, K. D., & Dikova, D. (2019). 25 years of real option empirical research in management. *European Management Review, 16*, 55–68.

Ismail, S. (2014). *Exponential organizations*. Singularity University Book.

Jacobides, M. G., Cernamo, C., & Gawer, A. (2018, March). Towards a theory of ecosystems. *Strategic Management Journal, 39*(8), 2255–2276.

Kallinikos, J., Aaltonen, A., & Marton, A. (2013). The ambivalent ontology of digital artifacts. *MIS quarterly*, 357–370.

Kane, G. C., Palmer, D., Phillips, A. N., Kiron, D., & Buckley, N. (2014). Strategy, not technology, drives digital transformation. *MIT Sloan Management Review*.

Kenney, M., & Zysman, J. (2016, Spring). The rise of the platform economy. *Issues in Science and Technology, XXXII*(3), 61.

Koller, T., Goedhart, M., & Wessels, D. (2010). *Valuation measuring and managing the value of companies*. Wiley.

Koprivnjak, T., & Oberman Peterka, S. (2020). Business model as a base for building firms' competitiveness. *Sustainability, 12*(21), 9278.

Korpela, K., Hallikas, J., & Dahlberg, T. (2017). Digital supply chain transformation toward blockchain integration. In *Proceedings of the 50th Hawaii International Conference on System Sciences*. https://scholarspace.manoa.hawaii.edu/handle/10125/41666

Lasher, W. (2010). *The perfect business plan made simple: The best guide to writing a plan that will secure financial backing for your business*. Broadway Books.

Lennard, A. (2018). *Intangibles: First thoughts*. Paper presented at IFASS meeting, Mumbai, 12–13 April 2018 Session 10.

Lòpez, L., Francisco, J., & Esteves, J. (2017). *Value in a digital world. How to assess business models and measure value in a digital world*. Palgrave Macmillan.

Maia Ferreire, R. J. (2018). *The venture capitalist investment decision: A dynamic real options approach* [Dissertation Master in Finance]. Universidade do Porto.

Miller, M. H. (1988, Fall). The Modigliani-Miller propositions after thirty years. *Journal of Economic Perspectives, 2*(4), 99–120.

Modigliani, F., & Miller, M. H. (1958, June). The cost of capital, corporation finance and the theory of investment. *American Economic Review, 1*, 3.

Morgan, M., Elbe, J., & De Esteban Curiel, J. (2009). Has the experience economy arrived? The views of destination managers in three visitors' dependent areas. *International Journal of Tourism Research, 11*, 201–216.

Moro Visconti, R. (2015). Leveraging value with intangibles: More guarantees with less collateral? *Corporate Ownership & Control, 13*(1), 241–252.

Moro-Visconti, R. (2021). *Startup valuation. From strategic business planning to digital networking*. Palgrave Macmillan.

Moro-Visconti, R. (2022a). *The valuation of digital intangibles. Technology, marketing, and the metaverse,* Palgrave Macmillan.

Moro-Visconti, R. (2022b). *Augmented corporate valuation. From digital networking to ESG compliance*. Palgrave Macmillan.

Moro-Visconti, R. (2022c). From physical reality to the Metaverse: A Multilayer Network Valuation. *Journal of Metaverse, 2*(1), 16–22.

Moro-Visconti, R., & Cesaretti, A. (2023). *Digital token valuation. Cryptocurrencies, NFTs, decentralized finance, and blockchains*. Palgrave Macmillan.

Odlyzko, A., & Tilly, B. (2005, March 2). *A refutation of Metcalfe's Law and a better estimate for the value of networks and network interconnections*. Manuscript.

Razgaitis, R. (2003). *Dealmaking using real options and Monte Carlo analysis*. Wiley.

Rochet, J. C., & Tirole, J. (2003). Platform competition in two-sided markets. *Journal of the European Economic Association, 1*(4), 990–1029.

Ross, S. A. (1988, Fall). Comment on the Modigliani-Miller propositions. *Journal of Economic Perspectives, 2*(4), 99–120.

Sahlman, W. A. (1997). How to write a great business plan. *Harvard Business Review, 75*(4), 98–109.

Schreieck, M., Hein, A., Wiesche, M., & Krcmar, H. (2018). The challenge of governing digital platform ecosystems. In C. Linnhoff-Popien, R. Schneider, & M. Zaddach (Eds.), *Digital marketplaces unleashed*. Springer.

Simon, P. (2011). *The age of the platform: How Amazon, Apple*. Motion Publishing.

Spagnoletti, P., Resca, A., & Lee, G. (2015). A design theory for digital platforms supporting online communities: A multiple case study. *Journal of Information Technology, 30*(4), 364–380.

Tiwana, A., Konsynski, B., & Bush, A. A. (2010). Platform evolution: Coevolution of platform architecture, governance, and environmental dynamics. *Information Systems Research, 21*(4), 675–687.

Trigeorgis, L., & Reuer, J. J. (2017). Real options theory in strategic management. *Strategic Management Journal, 38*, 42–63.

Weill, P., & Woerner, S. L. (2013, March). Optimizing your digital business model. *MIT Sloan Management Review, 1*(43), 123–131.

Westlake, S., & Haskel, J. (2017). *The rise of the intangible economy: Capitalism without capital*. Princeton University Press.

Williams, L. G., & Smith, C. U. (2004). *Web application scalability: A model based approach*. Software Engineering Research and Performance Engineering Services. http://www.spe-ed.com/papers/scale04.pdf

Yoo, Y., Henfridsson, O., & Lyytinen, K. (2010). Research commentary—the new organizing logic of digital innovation: An agenda for information systems research. *Information Systems Research, 21*(4), 724–735.

Zhang, J., Lichtenstein, Y., & Gander, J. (2015). Designing scalable digital business models. In *Business models and modeling, advances in strategic management* (Vol. 33, pp. 241–277). Emerald Group Publishing Limited.

CHAPTER 4

The Valuation of Artificial Intelligence-Driven Know-How and Patents

4.1 The Uncertain Perimeter of "Know-How", Between Organization and Technology

AI plays a crucial role in enhancing the safeguarding and utilization of proprietary data through the provision of sophisticated tools for the management and exploitation of intellectual assets. Using AI technologies facilitates a more effective identification, arrangement, and utilization of knowledge, boosting economic evaluation and potential benefits. Moreover, AI is essential in fortifying the protection of trade secrets from external entities, thereby improving the overall safety and confidentiality of critical information. Through the integration of AI in knowledge management, enterprises can enhance the sharing and transfer of knowledge, ultimately leading to improved commercial operations and increased value generation. Valuing AI-driven know-how and patents involves several key factors and considerations:

a. **Technological Uniqueness and Advancement**: The value of AI-driven patents often hinges on the uniqueness and advancement of the technology. Breakthroughs or significant improvements in AI can command high valuations, especially if they solve critical problems or open new possibilities in the field.

R. Moro-Visconti, *Artificial Intelligence Valuation*,
https://doi.org/10.1007/978-3-031-53622-9_4

b. **Market Application and Potential**: The broader the application of the AI technology, the higher its potential value. AI solutions that can be applied across multiple industries or offer solutions to widespread challenges can be particularly valuable. The size of the market and the potential revenue generated from the patented technology are crucial factors in valuation.
c. **Competitive Advantage**: Patents that provide a significant competitive advantage, such as reducing costs, improving efficiency, or enabling new capabilities, can be highly valuable. The degree to which the patented AI technology outperforms existing solutions or creates new market opportunities plays a significant role in its valuation.
d. **Intellectual Property (IP) Strength and Protection**: The strength of the IP rights, including the breadth and enforceability of the patent, is a critical aspect of valuation. Stronger IP rights that offer broad protection and are enforceable in key markets increase the value of AI-driven know-how and patents.
e. **Licensing Potential**: The potential for licensing the technology to other companies or industries is a major factor in valuation. Patents with high licensing potential can generate significant ongoing revenue streams, increasing their value.
f. **Research and Development Costs**: The investment made in research and development (R&D) to create the AI technology can impact its valuation. Patents that are the result of substantial R&D efforts may have higher valuations due to the sunk costs and the technological expertise embedded in them.
g. **Legal and Regulatory Landscape**: The legal and regulatory environment can significantly affect the valuation of AI-driven patents. Factors such as data privacy laws, AI-specific regulations, and the patentability of AI inventions in different jurisdictions can influence the perceived value and utility of AI patents.
h. **Scalability and Adaptability**: The ability of the AI technology to scale and adapt to different contexts and requirements is crucial. Technologies that are easily scalable and adaptable to various applications and industries can be more valuable.
i. **Future Growth Prospects**: The expected future growth of the field or application area of the AI technology influences valuation. Patents in rapidly growing fields or in areas anticipated to have substantial future impact can be valued higher.

j. **Risk Factors**: Finally, risk factors such as technological obsolescence, market uncertainties, and potential legal challenges can affect valuation. AI technologies in fast-evolving fields may face higher risks of becoming outdated, impacting their long-term value.

Valuing AI-driven know-how and patents is a complex process that requires consideration of both current market factors and future potentials. It often involves the expertise of valuation professionals who can assess the technology's technical merits, market potential, legal standing, and other relevant factors.

Many contents are readapted mostly from Moro-Visconti (2022a), or, occasionally, Moro-Visconti (2022b), or Moro-Visconti (2021), extending digital intangible, startup, or business planning applications to specific AI valuation patterns.

The uncertain perimeter of "know-how" at the intersection of organization and technology is further amplified by the integration of AI. AI technologies, including machine learning, natural language processing, and computer vision, have introduced new dimensions of complexity and opportunity in the way organizations operate. Here are some ways in which AI contributes to the uncertainty surrounding "know-how":

a. Rapid Technological Advancements: AI is advancing at a remarkable pace, with new algorithms, models, and tools being developed regularly. Staying up-to-date with these advancements and acquiring the relevant AI know-how is a challenge for organizations.
b. Data-Driven Decision-Making: AI heavily relies on data. Organizations must navigate the complexities of data collection, management, and analysis to leverage AI effectively. Understanding the intricacies of data science and AI is vital but can be uncertain due to evolving best practices.
c. Talent Shortage: There is a shortage of AI talent in the job market. Finding and retaining professionals with the necessary AI know-how can be difficult, leading to uncertainty within organizations about their AI capabilities.
d. Ethical and Regulatory Concerns: The use of AI raises ethical and regulatory questions. Organizations need to understand and comply with evolving regulations and ethical standards related to AI, which adds to the know-how complexity.

e. Integration Challenges: Implementing AI within an organization's existing processes and systems can be complex. Knowing how to integrate AI seamlessly is an area of uncertainty.
f. Interdisciplinary Nature: AI is highly interdisciplinary, requiring expertise in computer science, mathematics, data science, and domain-specific knowledge. This interdisciplinary nature can make it challenging to define clear boundaries of AI know-how.
g. Unpredictable Outcomes: AI can produce unexpected results, and understanding why AI models make specific decisions or predictions can be elusive. This unpredictability contributes to uncertainty in deploying AI effectively.

To address these challenges, organizations need a multifaceted approach:

1. **Continuous Learning**: Organizations should promote a culture of continuous learning and skill development, encouraging employees to stay updated on AI advancements.
2. **Collaboration**: Cross-functional teams with diverse skills should collaborate to bridge gaps in AI know-how and address interdisciplinary challenges.
3. **Ethical AI Practices**: Organizations must prioritize ethical AI practices and stay informed about evolving regulations to mitigate legal and reputational risks.
4. **Data Governance**: Robust data governance practices are essential to ensure data quality, security, and compliance.
5. **External Partnerships**: Partnering with external experts and AI service providers can help organizations access AI know-how when needed.
6. **Experimentation**: Organizations should be open to experimentation and willing to learn from both successes and failures in AI implementations.

The uncertain perimeter of "know-how" between organization and technology, driven by AI, requires organizations to be adaptable, proactive, and committed to knowledge acquisition and ethical use of AI technologies to thrive in an ever-evolving landscape.

According to OECD (2022) "*Know-how and trade secrets are proprietary information or knowledge that assist or improve a commercial activity, but that are not registered for protection in the manner of a patent or trademark. Know-how and trade secrets generally consist of undisclosed information of an industrial, commercial, or scientific nature arising from previous experience, which has practical application in the operation of an enterprise. Know-how and trade secrets may relate to manufacturing, marketing, research and development, or any other commercial activity. The value of know-how and trade secrets is often dependent on the ability of the enterprise to preserve the confidentiality of the know-how or trade secret. In certain industries, the disclosure of information necessary to obtain patent protection could assist competitors in developing alternative solutions. Accordingly, an enterprise may, for sound business reasons, choose not to register patentable know-how, which may nonetheless contribute substantially to the success of the enterprise. The confidential nature of know-how and trade secrets may be protected to some degree by (i) unfair competition or similar laws, (ii) employment contracts, and (iii) economic and technological barriers to competition*" (par. 6.20).

"*There are also intangibles that are not protectable under specific intellectual property registration systems, but that are protected against unauthorized appropriation or imitation under unfair competition legislation or other enforceable laws, or by contract. Trade dress, trade secrets, and know-how may fall under this category of intangibles*" (par. 6.38).

A trade secret is any information about a business that could give a competitive advantage to another person or business. A trade secret can include any of the following:

- formulas, practices, processes designs;
- instruments, patterns, algorithms;
- commercial methods, such as distribution or sales methods;
- advertising strategies,
- lists of suppliers or clients, or consumer profiles; and
- physical devices, ideas, compilations of information.

The know-how to do it is a concept characterized by a broad perimeter of definition. The problems of application and interpretation are complex, even in the phase of drafting contracts and protection of rights, primarily in the field of technology transfer or unfair competition.

"Know-how" means a wealth of non-patented practical information, resulting from experience and testing by the supplier, which is secret, substantial, and identified. In this context:

- "secret" means that the know-how, considered as a body of knowledge or in the precise configuration and composition of its components, is not generally known or easily accessible;
- "substantial" means that the know-how includes knowledge indispensable to the buyer for the use, sale, or resale of the contract goods or services; and
- "identified" means that the know-how must be described in a sufficiently comprehensive manner to make it possible to verify that it fulfills the criteria of secrecy and substantiality.

Most regulations relate know-how to products and processes and the performance of theoretical analyses, systematic studies, or experiments, including experimental production, technical checks of products or processes, the construction of the necessary facilities, and the obtaining of the relevant intellectual property rights.

Know-how (savoir-faire) consists of the production and organizational method, often embodied with technological applications as part of an industrialization process, and it consists of practical knowledge of how to do something, e.g., a product. The know-how exploits a wealth of knowledge and constructive artifices acquired through entrepreneurial talent, often by way of craftsmanship and not always formally codified, not in the public domain, and therefore such as to originate exclusive information asymmetries, which often encroach on trade secrets, intrinsically characterized by requirements of novelty and not accessible to third parties.

The work leading to know-how, through technical and organizational progress, is typically carried out in teams; in the legal field, for the know-how, there are significant problems of identifiability, traceability, and identifiability (which stem from the immateriality of the *res incorporales*, inapprehensible, and evanescent), as well as those of secrecy, substantiality, usefulness, and ownership.

The know-how, which can be considered an economic asset, and which represents a relational and knowledge heritage, can include tangible and substantial activities such as formulas, instructions, and specifications, codified procedures and archetypes, technical devices, production layouts using technology, design, molds or models or intangible activities such as marketing and communication strategies, quality testing techniques, production and organizational procedures and skills.

The know-how refers both to mass production, in which the organizational and production strategies are serially codified and standardized ("customized"), and to production by order, which represents "tailor-made clothes" in which the craftsmanship and creativity are enhanced. In any case, it is a matter of expertise and confidential internal knowledge linked to reproducible creativity of technical and/or commercial proprietary information, with an indefinite and potentially infinite useful life, which differentiates the know-how and trade secrets from patented inventions.

The extension of the concept, in its fundamental division between technical-industrial and commercial know-how (linked to marketing), is concomitant with the growing importance of innovation as a strategic driver. Insofar as patenting requires some form of disclosure, many inventions remain deliberately confined to the field of industrial secrets, where knowledge, as notorious, must be inaccessible; especially in process inventions, industrial secrecy typically offers greater guarantees (see Moro-Visconti, 2015), than patenting, against possible violations by third parties.

The know-how, through an orchestrated process of apprenticeship (learning by doing), involves process and product innovations, which at the strategic level can be a source of competitive advantage, understood by Porter (1998) as cost advantage and/or differentiation, in the context of competition between companies.

The voluntary cognitive dissemination of know-how is expressed in specific methods, practices, procedures, or processes, including technical assistance agreements. The know-how can be properly understood as a synergistic glue of the "organized complex of goods" that constitutes the firm, as a Coasian nexus of contracts, characterized by the ability to create, transfer, assemble, integrate, and economically exploit activities deriving (also) from knowledge. Its ambiguous perimeter does not always allow a clear separation concerning other intangible assets.

The know-how is the basis of R&D that can lead to the patenting of original inventions and sometimes can be associated with trademarks, considering their nature as distinctive signs that have qualitative characteristics largely based on know-how. And the know-how can be contiguous to the software or, sometimes, to the rights of use of the intellectual works.

The know-how is, in the broadest sense, the cognitive monitoring for the quality guarantee and the repair of the products, with an aftersales market, also concerning the reduction of defects, with consequent limitation of the product liability. Collateral value of know-how collapses in default conditions (see Moro-Visconti, 2015).

4.2 Galilean Replicability and Industrialization of the Experimental Scientific Method

The experimental scientific method, similar to the approach adopted by Galileo, highlights the importance of replicability and thorough documentation. Integration of AI in large scientific experiments plays a crucial role in automating the design and analysis processes, thereby improving reproducibility. AI models can provide more accurate estimations of replicability compared to conventional methods, consequently enhancing the quality of research and reducing associated expenses. Galileo's utilization of experiments and persuasive language mirrors Turing's reliance on idealizations and exploratory trials, illustrating the progression of scientific methodologies over time. The application of AI in streamlining scientific experimentation processes contributes to the industrialization of these practices, ensuring precise design and analysis in intricate experiments. Through the amalgamation of AI's computational prowess with human expertise, research self-assessment techniques can be optimized, leading to more scalable and efficient review procedures for the increasing number of publications. The integration of AI into the scientific method has the potential to enhance Galilean replicability and further industrialize the experimental scientific process. Here's how AI can impact these aspects:

1. **Automated Experimentation**:
    - **High-Throughput Experiments**: AI-powered robotics and laboratory automation can conduct experiments at a much higher rate and with greater precision than humans, facilitating replicability by ensuring that experiments can be repeated exactly.

- **Algorithmic Experiment Design**: AI can assist in designing experiments by optimizing variables and conditions, making experiments more efficient and reproducible.

2. **Data Collection and Analysis**:

   - **Big Data Analysis**: AI can process and analyze massive datasets generated by experiments quickly, identifying patterns and insights that may not be apparent through traditional methods.
   - **Real-Time Data Monitoring**: AI systems can continuously monitor experiments, detecting anomalies or deviations from expected results in real time, enhancing quality control and reliability.

3. **Simulation and Modeling**:

   - **AI-Powered Simulations**: AI-driven simulations can model complex physical phenomena, allowing scientists to conduct virtual experiments, explore various scenarios, and validate results in real-world experiments.

4. **Pattern Recognition and Prediction**:

   - **Predictive Analytics**: AI algorithms can predict experimental outcomes, guiding scientists in designing experiments that are more likely to yield desired results.
   - **Anomaly Detection**: AI can detect unexpected or anomalous results, helping identify potential issues in the experimental setup.

5. **Data Sharing and Collaboration**:

   - **AI-Powered Collaboration Platforms**: AI can facilitate collaboration by helping scientists share data, insights, and results across geographic and disciplinary boundaries.

6. **Replicability and Verification**:

   - **Digital Twin Experiments**: AI can create digital twins of experiments, allowing other researchers to replicate experiments virtually, thereby enhancing replicability.

- **Blockchain for Data Provenance**: Blockchain technology can be used to record and verify the entire experimental process, ensuring transparency and traceability in scientific research.

7. **Hypothesis Generation**:

   - **AI-Driven Hypothesis Generation**: AI can analyze existing scientific literature and data to generate hypotheses and research questions, accelerating the scientific discovery process.

8. **Ethical Considerations**:

   - **Ethical AI Governance**: As AI systems become integral to scientific research, ethical considerations around data privacy.

With the invention of the Galilean scientific method, the concept of reproducibility of experiments was introduced, which is the basis of the knowledge acquired through empirical attempts, then systematized, both in scientific theories and in a technological/organizational context of functional and industrialized replicability, to make each experiment productive and successful.

The scientific method uses an inductive and deductive approach and is aimed at achieving an objective—not arbitrary—knowledge of empirical reality, in a reliable, verifiable, shareable, and universally valid way. All this is based on heuristic analysis, i.e., on empirical intuition based on experience, including artisan experience, to be replicated on an industrial basis. Empirical observations, hypotheses, and deductions are used to draw replicable conclusions, through experiments inspired by know-why.

Everything is linked to the concepts of industrialization (mass production), replicability, scalability, and transferability which are of fundamental importance to fill the know-how with practical-application contents and to allow it to be exploited, shared, and negotiated.

The application of a Cartesian scientifically replicable method limits the subjectivity and irrationality of the know-how, favoring its industrialization, even if with the risk of weakening the creative vein, in favor of a replicating technicality. The know-how stems from the experience and the maieutic—Socratic—effort to bring out new industrial ideas, from the custom applied to making, inventing a method, codifying, and replicating it, using the technical archetype for mass production, and the systematic organization of the business model. This process follows iterative procedures based on often unsuccessful attempts, with the progressive refinement of knowledge and skills. The know-how understood as an engineered development of the technique, is a two-bladed scissor: deductive because it applies the first principles and inductive using the scientific method.

The formation of know-how is usually a slow and gradual process, based on small steps and empirical feedback often unsuccessful, with attempts and errors in constant evolution, which continuously redirect the strategies of incremental enhancement of the firm.

The incremental training of know-how, even in a process of value co-creation, can be inspired by reverse engineering processes, based on a detailed examination of the operation, design, and development of an invention applied by others, to produce a similar one, improving efficiency and quality.

4.3 Protection, Sharing, and Transfer of Know-How

Various innovative approaches have been suggested to tackle the challenges associated with safeguarding and disseminating AI-generated expertise. The development of cognitive aides is aimed at facilitating the transfer of implicit knowledge within dynamic intricate systems, underscoring the significance of efficient knowledge exchange. Progress in enhancing the security of information sharing through the utilization of recurrent neural networks has demonstrated a notable level of accuracy in identifying instances of information misuse, irregularities, and security responses, thereby indicating the efficacy of protective measures for sensitive data. AI improves the protection, sharing, and transfer of know-how within organizations. AI can be applied to these aspects, as shown in Fig. 4.1.

The steps are the following:

1. **Protection of Know-How**

    - **Data Encryption and Access Control**: AI can assist in securing sensitive knowledge by implementing robust encryption and access control mechanisms to ensure that only authorized personnel can access critical information.
    - **Anomaly Detection**: AI-powered anomaly detection systems can monitor knowledge repositories and alert organizations to

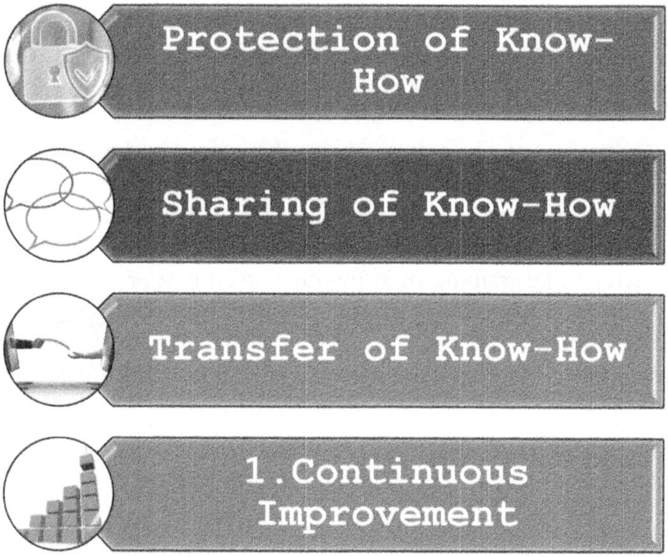

Fig. 4.1 Protection, sharing, and transfer of know-how

unusual or unauthorized access attempts, helping to protect against data breaches.

- **Content Classification**: AI can automatically classify and tag documents and data, making it easier to identify and protect confidential information.
- **Predictive Security**: AI can predict potential security threats and vulnerabilities by analyzing historical data and patterns of behavior within an organization, allowing for proactive protection measures.

2. **Sharing of Know-How**:

- **Knowledge Management**: AI-driven knowledge management systems can organize and index internal knowledge repositories, making it easier for employees to search for and access relevant information.
- **Content Recommendation**: AI can recommend relevant documents or experts based on a user's query or browsing history, facilitating knowledge sharing within an organization.

- **Chatbots and Virtual Assistants**: AI-powered chatbots and virtual assistants can provide instant answers to employee queries, helping to disseminate knowledge quickly and efficiently.
- **Collaborative Tools**: AI-enhanced collaborative tools can streamline communication and knowledge sharing among teams by suggesting relevant documents, scheduling meetings, or automating routine tasks.

3. **Transfer of Know-How**:

- **Skill Assessment and Gap Analysis**: AI can assess the skills and knowledge of employees and identify gaps, allowing organizations to tailor training and development programs accordingly.
- **Personalized Learning**: AI-driven learning platforms can provide personalized training content based on an individual's learning style and knowledge gaps.
- **Simulations and Virtual Reality**: AI-powered simulations and virtual reality can create immersive training experiences for employees, facilitating the transfer of practical know-how.
- **Natural Language Processing (NLP)**: NLP technologies can be used to automatically extract knowledge from unstructured documents and convert it into structured, transferable formats.
- **Machine Learning for Expertise Transfer**: Organizations can use machine learning algorithms to capture the expertise of experienced employees, making it available for future generations of workers.

4. **Continuous Improvement**:

- **Data Analytics and Feedback Loops**: AI can analyze the effectiveness of knowledge sharing and transfer initiatives.

The protection of industrial secrets, even in the absence of patents, is possible through instruments of protection and safeguarding as an inhibitory and compensatory measure, for example against unfair competition and its inherent abuses. The vulnerability of the know-how is connected to the technological innovations that allow recording images, forms, and processes—with elements of sophistication once unknown (through photocopies, scans, films, digital photographs, recordings, computer duplications …)—operating more and more through tools of technological piracy to unlawfully steal of data and sensitive information. There is a possibility to store data and transfer them via the web that allows a real-time migration of the wealth of the differential knowledge stolen.

The damages deriving from the subtraction of know-how are potentially significant and this imposes the adoption of cautions during the sharing of technologies (knowledge sharing), made necessary by increasingly interdependent value chains, where tacit knowledge becomes at least partially explicit.

In sharing know-how, strategic decisions to make or buy are marked by increasing specialization, which expands the scope of cooperation with other external parties, including business networks or technology parks. From the immateriality of the know-how comes the characteristic of an unrivaled good, in which the transfer to another subject involves the possibility of use by the assignor, with the consequent creation of a duopoly.

The technology transfer, by way of sharing through licensing contracts, or with final sales, often occurs in extraordinary operations, such as M&A, contributions or demergers of companies or their branches, asset swaps, etc.

The transfer of know-how requires its prior identifiability, at the perimeter level, and often entails the need to associate it with other tangible or intangible assets (machinery, patents, qualified personnel …), to which it appears connected.

Key managers represent a critical aspect of know-how, and the transfer of qualified personnel is the indispensable "software" governing the transfer of technologies. It must be accompanied by adequate training of new staff and, once again, the codification of procedures and knowledge, to preserve and depersonalize its use, making them fungible and interchangeable with knowledge management tools.

Contracts for the assignment or licensing of know-how may lead to unfair competition, even with criminal relevance, in the event of unlawful disclosure of industrial secrets.

The codification of tacit and routine procedures, mainly with advanced Enterprise Resource Planning management software, is an increasingly essential prerequisite for the preservation and transferability of know-how. The storage of sensitive and strategic data is increasingly using outsourcing and backup tools, such as cloud computing, with the outsourcing of security that solves some problems, but creates others, also in terms of responsibility.

The dissemination of know-how is based on the know-how of social networks, blogs, and chats, which allow exchanges of opinion and, more generally, the sharing of ideas within discussion forums. The libertarian nature of the network clashes with the entrepreneurial need to segregate knowledge, unlike what happens in academia, where free dissemination is a key principle of scientific thought, for its validation and refutability.

The diffusion of the know-how is stimulated by its frequent horizontal scalability (expanding its use in more companies with similar corporate purposes) and vertical scalability (with synergic crossings of know-how in functionally integrated companies). The extension of the value chain to more synergistically interconnected subjects and the assembly of the surplus value around shared know-how are at the origin of more refined competitive structures. This happens in an industrial district, which raises the competitive barriers to entry toward potential new competitors, preserving the incumbents' incomes. In this sense, know-how is the source of the competitive advantages, sometimes bringing to monopolistic rents (which tend to be increasingly ephemeral, as a result of increasing competitive pressure or antitrust provisions).

The implementation of a codified system of knowledge is important for large companies that repeatedly face the same problems, and that have a high turnover of staff, resulting in "skills traps".

The critical mass of continuous investment in skills is an essential strategic element, to the benefit of larger companies and/or those capable of doing systemic work. Investments in basic and applied research are based on market opportunities, the funding that can be obtained, including public funding, and the degree of legal protection.

The networking of know-how is an increasingly valuable driver for the creation of value, especially through the strategic sharing of economies of experience and scale (with minimization of fixed costs shared, first of all at the production level). This is relevant in intangible-intensive sectors intrinsically characterized by high scalability of economic margins (and the consequent financial flows).

The preservation of know-how is based on the preparation of remunerated non-competition agreements, also to limit the brain drain and, more generally, to retain the knowledge acquired within the firm perimeter.

Technology transfer refers to knowledge, technology, production methods, prototypes, patented inventions, or, more rarely, know-how on the part of governments, universities, public and private companies, research bodies, and individual inventors. Further considerations about the economic rationale of know-how, its impact on the financial structure of the firm, AI implications, and the overall consequences on valuation can be found in Abbel (2009), Aboody and Lev (2000), Advamed (Advanced Medical Technology Association) (2009), Allen and O'Shea (2014), Al-Najjar and Elgammal (2013), Amram (2005), Azzone and Manzini (2008), Banerjee et al. (2017), Bose (2007), Cassiman et al. (2000), Choi (2001), Cohen (2005), Còrcoles (2010), Dawson (2013), De Wit-De Vries et al. (2018), Degryse et al. (2012), Duffy (2005), Gambardella (2013), Jensen and Meckling (1976), Jun et al. (2015), Kristandl and Bontis (2007), Kynci (2017), Lee and Van Den Stein (2006), Leland and Pyle (1977), Mendi et al. (2016), Modigliani and Miller (1958), Mouritsen et al. (2004), Myers and Majluf (1984), Parchomovsky and Wagner (2004), Poston (2015), Roberts (2000), Smith and Warner (1979), Teece (2008), Thoma (2015), Vanacker and Manigart (2010), Vishwasrao (2007), Wu and Yeung (2012).

4.4 Economic and Financial Valuation

AI-driven know-how and patents are playing an increasingly important role in helping traditional firms improve their economic, financial, and market performance. Incorporating AI-powered expertise into economic, market, and financial appraisal procedures presents a substantial opportunity for augmenting decision-making and predictive precision. The impact of AI-driven expertise on economic growth is substantial, as it boosts productivity, expands consumer outreach, improves service quality, enhances work precision, and increases efficiency, ultimately resulting in heightened customer satisfaction. The influence of AI on economic growth is further enhanced by factors such as smart integration, extension of boundaries, generation of knowledge, and self-reinforcing effects, all of which contribute to the overall economic significance of AI technological innovation. Furthermore, the clustering of AI industries has been demonstrated to elevate economic complexity, primarily through the avenues of human resources and knowledge, underscoring the significance of talent and knowledge-driven AI clusters for sustainable economic progress. Moreover, the capital-intensive nature of AI concept development expedites technological progress, potentially accelerating overall economic growth by attracting more investments in AI-facilitated research and development.

a. Economic impact

AI-driven know-how and patents can help traditional firms improve their economic performance in several ways:

- Develop new products and services
- Improve the efficiency of manufacturing and logistics operations
- Automate tasks and reduce costs
- Make better business decisions.

For example, a traditional manufacturing firm could use AI to develop new products that are more customized to customer needs or that are more efficient to produce. AI could also be used to improve the efficiency of the manufacturing process by optimizing production schedules and inventory levels. Additionally, AI could be used to automate tasks such as customer service and order fulfillment.

b. Financial impact

AI-driven know-how and patents can also have a significant impact on the financial performance of traditional firms. AI can help to:

- Increase revenues
- Reduce costs
- Improve profitability.

For example, an AI powered sales forecasting system could help a traditional retail firm to more accurately forecast demand for its products, which could lead to increased sales. AI could also be used to reduce costs by automating tasks, improving efficiency, and reducing waste. Additionally, AI could be used to optimize pricing and inventory levels, which could improve profitability.

c. Market value impact

The economic and financial benefits of AI-driven know-how and patents can lead to a significant increase in the market value of traditional firms. Investors are increasingly recognizing the value of AI, and they are willing to pay a premium for firms that are successfully leveraging AI to improve their performance.

d. Challenges

While AI-driven know-how and patents offer several potential benefits for traditional firms, some challenges need to be addressed. For example, traditional firms need to invest in the necessary infrastructure and talent to develop and implement AI solutions. Additionally, traditional firms need to be careful to manage the ethical and social implications of using AI.

Despite the challenges, AI-driven know-how and patents have the potential to revolutionize traditional industries. By embracing AI, traditional firms can improve their economic, financial, and market performance, and position themselves for long-term success.

Here are some examples of how traditional firms are using AI-driven know-how and patents to improve their economic, financial, and market performance:

- General Electric (GE) is using AI to develop new medical imaging devices, improve the efficiency of its manufacturing operations, and automate tasks in its customer service centers.
- Siemens is using AI to develop new industrial automation systems, improve the efficiency of its energy grid operations, and automate tasks in its healthcare division.
- Microsoft is using AI to develop new cloud computing services, improve the efficiency of its software development process, and automate tasks in its customer support division.
- IBM is using AI to develop new Watson-powered cognitive computing solutions, improve the efficiency of its business consulting services, and automate tasks in its IT infrastructure.

AI can be a valuable tool for the economic and financial valuation of know-how, helping organizations assess the worth of their intellectual assets (Table 4.1).

Table 4.1 Artificial Intelligence-driven economic and financial valuation of know-how

Market Analysis and Competitive Intelligence	**Market Research**: AI can analyze market data, industry trends, and competitive landscapes to determine the demand for specific know-how or expertise **Competitor Analysis**: AI-powered tools can track and analyze competitors' strategies, technologies, and knowledge assets to assess their potential value
Knowledge Asset Valuation	**Knowledge Mapping**: AI can assist in mapping an organization's internal knowledge assets, including patents, trade secrets, proprietary data, and employee expertise **Patent Analysis**: AI can analyze patent databases to assess the uniqueness and potential value of intellectual property **Text Analytics**: AI-powered natural language processing (NLP) can extract valuable insights from unstructured data sources such as research papers, reports, and internal documents
Risk Assessment	AI can be used to model potential risks associated with knowledge assets, considering factors like legal risks, obsolescence, and competition **Sensitivity Analysis**: AI can perform sensitivity analysis to assess how modifications in market conditions or regulations might affect the value of intellectual assets
Predictive Analytics	**Machine Learning for Forecasting**: Machine learning algorithms can be used to forecast the future economic value of knowledge assets following past data and market trends **Scenario Analysis**: AI could simulate different scenarios to estimate the financial impact of various strategies for leveraging intellectual assets
Valuation Models	**AI-Powered Valuation Models**: AI can enhance traditional valuation models by incorporating a wider range of data sources and variables, making valuations more accurate and comprehensive

(continued)

Table 4.1 (continued)

Due Diligence	**AI-Assisted Due Diligence**: When organizations are involved in mergers, acquisitions, or partnerships, AI can assist in conducting due diligence by evaluating the knowledge assets of the target organization
Portfolio Management	**Optimizing Knowledge Portfolios**: AI can help organizations optimize their knowledge portfolios by identifying which assets to invest in, maintain, or divest based on their economic and financial potential
Decision Support	**AI-Driven Decision Support**: AI can provide decision-makers with data-driven insights and recommendations for maximizing the economic and financial value of knowledge assets
Monetization Strategies	**AI for Monetization Strategies**: AI can suggest strategies for monetizing knowledge assets, whether through licensing, partnerships, or commercialization
Compliance and IP Protection	**AI for IP Protection**: AI can monitor and protect intellectual property by identifying potential infringements or unauthorized use

The valuation of know-how, especially in the context of intellectual property, can be complex and may require the expertise of financial analysts, legal professionals, and AI specialists.

The estimate of the market value of the know-how must typically be placed in an evaluation context that considers not only the firm, but also its intangible resources, starting with those most contiguous to the know-how (i.e., patents and, residually, goodwill).

The exploitation of know-how stems from the value chain and the external sources of evaluation, as shown in Fig. 4.2.

Regarding intangible assets not registered or specifically protected, such as know-how, the valuation is subject to high inter-temporal variability, being anchored to provisions aimed at drawing up the strategic, industrial, and financial plans.

The breadth of the evaluation interval is demarcated, in its extremes, by upper and lower limits, in the hypothesis of (full) going concern (full

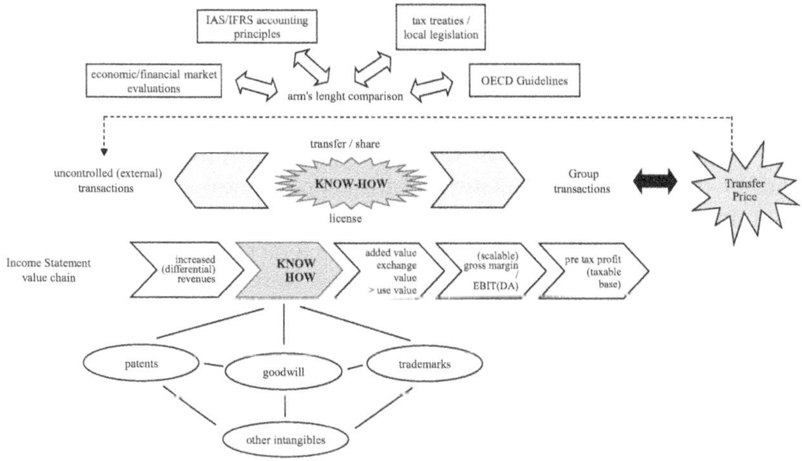

Fig. 4.2 Links between know-how, value chains, and external evaluation sources

business continuity) or in liquidation (break up) scenarios, in which traditionally intangible resources lose most of their value, especially if they are not independently negotiable or synergistically connected to other assets. In the hypothesis of discontinuity, the organized complex of assets that represents the firm is eliminated.

The choice of approaches depends on the intangible resource and the purpose and context of the evaluation, but also on the ease with which reliable information on the market in which it is strategically positioned can be found.

Of the different approaches, the complementarity in identifying—from different angles—the multifaceted aspects of the intangible object of evaluation, suitable to allow an integrated evaluation, must be grasped. For example:

- the relief from royalties is in the function of the incomes or incremental cash flows that derive from the exploitation of the know-how and that interact with the market surplus value or the multipliers of comparable companies;
- the incremental equity derives from an accumulation in the years of differential income; and

- the costs of reproduction estimate the future benefits and the independent estimate of the average differential goodwill between balance sheet-based versus income approaches.

The evaluation can be carried out for different purposes, even in litigation, in case of unfair competition with appropriation, replication, and/or undue imitation and usurpation of know-how.

The value of experimentation—with its practical implications—is a fundamental element of know-how. Know-how creates value if it is unconventional and if it is the result of engineered creative rationality that allows a mastering of complexity.

The risk of duplication in the valuation must always be borne in mind, where there is a lack of exclusivity (which is not limited by the intangibility of the know-how and its multiple reproducibility and transferability) and a clear segmentation and specificity of loyalty compared to other similar assets, represented by goodwill, patents, trademarks, and other intangible assets.

The evaluation time horizon must consider the nature of the know-how, which has a potentially indefinite duration but is forcibly ephemeral and subject to the unpredictability of the life cycle, which depends on the interaction of competitive pressures and external reactions.

The erosion of value, in the case of intangibles and know-how, in particular, derives from its potential obsolescence and technological decay, which eliminate its exclusive connotations, and not from a deterioration related to the use, which indeed increases the value, because of economies of experience, as well as visibility and synergistic sharing with other inventions or processes. The strategic value of the know-how must be appreciated in terms of uniqueness, specificity, non-permeability, and exclusivity, which are the basis of killer applications.

A. *The relief-from-royalty approach*

The relief-from-royalty approach is a common method used in the valuation of know-how, patents, and other intellectual property assets. This approach calculates the economic value of the intellectual property by estimating what it would cost an organization to license or acquire similar intellectual property if it did not already own it. AI can be a valuable tool in applying the relief-from-royalty approach to the valuation of know-how.

Relief from royalties follows these patterns, as shown in Table 4.2.

While AI can enhance the relief-from-royalty approach, the accuracy of the valuation still relies on the quality of the data used and the expertise of valuation professionals who interpret the results. Additionally, legal and contractual considerations, as well as market dynamics, can significantly impact the valuation process, and human judgment remains crucial in many aspects of intellectual property valuation.

An easily applicable empirical approach is based on the determination of the "presumed royalties" that the owner of the know-how would have required to authorize third parties to exploit it ("consent price" approach). The relief-from-royalties approach is indicated where one wants to arrive at the determination of the exchange value of the know-how.

This approach allows estimating the income of the know-how by deducting from the notional royalties that would be paid to a third party for the use of the know-how under license any direct and indirect costs of maintenance/development of the know-how itself not already deducted from the notional royalty.

The market value of know-how can be estimated as the sum of the relief from royalties (which the firm would pay as a licensee if the know-how were not owned) discounted over a time horizon of at least 3–5 years.

The concept of reasonable royalty can be relevant in the field of litigation in the quantification of damages for unlawful use of the know-how.

The presence of license agreements is appreciated by investors because it generates not occasional revenues and is a signal of the technological heritage and innovative capacity of the firm.

B. *The incremental income approach*

The incremental income approach is a commonly used method in the valuation of know-how and other intellectual property assets. This approach assesses the value of intellectual property by estimating the incremental income or cost savings it generates for a business when compared to a scenario where the intellectual property is not utilized.

Table 4.2 Relief from royalties

Data Analysis	**Market Data**: AI can analyze extensive market data to determine royalty rates for similar types of intellectual property in the industry or field of interest. This analysis can help establish a benchmark for the relief-from-royalty calculation Comparative Analysis: AI can identify and compare similar know-how assets by analyzing patent databases, research publications, and other relevant sources of data to find comparable technologies and their licensing rates
Risk Assessment	**Machine Learning for Risk Assessment**: AI can be used to determine the potential risks linked to the know-how, such as legal risks related to infringement or challenges to its validity **Scenario Analysis**: AI can perform scenario analysis to evaluate how variations in market conditions, competition, or legal factors may affect the royalty rate and, consequently, the valuation
Market Trends	**AI-Powered Market Trend Analysis**: AI can monitor market trends, technological advancements, and competitive developments that might impact the royalty rate and the value of know-how
Data Integration	**AI for Data Integration**: AI can integrate various data sources, including financial information, patent information, market evidence, and historical licensing agreements to create a comprehensive valuation model
Machine Learning Models	**Regression Analysis**: Machine learning algorithms, such as regression models, can be used to predict royalty rates based on multiple variables, including the uniqueness of the know-how, the market demand, and the competitive landscape **Neural Networks**: Complex neural network models can capture non-linear relationships between factors affecting royalty rates
Document Analysis	**Natural Language Processing (NLP)**: AI-powered NLP techniques can analyze licensing agreements, legal documents, and technical literature to extract valuable information regarding royalty rates, licensing terms, and industry practices
Predictive Analytics	**Predictive Modeling**: AI can build predictive models to estimate future royalty income streams based on historical data and assumptions about the know-how's potential market performance
Decision Support	**AI-Driven Decision Support**: AI can provide insights and recommendations to decision-makers regarding the fair value of the know-how, considering various scenarios and assumptions
Reporting and Visualization	**Data Visualization**: AI can generate visual reports and dashboards to present the valuation results, making it easier for stakeholders to understand the factors contributing to the estimated royalty rate and the overall value

AI can be leveraged to enhance various aspects of this valuation approach (Table 4.3).

The accuracy of the incremental income valuation using AI depends on the significance and quality of the input data, the assumptions made in the modeling process, and the expertise of valuation professionals who interpret the results. Additionally, legal and contractual considerations may be important in the valuation process, particularly if the know-how involves licensing agreements or contractual obligations.

The value of know-how is proportional to its expected economic results. Therefore, the contribution of know-how in terms of price and/or volume increases (and therefore economic margin) to the profitability of the business can be measured by the differential income approach, which determines the value of the know-how as the present value of the sum of the differential income that it is likely to produce in the future.

The know-how can, therefore, be evaluated if it gives rise to differential economic benefits, which are expressed in a premium price (the price differential of the product characterized by know-how).

The number of years of discounting the income from the exploitation of the know-how depends on its life cycle (useful life). A possible variant is based on the estimate of the incremental gross operating margin that the know-how contributes to obtaining, to which a reasonable multiplier derived from negotiations of comparable intangibles is applied. The additional cash flow generated by the know-how can also be considered.

The use of the know-how acts on the economic margins expressed by the differential between revenues and operating costs as it allows both to increase revenues (with higher direct sales or with royalties receivable from licenses) and to reduce costs, producing with less labor-intensive techniques and suitable to allow savings of other costs (production, organization, energy ...).

The stratification of differential incomes thanks to the know-how generates incremental equity, which expresses the differential between market value and the book value of the firm. It is a suitable element to express the surplus value of know-how. The lack of symbolic recognition and capitalization of know-how costs impacts the lack of amortization and the potential undervaluation of the equity, with a book value lower than the market value.

Both the approaches considered here, and the relief from royalties can be reconducted, in a broad sense, to the income approaches, based on a projection of normalized future income. This income is to be

Table 4.3 Artificial Intelligence, know-how, and the incremental income approach

Data Analysis	**Financial Data Analysis**: AI can analyze historical financial data, including revenue streams, cost savings, and profit margins associated with the use of the know-how **Market and Industry Data**: AI can process market and industry data to assess how the presence of the know-how impacts a business's competitive position and market share
Predictive Analytics	**Machine Learning Models**: Machine learning algorithms can build predictive models to estimate future income or cost savings generated by the know-how based on historical data and other relevant variables **Time-Series Analysis**: AI-powered time-series analysis can be used to identify trends and patterns in financial data related to the know-how
Market and Competition Analysis	**Competitive Intelligence**: AI can gather and analyze data on competitors' use of similar know-how or technologies to estimate how the know-how affects competitive positioning and potential market share **Market Trend Analysis**: AI can monitor market trends, customer preferences, and technological advancements to assess how the know-how's value might change over time
Scenario Analysis	**Monte Carlo Simulation**: AI-driven Monte Carlo simulations estimate the range of outcomes and uncertainties connected to the use of know-how under various scenarios **Sensitivity Analysis**: AI can perform sensitivity analysis to understand how modifications in key patterns, such as market demand, pricing, or cost structures, affect the incremental income

(continued)

Table 4.3 (continued)

Natural Language Processing (NLP)	**NLP for Document Analysis**: AI-powered NLP techniques can analyze contracts, licensing agreements, and other relevant documents to extract information regarding the use and impact of the know-how on business operations **Sentiment Analysis**: NLP can be used to analyze news articles and customer feedback to gauge public sentiment and reputation associated with the use of the know-how
Data Integration	**AI for Data Integration**: AI can integrate financial data, market data, and operational data to create a comprehensive model for assessing incremental income
Decision Support	**AI-Enhanced Decision Support**: AI can provide decision-makers with insights and recommendations based on the valuation results, helping them make informed decisions regarding the use, licensing, or sale of the know-how
Visualization and Reporting	**Data Visualization**: AI can generate visual reports and dashboards to present valuation results, making it easier for stakeholders to understand the financial impact of the know-how

discounted over a predefined (or unlimited) time horizon, consistent with the expected useful life of the know-how, at a reasonable rate, which incorporates the risk associated with the expected future manifestation of income.

C. The estimate of the cost incurred (or of reproduction)

The estimate of the cost incurred (or of reproduction cost) is a key element in the valuation of know-how and other intellectual property assets. This approach involves estimating the cost that would be required to recreate or reproduce the know-how using similar resources and expertise. AI can be applied to various aspects of this approach to foster the precision and efficiency of the valuation process (Table 4.4).

Table 4.4 Reproduction costs

Data Analysis	**Resource Cost Data**: AI can analyze data related to the cost of resources required to develop or reproduce the know-how, such as labor costs, material costs, and research and development expenses **Market Data**: AI can process market data to assess the availability and pricing of similar resources and expertise in the market
Market and Competition Analysis	**Competitive Intelligence**: AI can gather and analyze data on competitors or similar industry players to estimate the costs they might have incurred in developing comparable know-how **Market Trend Analysis**: AI can monitor market trends, technological advancements, and labor market conditions to assess how the cost of reproducing the know-how may change over time
Natural Language Processing (NLP)	**NLP for Document Analysis**: AI-powered NLP techniques can extract valuable information from documents related to the know-how, such as technical manuals, design specifications, and process documentation
Data Integration	**AI for Data Integration**: AI can integrate cost data, market data, and technical documentation to create a comprehensive model for estimating the reproduction cost
Decision Support	**AI-Enhanced Decision Support**: AI can provide decision-makers with insights and recommendations based on the reproduction cost estimate, helping them make informed decisions regarding the use, sale, or licensing of the know-how
Visualization and Reporting	**Data Visualization**: AI can generate visual reports and dashboards to present the reproduction cost estimate, making it easier for stakeholders to understand the factors contributing to the estimate

Legal and contractual considerations may be important in the valuation process, especially if the know-how involves licensing agreements or contractual obligations.

In the absence of reliable data on expected income capacity, a possible alternative is that of the cost incurred in the past to create the know-how and to occupy in the market the positions reached by the firm at the valuation date.

The identification of a historical cost of production, based on an analytical accounting that allows to functionally separate the costs for the know-how from the others, is preparatory to the estimate of a current cost of reproduction, having the nature of investment and oriented to the expected future benefits.

A limit of this estimate derives from the unfitness, of the historical costs to measure value later, due to the change in the purchasing power. A second limit is because the value of an asset is not only due to the costs necessary to obtain it, but also mainly to its expected benefits.

A step forward is represented by the process of reproducing functionally equivalent know-how, which replaces the historical costs with the costs of reproducing the asset from scratch, i.e., the costs that would have to be incurred at the time of valuation to reconstruct the same value that the know-how reached at that time.

However, in the procedure now examined, there is still the limit of not considering the profitability of the investment and the opportunity cost deriving from the immediate non-use of the know-how. The existence of high and uncertain fixed costs related to the reconstruction of know-how represents a barrier to entry that segregates the market and distances competitors.

D. *The complex balance sheet-based approach*

The complex balance sheet-based approach is a method used in the valuation of know-how and intellectual property. It involves assessing the value of these assets by considering their impact on a firm's balance sheet, including assets and liabilities. AI can be applied to various aspects of this approach to enhance accuracy and efficiency in the valuation process (Table 4.5).

The balance sheet-based approaches traditionally used in continental Europe (as shown in Chapter 2) are based on the analytical valuation of individual assets and liabilities, with a comparison with their book value, to adjust the book value of equity to arrive at a market value of equity. In this approach, in the so-called "second-degree complex" variant, there are

Table 4.5 Artificial Intelligence and the complex balance sheet-based approach

Data Analysis	**Financial Data Analysis**: AI can assess a firm's financial statements (balance sheet, income statement, and cash flow statement, as shown, for instance, in https://fastercapital.com/keyword/historical-financial-statements.html) to identify relevant information regarding the know-how's impact on the firm's financial position **Market Data**: AI can process market data to assess how the presence of the know-how impacts a firm's competitive position, market share, and financial performance
Asset and Liability Assessment	**Machine Learning Models**: AI can build predictive models to estimate the impact of know-how on a firm's assets (e.g., intangible assets) and liabilities (e.g., legal obligations related to the know-how) **Natural Language Processing (NLP)**: NLP can analyze legal contracts, licensing agreements, and other documents to identify any liabilities or obligations associated with the know-how
Market and Competition Analysis	**Competitive Intelligence**: AI can gather and analyze data on competitors to assess how their intellectual property assets impact their balance sheets and financial performance **Market Trend Analysis**: AI can monitor market trends, technological advancements, and competitive developments to assess how the value of know-how may change over time
Scenario Analysis	**Monte Carlo Simulation**: AI-driven simulations can help assess the range of potential impacts on a firm's balance sheet under different scenarios, considering factors like market demand, pricing, and legal risks **Sensitivity Analysis**: AI can perform sensitivity analysis to understand how modifications in key variables, such as market conditions or competitive dynamics, affect the valuation based on the balance sheet approach
Natural Language Processing (NLP)	**NLP for Document Analysis**: AI-powered NLP techniques can analyze legal documents, contracts, and financial reports to extract relevant information regarding the know-how's impact on the balance sheet

(continued)

Table 4.5 (continued)

Data Integration	**AI for Data Integration**: AI can integrate financial data, market data, legal documents, and technical documentation to create a comprehensive model for assessing the impact on the balance sheet
Decision Support	**AI-Enhanced Decision Support**: AI can provide decision-makers with insights and recommendations based on the valuation results, helping them make informed decisions regarding the use, sale, or licensing of the know-how
Visualization and Reporting	**Data Visualization**: AI can generate visual reports and dashboards to present the impact on the balance sheet, making it easier for stakeholders to understand how the know-how affects the firm's financial position

peculiar activities, such as know-how, which are not normally accounted for and do not typically have an independent market value. The capital gain should then be expressed net of potential tax liabilities, considering a tax profile that will only be applied when there is a need to move from an abstractly estimated value to a value-added price, monetarily negotiated.

E. *The mixed capital-income approach with an independent estimate of goodwill*

The mixed capital-income approach is a method used in the valuation of know-how and other intellectual property assets. It combines elements of both the capital approach and the income approach to estimate the value of these assets. In this approach, an independent estimate of goodwill is often a crucial component.

The main approach for estimating goodwill is based on the comparison between the extra yield that the firm can generate for a limited period (or, more rarely, unlimited) and the normal return on capital of comparable companies, within the product sector of reference.

To the extent that the goodwill is attributable to the know-how, the approach can be used to estimate this know-how; a critical point derives from the not easy separability of the know-how from other intangible resources.

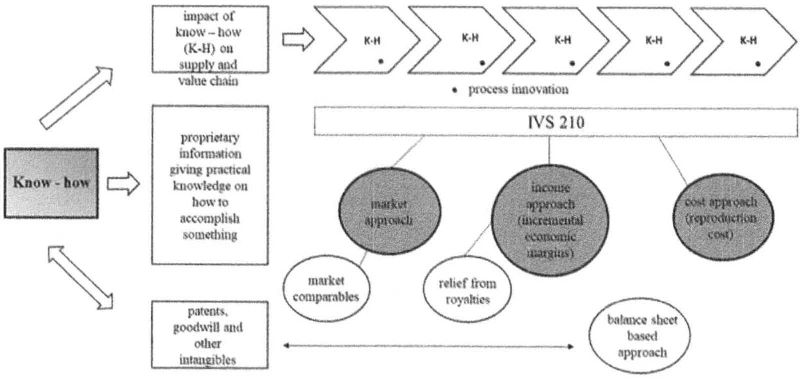

Fig. 4.3 Know-how valuation approaches

The extra income due to know-how is comparable to differential income and therefore the two approaches can find useful elements of convergence or, at least, complementarity.

Figure 4.3 summarizes the valuation approaches of know-how.

4.5 Product and Process Innovation

Product and process innovation are important in the valuation of know-how, as they can enhance the economic value and competitive advantage associated with intellectual property assets. AI-driven product and process innovation is a focal point in various sectors, such as manufacturing, process industries, and urban mobility. Studies underscore the advantages of AI in improving product quality, streamlining operations, and fostering continuous product innovation. AI facilitates extensive engagement among stakeholders, intelligent decision-making, and flexible innovation processes within manufacturing companies, underscoring the importance of establishing data management protocols and combining traditional expertise with online analysis. Moreover, integrating AI in innovation management plays a vital role in addressing the changing requirements of global markets, personalized solutions, and the push for digital transformation, providing specialized tools like machine learning and speech recognition to aid in innovation-related activities. AI can be applied to various aspects of the valuation process when considering the impact of product and process innovation on know-how:

1. **Data Analysis:**
    - **Market Data Analysis**: AI can process market data to assess the impact of product and process innovations on market demand, competitive positioning, and revenue potential.
    - **Competitor Analysis**: AI-driven competitive intelligence tools can analyze competitors' product and process innovations to gauge their impact on market share and pricing dynamics.
2. **Innovation Assessment**:
    - **Natural Language Processing (NLP)**: NLP techniques can analyze technical documentation, research papers, and patents to identify and quantify the innovative aspects of the know-how.
    - **Machine Learning for Innovation Metrics**: AI can be used to develop metrics that quantify the degree of innovation within the know-how based on factors such as novelty, uniqueness, and potential market impact.
3. **Market and Competition Analysis**:
    - **Market Trend Analysis**: AI can monitor market trends, emerging technologies, and competitive developments to assess how product and process innovations influence the valuation of know-how over time.
    - **Competitive Benchmarking**: AI can assist in benchmarking an organization's product and process innovations against industry standards and competitors, helping to identify areas of competitive advantage.
4. **Scenario Analysis**:
    - **Simulation Modeling**: AI-driven simulation models can project the potential financial impact of different product and process innovation scenarios on the valuation of know-how.
    - **Sensitivity Analysis**: AI can use sensitivity to understand how modifications in key variables, such as innovation success rates or market adoption rates, affect the valuation.

5. **Market Adoption Prediction**:

   - **Machine Learning for Market Adoption**: AI can develop predictive models to estimate the likely adoption rate of product and process innovations in the market, providing insights into their potential value.
   - **Consumer Sentiment Analysis**: NLP can be used to analyze consumer reviews, feedback, and sentiment data to gauge market receptiveness to innovative features or processes associated with the know-how.

6. **Data Integration**:

   - **AI for Data Integration**: AI can integrate financial data, market data, technical documentation, and innovation-related information to create a comprehensive model for assessing the valuation of know-how with product and process innovation considerations.

7. **Decision Support**:

   - **AI-Enhanced Decision Support**: AI can provide decision-makers with insights and recommendations based on the valuation results, helping them make informed decisions regarding the utilization, sale, or licensing of the know-how with innovations.

8. **Visualization and Reporting**:

   - **Data Visualization**: AI can generate visual reports and dashboards to present the impact of product and process innovations on the valuation, helping stakeholders to understand and act upon the findings.

By leveraging AI in these ways, organizations can better understand and quantify the contribution of product and process innovations to the value of their know-how. This enhanced understanding can inform strategic decisions, including investment priorities, licensing strategies, and negotiations in intellectual property transactions.

Innovation is one of the key elements of a firm's differentiation strategies, which allow it to become unique, acquiring a competitive advantage that can result in monopolistic rents. The innovations can be a product and/or process and are divided into main or derived: the former have an absolute degree of creativity and originality compared to the previous knowledge, while the latter has a relative character and may consist of progress or improvement of techniques. The derived inventions may be of:

- improvement (resolution in different and more convenient forms of technical problems previously solved in another way);
- translation (transposition of a known principle or a previous invention in a different sector and with a different result); and
- combination (ingenious and original coordination of elements and means already known with a technically new and economically useful result).

Also, "chain-linked" inventions, which form patent families along the same supply chain, are essential.

There may be cases of dependent and derived inventions, of selection, improvement, combination, and translation, whereby the original patent takes on higher value because of other inventions that depend on it, giving rise to significant synergies. Know-how is the "glue" that keeps together sequential inventions, presiding over their smooth interaction.

Differentiation helps to create barriers to entry into the market, limiting competition and the substitutability or comparability of the firm's assets. This can allow it to achieve high economic margins, even in the presence of an external demand that struggles to find satisfaction elsewhere and that may suffer the temporary monopolistic force of the leading firm that may activate price-maker strategies (with a specular price-taking clientele).

At a strategic level, the differential nature of inventions, which contributes to making the firm "unique", sheltering it from comparison and allowing it to avoid cost differentiation, is associated with their scalability, which allows its use—through industry and reproducibility in series—where costs are marginally decreasing as volumes increase. Low marginal costs and economies of scale are positive aspects of know-how, which are the result of often very costly initial investments and uncertain outcomes.

4.6 The Impact of Artificial Intelligence and Digitalization on Know-How

AI is now recognized as one of the main enablers of digital transformation in multiple industries. AI can help companies become more innovative, flexible, and adaptive than ever before, with an impact on robotics, and process automation.

With its ability to improve simulation, forecasting, and smooth proof-of-concept trials and errors, AI can boost (human) know-how, and its industrial applications. These technological advancements play a crucial role in enhancing processes, reducing timeframes, and improving decision-making. Nevertheless, challenges such as job displacement and the necessity for continuous education emerge as a result of AI and digitalization. The incorporation of AI and digitalization underscores the importance of providing support for employees to adjust to changes and cultivate essential soft skills. In essence, AI and digitalization are transforming industries, underscoring the significance of upskilling, adaptability, and organizational assistance in maneuvering through the ever-changing landscape of knowledge management and technological progress.

Digitalization is a further catalyst that fosters know-how through its input factors, easier to collect, store, and interpret (Fig. 4.4).

4.7 Patents: Definition and Rationale

A patent is a limited monopoly that is granted for 20 years in return for the disclosure of technical information (Benty & Sherman, 2014, p. 375). AI exerts a significant influence on the field of patents. The utilization of AI in conducting searches for prior art diminishes both the time expended and the costs incurred by proposing specific keywords, retrieving pertinent documents, and visually representing content. Various challenges surface in the realm of patenting innovations generated by AI, encompassing the identification of inventors and evaluating their originality and lack of obviousness. The bestowal of patents upon AI encounters legal complications, given that existing regulations mandate a "person" to secure a patent, thereby prompting inquiries into the rightful possession of financial entitlements linked to AI-driven patents. Within

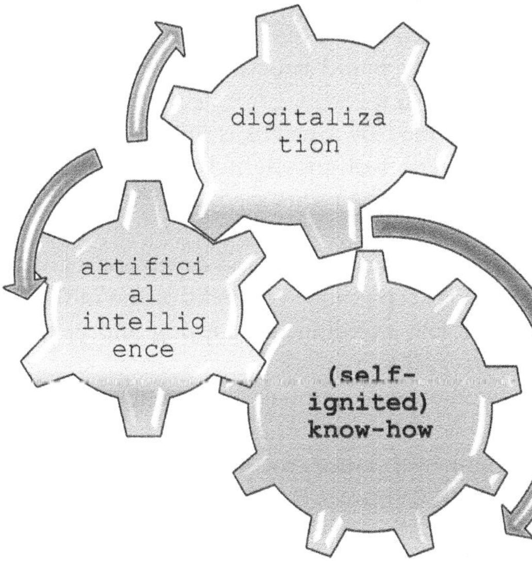

Fig. 4.4 Know-how, Artificial Intelligence, and Digitalization

the domain of European patents, safeguarding fundamental AI advancements such as novel algorithms and models proves intricate due to the rigorous demand for technical precision.

A patent is a set of exclusive rights granted by a sovereign state or intergovernmental organization to an inventor or assignee for a limited period in exchange for detailed public disclosure of an invention. An invention is a solution to a specific technological problem and is a product or a process (WIPO, 2008). The word patent originates from the Latin *patere*, which means "to lay open" (i.e., to make available for public inspection).

Patents are usually the result of risky and costly research and development, and the developer will try to recover its costs (and earn a return) through the sale of products covered by the patent, licensing others to use the invention (often a product or process), or through the outright sale of the patent.

The very fact that costs are incurred mainly before patentability for inventions may have important transactional implications: patents are ripe for sale or licensing even immediately after registration, considering their finite useful life, with typically soon peaking and then declining values.

The terminal value of an expiring patent is not necessarily zero if it can still be used as a distinctive, albeit no more protected, invention, during and after its phase-out. The brand associated with the expired patent (e.g., Aspirin) may still be worth it.

The protection provided by a patent is limited to 20 years, and so is shorter than the protection of copyright law or (potentially unlimited) trademark registration, but the rights are more extensive and cover most commercial uses.

Patents are granted only after a long and expensive registration process. Patent rights help firms keep unique competitiveness in the market, under the protection of the law, avoiding the copying and plagiarism of other competitors (Danchev, 2006).

Justifications and economic rationale for patents derive from:

- The natural right of inventors to the proceeds of their mental labor and
- The grant of a reward for the inventive activity that otherwise would lack proper incentives.

Patent valuation is required in many cases as:

1. M&A operations, spin-offs, demergers, joint ventures, etc.;
2. Bankruptcy;
3. Sale or license;
4. Patent conflicts and disputes;
5. Collateral for bank loans;
6. Accounting; and
7. Taxation (transfer pricing, patent box, etc.).

As shown in Table 4.6, a patent can be linked to AI in several ways.

AI is increasingly intertwined with the patent process from the creation and assessment of inventions to the management and protection of intellectual property. As AI technologies continue to advance, they will likely play an even more significant role in the patent landscape.

4.8 From Know-How to Patents

Patents represent the natural evolution of know-how.

Table 4.6 Artificial Intelligence and patents

AI-Based Inventions	Patents can be obtained for inventions that are based on or involve AI technologies. This includes inventions related to machine learning algorithms, neural networks, natural language processing, computer vision, and other AI techniques
AI as an Inventor	In some jurisdictions, there is debate over whether AI systems can be recognized as inventors on patent applications. Some argue that if an AI system autonomously generates a novel and non-obvious invention, it should be credited as the inventor
Patent Search and Analysis	AI and machine learning are employed to improve the efficiency and accuracy of patent searches. AI-powered algorithms can sift through vast patent databases to identify relevant prior art and help patent examiners and inventors determine the innovativeness of an invention
Infringement Detection	AI can assist patent holders in monitoring their patents and detecting potential infringements. Natural language processing and machine learning can be used to scan documents, websites, and databases for instances of unauthorized use
Patent Portfolio Management	AI tools can aid in managing a firm's patent portfolio by identifying which patents should be maintained, renewed, or divested. These tools can analyze market trends, competitive landscapes, and the potential value of patents
Automated Patent Drafting	AI-powered systems can assist patent attorneys and inventors in drafting patent applications. These systems can analyze the invention's technical details and generate patent claims and descriptions
Prior Art Analysis	AI algorithms can assist patent examiners and practitioners in assessing the relevance of prior art, making the patent examination process more efficient and accurate
Innovation and Research	AI can be used to accelerate the innovation process itself. By examining large data and identifying patterns, AI may help researchers and inventors generate new ideas and solutions that may be eligible for patent protection
IP Portfolio Strategy	AI can provide insights into an organization's intellectual property strategy by analyzing market dynamics, competitive landscapes, and technology trends. This information can inform decisions about where to focus patent efforts

> Know-how and trade secrets are proprietary information or knowledge that assists or improves a commercial activity, but that is not registered for protection in the manner of a patent or trademark. (OECD, Transfer Price Guidelines, 2022)

"Know-how is practical knowledge of how to get something done, as opposed to «know-what» (facts), «know-why» (science), or «know-who» (networking). Know-how is often tacit knowledge, which means that it is difficult to transfer to another person by means of writing it down or verbalizing it. The opposite of tacit knowledge is explicit knowledge. In the context of industrial property (now generally viewed as intellectual property), know-how is a component in the transfer of unpatented proprietary technology in national and international environments, co-existing with or separate from other Intellectual Property rights such as patents, trademarks, and copyright and is an economic asset" United Nations Industrial Development Organization (1996).

Know-how (to do it) is a key and trendy factor behind competitive and comparative advantage (Hall, 1993), representing the invisible glue behind strategies of product differentiation and innovation, creating ancillary value from other factor inputs.

If overall added value may be compared to an iceberg, know-how may well represent its gravitational sunk part. AI-driven patterns are of paramount importance in a variety of industries, shifting from conventional expertise to innovative approaches in patent strategies. The utilization of AI in the design of garment patterns, utilizing fuzzy logic and artificial neural networks, facilitates the development of knowledge-supported models, reducing the need for expert patternmakers and enhancing efficiency in the fashion sector. Additionally, the rise of design patterns specifically designed for AI systems tackles the challenges in attaining production readiness, with a focus on enhancing software quality characteristics and offering established solution frameworks for professionals and scholars. The examination of AI patents underscores the crucial role of intellectual property strategies in technology companies, illuminating the unique dilemmas faced by firms in the AI market.

4.9 Accounting as a Prerequisite for Valuation

The accounting treatment of patents is a crucial consideration when conducting economic, financial, and market valuations. Patents are considered intangible assets, and their proper accounting treatment impacts how they are reflected on a firm's financial statements and, subsequently, how they are assessed in valuation processes. Here's an overview of the accounting treatment of patents and its importance in valuation:

1. **Initial Recognition**:
   - When a firm incurs costs related to acquiring or developing a patent (e.g., research and development expenses), these costs are typically expensed as incurred, rather than capitalized on the balance sheet. This means that, initially, patents do not appear as assets on the balance sheet.
2. **Capitalization**:
   - However, once a patent is acquired or developed and meets specific criteria, it can be capitalized as an intangible asset. This typically occurs when future economic benefits are likely to be associated with the patent and its cost can be reliably measured.
   - The capitalized cost of the patent includes the purchase price (if acquired externally) or the direct costs incurred in developing it (if developed internally). This cost is amortized over its estimated useful life.
3. **Amortization**:
   - Patents are subject to amortization, which means that their recorded value on the balance sheet is systematically reduced over time. The amortization cost is recorded as an operating expense in the income statement, reducing the firm's net profit.
   - The amortization period for patents is typically their estimated useful life, which is determined based on factors like the expected duration of exclusivity and the anticipated technological or market changes that may affect the patent's value.

4. **Impairment Testing**:

    - Companies are required to periodically assess whether there has been any impairment in the value of their patents. If the carrying amount of a patent exceeds its recoverable amount (i.e., its value to the business), an impairment loss is recognized, reducing the asset's book value.
    - Impairment testing ensures that patents are carried at no more than their recoverable amount, preventing overstatement of their value on the balance sheet.

The accounting treatment of patents is important in valuation for several reasons:

- **Book Value**: The balance sheet value of patents affects the book value of the firm, which is a fundamental metric used in financial analysis and valuation.
- **Income Statement Impact**: The amortization of patents affects the firm's reported net income, which, in turn, affects various financial ratios and metrics used in valuation, such as price-to-earnings (P/E) ratios.
- **Impairment**: Recognizing impairments ensures that the value of patents is accurately reflected on the balance sheet, preventing overvaluation.
- **Useful Life**: The estimated useful life of patents influences the timing of expense recognition, which can impact cash flows used in valuation models.
- **Market Perception**: Investors and analysts consider the accounting treatment of patents when assessing a firm's financial health and growth potential.

When conducting economic, financial, and market valuations, it's crucial to consider both the book value and income statement impact of patents, as well as their expected future cash flows and market conditions. The appropriate treatment of patents in valuation models will depend on the specific purposes of the appraisal.

Accounting treatment and the consequent assessment of intangible capital are a prerequisite for financial performance appraisal and consequent bankability, combining economic margins, such as EBITDA, with debt-servicing cash flows (Metha & Madhani, 2008).

The slippery nature of intangibles and their consequent uneasy valuation boundaries represent a well-known problem.

According to IAS 38, the aggregate amount of research and development expenditure recognized as an expense during the period is required to be disclosed, but there are no specific requirements for disclosure of another spending on intangibles.

"*The academic and professional interest in Intangible Capital is underpinned by the idea that it can be considered one of the main levers to create value*" (Giuliani, 2013) and, according to Michael Porter's fundamental insights, value creation derives from the lasting competitive advantage over rival entities, embedded in continuously innovating business models, to be adequately designed and managed (Porter, 1998).

Competitive edge is increasingly driven by the catalyst presence of intangibles, which represents a pivotal breakthrough, and it occurs when an organization (painfully) develops core competencies and skills that allow it to outperform its competitors, especially for what concerns customized differentiation.

Patents, often underrepresented in the balance sheet, typically constitute a significant incremental EBITDA driver, which expresses the dominant income-driven cash flow source. Intangibles, which are the invisible "glue" behind going concern and value creation, not only enhance strategic differential value but are likelier to make results more sustainable in the future, thus easing proper debt service.

DCF or EBITDA calculus is currently used for the market valuation of patents. Even if academics and practitioners well know this fact, some further considerations, based on intangible-driven cash generation, may add originality to the discussion of intellectual capital valuation and debt servicing. Asset-less incremental EBITDA, driven by intangibles, reinforces debt service capacity, through "economic" liquidity, which originated in the income statement.

4.10 License or Sale?

Intangible transactions may temporarily or permanently transfer the property or the right to use the patent, being alternatively classified under a license or sale agreement. A patent can be used to protect or earn licensing revenues (Ignat, 2016).

The perimeter of a license is proportional to the value of the patent.

Even if many comparability problems are similar, some significant differences arise, and could be fiscally significant:

- (temporary) licenses are more common within the group, where information asymmetries are minimized, and synergies shared, and on an international basis, to bypass geographical exclusivity problems—and so making transfer price arm's length comparisons applicable but more difficult to estimate;
- definitive sales may conversely occur even outside (international) groups, especially when a small and independent firm, that owns a promising patent, is aware of its intrinsic value, but lacks the economic and financial soundness to properly exploit it, especially abroad;
- licensing may typically be riskier than selling for the owner of the patent since in many cases the royalty rate depends on unknown characteristics of the licensee (when the royalty is based on the licensee's output or sales, the rate may vary according to his or her turnover); and
- risk is asymmetrically transferred from the seller/licensor to the buyer/licensee, both in its dimension and timing, with a not negligible impact on the tax base and its repartition in different fiscal years. Albeit this parameter is difficult to estimate, it should be carefully investigated, together with its economic and fiscal impact. Risk transmission is definitive in sales (unless there are earn-out or other conditional clauses), being otherwise shared and diluted across time in license agreements.

A combination between licenses and sales is always possible, mainly when a license contract contains a put & call option, according to which after a certain period and at a stated price, the patent may be purchased by the licensee or sold by the licensor.

Legal ownership of the patent is not exclusively linked to its exploitation, not only because of possible licensing but also because of the versatility of the patent, which can be exploited with partnership agreements, risk sharing, common investments, etc., within an articulated international value chain, where it may prove difficult to estimate the value of each segment.

A license generally contains some or all of the following financial provisions:

- Upfront payments;
- Ongoing pre-commercial payments;
- Patent cost reimbursement;
- Milestone payments;
- Annual minimum royalties;
- Research support;
- Sublicense income sharing;
- Manufacturing; and
- Earned royalties or sales/profit sharing.

Most licenses include some form of upfront payment, variously called a license issue fee, a technology transfer fee, technology access fee (...).

The upfront payment reflects the value of the technology at the time is being transferred. For an embryonic academic technology that lacks both market and technology validation, this initial value will be relatively low, and so will the upfront fee.

For the academic institutions, a vital element of the upfront value of the technology is the investment in legal fees that they have put into turning scientific data and publications into an intellectual property portfolio that can be licensed to a corporate partner. Academic institutions usually insist on recouping that investment upfront, in part so they can redeploy the funds into new inventions.

Newly formed startups are usually illiquid. A wise licensor will typically not seek to suck much of that expensive cash out of the firm in upfront payments but will want to see those funds go into developing the technology. Instead, the licensor will generally agree to be compensated in shares of the licensee, purchased at nominal par value, and characterized by upside potential.

When a large firm licenses technology from a smaller, early stage company, the agreement normally includes the purchase of equity in the smaller firm by the large one.

From the licensor's perspective, the validation of their technology (demonstrated by the license fees) means that the firm has reached a significant value-added milestone.

Most licenses include several "pre-commercial" payments, made while the technology is still under development and before it is generating product revenues for the licensee.

Milestone payments reflect the increase in the value of the technology to the licensee as the licensee makes progress in developing the technology.

Developmental milestone payments are particularly common with life sciences inventions.

Annual minimum royalties ("AMR") refer to the payments that are made in advance, at the start of the license year. AMR typically starts low and escalates over time.

An AMR serves as a due diligence mechanism. If the licensee has lost interest in the technology, either because it does not work or because there is no market interest, then the licensee will terminate the license and return the technology to the licensor rather than make an AMR payment.

When technology is transferred at an early stage, the licensee frequently needs the licensor to help with the development of the technology. They can then share revenues by implementing value co-creating strategies.

There are two ways royalties are calculated:

1. A royalty fee based on the money value of the product's sales or
2. A royalty fee based on the units of product sold.

A royalty based on sales is expressed as a percentage of the monetary value of product sales.

4.11 Artificial Intelligence-Driven Patent Valuation Approaches

AI is transforming the methodologies used in patent valuation. Through the utilization of AI and big data analysis, it is possible to promptly identify patents of high value and introduce a hierarchical screening approach for the assessment of patent value, facilitating the swift screening of extensive patent data. The significance of AI in the determination of patent value, particularly in sectors such as healthcare where valuable patents can attract investments and foster innovation. Patent valuation methodologies driven by AI are transforming the assessment and valuation of patents across diverse industries. The valuation of patents involves assessing their economic, financial, and market value. Patents are considered intangible assets and determining their value is essential for various purposes, such as financial reporting, investment decisions, licensing, mergers and acquisitions, and legal disputes. AI is significant in enhancing the efficiency of the patent valuation process in all three dimensions:

1. **Economic Valuation**:
   Economic valuation focuses on assessing the intrinsic or fundamental value of a patent based on its potential economic benefits. AI can be applied as follows:
   - **AI-Enhanced Cash Flow Analysis**: AI-powered tools can assist in forecasting the future cash flows associated with a patent by analyzing historical financial data, market trends, and technological advancements.
   - **Market Demand Analysis**: AI can process vast amounts of market data to estimate the demand for products or services that incorporate the patented technology.
   - **Competitive Analysis**: AI can analyze competitive landscapes, including the presence of similar patents or technologies, to assess the uniqueness and competitive advantage of the patent.
   - **Scenario Analysis**: AI-driven simulation models can evaluate different scenarios and assumptions to understand how modifications in market conditions or technology trends affect the economic value of the patent.
2. **Financial Valuation**:
   Financial valuation considers the impact of a patent on a firm's financial statements and metrics. AI can be utilized in the following ways:

- **Amortization and Impairment Analysis**: AI can assist in estimating the appropriate amortization schedule for the patent and identifying impairment risks based on market and technological factors.
- **Financial Statement Impact**: AI can project the financial statement impact of a patent, including its effect on revenue, expenses, and net income.
- **Risk Assessment**: AI can analyze various financial risk factors associated with the patent, such as market risks, competitive risks, and legal risks.
- **Valuation Models**: AI can improve the accuracy of financial valuation models by incorporating a broader range of data sources and variables.

3. **Market Valuation**:
   Market valuation assesses the potential market value of a patent in terms of licensing opportunities, sale value, or strategic positioning. AI can be instrumental in market valuation by:

   - **Market Trend Analysis**: AI can monitor market trends, competitive developments, and patent licensing activities to gauge the market's perception of similar patents.
   - **Licensing Opportunities**: AI can identify potential licensing partners or opportunities by analyzing market dynamics and the patent's relevance to specific industries.
   - **Comparable Transactions**: AI can search and analyze databases of comparable patent transactions to benchmark the patent's potential market value.
   - **Market Sentiment Analysis**: AI-powered sentiment analysis can gauge the market's sentiment and perceptions regarding the patent's potential value.

AI can enhance the patent valuation process by providing access to vast amounts of data, improving the accuracy of financial projections, assessing market dynamics, and identifying licensing and strategic opportunities. AI-powered tools and models can help valuation professionals make more informed and data-driven decisions when assessing the economic, financial, and market value of patents.

Patents may be valued with many complementary approaches (cost-based; income-based or market-based, as shown below), whose practical implications go well beyond plain appraisals, concerning proper accounting, or the ability to promptly serve debt.

Intangible assets, such as patents or trademarks (Salinas & Ambler, 2009), are particularly difficult to evaluate (Moro-Visconti, 2012; Oestreicher, 2011), due to their intrinsic "immaterial" nature and many different—complementary—quantitative, and qualitative evaluation approaches (Andriessen, 2004; Lagrost et al., 2010) are traditionally used within the business community; valuation issues are even more complicated for non-tradable or not deposited non-routine intangibles, such as know-how (Moro-Visconti, 2013), trade secrets, and unpatented R&D (Ballester et al., 2003), goodwill, etc., characterized by limited if any marketability, higher and pervasive information asymmetries, and less defined legal boundaries, especially within increasingly specific businesses.

The main financial/market approaches (examined in Chapter 2) used for patents' fair pricing, with an appropriate rating and ranking, are consistent with IVS 210 prescriptions:

1. *Cost-based approaches*, with an estimate of the "what-if" cost to reproduce or replace intangibles from scratch if there is some relationship between cost and value (Moro-Visconti, 2015). This method ignores both maintenance and the opportunity cost of time (reproducing an intangible may take years, whereas its missed use is due to generating a lack of income) and is not very useful for income-generating assets, such as performing patents or trademarks. Cost-to-cost comparisons are difficult to imagine, especially if they are to be protracted over years; even if intangibles strongly depend on long-cumulated costs, their perspective value may hardly be inferred from past expenses and is volatile and cost differs from the value. To the extent that costs cannot typically be capitalized, their accounting track record may (partially) be detected from past income statement recordings.
2. *Income approaches*, based on the estimate of past and future economic benefits, assessing the ability of the patent to produce licensing income (royalties, which etymologically derive from "sovereign rents") or sale of the intangible; they may include:

- Capitalization of historic profits deriving from the exploitation of the intangible;
- Discounted Cash Flow (DCF), to estimate Net Present Value (NPV), duly incorporating risk factors in the discount rate, such as technology venture capital risk;
- Gross Profit Differential Approaches: They look at the difference in sales price between an "intangible backed" product (branded, patented, with embedded know-how ...) versus a generic one; the profit differential is then forecast and discounted;
- Excess or Premium Profit Approaches: Like the gross profit, it is determined by capitalizing the additional profits generated by the business over and above those generated by similar businesses, which do not have access to the intangible asset. Excess profits can be calculated by reference to a margin differential; and
- Relief-from-Royalty Method: Based on the assumption that the owner of the intangible is "relieved" from paying a royalty to obtain its use, the process considers the hypothetic "what-if" royalty that a potential user would be willing to pay and discounts its projection; a comparable market range of "reasonable" royalties may derive from careful arm's length benchmarking.

3. ***Market-based approaches***, evaluating an intangible asset by comparing it with sales of comparable/similar assets (considering their nature; using functional analysis ...). Information asymmetries often conceal the real (mostly secret) nature of the allegedly comparable transaction. A market-based variety may refer to the evaluation of the incremental equity, with indicators of the business surplus, given for example by the Tobin Q (1969), the ratio between the market value and replacement value of the same asset; a market value exceeding the replacement value may be a numerical consequence of valuable intangibles.

The purpose of the evaluation may change according to the context and the foreseen scenario, and could be targeted at the following different values:

- Fair Market Value—The price, expressed in terms of cash equivalents, at which property would change hands between a hypothetical willing and able buyer and a hypothetical willing and able seller. This fair value is assessed acting at arm's length in an open and unrestricted market when neither is under compulsion to buy or sell and when both have a reasonable knowledge of the relevant facts;
- Investment Value—The value the intangible would be worth, considering the specific buyer's intended use (and so with use-value higher than exchange value);
- Intrinsic Value—The value that an investor considers, based on an evaluation of available facts, to be the "true" or "real" value that will become the market value when other investors reach the same conclusion (Pratt, 2003); and
- Liquidation Value—The firm may pass from a going concern to a break-up context, this being a particularly conservative scenario for intangibles, especially if not autonomously tradable (Fig. 4.5).

While income and market-based approaches may theoretically seem based on accrual or, respectively, cash flow accounting, they tend to share standard parameters, softening the difference between these two accounting procedures.

Factors affecting the value of a patent include:

- Strength/weakness of the patent (how easily are they bypassed or engineered round);
- Characteristics of the patent (what the patent protects); and
- Other technology rights.

Market and income valuations need to consider patent risk factors like:

- R&D risk (the risk that the technology cannot be successfully developed into a functional product);
- FDA risk (the chance that the product will not be found safe and effective by the FDA or similar authorities);
- Standards risk (the likelihood that a standard-setting body will adopt a standard that is incompatible with the product);
- Manufacturability risk (the risk that the product can't be manufactured at an acceptable cost or with enough quality);

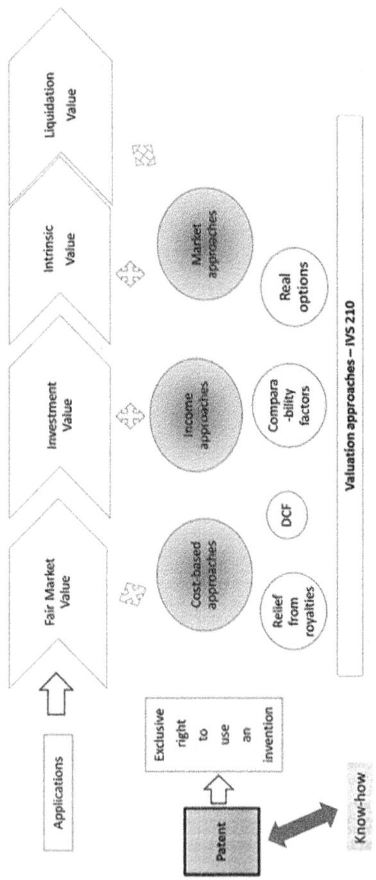

Fig. 4.5 Patent valuation approaches

- Marketing risk: the likelihood that the marketing launch of a product, which relies on patented technology, may be unsuccessful. Even if a company holds valuable patents, market acceptance of the product may not materialize due to factors such as poor marketing strategies, ineffective branding, or insufficient market demand;
- Competitive risk: the possibility that competitors, using different technical approaches or solutions, may develop similar products and enter the market first; and
- Legal risk: the risk that a competitor may obtain a patent that blocks others from entering the market and is unwilling to grant a license.

Valuation methodologies evolve and so need to adapt to changing circumstances.

4.12 Cost-Based Approaches

Cost-based approaches in the valuation of patents consider the historical or replacement cost of acquiring or developing a similar patent as the basis for estimating the patent's value. These approaches are linked to AI in various ways to enhance the accuracy and efficiency of the valuation process in the economic, financial, and market dimensions:

1. **Economic Valuation**:
    - **AI-Enhanced Cost Estimation**: AI can analyze past data and market trends to forecast the cost of developing a similar patent in today's environment. It considers factors such as labor costs, materials, research and development expenses, and technological advancements.
    - **Scenario Analysis**: AI-powered simulations can help assess different scenarios by varying cost inputs and estimating the economic value of the patent under various conditions.
2. **Financial Valuation**:

- **AI for Amortization**: AI can assist in determining the appropriate amortization schedule for the patent based on its estimated replacement cost. It can consider the patent's estimated useful life and expected cash flows.
- **Impairment Assessment**: AI can analyze market and technological factors to assess the risk of impairment by comparing the carrying amount of the patent (based on replacement cost) to its recoverable amount.
- **Financial Modeling**: AI can enhance financial models used for cost-based valuation by incorporating AI-generated cost estimates, which can be dynamic and updated based on real-time data.

3. **Market Valuation**:

- **AI-Powered Market Analysis**: AI can search market data and competitive landscapes to determine if the estimated cost of the patent aligns with market perceptions and licensing trends.
- **Market Trend Analysis**: AI can monitor market trends, including modifications in technology and competitive dynamics, to assess how the patent's replacement cost may vary over time.
- **Comparable Transactions**: AI can identify and analyze comparable patent transactions where similar patents were acquired or licensed, providing benchmarks for assessing the patent's market value relative to its replacement cost.
- **Licensing Opportunities**: AI can identify potential licensing partners or opportunities by considering both the patent's cost and its perceived market value within specific industries.

Incorporating AI into cost-based approaches for patent valuation helps valuation professionals access and analyze large volumes of data, consider dynamic factors affecting replacement costs, and make more data-driven decisions. AI-driven cost estimation and market analysis can improve the accuracy of cost-based valuations while considering economic, financial, and market dimensions. AI models and data sources used for cost estimation must be reliable and up-to-date to provide meaningful insights into patent valuation.

The cost approach to valuing patents involves quantifying the amount of money required to replace or reproduce the patented technology from scratch. However, this method is often not useful for valuing early stage technology because the cost of development is rarely relevant to its value. The cost approach relies on the assumption that the value of a patent is reflected in the cost of developing or reproducing it.

However, in the case of early stage technology, the cost of development may not accurately reflect its potential future benefits or market value. Factors such as market demand, competitive landscape, and intellectual property strength play a more significant role in determining the value of a patent.

While the cost approach can provide a starting point for valuing patents, particularly in cases where there are significant development costs involved, it should be complemented with other valuation methods that consider market factors, competitive dynamics, and potential future cash flows to arrive at a more accurate assessment of a patent's value.

4.13 Market Valuations and Net Present Value

Market valuations and Net Present Value (NPV) are fundamental elements in the assessment of patents, with the utilization of AI offering a substantial enhancement to the precision and efficiency of these procedures. Various AI-driven techniques, including sophisticated deep learning models and ensemble learning methodologies, have been suggested to augment patent valuation. These AI-centric strategies leverage extensive datasets to swiftly and cost-effectively execute quantitative assessments, effectively tackling the issues associated with the subjective nature of conventional valuation techniques. A more thorough and accurate appraisal of patent values can be attained through the integration of semantic data, market potential, and patent characteristics via artificial intelligence. AI assumes a critical role in transforming the landscape of patent valuation by furnishing more precise insights and empowering stakeholders to make well-informed choices concerning technology transactions. Market valuations and Net Present Value (NPV) are so critical aspects of patent valuation, and AI can be important in enhancing the accuracy and efficiency of these processes.

1. **Market Valuations**:

Market valuations assess the potential market value of a patent by considering its relevance, demand, licensing opportunities, and competitive landscape. AI can be linked to market valuations in the following ways:

- **Market Trend Analysis**: AI can monitor and analyze market trends, competitive developments, and patent licensing activities. This analysis helps gauge the market's perception of similar patents and their potential value.
- **Competitive Benchmarking**: AI can assist in benchmarking a patent against other patents or technologies in the same industry, helping identify the patent's competitive advantage and market positioning.
- **Licensing Opportunities**: AI-driven tools can identify potential licensing partners or opportunities by analyzing market dynamics, technological trends, and industry-specific data.
- **Market Sentiment Analysis**: AI-powered sentiment analysis can provide insights into the market's sentiment and perceptions regarding the patent's potential value, based on news articles, social media, and other sources.

2. **Net Present Value (NPV)**:
NPV is a financial metric that assesses the present value of future cash flows generated by a patent, considering the time value of money. It helps determine the economic value of the patent by discounting future cash flows to their present value. AI can be linked to NPV calculations in the following ways:

- **Cash Flow Analysis**: AI can assist in forecasting future cash flows generated by the patent. It can assess market trends, past financial data, and other key parameters to sort out more accurate cash flow projections.
- **Discount Rate Estimation**: AI can help determine the appropriate discount rate for NPV calculations by analyzing market risk factors, interest rates, and other financial variables. It can provide dynamic and data-driven discount rate recommendations.

- **Sensitivity Analysis**: AI may use sensitivity analysis to assess how modifications in key parameters (e.g., cash flow projections, discount rates) impact the patent's NPV. This helps understand the level of risk associated with the valuation.
- **Scenario Analysis**: AI-driven simulations can evaluate different scenarios and assumptions, allowing for a more comprehensive assessment of the patent's NPV under varying conditions.
- **Data Integration**: AI can integrate financial data, market data, and cash flow projections to create a comprehensive model for NPV calculations.

AI's role in both market valuations and NPV calculations is to provide better data-driven insights, enhance the accuracy of projections, and consider dynamic factors that may impact the patent's value over time. By leveraging AI in these processes, valuation professionals can make more informed decisions and reduce uncertainty when assessing the economic and market value of patents.

The market approach to valuing patents involves determining their present value based on what others in the marketplace have judged them to be worth. However, applying the market approach to startup technology can be challenging because such technology often lacks an active, public market, and comparable properties for exchange.

In cases where patents lack established market values, such as negotiated royalty rates, alternative methods may be used. One approach involves comparing the number of citations received by the patent to those received by other patents with established market values. However, this method may be less effective for recently issued patents (see Falk & Train, 2016) that have not had time to accumulate citations.

When conducting market valuations, two preferred approaches are commonly used: DCF analysis and the application of an EBITDA multiplier. DCF analysis is theoretically considered the optimal method as it follows the principle that "cash is king". However, EBITDA multipliers are also frequently employed, with the multiplier applied over a specific period (typically 2/3 up to 20 years). This approach results in an Enterprise Value (EV), which is attributed to debtholders and equity holders.

EV/EBITDA multipliers may be connected to price/book value or Tobin q parameters, which reflect the differential value of patents under a hypothetical cost reproduction hypothesis, so representing a precious bridge between the otherwise disconnected market and cost appraisal approaches.

As a rough calculation, the EV multiple serves as a proxy for how long it would take for the acquisition of the entire firm (including its debt) to earn enough to pay off its costs (assuming no change in EBITDA and a constantly added value contribution from the IC portfolio). Temporal mismatches between the numerator and the denominator may bias the ratio and should accordingly be minimized.

The market value of equity can be inferred from an EBITDA multiplier, which estimates EV. By deducting the market value of debt (Net Financial Position) from EV, the residual market value of equity can be derived. When the residual market value of equity exceeds its book value (price > book value; P/BV > 1), it suggests an implicit safety net for principal debt repayment.

Since EV serves as a proxy for the market capitalization (price), its relationship with the market-to-book ratio and Tobin's q, influenced by the presence of intangibles, becomes more apparent. Intangibles, such as patents, contribute to the overall value of a company and influence its market-to-book ratio and Tobin's q (Cheng et al., 2005; Valladares & Cuello de Oro, 2007).

The stream of Operating Cash Flows (OCF), which is marginally attributable to the strategic contribution of patents to the overall value, incorporates growth factors. These factors can include the expected growth (Tan et al., 2007) in revenue, market share, or profitability attributed to the patented technology.

Discounting OCF by the weighted average cost of capital (WACC) in the valuation process accounts for market risk, as recognized by debt and equity underwriters. WACC represents the blended cost of debt and equity financing, reflecting the risk associated with investing.

Being O_{CF} derived from EBITDA:

$$\Delta \text{EBITDA}_{\text{patent}} \pm \Delta \text{NWC} \pm \Delta \text{CAPEX} = O_{CF} \quad (4.1)$$

the link between key market approaches (possibly complementary, rather than alternative) is evident.

The estimate of future benefits with Net Present Value (NPV) corresponds to:

$$\text{NPV}_{\text{equity}} = \sum\nolimits_{t=1}^{n} \frac{\text{NCF}_t}{(1+\text{K}_e)^t} - \text{CF}_0 \quad (4.2)$$

where:
N_{CF} = Net Cash Flow for the shareholders;
t = time;
K_e = Cost of equity; and
CF_0 = initial investment.
Calculating the Net Present Value (NPV) of a patent or any investment should consider various factors beyond simple cash flows. Geographic limitations, restrictions, exclusivity, and other factors can significantly impact the potential cash flows generated by a patent.

One of the critical challenges in NPV calculation is accurately estimating cash flows, especially in the presence of unforeseeable events or flexibility options. Patents present this challenge because their value may depend on uncertain factors such as market demand, competitive landscape, and legal developments.

A patent can be likened to a real option because it provides its owner with the opportunity to choose between various courses of action, including commercializing the invention, licensing it to others, or not commercializing it at all. This optionality adds complexity to NPV calculations, as it requires assessing the probability and potential impact of different scenarios.

To address these challenges, sophisticated valuation techniques, such as real options analysis, can be employed to incorporate the flexibility inherent in patents and other investments. Real options analysis allows for the quantification of the value associated with the flexibility to adapt or change strategies in response to changing market conditions or new information.

By considering the uncertainty and flexibility inherent in patents, NPV calculations can provide a more nuanced assessment of their value, helping investors make informed decisions about patent acquisition, licensing, or commercialization strategies (see Cotropia, 2009).

According to Silberztein (2011) "There is currently no international consensus on the circumstances where financial valuation approaches and the Discounted Cash Flow ("DCF") may be appropriate for applying the arm's length principle", and again: "one of the main difficulties regarding the application of these approaches is that they are based on inherently uncertain projections".

4.14 Comparability Factors

Comparability factors are of paramount importance in the valuation of AI patents, exerting influence on the precision and dependability of the evaluation process. Various methodologies, such as those based on keywords, scientific references, and AI categorization systems such as WIPO and USPTO, exhibit differing capacities in categorizing patents as AI, thereby impacting their inherent growth, scope, and innovative synergies. Furthermore, evaluation techniques for patents that leverage artificial intelligence have the potential to improve accuracy through the inclusion of a comprehensive dimensional index framework, transaction systems reflecting market prices, and comparative patent assessments. A comprehensive economic assessment of AI patents necessitates a thorough understanding of the operational strategies of companies utilizing AI as well as the legal ramifications. Integration of these comparability factors into the valuation process enables stakeholders to make well-informed decisions regarding the value and potential of AI patents. Comparability factors are crucial in the valuation of patents as they help determine the appropriate benchmark and context for assessing a patent's value. These factors consider various aspects such as industry, technology, market, competitive landscape, and legal considerations when comparing a patent to similar assets or transactions. AI can be important in enhancing the assessment of comparability factors in patents' valuation:

1. **Technology and Technical Specifications**:
    - **AI-Powered Patent Search**: AI can assist in searching and identifying patents that are similar in terms of technology and technical specifications. Natural Language Processing (NLP) algorithms can scrutinize patent descriptions, claims, and technical documentation to select relevant patents based on similarities in technology.
2. **Industry and Market Dynamics**:
    - **Market Trend Analysis**: AI can monitor and analyze market trends and competitive developments within a specific industry. It can help identify how industry-specific factors may affect the value of a patent and its comparability to other patents.

- **Competitive Benchmarking**: AI can assist in benchmarking the patent against other patents or technologies within the same industry, providing insights into competitive advantages and positioning.

3. **Licensing and Transaction Data**:
   - **AI-Powered Database Searches**: AI can search databases of patent licensing agreements, sales transactions, and other relevant data sources to identify comparable patent transactions. This helps establish benchmarks for the patent's value in licensing or sales.

4. **Market Sentiment and Public Perception**:
   - **Sentiment Analysis**: AI-driven sentiment analysis can gauge public sentiment and market perception regarding patents, technologies, and innovations. This information can provide context for assessing the patent's value.
   - **News and Social Media Monitoring**: AI can continuously monitor news articles, social media discussions, and online forums to track discussions and opinions related to patents and their relevance in the market.

5. **Legal Considerations**:
   - **AI for Legal Document Analysis**: AI can analyze legal documents, including licensing agreements, patent portfolios, and litigation history, to assess the legal aspects of a patent's comparability. It can identify contractual obligations and restrictions that may affect the patent's value.

6. **Data Integration and Analysis**:
   - **AI for Data Integration**: AI can integrate sundry data, such as financial records, market data, technical documentation, or legal documents, to create a comprehensive model for assessing comparability factors.

7. **Machine Learning for Pattern Recognition**:

- Machine learning algorithms can identify patterns and similarities among patents, technologies, and transactions, helping valuation professionals make more informed decisions about comparability.

8. **Market and Industry Reports**:

   - AI can process market and industry reports, extracting relevant data and insights to inform the assessment of comparability factors.

By incorporating AI into the assessment of comparability factors, patent valuation professionals can access a wider range of data sources, analyze large volumes of information, and make more accurate comparisons. This, in turn, enhances the precision and reliability of patent valuations.

Comparing patents can be challenging due to their intrinsic uniqueness, as patents are granted for inventions that are novel and non-obvious. However, there are several factors that can be considered to assess the comparability of patents:

a. Expected Benefits: Assessing the potential benefits of the intangible property, often determined through net present value calculations, can provide insight into its value.
b. Geographic Limitations: Understanding any restrictions on the geographic area in which patent rights may be exercised is essential for evaluating its market potential.
c. Export Restrictions: Consideration of any export restrictions on goods produced using the patented technology is crucial for assessing its market reach and commercial viability.
d. Exclusive or Non-exclusive Rights: Determining whether the patent grants exclusive or non-exclusive rights can impact its value and marketability.
e. Capital Investment and Development Work: Evaluating the capital investment, startup expenses, and development work required for market entry provides context for the potential value of the patent.
f. Possibility of Sub-licensing: Whether the licensee has the right to sublicense the patented technology can affect its market reach and potential revenue streams.
g. Licensee's Distribution Network: Understanding the licensee's distribution network and market presence can help assess the market

potential and commercialization opportunities for the patented technology.

h. Right to Participate in Further Developments: Considering whether the licensee has the right to participate in further developments of the property by the licensor can impact the attractiveness of the patent to potential licensees.

The market price, depending on comparability factors, may be difficult to find, especially if the intangible is unique. This is the case, especially for patents that are affected by a paradox: the more they are exclusive, the higher their value—but also the lower their comparability, etc.

Market information may derive from composite sources as:

- internal (confidential) database;
- published surveys and research that may establish norm standards within an industry;
- public announcements of deals (of listed companies, etc.) and public databases (Liu et al., 2022);
- details from litigation and required disclosure of license terms;
- state of the art; and
- word-of-mouth.

Deal databases may derive from the following sources (for fee):

- RoyaltySource (www.royaltysource.com);
- TechAgreements (www.techagreement.com);
- Markables (markables.com);
- RoyaltyStat (www.royaltystat.com);
- Business Valuation Resources (www.bvresources.com);
- Recap by Deloitte (www.recap.com);
- PharmaDeals (www.pharmadeals.net);
- Orbis Intellectual Property (Bureau van Dijk); and
- Windhover (www.elsevierbi.com/deals).

4.15 Income Approach

The income approach (also examined in Chapter 2) is one of the primary methods used in the valuation of patents. It estimates the value of a patent by assessing the future income or economic benefits it is expected to generate. AI can be effectively linked to the income approach in patent valuation to enhance accuracy, efficiency, and depth of analysis. Here's how AI can be integrated into the income approach:

1. **Cash Flow Projections**:
    - **AI-Enhanced Cash Flow Forecasting**: AI can analyze market trends, past data, and other relevant information to sort out improved cash flow projections associated with the patent. AI can identify patterns and relationships in the data that humans might overlook, leading to more reliable forecasts.
    - **Natural Language Processing (NLP)**: NLP techniques can process large volumes of textual data, including patents, technical documents, and industry reports, to extract insights that inform cash flow projections. AI can analyze the patent's claims, descriptions, and technical specifications to assess its potential revenue streams.
2. **Discount Rate Estimation**:
    - **AI-Driven Risk Assessment**: AI can help determine the appropriate discount rate to apply in the income approach by assessing market risk factors, interest rates, and other financial variables. AI can provide dynamic and data-driven discount rate recommendations based on real-time data and market conditions.
3. **Scenario Analysis**:
    - **Simulation Modeling**: AI-driven simulation models can evaluate different scenarios by varying key assumptions, such as revenue growth rates, royalty rates, and market dynamics. This

allows for a more comprehensive assessment of the patent's value under varying conditions.

4. **Sensitivity Analysis**:
    - **AI-Powered Sensitivity Analysis**: AI can perform sensitivity analysis to understand how modifications in critical variables (e.g., revenue projections and discount rates) impact the valuation. AI can identify which variables influence the patent's value.
5. **Data Integration**:
    - **AI for Data Integration**: AI can integrate financial data, market data, technical documentation, and other relevant information to create a comprehensive model for the income approach. AI can ensure that the valuation model is up-to-date and considers more information.
6. **Market and Competitive Analysis**:
    - **AI-Enhanced Competitive Analysis**: AI can analyze competitive landscapes, market trends, and competitive developments to assess.

The income approach to patent valuation focuses on the potential income-producing capability of the patents over their useful life. This method measures the present worth of the net economic benefits expected to be received from the patent.

Key considerations in the income approach include evaluating the amount and pattern of the income stream, considering the duration of the income stream, and assessing the associated risks that may affect the realization of the predicted income.

In the traditional NPV approach, future cash flows are discounted back to their present value using a high discount rate. However, in the Risk-Adjusted NPV approach, risk is explicitly accounted for, and a "cost of money" discount rate is used instead of a risk-based discount rate. This approach considers trade-offs between near-term and long-term financial terms appropriately.

Limitations of the NPV-based valuation include its dependence on the quality of available data, the potential unavailability of critical data for early stage technologies, and susceptibility to the "garbage in, garbage out" issue.

Monte Carlo probabilistic approaches offer an alternative method for accounting for risk in patent valuation. This approach allows analysts to input ranges around various parameters, such as costs, revenues, and probabilities of success, and calculate NPV for each combination of estimated parameters. The results are presented as a distribution of the probability of NPV, providing a more sophisticated analysis of risk.

However, Monte Carlo approaches may also have limitations, particularly when data is unavailable for early stage academic technologies. Despite these limitations, they offer a more nuanced understanding of risk compared to traditional NPV or risk-adjusted NPV approaches.

Degnan and Horton (1997), in a dated by still inspiring publication, suggest these valuation methodologies and license valuations.

Table 4.7 presents the percentages of usage for different valuation methodologies in in-licensing and out-licensing scenarios. These percentages indicate the prevalence of each valuation methodology in both in-licensing and out-licensing situations. For example, the Discounted Cash Flow method is used in 56% of in-licensing cases and 49% of out-licensing cases. Similarly, the Profit-Sharing Analysis is utilized in 52% of in-licensing and 54% of out-licensing scenarios.

Profit Profit-sharing analysis is slightly more prevalent in out-licensing situations compared to in-licensing. Similarly, the 25% Rule as a Starting Point is used more frequently in out-licensing scenarios. Other methods, such as Return on Assets and Excess Return Analysis, show variations in usage between in-licensing and out-licensing but generally have lower percentages compared to Discounted Cash Flow and Profit-Sharing Analysis.

Table 4.7 License valuation

Valuation methodology	*In-Licensing (%)*	*Out-Licensing (%)*
Discounted Cash Flow	56	49
Profit-Sharing Analysis	52	54
Return on Assets	38	27
25% Rule as a Starting Point	24	30
Capital Asset Pricing Model	11	10
Excess Return Analysis	8	7

Table 4.8 Relationship of royalty rate to magnitude of improvement

Median royalty rates	*Pharma*	*Non-Pharma*
Revolutionary	10–15%	5–10%
Major Improvement	5–10%	3–7%
Minor Improvement	2–5%	1–3%

Royalty rates in the meaningful Pharma industry may be estimated as follows (Table 4.8).

This table provides orientation estimates for royalty rates based on the level of improvement introduced by the patented technology or innovation. The rates, inspired by ongoing empirical evidence in the pharma market, vary depending on whether the industry is pharmaceutical or non-pharmaceutical, and whether the improvement is considered revolutionary, major, or minor. For instance, in the pharmaceutical industry, revolutionary improvements typically warrant higher royalty rates ranging from 10 to 15%, while minor improvements may result in lower rates ranging from 2 to 5%. Conversely, in non-pharmaceutical industries, the royalty rates are generally lower across all categories compared to pharmaceuticals.

4.16 Real Options

Real Options Analysis (ROA) is a valuable technique for the valuation of patents, particularly when dealing with uncertainty and flexibility in decision-making. It allows for the assessment of the strategic value of a patent by considering the various options available to the patent holder over time. When integrating AI with Real Options Analysis for patent assessment, AI can perform a pivotal function in improving the precision and effectiveness of evaluating patent values. AI technologies have the capability to examine extensive datasets concerning patents, industry trends, and technological progressions, thus presenting valuable insights for decision-making procedures in patent assessment. Through the utilization of AI algorithms, patent proprietors can enhance their ability to assess the potential future repercussions and strategic alternatives linked to their patents, consequently refining their decision-making processes and optimizing the value of their intellectual property. AI can be linked to Real Options Analysis in patents valuation in the following ways:

1. **Market and Technology Trend Analysis**:
    - **AI-Enhanced Market Monitoring**: AI can continuously monitor market trends, technological advancements, and competitive developments. It can identify modifications in the market that may impact the future value of a patent, helping valuation professionals assess the options available based on evolving market conditions.
2. **Scenario Analysis**:
    - **AI-Driven Scenario Simulations**: AI-powered simulations can model different scenarios, including various market and technology trajectories. These simulations allow for the evaluation of multiple potential outcomes, helping assess the patent's value under different future states.
3. **Sensitivity Analysis**:
    - **AI-Powered Sensitivity Analysis**: AI-driven sensitivity analysis helps to understand how modifications in core variables, such as market demand, technological advancements, and competitive dynamics, affect the value of the patent and the options embedded within it.
4. **Data Integration**:
    - **AI for Data Integration**: AI considers many data sources that are eventually included into the Real Options Analysis model. This ensures that the model incorporates up-to-date and comprehensive information.
5. **Market and Competitive Analysis**:
    - **AI-Enhanced Competitive Intelligence**: AI can analyze competitive landscapes and identify potential competitors' strategies and actions. This information is crucial for assessing the competitive options available to the patent holder.

6. **Decision Support**:
    - **AI-Enhanced Decision Support**: AI can provide decision-makers with insights and recommendations based on Real Options Analysis results. AI can help patent holders make informed decisions regarding the exercise or abandonment of options related to the patent.
7. **Natural Language Processing (NLP)**:
    - **NLP for Document Analysis**: AI-driven NLP techniques can analyze legal contracts, licensing agreements, and technical documentation to identify and assess options and contingencies embedded in these documents.
8. **Machine Learning for Option Valuation**:
    - **Machine Learning Models**: AI can develop machine learning models to estimate the value of the options embedded within a patent. These models can consider a wide range of factors, including market volatility, technology advancement probabilities, and competitive actions.

AI's role in Real Options Analysis for patent valuation is to provide a more dynamic and data-driven approach that considers the complexities and uncertainties inherent in patent assets. By incorporating AI, valuation professionals can better assess the strategic value of patents and make more informed decisions about patent portfolio management, licensing, and strategic actions based on the flexibility and options available over time.

> *A fairly robust economics literature exists which analogizes patents to real options. Real options create the right, but not the obligation, to purchase the underlying asset at a defined exercise price. A patent is like a real option, economists say because it allows its owner to choose between exclusively commercializing the patented invention sometime during the patent term or foregoing commercialization altogether. Economists have taken this analogy and used real options analysis to place specific values on patents.* (Cotropia, 2009)

Real options theory can enhance the flexibility and accuracy of forecasts when evaluating investments or assets like patents (see Iazzolino &

Migliano, 2015) using NPV techniques. Real options refer to the rights, but not the obligations, to undertake certain business initiatives, providing managers with the flexibility to make strategic decisions in response to changing market conditions or uncertainties.

Real options theory recognizes that managers face tensions between commitment and flexibility, as well as between competition and cooperation. By incorporating real options into NPV analysis, managers can better assess the value of investment opportunities and make more informed decisions.

For example, when evaluating a patent, managers may have the option to defer commercialization until market conditions are more favorable, expand investment in the patent if demand exceeds expectations, or abandon the project if it proves unprofitable. These real options can significantly impact the overall value of the patent and should be considered in NPV analysis.

By incorporating real options theory into NPV techniques (see Trigeorgis & Reuer, 2017), analysts can capture the value of flexibility and strategic decision-making, leading to more accurate forecasts and better-informed investment decisions.

4.17 Quick and Dirty Valuation Techniques

Quick and dirty valuation techniques, often referred to as back-of-the-envelope calculations, provide a rough estimate of a patent's value without a comprehensive analysis. While these techniques are less precise than more rigorous methods, they can offer a preliminary sense of a patent's potential worth. AI can be linked to these quick and dirty valuation techniques in several ways to enhance their accuracy and efficiency:

1. **Market Data Analysis**:
    - **AI-Enhanced Market Research**: AI can quickly process and analyze vast amounts of market data to assess the demand for technologies or products related to the patent. It can provide insights into market size, growth rates, and competitive dynamics.
2. **Patent Database Search**:

- **AI-Powered Patent Search**: AI can help identify similar patents or prior art by analyzing patent databases and technical documentation. This information can be used to assess the uniqueness and relevance of the patent.

3. **Comparable Transactions**:
    - **AI-Driven Transaction Analysis**: AI can search and analyze databases of comparable patent transactions, such as licensing agreements or sales, to identify benchmarks for estimating the patent's value.

4. **Market Sentiment Analysis**:
    - **AI-Powered Sentiment Analysis**: AI can monitor news articles, social media discussions, and online forums to gauge market sentiment and public perception regarding the patent and its potential value.

5. **Financial Projections**:
    - **AI-Assisted Financial Forecasting**: AI can assist in generating quick financial projections based on historical financial data and market trends. This can help estimate potential revenue streams associated with the patent.

6. **Competitive Landscape**:
    - **AI-Enhanced Competitive Analysis**: AI can analyze the competitive landscape, identify potential competitors, and assess the patent's competitive advantage or uniqueness.

7. **Scenario Analysis**:
    - **AI-Powered Scenario Simulations**: AI-driven simulations can model different scenarios, allowing for a preliminary assessment of the patent's value under varying market conditions.

8. **Natural Language Processing (NLP)**:

- **NLP for Document Analysis**: AI-driven NLP techniques can analyze legal contracts, patent claims, and technical documentation to identify key factors that may influence the patent's value, such as licensing agreements or unique technical features.

9. **Data Integration**:

- **AI for Data Integration**: AI can integrate various data sources, such as market data, patent databases, financial records, and competitive intelligence, to assess the patent's potential value.

10. **Decision Support**:

- **AI-Enhanced Decision Support**: AI can offer preliminary insights and recommendations based on the quick and dirty valuation results, helping stakeholders make initial decisions regarding the patent.

While quick and dirty valuation techniques provide rough estimates, AI can help refine these estimates by providing access to a broader range of data sources, automating data analysis, and identifying relevant factors that may influence the patent's value. These AI-enhanced techniques can be particularly useful for preliminary assessments or initial screening of patent portfolios. However, they should be followed by more in-depth valuation methods for a comprehensive understanding of a patent's value.

Whereas the 25% rule of thumb has been widely used in licensing negotiations, it has come under scrutiny for its limitations and lack of empirical support. The rule suggests that the licensor should receive 25% of the pre-tax profit from a licensed product, while the licensee retains 75%. However, this rule has been criticized for several reasons:

a. Lack of Empirical Support: The 25% rule lacks empirical evidence to support its validity as a baseline royalty rate in licensing negotiations. Courts and experts have questioned its reliability and suitability for determining fair royalty rates.

b. Flawed Assumptions: The rule assumes a fixed percentage allocation of profits between the licensor and licensee without considering the specific circumstances of each licensing agreement. In reality, royalty rates should be determined based on factors such as the uniqueness of the technology, market demand, competitive landscape, and potential risks and rewards for both parties.
c. Allocation Over Multiple Technologies: In complex licensing agreements involving multiple technologies, the 25% rule may not accurately reflect the value contributed by each technology. Allocating 25% across all technologies may not be equitable or practical.
d. Resistance from Licensees: Licensees may resist agreeing to a 25% royalty rate if they perceive it as too high, especially if they need to make significant investments in developing and marketing the product. Negotiations should consider the licensee's costs, risks, and expected returns.

While the 25% rule of thumb may provide a starting point for negotiations, it should not be relied upon as the sole basis for determining royalty rates. Licensing agreements should be tailored to the specific circumstances and objectives of both parties, with consideration given to the value contributed by the licensed technology and the risks and rewards involved.

4.18 Forecasting Patent Outcomes with Big Data and Stochastic Estimates

Forecasting patent outcomes through the utilization of AI and big data entails the exploitation of cutting edge technologies for the analysis of patents, leading to a substantial enhancement of predictive models in the domain of patent valuation. The comprehension of the extent and quantity of patent activities associated with the utilization of big data for prediction purposes holds paramount importance, as it enables stakeholders to delve into timelines, geographical distributions, active assignees, technical classifications, and emerging themes encapsulated within the abstracts of patents. Predicting future outcomes, especially in the context of patents, can be challenging due to the inherent uncertainties involved. These uncertainties can lead to imprecise forecasts, resulting in significant differences between expected and realized outcomes, thus increasing risk. However, leveraging both big data and stochastic estimates can help mitigate these challenges and improve valuation estimates.

Big data analytics involves the analysis of large and complex datasets to uncover patterns, trends, and insights that can inform decision-making. Characteristics such as volume, velocity, variety, and veracity make big data particularly valuable for economic and financial planning. By analyzing diverse datasets from interoperable databases, big data analytics can provide a comprehensive understanding of various factors influencing the valuation of patents. This can include market trends, competitive dynamics, technological advancements, and consumer behavior, among others. Big data analytics can also help detect growth drivers and identify potential opportunities for innovation and investment.

Stochastic modeling, on the other hand, incorporates random variables into financial models to estimate the probability of different outcomes within a forecast. By considering uncertainty and variability in key parameters, stochastic modeling provides a more nuanced understanding of potential future scenarios. This allows decision-makers to assess the likelihood of various outcomes and develop strategies to mitigate risks or capitalize on opportunities.

When used in conjunction, big data analytics and stochastic modeling can complement each other, providing a more robust and comprehensive approach to predicting future outcomes and valuing patents. By integrating insights from both sources, decision-makers can make more informed and strategic decisions, reducing uncertainty and improving the accuracy of valuation estimates (see Moro-Visconti et al., 2018).

4.19 The Impact of Digitalization on Patents

Digitalization has had a profound impact on patents, transforming various aspects of patent creation, management, analysis, and enforcement. This impact is closely linked to AI, which plays a significant role in harnessing the power of digital technologies for patent-related activities. Digitalization contributes to the effectiveness of technology transactions, research, and development collaboration through the provision of a structured framework that incorporates technologies such as NLP and ML. This symbiosis between digitalization and patents is essential for the modernization of businesses, the diversification of economies, and the emergence of new prospects. Furthermore, the influence of digitalization on innovation is noteworthy, especially evident in the Euro Area nations where digitalization indicators positively impact innovation. The incorporation of novel digital technologies in the manufacturing sector not only boosts productivity and encourages innovation but also grants a competitive advantage to businesses. Hence, harnessing digitalization to support patents can result in improved technology transfer, research partnerships, and overall economic advancement. Here's how digitalization affects patents and its connection to AI:

1. **Digital Patent Filing and Management**:
    - **Electronic Filing**: Digitalization has made it possible to file patent applications electronically, streamlining the application process and reducing paperwork.
    - **Online Patent Databases**: Digital platforms provide access to extensive patent databases, allowing researchers, inventors, and patent professionals to search for prior art, review patent documents, and monitor patent activities more efficiently.
    - **AI-Powered Patent Search**: AI-driven algorithms enhance the effectiveness of patent searches by rapidly analyzing and categorizing vast amounts of patent data. These systems can identify relevant prior art and help patent examiners and applicants in the application process.
2. **Intellectual Property Portfolio Management**:
    - **Digital Portfolio Tools**: Digital platforms and software enable organizations to manage their intellectual property portfolios more effectively. These tools assist in tracking patent applications, maintenance, and licensing activities.
    - **AI-Enhanced Portfolio Analytics**: AI can analyze patent portfolios, identifying strategic opportunities, potential risks, and underutilized assets. AI-driven analytics help organizations make informed decisions regarding portfolio optimization and licensing strategies.
3. **Patent Analytics and Insights**:
    - **Big Data Analysis**: Digitalization generates large volumes of data related to patents, technology trends, and market dynamics. AI is used to analyze this big data to derive actionable insights for businesses and inventors.

- **Predictive Analytics**: AI-powered predictive analytics can forecast patent trends, technology developments, and market shifts, assisting organizations in making proactive decisions regarding research and development, patent filing, and strategic planning.

4. **Technology Watch and Surveillance**:
   - **Digital Surveillance Tools**: Digital platforms allow organizations to monitor patent activities, including patent grants, litigation, and infringement, in real time. This enables timely responses to emerging threats or opportunities.
   - **AI-Driven Alerts**: AI can be used to set up automated alerts that notify organizations of relevant patent events, such as new filings by competitors, patent expirations, or modifications in technology landscape.

5. **Intellectual Property Enforcement**:
   - **Digital Evidence Gathering**: Digitalization simplifies the process of gathering and presenting digital evidence in patent litigation. AI can assist in the analysis of vast volumes of electronic documents and data during legal proceedings.
   - **AI-Powered Prior Art Search**: AI algorithms are used to perform exhaustive searches of electronic documents and databases to uncover prior art relevant to patent validity challenges.

6. **Licensing and Technology** Transfer (see Moro-Visconti, 2018):
   - **Online Licensing Platforms**: Digital platforms facilitate patent licensing and technology transfer activities, enabling patent owners to reach a broader audience of potential licensees.
   - **AI-Enhanced Licensing Tools**: AI-driven tools can analyze patent portfolios and identify potential licensing partners.

Patents are an evolution of know-how. AI is now recognized as one of the main enablers of digital transformation in multiple industries. AI can help companies become more innovative, flexible, and adaptive than ever before, with an impact on robotics, and process automation.

With its ability to improve simulation, forecasting, and smooth proof-of-concept trials and errors, AI can boost the traditional patenting process and its industrial applications.

Digitalization smooths and catalyzes the patenting process:

1. it fosters know-how through its input factors, easier to collect, store, and interpret;
2. information, transformed into big data, is easier to collect and analyze;
3. proof-of-concept gets easier with digital prototypes;
4. digitalization eases knowledge transfer and sharing; and
5. as a service instruments and platforms (Software as a Service; Platform as a Service, etc.) reduce fixed costs and improve outsourcing efficacy.

4.20 Artificial Intelligence-Assisted Reverse Engineering

The utilization of AI tools has the potential to decrease costs and improve the effectiveness of tasks related to reverse engineering. Within the realm of network communication, AI models can accurately forecast the quality of experience based on quality-of-service parameters, thereby assisting in the creation of service level agreements. In the field of process engineering, there is a wide range of AI applications that focus on mechanistic models and hybrid modeling techniques, which include strategies for reverse engineering. Additionally, AI, especially through the use of neural networks, is employed in mechanical engineering to generate geometric CAD models from pre-existing objects, underscoring the significance of AI in streamlining the process of reverse engineering. In conclusion, AI-supported reverse engineering is transforming conventional methodologies in diverse sectors by providing effective resolutions to intricate challenges. AI-assisted reverse engineering (AIARE) represents a meaningful development in computer science, intertwining artificial intelligence, specifically machine learning, with traditional reverse engineering practices.

Traditional Reverse Engineering:

1. **Process**: Involves deconstructing a system, product, or process to understand its structure, design, and functionality.
2. **Applications**: Used for reproduction, modification, enhancing compatibility, or forensic examination.
3. **Challenges**: This method can be labor-intensive and time-consuming, particularly with complex systems.

AIARE Evolution:

1. **Integration of AI**: Incorporates machine learning algorithms to automate or enhance the reverse engineering process.
2. **Capabilities**:
   - Detects patterns, relationships, and structures within a system.
   - Identifies potential vulnerabilities.
   - Often exceeds human expertise in terms of speed and accuracy.
3. **Applications**:
   - Widely used in cybersecurity to identify and understand security flaws.
   - Crucial in software development for understanding and improving existing software.
   - Important in hardware design and analysis for better understanding of device functionality and structure.
4. **Benefits**:
   - Reduces the time and effort required compared to traditional methods.
   - Can provide more accurate and comprehensive analysis due to the advanced capabilities of AI and ML algorithms.

AIARE is a testament to the dynamic nature of technology, where the fusion of AI with established practices like reverse engineering is creating more efficient, accurate, and sophisticated tools and methodologies. Its impact is particularly notable in fields that require a deep understanding of complex systems, such as cybersecurity and hardware design.

4.21 The Impact of Knowledge Management on Artificial Intelligence

AI brings about a transformation in Knowledge Management (KM) by enhancing efficiency utilizing algorithms, addressing social and ethical concerns, and introducing novel technologies and theories. The collaboration between AI and KM plays a critical role in harnessing the potential of AI to propel knowledge innovation, enhance knowledge dissemination, and optimize organizational KM practices. The resurgence of AI and data analytics provides a chance to redesign KM systems, elevating them as potent elements of organizational infrastructure. Ultimately, the fusion of AI and KM results in the automation and enhancement of rationality in managerial decision-making, thereby revolutionizing established global management methodologies. The impact of knowledge management on the economic, financial, and market value of AI is significant and depends on the know-how that is embedded in the organization team and boosted by AI:

1. **Economic Impact**:
    - **Innovation and Efficiency**: Effective knowledge management in AI can lead to increased innovation and operational efficiency. AI systems that are well-fed with organized, relevant, and high-quality data can develop more accurate and sophisticated models. This improves their ability to automate complex tasks, leading to economic gains through increased productivity and cost savings.
    - **Market Expansion**: By leveraging well-managed knowledge, AI technologies can be adapted to new markets and applications more quickly. This expansion not only stimulates economic growth but also encourages the development of AI solutions tailored to specific industry needs.
2. **Financial Impact**:
    - **Return on Investment (ROI)**: Investments in AI become more profitable when backed by effective knowledge management. Businesses can see a higher ROI as AI systems become more efficient and capable, directly influencing their bottom line.

- **Cost Reduction**: Proper knowledge management in AI can significantly reduce costs associated with data processing, storage, and analysis. By optimizing these processes, companies can minimize wasted resources and allocate funds more effectively.

3. **Market Value**:

- **Competitive Advantage**: Companies that excel in knowledge management for their AI initiatives often gain a competitive edge. This advantage is reflected in their market valuation, as they are seen as more innovative and better equipped to handle future challenges.
- **Investor Confidence**: Effective knowledge management in AI signals to investors that a firm is capable of handling and maximizing the potential of cutting-edge technology. This can lead to increased investor confidence, attracting more investments and positively impacting market value.
- **Adaptability and Resilience**: AI systems supported by robust knowledge management are more adaptable and resilient to modifications in the market or industry trends. This adaptability is often valued highly by the market, as it suggests long-term stability and growth potential.

The integration of knowledge management in AI brings about significant economic benefits through innovation and efficiency, financial gains through better ROI and cost management, and an increase in market value by offering competitive advantages, investor confidence, and adaptability.

4.22 Artificial Intelligence and General Purpose Technologies

General-purpose technologies (GPTs) are a class of technological innovations, characterized by pervasiveness, innovation spawning, and high potential for subsequent improvements. Numerous methods of patent classification have been utilized to pinpoint AI patents, including keyword-based, scientific citations, WIPO, and USPTO approaches. The impact of AI pervades all societal facets, underscoring the crucial significance of reliable AI that is lawful, moral, and resilient, in addition to fostering effective collaboration between humans and AI. The European Union is actively engaged in the regulation of AI through the AI Act, concentrating on General Purpose AI Systems (GPAIS) and the necessity for precise definitions to govern these systems proficiently. General Purpose Technologies such as AI have traditionally exhibited considerable effects on productivity, potentially catalyzing a Fourth Industrial Revolution through the enhancement of research and development productivity. The impact of AI on GPTs and its influence on economic, financial, and market value is multifaceted and profound:

1. **Accelerating Innovation**: As a GPT itself, AI accelerates the development and improvement of other GPTs. It enhances their capabilities, efficiency, and applications.
2. **Enabling New Capabilities**: AI can unlock new functionalities in existing GPTs, allowing for innovative uses that were not previously feasible.
3. **Optimizing Efficiency**: AI improves the efficiency of other GPTs by enabling smarter, more efficient operational processes.
4. **Cross-Sectoral Integration**: AI fosters integration of different GPTs across various sectors, leading to more cohesive and interconnected technological ecosystems.

The Economic Impact involves:

1. **Productivity Growth**: AI significantly increases productivity by automating routine tasks, optimizing supply chains, and improving decision-making processes.
2. **Job Market Transformation**: While AI may displace certain jobs, it also creates new job opportunities, especially in tech-driven sectors. The nature of work shifts toward higher skilled roles.
3. **Innovation and Entrepreneurship**: AI stimulates innovation and entrepreneurship by providing tools for data analysis, market prediction, and streamlined product development.
4. **Global Economic Shifts**: Countries and companies that effectively leverage AI can gain significant competitive advantages, potentially leading to shifts in global economic power.

The main financial implications are the following:

1. **Investment Opportunities**: AI creates new investment opportunities, particularly in tech sectors, AI-driven startups, and companies that effectively integrate AI into their operations.
2. **Risk Management**: AI improves financial risk assessment and management through advanced predictive analytics and data modeling.
3. **Cost Reduction**: Implementing AI can lead to significant cost savings in various business operations, from manufacturing to customer service.

The Market Value Influence can be synthesized as follows:

1. **Valuation of Companies**: Companies that effectively utilize AI tend to have higher market valuations due to their increased efficiency, innovation potential, and future growth prospects.
2. **Sectoral Disruption**: AI disrupts traditional market sectors, leading to the rise of new leaders and the decline of businesses that fail to adapt.
3. **Consumer Behavior Analysis**: AI enhances market value by providing deep insights into consumer behavior, enabling more targeted marketing and product development.
4. **Data as a Valuable Asset**: AI-driven data analysis turns data into a crucial asset for businesses, influencing market strategies and decisions.

References

Abbel, M. (2009). Mixed know-how and patent licensing agreement. In D. Campbell & R. Proksch (Eds.), *International business transactions* (pp. 5–20). Kluwer Law International.

Aboody, D., & Lev, B. (2000). Information asymmetry, R&D, and insider gains. *Journal of Finance, 55*(2), 2747–2766.

Advamed (Advanced Medical Technology Association). (2009, January 7). *What is medical technology? Code of ethics on interactions with health care professionals*. https://www.advamed.org/sites/default/files/resource/112_112_code_of_ethics_0.pdf

Allen, T. J., & O'Shea, R. P. (2014, September 18). *Building technology transfer within research universities: An entrepreneurial approach*. Cambridge University Press.

Al-Najjar, B., & Elgammal, M. M. (2013). Innovation and credit ratings, does it matter? UK evidence. *Applied Economics Letters, 20*(5), 428–431.

Amram, M. (2005). The challenge of valuing patents and early—Stage technologies. *Journal of Applied Corporate Finance, 17*(2), 68.

Andriessen, D. (2004). IC valuation and measurement: Classifying the state of the art. *Journal of Intellectual Capital, 5*(2), 230–242.

Azzone, G., & Manzini, R. (2008). Quick and dirty technology assessment: The case of an Italian research centre. *Technological Forecasting and Social Change, 75*, 1324–1338.

Ballester, M., Garcia-Ayuso, M., & Livnat, J. (2003). The economic value of the R&D intangible asset. *European Accounting Review, 12*(4), 605–633. http://3ws-contabilidad.ua.es/trabajos/2024.pdf

Banerjee, A., Bakshi, R., & Kumar Sanyal, M. (2017). Valuation of patent: A classification of methodologies. *Research Bullettin, 42*(4), 158–174.

Benty, L., & Sherman, B. (2014). *Intellectual property law*. Oxford University Press.

Bose, S. (2007). Valuation of intellectual capital in knowledge-based firms: The need for new methods in a changing economic paradigm. *Management Decision, 45*(9), 1484–1496.

Cassiman, B., Pèrez Castrillo, D., & Veugelers, R. (2000, August). *Endogenizing know-how flows through the nature of R&D investments* (UPF Working Paper No. 512). Available at SSRN: http://ssrn.com/abstract=248683

Chen, M. C., Cheng, S. J., & Hwang, Y. (2005). An empirical investigation of the relationship between intellectual capital and firms' market value and financial performance. *Journal of Intellectual Capital, 6*(2), 159–176. https://mpra.ub.uni-muenchen.de/92888/1/MPRA_paper_92888.pdf

Choi, J. P. (2001). Technology transfer with moral hazard. *International Journal of Industrial Organization, 19*(1–2), 249–266.

Cohen, J. A. (2005). *Intangible assets: Valuation and economic benefit*. Wiley.

Còrcoles, Y. R. (2010). Towards the convergence of accounting treatment for intangible assets. *Intangible Capital, 6*(2), 185–201.

Cotropia, C. A. (2009). Describing patents as real options. *Journal of Corporation Law, 34*, 1127.

Danchev, A. (2006). Social capital and sustainable behavior of the firm. *Industrial Management & Data Systems, 106*(7), 953–965.

Dawson, P. C. (2013). *Royalty rate determination*. Working paper available at http://www.econ.uconn.edu/working/A2013-03.pdf

De Wit-De Vries, E., Dolfsma, W. A., Van Der Windt, H. J., & Gerkema, M. P. (2018, March). Knowledge transfer in university-industry research partnerships: A review. *The Journal of Technology Transfer, 44*(4), 1–20.

Degnan, A. A., & Horton, C. (1997). A survey of licensed royalties. *Les Nouvelles, XXXII*(2), 91–96.

Degryse, H., De Goeij, P., & Kappert, P. (2012). The impact of firm and industry characteristics on small firm's capital structure. *Small Business Economics, 38*(4), 431–447.

Duffy, J. F. (2005). *A minimum optimal patent term* (Paper 4). Berkeley Center for Law and Technology.

Falk, N., & Train, K. (2016). Patent valuation with forecasts of forward citations. *Journal of Business Valuation and Economic Loss Analysis, 12*(1), 101–121.

Gambardella, A. (2013, September). The economic value of patented inventions: Thoughts and some open questions. *International Journal of Industrial Organization, 31*(5), 625–633.

Giuliani, M. (2013). Not all sunshine and roses: Discovering intellectual liabilities "in action." *Journal of Intellectual Capital, 14*(1), 127–144.

Hall, R. (1993). A framework linking intangible resources and capabilities to sustainable competitive advantage. *Strategic Management Journal, 14*, 607–618.

Iazzolino, G., & Migliano, G. (2015). The valuation of a patent through the real options approach: A tutorial. *Journal of Business Valuation and Economic Loss Analysis, 10*(1), 99–116.

Ignat, V. (2016). *Modern evaluation of patents*. Paper presented at the 7th International conference on advanced concepts in mechanical engineering, IOP Conference Series: Materials Science and Engineering (Vol. 147, p. 012069).

Jensen, M., & Meckling, W. (1976). Theory of the firm: Managerial behavior, agency costs and ownership structure. *Journal of Financial Economics, 3*(4), 305–306. http://www.sfu.ca/~wainwrig/Econ400/jensenmeckling.pdf

Jun, S., Park, S., & Jang, D. (2015). A technology valuation model using quantitative patent analysis: A case study of technology transfer in big data marketing. *Emerging Markets Finance and Trade, 51*(5), 963–974.

Kristandl, G., & Bontis, N. (2007). The impact of voluntary disclosure on cost of equity capital estimates in a temporal setting. *Journal of Intellectual Capital, 8*(4), 577–594.

Kynci, M. (2017). *Methods of valuation intangible assets with emphasis on the valuation of know-how*. http://stc.fs.cvut.cz/pdf17/6598.pdf

Lagrost, C., Martin, D., Dubois, C., & Quazzotti, S. (2010). Intellectual property valuation: How to approach the selection of an appropriate valuation method. *Journal of Intellectual Capital, 11*(4), 481–503.

Lee, D., & Van Den Stein, E. (2006, December). *Managing know-how* (Unit Research Paper No. 07–039). HBS Technology & Operations Management.

Leland, H., & Pyle, D. (1977). Informational asymmetries, financial structure, and financial intermediation. *Journal of Finance, 32*(2), 371–387.

Liu, W., Yang, Z., Cao, Y., & Huo, J. (2022). Discovering the influences of the patent innovations on the stock market. *Information Processing & Management, 59*(3).

Mendi, P., Moner-Colonques, R., & Sempere-Monerris, J. J. (2016, June 1). Optimal know-how transfers in licensing contracts. *Journal of Economics/ Zeitschrift fur Nationalokonomie, 118*(2), 121–139.

Metha, A., & Madhani, P. M. (2008). Intangible assets—An introduction. *The Accounting World, 8*(9), 11–19.

Modigliani, F., & Miller, M. (1958). The cost of capital, corporation finance and the theory of investment. *American Economic Review, 48*(3), 261–297.

Moro-Visconti, R. (2012). Exclusive patents and trademarks and subsequent uneasy transaction comparability: Some transfer implications. *Intertax, 40*(3), 212–219.

Moro-Visconti, R. (2013). Evaluating know-how for transfer price benchmarking. *Journal of Finance and Accounting, 1*(1), 27–38.

Moro-Visconti, R. (2015). Leveraging value with intangibles: More guarantees with less collateral? *Corporate Ownership & Control, 13*(1), autumn 2015, continued – 2.

Moro-Visconti, R. (2018, April). Patent valuation. In G. Fusco & F. Musso (Eds.), *The Technology Transfer Cycle, University of Urbino Conference Paper*. https://press.uniurb.it/index.php/UrbinoUP/catalog/download/1/1/5?inline=1

Moro-Visconti, R. (2021). *Startup valuation: From strategic business planning to digital networking*. Palgrave Macmillan.

Moro-Visconti, R. (2022a). *The valuation of digital intangibles: Technology, marketing, and the metaverse*. Palgrave Macmillan.

Moro-Visconti, R. (2022b). *Augmented corporate valuation: From digital networking to ESG compliance*. Palgrave Macmillan.

Moro-Visconti, R., Montesi, G., & Papiro, G. (2018). Big data driven stochastic business planning and corporate valuation. *Corporate Ownership & Control, 15*(3), 189–204.

Mouritsen, J., Bukh, P. N., & Marr, B. (2004). Reporting on intellectual capital: Why, what and how? *Measuring Business Excellence, 8*(1), 46–54.

Myers, S. C., & Majluf, N. S. (1984). Corporate financing and investment decisions when firms have information that investors do not have. *Journal of Financial Economics, 13*(2), 187–221. http://www.nber.org/papers/w1396.pdf?new_window=1

OECD. (2022, July). *Transfer pricing guidelines for multinational enterprises and tax administrations*. https://www.oecd.org/tax/oecd-transfer-pricingguidelines-for-multinational-enterprises-and-tax-administrations-20769717.htm

Oestreicher, A. (2011). Valuation issues in transfer pricing of intangibles: Comments on the scoping of an OECD project. *Intertax, 39*(3), 126–131.

Parchomovsky, G., & Wagner, R. P. (2004). *Patent portfolios* (Paper 51). University of Pennsylvania Law School, Scholarship at Penn Law.

Porter, M. (1998). *Competitive advantage: Creating and sustaining superior performance*. Free Press.

Poston, T. (2015, December). Know how to transmit knowledge? *Nous, 50*(4), 865–878.

Pratt, S. P. (2003). *Business valuation body of knowledge: Exam review and professional reference*. Wiley.

Roberts, J. (2000, December). From know-how to show how? Questioning the role of information and communication technologies in knowledge transfer. *Technology Analysis & Strategic Management, 12*(4), 429–443.

Salinas, G., & Ambler, T. (2009). A taxonomy of brand valuation practice: Methodologies and purposes. *Journal of Brand Management, 17*(1), 39–61.

Silberztein, C. (2011). Transfer pricing aspects of intangibles: The OECD project. *Transfer Pricing International Journal, 8*, 4.

Smith, C. W., & Warner, J. (1979). On financial contracting: An analysis of bond covenants. *Journal of Financial Economics, 7*(2), 117–161.

Tan, H. P., Plowman, D., & Hancock, P. (2007). Intellectual capital and financial returns of companies. *Journal of Intellectual Capital, 8*(1), 76–95.

Teece, D. J. (2008). *The transfer and licensing of know-how and intellectual property: Understanding the multinational enterprise in the modern world*. World Scientific Publishing.

Thoma, G. (2015, January). The value of patent and trademark pairs. In *Academy of management proceedings* (Vol. 2015, No. 1, p. 12373). Academy of Management, 2015.

Tobin, J. (1969). A general equilibrium approach to monetary theory. *Journal of Money Credit and Banking, 1*(1), 15–29.

Trigeorgis, T., & Reuer, J. J. (2017). Real options theory in strategic management. *Strategic Management Journal, 38*, 42–63.

United Nations Industrial Development Organization. (1996). *Manual on technology transfer negotiation*. United Nations Industrial Development Organization. http://www.wipo.int/cgi-bin/koha/opacdetail.pl?bib=12398

Valladares Soler, L. E., & Cuello De Oro, C. D. J. (2007). Evaluating the scope of IC in firms' value. *Journal of Intellectual Capital, 8*(3), 470–493.

Vanacker, T. R., & Manigart, S. (2010). Pecking order and debt capacity considerations for high-growth companies seeking financing. *Small Business Economics, 35*(1), 53–69.

Vishwasrao, S. (2007). Royalties vs fees: How do firms pay for foreign technology? *International Journal of Industrial Organization, 25*(4), 741–759.

Wipo. (2008). *Wipo intellectual property handbook: Policy, law and use*. Fields of Intellectual Property Protection WIPO, Chap 2.

Wu, X., & Yeung, C. K. A. (2012). Firm growth and capital structure persistence. *Journal of Banking & Finance, 36*(12), 3427–3443.

CHAPTER 5

The Valuation of Artificial Intelligence-Driven Startups

5.1 Artificial Intelligence Startups

This chapter adapts the general valuation principles for traditional firms, shown in Chapter 2, and the scalability networking properties, analyzed in Chapter 3, to the startup environment. This adjustment should remember that "cash is king" anywhere. Even startups, sooner or later, must start generating enough liquidity to survive. Innovative AI startups, characterized by their high-growth potential and limited collateralizable assets, often encounter obstacles in obtaining conventional bank funding due to their absence of operational profits and history. The assessment of such startups follows conventional methodologies but also integrates distinctive elements pertaining to probabilistic scenarios and various exit strategies, which demonstrate the long-term value creation potential of AI driven enterprises. Moreover, the assessment process considers the technological footprint of these startups, encompassing aspects such as patents, know-how, and intangible assets specific to AI-driven sectors, which significantly influence their valuation.

Determining where value will accrue and choosing between Startups or Tech Giants is a key question, with deep consequences on where the value is created. This dilemma revolves around whether the financial benefits of these frontier technologies will primarily go to nimble startups, often backed by venture capital, or to established tech giants.

R. Moro-Visconti, *Artificial Intelligence Valuation*,
https://doi.org/10.1007/978-3-031-53622-9_5

This is a complex issue because it involves understanding not just the technology itself, but also market dynamics, customer behavior, and business strategies.

- **Startups**: They often focus on unexplored niches or entirely new markets, where they can innovate without direct competition from larger players. These smaller companies may initially target low-end markets or new market segments that are not attractive to bigger companies.
- **Technology Giants**: These incumbents generally focus on integrating new technologies into their product lines and customer bases. They are not necessarily slow or unaware of new technological developments. Rather, their strategies are typically aligned with maximizing current profits, which might inadvertently lead to overlooking disruptive innovations.

The dilemma is understanding the dynamics of technological adoption and market disruption. A head start in a novel technology (like having the best chatbot) does not always translate into long-term profitability. History is replete with examples where revolutionary innovations initially benefited smaller entities or new market entrants, while established giants either missed the opportunity or caught on too late.

The incumbents' focus on current customer needs and existing business lines, while logically profit-maximizing in the short term, can sometimes blind them to paradigm-shifting innovations. This phenomenon is well-documented in the business literature as the "Innovator's Dilemma", where companies fail to adopt new technologies or business models that will disrupt their existing products and market position.

In summary, the investment landscape in AI is highly dynamic and requires a nuanced understanding of both technological potential and market evolution. Investors need to assess not just what the next big technological breakthrough might be, but also who is best positioned to capitalize on it—nimble startups exploring new frontiers, or established giants with their vast resources and existing customer bases. This uneasy choice has deep implications in the timing and outcome of AI valuation:

where does value come from and how can it be foreseen, backing the most promising firms?

AI is a significant catalyst for startups, profoundly impacting their economic, financial, and market value in several ways:

1. **Enhanced Product and Service Innovation**: AI enables startups to develop innovative products and services. By incorporating AI into their offerings, startups can solve complex problems, automate processes, and create more personalized experiences for customers. This innovation can lead to a competitive advantage in the market and potentially higher valuations.
2. **Increased Efficiency and Cost Reduction**: AI can automate routine tasks, optimize operations, and improve decision-making processes. This increased efficiency often results in significant cost savings for startups, allowing them to allocate resources more effectively and potentially improve their financial performance.
3. **Data-Driven Insights and Decision-Making**: Startups leveraging AI can analyze large volumes of data to glean insights about market trends, customer preferences, and operational efficiencies. These insights can inform strategic decisions, leading to better-targeted products, marketing strategies, and operational improvements.
4. **Scalability**: AI systems can often scale more efficiently than traditional business models, allowing startups to handle increasing amounts of work or transactions without a proportional increase in costs. This scalability can significantly enhance a startup's growth potential and market value.
5. **Access to New Markets and Opportunities**: AI can open up new market opportunities for startups. By addressing previously unsolvable problems or creating new categories of products and services, AI-enabled startups can tap into new customer segments and revenue streams.
6. **Attracting Investment**: Startups that effectively utilize AI tend to attract more interest from investors. The promise of AI in driving future growth and innovation makes these startups appealing investment opportunities, potentially leading to higher funding amounts and valuations.
7. **Enhanced Customer Experiences**: AI can help startups provide superior customer experiences through personalization, predictive analytics, and improved customer service (e.g., through chatbots).

A strong customer experience can lead to higher customer retention, brand loyalty, and ultimately, improved financial performance.

8. **Risk Management**: AI can assist startups in identifying and managing risks more effectively. From financial risk assessments to cybersecurity, AI tools can provide startups with the capabilities to mitigate risks that they might not have been able to manage otherwise.
9. **Global Competitiveness**: AI can level the playing field for startups, allowing them to compete globally, even with larger enterprises. The use of AI can enable startups to offer unique products or services that can break into international markets.
10. **Talent and Human Capital Optimization**: AI can also help startups in human resource management, from hiring talent more efficiently to optimizing employee productivity and satisfaction. This can lead to better team performance and, subsequently, better company performance.

AI acts as a powerful catalyst for startups by driving innovation, improving efficiency, opening new markets, and attracting investment. This impact on startups not only enhances their economic and financial performance but can also significantly increase their market value and competitive positioning.

AI startups have become a significant force in the tech industry, driven by rapid advancements in technology and increasing demand for AI solutions across various sectors. Their impact on economic, financial, and market valuation landscapes is profound and multifaceted:

Main Features of AI Startups

a. **Innovative Technology**: AI startups are at the forefront of developing cutting-edge technologies like machine learning, natural language processing, and computer vision.
b. **Data-Driven Solutions**: They leverage large datasets to train AI models, providing innovative solutions across industries like healthcare, finance, retail, and more.
c. **Scalability**: AI startups often offer highly scalable products and services, enabling rapid growth and expansion into new markets.
d. **Talent Concentration**: They attract top-tier talent in software engineering, data science, and AI research.

e. **Venture Capital Attraction**: AI startups are often heavily reliant on venture capital for funding due to high initial R&D costs.

Trends in AI Startups

a. **Increased Specialization**: There is a trend towards specialized AI solutions targeting niche market segments or specific industry problems.
b. **Ethical AI and Regulation**: Growing emphasis on ethical AI and compliance with emerging regulations around data privacy and usage.
c. **AI Democratization**: Efforts to make AI tools more accessible to non-technical users, expanding the potential market.
d. **Cloud Integration**: Many AI startups are integrating their solutions with cloud platforms to enhance accessibility and scalability.
e. **Collaborations and Partnerships**: Partnerships with established companies for better market penetration and resource sharing.

Impact on Economic, Financial, and Market Valuation

1. **Economic Impact**:
    - **Job Creation**: AI startups contribute to job creation, particularly in high-tech sectors.
    - **Efficiency Gains**: Their solutions often increase efficiency and productivity in various industries.
    - **Innovation Drive**: They stimulate broader innovation across the tech ecosystem.
2. **Financial Impact**:
    - **Investment Flows**: Attract significant venture capital, influencing investment patterns in the tech sector.
    - **Market Disruption**: Potential to disrupt existing markets and financial models, particularly in sectors like finance, healthcare, and retail.
3. **Market Valuation**:
    - **High Valuations**: AI startups can achieve high valuations based on growth potential, technology ownership, and data assets.

- **Volatility**: Their valuations can be volatile, influenced by technology trends, regulatory changes, and market sentiment.
- **Acquisitions and IPOs**: High-profile acquisitions by larger tech companies or successful IPOs can significantly influence market valuations.

AI startups are reshaping industries by introducing advanced technologies that redefine how businesses operate. Their growth not only influences direct economic and financial outcomes but also drives broader trends in innovation, workforce development, and market dynamics. However, their path is also marked by challenges such as regulatory uncertainties, ethical considerations, and the need for sustainable business models.

Adaptation of the General Valuation Approaches

AI exerts a notable influence on traditional valuation methodologies for startup enterprises through the enhancement of precision and effectiveness. AI facilitates the integration of non-financial data into valuation procedures, enhancing the accuracy of evaluation for startups without historical financial records. Through the utilization of AI tools, startups can access more resilient valuation frameworks, which can assist stakeholders such as investors, entrepreneurs, and policymakers in making well-informed decisions and nurturing a more streamlined startup environment. Adapting general valuation approaches (shown in Chapter 2) to AI startups involves considering the unique characteristics, challenges, and opportunities associated with AI-based businesses. While traditional valuation methods can be applied, certain factors specific to AI startups should be considered. Traditional appraisal methodologies incorporate AI considerations, and refer to classic literature streams evidenced, for instance, by Damodaran (2018), Gao et al. (2013), Kenney and Zysman (2019), Moro Visconti (2019), Wang et al. (2017).

Most contents are readapted from Moro-Visconti (2021), or, occasionally, Moro-Visconti (2022a), or Moro-Visconti (2022b), extending startup, or business planning applications to specific AI valuation patterns.

The valuation of a startup and a seasoned firm differ significantly due to various factors related to their stages of development, risk profiles, and financial performance. These differences can influence the valuation patterns of AI-driven versus seasoned firms, as shown in Table 5.1.

Implications for AI-Driven Firms:

1. **Stage of Development Matters**: The stage of development of an AI-driven firm significantly influences its valuation. Startups with

Table 5.1 Valuation patterns of Artificial Intelligence-driven versus seasoned firms

Valuation of a startup	*Valuation of a seasoned firm*
1. **High Risk**: Startups are typically characterized by a high level of risk. They often have unproven business models, limited revenue, and uncertain market acceptance. Valuing a startup requires factoring in these risks 2. **Focus on Potential**: Startups are valued based on their growth potential, disruptive innovation, and scalability. Investors look at the startup's vision, market opportunity, and the team's ability to execute the business plan 3. **Reliance on Future Cash Flows**: Since startups may not have substantial historical financial data, valuation often relies on projections of future cash flows. Investors use methods like discounted cash flow (DCF) analysis and market comps to estimate the potential return on investment 4 **Emphasis on Technology and Intellectual Property**: In the case of AI-driven startups, the valuation heavily depends on the uniqueness of their AI technology, algorithms, and intellectual property. Patents and proprietary algorithms can significantly impact the valuation 5. **Limited Revenue and Profitability**: Startups often have limited or negative revenue and profitability in their early stages. Therefore, valuation metrics like Price-to-Earnings (P/E) ratios are less relevant for startups	1. **Established Track Record**: Seasoned firms have a history of financial performance and a track record of revenue generation and profitability. Their valuation is based on historical financial data and established market positions 2. **Lower Risk**: Compared to startups, seasoned firms are considered lower risk because they have already proven their ability to generate revenue and survive in the market 3. **Diverse Metrics**: Price-to-Earnings (P/E) ratios, Price-to-Sales (P/S) ratios, and Price-to-Book (P/B) ratios 4. **Market Share and Competitive Position**: In mature industries, valuation may depend on a firm's market share, competitive position, and ability to generate sustainable profits. Factors like barriers to entry and market concentration become important

promising AI technology may be valued based on their growth potential, while seasoned firms with established AI products or services may be valued based on their financial performance.
2. **Unique AI Technology**: For both startups and seasoned firms, the uniqueness and effectiveness of AI technology play a crucial role in valuation. Patents, proprietary algorithms, and AI capabilities can enhance valuation.
3. **Risk Perception**: Investors may perceive AI startups as riskier due to uncertainties associated with market adoption, competition, and technological hurdles. Therefore, startups may need to demonstrate a clear path to mitigating these risks to achieve favorable valuations.
4. **Revenue and Profitability**: Seasoned AI-driven firms with a history of revenue and profitability may command higher valuations based on traditional financial metrics. In contrast, startups may rely more on investor belief in the potential of their technology and market opportunity.

The valuation of AI-driven firms, whether startups or seasoned, is influenced by their stage of development, risk profile, and financial performance. While both types of firms emphasize the importance of unique AI technology, seasoned firms rely more on historical financial data and established market positions, whereas startups focus on growth potential and disruptive innovation.

Investors assess these factors when valuing AI-driven companies, which can lead to different valuation patterns for startups and seasoned firms in the AI sector.

The general valuation approaches (consistent with IVS 210 and with the principles illustrated in Chapter 2) can be adapted for AI startups:

1. **Income Approach**:
    - **Forecasting AI Revenue Streams**: AI startups often generate revenue through various channels, including software licensing, subscription models, consulting services, and data monetization. When using the income approach, consider the potential revenue streams specific to AI technologies and services.
    - **Data-Driven Projections**: AI relies heavily on data. Therefore, accurate data collection and analysis are crucial for revenue projections. Utilize AI and data analytics tools to make more

accurate forecasts based on historical data, market trends, and user behavior.

- **Scenario Analysis for AI Adoption**: AI adoption rates can vary widely across industries. Conduct scenario analysis to assess how different adoption rates and market conditions may impact revenue projections for AI startups.
- **AI-Specific Risk Factors**: Identify and assess AI-specific risks, such as data privacy and security concerns, regulatory compliance, and the availability of skilled AI talent. Adjust discount rates and growth rate assumptions accordingly.

2. **Market Approach**:

- **Analysis of Comparables**: When using the market approach, consider the market multiples of other AI startups or technology companies that are similar in terms of technology, customer base, and growth potential. AI-specific metrics, such as AI patent portfolios or proprietary algorithms, can be relevant for comparison.
- **AI Market Dynamics**: AI markets are dynamic and evolving rapidly. Be aware of market trends, competitive forces, and the potential for disruptive technologies. These factors can significantly influence the valuation of AI startups.

3. **Cost Approach**:

- **Intellectual Property Valuation**: AI startups often possess valuable intellectual property, including AI algorithms, models, and datasets. Assess the cost of developing or acquiring these assets when using the cost approach. AI-driven tools can help estimate the cost of developing AI algorithms.
- **Hardware and Infrastructure**: Consider the cost of AI-specific hardware and infrastructure, such as GPUs or cloud computing resources, which are essential for AI model training and deployment.

4. **Real Options Analysis**:

- **Flexibility and Scalability**: AI startups often have the flexibility to pivot or scale their offerings based on market feedback

and emerging opportunities. Incorporate real options analysis to capture the strategic value of these choices.
- **Technology Advancement**: Recognize that AI technologies can evolve rapidly. Assess the value of the option to upgrade or adapt AI models to stay competitive in a changing landscape.

5. **AI-Specific Factors**:
   - **AI Talent**: Consider the availability and expertise of AI talent within the startup. High-quality AI talent can be a significant asset and a factor in the startup's competitive advantage.
   - **Data Assets**: Evaluate the quality, quantity, and uniqueness of the startup's data assets, as they are often essential for AI model training and differentiation.
   - **Regulatory and Ethical Considerations**: AI startups may face regulatory challenges and ethical considerations related to AI, such as bias mitigation and data privacy. Assess the impact of these factors on the startup's valuation.
6. **AI-Specific Metrics**:
   - Utilize AI-specific metrics such as accuracy rates, model performance, user engagement, and customer retention when assessing the startup's growth potential and competitive positioning.
7. **Partnerships and Ecosystem**:
   - Consider the startup's strategic partnerships, collaborations, or integration with existing platforms or industry players, as these can impact the startup's valuation.

Adapting general valuation approaches to AI startups requires a deep understanding of the AI industry's unique dynamics, risks, and opportunities. AI-driven tools and data analytics can enhance the accuracy and relevance of valuation models for these startups, helping investors, entrepreneurs, and stakeholders make informed decisions in the rapidly evolving AI landscape. AI-driven startups employ a variety of economic, financial, and market valuation methodologies to optimize their performance and attract investment. Furthermore, providers of AI solutions play a role in advancing the economy by improving productivity and resource efficiency, broadening growth drivers, and strengthening local backward linkages. The adoption of segmented modeling in entrepreneurial finance further aids in the assessment of startup value, selection process, and survival probability analysis, taking into account variables like revenues, risks, company age, and prevailing macroeconomic circumstances.

The valuation of a startup (Achleitner, 2005; Batista de Oliveira & Perez Zotes, 2018; Berger & Köhn, 2017; Braun, 2009; Festela et al., 2013; Havard, 2018; Hering et al., 2006; IPEV, 2018; Jogekar, 2009; Koller & Goedhart, 2015; Nasser, 2016; Polimenis, 2018; Sassi, 2016; Sokol, 2018; Trichkova & Kanaryan, 2015; Venture valuation, 2019; Wasserman, 2017) follows the general appraisal rules illustrated in Chapter 8 with some important adaptations suggested by the peculiar nature of these innovative and still immature firms. Because of the peculiar features of early-stage companies, it is not easy to find an adequate method to assess their value. The valuation of a startup is complicated because of the newness of the business and industry, and because of the nature of the business structure (Ali & Khalidi, 2020). Traditional valuation methods are often unsuitable for startups. Therefore, over time, academic literature and experienced investors created alternative and innovative valuation models (Montani et al., 2020).

The various appraisal methods (Akkaya, 2020; Sivicka, 2018) include:

1. Discounted Cash Flow (DCF) Method (see also https://fastercapital.com/keyword/dcf-method.html).
2. Berkus Approach, considers five key success factors: (1) Basic value, (2) Technology, (3) Execution, (4) Strategic relationships in its core market, and (5) Production, and consequent sales.
3. Risk Factor Summation Method, an evolved version of the Berkus Method. It includes Management risk, Stage of the business risk, Legislation/Political risk, Manufacturing risk, Sales and marketing risk, Funding/capital raising risk, Competition risk, Technology risk, Litigation risk, International risk, Reputation risk, and Potential lucrative exit risk.
4. Reproduction Cost Approach. The cost to duplicate from scratch is a variant of the cost methodologies illustrated by the International Valuation Standard 210 (§ 130.1): the value [of an intangible asset] is determined based on the replacement cost of a similar asset or an asset providing similar service potential or utility.

5. Future Valuation Method, estimating the return on investment that the investors can expect shortly.
6. Market Multiple Approach (considering comparables, as illustrated in Sect. 8.6).
7. Real options, to assess the flexibility embedded in the startup's business model (Milanesi et al., 2013), as shown in Sect. 6.5.
8. Fair value is defined in IFRS 13 as "the price that would be received to sell an asset or paid to transfer a liability in an orderly transaction between market participants at the measurement date (an exit price)".

5.2 The IPEV Valuation Guidelines

The Valuation Guidelines of the International Private Equity and Venture Capital (IPEV) Board are essential when determining the value of startups driven by AI. These guidelines specifically emphasize the concept of Fair Value for the purpose of financial reporting, covering a wide range of private equity investments, which include investments in early stage businesses and growth capital. The assessment of startups, particularly those leveraging AI technology, introduces distinct challenges due to their substantial growth prospects and intangible assets. The evaluation of startups heavily relies on AI, as machine learning techniques are increasingly employed to estimate valuations based on funding rounds. The integration of AI in the valuation procedures of startups is a subject of great interest, with research studies shedding light on the advantages and disadvantages of AI applications in appraising startup enterprises. The utilization of AI in the valuation processes can improve precision and effectiveness, especially when dealing with startups that possess limited assets available as collateral. The IPEV Guidelines provide a framework for valuing private equity and venture capital investments. While they do not specifically address AI-driven startups, they offer general principles that can be applied to such startups. Here's how the IPEV Guidelines can be relevant when valuing AI-driven startups:

1. **Market Approach**:
    - See above

2. **Income Approach**:
    - See above
    - The IPEV Guidelines emphasize the importance of using reasonable assumptions when projecting cash flows. For AI startups, this means considering factors like the scalability of AI solutions, the cost of acquiring or developing AI algorithms, and potential regulatory or ethical considerations that could affect cash flows.
3. **Cost Approach**:
    - See above
4. **Exit Strategy**:
    - The IPEV Guidelines emphasize the consideration of exit strategies when valuing investments. For AI startups, explore potential exit scenarios, such as acquisition by a technology company looking to enhance its AI capabilities, initial public offering (IPO), or strategic partnerships. Assess the likelihood and timing of these exit events when estimating the startup's value.
5. **Risk Assessment**:
    - Consider the unique risks associated with AI startups, such as technological obsolescence, regulatory changes, data privacy concerns, and the availability of AI talent. The IPEV Guidelines stress the importance of appropriately adjusting discount rates and risk factors to reflect the specific risks of the investment.
6. **Documentation and Transparency**:
    - The IPEV Guidelines encourage transparency and proper documentation of valuation methodologies and assumptions. This is essential for AI-driven startups, as the valuation may rely on complex AI algorithms, proprietary models, and data sources. Transparent documentation helps stakeholders understand and assess the valuation process.

7. **External Inputs**:

   - When valuing AI startups, be prepared to incorporate external inputs such as market research reports, technology trends, and competitive analyses into the valuation process. These inputs can provide valuable context for assessing the startup's growth potential and competitive positioning.

While the IPEV Guidelines provide a valuable framework for valuing private equity and venture capital investments, adapting them to AI-driven startups requires a deep understanding of the AI industry's dynamics and unique factors. Collaborating with experts who have expertise in AI technologies and markets can enhance the accuracy and relevance of the valuation process for AI startups.

Assigning a valuation to a startup in the Venture Capital context is remarkably challenging because startup investments are characterized by high risk, high cash burn rates, and asymmetric information (Sahlman, 1990; Sievers et al., 2013). It is even more important to understand the different determinants that impact startup valuations.

The IPEV Guidelines are applicable across the whole range of Alternative Funds (seed and startup venture capital, buyouts, growth/development capital, infrastructure, credit, etc., collectively referred to as Private Capital Funds) and financial instruments commonly held by such Funds. They provide a basis for valuing Investments by other entities, including Fund-of-Funds, in these Private Capital Funds. Furthermore, the Valuation Guidelines have been prepared with the goal that Fair Value measurements derived when using these guidelines are compliant with both International Financial Reporting Standards (IFRS) and the United States Generally Accepted Accounting Principles (US GAAP).

According to the EVCA Guidelines, Fair Value is the price that would be received to sell an asset in an Orderly Transaction between Market Participants at the Measurement Date. It is the amount for which an asset could be exchanged between knowledgeable, willing parties in an arm's length transaction.

Fair Value measurement assumes that a hypothetical transaction to sell an asset takes place in the Principal Market or its absence, the Most Advantageous Market for the asset. For actively traded (quoted)

Investments, available market prices will be the exclusive basis for the measurement of Fair Value for identical instruments.

For Unquoted Investments, the measurement of Fair Value requires the Valuer to assume the Investment is realized or sold at the Measurement Date whether the instrument or the Investee Startup is prepared for sale or whether its shareholders intend to sell soon. Some Funds invest in multiple securities or tranches of the same Investee Startup. If a Market Participant would be expected to transact all positions in the same underlying Investee Startup simultaneously, for example, separate Investments made in series A, series B, and series C, then Fair Value would be estimated for the aggregate Investment.

Fair Value must be estimated using consistent Valuation Techniques from Measurement Date to Measurement Date unless there is a change in market conditions or Investment-specific factors, which would modify how a Market Participant would determine value. The use of consistent Valuation Techniques for Investments with similar characteristics, industries, and/or geographies would be expected. The Price of a Recent Investment, if resulting from an orderly transaction, generally represents the Fair Value as of the transaction date. At subsequent Measurement Dates, the Price of a Recent Investment may be an appropriate starting point for estimating the Fair Value. However, adequate consideration must be given to the current facts and circumstances, including, but not limited to, changes in the market or changes in the performance of the Investee Startup.

Inputs to Valuation Techniques should be calibrated to the Price of a Recent Investment, to the extent appropriate.

The valuation of a startup is consistent with its ability to produce expected cash flows, alternatively considering a debt-free or levered context.

In selecting the appropriate Valuation Technique, the Valuer should use one or more of the following Valuation Techniques as of each Measurement Date, considering Market Participant assumptions as to how Value would be determined, as anticipated:

1. Market Approach
    - Multiples
    - Industry Valuation Benchmarks
    - Available Market Prices

2. Income Approach

    - Discounted Cash Flows
    - Replacement Cost Approach
    - Net Assets

DCF is sometimes used even for startups, even if their liquidity forecasting is difficult. The general principles apply even to startups. According to Laitinen (2019), in general, DCF is found the most popular method in startup valuation followed by the internal rate of return (IRR) and the payback period methods. However, the consequences of using this method in startup valuation are rarely analyzed in financial research. The use of DCF favors startups that grow slowly and have a short payback period but that also exhibit a high IRR. The longer the time series of the startup used in the analysis, the more significant role IRR tends to play in DCF.

To identify the current value of a startup, before an investment is made (pre-money valuation), the Valuation Capital Method can be applied. This valuation approach was first described by Bill Sahlman in the late '80s.

The basic keywords are:

- Harvest year: the time (year) that the investor plans to exit the startup;
- Pre-money Valuation: the value of the startup before any investment has been made;
- Post-money Valuation: the value of the startup after the investment has been made;

The formula for post-money valuation is:

$$\text{Post-Money Valuation} = \text{Pre-Money Valuation} + \text{Investment Amount} \quad (5.1)$$

The Venture Capital Method is organized into a 2-step process:

- The terminal value of the business in the harvest year is derived

- The (desired) ROIC and the investment amount are used to derive the pre-money valuation. The return on investment can be estimated by determining what return an investor could expect from that investment with the specific level of risk attached.

In calculating the terminal value, the following inputs are required:

- Projected revenue in the harvest year;
- Projected (or industry average) profit margin in the harvest year;
- Industry P/E ratio.

The formula is:

$$\begin{aligned}\text{Terminal Value} &= \text{projected revenue} * \text{projected margin} * \text{P/E} \\ &= \text{earnings} * \text{P/E}\end{aligned} \tag{5.2}$$

In the same way, when calculating the pre-money valuation, the inputs needed are:

- Required Return on Investment Capital (ROIC)
- Investment amount

The formula is:

$$\begin{aligned}\text{Pre-Money Valuation} = &\text{Terminal value/ROIC} \\ &- \text{Investment amount}\end{aligned} \tag{5.3}$$

The advantages of the Venture Capital Valuation Method are linked to its simplicity in understanding and implementation.

5.3 The Fair Value of the Investments in the Target Firms

AI-driven startups are having a significant and growing impact on the global economy. The economic, financial, and market valuation of AI-driven startups is expected to continue to grow rapidly in the years to come.

The fair value of investments in target firms, particularly for AI-driven startups, is a critical consideration for investors, venture capitalists, and private equity firms. Determining the fair value involves assessing the worth of an investment based on various factors, including the startup's financial performance, growth prospects, market dynamics, and the inherent risks associated with AI technologies. The key considerations when determining the fair value of investments in AI-driven startups are reported in Table 5.2.

Determining the fair value of investments in AI-driven startups requires a comprehensive analysis of financial, technological, market, and regulatory factors. Collaboration with experts in AI, venture capital, and valuation can enhance the accuracy and reliability of the fair value assessment.

Additionally, regular monitoring and reassessment of fair value are essential as AI startups evolve in the dynamic technology landscape.

The valuation of target companies presupposes a startup valuation. The evaluation methodology should be referred to as the type of startup being evaluated. In most cases in which the appraisal refers to industrial, commercial, or service companies, the evaluation methodologies—even if different, depending on the type of startup—will be those typically adopted for such companies.

The general considerations made in Chapter 2 on balance sheet-based, income, mixed (capital-income), and market (empirical) approaches may apply to startups, with adaptations that presuppose a preliminary analysis of:

- The different business model applicable from time to time, with repercussions on value drivers, the value chain, strategic and market aspects (…);
- The financial statements (balance sheet, income statement, and cash flow statement);
- The presence of accounting parameters relevant to the valuation, such as EBIT, EBITDA, the Net Financial Position, etc.

In the evaluation of the target startup, especially when estimating the enterprise value, it is necessary to adequately consider the changes in the financial structure induced by the entry of private equity funds.

Leveraged buyouts are frequent, through which the fund finances part of its investment making the target startup indebted. Debt sustainability, subject to the startup's ability to generate adequate cash flows and the

Table 5.2 Fair value of investments in Artificial Intelligence-driven startups

Financial performance	• **Revenue and profitability**: Evaluate the startup's historical and projected revenue and profitability. Consider the revenue streams from AI-related products or services, such as software licensing, data monetization, or consulting • **Cost structure**: Assess the cost structure, including research and development expenses, marketing costs, and operational expenses related to AI development and deployment • **Cash flow analysis**: Analyze the startup's cash flows, including operating cash flow, free cash flow, and capital expenditures. Assess the adequacy of cash reserves to support AI development and growth
Market opportunity	• **Market size and growth**: Examine the size of the target market for the startup's AI solutions and the projected growth rates. Consider whether the startup is well-positioned to capture market share • **Competitive landscape**: Analyze the competitive dynamics within the AI sector, including the presence of dominant players, potential disruptors, and barriers to entry. Assess the startup's competitive advantages, such as proprietary algorithms or unique data assets
Technology and intellectual property	• **Intellectual Property (IP) portfolio**: Evaluate the strength and uniqueness of the startup's IP portfolio, including patents, trademarks, and proprietary algorithms. Consider the value of IP assets in protecting the startup's market position • **Technology differentiation**: Assess the startup's technology differentiation and its potential to provide a competitive edge in the AI market. Consider factors such as AI model accuracy, innovation, and scalability

(continued)

Table 5.2 (continued)

Regulatory and ethical considerations	• **Regulatory compliance**: Evaluate the startup's compliance with AI-related regulations, data privacy laws, and industry standards. Assess any potential regulatory risks and the startup's ability to navigate them • **Ethical framework**: Consider the startup's approach to ethical AI development, including bias mitigation, transparency, and responsible data use. Ethical considerations can impact the startup's reputation and long-term viability
Growth potential	• **User adoption and customer base**: Analyze the startup's user adoption rates and customer base. Assess whether the startup has a strong and growing customer base that can drive future revenues • **Product roadmap**: Consider the startup's product development roadmap, including plans for expanding AI offerings, entering new markets, or addressing emerging industry trends
Exit strategy	• **Exit opportunities**: Explore potential exit scenarios, such as acquisition by technology giants looking to enhance their AI capabilities or the possibility of going public through an IPO. Assess the likelihood and timing of these exit events
Risk assessment	• **Risk factors**: Identify and assess the specific risks associated with AI technologies, including technological obsolescence, data security, talent acquisition, and competitive pressures. Adjust discount rates and risk factors accordingly
External inputs	• **Market research**: Incorporate external market research reports, industry analyses, and expert opinions into the valuation process to provide context and validation for fair value assessments
Documentation and transparency	• **Valuation methodologies**: Transparently document the methodologies and assumptions used in the valuation process. Communicate the rationale behind the fair value determination

level of market interest rates, has a decisive impact in determining the overall risk level of the startup, which in turn influences its value.

In private equity buy-outs, debt is typically reshaped by type and maturity to make it compatible with the new business plans formulated with the contribution of the fund and is usually characterized by a strategic orientation more oriented towards the creation of value assisted by an extension of debt maturities.

Among the various approaches to estimating the fair value, the following matter:

- Price of recent investments, including those made by others (a reasonable estimate of fair value, the validity of which erodes rapidly over time);
- Income and market multiples (appropriate, sustainable, and equitable, usually applicable to consolidated businesses): P/E; EV/ EBIT; EV/ EBITDA...;
- Discounted cash flows, including terminal value;
- Sector benchmarks, whenever applicable (e.g., rate of occupancy of hotel rooms; the price per hospital bed; the price per subscriber to cable TV...);
- Market prices if the subsidiary is eventually listed.

If the fair value is challenging to estimate, the best estimate is often represented by the fair value referred to in the previous report, adjusted, if necessary, by applying the impairment test.

5.4 The Fair Value of the Investments in the Portfolio Companies

The valuation of the investment portfolio is the most critical aspect and the fundamental prerequisite for a valuation of the target startup. This valuation must refer first to the existing holdings in the portfolio and must not prudently consider possible future investments and the ability to expand the portfolio, which relates to purely potential goodwill.

In the estimate, the entire investee startup and its underlying business must first be evaluated, and then the fund's investment in that startup must be evaluated accordingly.

The estimate of the periodic performance of private equity funds is essential to establish portfolio benchmarks, and the fair remuneration of asset managers, and to analyze the degree of efficiency and sophistication of investors concerning unlisted companies.

Once the individual investee companies have been evaluated, the investments in these companies are estimated using a procedure that can be summarized as follows:

a. The starting point is the gross equity value of the investee startup, adjusted to consider the surplus assets and estimated by applying the approaches described above;
b. The pro-rata share of this Equity Value, based on the fund's percentage shareholding in the startup; the percentage is adjusted to consider the minority discount or majority premium; the net Equity Value is estimated.

If the target is to value a loan (bridge financing or mezzanine loan) instead of a shareholding, the market value of this financial loan must be estimated.

According to the valuation guidelines, in private equity, the value is usually crystallized by the sale or listing of the entire investment portfolio, rather than by the sale of individual holdings. The market value of the fund is determined by estimating the adjusted Enterprise Value of each startup, using the most appropriate valuation approaches, and then arriving at an estimate of the fair value of all the investments.

5.5 Startup Evaluation with Binomial Trees

Evaluation of startups using binomial trees is a valuable approach that can effectively tackle the challenges associated with conventional valuation methods for high-growth ventures. The utilization of binomial option pricing, particularly within the framework of single-asset Black-Scholes markets, presents efficient solutions; however, it encounters issues related to convergence and the application in multi-dimensional scenarios. The incorporation of binomial trees with optimal drift models and decoupling strategies enhances convergence rates and deals with irregularities in multi-asset markets, thus enhancing the accuracy of valuation. Moreover, the amalgamation of public information with decision tree algorithms assists venture capitalists in effectively screening startups, enabling the identification of promising projects for potential investment. Consequently, the integration of binomial trees with innovative valuation techniques and decision-making algorithms holds the potential to significantly improve the assessment process for startups, offering more precise insights into their value and potential. Evaluating an AI-driven startup using binomial trees involves applying a financial modeling technique to estimate the startup's value, considering various potential outcomes and uncertainties associated with the business. Binomial trees are commonly used for option pricing and can be adapted to assess the value of a startup. Startup evaluation can be performed with binomial trees:

Step 1: Define the Key Parameters

Before building the binomial tree model, identify the essential parameters and assumptions:

a. **Time Horizon**: Determine the period over which the startup's value has to be assessed. This could be, for example, the expected time to exit (e.g., acquisition or IPO).
b. **Potential Outcomes**: Identify the possible scenarios or outcomes for the startup's performance, considering factors like revenue growth, market adoption, and competitive positioning.
c. **Discount Rate**: Determine the appropriate discount rate to consider the startup's risk profile and the time value of money. This rate should reflect the required return on investment.
d. **Initial Valuation**: Estimate the startup's initial valuation which is the starting point for the binomial tree model.

Step 2: Build the Binomial Tree Model

A binomial tree model consists of nodes identifying different points in time and outcomes. Each node has two branches, typically representing an "up" or "down" scenario. In the context of startup valuation, these branches might represent different performance scenarios.

Here's how to build the model:

a. **Initial Node**: Start with the initial valuation of the startup as the first node.
b. **Branching**: At each time step, create two branches representing two possible outcomes. For an AI-driven startup, these outcomes

might be "successful market penetration" and "limited market penetration". Assign probabilities to these outcomes based on your assessment.

c. **Valuation Calculation**: Calculate the value of the startup at each node by discounting the potential outcomes to the present value through the discount rate. The valuation at a node is a weighted average of the values of its two child nodes.
d. **Continue Building the Tree**: Repeat the process for multiple time steps, branching at each step to account for different scenarios and potential outcomes.

Step 3: Calculate the Startup's Value
Once the binomial tree model is built, it is possible to calculate the startup's value at the initial node, which represents the current value of the startup and its potential scenarios. This calculated value is your estimate of the startup's fair value.
Step 4: Sensitivity Analysis
Perform sensitivity analysis to assess how changes in key parameters, such as discount rate, growth rates, or market adoption probabilities, affect the startup's value. This is useful to understand the valuation's sensitivity to various assumptions and risks.
Step 5: Risk Assessment
Consider the startup's specific risks and uncertainties related to AI technology, market competition, regulatory changes, and more. Incorporate these risk factors into your model and assess their impact on the startup's value.
Step 6: Interpretation and Decision-Making
Interpret the results of the binomial tree model in the context of your investment or decision-making process. Compare the calculated value to the startup's current valuation or investment opportunity to determine whether it represents a viable investment.

The valuation accuracy relies on the quality of assumptions, data, and probabilities assigned to different scenarios. Additionally, the binomial tree model provides a framework for assessing a range of potential outcomes, making it valuable for startups with uncertain prospects, such as AI-driven businesses. It is often used together with other valuation approaches.

The valuation of startup portfolios can be carried out with binomial trees (grids), frequently used in decision-making processes under uncertainty. Uncertain outcomes can be interpreted even with Monte Carlo methods, traditionally used to solve any problem having a probabilistic interpretation using randomness.

Suppose, for example, that a venture capital decides to invest in three startups at the same time, underwriting capital for 100 in each startup and with an exit after 2 years. The three startups have a different risk profile:

- The S1 startup has an expected variance in value, on an annual basis, of 20% (defensive investment);
- The S2 startup has an expected variance in value, on an annual basis, of 40% (risky investment);
- The S3 startup has an expected variance in value, on an annual basis, of 60% (highly speculative investment).

The payoff (expected results) is in Fig. 5.1.
The total payoff is in Table 5.3.
The total Net Present Value of the three projects, which are considered not mutually exclusive (since venture capital can take over all of them), nor with synergistic effects between them (which is possible, especially if the sectors and business models intersect), is positive if the rate at which they are discounted is less than 13.93%. This rate represents the watershed, which expresses the break-even point at which the Net Present Value of the project portfolio is zero, calculated through the iterative search for the Internal Rate of Return (which is the rate that makes the NPV = 0).

Venture capital must make a comparison between its cost of raising financial resources (weighted average cost of capital, which coincides with the cost of equity capital if the venture capital has not resorted to debt) and the return that the investments offer. In all cases where the expected return is lower than the cost of capital (IRR < WACC), it will not be convenient to undertake the investment.

Binomial networks (traditionally used as decision trees or to determine the pricing of options) are flexible: by adapting the parameters of the expected variance of the value and the probability that the value increases (upside potential) or decreases (downside risk), it is possible to estimate, with basically unlimited ramifications, a wide range of scenarios.

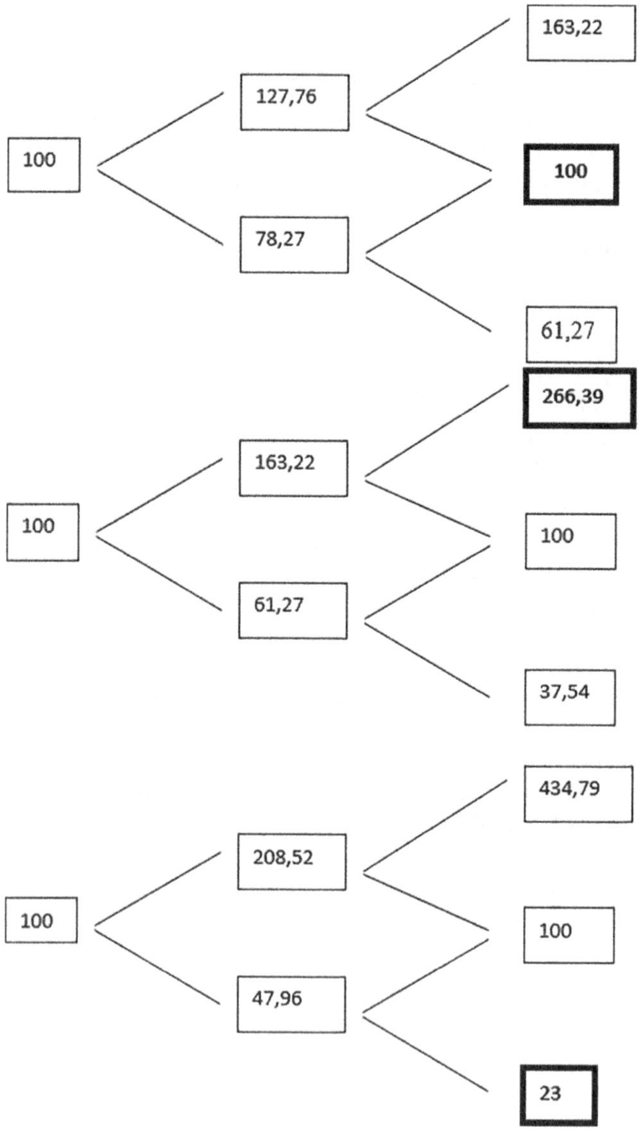

Fig. 5.1 Representation of the payoff

Table 5.3 Payoff calculation

		investment year 0	year 1	exit year 2	*capital gain (loss)*	Value i = 5%	actual i=10%	i=20%	net i=30%	IRR
Start up S1		-100	0	100	0	-9,30	-17,36	-30,56	-40,83	0,0%
Start up S2		-100	0	266,39	166,39	141,62	120,16	84,99	57,63	63,2%
Start up S3		-100	0	23	-77	-79,14	-80,99	-84,03	-86,39	(*)
Total investment portfolio		-300	0	389,39	89,39	**53,19**	**21,81**	**-29,59**	**-69,59**	
interest	5%									
Total Net Present Value						**53,19**				
interest	10%									
Total Net Present Value							**21,81**			
Internal Rate of Return	(NVP = 0)									13,93%
interest	20%									
Total Net Present Value								**-29,59**		
interest	30%									
Total Net Present Value									**-69,59**	

(*) individually not calculable because it is negative

The possibility of correcting the estimates along the way, refining them based on what happened in the portion of time passed (which declines a chronological process of time decay), represents a further element to improve the forecasts. Timely big data may conveniently be introduced in the model.

The Venture Capital Method

The Venture Capital Method is widely used for the startup evaluation, including those in the AI sector. The Venture Capital Method is a widely utilized strategy for assessing emerging AI companies Venture capitalists assume a pivotal role in the evaluation of entrepreneurial teams, employing diverse assessment methodologies like intuitive, systematic, and rational approaches. AI has been recognized as a game-changing technological advancement within the venture capital domain, facilitating informed investment judgments by VCs. Moreover, the utilization of decision tree algorithms in the risk analysis of substantial health industry startups exemplifies the incorporation of AI tools to prognosticate future business performance. Furthermore, examination of economic indicators for venture financing project appraisal underscores the significance of scrutinizing the economic potential of startups to attract venture capital. In essence, the Venture Capital Method plays a crucial role in molding the evaluation process of startups, particularly in cutting-edge sectors such as AI. This method is particularly suitable for early-stage AI-driven startups where cash flows and historical financial data may be limited. Here's how to apply the Venture Capital Method to evaluate an AI-driven startup:

Step 1: Gather Key Information

Before applying the Venture Capital Method, gather essential information about the AI startup:

1. **Investment Amount**: Determine the amount of investment the startup is seeking or the current round of financing.
2. **Exit Horizon**: Define the expected timeframe for the startup's exit event, such as an acquisition or IPO. This typically ranges from 3 to 7 years.
3. **Targeted Return**: Establish the investment's desired rate of return. Venture capitalists typically aim for high returns to offset the startup risk. Common target rates of return are 30% to 40% or higher.

Step 2: Estimate the Startup's Terminal Value
It expresses the estimated future value of the startup at the exit event. Calculate the Terminal Value using one of the following methods:

- **Multiple of Revenue**: Estimate the startup's future revenue at the exit event based on growth projections and industry benchmarks. Apply a multiple (e.g., 3× to 5×) of this revenue to determine the Terminal Value.
- **Market Capitalization**: If an IPO is the exit event, estimate the future market capitalization of the startup by multiplying projected earnings (EBITDA) by an industry-specific market multiple.
- **Comparable Transactions**: Consider recent acquisition deals or IPOs in the AI sector that are similar in terms of technology, size, and growth potential. Use the valuation multiples from these transactions to estimate the Terminal Value.

Step 3: Calculate the Pre-Money Valuation
It is the estimated startup value immediately before the current round of financing. To calculate it, subtract the investment amount from the estimated Terminal Value:

$$\text{Pre-Money Valuation} = \text{Terminal Value} - \text{Investment Amount}$$

Step 4: Calculate the Post-Money Valuation
It is the startup's estimated value after the current round of financing. To calculate it, add the investment amount to the Pre-Money Valuation:

$$\text{Post-Money Valuation} = \text{Pre-Money Valuation} + \text{Investment Amount}$$

Step 5: Determine Ownership Percentage
To determine the ownership percentage for the investor, divide the investment amount by the Post-Money Valuation:

$$\text{Ownership Percentage} = \frac{\text{Investment Amount}}{\text{Post Money Valuation}} * 100\% \qquad (5.4)$$

Step 6: Assess the Potential Return
To assess the return on the investment, utilize the ownership percentage to calculate the investor's proportion of the Terminal Value at the exit:

$$\text{Investor's Share of Terminal Value} = \text{Ownership Percentage}$$

$$\times \text{Terminal Value}$$

Then, estimate the expected return by comparing the investor's share of the Terminal Value to the investment amount:

$$\text{Expected Return} = \frac{\text{Investor's Share of Terminal Value}}{\text{Investment Amount}} * 100\% \quad (5.5)$$

Step 7: Evaluate the Investment Decision

Compare the expected return to the targeted return set in Step 1. If the expected return exceeds the targeted return, the investment may be considered attractive. However, consider the inherent risks associated with startups and perform due diligence to validate assumptions and projections.

The Venture Capital Method provides a structured methodology for evaluating AI-driven startups, considering their potential for high growth and uncertain future cash flows. Keep in mind that this method relies on various assumptions.

The valuation of a new venture is often considered to be a combative point of negotiation between venture capitalists and entrepreneurs. (Dhochak & Doliya, 2020).

How to value a new venture is critical in entrepreneurial financing. The attractiveness of the industry, the quality of the founder and top management team, as well as external relationships of a new venture significantly and positively affect its valuation by venture capitalists when it seeks venture capital financing in its early stages of development (Miloud et al., 2012).

Startup valuation in the venture capital (VC) context is often said to be more art than science (Köhn, 2018).

To identify the current value of a startup, before an investment is made (pre-money valuation), the Valuation Capital Method can be applied. This valuation approach was first described by Sahlman and Scherlis (1987).

The basic keywords used in this valuation approach are:

- Harvest year: the time (year) that the investor plans to exit the startup;
- Pre-money Valuation: the value of the startup before any investment has been made;
- Post-money Valuation: the value of the startup after the investment has been made;

The formula for post-money valuation is:

$$\text{Post-Money Valuation} = \text{Pre-Money Valuation} + \text{Investment Amount} \quad (5.6)$$

The Venture Capital Method is organized into a 2-step process:

1. The terminal value of the business in the harvest year is derived
2. The (desired) ROIC and the investment amount are used to derive the pre-money valuation. The return on investment can be estimated by determining what return an investor could expect from that investment with the specific level of risk attached.

In calculating the terminal value, the following inputs are required:

- Projected revenue in the harvest year;
- Projected (or industry average) profit margin in the harvest year;
- Industry P/E ratio.

The formula is as follows:

$$\text{Terminal Value} = \text{projected revenue} * \text{projected margin} * P/E$$

$$\text{Terminal Value} = \text{earnings} * P/E \quad (5.7)$$

In the same way, when calculating the pre-money valuation, the inputs needed are:

- Required Return on Investment Capital (ROIC)
- Investment amount
- The formula is as follows:

$$\text{Pre-Money Valuation} = \text{Terminal value}/\text{ROIC} - \text{Investment amount} \quad (5.8)$$

Besides the industry average P/E ratio, many of the required inputs are based on not-so-reliable assumptions. It follows that if one feeds the model with wrong assumptions, a wrong value will be derived.

5.6 The Break-Up Value of Venture-Backed Companies

Various factors can influence the break-up value of AI-driven companies that are backed by venture capital. The utilization of AI technologies is crucial in shaping business models and improving competitiveness. Machine learning is employed by venture capitalists to make investment choices, sometimes opting for poorly performing firms over those with a predictable track record of success. In the healthcare industry, AI companies that prioritize direct patient care tend to receive less funding in comparison to those that cater to research institutions or pharmaceutical corporations. Moreover, startups in the AI sector often highlight the enhancement of human capabilities rather than the replacement of jobs, resulting in a transformation of job responsibilities within companies. It is imperative to comprehend these dynamics in order to evaluate the break-up value of venture-backed AI-driven companies, taking into account the influence of AI technologies, investment strategies, funding sources, and implications on employment. Most venture-backed investments are directed towards companies that are unable to take off and that will never reach the stock exchange listing, which is the primary exit approach for the intermediary but is typically tricky to demobilize. When they are, the disposal of the investment typically takes place at a significant discount compared to the investments made by the venture capitalist.

This may be the case for startups in which a private equity fund has an interest, although in this case the target startup is typically at a more advanced stage of its life cycle and is generally more likely to limit losses in value, thanks to a more stable and well-established business model. If the going concern is irreparably compromised and no more shareholders are willing to recapitalize the startup, which is typically affected by cash and equity burnouts, different prospects open up. Scenarios range from a liquidation, with the disposal of attractive business units or sale of individual assets, to insolvency, if the market value of the assets realized is not sufficient to meet the liabilities (typical event of equity burnout, in which the shareholders' equity has zeroed or even become negative). The break-up value of the assets represents the lower limit in the valuations and is related to the possibility of selling them to third parties.

Venture-backed companies are typically represented by a composition of assets in which intangibles (that fuel the present value of growth opportunities) have a predominant weight.

The existence of intangible assets, especially if they are not included in the balance sheet, limits the startup's capacity for indebtedness because of the difficulty of establishing a guaranteed title on them and their uncertain or sometimes non-existent market value.

The idea that the capacity for indebtedness increases in the presence of tangible assets with collateral value on which a guarantee can be provided is confirmed by numerous studies. The fact that venture-backed startups have a portfolio of assets with a book value and—a fortiori—a market value represented essentially by intangibles sharply limits their ability to borrow but at the same time minimizes conflicts of interest between shareholders and third-party creditors, which are typical of situations of insolvency or prodromal to a state of crisis (Moro Visconti, 2015).

The transition from a going concern scenario to a break-up context implies the disappearance of the startup's income expectations. It only considers the market value of the individual assets (including the intangibles). The market value is usually well below the operating value and sometimes even below the book value (as is the case for intangibles without market value): using a concept introduced by Adam Smith, the exchange value is prevalent over the value in use of the individual asset. The presence in the startup of highly specialized activities (firm-specific) increases the difference between the value in use and exchange and, while it makes these activities more challenging to sell, it reduces agency costs between shareholders and creditors, since the former will have greater difficulties in making substitutions with other activities, making it more challenging—but less necessary—to collateralize them (Smith & Warner, 1979).

The market value of an intangible (as well as a tangible asset) mostly depends on the existence of a large and well-established secondary market. The secondary market is reduced by the more specific the intangible is, even though it is usually more value-added (Titman & Wessels, 1988).

Internally generated goodwill (not accounted for, as the startup has not paid a sum in this regard) of the venture capitalist is incorporated in the value of the investment in the venture-backed startup. In the case of badwill related to a startup in crisis, it emerges the need to write off the investment, with a significant impact on the shareholders' equity of the intermediary. Equity can be eroded substantially, especially if the write off is material compared to a portfolio of investments in other assets unable to offset the loss of some initiatives with the gains of others.

5.7 Stock Exchange Listing and Other Exit Procedures

Venture capital firms employ diverse exit strategies for AI-supported startups, with IPOs representing a significant route. Studies indicate that exit timing in VC firms is influenced by their specific characteristics and fund dynamics. The significance of IPOs as a means of exit is underscored. Comprehending these dynamics is paramount for AI startups backed by venture capital, as initial funds tend to retain shares for longer periods post-IPO, whereas funds satisfied with performance exit earlier following lockup periods. This intricate interplay of variables plays a pivotal role in shaping decisions related to stock exchange listings and other exit processes for AI-supported enterprises. AI startups often aim for successful exits to provide returns to their investors and founders. One exit strategy is through a stock exchange listing, such as an Initial Public Offering (IPO). Here are the steps involved in the stock exchange listing and other exit procedures for AI startups:

1. **IPO (Initial Public Offering):**
   - **Preparation Phase**:
     - **Hire Professionals**: Engage investment banks, legal advisors, auditors, and underwriters to assist with the IPO process.
     - **Financial and Operational Audit**: Conduct a thorough financial audit and ensure compliance with regulatory requirements.
     - **IPO Team Formation**: Form an IPO team within the company, including key executives responsible for the IPO.
   - **Documentation and Registration**:
     - **Draft Prospectus**: Prepare a prospectus that includes financial information, business details, risks, and plans. File the prospectus with the relevant regulatory authorities.

  - **Due Diligence**: Facilitate due diligence by regulators and underwriters, addressing any concerns or questions they may have.
- **Roadshow and Investor Outreach**:
  - **Roadshow**: Conduct a roadshow to meet with potential institutional investors and retail investors to generate interest in the IPO.
  - **Pricing**: Set the IPO price based on market demand and investor feedback.
- **Listing and Trading**:
  - **Listing Approval**: Obtain approval from the stock exchange to list the company's shares.
  - **Market Debut**: Execute the IPO, and the company's shares become publicly tradable.
- **Post-IPO**:
  - **Compliance**: Ensure ongoing compliance with stock exchange regulations, financial reporting requirements, and governance standards.
  - **Shareholder Relations**: Maintain relationships with shareholders, provide regular updates, and manage investor relations.

2. **Acquisition**:

- **Identify Potential Acquirers**: Identify companies that may have an interest in acquiring the AI startup, such as technology giants, competitors, or companies in related industries.
- **Engage in Negotiations**: Initiate discussions and negotiations with potential acquirers. Consider factors like valuation, terms, and the strategic fit of the acquisition.
- **Due Diligence**: Allow the acquiring company to conduct due diligence to assess the startup's assets, liabilities, technology, and team.
- **Agreement and Closing**: Finalize the acquisition agreement, obtain regulatory approvals, and complete the transaction.

3. **Merger**:

- **Merger Discussions**: Enter merger discussions with a suitable partner, which could be a complementary AI startup or a larger company.
- **Due Diligence**: Conduct due diligence to assess the compatibility of the two entities and identify potential synergies.
- **Merger Agreement**: Create a merger agreement outlining the terms and conditions of the merger.
- **Shareholder Approval**: Seek approval from shareholders of both companies to proceed with the merger.
- **Integration**: After the merger is approved, integrate the operations, technology, and teams of the two companies.

4. **Secondary Sale or Private Equity Investment**:

   - **Secondary Sale**: Existing investors or other financial institutions may purchase shares from early investors or founders.
   - **Private Equity Investment**: Consider raising additional capital from private equity investors to fuel growth and provide liquidity to existing stakeholders.

5. **Strategic Partnerships and Licensing**:

   - Explore opportunities to form strategic partnerships or licensing agreements with larger companies that can provide access to markets, distribution channels, or additional resources.

6. **Liquidation**:

   - In cases where other exit options are not viable, consider the liquidation of assets and distribution of proceeds to investors and stakeholders.

The choice of exit strategy depends on various factors, including the startup's growth stage, market conditions, investor preferences, and the founders' long-term vision. AI startups should work closely with legal and financial advisors to navigate the complexities of the exit process.

The listing of the venture-backed startup on the stock exchange is the traditional way for the venture capitalist to exit the investment.

The fact that this intermediary typically represents a minority facilitates the sale of the share package, on the Initial Public Offering and/or subsequently and does not help to signal to the market any feeling of distrust since the market knows in advance the nature and mission of the intermediary.

If the startup to be listed has a value that is strongly influenced by the permanence of some key managers (typically historical shareholders of the startup), it may require them to have a lock-up period. This constraint is not imposed on the intermediary, for the reasons mentioned above and for the disappearance of its strategic role (the financial resources are guaranteed by the stock market and the advisory service of the intermediary may continue, if necessary, through external consultancy). The stock market, when the time windows that allow divestments—usually fractioned—are opened to key managers bound by lock-up clauses, questions their behavior (often reacting negatively to their exit, knowing that they have privileged information).

The exit of some shareholders and, more generally, the purchases and sales, are influenced by the degree of liquidity of the stock, which is expressed in the ability to allow significant purchases or sales without having a significant impact on the price. In an illiquid market, which characterizes thin stocks and is typical of technological companies, strongly growing and with recent history, the price typically moves against the shareholder who carries out the transaction.

The intermediary plays an active role in assisting the startup in the listing process, not only because it is involved in the success of the operation but also because of its privileged relations with the financial community and with the intermediary that takes care of the IPO (Aggarwal et al., 2009).

With the quotation on the stock exchange (going public), the structure of the stakeholders is divided, and the process of fragmentation involves the passage from concentrated shareholders to a more intense fragmentation. This transition can preserve some reference shareholders, and expression of a majority (individually or—more frequently, especially as the size increases—through coalitions of shareholders through syndicate agreements). A public company model may apply, in which many small shareholders live together, none of whom can exert a significant influence on the former startup (in this context, the power of management is growing, and this can lead to a loss of value, counterbalanced by the value of the contestability of control).

The majority premium inherent in the controlling shareholding is gradually eroded with the splitting up of the equity until it tends to zero in a public company. Stock exchange listing creates intrinsic value not only by allowing the intermediary shareholder (or other shareholders, subject to any lock-up constraints) to sell all or part of their holding but—above all—by facilitating the search for a counterparty, to the point of making it anonymous and, in a liquid market, free of implicit costs.

With the listing, the so-called lack of marketability discount, which consists of the depreciation usually applied to unlisted companies, is eliminated. As a result, unlisted companies have traditionally been granted a discount resulting from the lack of marketability discount.

Empirical evidence allows for identifying a range of variations of the discount for lack of marketability (Novak, 2016).

5.8 Valuation of the Investment Portfolio with a Net Asset Value

Valuation of the investment portfolio of AI-driven startups through Net Asset Value entails the utilization of artificial intelligence models such as artificial neural networks (ANN) for predictive evaluation. These models have the capacity to improve conventional valuation approaches by integrating sector trends, macroeconomic factors, and startup-specific information to accurately forecast pre-money valuations, facilitating negotiations between venture capitalists and entrepreneurs. Furthermore, evaluation of the investment potential of startups in emerging sectors like autonomous driving can offer valuable insights into potential investment prospects and risks, underscoring the significance of comprehensive SWOT analysis for informed decision-making. The valuation of venture capital or private equity fund must be based on the book value of equity, to which the market value of the investments must be added, and the book value of the investments subtracted.

The market value of investments is based on their Net Asset Value and any capital gain over their book value must be expressed, whenever appropriate (where the participation exemption is not applicable ...), net of potential tax charges. In formulae:

$$
\begin{aligned}
\text{Net Asset Value} &= \text{NAV} \\
&= \text{Market Value of the Fund} \\
&= \text{Book Value of the Fund}
\end{aligned}
$$

$$+ \text{ (market value} - \text{book value of the investments)} \\ (1 - \text{tax rate}) \quad (5.9)$$

The valuation of equity investments at fair value, applying international accounting standards (IAS/IFRS), should decrease the difference between the market and the book value of equity investments and the book value of shareholders' equity will already reflect the market value of the venture capital or private equity fund.

In the case of the valuation of venture capital or private equity funds, the following aspects should be considered:

- The value of each subsidiary must be estimated by discounting it at the cost of capital that incorporates the systematic risk of the most similar stock index (Nasdaq, Numtel ...), increased by a firm-specific risk premium, as to include the lack of marketability, the volatility of economic and financial flows (higher in startups ...);
- The valuation of the shareholding must sometimes consider the size of the package, which may be subject to a minority discount (i.e., less frequently—a specular majority premium) in the absence of co-sale options, non-participation in syndicate agreements, etc.;
- The financial flexibility of the intermediary, which may or may not intervene in the event of cash or equity burnout of the investee startup, with the possibility of retaining at least part of its value (post-equity recapitalization burnout involves a reshuffling of the shareholding structure, in the event of failure by all shareholders to exercise the option right);
- There may be a synergistic value of the investment portfolio (if it relates to vertically integrated companies operating in contiguous segments of the value chain ...), such that the market value of that portfolio is higher than the sum of the NAVs per share of each holding. This synergistic value expresses goodwill not accounted for but considered in the estimate of the market value;
- The holding of a stake can generate management consulting services, placement fees, and intermediation, which must be independently evaluated;
- The intermediary has its intrinsic value linked to its portfolio of holdings but is dependent on its reputation (which is an asset of primary importance for any financial intermediary).

5.9 Boom and Bust Cycles

The fluctuations in the valuation of AI-driven startups go through boom and bust cycles due to a multitude of factors, including the incorporation of AI in assessment procedures, the business strategies adopted by AI-centric companies, the asymmetric interplay between actual performance and future expectations, as well as the triumphs and apprehensions associated with AI technologies. The swift emergence of AI technologies has sparked substantial investments in AI startups, characterized by periods of initial achievements succeeded by criticisms and obstacles, mirroring historical trends in the evolution of AI. Furthermore, tools such as Artificial Neural Networks (ANN) are now employed for forecasting startup valuations, offering a competitive edge in funding determinations and negotiations between venture capitalists and entrepreneurs. In 2023, as indicated by statista.com, the total AI startup funding worldwide had slumped to a low not seen since early 2018. This is a correction from the incredible levels of startup funding in 2021 and 2022 following the COVID-19 pandemic. As a broader economic crisis looms in 2023, the funding for less reliable and forward-looking projects like startups shrinks.

This trend aligns with broader economic patterns often seen in the aftermath of significant global events like the COVID-19 pandemic. The surge in AI startup funding in 2021 and 2022 likely reflected a combination of factors, including:

a. **Post-Pandemic Digital Transformation**: Many businesses accelerated their digital transformation initiatives in response to the pandemic, leading to increased investment in AI and related technologies.
b. **Innovation Surge**: The pandemic period saw a surge in innovation and new startups, as organizations sought new ways to adapt to changing circumstances.
c. **Investor Enthusiasm**: The potential of AI technology likely fueled investor enthusiasm, leading to increased funding for AI startups.

The decline in AI startup funding in 2023—the lowest since early 2018—suggests several shifts:

1. **Economic Realignment**: As the immediate impacts of the pandemic wane, there may be a realignment of investment priorities. The

initial rush to invest in AI startups might be normalizing as investors reassess the long-term viability and profitability of these ventures.

2. **Broader Economic Concerns**: With looming economic challenges in 2023, investors might be more cautious, focusing on more reliable and immediate returns. This shift often leads to a reduction in funding for sectors perceived as high risk or long term, like startups, especially in cutting-edge fields like AI.
3. **Market Saturation and Competition**: The AI field has become increasingly crowded, and with many startups now competing for market share and investment, it is possible that only the most promising or well-established ones are attracting significant funding.
4. **Return to Pre-Pandemic Levels**: It is also possible that the funding levels are simply returning to pre-pandemic norms, suggesting a correction in the market rather than a decline in interest in AI technology.

This trend reflects the natural ebb and flow of investment in emerging technologies, influenced by broader economic conditions and the evolving maturity of the technology sector. While AI remains a field of great potential, the pattern of investment will likely continue to fluctuate based on these external factors.

5.10 A Practical Valuation Case

This valuation example is taken from a real case, duly anonymized. The startup is represented by an AI-driven food processing firm that operates in a mature market with an innovative business model. Its scalability is somewhat limited but the same applies to the overall market risk.

This template can be easily extended to other startups, even operating in different businesses.

The two methodologies used are the DCF_{equity} and the market comparables (to assess the Enterprise Value and then the Equity Value). The target of this estimate is to assess the fair (equity) market value for potential new investors.

Startup Epsilon is evaluated at the end of year 0 and has a business plan forecast for the following five years.

The two methodologies are described below.

Table 5.4 Mean forecast EBITDA

	Year 1	*Year 2*	*Year 3*	*Year 4*	*Year 5*
EBITDA	€ 12,87,000	€ 16,44,000	€ 20,08,000	€ 21,45,000	€ 22,94,000
Mean year 1 to year 5	€ 18,75,600				

To Estimate the DCF_{equity}, we first need to estimate the forecast EBITDA, considering both the (short) history of the startup and its market perspectives. The EBITDA is the key variable that brings to the operating and then net cash flow that must be discounted using the cost of equity, to estimate the DCF_{equity} (Table 5.4).

The EBITDA brings to the net cash flow following the passages described in Sect. 2.4. The net cash flow is then discounted year after year with a (constant) cost of equity (Ke) that is calculated with the Capital Asset Pricing Model formula:

$$E(R_i) = R_f + \beta_i\left[E(R_m) - R_f\right] \tag{5.10}$$

where:

$E(R_i)$	expected return of investment
R_f	isk-free rate
β_i	beta of the investment (sensitivity to the market index)
$E(R_m) - R_f$	market risk premium

It is normal to assess a terminal value since the business model goes beyond the proposed five-year "gosplan" (already difficult to estimate). As shown below, the Terminal Value is calculated with the "exit multiple" methodology (Ouidad, 2010).

Exit multiple is one of the methods used to calculate the terminal value of the free cash flows of a startup. Terminal value refers to the value at a future point in time of all future cash flows of a company when the growth rate is expected to be consistent and stable. However, terminal value limits the cash flow projections to a several-year period. Usually, predicting the value of a business (Krihna et al., 2016) beyond such a period is often impossible, and it exposes such a process to a variety of risks that question the validity of the forecast. Terminal value addresses such limitations by allowing the inclusion of future cash flow values beyond the projection period while mitigating any issues that may arise from using the values of such cash flows.

The very fact that the Terminal Value represents most of the total value, as shown in this case, is frequent in startup valuation, but should be considered with caution, and periodically rechecked updating the estimates. Overwhelming Terminal Value is a typical matter of discussion between existing shareholders and potential newcomers. While the former stick on it to back what they consider a minimum value, incoming shareholders tend to be skeptical, and unwilling to pay for mighty future value. A possible compromise solution may consist of an earn-out clause (linked to real options), according to which the Terminal Value is paid to historic shareholders only when and if it concretely materializes. The business planned milestones represent the expected hard evidence that backs earn-out triggering.

The discounting passages of the Net Cash Flow are in Table 5.5.

The comparables are found using the Nace Rev. 2 industry code and then selecting them from a databank after careful scrutiny for effective comparability (Table 5.6).

The Net Financial Position (NFP) at the end of year 0 (reference date of the estimate) is considered to pass from the Enterprise Value (estimated through DCF of operating flows—not reported here for simplicity—or through market multipliers of the EBITDA) to the Equity Value that corresponds to the final target of the appraisal. It should be noted that NFP is the only "punctual" parameter with a "photo" at the reference date of the estimate. All the other sensitive parameters are perspective. It may also be possible to estimate a perspective NFP, but this assessment is arbitrary for a startup with little history and a volatile outlook (Table 5.7).

The adjusted multiple (taken from the Orbis database) originates from the average of the selected sample and then incorporates a dimensional and illiquidity discount for lack of marketability. This is often necessary since it may be inappropriate to compare established listed firms with a promising but still unlisted and small startup (Table 5.8).

The valuation is reported in Table 5.9.

It is also advisable to make a sensitivity analysis. Startup estimates are, as known, difficult and volatile, and they need constant refreshing, possibly exploiting real-time big data sources and augmented business planning (see Sect. 2.12).

Table 5.5 From the net cash flow to the equity value

DCF	*Year 1* 1	*Year 2* 2	*Year 3* 3	*Year 4* 4	*Year 5* 5	*Terminal value* 6	
Net Cash Flow (NCF)	€ 6000	€ 2,77,000	€ 6,09,000	€ 7,14,000	€ 9,94,000	€ 43,26,359	exit multiple
Discount factor	0.933415723	0.871264912	0.813252367	0.759102546	0.708558252	0.661379413	
Discounted NCF	€ 5600	€ 2,41,340	€ 4,95,271	€ 5,41,999	€ 7,04,307	€ 28,61,365	
Equity value	€ 48,49,883						
Ke							
Beta			0.71			Damodaran [2020]	
Risk free rate			0.36%			Long-Term Treasury Bonds	
Market risk premium			9.54%			Damodaran [2020]	
Ke			**7.13%**				

Sources

Beta: http://pages.stern.nyu.edu/~adamodar/New_Home_Page/datacurrent.html [Total beta by industry sector, Europe, Jan 2020, Food Processing, Average Levered Beta]

Risk free: http://www.dt.mef.gov.it/export/sites/sitodt/modules/documenti_it/debito_pubblico/risultati_aste/risultati_aste_btp_5_anni/BTP_5_Anni_Risultati_Asta_del_27-28.02.2020.pdf

MRP I: http://pages.stern.nyu.edu/~adamodar/New_Home_Page/datafile/ctryprem.html [Risk premium for other markets, Jan 2020, ERP + CRP, Italy]

Table 5.6 Listed comparables

Comparables	*Country*	*Nace Rev. 2*	*EV/EBITDA*			*Average*
			Year 0	*Year −1*	*Year −2*	
Listed Competitor Alpha	US	4632	5.28	5.56	5.82	5.55
Listed Competitor Beta	IT	4729	13.49	n.a	9.00	11.25
Listed Competitor Gamma	JP	4617	7.14	8.40	6.91	7.48
					Average	**8.09**

Table 5.7 Net financial position

Net financial position	End of year 0
Item	**Value**
Debts owed to quotaholders	−€ 2,12,000
Short-term Debts owed to banks	−€ 10,07,000
Long-Term Debts owed to banks	−€ 5,27,000
Liquidity	0
Total NFP (end of year 0)	*−€ 17,46,000*

The sensitivity starts from the "base case" estimating EBITDA variations from −20% to +20% and cost of equity (ke) variations from −2% to +2%, as shown in Table 5.10.

Cost of equity (ke) variations are calculated in Table 5.11.

Wise evaluators are aware of the difficulties in making a fair market value estimate. The caveats may be softened with periodical updating (refreshing) of the appraisal, incorporating in the model the timely market evidence with bottom-up feedback.

This sample starts from the EBITDA but what mostly matters is represented but its constituting elements, expressed by the difference between expected revenues and monetary OPEX. The assessment of the revenue model is, probably, the most difficult but also fascinating task.

Table 5.8 Adjusted Multiple of the EBITDA

EBITDA		
EBITDA [year 1 to year 5]	€ 18,75,600	
* adj. multiple [EV/EBITDA]	3.24	
= *Enterprise value*	*€ 60,72,359*	
± Net Financial Position	–€ 17,46,000	end of year 1
= Equity value	**€ 43,26,359**	

MULTIPLE (EV/EBITDA)	*Orbis* *Years from −2 to 0*
Listed Competitor Alpha	5.55
Listed Competitor Beta	11.25
Listed Competitor Gamma	7.48
Average	*8.09*
Dimensional discount	25%
Illiquidity discount	35%
Total discount	*60%*
Adjusted multiple	**3.24**

	Year 1	*Year 2*	*Year 3*	*Year 4*	*Year 5*
EBITDA	€ 12,87,000	€ 16,44,000	€ 20,08,000	€ 21,45,000	€ 22,94,000
Mean year 1 to year 5	€ 18,75,600				

Table 5.9 Synthetic valuation

Synthesis		
Fair Value at year 0 (end)		
Method	**Value**	**Rounded value**
Multiple	€ 43,26,359	€ 43,20,000
DCF	€ 48,49,883	€ 48,40,000
Average	*€ 45,88,121*	*€ 45,80,000*

Table 5.10 Sensitivity analysis

Sensitivity analysis					
EBITDA method	*EBITDA variations*				
	−20%	*−10%*	*Base case*	*+10%*	*+20%*
EBITDA [mean]	€ 15,00,480	€ 16,88,040	€ 18,75,600	€ 20,63,160	€ 22,88,232
* adj. multiple [EV/EBITDA]	3.24	3.24	3.24	3.24	3.24
= Enterprise value	€ 48,57,887	€ 54,65,123	€ 60,72,359	€ 66,79,595	€ 74,08,278
± NFP	−€ 17,46,000	−€ 17,46,000	−€ 17,46,000	−€ 17,46,000	−€ 17,46,000
= Equity value	€ 31,11,887	€ 37,19,123	€ 43,26,359	€ 49,33,595	€ 56,62,278
DCF method	*Ke variations*				
	−2%	*−1%*	*Base case*	*+1%*	*+2%*
Ke	5.13%	6.13%	7.13%	8.13%	9.13%
Equity value	€ 53,42,620	€ 50,88,784	€ 48,49,883	€ 46,24,888	€ 44,12,856

Table 5.11 Cost of equity (ke) sensitivity

	Year 1	*Year 2*	*Year 3*	*Year 4*	*Year 5*	*Terminal value*
Year	*1*	*2*	*3*	*4*	*5*	*6*
Ke	*5.13%*					
Levered Cash Flow (LCF)	€ 6000	€ 2,77,000	€ 6,09,000	€ 7,14,000	€ 9,94,000	€ 43,26,359
Discount factor	0.95117251	0.904729144	0.860553492	0.818534825	0.778567824	0.740552312
Discounted LCF	€ 5707	€ 2,50,610	€ 5,24,077	€ 5,84,434	€ 7,73,896	€ 32,03,895
Equity value	€ 53,42,620					
Ke	*6.13%*					
Levered Cash Flow (LCF)	€ 6000	€ 2,77,000	€ 6,09,000	€ 7,14,000	€ 9,94,000	€ 43,26,359
Discount factor	0.942210463	0.887760557	0.836457286	0.788118807	0.742573787	0.699660792
Discounted LCF	€ 5653	€ 2,45,910	€ 5,09,402	€ 5,62,717	€ 7,38,118	€ 30,26,984
Equity value	€ 50,88,784					
Ke	*8.13%*					
Levered Cash Flow (LCF)	€ 6000	€ 2,77,000	€ 6,09,000	€ 7,14,000	€ 9,94,000	€ 43,26,359
Discount factor	0.924783647	0.855224794	0.790897903	0.731409447	0.676395496	0.625519494
Discounted LCF	€ 5549	€ 2,36,897	€ 4,81,657	€ 5,22,226	€ 6,72,337	€ 27,06,222
Equity value	€ 46,24,888					
Ke	*9.13%*					
Levered Cash Flow (LCF)	€ 6000	€ 2,77,000	€ 6,09,000	€ 7,14,000	€ 9,94,000	€ 43,26,359
Discount factor	0.916309764	0.839623584	0.769355288	0.704967762	0.645968844	0.591907559

	Year 1	*Year 2*	*Year 3*	*Year 4*	*Year 5*	*Terminal value*
Year	*1*	*2*	*3*	*4*	*5*	*6*
Discounted LCF	€ 5498	€ 2,32,576	€ 4,68,537	€ 5,03,347	€ 6,42,093	€ 25,60,805
Equity value	€ 44,12,856					

References

Achleitner, A. K. (2005). First Chicago method: Alternative approach to valuing innovative startups in the context of Venture Capital Financing rounds. *Betriebswirtschaftliche Forschung Und Praxis, 57*(4), 333–347.

Aggarwal, R., Bhagat, S., & Rangan, S. (2009). The impact of fundamentals on IPO valuation. *Financial Management, 38*(2), 253–284.

Akkaya, M. (2020). *Startup valuation: Theories, models, and future, valuation challenges and solutions in contemporary businesses*. ICI Global Publisher.

Ali, S. B., & Khalidi, M. A. (2020). Valuation of equity securities, private firms, and startups. *IBT Journal of Business Studies, 16*, 125–140.

Batista de Oliveira, F., & Perez Zotes, L. (2018). Valuation methodologies for business startups: A bibliographical study and survey. *Brazilian Journal of Operations & Production Management, 15*(1), 96–111.

Berger, E. S. C., & Köhn, A. (2017, November). *Exploring differences in early-stage startup valuation across Countries*. Academy of Management.

Braun, R. (2009). Risk of private equity fund-of fund investments—A detailed cash flow-based approach. *SSRN Electronic Journal*. https://ssrn.com/abstract=1368277

Damodaran, A. (2018). *The dark side of valuation*. Pearson FT Press PTG.

Dhochak, M., & Doliya, P. (2020). Valuation of a startup: Moving towards strategic approaches. *Journal of Multi-Criteria Decision Analysis, 27*(1–2), 39–49.

Festela, G., Wuermseherb, M., & Cattaneo, G. (2013). Valuation of early-stage high-tech startup companies. *International Journal of Business, 18*(3), 216.

Gao, X., Ritter, J. R., & Zhu, Z. (2013). Where have all the IPOs gone? *Journal of Financial and Quantitative Analysis, 48*(6), 1663–1692.

Havard, E. (2018). *Internet Startups' Profit Dilemma: A theoretical paper on using two-sided markets theory as a framework in a valuation setting*. The Arctic University of Norway.

Hering, T., Olbrich, M., & Steinrucke, M. (2006). Valuation of startup internet companies. *International Journal of Technology Management, 33*(44), 406–419.

IPEV. (2018). *IPEV Guidelines*. http://www.privateequityvaluation.com/Portals/0/Documents/Guidelines/IPEV%20Valuation%20Guidelines%20-%20December%202018.pdf?ver=2018-12-21-085233-863

Jogekar, N. (2009). *Marketing R&D, and Startup valuation*. IEEE Transaction on engineering management.

Kenney, M., & Zysman, J. (2019). Unicorns, Cheshire cats, and the new dilemmas of entrepreneurial finance. *Venture Capital, 21*.

Köhn, A. (2018). The determinants of startup valuation in the venture capital context: A systematic review and avenues for future research. *Management Review Quarterly, 68*, 3–36.

Koller, T., & Goedhart, M. (2015). *Valuation: Measuring and managing the value of companies*. McKinsey & Company.

Krihna, A., Agrawal, A., & Choudhary, A. (2016). *Predicting the outcome of startups: less failure, more success*. Paper presented at IEEE 16th International Conference on Data Mining workshops (ICDMW).

Laitinen, E. K. (2019). Discounted Cash Flow (DCF) as a measure of startup financial success. *Theoretical Economics Letters, 9*(8), 2997.

Milanesi, G., Pesce, G., & Alabi, E. E. (2013). Technology-based startup valuation using real options with Edgeworth expansion. *Journal of Finance and Accounting, 1*(2), 54–61.

Miloud, T., Cabrol, M., & Aspelund, A. (2012). Startup valuation by venture capitalists: An empirical study. *Venture Capital, an International Journal of Entrepreneurial Finance, 14*(2–3), 151.

Montani, D., Gervasio, D., & Pulcini, A. (2020). Startup Company Valuation: The state of art and future trends. *International Business Research, 13*(9), 31–45.

Moro Visconti, R. (2015). Leveraging value with intangibles: More guarantees with less collateral? *Corporate Ownership & Control, 13*(1), 241–252.

Moro Visconti, R. (2019, June 1). *How to prepare a business plan with excel*. https://ssrn.com/abstract=2039748

Moro-Visconti, R. (2021). *Startup valuation*. Palgrave Macmillan.

Moro-Visconti, R. (2022a). *The valuation of digital intangibles. Technology, marketing, and the metaverse*. Palgrave Macmillan.

Moro Visconti, R. (2022b). *Augmented corporate valuation*. Palgrave Macmillan.

Nasser, S. (2016). *Valuation for startups—9 methods explained*. ICT Strategic Consulting.

Novak, N. P. (2016). Measuring the discounts for lack of marketability for Noncontrolling Nonmarketable Ownership interests. *Insights*.

Ouidad, Y. (2010). Exit routes in LBO projects (March 20). SSRN: https://ssrn.com/abstract=1552316

Polimenis, V. (2018). *Valuation issues with early equity finance*. NUP Academic Publications, School of Economic Sciences and Business.

Sahlman, W. A. (1990). The structure and governance of venture-capital organizations. *Journal of Financial Economics, 27*(2), 473–521.

Sahlman, W. A., & Scherlis, D. R. (1987, July). A Method for valuing high-risk, long-term investments: The "Venture capital method". *Harvard Business School Background Note 288-006* (Revised October 2009).

Sacci, R. (2016). *An improved valuation method for startups in the social-media industry*. RUN Nova School of Business and Economics (NSBE).

Sievers, S., Mokwa, C. F., & Keienburg, G. (2013). The relevance of financial versus non-financial information for the valuation of venture capital-backed firms. *European Accounting Review, 22*(3), 467–511.

Sivicka, J. O. (2018). Features of valuation of startup companies. *Economic Scope, 132*, 163.

Smith, C. W., & Warner, J. (1979). On financial contracting: An analysis of bond covenants. *Journal of Financial Economics, 7*(2), 117–161.

Sokol, M. (2018). What drives the magic of startups? *People & Strategy*, 4.

Venture valuation. (2019). *Valuation methods*. https://www.venturevaluation.com/en/methodology/valuation-methods

Titman, S., & Wessels, R. (1988). The determinants of capital structure choice. *Journal of Finance, 43*(1), 1–19.

Trichkova, R., & Kanaryan, N. (2015). Startups valuation: Approaches and methods. Paper presented at 1st Balkan Valuation conference. *Best Valuation Practices* (pp. 19–21).

Wang, L., Zhou, F., & An, Y. (2017). Determinants of control structure choice between entrepreneurs and investors in venture capital-backed startups. *Economic Modelling, 63*, 215–225.

Wasserman, N. (2017). The throne vs. the kingdom: Founder control and value creation in startups. *Strategic Management Journal, 11*(3), 326–343.

CHAPTER 6

The Valuation of Software as a Prerequisite for Artificial Intelligence

6.1 Definition and Main Features

In general terms, the software is a sequence of computer instructions, written in a programming language (C, Visual Basic …), to obtain a certain result and to perform functions in an electronic device. These instructions form the source code, transformed through a compiler into an object code, which the CPU (Central Processor Unit) can process. In other words, the software is represented by information (data) and rules (programs) to manage the given data. This information can, therefore, be represented by one or more programs, or by one or more data, or by a combination of the two.

The source code of the proprietary software is usually not distributed and is considered a trade secret, following know-how valuation patterns. In this context, there is proprietary software, as opposed to open-source software (free software), in which the source code is made public by the authors, enabling independent programmers to make changes and extensions.

Software represents a fundamental element in computer science, which deals with the processing of information through automated procedures, using algorithms, i.e., formal procedures that solve problems (procedural, computational, etc.), interpreting the computability through a finite number of steps. Algorithms, usually based on mathematical concepts,

R. Moro-Visconti, *Artificial Intelligence Valuation*,
https://doi.org/10.1007/978-3-031-53622-9_6

are thus a key aspect in the programming phase of software development which uses IT languages then executed by a computer.

The theoretical concept of software, not without ambiguity (because of its constantly evolving technical characteristics), turns out to be instrumental to its legal framework. According to the first definition, provided by the World Intellectual Property Organization (WIPO) in 1984, software is "the expression of an organized and structured set of instructions in any form or on any medium capable, directly or indirectly, of having a function or task performed or of obtaining a specific result utilizing an electronic information processing system".

In the English language "software" is born in contrast to the term "hardware"[3] and from the composition of the words "soft" and "ware".

According to their different characteristics, the software can be classified according to:

- The functions it fulfills (accounting, document consultation, document video-writings, spreadsheets, payroll management, databases, graphics, etc.);
- The degree of openness of the license (free use or ownership);
- The installation of hardware or portability equipment, with Internet evolutions which have opened the space to cloud computing. Remote storage allows to backup of data and process of information remotely (Data as a Service—DaaS), or to use of programs always from remote, outside the physical computer or the local LAN (software as a service), through an external cloud provider using mass storage in outsourcing;
- The operating system on which they can be used (DOS, Unix, Mac OS, Linux, Windows, Android, iOS ...);
- The type of interface which uses them (single PCs or networked, textual or graphical);
- The criticality of the processes they govern.

The term "suite" refers to software structured in different programs/modules, usually configurable separately but forming part of a single IT solution (such as, for example, office automation application packages or antivirus).

The realization of software is a complex activity articulated in several phases, starting from a basic platform of programs (e.g., Java) on which applications and customizations are developed, within an environment of execution, and for this reason, the software is generally associated with an engineering product, but differing mainly for its formability according to the need.

Many contents are readapted mostly from Moro-Visconti (2022a), or, occasionally, Moro-Visconti (2022b), or Moro-Visconti (2021), extending digital intangible, startup, or business planning applications to specific software-driven AI valuation patterns. The literature on software valuation dates back to the last twenty years and is represented, for instance, by Amran (2005), Azura et al. (2015), Ben-Menachem (2007), Bernaroch and Appari (2010), Boehm and Valerdi (2008), Brown and Boehm (2010), Contractor (2001), Cusumano (2008), Degenne and Forsè (2006), Groot et al. (2012), Denne and Cleland-Huang (2004), Dhillon and Mahmoud (2015), Du et al. (2013), Erdogmus et al. (2008), Garcia and Magdaleno (2013), Head and Nelson (2012), Jiang et al. (2007), Kalaiselvi (2009), King (2007), Puntambekar (2009), Ramzan et al. (2009), Reilly and Schweihs (2014), Saunders and Brynjolfsson (2015), Tansey and Stroulia (2007), Thurman (2018), Tockey (2014). AI has a significant impact on the value co-creation patterns of companies that invest in it to improve their value. The utilization of AI innovation, through customized software, plays a vital role for manufacturing businesses that aim to gain a competitive edge in the era of the digital economy by reducing risks specific to enterprises and improving their fundamental competitiveness. The incorporation of AI in various companies around the world demonstrates that users of AI, particularly in the fields of ICT and Professional Services, display higher levels of productivity, underscoring the crucial importance of supplementary resources such as ICT expertise and digital infrastructure in augmenting productivity.

6.2 Accounting and Fiscal Aspects

The accounting aspects related to the recording of the software in the financial statements play an important role in its economic evaluation, for the estimate of the damages due to counterfeiting, which may include the accounting of the counterfeiter for the estimate of his marginality. In a broad sense, accounting evaluates the impact:

- On revenues, costs, and differential economic margins (EBITDA; EBIT; pre-tax profit ...);
- On provisions for assets (of profit reserves ...);
- On incoming, outgoing operating, and net cash flows.

The accounting discipline, dictated by the national accounting principles or by the international accounting principles (IAS/IFRS), is increasingly adopting new valuation standards, providing for the alignment of the book values recorded in the balance sheet and based on the fair value cost.

Accounting standards distinguish software, based on its intrinsic characteristics, in:

a. Basic software: consisting of the set of instructions required for the computer operation (hardware);
b. Application software: the set of instructions enabling the use of basic software functions to meet specific user requirements.

Since the basic software is closely related to the hardware, this one is treated as a core component of a tangible asset. Costs incurred for the internal production of "unprotected" application software can either be charged to the income statement in the period in which they are incurred or can be recognized under "other" intangible assets, linked to programs that can be used for a certain number of years within the firm and have the characteristics specified below. Capitalized costs include direct and indirect costs that relate to the development of the software. Indirect costs attributable to the project, such as rents, depreciation and amortization, supervisory personnel costs, and other similar items, are excluded.

Capitalization of costs begins only after the firm is reasonably certain of the completion and suitability for the expected use of the new software. This moment may vary depending on the nature of the project.

The amortization of the cost of the unprotected software is made within its foreseeable period of use.

As far as fiscal aspects are concerned, a distinction is made between software entered under the intellectual property or licenses of assets: concerning tax amortization, only a limited number of financial years are recognized for the former, while for the latter the tax amortization follows the duration of the license agreement.

The tax aspects are relevant for transfer price problems, within international corporate groups, for instance when the software is concentrated in foreign royalty companies, which charge the fees back to other group companies for the license of the same.

6.3 Legal Protection of Software: Introductory Remarks

Legal protection of software is crucial for software developers and companies, including those in the AI sector. It involves establishing and enforcing intellectual property rights and complying with relevant laws and regulations. The legal safeguarding of AI driven software presents a multifaceted challenge that demands a meticulous examination of intellectual property rights and regulatory structures. Acknowledging AI as a legal entity prompts inquiries into its legal standing and accountabilities, potentially entailing the acknowledgment of AI as a legal entity with its own entitlements and duties, thereby necessitating mechanisms for accountability and safeguarding of AI entitlements. These deliberations underscore the necessity of adjusting legal safeguards to the dynamic landscape of AI technology to promote innovation while upholding rights and accountabilities in AI-driven software progression. The level of protection can impact the valuation of AI companies in several ways, as shown in Table 6.1.

The legal protection of software, including AI technology, is a critical aspect of an AI firm's overall value proposition. Strong protection can enhance a firm's competitiveness, reduce risks, open revenue opportunities, and positively influence valuation. Therefore, AI companies should invest in legal strategies and compliance efforts to maximize their intellectual property protection and overall market value.

Regarding the possible forms of protection, the software, given its nature, could be qualified both as an industrial invention, thus enjoying patent protection, as well as intellectual work, with the consequent traceability to the protection of copyright. In the past, the protection of software using copyright or patents has been the subject of a wide doctrinal and jurisprudential debate.

There are still discrepancies between the U.S. and the European Union.

The choice of copyright for the protection of computer programs has been, since the '60s, strongly advocated by the manufacturers of

Table 6.1 Level of protection

Intellectual Property Protection	• **Patents**: Patents can protect novel and non-obvious AI algorithms, methods, or applications. Having patented AI technology can enhance a firm's valuation, as it demonstrates a competitive advantage and potential revenue streams through licensing • **Copyright**: Copyright protects the specific code and software architecture. While it doesn't protect the underlying idea or functionality, it safeguards against direct copying. A strong copyright portfolio can add value to an AI firm by safeguarding its proprietary codebase • **Trade Secrets**: Protecting trade secrets, including AI algorithms and data sets, can be critical. Companies with well-protected trade secrets may have a competitive edge, which can positively affect their valuation • **Trademarks**: Trademarks protect branding elements, such as the firm name and logo. Strong branding can enhance the market perception of an AI firm and potentially increase its valuation
Competitive Advantage	• Strong legal protection can provide a competitive advantage by deterring potential infringers or competitors from replicating AI technology. This advantage can lead to market dominance, increased market share, and higher valuation
Regulatory Compliance	• **Data Privacy**: Compliance with data privacy regulations, such as GDPR or CCPA, is essential for AI companies that handle personal data. Non-compliance can lead to legal issues and a decrease in valuation due to regulatory risks • **Ethical Considerations**: Adherence to ethical guidelines for AI, including bias mitigation and transparency, can enhance a firm's reputation and valuation. Ethical AI practices reduce the risk of public backlash or regulatory scrutiny
Risk Mitigation	• Strong legal protection reduces the risk of intellectual property disputes, which can be costly and time-consuming. Investors often view well-protected AI companies as lower-risk investments, potentially resulting in higher valuations

(continued)

Table 6.1 (continued)

Licensing and Revenue Streams	• Companies with robust intellectual property portfolios can generate revenue through licensing agreements. Licensing AI technology to other companies or industries can create additional income streams, positively impacting valuation
Due Diligence	• During mergers and acquisitions (M&A) or investment rounds, potential investors or acquirers conduct due diligence to assess the legal status of a firm's software assets. Having solid legal protection in place can expedite the due diligence process and instill confidence in stakeholders, possibly leading to a favorable valuation

hardware, since in those days the software was supplied with it and in source format so that the user could adapt it to his needs. It is only with the birth, in the '70s, of companies producing only software that it acquires its independence and therefore requires a legal effort for better protection.

The aspect of the originality of software is of decisive importance for those who produce and develop such products, especially if third parties market products with similar characteristics and content.

6.4 Software as a Prerequisite for Artificial Intelligence

Valuing software is a critical prerequisite for the successful implementation and integration of artificial intelligence (AI) in any system or business. The incorporation of software, notably AI, has notably influenced the economic, financial, and market value domains. The involvement of AI in the process of digitalization has resulted in swift changes within establishments and business frameworks, enriching efficiency and decision-making procedures. Productivity is heightened by generative AI tools, underscoring the interconnectedness between humans and AI in software development. Despite being perceived as a source of escalated productivity and economic advancement, apprehensions persist regarding the potentially disruptive impacts of AI on the economy and society, including the exacerbation of inequality and repercussions on the labor market. The ongoing progressions in AI software are redefining approaches in various sectors, accentuating the escalating importance of AI in propelling economic expansion and market value. The valuation of AI-driven software, concerns several aspects:

a. **Development Costs**: costs incurred in the design, development, and testing. For AI, this might involve the expense of acquiring or generating training data, the development of algorithms, and the cost of computational resources.
b. **Technology and Intellectual Property**: The uniqueness and sophistication of the technology, including any patents or proprietary algorithms, add to the software's value. AI software that offers innovative solutions or advanced capabilities may have a higher valuation.
c. **Market Demand and Application**: The potential market size and application scope of the software influence its value. AI software that can be applied across various industries or addresses a significant market need can be more valuable.
d. **Revenue Generation Potential**: The ability of the software to generate revenue, either through direct sales, subscriptions, or licensing, is a key factor in its valuation. AI software that can open new revenue streams or enhance existing ones is particularly valuable.
e. **Competitive Advantage**: If the software provides a significant competitive edge, such as improving efficiency, reducing costs, or enabling new capabilities, it can be highly valuable. AI software that empowers a business to outperform its competitors is a valuable asset.
f. **Scalability and Performance**: The ability of the software to scale and perform reliably under different conditions is crucial, especially for AI which may require extensive computational resources as it scales.
g. **User Base and Adoption**: Software that has a large and growing user base is typically more valuable. For AI software, the rate of adoption and the user base's growth trajectory can significantly impact valuation.
h. **Regulatory Compliance and Risks**: Compliance with relevant regulations, especially in areas like data privacy and security, is crucial. AI software that meets these regulatory requirements without significant additional investment is more valuable.

i. **Integration and Compatibility**: The ease with which the software can be integrated with existing systems and its compatibility with other technologies affect its value. AI software that is easily integrable can add more value to a business.
j. **Future Potential and Upgradability**: The potential for future enhancements, adaptability to emerging technologies, and the software's ability to evolve with the AI field are important for long-term value.

In the context of AI, these factors take on additional complexity due to the rapidly evolving nature of the technology, the specialized skills required for development and maintenance, and the potential for significant impact on business operations and strategies. The valuation of AI-driven software, therefore, not only reflects its current utility and performance but also its potential to drive future growth and innovation.

The relationship between software and AI is intricate and evolving, as shown in Table 6.2.

AI and software are deeply intertwined, with AI representing a complex and advanced area of software development that pushes the boundaries of what software can achieve, often requiring new approaches and tools compared to traditional software development.

The economic, financial, and market valuation of AI driven software is significant and growing rapidly:

a. Economic impact

AI-driven software is having a significant impact on the global economy in a number of ways. For example, AI-driven software is being used to.

- Automate tasks, reducing costs
- Improve the efficiency of manufacturing and logistics
- Develop new products and services
- Improve business decisions

b. Financial impact

Table 6.2 Relationship between software and artificial intelligence

AI as a Subset of Software	AI is a specific subset of software. All AI systems are software, but not all software systems are AI. AI software is designed to perform tasks that would normally require human intelligence, such as recognition of images, speech, and patterns, and decision-making
Development and Implementation	AI algorithms and models are developed using programming languages and software development tools. This process involves coding, testing, and deploying AI models within software applications
Enhancing Software Capabilities	AI can significantly enhance the capabilities of traditional software. For example, AI can be integrated into software applications to provide personalized user experiences, automate processes, and analyze large datasets
Machine Learning	A significant part of AI involves machine learning (ML), where algorithms learn from data. This learning process is facilitated by software tools and frameworks specifically designed for ML development
Data Processing and Storage	AI systems often require vast amounts of data for training and operation. Software is used to collect, process, store, and manage this data. Databases, data processing frameworks, and cloud computing platforms are integral parts of an AI system's software stack
Ethical and Governance Considerations	As AI becomes more prevalent, software developers and AI practitioners must consider ethical implications and governance issues. This includes ensuring that AI systems are fair, transparent, and respect privacy, which often involves developing and implementing specific software controls and audit mechanisms

(continued)

Table 6.2 (continued)

Evolution of Software Development Practices	The rise of AI has led to new methodologies in software development, including the use of AI for code generation, testing, and optimization. AI is increasingly being used to enhance software development processes themselves
Interdisciplinary Nature	The development of AI software often requires a blend of expertise from computer science, mathematics, domain-specific knowledge, and other fields. This interdisciplinary approach is reflected in the software tools and methodologies used in AI

AI-driven software is also having a significant impact on the financial performance of businesses. For example, AI-driven software can help businesses to:

- Increase revenues
- Reduce costs
- Improve profitability

c. Market valuation

The market valuation of AI-driven software is also growing rapidly.
Some of the main AI software companies are:

- Google AI
- Microsoft AI
- IBM AI
- Amazon AI

These BigTechs develop many AI software products and services, such as.

- Natural language processing (NLP) software
- Machine learning (ML) software

- Computer vision software
- Robotic process automation (RPA) software
- AI-powered decision support systems

AI-driven software is automating tasks, improving efficiency, developing new products and services, and making better business decisions. As a result, AI-driven software is boosting economic growth, creating new jobs, and improving the financial performance of businesses. The market valuation of AI-driven software is also growing rapidly.

Software valuation refers to the financial worth or value of a software product or firm. In the case of AI, software is the underlying technology that enables AI to function. Some key considerations when valuing software as a prerequisite for AI are shown in Table 6.3.

Software valuation as a prerequisite for AI involves a comprehensive assessment of technical, financial, market, and strategic factors. It requires a nuanced understanding of the software's unique attributes and its potential to drive AI-driven solutions in various sectors. Valuation methodologies may vary, but they aim to provide a fair estimate of the software's worth in the context of AI innovation and market dynamics.

Software acts as a prerequisite for AI development and deployment. The main features of software that represent a foundation for AI include:

1. **Flexibility and Adaptability**:
    - AI software must be flexible and adaptable to accommodate various AI algorithms, models, and techniques. It should allow for easy integration of new AI components and frameworks as technology advances.
2. **Scalability**:
    - Scalability is crucial as AI applications often require significant computational resources. Software should scale horizontally (across multiple machines) or vertically (on a single machine) to handle large datasets and complex computations efficiently.
3. **Data Management**:
    - Effective data management capabilities are essential. AI relies on vast amounts of data, and software must support data ingestion, storage, retrieval, and preprocessing efficiently. It

Table 6.3 Valuing software as a prerequisite for artificial intelligence

Intellectual Property (IP) and Technology Assets	The value of AI software often lies in its intellectual property, algorithms, proprietary data, and technology assets. Valuation considers the uniqueness and competitiveness of these assets
Market Demand	The demand for AI software in the market can significantly impact its valuation. High demand for AI solutions in specific industries or use cases can drive up the value of AI software companies
Revenue and Profitability	Traditional financial metrics such as revenue and profitability play a crucial role in determining the valuation of software companies, including those in the AI space. Investors and acquirers assess the potential for generating revenue and achieving profitability
User Base and Adoption	The number of users, customers, or clients using the AI software can influence its valuation. Widespread adoption and a large user base can demonstrate the software's value and potential for growth
Competitive Landscape	The competitive landscape within the AI sector can impact valuation. The presence of strong competitors or the potential for disruption can affect how investors perceive the value of the software
Intellectual Property Protection	The extent to which the software's IP is protected through patents, copyrights, or trade secrets can influence valuation. Strong IP protection can enhance a firm's value
Growth Potential	Valuation also considers the growth potential of the software. AI software that can expand into new markets, industries, or use cases may be valued higher due to its growth prospects
Team and Talent	The expertise and talent of the team behind the software can be a significant factor in valuation. Experienced and skilled AI professionals can add value to the firm

(continued)

Table 6.3 (continued)

Market Trends and Future Outlook	The valuation of AI software is influenced by broader market trends and the outlook for the AI industry. Investors assess the software's position in a rapidly evolving field
Strategic Fit	For potential acquirers, the strategic fit of the AI software with their existing business or product portfolio can impact the valuation. The software's ability to enhance an acquirer's capabilities or address specific strategic goals may justify a higher valuation
Risks and Challenges	Valuation also considers the risks and challenges associated with the AI software, including regulatory compliance, data privacy concerns, and technical limitations
Comparable Transactions	Valuation analysts often look at comparable transactions in the industry to gage the market value of AI software companies. This involves studying similar acquisitions, investments, or IPOs

should also enable data versioning, data quality control, and data integration from diverse sources.

4. **High-Performance Computing**:
    - AI software should be optimized for high-performance computing, capable of leveraging multi-core processors, GPUs, and distributed computing frameworks to process data and train AI models quickly.
5. **Compatibility**:
    - Compatibility with various platforms and operating systems is critical to ensure that AI applications can run on different environments, including cloud platforms, edge devices, and data centers.
6. **Open Source and Libraries**:
    - Many AI projects benefit from open-source software (see https://fastercapital.com/keyword/open-source-technology.html) and libraries that provide prebuilt AI components,

frameworks, and tools. Access to a wide range of open-source resources can accelerate AI development.

7. **Interoperability**:
    - AI software should be able to interact with other software components and systems seamlessly. It should support common data exchange formats and APIs to integrate AI capabilities into existing workflows and applications.
8. **Modularity**:
    - Modular software architecture allows developers to build, test, and update AI components independently. It simplifies the development and maintenance of AI systems, making it easier to add or replace specific functionalities.
9. **Security**:
    - Robust security features are crucial to protect AI models and data. This includes encryption, authentication, access control, and mechanisms to guard against adversarial attacks on AI systems.
10. **Real-time Processing**:
    - Some AI applications require real-time or near-real-time processing capabilities. Software should be designed to support low-latency data processing and decision-making.
11. **Monitoring and Logging**:
    - Effective monitoring and logging capabilities are necessary to track the performance, behavior, and health of AI systems. This aids in troubleshooting, optimization, and compliance with regulatory requirements.
12. **Ease of Development and Deployment**:

- AI software should provide development tools, libraries, and frameworks that simplify the creation of AI applications. Additionally, it should support easy deployment to production environments, cloud platforms, and edge devices.

13. **Customization and Extensibility**:
    - The capacity to tailor-make and extend AI software to match peculiar business or research necessities is essential. It should support the development of proprietary AI models and algorithms.
14. **Documentation and Support**:
    - Comprehensive documentation and robust support resources, such as user guides, tutorials, and forums, are crucial for developers and data scientists working with AI software.
15. **Compliance and Ethics**:
    - AI software should provide features for ethical AI development, such as fairness, bias detection and mitigation, transparency, and compliance with privacy regulations.

AI software plays a vital role in enabling the development, deployment, and successful operation of AI systems across various domains and industries.

6.5 Economic and Financial Valuation

AI-driven software from an economic and financial perspective represents a critical element in contemporary business strategies, as illuminated in several academic studies. AI technologies, characterized by their autonomous and predictive functionalities, are reshaping sectors like financial services, fostering profitability, expansion, and digital innovation, while also presenting regulatory hurdles and influencing competitive dynamics and employment trends. Moreover, AI-powered management systems assume a crucial role in organizing economic endeavors, furnishing valuable data for financial assessments, and sound decision-making within organizations. These observations highlight the escalating significance of AI in steering economic and financial appraisals across diverse industries. The assessment of software's economic and financial worth, especially using AI, is a subject that is garnering increasing attention and importance. The utilization of generative AI tools has the potential to notably boost efficiency by having users incorporate part of recommended code. The software is classified as an intangible asset and, therefore, its valuation is based on the IVS 210 valuation principles normally applicable to intangible assets, to be adapted to the case.

The evaluation of the software must be carried out with an interdisciplinary approach, which considers different aspects together, appreciating its impact from an economic and financial point of view.

The main approaches to evaluating software will be summarized below. In the following paragraphs, a specific analysis will be dedicated to software, as well as to the development companies (software houses).

The distinction between proprietary and open-source software has an impact on the valuation, given that only the proprietary closed code model allows a remuneration based on the exploitation by the user.

The open-source code is not however entirely devoid of potential remuneration, which is based on nonproprietary licensing models or on value co-creation mechanisms in which external developers contribute to improving the software, which can then serve as a basic IT platform for the sale of other related products (e.g., Mobile Apps) to support-oriented buyers.

The evaluation is typically limited to software only, as a separate legal entity, even if in some cases it is associated with other activities—primarily immaterial—which have characteristics of contiguity and affinity with the software.

These complementary assets can represent a synergistic portfolio of intellectual property, expressing an entire firm—as an organized complex of assets—or an organic branch. Among the intangibles closest to software, there are, first, patents (to the point that the software is considered patentable in some systems) or trademarks with which software can be associated. If the software is not yet completed, its nature is similar, first from an economic point of view and always from an evaluative point of view, with the know-how and industrial secrets.

The main approaches—used individually or in a complementary way—of professional practice for estimating the value of intangible resources have already been described in Chapter 2.

The choice of the approaches depends on the type of intangible and the purposes and context of the evaluation, but on the ease with which reliable and significant information can be found on the resource and on the market in which it is strategically positioned.

Figure 6.1 shows the main valuation approaches.

The valuation of the software may conveniently follow these patterns:

a. **Classification as an Intangible Asset**: Software is considered an intangible asset, and its valuation follows the principles outlined in IVS 210 for intangible assets.
b. **Applications of Software Valuation**: Software valuation can be applied in various contexts, including contractual disputes, extra-judicial matters, and cases involving counterfeiting or unfair competition.
c. **Interdisciplinary Approach**: The evaluation of software should take an interdisciplinary approach, considering both economic and financial aspects to assess its impact comprehensively.
d. **Main Approaches to Software Valuation**: valuing software may include market-based, income-based, and cost-based approaches.

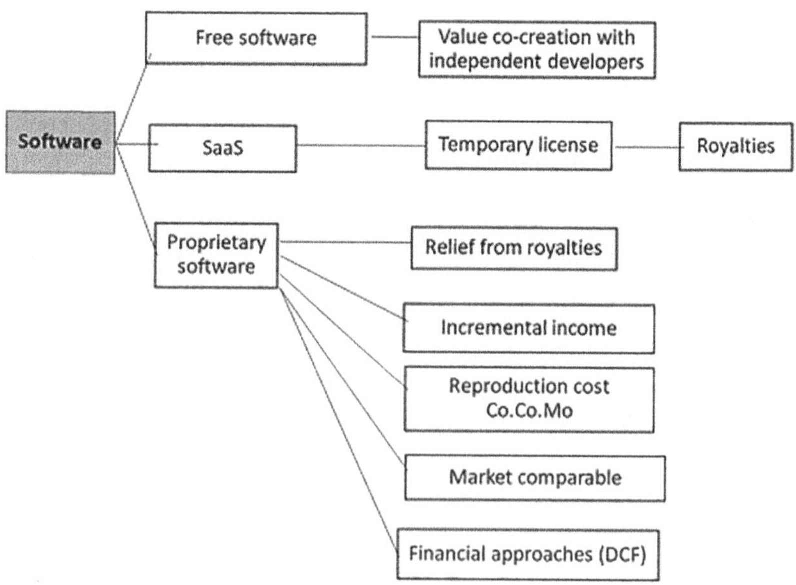

Fig. 6.1 Software valuation approaches

e. **Proprietary vs. Open-Source Software**: The distinction between proprietary and open-source software affects valuation. Proprietary software can generate revenue through user exploitation, while open-source software may generate revenue through nonproprietary licensing models or value co-creation mechanisms.
f. **Focus on Software**: Typically, software is evaluated as a separate legal entity, even if it is associated with other activities. Complementary assets like patents, trademarks, know-how, and industrial secrets can be considered.
g. **Choice of Valuation Approaches**: The choice of valuation approaches depends on the specific type of intangible asset, the purpose of the evaluation, and the availability of reliable market and resource information.

Valuing software-driven AI patterns presents unique challenges and considerations compared to traditional software valuation, as shown in Table 6.4.

Valuing software-driven AI patterns is a complex process that requires a multidisciplinary approach, involving experts in AI, data science, legal, and business domains. The valuation methodology chosen should align with the specific characteristics and market dynamics of the AI patterns in question to provide an accurate assessment of their value. Additionally, given the rapidly evolving nature of AI, regular reassessment of the patterns' value may be necessary to account for changes in the market and technology landscape.

Software House Revenue Model

Software houses are companies specialized in the production of software and applications (operating systems, office automation, design systems, video games ...), both for computers and for other devices (tablets, smartphones, machinery ...).

Among the most famous software houses, are, for example, Adobe Systems, Apple, IBM, Microsoft, Oracle, Symantec ...

The software houses can be distinguished according to the type of product developed (commercial customized, on-demand, individual components, hosting providers ...) and according to the activity carried out (specific products on order or products in series ready-to-use).

Table 6.4 Valuing software-driven artificial intelligence patterns

Data Quality and Quantity	The quality and quantity of data used to train AI models are crucial. High-quality training data can significantly impact the accuracy and effectiveness of AI patterns. Valuation should account for the costs associated with data acquisition, cleaning, and curation
Model Complexity	The complexity of AI models can vary widely, from simple algorithms to deep neural networks with millions of parameters. More complex models may require higher development costs and computational resources, impacting their valuation
Intellectual Property and Patents	If the AI patterns involve unique algorithms, methodologies, or techniques, intellectual property rights and patents may come into play. Valuation should consider the potential value of patents and any licensing agreements
Market Demand	The demand for specific AI patterns in the market plays a significant role in their valuation. Patterns that address critical industry needs or have a competitive advantage may have a higher value
Commercial Viability	The potential commercial applications of AI patterns are essential. Valuation should assess their ability to generate revenue through licensing, subscription models, or integration into products and services
Ethical Considerations	Ethical and regulatory factors may impact the valuation of AI patterns. Compliance with data privacy regulations and ethical AI practices is critical and can affect the legal and reputational value of the patterns
Development and Maintenance Costs	The ongoing costs associated with AI pattern development, maintenance, and updates should be considered. These costs may include the need for continuous training and monitoring
Market Comparables	Comparable transactions in the AI pattern market can provide benchmarks for valuation. Analyzing similar deals and their associated valuations can help assess the relative value of specific patterns

(continued)

Table 6.4 (continued)

Risk Assessment	Valuation should account for the risks associated with AI patterns, such as technological obsolescence, changing market dynamics, and competition from other AI solutions
Team Expertise	The expertise of the development team and their ability to innovate and adapt can influence the valuation. Experienced teams may have a track record of successful AI pattern development
Use Cases and Industries	The applicability of AI patterns across various industries and use cases should be considered. Patterns with broad utility may have higher value than those limited to specific niches
Licensing and Royalties	If the AI patterns are licensed to third parties, the terms of licensing agreements and royalty structures can impact their valuation

Revenues from software houses mainly refer to the sale of software or its licensing, as well as those related to maintenance and periodic customer service contracts (theoretically constant and less volatile).

The license is the contract of use by which the owner of the proprietary software (closed source), defines the legal regime of circulation and limitations in its use and transfer. In the case of free software (open-source), there is no fee for its use. A recent trend followed by some large companies (such as Adobe Systems, for example) is to direct their revenue model more towards temporary (renewable) licensing of program packages rather than to the sale of individual software for perpetual use. In many cases, the software is freely available and is distributed free of charge (freeware) or in shared mode (shareware), with downloads from the Internet.

Many applications (mobile apps installed on the user's device) for smartphones or tablets are free of charge and find their economic rationale in the fact that they allow the user to channel quickly and intuitively towards the use of paid services of e-commerce (App stores) or linked to advertising banners or other revenue models. In many cases, apps are not developed by specialized software houses, but by individual inventors, who sell them or make them available, even for free, on the web, with viral interactions often associated with social networks.

The evaluation of a single (stand-alone) software, generally to be pursued through the approaches of appraisal of intangible resources, tends to differ from the evaluation of software houses, for which it is possible to apply the canonical approaches of evaluation of companies, considering the specificity of their revenue model.

An intrinsic characteristic of the software—and many other intangible resources—is its scalability, as shown in Chapter 3. Its fruition, mainly linked to a download from the web (free or paid or with other indirect remuneration approaches, for example, linked to the fruition of editorial contents or linked to other media), entails, for the owner of the rights, the incurrence of fixed costs associated with negligible variable costs (deriving from each incremental fruition of the software, by new users).

Scalability means that the software house that sells proprietary software, once it has reached an economic break-even point in which revenues equal fixed costs incurred, at that point has additional and incremental revenues, in fact, unrelated to costs that have already been incurred, with significant profiles of economic marginality.

This is not the case for firms that provide software customization services, adapt their platforms to the personalized needs of users, and charge customers for man-hours (body rental), in the absence of the scalability requirements described above.

Replication of software licenses is almost costless for the producer. Hence the direct impact of revenues on the EBIT, and the consequent scalability of the business model.

Applicability of Empirical and Analytical Evaluation Approaches to Software

The applicability to the software of the different evaluation approaches illustrated in Chapter 2 requires an adaptation that considers its intrinsic characteristics, considering the revenue model previously described, if necessary, in a stand-alone perspective, in which the software is considered extractable by the firm and distinctly appraisable.

The evaluation can be carried out for different purposes, even in litigation, in case of unfair competition with appropriation, replication, and/or undue imitation and usurpation of software, in violation of the right of exclusivity.

In this context, the traditional legal concepts based on the emerging damage and, in a perspective, on the loss of profit, are used, projecting the prospective market shares and their contraction, considering the failure to recover the investments made.

The erosion of value derives from its obsolescence and technological upgrades, which eliminate exclusive connotations. The strategic value of software should be appreciated in terms of uniqueness, specificity, non-permeability, and exclusivity, which must be associated with flexible versatility, even in terms of applications to multiple sectors, with customized adaptations.

The main valuation approaches (consistent with the description made in Chapter 2) are:

A. The relief from royalties' approach

The market value of software can be estimated as the sum of the relief from royalties (which the firm would pay as a licensee if the software were not owned) discounted over a given period.

The concept of *reasonable royalty* can be relevant in the field of litigation in the quantification of damages from counterfeiting.

In the evaluation of a firm with software, the presence of license contracts is particularly appreciated by investors, because it generates revenues that are not occasional and constitutes a signal of the technological equity and the innovative capacity of the firm.

The exploitation of the software is alternatively linked to the payment of periodic royalties, one-off amounts, use on consumption (pay per use), periodic maintenance, technical support, updates, etc. Revenues from maintenance, updating, services, etc., in many cases, tend to exceed those related to the product license. This must be considered in the economic estimate, even in the case of counterfeiting

B. The incremental income approach

The value of software depends on its expected economic and financial margin. Therefore, if a going concern is considered, the contribution of software in terms of price and/or volume increases (and therefore of economic margin) to the profitability of the business can be measured through the differential income approach. The value of the software corresponds to the present value of the sum of the differential income that it will presumably produce in the future. The software can, therefore, be evaluated considering its contribution to tangible differential economic benefits and potential future benefits, which are expressed at a premium price.

The number of years of exploitation of the software depends on its life cycle (useful life). A possible variant is based on the estimate of the incremental gross operating margin or other partial economic margins that the software allows obtaining, to which a suitable multiplier is applied, derived from negotiations of comparable software. In addition to or as an alternative to the incremental income, the additional (operating or net) cash flow generated by the software can be considered.

The use of the software acts on the economic margins expressed by the differential between revenues and operating costs since it ideally allows both to increase revenues (with greater direct sales or with royalties from licenses) and to reduce costs, producing with less labor-intensive techniques and savings of other costs (production, organizational, energy ...). The stratification of differential income thanks to the software generates incremental equity, which expresses the differential between the market value and the book value of the firm; it is a suitable element to express the surplus-value of software.

Both the approaches considered here, including the relief from royalties, can be traced, in a broad sense, to the income approaches. They are based on a projection of normalized future incomes, to be discounted in a predefined (or unlimited) time horizon, consistent with the expected useful life of the software, at a reasonable rate. Such a rate incorporates the risk connected to the expected future manifestation of the income, in terms of both "if" and "how much".

C. The estimate of the cost incurred (or of reproduction)

In the absence of available data on income capacity, a possible alternative is that of the cost incurred in the past to create the software and to occupy in the market the positions reached by the same software at the valuation date. It is, therefore, necessary to identify the most significant costs incurred, considering the percentage of sales:

- Research and development costs;
- Costs for raw materials;
- Hours worked;

- Other accessory charges.

The identification of a historical cost of production, based on analytical accounting that allows the functional separation of the costs for the software from the others, is preliminary to the estimate of a current cost of reproduction, having the nature of investment and being oriented to the future economic returns.

A step forward is constituted by the cost of reproduction of a functionally equivalent software that substitutes the historical costs for the costs of reproduction *ex novo*, i.e., the costs that it would be necessary to sustain at the moment of the evaluation to rebuild the same value that the software has reached that very moment.

In this procedure, there is still the limit of not considering the return on investment and the opportunity cost resulting from the immediate failure to use the software. Reproduction costs can potentially be expressed in terms of emerging damage and loss of profit for lost revenues.

The existence of high and uncertain fixed costs connected to the reconstruction of the software represents an entry barrier, which segregates the market and distances competitors.

Among all the intangibles, the software is possibly the most versatile, as it is ubiquitous and indispensable for any application.

Figure 6.2 synthetizes the links of software with the other intangibles and its pivoting role, like that of a digital hub (main link) within a network.

CO.CO.MO Method and Putnam Model

The catalytic influence of AI on the COCOMO software valuation process holds significant importance. By utilizing Artificial Neural Networks alongside backpropagation learning algorithms, scholars have enhanced the forecasting of software development efforts, resulting in superior performance compared to conventional methods. The integration of AI within COCOMO models has displayed encouraging outcomes in decreasing uncertainty and vagueness in software attribute estimations. Furthermore, AI has facilitated the automation of early size estimation techniques, enhancing the precision and efficiency of the process. In general, the fusion of AI with COCOMO models has transformed software cost estimation by offering more precise and dependable forecasts,

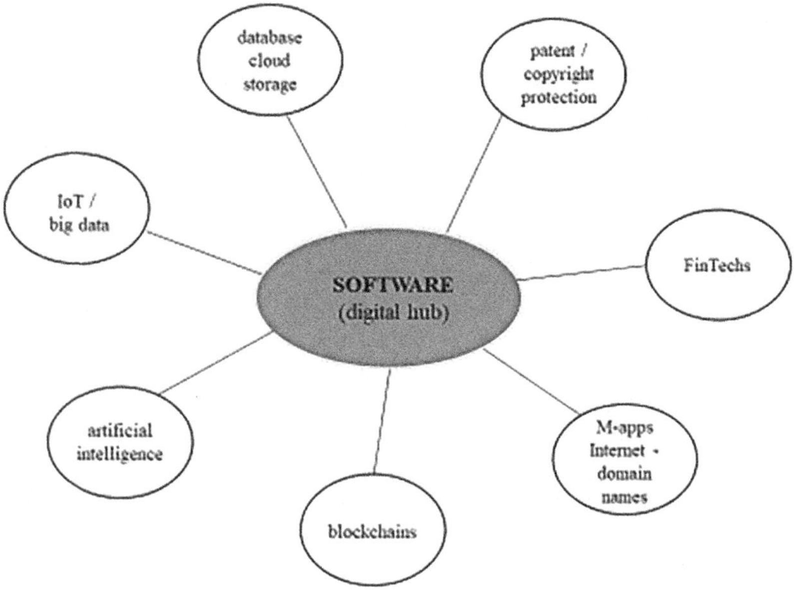

Fig. 6.2 Software as a digital hub

ultimately streamlining the software development process. CO.CO.MO. (COnstructive COst MOdel) is a mathematical model created by Barry Boehm (initially in 1981 and later implemented; see Boehm et al., 2005) to estimate some basic parameters (such as delivery time and man-months) necessary for software development. The model is based on the study of sixty projects (with different lines of code and programming languages) of a Californian automation and software development firm. CO.CO.MO. is considered a static and analytical model; static because the input and output variables are well defined and fixed, analytical because it can be used not necessarily to a project in its entirety but also to its parts. There are three different versions of the model, which differ in the precision with which the different values are estimated:

- Basic—the estimate is made starting from the size of the software to be developed and calculated in KNCSS.
- Intermediate—it calculates the software development effort as a function of the size of the program, always expressed in KNCSS,

and on a set of cost drivers, which include the subjective assignment of product, hardware, design, and personal attributes evaluations;

- Advanced/detailed—incorporates all the features of the intermediate version, with an assessment of the impact of the various costs for each step (analysis, design ...) of the software engineering process.

CO.CO.MO. can be applied to the following three classes of software projects:

- Organic: small projects, where teams of a few people work on a set of strict requirements;
- Semi-detached—are in the middle of the three types (both in size and complexity) are suitable for software projects in which teams with average experience work on medium-level requirements.
- Embedded—are projects that need to be developed with limited hardware and with software and operational constraints.

The CO.CO.MO. basic equation expresses the number of people required for the development of software as a ratio between the effort applied per person/month (depending on the estimate of lines of code for the project) and the development time in months, based on empirical coefficients, different according to the class of project (above mentioned).

The Constructive Cost Model (COCOMO) is a well-known and widely used method for estimating the effort, time, and cost required to develop software projects. It was developed by Barry Boehm in the 1980s and has since undergone several updates. COCOMO is primarily used for software project estimation and planning. The main features of the COCOMO method are:

1. **Three Models**:
   - COCOMO is divided into three models, each tailored for different levels of project complexity and development stages:
     - COCOMO I: Basic model for early-stage project estimation.
     - COCOMO II: Intermediate model for more detailed and accurate estimates.
     - COCOMO III: Advanced model for complex, distributed, and real-time software systems.

2. **Effort Estimation**:
    - COCOMO estimates the amount of effort (usually measured in person-months) required to complete a software project. Effort estimation is a central feature of the method.
3. **Cost Estimation**:
    - The method provides estimates of the total project cost based on the estimated effort and cost rates for personnel.
4. **Time Estimation**:
    - COCOMO includes estimates of the project's development time, typically measured in months.
5. **Inputs and Outputs**:
    - COCOMO relies on various input parameters, such as lines of code, development mode, personnel characteristics, and project attributes.
    - It produces output estimates for effort, cost, and time.
6. **Development Modes**:
    - COCOMO considers different development modes, including organic, semi-detached, and embedded. These modes reflect variations in project size, complexity, and team dynamics.
7. **Size Estimation**:
    - COCOMO uses different size metrics, such as lines of code (LOC) or function points, to quantify the size of the software project. The size metric chosen depends on the model and project specifics.
8. **Risk Management**:
    - The method incorporates risk management factors that account for project uncertainties and potential risks. Risk analysis is an important feature of COCOMO II and III.
9. **Personnel Factors**:

- COCOMO considers various personnel factors, including experience, capability, and team cohesion, to adjust effort and cost estimates based on the project team's characteristics.

10. **Lifecycle Phases**:
    - COCOMO II and III recognize different phases of the software development lifecycle, such as requirements analysis, design, implementation, testing, and maintenance. Estimates are provided for each phase.
11. **Customization**:
    - COCOMO can be customized to fit the specific characteristics of a project, industry, or organization. Customization allows for more accurate estimates.
12. **Parametric Model**:
    - COCOMO is a parametric model, meaning that it relies on mathematical equations and coefficients to generate estimates based on input values.
13. **Accuracy Improvement**:
    - COCOMO II and III are considered more accurate and comprehensive than the original COCOMO I model, as they account for a wider range of factors.
14. **Documentation and Tools**:
    - Several software tools and documentation support the application of COCOMO, making it more accessible to practitioners.

COCOMO is widely used in the software engineering industry for project planning, budgeting, and resource allocation. It provides a structured approach to estimating the size and effort required for software development projects, helping organizations make informed decisions and manage project risks.

The Putnam model (1978) stands as a pioneering empirical approach to estimating software development effort and time. This model, deeply rooted in the application of mathematical and statistical principles, provides a framework for forecasting the resources necessary to complete a software project based on its anticipated size. The utilization of the Putnam model, specifically the CDP algorithm, has been employed in AI to tackle the computational intricacies associated with counting models of propositional formulas. A comprehensive strategy for model-centric software development tailored for AI-powered systems, encompassing IoT, can be realized, thereby boosting the effectiveness and performance of such systems. The Putnam Model considers various essential components, such as the project's size (quantified in lines of code or function points), the productivity rate of the development team, the total effort needed, the calendar time required for project completion, the number of resources within the team, and a productivity adjustment factor that considers project-specific factors like software complexity and team experience. The model highlights the direct correlation between project size, team productivity, and the overall effort necessary for project completion. Although the Putnam Model and its adaptations offer a fundamental structure for project estimation and resource distribution, it is crucial to complement it with additional project management strategies and risk assessment techniques to enhance the accuracy of predictions and facilitate effective decision-making in software development initiatives.

The model also introduces the concept of a "time to develop" equation, linking the effort needed with the time span of the project, emphasizing the non-linear relationship between project size, and required effort/time. This relationship illustrates that as software projects grow, they require disproportionately more effort and time to complete, a reflection of the increasing complexity and communication overhead associated with larger projects. The Putnam model's reliance on historical data for calibration is one of its distinguishing characteristics. Calibration involves adjusting the model's parameters based on past project data to improve its accuracy for future project estimations. This process acknowledges that productivity can vary significantly between organizations or even within an organization over time, influenced by factors such as team experience, technology used, and process maturity. One of the key features of the Putnam model is its use of the equation:

$$Process\ Productivity = \frac{Size}{\frac{Effort}{B}^{1/3}\ Time^{4/3}} \tag{6.1}$$

By focusing on easily measurable factors such as project size, effort, and duration, the model provides a straightforward framework for estimating software project effort. This simplicity allows software development organizations of varying maturity levels to collect and utilize relevant data from past projects effectively.

The distinction between conventional productivity (based on size/effort) and process productivity is another key aspect of Putnam's model. By separating these two components, Putnam provides a more nuanced understanding of productivity within software development projects. Process productivity, which accounts for factors such as team experience, tools, and methodologies, is crucial for accurately estimating effort requirements.

Here are the key components of the Putnam Model:

1. **Size of the Project (S)**: This is typically measured in lines of code (LOC) or function points. It represents the scale or scope of the software project.
2. **Productivity Rate (P)**: This is the rate at which the development team can produce lines of code or function points. It is often expressed in terms of LOC per person-month or function points per person-month.
3. **Effort (E)**: Effort is the total human effort required to complete the project.
4. **Calendar Time (T)**: Calendar time is the total duration required to complete the project.
5. **Number of Resources**: This represents the size of the development team working on the project. It can impact both effort and duration.
6. **Productivity Adjustment Factor (PAF)**: it considers project-specific factors that affect productivity.

6.6 Artificial Intelligence-Driven Economic and Financial Valuation of Software

AI plays a crucial role in the economic and financial assessment of software by facilitating sophisticated analysis and decision-making procedures. AI-driven systems, such as personalized digital replicas and valuation systems based on deep learning technology, substantially contribute to evaluating the economic worth of innovative technologies and assist in making strategic decisions for organizations. The collaborative concept of co-creating value between AI and developers highlights the potential for automating AI in software development, underscoring the synergy between AI and human knowledge in generating value for businesses and society through software systems. The economic and financial valuation of software has a significant impact on the valuation of AI initiatives:

1. **Economic and Financial Valuation of Software**:
   - **Asset Valuation**: Software is considered an intangible asset on a firm's balance sheet. Its valuation involves assessing the cost of development or acquisition, ongoing maintenance costs, and estimating its useful life.
   - **Revenue Generation**: In some cases, software generates revenue directly through licensing or subscription models. Its financial valuation considers the software's revenue streams, customer base, and growth potential.
   - **Cost–Benefit Analysis**: Organizations evaluate the economic value of software by conducting cost–benefit analyses. This implies comparing the costs of developing, maintaining, and licensing software to the benefits, such as increased efficiency, productivity, and revenue generation.
   - **Market Comparables**: For software companies, market comparables play a role in valuation. This involves looking at the valuations of similar software companies in the market to determine a fair market value.
2. **Impact on AI Valuation**:
   - **AI Software Assets**: AI initiatives often heavily rely on software, including AI algorithms, machine learning frameworks, and data processing software. The economic and financial valuation of these software assets is crucial in determining the overall value of an AI project.
   - **Revenue Generation**: AI applications, especially those involving AI-driven products or services, can have a direct impact on revenue generation. The financial valuation of AI projects considers their potential to increase revenue, reduce costs, or create new revenue streams.

- **Cost of Development**: AI development typically requires significant investment in software development, data acquisition, and hardware infrastructure. The cost of developing AI software components is factored into the overall valuation of AI projects.
- **Market Opportunity**: The market opportunity for AI-driven products and services is assessed as part of AI valuation. Software plays a critical role in delivering AI solutions to the market, and the quality, scalability, and uniqueness of the underlying software impact the valuation.
- **Intellectual Property**: AI projects often involve the creation of unique algorithms, models, and software. The intellectual property associated with AI software can have a substantial impact on valuation, especially if it is protected and has commercial potential.
- **Data Assets**: AI relies on data, and the software used to manage, process, and analyze data is a crucial component. Data assets and the software associated with them contribute to the overall value of AI projects.
- **Operational Efficiency**: AI-driven software can significantly improve operational efficiency. The economic valuation of AI considers how software-driven AI solutions reduce costs and enhance productivity within an organization.
- **Scalability**: The scalability of AI software assets can influence valuation. Software that is easily scalable to accommodate growing data volumes and user loads is seen as a valuable asset.

The economic and financial valuation of software is intertwined with the valuation of AI. AI projects often rely heavily on software components, and their success and potential value are closely tied to the quality, effectiveness, and marketability of the underlying software. A comprehensive valuation of AI includes an assessment of the software assets and their contribution to the overall economic and financial value of the project.

6.7 Open-Source Software

Open-source software is open-source meaning that its source code is left to the availability of any developers, with a free circulation of information about the programs, freely modifiable.

Open-source software (OSS) has distinct features that impact the development and deployment of AI applications:

1. **Accessible Source Code**:
    - Open-source software is its source code's gate, enabling developers to view, change, and distribute it freely. This openness fosters transparency and collaboration within the AI community.
2. **Community Collaboration**:
    - OSS projects often have large and diverse developer communities. In the context of AI, this means that a global network of experts can collaborate on improving AI algorithms, libraries, and tools.
3. **Cost-Effective**:
    - Open-source AI tools and frameworks are typically free to use, reducing the financial barriers to AI development and research. This affordability encourages experimentation and innovation.
4. **Customization**:
    - Developers can customize open-source AI software to meet specific project requirements. This flexibility is invaluable for tailoring AI models and algorithms to unique use cases.
5. **Rapid Innovation**:
    - Open-source AI projects evolve quickly due to community contributions. This rapid pace of innovation results in continuously improved AI algorithms and tools.
6. **Peer Review**:
    - The open-source model promotes peer review of code and algorithms, enhancing the quality and reliability of AI solutions. Bugs and vulnerabilities are often identified and fixed promptly.

7. **Interoperability**:
    - Many open-source AI libraries and tools are designed to work well together. This interoperability simplifies the integration of various AI components into comprehensive solutions.
8. **Large Ecosystem**:
    - A vast ecosystem of open-source AI software exists, encompassing deep learning frameworks, as well as AI libraries for natural language processing (NLP) and computer vision.
9. **Reduced Vendor Lock-In**:
    - Organizations can avoid vendor lock-in by using open-source AI tools. They have the freedom to switch between software solutions and service providers without constraints.
10. **Global Adoption**:
    - Open-source AI tools enjoy widespread adoption across industries, making them well-supported and maintained. This global adoption ensures their longevity and relevance.
11. **Ethical Considerations**:
    - Open-source AI aligns with ethical considerations of transparency, fairness, and accountability. It allows scrutiny of AI algorithms and models to identify and mitigate biases and ethical concerns.
12. **Educational Resources**:
    - OSS provides educational resources such as tutorials, documentation, and online communities that help individuals and organizations learn and adopt AI technologies effectively.
13. **AI Research**:
    - Open-source AI frameworks and datasets facilitate AI research by providing a common foundation for experimentation and benchmarking.
14. **Innovation in AI Applications**:

- Open-source AI accelerates innovation in AI applications by enabling developers to leverage cutting-edge algorithms and tools without reinventing the wheel.

Open-source software's features greatly impact the development, accessibility, and democratization of AI applications. They foster collaboration, reduce costs, and drive innovation within the AI community, ultimately leading to the widespread adoption and advancement of AI technologies across various industries.

Open-source AI software is characterized by several key features and has brought about various positive impacts:

6.8 Impact of Open-Source AI Software

1. **Accessibility**, as shown above.
2. **Community Collaboration**: Open-source projects have a worldwide community of developers, researchers, and enthusiasts who cooperate to improve and enhance the software. This collective effort accelerates development and ensures robustness.
3. **Transparency**: Open-source AI software is transparent, enabling users to examine the code and algorithms. This transparency builds trust, encourages scrutiny, and helps identify and rectify potential biases or errors.
4. **Customization and Flexibility**: Users can change and customize open-source AI software. This adaptability is crucial for a wide range of applications and industries.
5. **Cost Savings**: Open-source AI software eliminates licensing fees, making it cost-effective for organizations and individuals. This can lead to significant cost savings in AI development projects.
6. **Education and Learning**: Open-source AI software provides valuable resources for learning and skill development. Students, researchers, and aspiring AI practitioners can gain hands-on experience and knowledge.
7. **Innovation**: Open-source AI fosters innovation by enabling rapid experimentation and collaboration. It plays a pivotal role in advancing AI research and development.

Main Features of Open-Source AI Software:

1. **Open Licensing**: Open-source AI software is typically released under licenses, such as the GNU General Public License (GPL) or the Apache License, that grant users the freedom to use, change, and distribute the software.
2. **Collaborative Development**: Open-source AI projects often have a decentralized, collaborative development model. Contributions come from individuals and organizations.
3. **Community Support**: Open-source projects typically involve active online networks where users and developers can seek help, share knowledge, and discuss improvements.
4. **Version Control**: Open-source projects use version control systems, like Git, to manage and track changes to the codebase, ensuring transparency and collaboration.
5. **Documentation**: Good open-source projects make comprehensive documentation available, together with tutorials, and guides to help users run the software effectively.
6. **Regular Updates**: Active open-source projects receive regular updates and bug fixes, ensuring that the software remains reliable and secure.
7. **Wide Range of Libraries and Tools**: Open-source AI ecosystems offer a wide array of libraries and tools, catering to various AI needs.
8. **Interoperability**: Many open-source AI tools and libraries are designed to be interoperable, enabling users to combine and use them in conjunction with one another.
9. **Ethical and Responsible AI**: Some open-source AI projects focus on ethical and responsible AI development, incorporating fairness, transparency, and accountability principles into their code and documentation.

Open-source AI software has democratized access to AI technology, accelerated AI development, and facilitated a collaborative and transparent approach to building AI solutions. It continues to play a vital role in shaping the AI landscape and driving innovation in the field.

6.9 Software as a Service (SaaS)

Software as a Service (SaaS) is a prominent software distribution model in cloud and fog computing. It involves a third-party provider hosting applications and making them available to customers over the Internet. This model offers various advantages such as accessibility from any location with an internet connection, scalability to accommodate changing user needs, and reduced IT infrastructure and maintenance costs for users. The convergence of AI and developers in collaboratively creating software for both business and societal advantages represents a hopeful vision that underscores the partnership between AI and human proficiency. AI-enhanced service operations have demonstrated notable improvements in service provision, response time reduction, enhanced customer satisfaction, and cost savings generation, underscoring the considerable business value that AI contributes to IT service operations. Assessing the business ramifications of AI-driven IT service operations is imperative for organizations seeking to streamline procedures and fortify resilience in swiftly evolving landscapes. Appraising the value of AI-powered SaaS necessitates a sophisticated approach that acknowledges the distinct attributes of SaaS frameworks and the transformative capacity of AI in software development and operations.

SaaS is part of the broader spectrum of cloud computing services, with Infrastructure as a Service (IaaS) and Platform as a Service (PaaS) being the other two main categories. While IaaS provides virtualized computing resources over the internet, and PaaS offers a platform for developing, running, and managing applications, SaaS focuses on delivering software applications directly to end-users.

The concept of SaaS is not entirely new and is closely related to earlier models such as Application Service Provider (ASP) and on-demand computing software delivery. However, SaaS has gained significant traction due to advancements in internet connectivity, improved security measures, and the growing demand for flexible and cost-effective software solutions.

SaaS has revolutionized the way businesses and individuals' access and utilize software applications, offering convenience, flexibility, and cost-effectiveness in comparison to traditional software deployment models.

SaaS has emerged as a major force in the software industry, challenging traditional perpetual software vendors with its unique business model and advantages. One key aspect of SaaS is its pricing model, which typically charges customers based on usage or subscription rather than a one-time licensing fee. This approach offers greater flexibility for customers, allowing them to scale their usage up or down as needed, while also potentially reducing upfront costs. SaaS providers often deliver continuous updates and improvements to their software (Guo & Ma, 2018), enhancing its quality and functionality over time. This ongoing innovation can provide significant value to customers, ensuring that they have access to the latest features and capabilities without the need for expensive upgrades or migrations.

SaaS offers organizations the opportunity to streamline their IT operations. By offloading the responsibility for software maintenance, updates, and infrastructure management to the SaaS provider, organizations can focus their resources on core business activities rather than IT management tasks. This can lead to cost savings (Safari et al., 2015), improved efficiency, and greater agility in responding to changing business needs. SaaS represents a transformative shift in the software industry, offering organizations a flexible, cost-effective, and efficient way to access and utilize software applications. As SaaS continues to evolve and mature, its impact on businesses of all sizes is likely to grow, driving further innovation and adoption in the years to come.

SaaS represents an opportunity for trendy software houses to expand traditional business models, reaching new clients with digital (cloud) scalability.

SaaS is a cloud computing model. SaaS has specific features that influence its impact on AI applications, as shown in Table 6.5.

SaaS offers features that impact on AI applications, making AI more accessible, cost-effective, and scalable for organizations and individuals. SaaS platforms provide the infrastructure, tools, and services necessary to build, deploy, and manage AI solutions, enabling businesses to leverage AI's capabilities without the need for extensive in-house resources.

6.10 Databases and Artificial Intelligence

In computer science, the term database means a set of data, homogeneous in content and format, stored in a computer and interrogated via a terminal using the access keys provided. The assessment of databases and AI encompasses the evaluation of the value and influence of these technologies in different fields. Machine learning within AI plays a vital role in the enhancement of database structures and performance optimization. The amalgamation of AI with big data offers decision-makers a broader perspective and valuable insights, notwithstanding the challenges related to uncertainty management and the creation of new models to address the intricacies of data-centric choices. The rapid expansion of AI applications

Table 6.5 Software as a service and artificial intelligence

Accessibility and Availability	SaaS applications are accessible from anywhere with an internet connection, making AI tools and solutions available to a broader audience of users and devices
Scalability	SaaS platforms can scale computing resources as needed, which is crucial for AI applications that may require significant computational power for tasks like machine learning model training
Cost Efficiency	SaaS eliminates the need for organizations to invest in and maintain on-premises hardware and software infrastructure. This reduces ongoing maintenance expenses and upfront costs for AI projects
Frequent Updates and Improvements	SaaS providers often release regular updates and enhancements to their software, ensuring that AI applications stay current with the latest features, security patches, and improvements
Data Management and Integration	SaaS platforms often include tools for data storage, management, and integration. This is critical for AI applications that rely on large datasets for training and analysis
Collaboration and Sharing	SaaS applications enable collaboration among distributed teams, making it easier for data scientists, developers, and other stakeholders to work together on AI projects
Real-Time Processing	Some SaaS platforms offer real-time processing capabilities, which are valuable for AI applications that require immediate analysis and decision-making
AI Integration	SaaS providers may offer AI-specific services and integrations, such as AI APIs, to simplify the incorporation of AI capabilities into applications
Security and Compliance	Reputable SaaS providers invest in robust security measures and compliance certifications, addressing concerns related to data security and privacy in AI applications
Cost-Effective AI Services	SaaS providers may offer AI-specific services, such as AI model deployment, natural language processing (NLP) APIs, and image recognition services

(continued)

Table 6.5 (continued)

Accessibility of AI Tools	SaaS-based AI tools and platforms make advanced AI capabilities, like machine learning and data analytics, more accessible to businesses and individuals without requiring deep technical expertise
Rapid Prototyping and Development	SaaS platforms allow developers to rapidly prototype and develop AI applications, accelerating time-to-market for AI-powered solutions
Reduced IT Burden	SaaS offloads the burden of software maintenance, updates, and infrastructure management from IT teams, enabling them to focus on AI development and integration
Subscription-Based Pricing	SaaS typically follows a subscription-based pricing model, which can align AI costs with actual usage and scale as needed, reducing financial risk in AI projects

exploits self-learning capabilities and collaborations with human intelligence to achieve exceptional results, particularly in sectors such as real estate appraisal, where AI models demonstrate potential but necessitate further refinement and investigation to improve precision and practicality. The joint consideration of databases and AI entails comprehending their possibilities, constraints, and evolving significance in influencing decision-making processes across diverse sectors.

The most similar intangible asset to the database is the software, which consists of information used by computer systems, stored on a computer medium (hardware, as a physical component of a computer system), and represented by one or more programs.

The database is incorporated in hardware (physical or more and more frequently in the cloud) and is fed and interrogated with specific software. The connection between these types of intangible assets, which are highly complementary, is important for their legal framework and economic development.

Users interface with databases through so-called query languages (search or query queries, insertion, deletion, updating, etc.) and thanks to special dedicated software applications (DBMS).

The databases may have various structures (computer architectures), including the following:

1. Hierarchical (represented by a tree);
2. Reticular (represented by a graph);
3. Relational (currently the most widespread, representable through tables and relations between them);
4. Object-oriented (extension to databases of the "object-oriented" paradigm, typical of object-oriented programming);
5. Semantic (representable with a relational graph).

In the field of database use/administration, any operation on the database by the user/administrator on DBMS can be obtained through an appropriate language through a DBMS manager with a graphical interface or a command-line interface.

The server is the part of the DBMS that provides the services of the use of the database to other programs and other computers, according to the client/server mode. The server stores data receives client requests and processes appropriate responses.

The features of databases play a significant role in influencing the performance and functionality of AI applications. Table 6.6 shows some key features of databases and how they impact AI applications.

Databases are foundational to AI applications by providing a structured and efficient means of storing and accessing data. The features of databases impact AI applications by influencing data quality, availability, and processing speed, all of which are critical for the development and deployment of AI models and systems. The utilization of AI in financial domains such as asset management, risk mitigation using extensive data, and insurance has transformed the financial sector. The advent of AI has resulted in the generation and dissemination of copious amounts of data within financial market frameworks, catering to the escalating demand fueled by AI applications in finance. As AI continues to progress, its influence on society, enterprises, cultural norms, and individuals is profound, carrying implications for data protection and the potential expenses linked to ensuring security in the digital era.

6.11 Legal Protection

Legal protections have a significant impact on AI-driven databases. Various legal frameworks, such as data protection laws, database rights, and regulations like the EU GDPR and the proposal for the Artificial

Table 6.6 Databases and artificial intelligence

Data Storage	Databases store large volumes of structured and unstructured data, including text, images, videos, and more. This diverse data can be used as input for AI algorithms
Data Retrieval	Databases offer efficient mechanisms to retrieve specific data quickly. This is crucial for AI applications that need to access and process data in real-time or with low latency
Data Indexing	Indexes in databases accelerate data retrieval by creating a data structure that allows for quick lookup of records. AI applications benefit from faster data access when using indexed databases
Data Consistency	Databases ensure data consistency and integrity through ACID (Atomicity, Consistency, Isolation, Durability) properties. This ensures that AI models are trained on reliable and accurate data
Data Security	Databases offer security features such as access control and encryption, which are essential for safeguarding sensitive data used by AI systems
Data Scalability	Scalable databases can handle increasing amounts of data, which is essential as AI applications often require access to ever-expanding datasets
Data Versioning	Version control features in some databases help AI teams track changes to data over time, allowing for reproducibility and auditing of experiments and model training
Data Integration	Databases can integrate with various data sources, making it easier to gather and preprocess data from different systems, which is often necessary for AI applications
Query Language Support	SQL (Structured Query Language) and NoSQL databases provide query languages that allow developers to extract, transform, and load (ETL) data for AI model training and inference
Real-time Processing	Some databases offer real-time data streaming and processing capabilities, which are crucial for AI applications that require immediate responses or real-time insights
Data Warehousing	Data warehousing databases can store historical data, enabling AI applications to perform analytics and predictions based on long term trends

(continued)

Table 6.6 (continued)

Replication and High Availability	Databases with replication and high availability features ensure that AI applications have continuous access to data, even in the event of hardware failures
Support for Large Models	AI applications that use large models may require databases with high I/O performance and the ability to store and serve model parameters efficiently

Intelligence Act, play a crucial role. These regulations affect AI development, training, and utilization by imposing responsibilities on those constructing datasets to ensure compliance with the law. Moreover, the transparency of AI systems is a significant concern under data protection laws, prompting inquiries into acceptable usage and the entitlement to an explanation for individuals impacted by AI decisions. Additionally, European regulations concerning the protection of databases may restrict the reusability of data for AI advancement, thereby requiring reforms such as introducing rights for data users to improve access and the reuse of non-personal data by startups and small to medium-sized enterprises. The problem of creating databases populated by progressively accumulated and ordered information, together with access to it, is intertwined with copyright protection and with software, within an international framework.

According to the provisions of Dir. 96/9/EC, there is a double track of protection for databases: on the one hand, there is a reference to copyright, so that "databases which, because of the choice or the arrangement of the material, constitute a creation of the author's intellectual property are protected as such by copyright"; this protection under copyright "does not extend to their content and does not affect existing rights on such content".

According to Recital 15, "the criteria to be applied to determine whether a database is protected by copyright should be limited to the fact that the choice or arrangement of the content of the database constitutes an intellectual creation, which is the author's own; that this protection concerns the structure of the database" and "no criteria other than originality, in the sense of intellectual creation, should be applied to determine whether or not a database is protected by copyright, and in particular no assessment of the quality or aesthetic value of the database should be made".

A very important aspect concerns the protection of privacy, especially considering databases that collect sensitive data (such as health data, bank details, etc.). In this context, they detect cybersecurity issues related to improper access or blockages of databases and the inherent liability profiles of different subjects, with civil and/or criminal profiles.

6.12 Information Value Chain, *Data Mining* and Interaction with Networks, Big Data, and the Internet of Things

The value chain relating to the information supply chain is based on a series of steps and processes (organizational, managerial, etc.), individually represented by consequential links, which can be expressed at the IT level through algorithms. Each link in the chain represents a point of connection with the previous and subsequent steps, with incremental added value taking on economic and legal significance (at the contractual level and, if necessary, in the case of litigation). AI, through the utilization of deep learning algorithms, plays a crucial role in enhancing decision making processes by minimizing bounded rationality, optimizing managerial decisions, and automating tasks. It serves as a means of innovation, altering innovation processes towards more data-centric research and encouraging the procurement of extensive datasets for competitive advantages. The capabilities of AI, such as comprehension of text, decision-making, and predictive analytics, are transforming fields like cancer detection, drug development, and nuclear fusion regulation, signifying a revolutionary technological influence across social and economic sectors. AI-driven service operations enhance efficiency, lower costs, and boost customer satisfaction in IT service management, demonstrating the concrete business value that AI contributes to operational processes. Within the supply chain, AI's compatibility with natural language processing, machine learning, and decision-making plays a role in establishing sustainable competitive advantages through enhanced forecasting, planning, and resource management, underlining the essentiality of AI for future supply chain structures and value generation. What is important is the synergistic contribution of the individual links to the composition of a unitary chain. The logical-sequential steps (relevant from a legal point of view) for the databases are as follows:

1. Data collection;
2. Organization of the data;
3. Data processing;
4. Analysis of the results;
5. Archiving (storage, basically in the cloud) and indexing;
6. Usability and sharing.

Data collection is the first—fundamental—link in the value chain and takes place by attracting, often in a complementary way, to different sources, among which the following ones are collected:

- Digital platforms (for the intermediate interchange of data, transactions, etc.);
- Sensors/Internet of Things (IoT);
- (Social) networks;
- New media;
- Wireless protocols;
- Encrypted and tracked internet access.

The next steps (organization, processing, analysis, archiving, sharing) take place through increasingly automated algorithms in a sequential perspective, also through automatisms driven by AI.

The organization of the data is based on:

- Classification;
- Coupling/correlation;
- Connectivity.

Data processing, on the other hand, is based on:

- Computational methods;
- Calculation tools.

Archiving is increasingly based on cloud storage technologies in remote archives (with delicate legal issues, such as data retention, access restrictions, real-time usability, privacy protection, etc.).

The use of the information that populates the databases is in perspective, increasingly relevant for procedures:

- Strategic planning and management;
- Descriptive, prescriptive, and predictive analyses;
- Performance monitoring;
- Functional analysis;
- Support in experimental analysis;
- Production optimization.

The progressive increase in the size of the data that populate the databases (big data) is linked to the need for analysis of a single set of data, to extract additional information compared to that which could be obtained by analyzing small series, with the same total amount of data.

In this context, databases exploit data mining, a set of techniques and methodologies that have as their object the extraction of knowledge, starting from large quantities of data (through automatic or semi-automatic methods), and the scientific, industrial, or operational use of this knowledge. Data mining is often preceded by harmonization of the same data, especially if derived from heterogeneous and unstructured sources, through data fusion processes.

Data analysis technologies are becoming part of many aspects of everyday life (sensors, biometrics, domotics, communications...). The Internet of Things (IoT) interacts with databases, especially in the phase of feeding information flows. It is based on a family of innovative technologies (chips, wired and wireless sensors, tags, QR codes, radio frequency RFID identifications, etc.), which connect inanimate objects (gadgets ...) in smart devices always connected to the web (such as mobile phones), to collect, exchange and process data in real-time.

The innovative paradigms that govern the IoT move around networks that connect sensors and actuators with the Internet.

The examination of the information value chain, subdivided into its fundamental components, is important in the legal sphere, to understand the problems of causal links, and the responsibility, from a contractual point of view or in litigation. Investments in AI may result in diverse effects on economic, financial, and market values. The significance of Information Value within the context of the IoT environment, in combination with AI, brings about complexities in the process of value extraction owing to the overwhelming volume of information and the inherent intelligence of the system.

6.13 Economic Valuation of Database and Links with Cloud Computing

Assessing the economic value of AI-driven databases holds great importance in the contemporary data-centric commercial environment. The combination of AI and big data presents substantial prospects for generating value. Organizations that utilize AI technologies can optimize business operations, improve decision-making processes, and generate additional revenue streams through efficient data monetization. Within the healthcare industry, for instance, AI tools such as diabetic retinopathy screening demonstrate cost-effectiveness, underscoring the potential economic advantages of AI integration. Moreover, AI-driven solutions facilitate digital transformation, empowering businesses to maximize their value proposition and revolutionize their operational frameworks. Comprehending the economic consequences of AI in database management is imperative for enterprises seeking to remain competitive and leverage the prevailing data-focused market dynamics. The value of a database cannot always be estimated considering it as an independent "legal asset" (in this case, the declination of software) since it is within a wider context that it finds a complete framework.

The database can, therefore, be estimated within a portfolio of intangible resources and be linked to patents or trademarks and logos (think, for example, of the value of the Bloomberg brand in the field of economic and financial information).

Cloud computing revolutionizes how businesses and individuals' access and utilize computing resources, offering a shift from traditional on-premises IT infrastructure to services hosted on the Internet. This model provides several key advantages:

a. **Cost Efficiency**: One of the primary benefits of cloud computing is the reduction in capital and operational expenses. Users don't need to invest heavily in hardware, software, or the maintenance of their

IT infrastructure. Instead, they pay for only what they use, which can significantly lower operating costs.

b. **Scalability**: Cloud services are inherently scalable, offering flexibility that traditional IT cannot match. Users can easily increase or decrease their computing resources based on demand, ensuring that they always have the right amount of capacity without paying for idle resources.
c. **Innovation and Agility**: With cloud computing, businesses can deploy and iterate on applications more quickly than if they had to manage infrastructure and software updates themselves. This agility allows for faster innovation and the ability to respond to market changes or customer needs with minimal delay.
d. **Global Reach**: Cloud providers typically have data centers located around the world. This global presence enables users to deploy their applications in locations closest to their customers, improving performance and user experience due to reduced latency.
e. **Performance and Reliability**: Major cloud service providers invest heavily in securing their infrastructure and ensuring high levels of service availability. They offer a reliable environment with guarantees around uptime, data protection, and disaster recovery.
f. **Security**: While security remains a top concern, cloud providers often have robust security measures in place that can exceed what businesses might afford on their own. This includes physical security of data centers, cybersecurity measures, and compliance with various regulatory standards.
g. **Advanced Services**: Beyond basic computing resources, cloud platforms offer a wide range of services, including advanced analytics, artificial intelligence, machine learning capabilities, and Internet of Things (IoT) integration. These services allow users to build and deploy sophisticated applications and insights that would be challenging to implement on-premises.

The main features of cloud computing are synthesized in Fig. 6.3.

Numerous industries are implementing cloud computing as part of their business processes. Valuation patterns may be concerned not only with public or private cloud but also with their impact on traditional businesses.

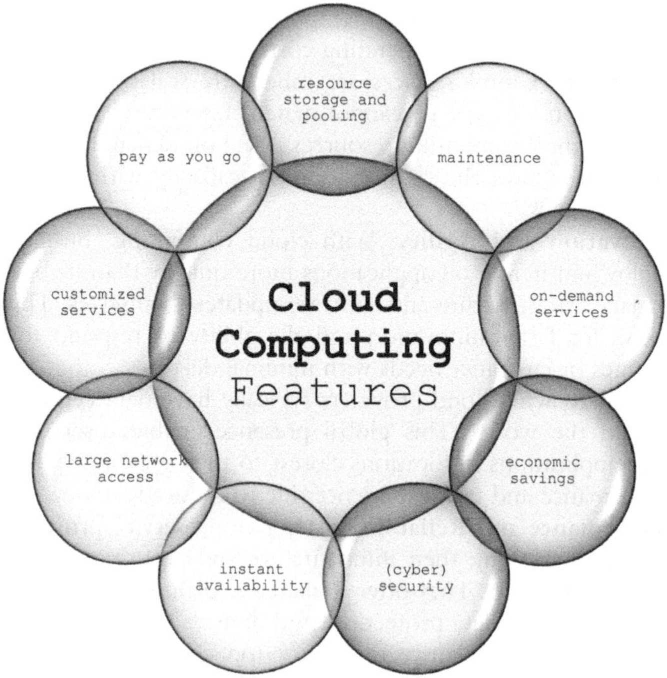

Fig. 6.3 Features of cloud computing

As a Service models (Hajipour et al., 2023) represent a primary outsourcing option for end-users and may be synthesized in Fig. 6.4. They may also include Infrastructure as a Service (IaaS).

Cloud computing can be represented as a digital node that masters a virtual ecosystem, as shown in Fig. 6.5.

For the economic evaluation of the databases, first, the most well-known approaches of estimating the value of the intangibles used by the applicative practice can be the starting point, appropriately adapted. The approaches are those foreseen by IVS 210.

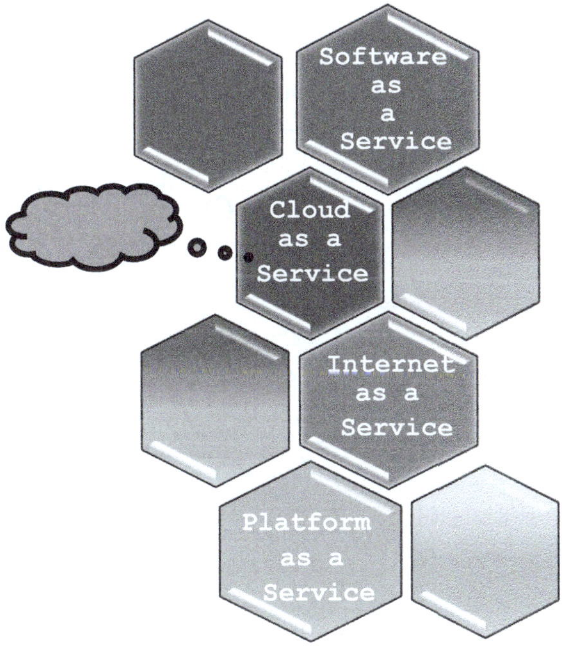

Fig. 6.4 As a service models

The Cost Approach

According to this approach (already examined in Chapter 2), the value can be obtained by estimating the costs incurred for the realization of the software or to be incurred for its reproduction.

Still, in the context of the cost approach, the already mentioned "CO.CO.MO". approach applies.

The cost approach has a significant semantic value for the estimation process but does not always allow for sorting out a precise correlation between costs incurred and potential value, which depends essentially on other variables (such as the expected marginality at an economic-financial level). The costs incurred by individual developers, insofar as they are comparable, represent a reference point for the analysis of the break-even point between operating costs and revenues.

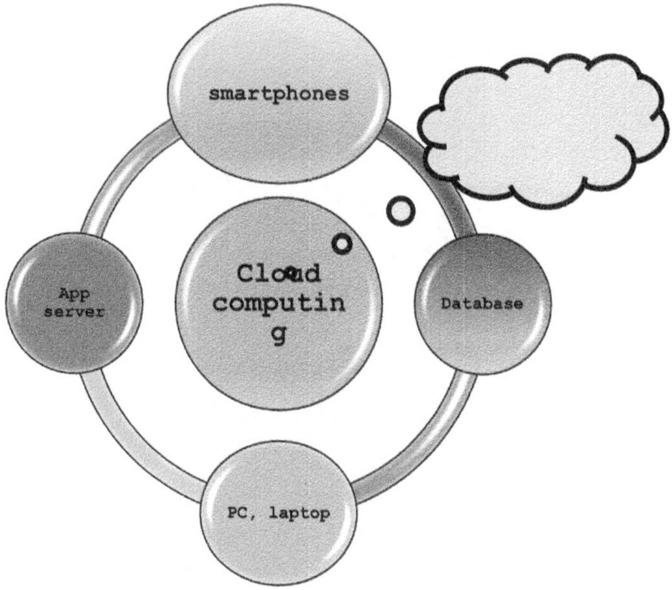

Fig. 6.5 Cloud computing ecosystem

A trended historical cost model evaluates recent software through a cost accounting system, considering historical costs of development indexed to incorporate inflation.

A variant is represented by the Putnam model (1978), examined in Sect. 5.3, which describes the time and effort required to finish a software project of a specified size, bringing it to SLIM (Software Lifecycle Management). The non-linear mathematical model estimates the cost of the software combining a productivity index with a workforce build-up index to estimate the software efficiency.

The Income-Financial Approach

The use of the database acts on the economic margins expressed by the differential between revenues and operating costs (EBIT) in that it ideally allows both to increase revenues (with greater direct sales or with royalties from licenses) and to reduce costs, producing with less labor-intensive techniques and suitable to allow savings of other costs (production, organizational, energy...).

Another economic-financial margin is the EBITDA, from which operating cash flow and DCF derive.

The Empirical Approach

The estimate of the market value is based on the screening of market multipliers from comparable transactions involving software or other intangibles, by way of sale or license, using the international databases available on the web can provide useful clues on their value (in terms of price comparison).

The analysis of comparability between different databases can provide information about any capital gain resulting from their originality (intended as a requirement for patentability).

Comparability is easier if databases are interoperable and perform similar tasks.

6.14 Data Validating Blockchains

AI-driven Data Validating Blockchains have a notable economic and financial influence through the enhancement of security, efficiency, and trust within various sectors. The amalgamation of AI and blockchain technology allows entities to enhance data validation procedures, decrease energy consumption, and bolster the security of financial transactions. This fusion facilitates the emergence of novel financial service paradigms, elevating the efficiency of banking services, asset management, and lending capacities. Leveraging machine learning algorithms within blockchain technology guarantees precise identification of block data sensitivity, hence refining decision-making processes and the selection of suitable consensus mechanisms. The incorporation of blockchain in financial sectors can rationalize operations, boost competitiveness, and fortify the stability of capital flow, thereby ultimately enriching the economy. Data validation on blockchains plays a vital role in ensuring the integrity and reliability of data stored on distributed ledger technology. While the immediate impact of blockchain technology on AI is not always direct, it can have several important implications, particularly in the context of data quality and trustworthiness, which can subsequently affect AI applications in economic, financial, and market value contexts. Here's how data validation on blockchains can impact AI:

1. **Data Quality Assurance:** Blockchain's immutable and decentralized nature can help ensure the accuracy and integrity of data. This high level of data quality is crucial for AI systems that rely on clean and reliable data for training and decision-making.
2. **Enhanced Trust:** Blockchain's transparency and traceability can enhance trust in data sources. This is especially important in AI applications, such as supply chain management and fraud detection, where data provenance and authenticity are critical. By providing a verifiable history of data, blockchain can increase confidence in AI-driven insights and actions.
3. **Data Sharing and Monetization:** Blockchain can facilitate secure and transparent data sharing among multiple parties while maintaining data privacy and control. This can open up new opportunities for AI applications that require access to diverse datasets, such as medical research or financial analysis. Improved data sharing can lead to more accurate AI models and insights.
4. **Smart Contracts:** Blockchain-based smart contracts can automate and enforce agreements related to data sharing, access, and usage. AI applications that rely on data from multiple sources benefit from smart contracts that ensure fair compensation and compliance with data-sharing agreements, potentially creating new economic models for data monetization.
5. **Decentralization:** Blockchain's decentralized architecture can reduce the reliance on central authorities, making data more accessible and secure. In financial and economic applications, decentralized AI systems can provide more resilient and transparent solutions for tasks like algorithmic trading or risk assessment.
6. **Reducing Bias:** Blockchain technology create decentralized and unbiased AI models. By preventing centralized control over training data and model development, blockchain can help mitigate issues of bias and discrimination in AI, which is essential for fair and ethical AI applications.

The impact of data validation on blockchains on AI applications in terms of economic, financial, and market value can be significant:

a. **Economic Value:** Improved data quality and trust can lead to more accurate AI models, reducing errors and inefficiencies in various industries. This can result in cost savings, increased productivity, and new revenue streams through innovative AI-driven products and services.
b. **Financial Value:** In finance, blockchain-powered data validation can enhance the accuracy of risk assessments, fraud detection, and trading strategies. This can lead to reduced financial losses and improved investment decisions, which can have a direct impact on financial market performance.
c. **Market Value**: AI applications powered by trustworthy data and blockchain technology can gain a competitive edge in the market. This can drive market share growth, increased customer trust, and potentially higher valuations for AI-focused companies.

Data validation on blockchains can have a positive impact on AI by improving data quality, enhancing trust, enabling secure data sharing, and reducing bias. These improvements can, in turn, lead to economic efficiencies, financial benefits, and increased market value for AI applications across various sectors. However, it's essential to consider the challenges and complexities associated with integrating blockchain and AI technologies to fully realize these potential benefits.

6.15 New Assessment Scenarios and Monetization Strategies

In addition to the traditional approaches highlighted above, there are peculiarities, typical of databases, which affect their use, with consequences on the evaluation. This refers, for example, to ways of co-creating value between database owners and users, when the latter do not just draw on information sources, helping to feed the databases with feedback, information, data sharing, etc.

Value co-creation does not always go hand in hand with its sharing, due to the presence of asymmetries in the database business model, which often does not appropriately reward users for their function as data providers. Privacy issues related to the use of personal data are very delicate, and the individuals directly concerned are not always fully aware of this issue (see the example of social networks that steal personal data even without the users' knowledge).

An element that can increase the value of databases relates to their interoperability, which allows different databases to communicate with each other, implementing a sharing of digital information, appropriately harmonized. In this context, they detect data fusion procedures, typical of the value chain that rotates around big data.

Databases are increasingly used as a source of information for economic and financial planning (business planning) and in this context, information data becomes a real asset (an intangible asset with its intrinsic value), which can be the subject of a sale, license, or sharing, showing economic exploitation that can be used in comparable transactions.

The strategies of monetization of the databases can be declined in the following cases:

1. Use of data for internal purposes, maintaining ownership and exclusive use;
2. Use to facilitate entry into new businesses, through product differentiation;
3. Exclusive or shared licenses to third parties, with subscriptions or pay-per-use services over multi-year time frames;
4. Interchange and sharing of data (also with commercial partners);
5. Sale of premium products associated with the exclusive use of data (data vending; through digital platforms);
6. Free provision of data (with advertising or other income);
7. Selective use of data for vertical advertising purposes (profiled advertising).

6.16 Artificial Intelligence and Technical Debt in Software Development

The intersection of artificial intelligence and technical debt in software development is a useful and increasingly popular application that follows these steps:

a. **Understanding Technical Debt in Software Development**

1. **Definition**: Technical debt refers to the cost of additional rework in software caused by choosing an easy, often quick solution over a better approach that would take longer.
2. **Consequences**: It can lead to decreased software quality, maintainability issues, and reduced performance over time.
3. **Common Sources**:
   - Rushed coding.
   - Lack of documentation.
   - Incomplete testing.
   - Outdated technology or dependencies.

b. **The Role of AI in Managing Technical Debt**

1. **Early Detection**:
   - AI tools can analyze code and identify potential areas of technical debt early in the development process.
   - Machine learning algorithms can learn from past projects to predict where technical debt might occur.
2. **Automated Refactoring**:
   - AI can suggest or even automatically implement refactoring strategies to improve code quality and reduce technical debt.
   - It can identify obsolete code or dependencies and suggest updates or replacements.
3. **Code Quality Analysis**:
   - AI algorithms can assess code quality in real-time, providing feedback to developers to prevent the accumulation of technical debt.
   - They can analyze code complexity, adherence to coding standards, and potential security vulnerabilities.
4. **Predictive Analytics**:
   - AI can predict the future impact of technical debt on a project, helping teams make informed decisions about when and how to address it.

c. **Challenges and Considerations**

1. **Accuracy of AI Tools**: The effectiveness of AI in managing technical debt depends on the accuracy and sophistication of the algorithms used.
2. **Integration with Existing Workflows**: Successfully integrating AI tools into existing software development workflows can be challenging.
3. **Training Data**: The quality of machine learning models depends on the availability of high-quality, relevant training data.
4. **Understanding AI Recommendations**: Developers need to understand and interpret the recommendations made by AI tools, which requires a certain level of expertise.

d. **Future Directions**

1. **Enhanced Machine Learning Models**: Continuous improvement in machine learning models can provide more accurate predictions and suggestions.
2. **Customization for Specific Projects**: AI tools that can be customized to the specific needs and characteristics of a project could be more effective in managing technical debt.
3. **Integrated Development Environments (IDEs)**: Incorporating AI tools directly into IDEs for real-time assistance.

AI provides promising avenues for managing technical debt in software development, offering tools for early detection, automated refactoring, code quality analysis, and predictive analytics. However, challenges like the accuracy of AI tools, integration into existing processes, and the need for quality training data must be addressed to fully realize its potential. Continued advancements in AI and machine learning are expected to further enhance its effectiveness in this domain.

References

Amran, M. (2005). The challenges of valuing patents and early-stage technologies. *Journal of Applied Corporate Finance, 17*(2), 68–81.

Azura, Z. N., Suhaimi, I., & Mohd, N. M. (2015). *A survey of value-based factors in software development*. American Scientific Publishers.

Ben-Menachem, M. (2007). Accounting software assets. A valuation model for software. *Journal of Information Systems, 21*(2), 117–132.

Bernaroch, M., & Appari, A. (2010). Financial pricing of software development risk factors. *IEEE Software, 27*(5).

Boehm, B., & Valerdi, R. (2008). Achievements and challenges in COCOMO-based software resource estimation. *IEEE Software, 25*(5).

Boehm, B., Valerdi, R., Lane, J. A., & Winsor Brown, A. (2005, April 20). COCOMO suite methodology and evolution. *The Journal of Defense Software Engineering, 18*(4).

Brown, W., & Boehm, B. (2010). Software cost estimation in the incremental commitment model. *Systems Research Forum, 4*(1), 45–55.

Contractor, F. J. (2001). *Valuation of intangible assets in global operations*. British Library Cataloguing, Permanent Paper Standard issued by the National Information Standards Organization.

Cusumano, M. A. (2008). The changing software business: Moving from products to services. *Computer, 41*(1), 20.

Degenne, A., & Forsè, M. (2006). *Introducing social networks*. Sage.

De Groot, J., Nugroho, A., Back, T., & Visser, J. (2012). What is the value of your software? In *MDT'12 Proceedings of the Third International Workshop on Managing Technical Debt* (pp. 37–44). LIACS Leiden University.

Denne, M., & Cleland-Huang, J. (2004). *Software by numbers*. Prentice Hall.

Dhillon, S., & Mahmoud, Q. H. (2015). An evaluation framework for crossplatform mobile application development tools. *Software: Practice and Experience, 45*(10), 1331–1357.

Du, W. L., Capretz, L. F., Nassif, A. B., & Ho, D. (2013). A hybrid intelligent model for software cost estimation. *Journal of Computer Science, 9*, 1506–1513.

Erdogmus, H., Favaro, J., & Halling, M. (2008). Valuation of software initiatives under uncertainty: Concepts, issues, and techniques. *Value-based software engineering* (pp. 39–66). Springer.

Garcia, J., & De Magdaleno, M. I. A. (2013). *Valuation of open-source software: How do you put a value on free?* (Vol. 3, No. 1). Revista de Gestao, Financas e Contabilidade.

Guo, Z., & Ma, D. (2018). A model of competition between perpetual software and software as a service. *MIS Quarterly, 42*(1), 101–120.

Hajipour, V., Siavash Hekmat, & Mohammad Amini. (2023). A value-oriented artificial intelligence-as-a-service business plan using integrated tools and services. *Decision Analytics Journal, 8*, 100302.

Head, S. J., & Nelson, J. B. (2012). *Data rights valuation in software acquisitions*. Center for Naval Analyses.

Jiang, B., Chan, P., & Mukhopadhyay, T. (2007). *Software licensing: Pay-per-use versus perpetual*. SSRN.

Kalaiselvi, S. (2009). *Financial performance in software industry*. Discovery Publishing House Pvt Ltd., Vellalar College for Women.

King, K. (2007, January). A case study in the valuation of a database. *Journal of Database Marketing & Customer Strategy Management, 14*(2), 110–119.

Moro-Visconti, R. (2021). *Startup valuation. From strategic business planning to digital networking*. Palgrave MacMillan.

Moro-Visconti, R. (2022a). *The valuation of digital intangibles. Technology, marketing, and the metaverse*. Palgrave MacMillan.

Moro-Visconti, R. (2022b). *Augmented corporate valuation. From digital networking to ESG compliance*. Palgrave MacMillan.

Puntambekar, A. A. (2009). *Software engineering*. Technical Publications.

Putnam, L. H. (1978). A general empirical solution to the Macro software sizing and estimating problem. *IEEE Transactions on Software Engineering, SE-4*(4), 345–361.

Ramzan, M., Anwar, S., & Shahid, A. A. (2009). Need to redefine "value" and case for a new "software valuation" technique: An analytical study. In *Proceedings of International Conference on Computer Engineering and Applications*.

Reilly, R. F., & Schweihs, R. P. (2014). *Guide to intangibles asset valuation*. AICPA American Institute of Certified Public Accountants Inc.

Safari, F., Safari, N., & Hasanzadeh, A. (2015). The adoption of software as a service (SaaS): Ranking the determinants. *Journal of Enterprise Information Management, 28*(3), 400–422.

Saunders, A., & Brynjolfsson, E. (2015). Valuing IT-related intangible assets. *MIS Quarterly, 40*(1), 83–110.

Tansey, B., & Stroulia, E. (2007). Valuating software service development: Integrating COCOMO II and real options theory. In *Paper presented at 2008 1st International Workshop on the Economics of Software and Computation*. IEEE Xplore.

Thurman, C. J. (2018). *Application of the cost approach to value internally developed computer software*. http://www.willamette.com/insights_journal/18/summer_2018_4.pdf

Tockey, S. (2014) Aspects of software valuation. In *Economics-driven software architecture*. Science Direct.

Ullrich, C. (2013). Valuation of IT investments using real options theory. *Business & Information Systems Engineering, 5*(5), 331–341.

CHAPTER 7

The Valuation of Artificial Intelligence

7.1 The Fundamentals of Artificial Intelligence

AI exerts a significant impact on conventional enterprises that invest in AI-related products. The utilization of AI technologies not only boosts the firm's value but also has a favorable influence on cost structures, mainly through the automation capabilities of AI. Nevertheless, the impact of augmentation AI on profit and cost frameworks remains unclear. Moreover, AI's capacity to optimize decision making processes and harness big data leads to heightened productivity and economic expansion. This shift underscores the imperative for traditional corporations to strategically integrate AI in order to sustain competitiveness and navigate legal, financial, market, and economic evaluation frameworks. AI encompasses the development of computer systems capable of performing tasks that would typically require human intelligence. These tasks span a wide range of capabilities, including problem-solving, learning from data, recognizing patterns, understanding natural language, and making decisions based on complex information. AI systems are designed to simulate various aspects of human cognition, enabling machines to analyze data, draw insights, and execute tasks with a level of autonomy and intelligence. The ultimate goal of AI is to create machines that can perceive their environment, adapt to changing circumstances, and interact with humans in a manner that is both efficient and intelligent.

R. Moro-Visconti, *Artificial Intelligence Valuation*,
https://doi.org/10.1007/978-3-031-53622-9_7

AI is a broad and varied concept, based on processes and reasoning of thought and behavioral dynamics, faithful to human performances and tending toward rationality. Russell and Norvig (2016) recall complementary definitions, according to which AI consists of designing computers and machines that think and act as human beings (even though limited to specific predefined applications, such as decision-making, problem-solving, and learning). AI consists, therefore in the study of mental faculties through computational models making possible actions such as learning, reasoning, and action, to design intelligent agents. These agents must be able to act humanely and to this end must be able to communicate with human beings through processes defined by the Turing test, as shown in Fig. 7.1.

To pass the Turing test (a method of inquiry for determining whether or not a computer is capable of thinking like a human being), the computer needs computer vision to frame the objects and robotic capabilities to manipulate and move them.

One of the biggest criticalities of AI concerns its flexibility and resilience: differently from the plasticity inherent in human intelligence, AI cannot easily reinvent new strategies or patterns with collateral thinking, etc. Cooperation with other devices and humans can also be limited. Another issue is represented by empathy: AI is hardly able to

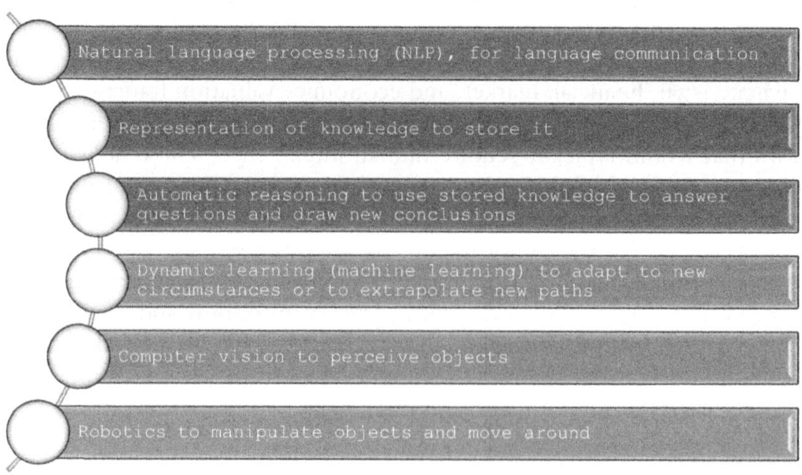

Fig. 7.1 Turing test

"cook the ingredients of emotions", incorporate them in an algorithm, or establish social ties. Artificial emotional intelligence (AEI) has the potential to transform human–computer interactions, making technology more intuitive, empathetic, and responsive to human needs and emotions. As AEI continues to advance, it will play an increasingly significant role in shaping the future of human–machine collaboration and communication.

Harari (2015) explores the transformative "cognitive revolution" that occurred approximately 70,000 years ago, marking a significant turning point in human history. During this period, Homo sapiens distinguished themselves from other hominid species by developing sophisticated language skills, forming complex social structures, and exhibiting advanced cognitive abilities. Harari's work delves into the implications of this cognitive revolution and examines the possible trajectories of human evolution in the face of emerging biotechnological advancements. He speculates on the profound implications of fields such as genetic engineering and artificial intelligence, which have the potential to redefine what it means to be human.

In Harari's vision of the future, humans may gain unprecedented control over their biology and cognition, enabling them to enhance their physical and mental capabilities in ways previously unimaginable. This could include the ability to manipulate genetic code to eliminate disease, enhance physical strength, or even extend lifespan. Furthermore, Harari contemplates the integration of humans with advanced technologies, blurring the boundaries between organic and synthetic entities. He envisions scenarios where humans merge with artificial intelligence, augmenting their cognitive abilities and potentially transcending the limitations of biological existence. Harari's exploration of these speculative futures prompts reflection on the ethical, social, and existential implications of biotechnological advancements. It raises profound questions about identity, consciousness, and the nature of humanity in an increasingly technologically mediated world.

Genetic engineering holds the promise of allowing humans to manipulate their own DNA, potentially curing diseases, enhancing physical attributes, and extending lifespan. Additionally, Harari discusses the possibility of technologies like brain computer interfaces enabling direct communication between the human brain and computers, opening up new avenues for cognitive enhancement and information processing.

Harari contemplates the creation of non-organic entities, such as advanced AI systems, that operate independently of biological bodies.

These AI entities could possess intelligence and capabilities far surpassing those of humans, potentially reshaping society, and the nature of human existence.

Harari's ideas prompt reflection on the ethical, social, and philosophical implications of these technological advancements, highlighting both the opportunities and challenges they may bring as humanity navigates the uncharted territory of the future.

A still largely unanswered question concerns self-learning (a key feature of AI) and its capacity to improve flexibility or increase scope.

AI is a discipline that over the years has made an important contribution to the progress of computer science. It has been influenced by numerous disciplines including philosophy, neurology, mathematics, psychology, cybernetics, and cognitive sciences.

AI is not to be considered a single intangible asset, but rather a product and process innovation, intersecting with typical intangible assets such as software, patents, and know-how, other intangible internet-driven (M-App, etc.), and input data derived from big data or sensors IoT.

The pervasiveness of AI and its applicability to wider solutions and business models represents a strong element of innovation, which can operate within a portfolio of intangible resources, enhancing their characteristics and potential.

AI studies the theoretical foundations, methodologies, and techniques that allow the design of hardware systems and software program systems capable of providing the computer with performances that, to an ordinary observer, would seem to be the exclusive competence of natural (human) intelligence.

The purpose of AI is not to replicate this intelligence, an objective which for some is even inadmissible, but rather to reproduce or emulate certain functions of it. There is no reason why certain (but not all) performances of human intelligence—for example, the ability to solve problems through inferential processes—should not be provided by a machine. In the case of emulation, intelligent performance is achieved by using the machine's mechanisms, to provide performance that is qualitatively equivalent and quantitatively superior to human performance.

One of the fundamental contributions that AI has given to computer science has been to place the accent on the notion of the problem, positioning it side by side with those of algorithms and data, studying and highlighting the various modalities for its modeling.

Augmented reality has become public knowledge thanks to the introduction of Google Glass which, through a small display positioned above the eye, fills the field of view with data and information on the surrounding environment of the wearer. However, even before conquering the entire mobile sector (smartphones, laptops, tablets, glasses, and viewers combined with special software or applications), it took its first steps in much more technical and specific areas, such as military, scientific research, and medicine.

The first examples of augmented reality, not by chance, have been introduced in the field of military aeronautics in the form of head-up displays (HUD). This technology was later adopted by civil aviation.

7.2 Applications and Business Models

AI applications have become essential components of contemporary business frameworks, presenting a diverse range of advantages across multiple sectors. Through advancements in productivity enhancement and cost reduction, as well as the transformation of business processes utilizing AI-based frameworks, the integration of AI technologies is reforming conventional business methodologies. Startups are capitalizing on AI to establish innovative value propositions, effectively utilize data, and redefine overarching business strategies. The era of digitalization, characterized by innovations like AI, Big Data, and the Internet of Things, is propelling the fourth industrial revolution, with AI emerging as a pivotal catalyst for fostering innovation and competitiveness. AI is a transformative technology that can significantly influence how businesses operate and compete through:

a. **Operational Efficiency and Automation:** AI's capacity to automate tasks and processes can lead to increased efficiency and cost savings. This can be especially beneficial for traditional companies with legacy systems and processes.
b. **Personalized Customer Experiences:** AI-driven customer insights can help companies tailor their offerings and marketing efforts to individual preferences, enhancing customer satisfaction and loyalty.
c. **New Revenue Streams:** AI fosters the development of new products and services, with new revenue streams and business opportunities.

d. **Data-Driven Decision-Making:** AI analytics provide valuable insights from data, facilitating decision-making and reactions to market changes.
e. **Competition and Disruption:** Traditional firms face the challenge of competition from AI-native startups.
f. **Business Model Innovation:** AI reshapes business models, for example represented by subscription-based offerings, outcome-based pricing, and data monetization.
g. **Collaboration with AI Startups:** Partnering with AI startups can inject innovation into traditional businesses and help them access cutting-edge technology and expertise.
h. **Reskilling and Workforce Transformation:** Preparing the workforce for AI integration is crucial. Companies must invest in training and foster a culture that embraces change.
i. **Ethical and Regulatory Considerations:** As AI use grows, addressing ethical concerns and complying with regulations is vital to maintain trust and avoid legal issues.
j. **Risk Management and Security:** AI may shelter firms from cyber threats.

The impact of AI on business models will vary depending on the specific industry (as shown in Chapter 10) and firm. Those who proactively embrace AI and incorporate it strategically into their operations are likely to be better positioned for long-term success. Additionally, a thoughtful approach to ethical and regulatory considerations is essential to ensure responsible AI adoption.

AI firms can be divided into:

1. Infrastructure: firms that run in the back office and provide computational services to others.
2. Application: Firms active in the B2B and B2C segments. In the B2B ecosystem, they may offer SaaS-based subscription services. These companies generally develop applications for specific use cases defined by their clients.

Table 7.1 shows some examples of the application of AI in the field of business solutions. The applications of AI systems are innumerable, and their complete cataloging is very difficult because of the quantity and heterogeneity of the sectors involved, and due to constant evolution.

Key fundamentals and definitions of AI include:

a. **Machine Learning**: A subfield of AI that focuses on the development of algorithms and models that enable machines to improve their performance on a specific task through data-driven learning. Machine learning algorithms learn from data and adapt their behavior based on patterns and insights.
b. **Deep Learning**: A subset of machine learning that utilizes neural networks with multiple layers (deep neural networks) to process and analyze complex data, such as images, audio, and text. Deep learning has been instrumental in many AI breakthroughs, including image and speech recognition.
c. **Natural Language Processing (NLP)**: NLP is a branch of AI that deals with the interaction between computers and human languages. It facilitates tasks like language translation, sentiment analysis, and chatbots.
d. **Computer Vision**: Focuses on teaching machines to interpret and understand visual information, such as images and videos. Computer vision enables applications like facial recognition, object detection, and autonomous driving.
e. **Robotics**: AI enables robots to perceive their environment, make decisions, and execute tasks autonomously. Robotic AI is used in manufacturing, healthcare, logistics, and more.
f. **Artificial General Intelligence (AGI)**: This strong form of AI, represents machines or systems with the ability to understand, learn, and apply knowledge at a level comparable to human intelligence.
g. **Narrow AI (Weak AI)**: Narrow or weak AI systems are still the most popular, and they are designed to perform specific tasks or solve particular problems. They excel in their designated area but lack the general intelligence of humans.
h. **Supervised Learning**: A common machine learning paradigm in which algorithms are trained on labeled data, with input–output pairs. The algorithm learns how to make predictions based on examples from the training data.

Table 7.1 Examples of the application of artificial intelligence in the field of business solutions

Technology	*Definition*	*Example of solution*
Computer Vision—Image Recognition	Acquisition, processing, analysis, and understanding of images and objects	Video analysis integrated with cameras for video surveillance systems. Analysis of consumer behavior in shops. Scan and diagnosis of X-rays. Photo tagging of friends
Audio Processing	Identification, recognition, and analysis of sounds and languages	Integrated language recognition in call centers
Sensor Processing	Processing and analysis of information from camera sensors and microphones	In the agricultural sector, sensors in the fields can be integrated with software that can communicate information about temperature, humidity, etc
Natural language processing	Understanding and formulation of spoken and written languages	Personal assistants on mobile devices
Knowledge representation	Representation and communication of knowledge to facilitate forecasting and decision-making	Knowledge-based tools that correlate content with related topics across the web
Inference Engines	Identification of answers from basic knowledge such as business rules	Automatic approval for financing concessions; issuing of visas, and decisions on credits
Expert Systems	Emulation of human problem-solving and decision-making skills by reasoning with the information available in the basic knowledge	Medical diagnostics and legal research can be improved through the ability of an expert system to use millions of pieces of data, summarizing the information to be presented to the user
Augmented reality—3D applications	Enrichment of human sensory perception with additional data in digital format	Head-up display (HUD): Overlay display for pilots

(continued)

Table 7.1 (continued)

Technology	*Definition*	*Example of solution*
Machine Learning	Changing the decision-making process based on experience	Software tools and personal assistants can learn from users (email classification, calendar updates, etc.) to increase productivity
Web search Engines	A web search engine or internet search engine is a software system that is designed to carry out web searches (internet search)	The system learns how to rank pages through a complex learning algorithm
Email Spam Detector	Email spam, also known as junk email, is unsolicited messages sent in bulk by email. There are different approaches to spam detection. These approaches include blacklisting, detecting bulk emails, scanning message headings, grey-listing, and content-based filtering	The machine learning system operates by classifying the mails and moving the unwanted emails to a spam folder. This is again achieved by a spam classifier running in the back end of a mail application
Virtual personal assistant	Help to find relevant information when requested using voice. AI fosters these applications, as they gather data on the user's request and utilize them to detect speech and serve the user with answers that are customized to his inclination	Virtual assistants can provide a wide variety of services. • Provide information such as weather, and facts set the alarm, make to-do lists and shopping lists • Play music from streaming services; • read audiobooks; • Play videos, TV shows, or movies on televisions, • Conversational commerce; • Complement and/or replace customer service with humans
Robotic Vehicles	Proposing driverless solutions	Self-driving cars where AI improves driving patterns

i. **Unsupervised Learning**: In this machine learning approach, algorithms use unlabeled data and tasked with finding patterns, structures, or groupings within the data without specific guidance.
j. **Reinforcement Learning**: Agents interact with an environment and learn to make sequential decisions through trial and error. Agents receive feedback in the form of rewards or penalties, enabling them to maximize their behavior.
k. **AI Ethics**: The ethical considerations of AI, including issues related to fairness, privacy, bias mitigation, transparency, accountability, and the responsible use of AI technology.

AI has a wide range of applications across industries, including healthcare (diagnosis and drug discovery), finance (algorithmic trading and fraud detection), autonomous vehicles, virtual assistants, and more. As AI technology continues to advance, it holds the potential to revolutionize various aspects of society and business, making it a topic of great interest and importance.

An important aspect of AI is represented by the ability to formulate forecasts, which play a fundamental role in decision-making. A reduction in the cost of forecasts impacts the increase in the value of the data. Better accuracy reduces risk (the denominator of the DCF formulation), improving value.

AI relates to big data usually stored in the cloud that provides essential real-time input data, which is then processed through algorithms for different purposes.

Figure 7.2 shows the links between AI and its main business models.

AI has a profound impact on the business models of traditional brick-and-mortar firms across various industries. The main effects of AI on these businesses are reported in Table 7.2.

While AI offers significant benefits to brick-and-mortar firms, successful adoption requires careful planning, investment, and ongoing adaptation to changing business dynamics. Companies that strategically integrate AI into their operations are better positioned to remain competitive and thrive in a rapidly evolving business landscape.

The machine learning workflow represents another popular AI application and is often referred to as the model evaluation phase:

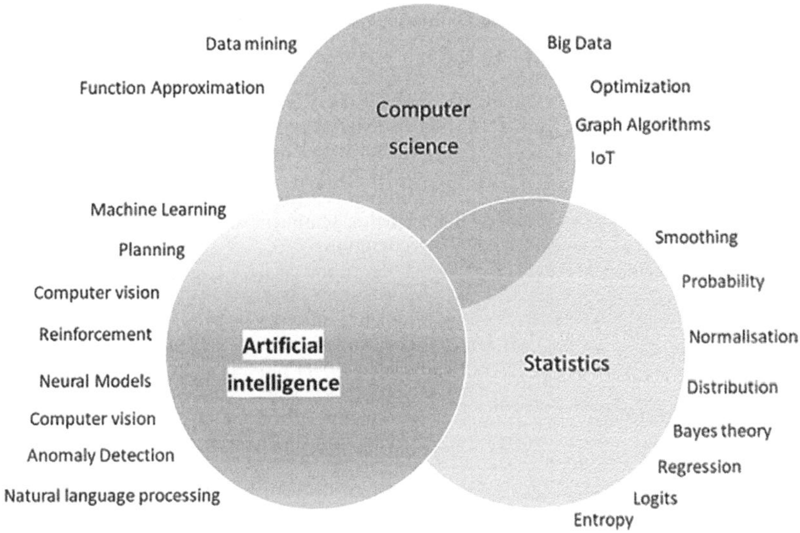

Fig. 7.2 AI and business models

1. **Model Development**: Data scientists start by developing machine learning models designed to solve specific tasks. This includes selecting the appropriate algorithms, architectures, and features to build and train the models.
2. **Training**: The models are trained on labeled data. During training, the model learns from the data to make predictions.
3. **Testing and Evaluation**: After training, the models need to be evaluated to assess their performance. The key metrics used for evaluation include:

   - **Accuracy**: The proportion of correctly classified instances out of all instances.
   - **Precision**: Correctly predicted positive instances out of all instances predicted as positive.
   - **Recall**: The percentage of correctly predicted positive instances out of all actual positive instances. It measures the model's ability to find all relevant instances.

Table 7.2 Artificial Intelligence's impact on business models

Enhanced Customer Experience	AI-powered chatbots and virtual assistants provide 24/7 customer support and assistance Personalized product recommendations and content based on customer data improve engagement Improved customer service through AI-driven analytics, sentiment analysis, and voice recognition
Data-Driven Decision-Making	AI algorithms analyze large volumes of data to inform strategic decisions Predictive analytics helps maximize inventory management, pricing, and marketing strategies Real-time data monitoring enhances supply chain efficiency and reduces operational costs
Operational Efficiency	Automation of routine tasks, such as inventory tracking and order processing, reduces labor costs AI-driven demand forecasting and dynamic pricing increase revenue and profit margins AI-powered robots and autonomous vehicles improve warehouse and logistics operations
Inventory Management	AI systems maximize inventory levels, reducing carrying costs and minimizing stockouts Predictive maintenance prevents equipment breakdowns, minimizing downtime
Personalized Marketing:	AI-driven customer segmentation and targeting enable hyper-personalized marketing campaigns Chatbots engage with customers, answer questions, and guide them through the purchase process
E-commerce Integration	Many brick-and-mortar retailers expand into e-commerce and use AI to bridge the online and offline customer experience AI-driven virtual showrooms and augmented reality enhance online shopping
Supply Chain Optimization	AI enhances supply chain visibility, enabling real-time tracking and efficient routing Predictive analytics reduces waste, improves procurement, and streamlines logistics
Predictive Maintenance	AI monitors equipment and infrastructure for maintenance needs, reducing downtime and costs Sensors and IoT devices transmit real-time data for analysis

(continued)

Table 7.2 (continued)

Cost Reduction	Labor cost savings through automation and AI-powered robotics Energy efficiency improvements through AI-driven HVAC and lighting systems
Competitive Advantage	AI allows traditional firms to compete with tech-native companies by leveraging data analytics and automation Enhanced customer service and convenience differentiate them from competitors
New Revenue Streams	AI enables the creation of new products and services, such as AI-powered virtual consultants Licensing AI technology or data analytics services to other businesses can generate additional income
Business Model Evolution	Traditional firms may transition from product-centric to service-centric models, offering AI-driven services alongside their core products Subscription-based models or pay-per-use pricing become viable options
Regulatory Compliance	Firms must navigate AI-related regulatory challenges, such as data privacy and ethics, impacting business models and practices
Human-AI Collaboration:	Traditional firms increasingly rely on human-AI collaboration, with AI supporting employees in decision-making and enhancing productivity
Market Expansion	AI can help traditional firms identify new market opportunities and customer segments, leading to expansion and diversification

- **F1-Score**: The harmonic mean of precision and recall, which balances both metrics. It's useful when there's an imbalance between positive and negative classes.
- **Confusion Matrix**: A matrix that summarizes the model's performance, showing true positives, true negatives, false positives, and false negatives.

4. **Logging and Analysis**: The evaluation metrics, along with other relevant information, are logged and recorded for each model. This logging helps data scientists and stakeholders analyze the performance of different models and approaches.

5. **Model Selection**: Based on the evaluation results, data scientists can choose the best-performing model or combination of models for the given task.
6. **Fine-Tuning**: If the selected model doesn't meet the desired performance criteria, data scientists may go back to the development and training phases, fine-tune hyperparameters, adjust features, or collect more data to improve the model's performance.
7. **Deployment**: Once a satisfactory model is selected, it can be deployed for real-world use, such as making predictions on new, unseen data.
8. **Monitoring**: After deployment, it is vital to monitor the model's performance.

The iterative nature of the machine learning workflow means that data scientists often go through multiple cycles of model development, training, and evaluation to achieve the best results for a given task. The choice of evaluation metrics depends on the specific problem and business goals, and it's essential to consider both the quantitative metrics and qualitative aspects of model performance when making decisions.

The emphasis on data integration products reflects the evolving landscape of data-driven decision-making within firms:

a. **Growing Importance of Trusted Datasets**: Reliable and high-quality datasets are the foundation of successful DS/ML projects. Ensuring data quality and integrity is crucial for meaningful analytics and machine learning.
b. **Investment in Newer Data Integration Products**: To address the demand for trusted datasets, companies are investing in newer data integration products. These tools help organizations aggregate, transform, and prepare data from various sources for analysis and modeling.
c. **Shift Toward Data-Driven Initiatives**: The prioritization of DS/ML initiatives shows a broader trend where firms leverage data and AI to drive decision-making, gain a competitive edge, and maximize operations. Data integration is a critical step in making this transition successful.

d. **Challenger Tools in Data Integration**: The data integration market is dynamic and competitive, with new entrants and innovative solutions challenging established players. These tools focus on addressing specific pain points or offering unique features that resonate with organizations seeking efficient data integration solutions.

The rise of data integration products reflects the changing landscape of data-driven decision-making within companies. The focus on trusted datasets, automation, and the growth of challenger tools all highlight the evolving priorities and strategies of organizations as they continue to invest in DS/ML initiatives to stay competitive and innovative. Data integration is a critical enabler of these initiatives, ensuring that data is accessible, reliable, and ready for analysis and modeling.

Artificial Intelligence-driven Productivity Growth

AI has demonstrated considerable potential in augmenting productivity across a range of sectors. Through the automation of repetitive tasks and facilitating quicker decision-making processes, AI can release human resources for more strategic endeavors, thereby fostering productivity growth. Productivity growth plays a crucial role in shaping long-term prosperity and overall welfare within an economy. When productivity increases, it means that more output is being generated with the same or fewer inputs, such as labor and capital. This leads to higher levels of efficiency, innovation, and economic growth, ultimately benefiting individuals and society (see, for instance, Baily et al., 2023). AI has the potential to significantly impact productivity in various ways, as shown in Table 7.3.

AI boosts productivity by automating tasks, improving decision-making, enhancing personalization, and optimizing various processes across industries. However, the extent and pace of AI's impact on productivity growth will depend on the specific applications of this troublesome technology.

Table 7.3 Artificial Intelligence's impact on productivity

Automation	AI technologies, including machine learning and robotics, can automate routine and repetitive tasks in various industries, such as manufacturing, logistics, and customer service. This can lead to increased efficiency, reduced labor costs, and higher overall productivity
Improved Decision-Making	AI can analyze vast amounts of data and provide valuable insights to support better decision-making in business and government. This can lead to more informed and efficient resource allocation and strategy development
Personalization	AI can enhance the customization of products and services by analyzing individual preferences and behavior. This can lead to more satisfied customers and higher productivity by tailoring offerings to specific needs
Enhanced Research and Development	AI can accelerate research and development processes by simulating experiments, optimizing designs, and identifying potential breakthroughs. This can lead to faster innovation and increased productivity in industries like pharmaceuticals and materials science
Predictive Maintenance:	AI-powered predictive maintenance systems can help businesses maximize the maintenance of equipment and infrastructure, reducing downtime and increasing operational efficiency
Supply Chain Optimization	AI can maximize supply chain management by predicting demand, optimizing inventory levels, and improving logistics. This can reduce costs and increase productivity in the manufacturing and distribution sectors

(continued)

Table 7.3 (continued)

Healthcare Efficiency	AI can improve healthcare by enhancing diagnostic accuracy, streamlining administrative tasks, and supporting personalized treatment plans. This can lead to improved healthcare outcomes and more efficient use of resources
Natural Language Processing (NLP)	NLP technologies enable AI systems to understand and generate human language. This can be applied in customer service, content generation, and translation services, improving communication and efficiency

7.3 Legal Aspects: Introductory Notes

The principal legal considerations surrounding AI pertain to the necessity of an appropriate legal structure for delineating AI within legal relationships involving subjects and objects, acknowledging AI as a novel subject for legal oversight. AI advancements present challenges to individual autonomy, the interpretation of contracts, and mechanisms for enforcement, underscoring the need for a gradual adjustment of regulatory frameworks to keep pace with the evolving nature of AI, which in turn affects civil liability and the insurance industry. The ethical dilemma emerges from the wide-ranging applications of AI and the imperative to establish an ethical rapport between AI entities and humans, with endeavors underway to instill AI systems with human principles. These legal considerations have a profound impact on economic, financial, and market assessments by influencing aspects such as the protection of intellectual property, cross-border data transfers, and the modification of current regulations to accommodate AI innovations. The legal aspects of AI play a significant role in influencing the economic, financial, and market valuation of AI-related companies and technologies. Legal considerations can impact valuation in various ways:

1. **Intellectual Property Rights**:
    - **Patents**: AI companies may hold patents for innovative algorithms, technologies, or applications. The strength and breadth of these patents can enhance a firm's competitive advantage and valuation.

- **Copyright**: Copyright protects the original code, datasets, and software architectures used in AI systems. Companies with strong copyright protections can secure their software assets and maintain their competitive position.
- **Trade Secrets**: AI companies often rely on proprietary algorithms and data. Protecting these trade secrets can prevent competitors from replicating their technology, thus preserving their market value.

2. **Regulatory Compliance**:

   - **Data Privacy**: AI companies that handle personal data must comply with data privacy regulations like GDPR or CCPA.
   - **Ethical Considerations**: AI systems must adhere to ethical guidelines to avoid legal and reputational risks. Ethical violations can lead to legal actions, public backlash, and damage to a firm's brand and valuation.
   - **Antitrust and Competition Laws**: As AI markets evolve, antitrust and competition authorities may scrutinize the actions of dominant AI companies. Legal challenges related to monopolistic practices can affect market valuation.

3. **Liability and Accountability**:

   - **Product Liability**: AI companies must consider the potential for liability claims arising from AI system errors or biases.

4. **Contracts and Licensing**:

   - **Licensing Agreements**: Companies often enter into licensing agreements for AI technology. The terms of these agreements can impact revenue streams and overall financial health.
   - **Customer Contracts**: The terms of customer contracts, particularly in enterprise AI solutions, can affect revenue predictability and long-term financial stability.

5. **Data Ownership and Intellectual Property Licensing**:

   - **Data Ownership**: Clarifying data ownership rights and licensing terms for data used in AI applications is crucial. Disputes over data ownership can have legal and financial ramifications.

- **IP Licensing**: AI companies may engage in licensing their technology to others. Licensing agreements can generate revenue and enhance the firm's valuation.

6. **Cybersecurity and Data Protection**:
   - **Data Breaches**: Legal and financial liabilities can result from data breaches or cybersecurity incidents. The costs associated with data breaches can impact a firm's bottom line and reputation.
7. **Regulatory Environment**:
   - **Government Regulations**: Changes in government regulations and policies related to AI can impact the market landscape and the compliance costs for AI companies. This can influence their financial performance and valuation.
8. **Export Control and National Security**:
   - Export controls on AI technologies due to national security concerns can affect market access and global expansion opportunities, thereby influencing financial projections and valuation.
9. **AI Liability Framework**:
   - Establishing a legal framework for AI liability, including defining responsibility in cases of AI-related harm or errors, can provide clarity for investors and insurers, influencing risk assessments and valuation.
10. **Anti-Bias and Fairness Regulations**:
    - Legal requirements to mitigate bias in AI algorithms may impact the development and deployment of AI systems. Companies that proactively address bias and fairness issues may face fewer legal challenges.

Ensuring compliance with regulations, protecting intellectual property, managing liability risks, and addressing ethical concerns are essential elements of an AI firm's legal strategy.

The radical changes brought in by AI and machine learning inevitably impact regulatory and social practices. One of the most complicated aspects concerns the legal personality of intelligent systems.

Specifically, the risks associated with the development of AI methodologies (Giudici et al., 2024) and technologies include "cause-driven" and "data-driven" risks. Risks "determined by causality" refer to how questions relating to the attribution of human responsibility are decided. Risk is based on the attribution of the factual consequences of a subjective condition, fault, or malice, to a human being, identified through the application of the principle of causality.

The limit of natural causality to phenomena related to algorithmic decision-making processes of machine learning lies in the fact that the decisions that the machine adopts or the acts it performs can become increasingly distant from any logic implemented by the human being in the software code.

The European Union's digital strategy to regulate AI (first regulation on artificial intelligence—European Parliament (europa.eu) is a significant step in addressing the rapidly evolving landscape of AI technology. By proposing a regulatory framework, the EU aims to harness the benefits of AI while ensuring safety, reliability, and ethical use. This initiative reflects the growing awareness of the potential impacts of AI on various sectors such as healthcare, transportation, manufacturing, and energy.

The key aspects of this framework include:

a. **Risk-based Classification**: The EU's approach categorizes AI systems based on the level of risk they pose to users. This risk assessment is crucial as it determines the extent of regulation required for each AI application.
b. **Benefits of AI**: The EU recognizes the transformative potential of AI in improving various aspects of life and industry. AI can revolutionize healthcare through advanced diagnostics and personalized treatment, enhance transportation safety and efficiency, boost manufacturing productivity, and contribute to sustainable energy solutions.
c. **World's First AI Rules**: These regulations will set a global precedent as the first comprehensive legal framework for AI.
d. **Balancing Innovation and Regulation**: To foster innovation in AI while ensuring that it is developed and used responsibly. By setting

clear rules, the EU hopes to create a conducive environment for AI development, ensuring that the technology benefits society.

This initiative indicates a proactive approach to managing the challenges and opportunities presented by AI. By creating a structured regulatory environment, the EU is seeking to encourage responsible AI innovation that aligns with ethical standards.

A useful normative reference, in addition to the provisions of the General Regulation about the protection of personal data (GDPR), in the EU Directive 680 of 27 April 2016, about protection of natural persons concerning the processing of personal data by the competent authorities for prevention, investigation, detection, and prosecution of crimes or execution of criminal sanctions. Article 11 of that directive states that the automated decision-making process about natural persons requires the Member States to provide that a decision based solely on automated processing, including profiling, which produces adverse legal effects or significantly affects the data subject, is prohibited unless explicitly authorized by European Union law or by the law of the Member State to which the data controller is subject. In addition, it must provide adequate safeguards for the rights and freedoms of the data subject, at least the right to obtain human intervention from the data controller.

The flow of data generated by intelligent devices and the availability of machine learning models and algorithms for predictive analysis are risk factors for privacy and personal data protection. Smart data streaming is already the subject of regulatory attention.

For example, the European Commission has published its Strategy on Co-Operative Intelligent Transport Systems (CITS) for the development of an intelligent transport infrastructure that allows vehicles to communicate with each other and with a centralized traffic management system, as well as with other transport systems agents. The potential risk of misuse of data is evident, as the intelligent infrastructure can identify each vehicle in real time along its route, know its destination, and report the driver's behavior and any possible infringement of traffic rules.

If a self-driving car led by AI applications causes an accident, who is responsible? Legal solutions to questions like this are a prerequisite for the large-scale implementation of AI.

The growing focus on AI governance by intergovernmental, national, and regional organizations has several economic, financial, and market impacts on the valuation of AI:

1. Economic Impact:

   - Regulatory Compliance Costs: Organizations operating in the AI space may incur costs associated with complying with AI governance regulations. These costs can include investments in ethical AI development, compliance audits, and reporting requirements.
   - Legal and Regulatory Certainty: Clear and robust AI governance frameworks can provide legal and regulatory certainty for businesses. This can reduce legal risks and uncertainties, leading to more stable economic conditions for AI-related companies.
   - Stakeholder Confidence: Ethical and responsible AI governance can build stakeholder confidence, including investors, customers, and partners. A more confident stakeholder base can lead to greater economic stability and investment in AI technologies.

2. Financial Impact:

   - Market Entry and Exit: AI governance regulations can affect market entry and exit strategies for AI companies. Companies that align with ethical and regulatory standards may find it easier to enter new markets or attract investors.
   - Risk Mitigation: Robust AI governance can help mitigate legal and reputational risks for AI businesses. Reduced risks can translate into better financial performance and a more positive outlook for investors.

3. Market Valuation Impact:

   - Investor Sentiment: AI companies that demonstrate a commitment to ethical AI practices and compliance with governance standards may be viewed more favorably by investors. Positive investor sentiment can contribute to higher market valuations.
   - Competitive Advantage: Companies that proactively implement AI governance measures may gain a competitive advantage by differentiating themselves from competitors with weaker governance practices. This competitive edge can influence market valuations.
   - Long-Term Sustainability: AI companies that prioritize ethical and responsible AI governance are more likely to be viewed as

sustainable and resilient in the long term. This perception can positively impact their market valuations.

4. Innovation and Industry Growth:

- Innovation Funding: Governments and organizations supporting AI governance may allocate funding and resources to promote ethical AI innovation. This funding can stimulate research and development activities, potentially leading to technological breakthroughs and increased market valuations.
- Industry Standardization: Governance efforts can lead to the standardization of ethical AI practices. Standardization can enhance interoperability and collaboration within the AI industry, potentially spurring growth and market valuation.

The increasing focus on AI governance has multifaceted economic, financial, and market valuation impacts. While regulatory compliance may entail costs, it can also provide legal certainty and build stakeholder confidence. AI companies that embrace ethical governance may benefit from improved investor sentiment and competitive advantages, potentially leading to higher market valuations.

Additionally, governance efforts can stimulate innovation, industry growth, and industry standardization, further influencing market dynamics and valuations in the AI sector.

AI-related legal cases can have various economic, financial, and market valuation impacts, depending on the nature of the case and its outcome, as shown in Table 7.4.

AI-related legal cases can have economic and financial impacts in the form of legal expenses, fines, compensation payments, and adjustments to business practices. These impacts can affect the financial performance of AI companies and organizations. Additionally, legal cases can influence market valuation by affecting a firm's reputation, customer trust, and investor sentiment. Therefore, managing legal risks and compliance with AI-related laws and regulations is crucial for the long-term economic and market success of AI businesses.

The evolving landscape of AI regulation and the challenges that policymakers and technology companies face in addressing the risks associated with AI technologies:

Table 7.4 Artificial Intelligence-related legal cases

Data Privacy and Security Cases	Impact on Economic and Financial Aspects: Legal cases related to data breaches, unauthorized data collection, or inadequate data security measures can result in financial penalties, legal fees, and compensation payments to affected parties. These costs can have a direct impact on the financial health of AI companies and organizations Market Valuation Impact: Publicized data privacy breaches can damage a firm's reputation and lead to a loss of customer trust. This can result in decreased market valuation as investors may view the company as a higher risk
Intellectual Property Cases	Impact on Economic and Financial Aspects: AI-related IP disputes, such as patent infringement or copyright violations, can lead to legal expenses, damages, and licensing fees. These costs can affect a firm's financial performance Market Valuation Impact: IP disputes can create uncertainties around a firm's ability to operate or its competitive position. This uncertainty can negatively impact market valuation, as investors may perceive higher legal risks
Algorithmic Bias and Discrimination Cases	Impact on Economic and Financial Aspects: Legal cases related to algorithmic bias and discrimination can result in fines, legal expenses, and the need to adjust algorithms or business practices. These costs can have financial implications Market Valuation Impact: Publicized cases of algorithmic bias and discrimination can harm a firm's reputation and brand image. This can lead to a loss of customers and investors, affecting market valuation

(continued)

Table 7.4 (continued)

Liability Cases	Impact on Economic and Financial Aspects: Cases involving AI-related accidents or failures that result in harm may lead to legal liabilities and compensation payments. These costs can have a direct financial impact Market Valuation Impact: High-profile liability cases can damage a firm's reputation and investor confidence. This can result in a lower market valuation as investors may perceive increased legal and operational risks
Regulatory Compliance Cases	Impact on Economic and Financial Aspects: Non-compliance with AI-related regulations and governance standards can lead to fines, legal expenses, and the need for compliance measures. These costs can affect financial performance Market Valuation Impact: Regulatory cases can signal to investors that a firm may not be fully compliant with evolving AI regulations. This can lead to concerns about legal and operational risks and potentially impact market valuation

1. Changing Attitudes of Tech Companies: Traditionally, the technology industry opposed regulation, but now major tech companies like Alphabet, Microsoft, and AI startups like Anthropic and OpenAI are advocating for AI regulation. They are concerned that unregulated competition might lead to the reckless release of AI models that could be misused or become uncontrollable.
2. Lack of Consensus: While there is a willingness to regulate AI, there is no consensus on the problems that need to be addressed and how to govern them effectively. This lack of consensus is a significant challenge in AI rulemaking diplomacy.
3. Regulation Goals: Determining the goals of AI regulation is challenging due to the rapid evolution of AI technology. Tech companies prefer narrow regulation that targets extreme risks, while others argue that the focus should be on broader issues such as threats to democracy.
4. What to Regulate: The debate over what exactly should be regulated is ongoing. Some suggest regulating the most powerful AI models,

while others focus on regulating the applications of these models rather than the models themselves.

5. Regulatory Bodies: There are differing opinions on who should be responsible for regulating AI. Some countries believe existing government agencies can handle the job, while the EU is considering creating a new regulatory body.
6. Recent Developments: The rise of large language models (LLMs) like ChatGPT has prompted a reevaluation of AI regulation approaches. There is growing recognition of the need for AI regulation, but also the complexity and lack of consensus in addressing the challenges associated with AI technology. Different stakeholders have varying perspectives on the goals, scope, and enforcement of AI regulations, making it a complex and ongoing debate.

Holistic regulation refers to a regulatory approach that considers the entire system or context in which a particular industry or activity operates, rather than just focusing on isolated aspects or individual components. It emphasizes a comprehensive understanding of the interconnections and dependencies within a system to create more effective and sustainable regulations.

This approach recognizes that various factors, such as economic, social, environmental, and technological aspects, can influence and be influenced by regulatory decisions. By taking a holistic view, regulators aim to promote the well-being of society, protect the environment, and support economic growth in a balanced and integrated manner.

Holistic regulation often involves collaboration between different government agencies, stakeholders, and experts to develop policies and regulations that address complex and multifaceted challenges. It's particularly relevant in fields like environmental protection, healthcare, and financial services, where the impact of regulatory decisions can have far-reaching consequences.

Holistic regulation can indeed help align AI interests more effectively. When regulating AI, considering the broader context and impacts of AI systems is essential:

a. Ethical Considerations: Holistic regulation can consider ethical principles and societal values when shaping AI policies. This helps ensure that AI systems are developed and used in ways that respect human rights, privacy, and fairness.

b. Safety and Security: Holistic regulation can address not only the immediate safety of AI systems but also their broader implications for cybersecurity and national security. It can help establish standards for securing AI technologies against potential misuse or attacks.
c. Interdisciplinary Approach: AI's impact extends beyond technology to various sectors like healthcare, finance, transportation, and more.
d. Data Privacy: Holistic regulation can integrate data protection and privacy considerations into AI regulation.
e. Socioeconomic Effects: Regulators can assess how AI adoption may impact the job market, economic disparities, and social cohesion.
f. International Collaboration: AI is a global technology, and international cooperation is crucial for setting common standards and guidelines. Holistic regulation can facilitate collaboration among countries to ensure consistency and interoperability in AI regulations.

Holistic regulation takes a comprehensive view of AI, considering its ethical, safety, economic, and societal implications. By doing so, it can help align AI interests with broader societal goals and values, fostering responsible and beneficial AI development and deployment. The EU Artificial Intelligence act is being approved (https://artificialintelligenceact.eu/ai-act-explorer/). This regulation will lay the foundations for the regulation of AI in the EU, representing a cornerstone for other countries.

7.4 Valuation Metrics

AI implementation affects companies' economic and financial performance through various assessment metrics and approaches. The adoption of AI has a positive impact on the value of companies, particularly with the integration of AI automation leading to significant improvements in cost structures. Nevertheless, the announcement of investments in AI may decrease market value, especially for companies in non-manufacturing sectors with limited IT capabilities. The societal value of AI, which involves weighing the advantages and disadvantages for various stakeholders, is projected to increase over time due to declining technology expenses, enhanced AI expertise, and regulation advancements. Many contents are readapted mostly from Moro-Visconti (2022a), or, occasionally, Moro-Visconti (2022b), or Moro-Visconti (2021), extending digital intangible, startup, or business planning applications to specific AI valuation patterns. Further interdisciplinary references can be found in the studies of Anzai (2012), Ertel (2018), IFRS 3 (2008), Li and Du (2017), Mariusz (2016), Müller and Bostrom (2016), Nilsson (1980), Parag and Prachi (2015), Pedersen (2016), Short and Adams (2017), Skansi (2018), Stein (2020), Stuart and Norvig (2016).

The main economic, financial, and market valuation patterns of AI are shown in Table 7.5.

The target of AI value chains is represented by digital applications (social networks; the metaverse; eCommerce and other digital platforms; NFTs; telemedicine, etc.), even concerning Industry 4.0. (Popkova & Sergi, 2020). Institutions that use AI generate added business value gains, through increased sales, and cost reduction, with an impact on cost/benefit analysis. Business efficiency is also improved (AlSheibani et al., 2020).

The valuation metrics of AI must consider that:

Table 7.5 Economic, financial, and market valuation patterns of artificial intelligence

Economic patterns	AI is driving economic growth by automating tasks, improving efficiency, and developing new products and services AI is creating new jobs in fields such as AI development, data science, and machine learning AI is displacing some jobs, particularly in industries where tasks can be easily automated AI is increasing productivity and reducing costs for businesses AI is boosting innovation and creating new opportunities for businesses
Financial patterns	Investment in AI is growing rapidly The market valuation of AI companies is also growing rapidly AI is helping businesses to increase revenues, reduce costs, and improve profitability
Market valuation patterns	The market valuation of AI companies is typically high relative to their earnings This is because investors are betting on the future growth potential of AI The market valuation of AI companies can be volatile, as investors react to news about AI developments and the performance of AI companies

a. Standard firms, based on traditional business models, use some AI tools to expand their business or improve efficiency targets;
b. Born-digital firms are built around AI and other related intangibles.

These two typologies of firm interact, sharing an evolving marketplace where innovative companies propose new solutions often as unconventional answers to well-known problems. Traditional firms, on their side, provide unmet demand, market potential, and hints for customer upgrades.

AI can play a significant role in maximizing data value, improving enterprise adoption rates, accelerating time to insight, and providing smart and contextual data-driven advice, as shown in Table 7.6

AI's role in maximizing data value is crucial as businesses increasingly rely on data to make informed decisions, improve processes, and stay competitive in today's data-driven world. By integrating AI into their data strategies, organizations can unlock new opportunities and gain a competitive edge.

The economic, financial, and market valuation of AI technologies and companies can be influenced by a variety of metrics and appraisal approaches. These metrics and approaches help investors, analysts, and stakeholders assess the value and potential of AI investments:

Metrics:

a. **Revenue Growth**: The rate at which an AI firm's revenue is increasing is a fundamental metric. Rapid revenue growth is linked to higher valuations, as it suggests strong market demand and scalability.
b. **Customer Acquisition Cost (CAC)**: The cost to acquire new customers relative to the revenue generated from those customers represents the efficiency of a firm's sales and marketing efforts. Lower CAC relative to customer lifetime value is typically favorable.
c. **Customer Lifetime Value (CLTV)**: CLTV represents the total expected revenue from a customer over their lifetime as a customer. A higher CLTV can positively impact valuation.
d. **Churn Rate**: The rate at which customers stop using a firm's AI products or services can affect long-term revenue projections. Lower churn rates are generally preferred.

Table 7.6 Artificial intelligence and data value

Data Analysis and Insights	AI excels at analyzing vast volumes of data rapidly and efficiently, identifying valuable insights, trends, and patterns that might be difficult for humans to discover manually
Automation and Efficiency	AI can automate labor-intensive data processing, cleansing, and integration tasks. This not only improves the accuracy of data management but also saves time and resources, allowing employees to focus on more strategic tasks
Personalization and Contextual Advice	AI can provide personalized recommendations and advice tailored to individual or organizational needs, enhancing decision-making and user experiences
Natural Language Interfaces	AI-powered natural language interfaces, such as chatbots, enable users to interact with data in a conversational and user-friendly manner, making data more accessible to a broader audience
Continuous Learning and Adaptability	AI algorithms continuously learn and adapt to changing data and business conditions
Enhanced Decision Support	AI can assist decision-makers by running simulations, predictive models, and what-if analyses, helping organizations make informed and data-driven decisions
Augmented Analytics	AI augments human data analysis capabilities by automating routine tasks, offering data-driven suggestions, and providing deeper insights, thus improving the quality and speed of data analysis
Unlocking Data Potential	By harnessing AI technologies effectively, organizations can tap into the full potential of their data. This not only leads to enhanced operational efficiency but also provides valuable insights that drive innovation and growth

e. **Gross Margin**: Gross margin measures the profitability of a firm's products or services. High gross margins are often associated with strong valuations.
f. **Operating Margin**: Operating margin reflects the profitability of a firm's core operations after accounting for operating expenses. Improving operating margins can enhance valuation.

g. **Customer Retention Rate**: A high rate of customer retention can lead to predictable revenue streams and may positively influence valuation.
h. **Market Share**: The percentage of the market that an AI company captures can impact its valuation. A growing market share can be a sign of competitive strength.
i. **User Engagement Metrics**: For AI-driven consumer products, user engagement metrics such as daily active users, session duration, and retention rates can be critical indicators of product success and valuation.
j. **Licensing and Royalty Income**: For AI companies that license their technology, revenue from licensing agreements can be a significant metric affecting valuation.

Appraisal Approaches Include:

a. **Discounted Cash Flow (DCF) Analysis**: DCF (see www.fastercapital.com) is a fundamental valuation method that estimates the present value of expected future cash flows generated by AI technology or a company. It considers revenue projections, growth rates, and discount rates to arrive at a valuation.
b. **Comparable Firm Analysis (CCA)**: CCA involves comparing the AI firm's financial metrics, such as revenue multiples, profitability, and growth rates, to those of similar AI companies that are publicly traded or have been acquired recently.
c. **Market Opportunity Analysis**: Assessing the size and growth potential of the AI market segment the firm operates in can provide insight into its future revenue potential and valuation.
d. **Risk-Adjusted Return Analysis**: Investors often consider the level of risk associated with AI investments and adjust their valuation expectations accordingly. This approach may involve incorporating a risk premium into the valuation.
e. **Intellectual Property Valuation**: For AI companies with significant intellectual property, valuing patents, proprietary algorithms, and data assets is an essential component of the overall valuation.
f. **Scenario Analysis**: Evaluating multiple deterministic/stochastic scenarios with different assumptions, such as high and low growth

rates or varying competitive landscapes, can provide a range of potential valuations to account for uncertainty.

g. **Venture Capital Method**: This method, often used in early stage AI startups, considers the desired rate of return for investors and the expected exit value of the firm, factoring in the number of years to exit.
h. **Option Pricing Models**: For startups and research projects with significant uncertainty, option pricing models, such as real options analysis, may be used to assess the value of AI projects and technologies.
i. **Blockchain and Token Valuation**: When AI companies are involved in blockchain or token-based projects, valuation may consider factors like token utility and adoption.
j. **AI-Specific Metrics**: AI-specific metrics such as model accuracy, data quality, and training efficiency can influence valuation, especially for companies heavily focused on AI technology development.

The choice of metrics and valuation approaches can vary depending on the stage of the AI firm, its business model, and the specific industry it operates in. A comprehensive evaluation typically involves considering a combination of these metrics and approaches to arrive at a reasonable and defensible valuation.

A valuation metric for traditional firms may consider the "with or without" methodology explained in the International Valuation Standard 210, showing the incremental EBITDA given by AI (in the form of higher revenues deriving from new market opportunities and lower monetary OPEX consequential to efficiency gains).

Figure 7.3 shows the link between the main AI business models and the valuation approaches.

The utilization of AI and digital technologies within value chains is a pivotal component of contemporary dialogues regarding economic development and the transformation of work. The integration of AI-driven changes and efficient management of data are progressively being incorporated within the public sector to bolster decision-making procedures and heighten operational effectiveness. The substantial role of Artificial Intelligence in amplifying production procedures through the augmentation of flexibility and efficiency is particularly evident when interwoven into digital value chains that interconnect various collaborators within the

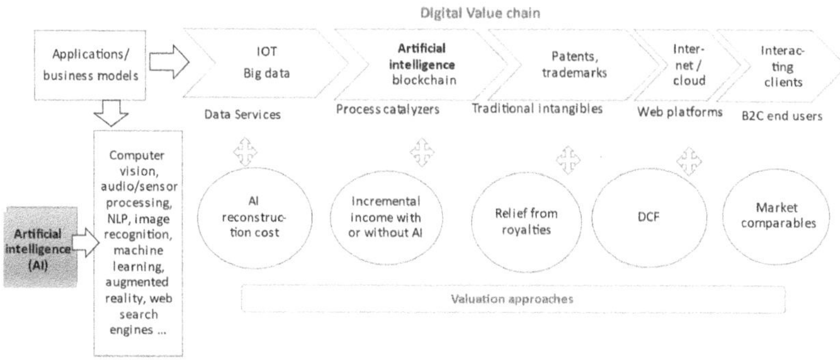

Fig. 7.3 Application of AI, digital value chains, and valuation approaches

production framework. In addition, blockchain technology is fundamentally altering conventional business structures by furnishing decentralized and secure digital records that expedite the co-creation of value and remove the necessity for intermediaries in transactions. Moreover, the application of digital twins and AI technologies in the manufacturing domain is enriching comprehension of processes, as well as improving agility and resilience, albeit encountering challenges associated with data scalability and uncertainties in modeling. The assessment metrics of the business models connected to the AI must first consider their nature: such models can be the basis of entrepreneurial realities for which the AI constitutes the primary mission (prevailing social object) or a mere accessory activity.

In the first case, the objective is to estimate the overall value of companies that are mainly focused on AI, while in the second case, the estimate is limited to identifying, where possible, the differential (incremental) value made possible by traditional business models by the introduction of AI, to stimulate product or, more frequently, process innovation.

The incremental economic and financial marginality induced by AI directly influences the evaluation parameters and must consider the possibility that these parameters can be subject to (digital) scalability, with a multiplying impact on the evaluation. First, it is possible to refer to the economies of scale and experience (linked to learning curves that are inherent to AI) that allow cost savings and increases in revenues, thus expanding the economic marginality and with it, the cash flows produced (EBITDA impacts on operating cash flows and DCF metrics).

Scalability is typical of unrivaled intangible assets (i.e., assets that can be used simultaneously by several parties) and allows operating revenues to be increased while minimizing variable extra costs, thus giving the business model plasticity that enhances its key value drivers.

The use of traditional methods of valuation of intangible assets (cost, income, or market approach, following IVS 210 prescriptions) can be adapted, especially when the valuation of AI is part of a synergistic portfolio of intangible assets. They may be linked, for example, to big data or IoT sensors as input data, to databases in the archiving phase, to software and development algorithms, etc.

Software is the one that has the greatest affinity with AI, which in many ways represents an advanced declination of it, as shown in Chapter 6. In the use of the reconstruction or replacement cost approach, the accounting aspects ease the search for clues on the costs sustained for investments in AI.

Development costs, also related to AI, can be recorded as assets in the balance sheet (CAPEX) if they refer to a process or product that is clearly identifiable, measurable, and technically feasible; they must be costs that can be recovered in the future with adequate revenues.

The income approach is based on the expected incremental profit made possible using AI, for example with a differential "with or without" comparison in which the firm is compared in the presence or absence of AI. The income approach is linked through the EBITDA to the financial approach, based on the estimate of incremental cash flows. The method of relief from royalties that the firm would collect to license its portfolio of AI applications can find applications, always in the sphere of income approaches.

Both for the companies that base their mission on AI and for the others that use it as a complement to more traditional business models, it is considered appropriate to use a valuation methodology that converges on these two approaches, already mentioned in Chapter 2:

a. The discounted cash flow (DCF);
b. The market method of the EBITDA multipliers.

Both approaches lead to the estimation of the enterprise value, intended as the total market value of a firm (shareholders' equity and debt).

To estimate the equity value only, the evaluator must subtract the (typically negative) net financial position from the enterprise value, meaning the algebraic sum of financial receivables, cash and cash equivalents, and financial payables.

Business models introducing AI have a positive impact on incremental revenues or a reduction in costs, with a consequent improvement in economic and financial marginality, showing greater efficiency.

Always from an incremental point of view, the impact on economic marginality can be examined through the so-called with or without technique, which compares situations in which AI has been introduced, concerning pre-existing scenarios.

Excess returns are related to the applicability of real options (of expansion or development), linked to the concept of augmented reality. AI increases the scope of existing technologies and opens new markets.

The real options are connected to the use of big data giving real-time information on the underlying reality, allowing the exercise of strategic options (development, expansion, temporary suspension, abandonment, deferral, etc.). The valuation approach based on the combined use of real options and big data is bottom-up in that it uses empirical evidence of the underlying reality to reformulate and update (in real time, thanks to big data) the business plans to which the valuation parameters are linked.

In the evaluation, the distinction between companies providing AI services as their core business is compared to companies (much more numerous) that just use single applications to integrate their strategies. Only in the first case, the surplus value of the AI constitutes the principal asset of the enterprise, while in the second case, the autonomous identification of the AI applications is more complex and can follow the "with or without" differential methodologies.

In this context, AI interacts with big data (as cited above) and impacts information asymmetries, which affect corporate governance and bankability issues (also in terms of rating).

The Financial Method

The methodology of discounted cash flow (DCF) is of paramount importance in determining the valuation of AI companies and investments. Through the application of DCF, a firm's Enterprise Value is initially computed, following which adjustments are made to ascertain the Equity Value through the deduction of Net Debt. This approach takes into account various elements such as cash inflows, discount rates (Weighted Average Cost of Capital), and terminal value in evaluating the worth of a corporation. The financial method for AI firm's valuation, based on operating or net DCF, is widely used in the appraisal of businesses, including those in the AI sector. DCF analysis estimates the present value of the firm's expected cash flows, accounting for the time value of money:

Step 1: Forecast Cash Flows

a. **Revenue Projections**: Estimate the firm's future revenue, considering historical performance, market growth rates, and potential adoption of AI products or services.
b. **Operating Expenses**: Project operating expenses, including research and development costs, sales and marketing expenses, and general and administrative costs.
c. **Capital Expenditures (CAPEX)**: Consider capital investments for AI technology development, infrastructure, or expansion.
d. **Taxation**: Calculate taxes based on the firm's expected profitability.
e. **Working Capital Changes**: Consider changes in working capital, including changes in accounts receivable, accounts payable, and inventory.

Step 2: Determine the Discount Rate

a. **Cost of Capital (Discount Rate)**: Estimate the firm's cost of capital, which reflects the risk associated with the AI industry and the firm's specific risk profile.

Step 3: Calculate Present Value

1. **Discount Cash Flows**: Discount projected cash flows back to their present value. The formula for discounting cash flows is:

$$PV = (1 + r)nCF \tag{7.1}$$

where:

- PV is the present value of cash flow each year.
- CF is the cash flow in that year.
- r is the discount rate.
- n is the year.

2. **Sum the Present Values**: Sum up the present values of all projected cash flows to get the total present value.

Step 4: Calculate the Terminal Value

1. **Terminal Value**: Estimate the value of the firm at the end of the forecast period. This can be done using the perpetuity growth method (Gordon Growth Model) or the exit multiple method.
   - **Perpetuity Growth Method**: Assumes that cash flows will continue to grow at a constant rate indefinitely beyond the forecast period. The formula is:

$$TerminalValue = FCFF/(d - g) \tag{7.2}$$

where:

- FCF is the free cash flow to the firm (operating cash flow) in the last forecasted year.
- g is the perpetual growth rate
- d = discount rate (which is usually the weighted average cost of capital)

Step 5: Add Present Value and Terminal Value

1. **Total Enterprise Value**: Sum up the present value of projected cash flows and the terminal value to obtain the total enterprise value (TEV).

Step 6: Subtract Debt and Add Cash

1. **Equity Value**: Adjust the TEV by subtracting debt and adding cash to calculate the equity value.

Step 7: Calculate Per-Share Value

Per-Share Value: Sub-divide the equity value by the total number of shares outstanding to determine the per-share value.

Step 8: Sensitivity Analysis

A DCF analysis provides a comprehensive view of an AI firm's value, considering its projected financial performance and risk factors. It's essential to use realistic and well-supported assumptions and to consider the uncertainty inherent in forecasting cash flows. Additionally, obtaining a comprehensive understanding of the AI industry and dynamics is crucial for accurate valuation.

The financial method is based on the principle that the market value of a firm is equal to the discounted value of the cash flows that it will be able to generate.

Operating cash flows (unlevered) and net cash flows for shareholders (levered) are determined by comparing the last two balance sheets (to make changes in operating net working capital, fixed assets, financial liabilities, employee severance indemnities, and shareholders' equity available) with the income statement for the last year.

The cash flows to be used can be the operating cash flow or the net cash flow for the shareholders. Cash flows from operating activities are discounted to present value at the weighted average cost of capital (WACC). This flow configuration offers an evaluation of the whole firm, independent of its financial structure.

Net cash flows are discounted to present value at the cost of equity (Ke).

Once the present value of the cash flows has been determined, the calculation of the economic value (W) may correspond:

a. to the unlevered cash flow method:

$$W = \sum \frac{CF_0}{WACC} + VR - NFP \tag{7.3}$$

b. to the levered cash flow method:

$$W = \sum \frac{CF_n}{K_e} + TV \tag{7.4}$$

where:

- $\sum CF_0 / WACC$ = present value of operating (debt-free) cash flows;
- $\sum CF_n / K_e$ = present value of net cash flows;
- TV = terminal value;
- NFP = net financial position (cash + financial receivables – financial payables).

A decomposition of formula (7.1), useful to understand its main constituents, brings to the following Enterprise Value of the AI-adopting firm:

$$W \approx DCFoperating \sum \frac{CF_0}{WACC} = \sum_{i=1}^{n} \frac{(AIdrivenSales) - (AIdrivenOPEX) = (AIdrivenEBITDA)}{WACC} \frac{\pm \Delta OperatingNWC \pm \Delta CAPEX = CFo}{WACC} \tag{7.5}$$

The cash flow statement used in the estimate of DCF and reproduced in Table 7.7 (already explained in Chapter 2) considers both the EBITDA and the Operating Cash Flows (see Moro Visconti, 2022b). CAPEX and Net Working Capital change with respect to the previous year.

An analytical representation of the EBITDA, showing the impact of AI, is the following (Table 7.8):

The cost of capital (see: https://fastercapital.com/keyword/dcf-method.html) associated with AI investments can vary depending on various

Table 7.7 Cash flow statement and link with the cost of capital

Sales (monetary revenues)	
- OPEX	
= EBITDA (A)	
± □Operating Net Working Capital	
± □fixed assets (CAPEX)	
= Operating cash flow (unlevered cash flow to the firm - FCFF) (B)	
- Financial charges	debt service/bankability
± □net financial liabilities	
± Extraordinary income and charges	
- Taxes	
± □Equity	
= Net (free) cash flow to the shareholders (levered cash flow - FCFE) (C)	

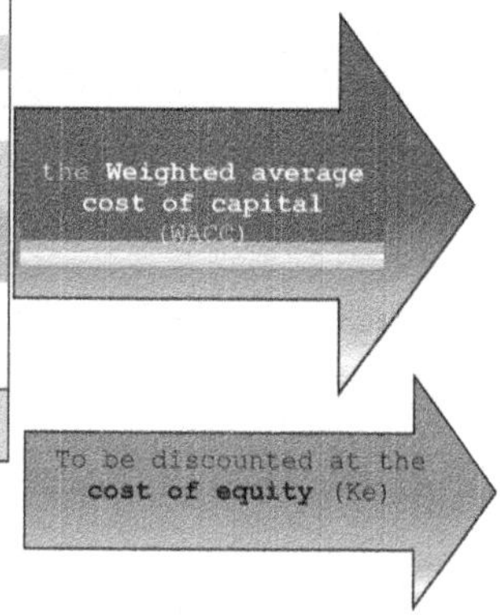

Table 7.8 EBITDA determination

Income statement (input data)	*Impact of AI*
Monetary revenues (sales)	AI improves sales (new AI-based products and markets; new clients with customer segmentation and service analytics, etc.)
- Monetary OPEX	AI improves the supply chain efficiency, optimizing the service operations, and reducing the OPEX
= EBITDA	EBITDA improves

factors, including the nature of the AI project, the industry, the risk profile, and the source of funding:

1. **Cost of Capital for AI Investments**:
    - **Equity Capital**: The cost of equity capital for AI investments is typically higher than other sources of funding. Investors expect a higher return for the perceived risk associated with AI projects, which can include technological uncertainty, regulatory hurdles, and competition.
    - **Debt Capital**: Debt financing, such as loans or bonds, can offer a lower cost of capital compared to equity. However, AI

projects may face challenges in obtaining debt financing due to their speculative and high-risk nature.

- **Venture Capital and Private Equity**: Many AI startups and companies secure funding from venture capital (VC) and private equity (PE) firms. These investors often seek significant returns to compensate for the high risk of early stage AI projects.

2. **Economic Impact**:
    - The cost of capital influences a firm's investment decisions in AI. A high cost of capital can deter companies from pursuing AI projects, as the expected ROI may not justify the expense.
    - Conversely, a lower cost of capital can incentivize more AI investment, leading to increased innovation, productivity gains, and economic growth.

3. **Financial Impact**:
    - The cost of capital affects a firm's financial statements, particularly its profitability and financial performance. Higher costs of capital can lead to lower net income and reduced shareholder returns.
    - Companies that successfully implement AI and generate substantial returns on investment may see their cost of capital decrease as investors become more confident in the technology and its potential.

4. **Market Valuation**:
    - The cost of capital is a critical factor in determining the discount rate used in discounted cash flow (DCF) analysis, which is a common method for valuing companies. A higher cost of capital leads to a lower current value of expected cash flows, bringing to a lower market valuation.
    - A lower cost of capital can lead to a higher market valuation as the DCF analysis yields a higher present value of expected cash flows.

5. **Risk Perception**:
    - The cost of capital also reflects the risk associated with AI investments. If investors perceive AI projects as highly risky,

they may demand a higher cost of capital, which can lead to higher financing costs for companies.
- Successful AI implementations and a track record of ROI reduce risk perception and lower the cost of capital over time.

The cost of capital associated with AI investments can significantly impact economic, financial, and market valuation outcomes. Companies and investors need to carefully consider the risk and return trade-offs associated with AI projects and adapt their financing strategies accordingly to maximize their capital allocation and market position.

The residual value, if subject to appreciation, is the result of discounting the value attributed to the capital of the firm operating at the time n (before which the cash flows were estimated analytically). IT is often a significant component of the overall value W and tends to zero if the time horizon of capitalization is infinite (VR/$\infty \rightarrow 0$).

The terminal value (TV) corresponds to:

$$TV = [F_m/(i - g)] * (1 + i)^{-(n+1)} \quad (7.6)$$

where:

- F_m = the average flow that the firm expects to obtain in the explicit planning period (the flow relative to the last year of the explicit forecast is often used);
- i = the discount rate of the flows;
- g = expected growth rate in the period following the explicit planning period;
- n = number of years of explicit planning.

If the evaluator opts for a perpetual capitalization horizon, the terminal value formula corresponds to:

$$TV = [F_m * (i + g)]/(1 - g) \quad (7.7)$$

The Empirical Method of Market Multiples

Synthetic approaches, based on indicators and market multiples, allow the estimate of the value based on the observation of specific parameters, in similar companies listed on regulated markets.

Market multiples are frequently utilized to evaluate companies' economic, financial, and market worth, particularly those incorporating AI technologies. The introduction of AI integration results in substantial positive abnormal returns, with discernible distinctions between companies within the IT and non-IT sectors. Furthermore, models can be used to forecast corporate wealth, with factors such as Market Capitalization, Debt Asset Ratio, ROI, and Beta Value playing pivotal roles. Moreover, using regularization methods in machine learning has proven to be efficient in assessing companies spanning various industries such as Automobile, Banking, and Steel, underscoring the relevance of standard variables in the appraisal of corporate valuation. The empirical method of market multiples assesses the value of an AI firm by comparing it to the market prices or valuations of similar publicly traded AI companies. Companies in the same industry with comparable financial and operational characteristics should have similar valuations. Here's how to perform a valuation using market multiples for an AI firm (Table 7.9):

The market multiples method relies on the availability of comparable publicly traded companies. This approach is typically unsuitable for early stage or private AI companies with limited financial data or when there are not directly comparable publicly traded peers. In such cases, other valuation methods, such as the DCF analysis or the Venture Capital Method (examined in Chapter 5), may be more appropriate.

Additionally, due diligence and careful selection of comparable companies are critical for the accuracy of this valuation method.

Comparability profiles can be hampered by increasingly unique business models, even if the growing spread of databases accelerates and stimulates the digital dissemination of information, allowing for increasingly sophisticated and capillary databases.

Among the empirical criteria, the approach of the multiplier of the EBITDA is widely diffused, to which the net financial position must be added algebraically, to pass from the estimate of the enterprise value (total value of the firm) to that of the equity value (value of the net assets), according to the following formula:

$$W = \mathrm{p} * \mathrm{m} +/- \mathrm{NFP} \tag{7.8}$$

Table 7.9 Comparable companies

Identify Comparable AI Companies	**Industry Classification**: Identify publicly traded AI companies that are in the same or similar subsector within the technology industry. These companies should be involved in AI-related activities, such as AI software development, AI services, or AI hardware **Size and Scale**: Choose companies that are similar in size and scale to the target AI firm. Market capitalization, revenue, and other financial metrics should be in the same range **Business Model**: Select comparable companies with a similar business model. For example, if the target firm specializes in AI software for healthcare, focus on publicly traded AI software companies in the healthcare sector
Gather Financial Data	**Financial Metrics**: Gather economic and financial data for the target AI firm and the selected comparables. Key financial metrics include revenue, EBITDA, net income, and other relevant financial ratios **Market Metrics**: Gather market metrics for the selected comparable companies, such as their market capitalization, enterprise value, and share price
Calculate Market Multiples	**Determine the Appropriate Multiple**: Choose a relevant financial multiple for the valuation. Common multiples used in AI firm valuations include the Price-to-Sales (P/S) ratio, Price-to-EBITDA (P/EBITDA) ratio, Price-to-Earnings (P/E) ratio, and Enterprise Value-to-Revenue (EV/Revenue) ratio **Calculate Multiples**: Calculate the selected multiples for both the target AI firm and the comparable companies. Divide the market metrics (e.g., market capitalization or enterprise value) by the corresponding financial metrics (e.g., revenue or EBITDA) to compute the multiples

(continued)

Table 7.9 (continued)

Apply the Multiples to the Target AI Firm	**Adjust for Differences**: Consider any differences between the target AI firm and the selected comparables. Adjust the multiples if there are significant variations in growth rates, risk profiles, or other factors **Calculate Valuation**: Multiply the relevant market multiple by the financial metric of the target AI firm to estimate its valuation. For example, if the average P/S ratio of the comparables is 5x, and the target firm has $10 million in annual revenue, the estimated valuation would be $50 million
Sensitivity Analysis	**Sensitivity Analysis**: Perform sensitivity analysis by applying a range of multiples or testing different scenarios. This helps account for variations in market sentiment and potential outliers among the comparables
Final Valuation	**Final Valuation**: After conducting a sensitivity analysis and considering all relevant factors, arrive at a final estimated valuation for the target AI firm based on market multiples

where:

- W = market value;
- p = income parameter;
- m = multiplier;
- NFP = net financial position.

Valuations based on the application of multiples derived from stock market prices require the identification of a sample of comparable firms. EBITDA, expressed as the difference between operating revenues (sales revenues, changes in inventories of finished products, and other operating revenues) and operating costs gross of amortization/depreciation and provisions, is often used as the basic parameter of operating profitability.

The functional link between the financial approach and the multiples approach is provided, once again, by the EBITDA, which is the basis of both the operating cash flow and the application of market multipliers.

7.5 Forecasting Rational Expected Outcomes: Sales Prediction

Forecasting sales with AI algorithms involves leveraging historical data, market variables, and machine learning techniques to predict future sales accurately, as shown in Table 7.10.

Sales prediction with AI algorithms can be are a valuable tool for businesses to maximize operations, allocate resources efficiently, and make data-driven decisions. AI models are not infallible, and the accuracy of forecasts depends on data quality, feature engineering, and model selection.

In AI, economics, game theory, or decision theory, a rational agent (software, person, machine, firm, etc.) has clear-cut preferences, models uncertainty through expected values of variables, and always chooses to act with the optimal expected outcome.

The rational agent acts with the best outcome after considering past and current input data.

The rational agent is a theoretical entity based on a realistic evolutionary model and prefers advantageous outcomes that maximize its performance targets and will seek to achieve them in a (machine) learning scenario.

Intelligent agents interact with the environment through sensors and actuators.

The relationship between AI and standard valuation approaches is two-sided: whereas AI follows the same valuation criteria that concern standard firms and their intangibles, the basic features of AI can help to improve forecasts—one of the critical points of any appraisal. Forecasts may concern episodic or sequential task environments in a static or dynamic environment whose evolution can be deterministic or stochastic (following probabilistic patterns that AI can model and autonomously refine).

AI can nurture future patterns that follow rational outcomes with autonomous learning; milestones and occurrences can be detected in real time and automatically included in a self-learning software that continuously improves. The tendency is to embed AI in valuation methodologies.

Table 7.10 Forecasting sales with Artificial Intelligence

Data Collection and Preparation	**Data Sources**: Gather historical sales data, including date, product, location, pricing, and any other relevant factors. Additionally, collect external data sources like economic indicators, customer demographics, and competitor data if applicable **Data Cleaning**: Clean and preprocess the data to handle missing values, outliers, and inconsistencies. Ensure data is in a format suitable for machine learning
Feature Selection and Engineering	**Feature Selection**: Identify which features or variables are most relevant to sales prediction. Features may include past sales, marketing expenditures, seasonality, and more **Feature Engineering**: Create new features or transform existing ones that could enhance the predictive power of the model. For example, create lag features to capture trends or incorporate categorical variables through one-hot encoding
Data Splitting	**Training and Testing Data**: Split the dataset into training and testing sets. The training set is used to train the AI model, while the testing set is reserved to evaluate the model's performance
Model Selection	**Regression Algorithms**: Common AI algorithms for sales prediction include linear regression, decision trees, random forests, support vector machines, and neural networks. Choose an algorithm that best fits your data and problem
Model Training	**Training the Model**: Feed the training data into the chosen AI algorithm to train the model. The model learns the relationships between the input features and sales
Model Evaluation	**Testing the Model**: Use the testing dataset to evaluate the model's performance. Common evaluation metrics include Mean Absolute Error (MAE), Mean Squared Error (MSE), Root Mean Squared Error (RMSE), and R-squared (R^2) **Cross-Validation**: Consider using cross-validation techniques, such as k-fold cross-validation, to assess the model's stability and reliability

(continued)

Table 7.10 (continued)

Hyperparameter Tuning	Maximize the model's hyperparameters to improve its predictive performance. This may involve adjusting parameters like learning rate, tree depth, or neural network architecture
Seasonality and Time-Series Forecasting	If sales data exhibits seasonality or time-dependent patterns, consider using specialized time-series forecasting models like ARIMA (AutoRegressive Integrated Moving Average), Exponential Smoothing, or Prophet. These models are designed to capture temporal dependencies
Predictions and Interpretability:	Once the model is trained and validated, use it to make sales predictions for future periods. Ensure that the model's predictions are interpretable and actionable
Monitoring and Updating	Continuously monitor the model's performance and retrain it periodically with new data. Markets and customer behaviors change over time, so keeping an up-to-date model is essential for accurate sales predictions
Business Insights	Translate the AI-generated sales predictions into actionable business insights. Consider how the predictions can inform marketing strategies, inventory management, pricing decisions, and sales forecasting
Visualization	Create visualizations and dashboards to communicate sales forecasts and insights effectively to stakeholders within the organization
Scenario Analysis	Conduct scenario analysis by adjusting input variables to explore how changes in marketing budgets, pricing strategies, or external factors might impact future sales

AI-driven sales prediction, with its temporal granularity, is a key part of the planning process, as the revenue model is the basis for the forecast of cash flows. Tsoumakas (2019) shows that food sales prediction is concerned with estimating future sales of companies in the food industry. Accurate short-term sales prediction allows companies to minimize stocked and expired products inside stores and at the same time avoid missing sales.

AI is fully consistent with the research scope of this chapter since it impacts predictive analytics. AI can ideally automize the value creation process, making it self-fulfilling and automatically increasing its potential with self-learning patterns that boost scalability and real options. The reality is, however, harder than these ideal targets, and the AI setup needs careful tailor-made configuration, still characterized by limited applications. Digitalization is a prerequisite for the usability of (preferably, numerical) big data. Different approaches such as time series analysis, artificial neural networks, and machine learning algorithms are utilized for precise sales prediction in the retail industry, with machine learning demonstrating superior accuracy owing to its capability to recognize concealed demand patterns and market trends. Machine learning methodologies, especially Convolutional Neural Networks (CNN), have surfaced as valuable instruments for enhancing sales prediction accuracy over time, outperforming conventional techniques such as Excel functions or subjective estimations. Furthermore, the incorporation of AI in sales prediction not only enriches forecasting precision but also safeguards data integrity through sophisticated encryption techniques, essential for decision-making and strategizing in retail enterprises. By harnessing AI technologies like neural networks and machine learning, organizations can make well-informed decisions, optimize inventory management, and propel business expansion based on logical anticipated outcomes.

AI fosters data analytics that impact cash flow forecasting, as shown in Table 7.11 which represents just an example of the possible AI applications.

7.6 Network Theory Applications (Artificial Intelligence-driven Nodes and Edges)

Network theory, especially within AI applications, provides valuable perspectives for traditional companies leveraging AI technologies. By utilizing network models that integrate various AI algorithms, companies can enhance their comprehension of algorithms' suitability for their data and effectively compare their performance. Network theory, particularly in AI applications, is significant for assessing the market, economic, and financial value of conventional companies that are integrating AI technologies. This methodology can aid regulators, judicial authorities, and insurance providers in visualizing intricate legal inquiries pertaining to emergent technologies such as AI. The societal value of AI, which

Table 7.11 Impact of data analytics on cash flow forecasting

AI-driven data analytics	*Discounted cash flow forecasting*
AI can improve the following processes, in particular predictive analytics • Descriptive Analytics illustrates what happened in the past and is widely used in traditional business planning • Diagnostic Analytics helps to understand why something happened in the past • Predictive Analytics uses data mining to predict what is most likely to happen in the future • Prescriptive Analytics recommends actions to affect those outcomes	Cash flow forecasts are fueled by data analysis, a process of inspecting, cleansing, transforming, and modeling data to discover useful information, inform conclusions, and support decision-making
Customer analytics • Client profiling • Client experience/feedback • Market segmentation • Social Network Analysis • Brand awareness • Marketing mix optimization	Client profiling eases cash flow forecasting, responses to unexpected positive or negative events (incorporating real options), experience sharing to foster value co-creation, and viral networking through social media. Customer analytics mainly impacts revenues, easing their prediction and leveraging the scalability of the business model which becomes more reactive and timelier
Supply Chain Analytics • Demand forecasting • Optimization of inventory • Pricing • Scheduling • Transportation and Storage • Human Capital / Workforce Analytics	Optimization of the supply chain improves demand forecasting and stock turnover, providing useful insights for reactive pricing Operating costs can be reduced, improving the efficiency and efficacy of used resources, and productivity. Lower Operating expenditure (OPEX) increases the EBITDA, and maximizes Net Working Capital Management, with a positive impact on the Operating Cash Flows
Risk analytics • Market risk • Operational risk • Credit scoring • Macroeconomic risk (interest rates, currency rates, country, and political risk, inflation, GDP forecasts, etc.)	Improved forecasting of future events reduces risk, incorporated in the denominator of DCF metrics

includes advantages for internal stakeholders, business clients, supply chain collaborators, and the broader community, underscores the significance of AI adoption in augmenting decision-making processes and operational efficiencies within organizations.The integration of AI and network theory holds significant potential for optimizing and managing various aspects of modern ecosystems, especially in handling large datasets. Here's a more detailed exploration of the points you've raised:

1. **Efficient Resource Allocation:** AI-powered networks can help in the efficient allocation of computational resources. Machine learning algorithms can be used to analyze the characteristics of data nodes and determine the most suitable computing resources for processing them. This ensures that resources are allocated optimally, leading to improved performance and cost savings.
2. **Data Matching and Interpretation:** AI plays a critical role in matching dataset nodes with computing links. Machine learning models are trained to understand the relationships between different data points, enabling better matching and interpretation of data. This is particularly important in scenarios where data nodes are heterogeneous and complex.
3. **Quantitative Nodes and Qualitative Links:** The concept of representing quantitative nodes with qualitative links aligns with the idea of using AI to extract meaningful insights from data. AI techniques like natural language processing and sentiment analysis can convert numerical data into qualitative information, making it easier to understand and act upon.
4. **Synergistic Interactions:** AI and network theory can complement each other in various ways. Network theory provides a framework for understanding the structure and connectivity of data, while AI can uncover patterns and anomalies within that structure. The synergy between these two fields can lead to more effective data analysis and decision-making.
5. **Scalability:** AI's ability to automate tasks and analyze large volumes of data makes it instrumental in scaling up data processing and analysis. As datasets continue to grow and complexity, AI-powered networks can adapt and handle the increased workload, ensuring scalability.

6. **Theoretical and Practical Insights:** The interaction between AI and network theory represents an intriguing theoretical perspective with practical implications. Researchers and practitioners can explore how AI algorithms can enhance network analysis and vice versa. For example, AI can assist in identifying critical nodes in a network, while network theory can help in optimizing AI algorithms for distributed computing.
7. **Challenges:** It's important to note that integrating AI and network theory also comes with challenges. Ensuring the accuracy and reliability of AI-driven insights in network analysis is crucial. Additionally, privacy and security considerations must be addressed when dealing with sensitive data within network ecosystems.

The combination of AI and network theory holds great promise in optimizing and managing modern ecosystems, particularly in handling large datasets. This interdisciplinary approach can lead to innovative solutions and improved decision-making in various domains, from healthcare and finance to transportation and telecommunications. Further research and practical applications in this area are likely to yield valuable insights and benefits.

Network theory, often associated with graph theory, provides a framework for analyzing and understanding the structure, connectivity, and dynamics of networks. Here are some main features of network theory and how they can contribute to the growth of additional nodes and more intense edges in a network, thereby increasing its market value:

1. **Nodes and Edges:** In network theory, nodes represent individual entities or elements, and edges represent the connections or relationships between them. The addition of new nodes and edges expands the network's scope and potential.
2. **Scale-Free Networks:** One notable feature of many real-world networks is their scale-free nature. In scale-free networks, a small number of nodes, known as hubs, have a disproportionately high number of connections. This feature can promote the growth of additional nodes and edges because new nodes tend to connect to existing hubs, enhancing the network's connectivity and value.

3. **Small World Phenomenon:** The small-world property suggests that in many networks, any two nodes can be connected through a relatively small number of intermediate nodes. This feature fosters the rapid spread of information, innovation, and interactions, attracting more nodes and edges as the network becomes more efficient and accessible.
4. **Clustering and Community Detection:** Network theory also enables the identification of clusters or communities within a network, where nodes are densely connected. The presence of such clusters can encourage the formation of more edges within these communities and the addition of new nodes to strengthen community ties, thus increasing overall market value.
5. **Centrality Measures:** Centrality metrics like degree centrality, betweenness centrality, and closeness centrality help identify the most important nodes in a network. These nodes often play key roles in information dissemination and influence, making them attractive for new connections and partnerships, which can drive the growth of additional nodes and edges.
6. **Resilience and Robustness:** Network theory allows for the analysis of a network's resilience and robustness to various disruptions. Networks that can adapt to perturbations by forming new connections or nodes are more likely to grow and maintain their market value in dynamic environments.
7. **Innovation and Knowledge Transfer:** Networks facilitate the exchange of ideas, information, and resources. When nodes (representing individuals, organizations, or entities) can easily share knowledge and collaborate, innovation and value creation tend to flourish, attracting more participants and fostering the growth of additional nodes and edges.
8. **Economic and Social Networks:** In economic and social contexts, networks play a crucial role in forming business partnerships, collaborations, and social relationships. As the network expands and more actors join, the potential for value creation and market growth increases through enhanced interactions and opportunities.
9. **Emergent Properties:** Networks often exhibit emergent properties, where the collective behavior of nodes and edges leads to outcomes that cannot be predicted by looking at individual components. These emergent properties can drive market value by enabling new functionalities or services within the network.

Network theory provides valuable insights into the structure and dynamics of networks. Its features, such as scale-free networks, small-world properties, and centrality measures, can contribute to the growth of additional nodes and more intense edges, leading to increased market value. Networks that are adaptable, efficient, and conducive to collaboration tend to attract more participants and thrive in various domains, ultimately generating economic and social value.

Network theory and digital scalability are closely linked, and their synergy can indeed create significant value in various domains, as shown in Table 7.12.

The link between network theory and digital scalability lies in their shared principles of efficient resource management, adaptability, and resilience. When applied in tandem, these concepts can help digital systems and platforms create value by accommodating growth, enhancing performance, and fostering network effects, ultimately leading to increased user satisfaction and economic benefits.

Figures 7.4 and 7.5 represent by way of example:

- a traditional network in which four nodes (stakeholders, etc.) interact with each other, with direct links (for example, from A to B or D) or mediated (from A to C);
- a scalable network, in which, thanks to the presence of AI, the number of nodes (big data, etc.) and the links (primarily epistemological) between the nodes increases (even exponentially), thanks to the interpretative/qualitative properties of the AI.

7.7 Risk Assessment and SWOT Analysis

Risk assessment and SWOT analysis can be significantly improved by incorporating AI methodologies. AI-driven algorithms can offer predictive risk analysis, which can thoroughly evaluate risks and pinpoint deficiencies in control measures. When applied to established risk assessment techniques such as Process Hazard Analysis (PHA) and Hazard Identification (HAZID), AI can amalgamate encoded human expertise to

Table 7.12 Network theory and digital scalability

Scalability in Network Theory	In network theory, scalability refers to a network's ability to handle an increasing number of nodes, edges, or interactions without a proportional decrease in performance or efficiency Scalability is essential in various networked systems, such as computer networks, social networks, transportation networks, and more. It ensures that these systems can grow to accommodate new users, data, or resources
Scalability in Digital Systems	In the digital world, scalability refers to the ability of a system or application to handle growing workloads and user demands gracefully Digital systems often need to scale to accommodate increased data volumes, user traffic, or computational requirements without experiencing performance degradation or service disruptions
The Link between Network Theory and Digital Scalability	Network theory provides valuable insights into how networks grow and adapt as they scale. It offers principles and models for understanding the dynamics of connections, which can be applied to various digital systems Many digital systems can be conceptualized as networks, where nodes represent users, devices, or components, and edges represent interactions or data flows. Network theory can help analyze and maximize the scalability of these systems

(continued)

Table 7.12 (continued)

Creating Value through Joint Efforts	Leveraging network theory in digital scalability efforts can create value in several ways: a. **Efficient Resource Allocation:** Network theory can inform the allocation of resources in digital systems, ensuring that computational resources, data storage, and bandwidth are optimally distributed as the system scales. This efficiency contributes to cost savings and improved performance b. **Load Balancing:** Understanding network theory concepts like load distribution and routing algorithms can aid in distributing workloads evenly across digital infrastructure, preventing bottlenecks and ensuring a smooth user experience c. **Redundancy and Resilience:** Network theory can guide the design of redundant connections and failover mechanisms in digital systems. This enhances system resilience and availability, minimizing downtime and preserving user trust d. **Scalable Architectures:** Digital systems can be designed with scalable architectures that mimic the characteristics of scale-free networks or small-world networks, allowing them to grow organically as demand increases e. **Data Analysis and Optimization:** Network theory techniques can be applied to analyze the flow of data within digital systems, leading to insights that can maximize data processing, reduce latency, and improve the user experience f. **Network Effects:** As digital systems scale and attract more users or participants, they often benefit from network effects, where the value of the system increases as more users join. This can lead to exponential growth in value as the network expands

(continued)

Table 7.12 (continued)

Examples of Value Creation	Social media platforms (Facebook, Twitter, etc.) leverage network theory to connect users and facilitate interactions, resulting in tremendous value through user engagement and advertising revenue Cloud computing providers use scalable network architectures to accommodate the increasing demands for data storage and processing, creating value for businesses by offering flexible and cost-effective services

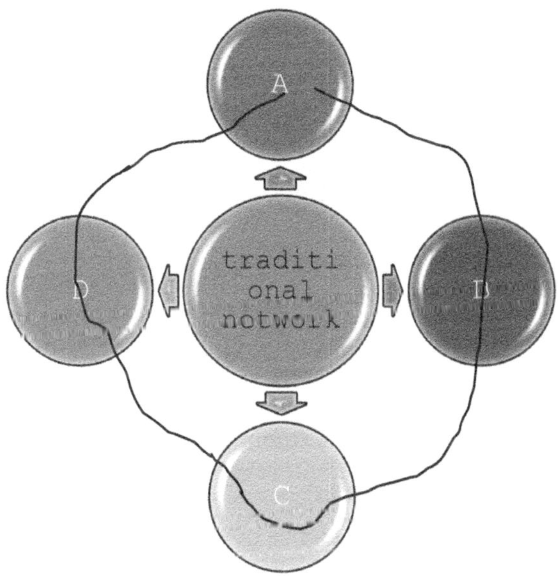

Fig. 7.4 Node interaction in a traditional network

enhance decision-making processes and promote the development of safer designs and operational practices. The utilization of AI in SWOT analysis can introduce a dynamic element through the use of fuzzy cognitive maps, facilitating a more interactive and real-time evaluation of projects and their interconnections. By utilizing machine learning techniques on

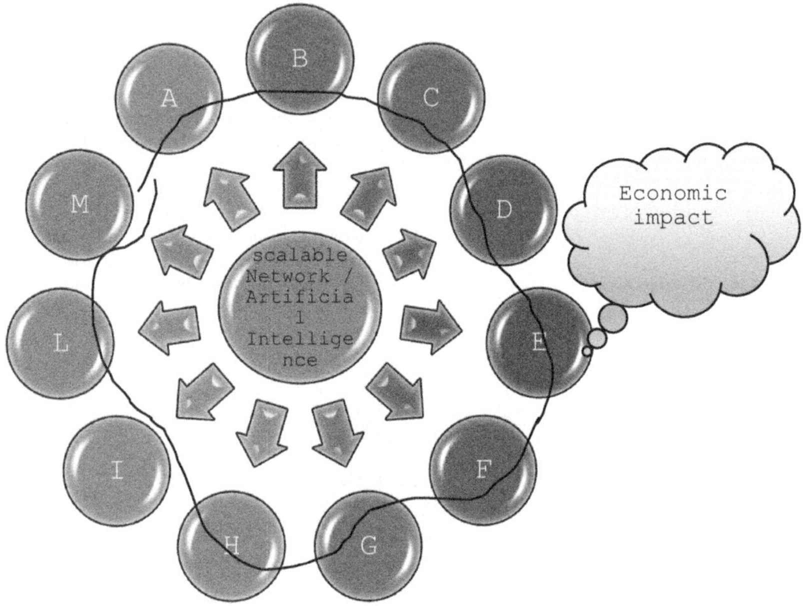

Fig. 7.5 Node interaction in a network made scalable by AI

analogous scenarios, AI can boost the intelligence and precision of risk assessment models, thereby ensuring domain specificity and enhancing the overall effectiveness of assessments. Risk assessment and SWOT analysis (Strengths, Weaknesses, Opportunities, Threats) are valuable strategic tools used to evaluate the impact of various factors on AI initiatives, and they can significantly affect the economic, financial, and market valuation of AI projects and companies. Here's how these analyses work and their implications:

Risk Assessment in AI:

Risk assessment in AI involves identifying and evaluating potential risks associated with AI projects or implementations. These risks can be categorized into various dimensions:

a. **Technical Risks:** These relate to the technology itself, including issues like model accuracy, scalability, and robustness. Technical risks can impact project timelines, costs, and overall success.

b. **Ethical and Regulatory Risks**: These involve concerns related to bias, fairness, privacy, and compliance with relevant regulations such as GDPR. Violations of ethical principles or regulatory non-compliance can lead to legal and reputational risks.
c. **Market Risks:** These consider factors like competition, changing market dynamics, and customer adoption rates. Failure to meet market expectations can lead to financial losses.
d. **Operational Risks:** These pertain to the day-to-day management of AI projects, including issues like data quality, data security, and system uptime. Operational disruptions can affect project outcomes and financial performance.
e. **Financial Risks:** These encompass budget overruns, unexpected costs, and ROI uncertainties. Financial risks can impact the economic viability of AI initiatives.
f. **Strategic Risks:** These involve the alignment of AI strategies with broader business goals. Misalignment can lead to inefficiencies and reduced market competitiveness.

SWOT Analysis in AI:

SWOT analysis assesses the internal strengths and weaknesses of an AI project or firm, along with external opportunities and threats in the broader environment. The analysis typically covers the aspects illustrated in Table 7.13.

Table 7.13 SWOT analysis

Strengths	These are internal advantages or assets that can enhance the success of AI initiatives. Strengths might include a talented AI team, proprietary algorithms, access to quality data, or a strong brand reputation
Weaknesses	These are internal limitations or shortcomings that can hinder AI projects. Weaknesses could include a lack of expertise, data limitations, or outdated technology infrastructure
Opportunities	These are external factors or trends that can be leveraged for AI success. Opportunities might include growing market demand for AI solutions, emerging technologies, or strategic partnerships
Threats	These are external challenges or risks that could negatively impact AI initiatives. Threats may include competition from established players, regulatory changes, or economic downturns

Impact on Economic, Financial, and Market Valuation:

a. **Economic Valuation:** Risk assessment helps estimate the economic viability of AI projects. Identifying and mitigating risks can lead to more accurate financial projections, reducing the likelihood of budget overruns and financial losses.
b. **Financial Valuation:** AI projects or companies with well-managed risks and a favorable SWOT profile are more attractive to investors. Lower risk profiles can lead to higher valuation multiples and lower discount rates in financial models, potentially increasing the project or firm's valuation.
c. **Market Valuation:** Market valuation is influenced by a firm's competitive position and growth prospects. A positive SWOT analysis can highlight a firm's strengths and opportunities, enhancing its market perception and valuation.
d. **Investor Confidence:** Comprehensive risk assessment and SWOT analysis can instill investor confidence. Investors may be more willing to provide funding or invest in companies with a clear understanding of risks and strategies to address them.

Risk assessment and SWOT analysis contribute to shaping the economic, financial, and market valuation of AI projects and companies. By identifying and mitigating risks, leveraging strengths, capitalizing on opportunities, and addressing weaknesses and threats, organizations can enhance their chances of successful AI implementations and positively impact their valuation.

7.8 The Valuation of Listed Artificial Intelligence Firms

AI companies ascertain their market worth by considering various factors, including the impact of AI investments, success in innovation, societal contribution, disclosure of AI implementation, and awareness of potential risks. The success of innovation in the field of AI is linked to previous advancements in information and communication technology (ICT), as the productivity of AI patents tends to increase alongside the scale of innovation within a company. The disclosure of AI implementation details and identification of risks associated with AI are deemed significant in terms of value, indicating that investors tend to view those companies that demonstrate a clear understanding of AI-related risks positively. Furthermore, companies with stronger IT governance tend to receive higher investor valuation when disclosing factors related to AI risks. In essence, the market value of AI enterprises is shaped by their investments in AI, track record of innovation, societal impact, and level of awareness regarding potential risks. The valuation patterns of listed AI Firms are characterized by the following features:

1. **Market Capitalization**: The market capitalization of AI firms can vary significantly depending on various factors like their size, revenue, growth potential, and market sentiment. Companies with strong growth prospects and innovative AI technologies often have higher valuations.
2. **Revenue Growth**: Investors often look at the revenue growth rate as a key indicator of the valuation of AI firms. Companies that can demonstrate rapid revenue growth tend to command higher valuations.
3. **Profitability**: While many AI companies focus on growth over profitability in their early stages, profitability or a clear path to profitability can positively impact their valuation.
4. **Competitive Position**: The competitive position of an AI firm in its respective industry can influence its valuation. Companies that are leaders in their niche or have a strong competitive advantage tend to be valued more highly.
5. **AI Technology**: The uniqueness and effectiveness of an AI firm's technology can play a significant role in its valuation. Proprietary algorithms, datasets, and cutting-edge AI solutions can drive higher valuations.

Important Listed AI Firms include:

a. **NVIDIA Corporation (NVDA)**: NVIDIA is known for its graphics processing units (GPUs) that are widely used in AI and machine learning applications. Its main business model includes selling GPUs and providing AI hardware and software solutions.
b. **Alphabet Inc. (GOOGL)**: Alphabet is the parent company of Google and owns various AI-related businesses, including Google

AI and Waymo (self-driving cars). Alphabet generates revenue primarily through online advertising and cloud services.

c. **Microsoft Corporation (MSFT)**: Microsoft has a significant presence in the AI space through its Azure cloud platform and AI services. It generates revenue from software, cloud services, and hardware.
d. **Amazon.com Inc. (AMZN)**: Amazon uses AI extensively in its e-commerce operations and its Amazon Web Services (AWS) cloud platform. Its main business model includes e-commerce, cloud computing, and digital streaming.
e. **IBM Corporation (IBM)**: IBM has been involved in AI research for decades and offers AI-related services through its IBM Watson platform. Its main business model includes IT services, software, and hardware.
f. **Tesla, Inc. (TSLA)**: While primarily known for electric vehicles, Tesla also incorporates AI in its self-driving technology, known as Autopilot. Tesla generates revenue from the sale of electric vehicles and solar energy products.
g. **Salesforce.com, Inc. (CRM)**: Salesforce uses AI in its customer relationship management (CRM) software, enhancing customer insights and automation. Its main business model is subscription-based CRM software and services.
h. **Facebook, Inc. (now Meta Platforms, Inc., META)**: Facebook, now Meta, utilizes AI for content recommendation and virtual reality (VR) applications. Its primary source of revenue is advertising.

The valuation patterns of listed AI firms and traditional unlisted AI companies (often represented by startups) can differ significantly due to various factors related to their stage of development, access to capital markets, and investor expectations. Here are some key differences:

1. **Access to Public Capital Markets**:
    - **Listed AI Firms**: Listed AI companies have access to public capital markets through stock exchanges, allowing them to raise funds by selling shares to a broad range of investors. This access to liquidity can lead to more significant capital infusions.

- **Startup AI Companies**: Unlisted startups typically rely on private funding sources, such as venture capital, angel investors, or corporate investors. This limited access to capital can constrain their growth potential until they reach a stage where they can consider an IPO (Initial Public Offering).

2. **Valuation Metrics**:

- **Listed AI Firms**: Publicly traded companies are subject to daily market valuation, which is often based on metrics like price-to-earnings (P/E) ratios, price-to-sales (P/S) ratios, and market capitalization. Valuations are transparent and based on market sentiment.
- **Startup AI Companies**: Valuations of startups are less transparent and may rely on negotiations between founders and investors. They often use metrics like pre-money and post-money valuations in the context of funding rounds. Valuations can be more subjective and may depend on investor expectations and the startup's growth potential.

3. **Financial Reporting**:

- **Listed AI Firms**: Public companies are required to adhere to strict financial reporting standards and provide regular updates to shareholders. They must disclose financial results, including revenue, profit, and cash flow, on a quarterly and annual basis.
- **Startup AI Companies**: Private startups have fewer reporting obligations and can keep financial information confidential. They typically share financial details with a limited circle of investors and stakeholders.

4. **Risk and Reward Profile**:

- **Listed AI Firms**: Publicly traded AI companies often face higher scrutiny from investors and regulatory bodies. They may be subject to market volatility and shareholder pressure, but they also have the potential to access a broader investor base and raise substantial capital.

- **Startup AI Companies**: Startups, especially in the early stages, carry higher risk and uncertainty. They have the potential for significant rewards if they succeed, but they also face a higher likelihood of failure. Investors in startups are typically willing to accept higher risk in exchange for the potential for outsized returns.

5. **Exit Strategies**:

- **Listed AI Firms**: Listed AI companies may consider various strategies for growth, including mergers and acquisitions (M&A) and global expansion. They can also be attractive targets for acquisition by larger technology firms.
- **Startup AI Companies**: Unlisted startups often consider exit strategies such as being acquired by larger companies or eventually going public through an IPO. These exit strategies can significantly impact their valuation and the returns for early stage investors.

6. **Regulatory Compliance**:

- **Listed AI Firms**: Publicly traded companies must adhere to stringent regulatory requirements, including financial reporting, corporate governance, and compliance with securities laws.
- **Startup AI Companies**: Startups have more flexibility in their operations and may not be subject to the same level of regulatory scrutiny until they reach a certain size or consider going public.

The main differences in valuation patterns between listed AI firms and traditional unlisted AI startups revolve around access to capital, transparency, risk profiles, and regulatory requirements. Publicly traded companies have more liquidity but face greater regulatory and reporting obligations, while startups operate in a less transparent and often riskier environment but have the potential for substantial growth and returns. The choice between being listed or staying private depends on the firm's specific goals, stage of development, and investor strategy.

7.9 The Valuation of Artificial Intelligence-adopting Traditional Firms

The assessment of conventional companies that integrate AI is subject to a range of factors underscored in scholarly investigations. Research indicates that the incorporation of AI has a favorable effect on the operational efficiency of firms, resulting in noteworthy abnormal returns following the disclosure of AI adoption initiatives. AI integration is viewed as a supplement to mutable inputs, enriching forecasting capabilities and potentially decreasing prices in the extended term, thereby yielding advantages for both adopting and non-adopting enterprises. The attributes of AI adopters, such as heightened productivity, larger scale, and specific geographical locations, influence their assessment. Moreover, the availability of intellectual capital and supplementary resources like ICT expertise and digital infrastructure further enhance the operational effectiveness of AI users, thereby impacting their overall appraisal in the marketplace. The valuation patterns of traditional firms that adopt AI, as shown in Moro-Visconti et al. (2023), can vary based on several factors. AI adoption can indeed have an impact on operating revenues, operating expenses, and scalability, as shown in Table 7.14. Here's an overview of how AI adoption can affect valuation and these key business metrics:

The adoption of AI can positively impact the valuation of traditional firms by increasing their growth potential, profitability, and efficiency. Investors often perceive companies that effectively harness AI as having a competitive edge in their respective industries.

Firms need to communicate their AI initiatives and their potential to drive revenue growth and cost savings to investors and stakeholders. Demonstrating a clear strategy for AI adoption and highlighting the benefits it can bring is key to maximizing the positive impact on valuation patterns.

AI has the potential to be a transformative force for businesses, not only by improving financial margins but also by enabling efficient scaling and fostering innovation. By leveraging AI technologies effectively, companies can position themselves for sustainable and accelerated growth in an increasingly competitive business environment.

When conducting sensitivity analysis to compare AI-adopting traditional firms versus non-AI adopters, a "with or without" approach is consistent with the International Valuation Standard 210 (IVS 210),

Table 7.14 Impact of Artificial Intelligence adoption on valuation metrics

Impact on Operating Revenues	Revenue Growth Potential: AI can enable traditional firms to enhance their products and services, create new revenue streams, and improve customer experiences. AI-powered recommendation systems can boost sales in e-commerce, while predictive analytics can maximize pricing strategies Customer Retention: AI can help improve customer retention by personalizing interactions and providing proactive customer support. Loyal customers contribute to sustained revenue streams New Market Opportunities: AI can uncover new market opportunities through data analysis and market segmentation, potentially expanding the customer base and revenue sources Cross-selling and Upselling: AI-driven insights can identify cross-selling and upselling opportunities, increasing the average transaction value and overall revenue
Impact on Operating Expenses	Cost Reduction: AI can automate repetitive tasks, streamline operations, and reduce labor costs. For example, chatbots and virtual assistants can handle customer inquiries, reducing the need for customer support staff Enhanced Efficiency: AI can maximize supply chain management, inventory control, and resource allocation, leading to cost savings Improved Decision-Making: AI provides data-driven insights that can lead to better decision-making, reducing costly mistakes and inefficiencies Predictive Maintenance: In industries like manufacturing, AI can enable predictive maintenance, preventing costly equipment breakdowns and minimizing downtime

(continued)

Table 7.14 (continued)

Impact on Scalability	Scalability Enhancement: AI-driven processes and systems can scale more efficiently than manual processes. This scalability can accommodate increased demand without proportionally increasing operating expenses Global Expansion: AI can assist firms in expanding globally by facilitating market research, localization, and customer engagement on a larger scale Personalization at Scale: AI enables firms to provide personalized experiences to a large customer base, fostering customer loyalty and satisfaction as the business scales Data Handling: Scalable AI systems can handle vast amounts of data, which is crucial in today's data-driven business landscape
Informed Decision-Making	AI provides real-time data analysis, assisting companies in making more informed decisions to support scalability It can help identify areas where investments are most needed for growth
Innovation and Growth	AI enables companies to analyze data from various sources, uncovering trends and patterns that can lead to innovation and the development of new products and services This innovation can drive long-term scalability and sustainable growth

which is often used as a framework for valuing businesses and assets. Here's how such an approach might be applied:

1. Identify the Variables: Start by identifying the key variables that are likely to be influenced by AI adoption. In the context of AI integration, this would include variables related to revenue enhancement and operating cost reduction.
2. Establish Baseline Scenarios: Develop a baseline scenario for both AI-adopting firms and non-AI adopters. These scenarios should reflect the current financial performance and operational dynamics of each group.
3. Introduce Sensitivity Factors: Introduce sensitivity factors that represent the potential impact of AI adoption on these key variables. For example:

- For revenue enhancement, you might consider different scenarios of revenue growth rates, considering AI-driven improvements.
- For operating cost reduction, you could assess various levels of cost savings achievable through AI implementation.

4. Conduct Comparative Analysis: Conduct a comparative analysis between AI-adopting firms and non-AI adopters by applying the sensitivity factors to each group's baseline scenario. This will help quantify the potential financial impact of AI adoption.
5. Evaluate Risks: Consider the inherent uncertainties and risks associated with AI adoption. Sensitivity analysis should account for a range of scenarios, including best-case and worst-case outcomes, to provide a comprehensive view of potential risks and rewards.
6. Make Informed Decisions: The results of the sensitivity analysis will assist decision-makers in evaluating the financial implications of AI adoption.

By following this approach, businesses can gain a clearer understanding of how AI adoption might affect their financial performance compared to non-adopters. It also helps stakeholders, including investors and management, assess the benefits and risks associated with AI integration and make strategic decisions accordingly.

The adoption of AI by traditional brick-and-mortar firms, when it leads to increased revenues and reduced operating expenses (OPEX), impacts the financial valuation metrics, including EBITDA, economic performance, financial health, market valuation, and bankability:

1. **Incremental EBITDA**:
   - AI adoption can boost revenues and reduce operating costs, resulting in higher EBITDA. The incremental EBITDA represents the additional EBITDA generated as a direct result of AI adoption. This can be a key indicator of the financial benefits of AI integration.
2. **Economic Performance**:
   - Improved EBITDA contributes to enhanced economic performance, as it signifies increased profitability. AI can drive

higher margins, better resource allocation, and revenue growth, leading to improved financial health.

3. **Financial Health**:
   - Better economic performance, reflected in higher EBITDA, can strengthen the financial health of the brick-and-mortar firm. This can lead to improved liquidity, reduced financial risk, and greater financial stability.
4. **Market Valuation**:
   - The positive impact of AI on revenues and profitability can enhance the market valuation of the firm. Investors often place a premium on firms that demonstrate sustainable revenue growth and profitability driven by technological advancements like AI.
5. **Bankability**:
   - Banks and financial institutions may view brick-and-mortar companies with successful AI adoption more favorably when considering lending or investment opportunities. Improved financial health and profitability can enhance the firm's bankability, making it more attractive to lenders and investors.
6. **Competitive Advantage**:
   - AI adoption can provide a competitive advantage in the market, which can be an important factor for valuation. Companies that leverage AI effectively may outperform competitors, leading to a higher market share and valuation.
7. **Long-Term Viability**:
   - Demonstrating adaptability and innovation through AI adoption can signal to stakeholders that the firm is forward-thinking and well-positioned for long-term success. This can positively impact market valuation and bankability.
8. **Risk Mitigation**:
   - Effective AI adoption can help mitigate certain risks, such as supply chain disruptions or customer churn, which can be important for both financial health and market valuation.

The impact of AI adoption on various factors such as revenue growth, operating expenses, profitability, and overall corporate valuation can indeed be significant, as highlighted in studies such as Moro-Visconti et al. (2023).

By integrating AI technologies into their operations, companies can experience improvements in revenue generation and cost reduction, leading to enhanced financial performance. These improvements are often reflected in key financial metrics such as EBITDA (earnings before interest, taxes, depreciation, and amortization), which serves as a measure of operational profitability.

Specifically, AI can help optimize processes, enhance decision-making, and improve efficiency across various business functions, leading to increased productivity and reduced costs. For example, AI-driven automation can streamline repetitive tasks, reduce errors, and enable more accurate demand forecasting, ultimately contributing to higher revenues and lower operating expenses. Furthermore, the adoption of AI technologies may also have a positive impact on corporate valuation. As companies demonstrate their ability to leverage AI effectively to drive growth and profitability, investors may perceive them as more valuable and potentially offer higher valuations in the marketplace.

The integration of AI into business operations has the potential to deliver significant benefits in terms of financial performance and value creation. However, the specific impact will vary depending on factors such as the industry, the quality of AI implementation, and the competitive landscape. Conducting sensitivity analyses, as described in the study, can help organizations better understand and quantify the potential benefits of AI adoption and make informed strategic decisions accordingly.

A brief comparison is illustrated in Table 7.15. where a sensitivity analysis applied to the base case, 5%, and 10% growth in operating revenues (and a corresponding reduction in operating costs, mostly monetary OPEX) is reported in each column.

The first column shows the base case of a standardized firm that consequently adopts AI solutions, with increasing economic marginality.

The first column shows the base case of a standardized firm that consequently adopts AI solutions, with increasing economic marginality.

Table 7.15 Impact of Artificial Intelligence on the firm's key parameters

		AI intervention	
	Base Case	Sales +5% Opex −5%	Sales +10% Opex +10%
Average Sales t1–t3	€12,136,667	€13,311,250	€14,560,000
Average Opex t1–t3	€9,709,333	€8,827,000	€8,000,000
Average EBITDA t1–t3	€2,427,333	€4,484,250	€6,560,000
Average Net result t1–t3	€1,318,203	€2,770,397	€4,235,000
Average Net Financial Position t1–t3	€199,549	€2,240,533	€4,220,977
Average Equity t1–t3	€5,448,563	€7,791,670	€10,149,333
Equity Value (DCF)	€18,599,227	€36,411,256	€54,376,197
Equity Value (Multiples)	€17,806,273	€34,590,713	€51,528,833
Enterprise Value (DCF)	€20,599,994	€38,412,023	€56,376,964
Enterprise Value (Multiples)	€19,807,040	€36,591,480	€53,529,600

7.10 Economic, Financial, and Market Benefits and Concerns

Economic evaluation patterns

AI is able to increase productivity. AI can automate tasks that are currently performed by humans. This could lead to significant economic growth.

Another economic benefit of AI is its potential to create new jobs. As AI is deployed in new and innovative ways, it is likely to lead to the creation of new industries and occupations. For example, AI is already being used to develop new medical treatments, financial products, and transportation systems.

However, there are also some potential economic risks associated with AI. One of the biggest concerns is that AI could lead to widespread job displacement. As AI becomes more sophisticated, it is likely to be able to perform many tasks that are currently done by humans. This could lead to millions of people losing their jobs.

Another concern is that AI could lead to increased inequality. AI is likely to benefit those who own and control the technology, while those who do not may be left behind.

Financial evaluation patterns

AI is also having a significant impact on the financial sector and is employed to develop innovative financial products and services, improve risk management, and automate back-office tasks.

For example, AI is being used to develop robo-advisors, which are automated investment platforms that can help people manage their investments.

In addition, AI is being used to improve risk management in the financial sector. AI can help financial institutions to identify and manage risks more effectively. This can help to reduce losses and improve financial stability.

One of the most significant financial applications of AI is algorithmic trading. Algorithmic trading is the use of computers to automatically execute trades based on pre-programmed rules. Algorithmic trading is already being used to execute a significant portion of trades on major financial markets.

Finally, AI is also being used to automate back-office tasks in the financial sector. This can help financial institutions to reduce costs and improve efficiency.

Market evaluation patterns

AI also impacts the way markets are evaluated. AI is utilized to develop new tools and techniques for market research, market analysis, and portfolio management.

One of the most significant market evaluation applications of AI is the use of AI to analyze large amounts of data. AI can be used to identify trends and patterns in market data that would be difficult or impossible for humans to identify on their own. This information can then be used to make better investment decisions.

AI is also being used to sort out new trading strategies. AI can be used to identify trading opportunities that would be difficult or impossible for humans to identify on their own. This can help investors to generate higher returns and reduce their risk.

Finally, AI is also being used to develop new portfolio management tools. AI can be used to automatically construct and manage portfolios based on an investor's individual risk preferences and financial goals. This can help investors to save time and improve their investment performance.

AI is having a significant impact on the economy, finance, and markets. AI is being used to develop new products and services, improve efficiency, and reduce costs. As AI continues to develop, it is likely to have an even greater impact on these sectors in the years to come. Firms' adoption of AI yields a multitude of economic, financial, and market advantages and reservations. From an economic standpoint, the integration of AI augments forecasting capabilities, influencing the flexibility of supply and potentially reducing prices in competitive markets. From a financial perspective, companies that implement AI tend to exhibit higher levels of efficiency, particularly those of a larger scale, and capitalize on supplementary resources such as ICT proficiency and digital infrastructure. Within the financial industry, the adoption of AI is deemed essential for adapting to the information age, although varying viewpoints exist regarding its implications from operational and strategic standpoints. In essence, while the adoption of AI presents notable benefits, it also gives rise to issues such as implementation costs, data security vulnerabilities, and ethical considerations, underscoring the imperative need for meticulous oversight. AI plays a vital role in economic and financial assessments, presenting advantages as well as posing challenges. The progressing relationship between humans and AI underscores the significance of reassessing perceptions of cost-value and problem-solving approaches to ensure the creation of reliable machines and the efficient resolution of real-world issues. AI-powered assessments offer notable advantages but also call for a comprehensive comprehension of the economic, financial, and market consequences to fully exploit their potential.

7.11 Gamification and Artificial Intelligence

Gamification can have a significant impact on AI and can improve its economic, financial, and market value in various ways:

Impact of Gamification on AI:

1. **Enhanced User Engagement**: Gamification makes AI applications more engaging by incorporating game elements like points, badges, rewards, and leaderboards. This increased engagement can lead to more active usage of AI systems, which in turn can generate more user data for AI training and refinement.
2. **Data Collection and Quality Improvement**: Gamification can incentivize users to provide valuable data and feedback. Users may

willingly participate in activities that help improve AI models, such as tagging images, providing ratings, or contributing annotations. This user-generated data can enhance the quality of AI training datasets.

3. **Behavioral Insights**: Gamification provides AI systems with insights into user behavior and preferences. By analyzing how users interact with gamified elements, AI algorithms can tailor recommendations and user experiences, making them more personalized and effective.
4. **Training AI Agents**: Gamification can be used as a training mechanism for AI agents, especially in reinforcement learning scenarios. Games can serve as simulation environments where AI agents learn and maximize their decision-making strategies.
5. **Employee Training**: Gamification can be employed for employee training in AI-related skills and tasks. It can improve workforce competency, leading to more effective AI utilization within organizations.

Impact on Economic, Financial, and Market Value:

1. **Increased User Adoption**: Gamification can attract more users to AI applications, leading to increased user adoption. This broader user base can result in higher revenue potential, improved economic value, and enhanced market positioning.
2. **Monetization Opportunities**: Gamified AI applications can create revenue streams through in-app purchases, subscriptions, or premium content. This can contribute to the financial value of AI ventures.
3. **User Loyalty and Retention**: Gamification can foster user loyalty and retention by making AI applications more enjoyable and satisfying. Users who have positive experiences are more likely to continue using AI services, which can contribute to long-term financial value.
4. **Brand Recognition**: Companies that successfully implement gamification in AI can differentiate themselves in the market, enhancing

their brand recognition. A well-received gamified AI product or service attracts potential customers and investors.

Impact of Game Theory Patterns on AI:
Game theory patterns can also influence AI in several ways, particularly in multi-agent systems and strategic decision-making scenarios:

1. **Strategic Planning**: Game theory can help AI agents make strategic decisions in competitive environments. It provides a framework for modeling interactions among rational agents and predicting their behavior.
2. **Multi-Agent Systems**: In scenarios where multiple AI agents interact, game theory can guide agents in achieving desirable outcomes, such as cooperation, competition, or negotiation, based on the strategies of other agents.
3. **Resource Allocation**: Game theory can be used to maximize resource allocation in AI systems, such as allocating computing resources in a cloud computing environment efficiently.
4. **Market Dynamics**: Game theory is relevant in AI applications related to pricing, auctions, and market competition. It can help companies set competitive pricing strategies and make informed decisions in dynamic markets
5. **Security and Adversarial Scenarios**: Game theory is crucial in cybersecurity and adversarial AI, where AI systems must defend against attacks or make strategic decisions in response to threats.

Gamification can enhance user engagement, data collection, and user loyalty, contributing to the economic, financial, and market value of AI. Additionally, game theory patterns provide AI with strategic decision-making tools for multi-agent scenarios, resource allocation, market dynamics, and security. Both gamification and game theory can play vital roles in shaping the future of AI. Gamification and AI have profound implications for valuation. The intersection of gamification with Machine Learning algorithms offers a multitude of opportunities in various sectors such as e-commerce, ed-tech, and medicine. The utilization of AI by financial institutions is instigating a transformative shift in the industry, reshaping business models through the implementation of data-centric strategies and cutting-edge algorithms. The success of companies that invest in AI is contingent upon various factors including the development of use cases, patterns of adoption, and the regulatory landscapes, underscoring the necessity for a comprehensive comprehension of AI's influence on valuation and strategic decision-making. The utilization of AI in gaming is a means to enrich the overall player experiences, with AI assuming a pivotal position in the design of gaming interfaces. The perspective on value co-creation by AI and developers accentuates the synergistic endeavors between AI systems and developers aimed at generating economic and societal values through software development and operational processes, thus emphasizing the prospective role of AI automation in software engineering. The intricate dynamics of competition and collaboration in the establishment of global AI standards also wield a notable influence on the governance framework of AI, underscoring the essentiality of shared standards for universal AI frameworks and the repercussions of geopolitical competitions on international collaborations concerning AI standards.

7.12 Model Collapse and Other Value Destroying Patterns

In AI, the emergence of value destruction patterns is observed in various fields. For example, within the realm of art, some contemporary artists are challenging conventional perceptions of cultural value, highlighting the fluid and progressive nature of artistic interpretation. Furthermore, in financial markets, the issue of unpredictable returns is tackled by expert traders who employ artificial neural networks to eliminate systematic patterns, resulting in the volatility of prices. Moreover, the potential future impact of AI on traditional marital values is brought to attention, as dilemmas surface from AI's involvement in decision-making procedures, the impact of genetic technology on extending human lifespan, and the ethical considerations surrounding bioengineering's role in human reproduction. These instances emphasize the diverse ways in which AI can disturb established norms and values in various sectors. Model collapse in AI, particularly in machine learning, refers to a phenomenon where a model, often a generative model like a Generative Adversarial Network (GAN), starts producing outputs that are less diverse and increasingly like each other. This typically happens when the model fails to learn a broad representation of the input data and instead focuses on a narrow aspect of the data. Here's a breakdown of the key aspects of model collapse:

1. **Loss of Diversity in Outputs**: The most evident sign of model collapse is when the outputs of the model become very repetitive and lack diversity. For instance, if a GAN trained to generate images of various objects starts producing variations of the same object repeatedly, it's indicative of model collapse.
2. **Echo Chamber Effect**: In model collapse, the AI system essentially becomes an echo chamber. It repeats the same patterns or data points over and over again. This is contrary to the goal of many AI systems, especially generative models, which aim to produce novel, varied outputs.
3. **Causes**: Model collapse can occur due to various reasons, such as:
   - **Insufficient or Biased Training Data**: If the model is trained on a limited or biased dataset, it may not learn to generate a wide variety of outputs.
   - **Model Architecture and Parameter Issues**: Sometimes, the design of the model or the choice of parameters may lead to model collapse. For example, if a GAN's discriminator becomes too strong, it might force the generator into a narrow path of output generation.
   - **Training Process Issues**: Issues in the training process, such as improper learning rate settings or inadequate training time, can also contribute to model collapse.
4. **Impact on Generative Models**: Generative models like GANs are particularly susceptible to model collapse because their objective is to generate new data instances that are indistinguishable from real data. If they start generating only a specific type of output, their utility diminishes significantly.
5. **Mitigation Strategies**: To prevent model collapse, researchers and practitioners employ various strategies like:
   - **Regularization and Normalization Techniques**: To ensure that the model doesn't overfit a particular aspect of the data.
   - **Diverse and Comprehensive Datasets**: Using datasets that are well-rounded and cover a wide variety of scenarios.

- **Monitoring and Adjusting Training Process**: Keeping an eye on the training process and making adjustments as needed to ensure the model learns a broad representation of the data.

Model collapse is a critical challenge in the field of AI, especially in unsupervised learning models like GANs, where the goal is to explore and generate diverse outputs without explicit labels or guidance.

The misuse and manipulation of Artificial Intelligence (AI) can lead to several economic, financial, and value-destroying patterns. These negative impacts are important to consider as AI becomes increasingly integrated into various sectors:

1. **Economic Impacts**:
    - **Job Displacement and Unemployment**: One of the most discussed economic impacts of AI is the potential for job displacement. Automation through AI can lead to significant changes in the job market, potentially rendering certain skills or roles obsolete. While AI can create new job opportunities, the transition may not be smooth, leading to unemployment or underemployment in certain sectors.
    - **Market Concentration and Monopolies**: AI can reinforce market dominance for large corporations, especially tech giants with the resources to invest heavily in AI research and development. This could lead to increased market concentration and monopolistic behavior, stifling competition and innovation.
    - **Inequality and Bias**: AI systems, if not designed carefully, can perpetuate and even exacerbate existing social and economic inequalities. Biased algorithms can lead to unfair practices in hiring, lending, and law enforcement, disproportionately affecting marginalized groups.
2. **Financial Impacts**:
    - **Investment Risks**: The hype around AI can lead to irrational investment behaviors, where funds are funneled into ventures without a sustainable or practical business model. This can create financial bubbles and lead to significant losses when these ventures fail.

- **Operational Risks in Financial Services**: In the financial sector, AI-driven decision-making systems, if not properly regulated and monitored, can lead to operational risks. These include erroneous trading decisions or mismanagement of financial products, potentially destabilizing markets.

3. **Value Destruction**:

- **Erosion of Trust**: The misuse of AI, such as in spreading misinformation or conducting surveillance without consent, can erode public trust in technology and institutions. This loss of trust can have long-term negative consequences for societal cohesion and the ethical development of technology.
- **Reduced Human Agency and Creativity**: Over-reliance on AI for decision-making can undermine human agency and creativity. In a world where algorithms make most decisions, human judgment and innovation could be undervalued, leading to a stagnation in creative problem-solving skills.
- **Security Risks**: AI systems are vulnerable to manipulation and hacking. Malicious use of AI in cyberattacks can lead to significant value destruction, impacting critical infrastructure, personal data security, and national security.

4. **Regulatory and Ethical Challenges**:

- **Lack of Adequate Regulation**: The rapid development of AI has outpaced the establishment of regulatory frameworks. This lag can lead to misuse and manipulation of AI technologies in harmful ways.
- **Ethical Dilemmas:** AI poses complex ethical dilemmas, such as the delegation of life-impacting decisions to machines (e.g., in healthcare or criminal justice). Misuse in these areas can have grave consequences for individuals and communities.

To mitigate these issues, policymakers, industry leaders, and the AI research community must work together. This collaboration should focus on creating ethical guidelines, robust regulatory frameworks, and continuous monitoring mechanisms to ensure AI is used responsibly and for the greater good. Additionally, there should be an emphasis on education and reskilling programs to prepare the workforce for an AI-driven future.

AI holds immense potential for transforming various sectors, but it also presents several criticalities or challenges. These challenges can significantly impact the economy, finance, and overall market value in various ways:

1. **Data Privacy and Security**:
    - **Impact**: AI systems often rely on vast amounts of data, raising concerns about privacy and data security. Breaches or misuse of data can produce significant financial losses, damage to firm reputations, and erosion of consumer trust.
    - **Economic Implications**: Companies may incur high costs for data protection and face regulatory penalties for breaches. Moreover, consumer mistrust can lead to reduced adoption of AI services.
2. **Bias and Fairness**:
    - **Impact**: AI algorithms can exacerbate biases if they are trained on biased datasets. This can lead to unfair decisions in areas like hiring, lending, and law enforcement.
    - **Economic Implications**: Biased AI systems can result in legal challenges and loss of public trust. In finance, biased algorithms could lead to unfair credit assessments, impacting market inclusivity and stability.
3. **Lack of Transparency and Explainability**:
    - **Impact**: Many AI models, especially deep learning models, are often seen as "black boxes" due to their complex and opaque decision-making processes. This lack of transparency can be problematic in critical applications.
    - **Economic Implications**: Industries like finance and healthcare, where decision accountability is crucial, may be hesitant to fully adopt AI. This can slow down innovation and market growth in these sectors.
4. **Job Displacement and Workforce Transformation**:
    - **Impact**: Automation and AI technologies can displace workers, particularly in routine or manual jobs, leading to unemployment and income inequality.

- **Economic Implications**: While AI can increase productivity, job displacement can lead to social unrest and economic instability. There is also the need for significant investment in retraining and education.

5. **Regulatory Challenges**:
   - **Impact**: The fast-paced development of AI technologies often outpaces the development of regulatory frameworks, leading to a lack of clear guidelines and standards.
   - **Economic Implications**: Uncertain regulatory environments can hinder investment and innovation in AI. Overregulation can stifle growth, while under-regulation can lead to misuse and public mistrust.
6. **Dependency and Systemic Risks**:
   - **Impact**: Over-reliance on AI systems can create vulnerabilities, especially if these systems malfunction or are manipulated.
   - **Economic Implications**: In finance, for example, AI-driven trading systems could contribute to systemic risks if they all react similarly to certain market conditions, potentially leading to market crashes or volatility.
7. **Ethical and Societal Concerns**:
   - **Impact**: AI raises ethical questions regarding autonomy, consent, and the role of machines in society.
   - **Economic Implications**: Ethical lapses in AI deployment can lead to public backlash and resistance, impacting market adoption and value.

7.13 Artificial Intelligence-Driven Goodwill

AI plays a crucial role in the assessment and enhancement of goodwill within organizations. The consideration of factors beyond traditional fixed asset methods in goodwill evaluation with the help of AI leads to more precise assessments. The incorporation of AI into the process of evaluating goodwill offers a more comprehensive and dynamic approach, ultimately contributing to enhanced decision-making and organizational performance. AI is essential in the operations of organizations, influencing various areas including employee responsibilities, the development of international norms, enhancing productivity through automation, integrating AI for better business insights and innovations, and including AI in business strategies to enhance decision-making and performance. The utilization of AI in the assessment of goodwill goes beyond traditional methods, offering a more exact and dynamic approach that contributes to improved decision-making and overall organizational performance. AI's capacity to analyze intricate data sets enables a thorough evaluation of goodwill, resulting in more precise assessments and strategic choices within organizations. AI influences the goodwill of its users, hopefully improving their competitive advantage and economic returns.

The economic valuation of goodwill requires a multifaceted approach that encompasses several disciplines, concerning legal aspects, accounting practices, fiscal implications, and strategic factors. AI-driven goodwill is linked to digital assets like technology, software, online presence, and digital customer relationships. Valuing AI-driven goodwill is complex due to the rapidly changing digital landscape and the difficulty in making market comparisons. The value derived from competitive advantages is often short-lived, as market conditions, technology, and consumer preferences change rapidly. This ephemerality can make it challenging to assess the long-term value of goodwill.

The Controversial Concept of Goodwill

IVS 210 § 20.6. indicates that "Goodwill is any future economic benefit arising from a business, an interest in a business or from the use of a group of assets which has not been separately recognized in another asset. In general terms, the value of goodwill is the residual amount remaining after the values of all identifiable tangible, intangible, and monetary assets, adjusted for actual or potential liabilities, have been deducted from the value of a business. It is typically represented as the excess of the price paid in a real or hypothetical acquisition of a firm over the value of the firm's other identified assets and liabilities".

According to OECD (2022) "Depending on the context, the term goodwill can be used to refer to several different concepts. In some accounting and business valuation contexts, goodwill reflects the difference between the aggregate value of an operating business and the sum of the values of all separately identifiable tangible and intangible assets. Alternatively, goodwill is sometimes described as a representation of the future economic benefits associated with business assets that are not individually identified and separately recognized. In still other contexts goodwill is referred to as the expectation of future trade from existing customers. The term ongoing concern value is sometimes referred to as the value of the assembled assets of an operating business over and above the sum of the separate values of the individual assets. It is generally recognized that goodwill and ongoing concern value cannot be segregated or transferred separately from other business assets" (par. 6.27).

Goodwill indicates the ability of a firm or one of its branches to generate an extra profit (new incremental wealth or excess capital), that is the concrete attitude to produce profits higher than the average of the reference sector; this is represented by a typically indistinct set of intangible conditions (the image and the prestige of the firm, the clientele, the organization, the management, the quality of the products, the commercial network, etc.) that express the competitive capacity of the firm on the market.

Goodwill Valuation, Competitive Advantage Period, and Monopolistic Rents

AI-driven goodwill valuation entails the utilization of AI to optimize the evaluation of a company's intangible assets, as deliberated in various contexts. Through embedding AI in organizational operations such as grounding, bounding, and recasting, enterprises can cultivate AI-driven competencies that are tailored to the organization, cost-efficient, and strategically congruent, leading to competitive advantages. The utilization of business intelligence software in goodwill valuation can profoundly influence a company's adjusted net assets value, providing a more precise representation of its value. Additionally, within a monopolistically competitive market, the valuation of future technology rents plays a pivotal role in stock market valuation, as announcements regarding prospective technological advancements impact firms' forthcoming profits and equity value. By amalgamating AI-driven goodwill valuation with strategies for competitive advantage and comprehending monopolistic rents, organizations can adopt a holistic approach to enriching their valuation processes and strategic positioning in the marketplace. The estimation of goodwill in corporate finance involves a blend of objective analysis and subjective judgment, influenced by various psychological and market factors. Here's an overview of the complexities involved in goodwill valuation and the common approaches used:

1. **Subjectivity and Psychological Influences**:
    - **Human Psyche**: Factors like megalomania or a sense of immortality can lead to an overestimation of goodwill. This psychological aspect can result in valuing goodwill higher than its realistic market value.
    - **Perceived Perpetuity**: There's often a tendency to view goodwill as perpetual, but any competitive advantage it represents is typically transient.
2. **Ephemerality of Competitive Advantage**:
    - **Decay of Extra-Returns**: Over time, the extra returns generated by goodwill can diminish due to various factors like market saturation, competitive pressure, or changes in consumer preferences.
    - **Antitrust Pressures**: High perceived value, especially in cases of monopolistic rents, can attract antitrust scrutiny, leading to regulatory pressures that might erode goodwill value.
3. **Valuation Approaches for Goodwill**:
    - **Mixed Capital-Income Approach**: This is a common method for independently estimating goodwill. It involves two components:

    - **Adjusted Net Equity (Capital)**: This is determined using a balance sheet-based approach, either simple or complex, to calculate the firm's net equity after necessary adjustments.
    - **Value of Goodwill (Excess Economic Margin)**: This represents the additional income the firm can generate over its competitors. If this excess income is negative, indicating an excess loss, it leads to badwill.
4. **Goodwill Impairment Testing (IAS/IFRS)**:
    - **Financial Approaches**: International accounting standards, such as IAS/IFRS, mandate the use of financial approaches for goodwill impairment testing. This involves assessing whether

the carrying amount of goodwill exceeds its recoverable amount.

- **The objective of Impairment Testing**: The aim is to ensure that the value of goodwill on the balance sheet accurately reflects its current market value and is not overstated.

5. **Challenges in Valuation**:

- **Market and Competitive Dynamics**: Estimating the future profitability and competitive advantage associated with goodwill involves analyzing market trends, competitive dynamics, and consumer behavior.
- **Regulatory Environment**: The regulatory landscape can significantly influence the value of goodwill, especially in industries prone to antitrust actions.

The estimation of goodwill, whether positive or negative, requires a nuanced approach that balances objective financial metrics with subjective judgments and market insights. This process is crucial for ensuring accurate financial reporting and strategic decision-making in corporate acquisitions and management.

The Competitive Advantage Period (CAP) is a key concept in understanding and valuing the positive goodwill of a firm. It reflects the period during which a firm can expect to earn returns on its invested capital that are higher than its weighted average cost of capital (WACC). Here's a detailed look at the various aspects of CAP:

1. **Definition and Significance of CAP**

- **Returns vs. Cost of Capital**: CAP is defined by the duration during which a firm's return on invested capital (ROIC) exceeds its WACC, indicating a period of positive goodwill. See also Pandey et al. (2021) for a comparison between ROIC and AI.
- **Indicator of Goodwill**: This period is a critical measure of the firm's capacity to generate value beyond the normal expectations of the market.

2. **Strategic and Economic Components**:

   - **Competitive Advantages**: CAP is influenced by factors like product differentiation, cost advantages, and the firm's specific resources and skills in technology, marketing, and organization.
   - **Industry Attractiveness**: The attractiveness of the industry in which the firm operates also plays a role in determining the CAP.
   - **Economic and Financial Aspects**: The incremental EBITDA margin is a key financial metric related to CAP.

3. **Resource-Based Approach**:

   - **Intangible Characteristics**: CAP is often based on intangible aspects such as rarity, inimitability, distinctive capabilities, and the ability to effectively utilize resources.
   - **Resource-Picking and Capability-Building**: These mechanisms are fundamental to creating and maintaining competitive differentiation.

4. **Influence of Market Dynamics**:

   - **Economies of Scale and Experience**: CAP can be influenced by the firm's scale of operations and its accumulated experience.
   - **Monopolistic Rents**: Companies with unique market power, such as those enjoying natural monopolies or possessing unique inventions, can leverage this to achieve higher returns.

5. **Types of Economic Rents**:

   - **Ricardian Rents**: Derived from limited intangible resources that provide a competitive edge.
   - **Schumpeterian Rents**: Based on innovative products or services that lead to high economic margins.
   - **Paretian Rents**: Stem from optimal resource utilization.

6. **Diminishing Returns Over Time**:

   - **Impact of External Pressures**: Over time, external competitive pressures, new standards, and innovations can erode the initial competitive advantage.

- **Importance of Realistic Estimation**: Valuation procedures must avoid overestimating the ability of goodwill to persist indefinitely.

7. **Growth Rate and Sustainability**:

   - **Transition to Sustainable Growth**: High-growth rates, especially in startups, typically converge toward a more stable, sustainable growth rate in the medium to long term.

8. **Creditworthiness and Monitoring**:

   - **Strong Borrowing Capacity**: Companies with positive economic rents and CAP usually have sound creditworthiness.
   - **Need for Periodic Monitoring**: Regular impairment testing is necessary to assess the residual useful life and current value of the goodwill.

9. **Valuation of Surplus Value**:

   - **Intensity and Duration of CAP**: These factors are central to the valuation models of implicit goodwill.
   - **Focus on Intangible Sources**: The valuation considers the intangible sources of expected competitive advantages that allow reinvestments at an ROIC higher than the WACC.

In essence, the CAP is a critical factor in assessing and valuing a firm's goodwill. It encapsulates the expected duration of a firm's competitive edge and is heavily influenced by intangible assets and market dynamics. Understanding and accurately estimating the CAP is crucial for realistic goodwill valuation and strategic business planning.

The sustainable enterprise value corresponds to the valorization of the existing assets, added to the (typically intangible) value of growth opportunities, as shown in Fig. 7.6

Goodwill Determinants

The development of the AI-driven economy significantly impacts how goodwill is perceived, valued, and accounted for. The evolution of AI-driven goodwill (Tiesheva & Smyrnov, 2023) has deep implications for accounting and strategic asset management:

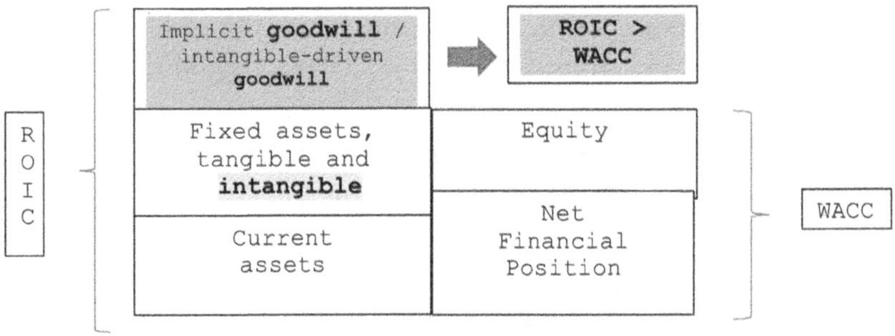

Fig. 7.6 Goodwill as a positive differential between the return and the cost of invested capital

1. **Expansion of Factors Influencing Goodwill Formation**:
   - **Digital Economy Impact**: The rise of the digital economy has expanded the range of factors influencing the formation of goodwill. This includes digital assets like online presence, customer data, digital platforms, and intellectual property.
   - **Changing Valuation Landscape**: The methods and approaches for valuing these AI-driven assets and the resulting goodwill are evolving, reflecting the unique characteristics of the AI-driven economy.
2. **Goodwill in the Landscape of Intangible Assets**:
   - **Increased Importance**: In the AI-driven economy, the role of goodwill has become more prominent, particularly in relation to other intangible assets.
   - **Need for Clear Understanding**: There is a growing need to clearly understand and formulate the concept of goodwill, especially as it relates to AI-driven assets.
3. **Market Value of AI-driven Companies**:
   - **Rapid Increase Since 21st Century**: Digital companies have seen a sharp increase in market value, largely due to the valuation of their intangible assets, including AI-driven goodwill.

- **Shift in Value Factors**: There has been a significant shift toward intangible assets in the overall value composition of companies, particularly in the AI-driven sector.

4. **Accounting and Regulatory Challenges**:

   - **Lack of Public Comprehension**: Despite its growing importance, there is still a lack of widespread understanding of AI-driven goodwill, both in terms of its nature and its accounting treatment.
   - **Need for Regulatory Improvement**: The regulatory and legislative framework for accounting for intangible assets, including AI-driven goodwill, needs further development to capture the nuances of the AI-driven economy.

5. **Valuation Techniques and Methods**:

   - **Emerging Techniques**: New techniques and methods for evaluating intangible assets and AI-driven goodwill are emerging, but their integration into standard accounting practices is still in progress.
   - **Rationalization of Accounting Practices**: There is a need to rationalize these emerging valuation techniques and incorporate them into standard accounting and regulatory frameworks.

6. **Strategic Asset Management Implications**:

   - **Asset Management Challenges**: The rise of AI-driven goodwill presents new challenges for strategic asset management, particularly in how AI-driven assets are leveraged for long-term value creation.
   - **Importance of Adaptation**: Companies must adapt their asset management strategies to effectively incorporate and capitalize on AI-driven goodwill.

7. **Research and Practical Significance**:

   - **Need for Ongoing Research**: Continuous research is essential to deepen the understanding of AI-driven goodwill and its impact on business valuation and strategy.

- **Practical Applications**: Understanding AI-driven goodwill has practical implications for business decisions, investment strategies, and financial reporting.

The AI-driven economy has fundamentally altered the landscape of goodwill, especially in terms of its formation, valuation, and accounting. This shift necessitates a deeper understanding and adaptation of accounting practices and strategic asset management to effectively capture and leverage the value of AI-driven goodwill.

AI-driven goodwill valuation, a relatively new and evolving area in corporate finance, involves estimating the value of goodwill generated by AI-driven assets and capabilities. Here are the main features that distinguish AI-driven goodwill valuation from traditional goodwill valuation:

1. **Nature of AI-driven Assets**: AI-driven goodwill is often associated with assets like online brand presence, customer data, digital platforms, software, algorithms, and social media influence. These assets are typically intangible and rapidly evolving, making their valuation more complex and dynamic.
2. **Measurement of Online Presence and Reputation**: The value of a firm's online presence, including its website traffic, social media engagement, and online customer reviews, plays a significant role in AI-driven goodwill. Measuring and valuing these aspects require different approaches compared to traditional physical or financial assets.
3. **Reliance on Data and Analytics**: AI-driven goodwill valuation often depends heavily on data analytics to assess the performance and potential of AI-driven assets. This includes analyzing customer data, online user behavior, and AI-driven marketing effectiveness.
4. **Influence of Technological Innovation**: The rapid pace of technological change and innovation can significantly impact the value of AI-driven goodwill. New technologies can either enhance the value of AI-driven assets or render them obsolete.
5. **Importance of Intellectual Property**: AI-driven goodwill is closely tied to the value of a firm's intellectual property related to AI-driven content and technology.
6. **Scalability and Network Effects**: AI-driven assets often have high scalability, meaning they can serve a growing number of users or transactions with relatively low incremental costs. Network effects,

where the value of an AI-driven asset increases with the number of users, also play a crucial role in AI-driven goodwill valuation.

7. **Regulatory and Privacy Concerns**: The regulatory environment, particularly concerning data privacy and cybersecurity, can significantly impact the value of AI-driven assets. Changes in regulations or breaches in data security can affect the perceived value of AI-driven goodwill.
8. **Market Comparison Challenges**: Comparing AI-driven assets to market benchmarks or competitors can be challenging due to the uniqueness and rapid evolution of AI-driven technologies. This can make it difficult to find comparable market data for valuation purposes.
9. **Volatility and Uncertainty**: The value of AI-driven assets can be more volatile and uncertain compared to traditional assets. This is due to the fast-changing nature of AI-driven markets and consumer preferences.
10. **Importance of Strategic Vision**: The strategic vision of a firm in leveraging its AI-driven assets is crucial. The ability to innovate and adapt AI-driven strategies can significantly influence the future value of AI-driven goodwill.

AI-driven goodwill valuation requires a nuanced understanding of the AI-driven landscape, including the unique characteristics of AI-driven assets, the role of technology and innovation, and the importance of data and analytics in assessing value. The process involves balancing traditional valuation methods with new approaches tailored to the AI-driven context.

AI-driven goodwill valuation needs to consider the intricate balance between objective financial analysis and subjective factors that influence the valuation process:

1. **Integration of Subjective and Objective Factors**:
   - The challenge in goodwill valuation lies in effectively integrating subjective elements like management's expectations, market perceptions, and psychological factors with objective financial data.

2. **Role of Professional Judgment**:
    - The valuation process often relies heavily on the professional judgment of accountants, financial analysts, and auditors.
    - This judgment is guided not only by financial data but also by experience and insights into market and industry trends.
3. **Importance of Regular Reassessment**:
    - Given the transient nature of the factors contributing to goodwill, regular reassessment is critical to ensure its carrying value remains aligned with its realizable value.
    - This is where impairment testing plays a key role, as it allows for adjustments based on current market conditions and business performance.
4. **Impact of External Factors**:
    - External factors such as economic shifts, technological advancements, and changes in consumer behavior can significantly impact goodwill.
    - Companies need to be agile and responsive to these changes to maintain the accuracy of their goodwill valuation.
5. **Implications for M&A Strategies**:
    - Understanding the nuances of goodwill valuation is crucial for informed decision-making in mergers and acquisitions.
    - Overvaluation or undervaluation of goodwill can have significant strategic and financial consequences for both acquiring and acquired companies.
6. **Educating Stakeholders**:
    - Companies need to educate their stakeholders, including investors and board members, about the nature of goodwill and its impact on financial statements.

- Transparency in reporting and communication about the factors affecting goodwill valuation can enhance stakeholder trust and confidence.

In conclusion, the estimation of goodwill is a complex process that requires a careful blend of financial expertise and a nuanced understanding of market dynamics and psychological factors. It's a critical aspect of financial reporting and strategic decision-making in corporate finance.

7.14 Residual Income and Artificial Intelligence

Residual income is a form of passive income that continues to generate earnings after the initial effort or investment has been made. This type of income can be earned through various means such as rental properties, royalties from books or patents, or earnings from investments. It is essentially income that one receives regularly, with little to no effort required to maintain it. Residual income (RI) is employed for the purpose of analyzing earnings expansion, making a distinction between the growth in RI, the growth in invested capital, and other elements. This approach offers an improved level of elucidation for stock returns when compared to conventional methodologies. RI is more highly esteemed by the market in comparison to the growth in invested capital. The growth in RI demonstrates greater persistence and a positive correlation with future returns, whereas the growth in invested capital is more prone to reversal and has a negative impact on future returns. AI systems utilize AI algorithms to forecast pregnancy outcomes in single embryo transfer cycles post preimplantation genetic testing for aneuploidy. This underscores the potential of AI in enriching decision-making processes across diverse domains.

The impact of AI on residual income can be significant, particularly in the context of investments:

a. **Efficient Investment Strategies**: AI can analyze vast amounts of data to identify investment opportunities that might yield higher residual income. This could include identifying profitable stocks, real estate investments, or other income-generating assets.
b. **Automated Trading**: AI algorithms can manage investment portfolios, buying and selling assets to maximize returns. This automation

can lead to more effective investment strategies that can increase residual income.

c. **Cost Reduction**: AI can reduce costs in managing investments by automating processes that were previously done manually. This increased efficiency can translate into higher net returns for investors.
d. **Predictive Analysis**: AI can predict market trends and consumer behavior, which can be crucial for making informed investment decisions that could lead to higher residual income.
e. **Diversification Opportunities**: AI can identify new and emerging markets or sectors that might not be obvious to human investors. Investing in these areas could provide new sources of residual income.
f. **Risk Management**: AI can better assess and manage risks associated with investments, potentially protecting the residual income streams from market volatility or other financial risks.

While AI can enhance investment strategies for generating residual income, it also introduces new complexities and risks, such as the need for understanding AI-driven investment decisions and the potential for AI-related market disruptions.

7.15 Impact of Artificial Intelligence on the Economic Value Added and Market Value Added

Economic Value Added (EVA) and Market Value Added (MVA) are two important financial metrics used to assess a firm's performance. AI has a significant influence on both EVA and MVA. According to research findings, the implementation of AI results in favorable abnormal returns, particularly in IT firms, following its announcement. The economic ramifications of AI are broad, impacting aspects such as productivity, labor market participation, and income distribution, underscoring the necessity for well-designed public policies to counteract adverse consequences. The behavior of AI algorithms in market transactions, influenced by their learning mechanisms, has implications for pricing dynamics, potentially leading to competitive market structures or monopolistic tendencies. In a comprehensive view, the integration of AI across various sectors serves to elevate efficiency, service standards, and customer satisfaction levels, thereby making a positive contribution to sustained economic expansion.

Economic Value Added is a measure of a firm's financial performance based on the residual wealth calculated by deducting its cost of capital from its operating profit, adjusted for taxes on a cash basis. It can be calculated as follows:

$$\text{EVA} = \text{Net Operating Profit After Taxes(NOPAT)} - (\text{Capital Invested} \times \text{Cost of Capital}) \quad (7.9)$$

where:

- **Net Operating Profit After Taxes (NOPAT)** is the profit a firm generates from its operations after taxes but before financing costs and non-cash bookkeeping entries.
- **Capital Invested** refers to the total amount of money that is being used in the firm, which can include both equity and debt.
- **Cost of Capital** is the rate of return that capital could be expected to earn in an alternative investment of equivalent risk.

EVA is a measure of the true economic profit of a firm. If a firm's EVA is positive, it means the firm is generating value over and above the cost of the capital it has employed.

Market Value Added is a calculation that shows the difference between the market value of a firm and the capital contributed by all its investors. It is essentially the sum of all capital claims held against the firm plus the market value of its equity, less the amount of capital invested. MVA can be expressed as:

$$\text{MVA} = \text{Market Value of the Firm} - \text{Capital Invested} \quad (7.10)$$

where:

- **Market Value of the Firm** typically refers to the total market capitalization in the case of a publicly traded firm, which is calculated as the share price times the number of outstanding shares.
- **Capital Invested** here also includes both equity and debt capital.

A high MVA indicates that the firm has added a lot of value for its shareholders. In contrast, a negative MVA suggests that the value of the firm is less than the sum of the capital that has been invested into it.

EVA focuses on operational efficiency and profit generation against the cost of capital, while MVA looks at the value creation from the perspective of shareholders and investors as reflected in the market value of the firm.

The impact of AI on EVA and MVA is multifaceted and significant:

a. Economic Value Added (EVA)

1. **Operational Efficiency**: AI can significantly improve efficiencies in businesses by automating processes, optimizing supply chains, and enhancing decision-making. This leads to reduced operational costs and increased productivity, positively impacting EVA.
2. **Innovation and Product Development**: AI-driven innovation can lead to the development of new products and services, opening up new revenue streams and improving the profitability of a business.
3. **Risk Management**: AI enhances risk assessment and management capabilities, leading to better investment decisions and cost savings, which in turn can boost EVA.
4. **Employee Productivity**: With AI handling routine tasks, employees can focus on higher-value activities, leading to improved productivity and, consequently, higher EVA.
5. **Customer Satisfaction**: AI tools like chatbots and personalized recommendations enhance customer experience, potentially leading to increased customer loyalty and higher revenue.

b. Market Value Added (MVA)

1. **Investor Perception**: The adoption of AI can enhance a firm's image as a forward-thinking and innovative entity, potentially leading to a higher market valuation.
2. **Competitive Advantage**: Companies leveraging AI effectively may gain a competitive advantage, leading to better market positioning and increased market share, positively affecting MVA.
3. **Revenue Growth**: AI can enable businesses to tap into new markets and customer segments, driving revenue growth and positively impacting MVA.
4. **Cost of Capital**: AI can reduce the risk profile of a business, potentially lowering its cost of capital. A lower cost of capital can increase net present value of future cash flows, thus enhancing MVA.

5. **Scalability**: AI-driven solutions are often highly scalable, allowing businesses to expand rapidly without proportional increases in costs, positively impacting MVA.

c. Challenges and Risks

- **Implementation Costs**: The initial investment in AI can be substantial, which might temporarily affect EVA negatively.
- **Regulatory Compliance**: Adhering to evolving regulations around AI can be costly and complex.
- **Dependence on Data**: AI's effectiveness is contingent on the quality and quantity of data, which can be a limiting factor.
- **Workforce Disruption**: AI implementation can lead to workforce displacement, necessitating retraining and potentially affecting morale.

The integration of AI into business operations has the potential to significantly enhance both EVA and MVA by improving operational efficiencies, fostering innovation, and enhancing market positioning.

The graphical representation of the AI-driven evolution from EVA to cumulated MVA is the following (Fig. 7.7):

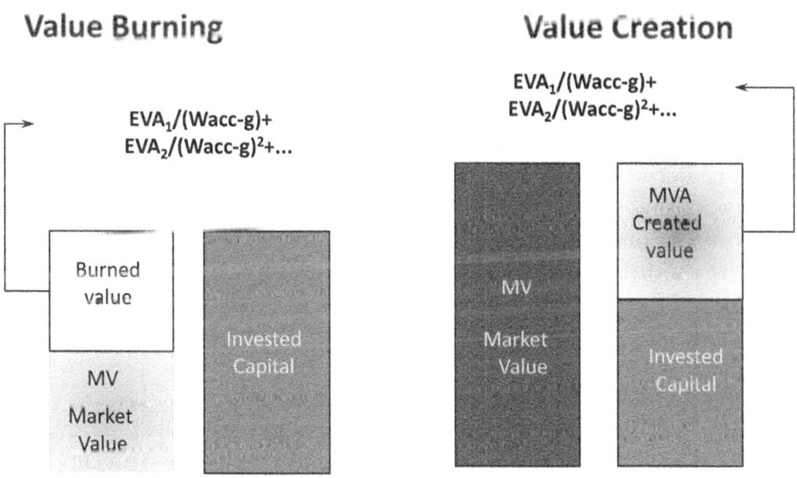

Fig. 7.7 From EVA to MVA

7.16 Artificial Intelligence and the Franchise Factor Model

AI can improve the franchise value and future growth opportunities in several ways. By enhancing various aspects of the franchise's operations and strategy, AI can increase the present value of expected future cash flows:

a. **Improved Decision-Making**: AI enables more accurate and data-driven decision-making. By analyzing many data, AI can provide insights into consumer behavior, market trends, and productivity. This leads to better strategic decisions, positively impacting the franchise's growth and profitability.
b. **Enhanced Customer Experience**: AI technologies like chatbots, personalized recommendations, and AI-driven customer service tools can boost the customer experience. Higher customer satisfaction and loyalty are critical drivers of repeat business and long-term revenue streams.
c. **Operational Efficiency**: AI can streamline operations, from inventory management to staffing and supply chain optimization. These efficiencies can reduce costs and improve margins, thereby increasing the DCF.
d. **Marketing and Sales Optimization**: AI can analyze customer data to identify targeted marketing campaigns, improve sales strategies, and maximize product offerings. This leads to more effective marketing, higher conversion rates, and increased sales.
e. **Predictive Analytics for Expansion**: AI can identify the most promising markets for expansion and predict the success of new locations or products. This helps in minimizing the risks associated with expansion and maximizes the chances of success in new ventures.
f. **Risk Management**: AI helps in better risk assessment and management by predicting potential market shifts, economic changes, and other factors that might affect the business. This proactive risk management can safeguard future cash flows.
g. **Innovation and Competitive Advantage**: AI drives innovation, helping franchises stay ahead of the curve in terms of technology, product offerings, and customer service.

h. **Franchisee Performance and Support**: AI tools can assist in monitoring and supporting franchisee performance, ensuring that each unit operates optimally. This uniform success across the franchise network contributes to overall brand strength and value.
i. **Labor and Human Resource Optimization**: AI can maximize staffing, reduce labor costs, and improve employee training and retention strategies. A more efficient workforce directly contributes to better operational performance and profitability.
j. **Sustainability and Compliance**: AI can also aid in ensuring sustainability and regulatory compliance, which are increasingly important for maintaining a positive brand image and avoiding potential legal issues.

AI's impact on franchise value lies in its ability to enhance decision-making, operational efficiency, customer experience, and market competitiveness, all of which are crucial for driving future growth opportunities. By integrating AI into various aspects of the franchise system, franchises can not only improve their current operations but also position themselves for sustained growth and value creation in the future.

7.17 Minimizing Value Destruction and Financial Distress with Artificial Intelligence

AI models are of paramount importance in mitigating value erosion and financial turmoil across diverse industries. Through the application of AI methodologies such as Artificial Neural Networks and ensemble models, precise forecasts can be generated concerning potential financial insolvencies, empowering firms to proactively avert distress. These models not only deliver heightened precision in anticipating distress but also furnish transparency and interpretability via additive explanations and counterfactual explanations. The implementation of AI-driven preemptive alert systems grounded in financial metrics and additional indicators holds the capacity to notably diminish the likelihood of value depletion and financial crisis, thereby accruing advantages for both enterprises and stakeholders. AI can have a significant relationship with corporate financial distress, particularly in the context of insolvent firms. AI can play a role both in predicting financial distress and in managing it once it occurs:

a. **Early Detection of Financial Distress**: AI algorithms can analyze various financial indicators, market trends, and other relevant data to identify early signs of financial distress. AI can detect patterns and anomalies that might indicate a firm is heading toward insolvency.
b. **Risk Assessment and Management**: AI can provide advanced tools for assessing and managing risks, including credit risk, market risk, and operational risk. By accurately identifying and quantifying these risks, companies can take proactive steps to mitigate them, potentially avoiding insolvency.
c. **Improving Financial Decision-Making**: AI can enhance decision-making processes by providing more accurate financial forecasts, scenario analysis, and stress testing. This can help firms make better-informed decisions about investments, cost-cutting, debt management, and other critical financial matters.
d. **Optimization of Operations**: AI can identify inefficiencies in business operations, supply chain management, and resource allocation. Addressing these inefficiencies can improve profitability and cash flow, which are crucial for firms facing financial challenges.
e. **Debt Restructuring and Negotiations**: AI tools can assist insolvent firms in analyzing their debt situation and exploring restructuring options. They can also support negotiations with creditors by providing detailed financial projections and risk assessments.
f. **Bankruptcy Prediction Models**: AI-powered bankruptcy prediction models can forecast the likelihood of a firm becoming insolvent. These models use various financial ratios, market data, and other relevant variables.
g. **Asset Management and Liquidation**: In cases where a firm is insolvent, AI can help in efficiently managing and liquidating assets. It can analyze which assets should be sold and at what price, maximizing the return for creditors and stakeholders.
h. **Monitoring Market and Economic Indicators**: AI systems can continuously monitor market and economic indicators that might impact a firm's financial health. This ongoing monitoring can provide early warnings of conditions that may lead to financial distress.
i. **Enhancing Compliance and Reporting**: AI can ensure that financially distressed firms remain compliant with regulatory requirements and financial reporting standards, which is crucial during periods of financial uncertainty.

j. **Stakeholder Communication**: AI can aid in managing communication with stakeholders, including investors, creditors, and employees, particularly in times of financial distress, providing timely and accurate information about the firm's situation and plans.

AI can play a critical role in both preventing and managing corporate financial distress. It offers tools for early detection, risk management, operational optimization, and informed decision-making, which can be vital for firms facing or at risk of insolvency. While AI can significantly aid in these areas, the effectiveness of AI depends on the quality of the data it processes and the expertise of those interpreting its outputs.

References

Alsheibani, S., Messom, D., Cheung, Y., & Alhosni, M. (2020). Reimagining the strategic management of artificial intelligence: Five recommendations for business leaders. In *26th Americas Conference on Information Systems, AMCIS 2020, Virtual Conference*. Association for Information Systems.

Anzai, Y. (2012). *Pattern recognition and machine learning*. Elsevier.

Baily, M. N., Brynjolfsson, E., & Korinek, A. (2023, May 10). *Machines of mind: The case for an AI-powered productivity*. https://hai.stanford.edu/news/machines-mind-case-ai-powered-productivity-boom

Ertel, W. (2018). *Introduction to artificial intelligence*. Springer.

Giudici, P., Centurelli, M., & Turchetta, S. (2024). Artificial intelligence risk measurement. *Expert Systems with Applications, 235*, 121220.

Harari, Y. N. (2015). *Sapiens: A brief history of humankind*. Vintage Publishing.

IFRS 3. (2008). *Business combinations*. https://www.iasplus.com/en/standards/ifrs/ifrs3

Li, D., & Du, Y. (2017). *Artificial intelligence with uncertainty*. CRC Press.

Mariusz, F. (2016). *Introduction to artificial intelligence*. Springer.

Moro-Visconti, R. (2021). *Startup valuation. From strategic business planning to digital networking*. Palgrave MacMillan.

Moro-Visconti, R. (2022a). *The valuation of digital intangibles. Technology, marketing, and the Metaverse*. Palgrave MacMillan, Cham.

Moro-Visconti, R. (2022b). *Augmented corporate valuation. From digital networking to ESG compliance*. Palgrave MacMillan.

Moro-Visconti, R., Cruz Rambaud, S., & López Pascual, J. (2023, November). Artificial intelligence-driven scalability and its impact on the sustainability and valuation of traditional firms. *Humanities & Social Sciences Communications, 10*, 1–14.

Müller, V. C., & Bostrom, N. (2016). Future progress in artificial intelligence: A survey of expert opinion. In V. Müller (Eds.), *Fundamental issues of artificial intelligence*. Synthese Library (Studies in epistemology, logic, methodology, and philosophy of science, Vol. 376). Springer.

Nilsson, N. J. (1980). *Principles of artificial intelligence*. Morgan Kaufmann Publishers.

OECD. (2022). *Transfer pricing guidelines for multinational enterprises and tax administrations*. https://www.oecd.org/tax/oecd-transferpricing-guidelines-for-multinational-enterprises-and-tax-administrations-20769717.htm

Pandey, S., Gupta, S., & Chhajed, S. (2021). ROI of AI: Effectiveness and measurement. *International Journal of Engineering Research & Technology, 10*(5).

Parag, K., & Prachi, J. (2015). *Artificial intelligence: Building intelligent systems*. PHI Learning.

Pedersen, M. (2016). *Artificial intelligence for long-term investing*. SSRN. https://ssrn.com/abstract=2740218

Popkova, E. G., & Sergi, B. S. (2020). Human capital and AI in industry 4.0. Convergence and divergence in social entrepreneurship in Russia. *Journal of Intellectual Capital, 21*(4), 565–581.

Russell, S., & Norvig, P. (2016). *Artificial intelligence: A modern approach*. Pearson.

Short, T., & Adams, T. (2017). *Procedural generation in game design*. CRC Press.

Skansi, S. (2018). *Introduction to deep learning: From logical calculus to artificial intelligence*. Springer.

Stein, S. S. (2020). *Blockchain, artificial intelligence and financial services*. Future of Business and Finance. Springer.

Stuart, R., & Norvig, P. (2016). *Artificial intelligence: A modern approach* (Global). Pearson.

Tiesheva, L., & Smyrnov, I. (2023). A company's digital goodwill: The concept and valuation possibilities. *Economic Affairs, 68*(2), 1279–1290.

Tsoumakas, G. (2019). A survey of machine learning techniques for food sales prediction. *Artificial Intelligence Review, 52*, 441–447.

CHAPTER 8

Chatbots and Generative Artificial Intelligence

8.1 Introduction

Chatbots, driven by AI and natural language processing, simulate human dialogue to aid users effectively. They diminish expenses, improve customer support, and manage numerous inquiries concurrently. The progression of these artificial intelligence systems is swift, characterized by a transition to more intricate models incorporating neural networks. The development of business frameworks for chatbots holds significance in economic assessment, considering elements such as cost-effectiveness, return on investment, customer contentment, and revenue generation. The assessment may prioritize the market worth of chatbot platforms or the advantages they deliver to users. Despite the benefits like prompt customer support and task streamlining, obstacles such as inaccuracies, absence of empathy, and maintaining a balance between automation and human interaction necessitate careful consideration. Generative AI (Gartner, 2023) impacts the business as it relates to content discovery, creation, authenticity, and regulations. It also can automate human work, as well as customer and employee experiences. The critical technologies that fall into this category include the following:

- Artificial general intelligence (AGI) is the (currently hypothetical) intelligence of a machine that can accomplish any intellectual task that a human can perform.

R. Moro-Visconti, *Artificial Intelligence Valuation*,
https://doi.org/10.1007/978-3-031-53622-9_8

- AI engineering is foundational for enterprise delivery of AI solutions at scale. The discipline creates coherent enterprise development, delivery, and operational AI-based systems.
- Autonomic systems are self-managing physical or software systems performing domain-bounded tasks that exhibit three fundamental characteristics: autonomy, learning, and agency.
- Cloud AI services provide AI model-building tools, APIs for prebuilt services, and associated middleware that enable the building/ training, deployment, and consumption of machine learning (ML) models running on prebuilt infrastructure as cloud services.
- Composite AI refers to the combined application (or fusion) of different AI techniques to improve the efficiency of learning to broaden the level of knowledge representations. It solves a wider range of business problems in a more effective manner.
- Computer vision is a set of technologies that involves capturing, processing, and analyzing real-world images and videos to extract meaningful, contextual information from the physical world.
- Data-centric AI is an approach that focuses on enhancing and enriching training data to drive better AI outcomes. Data-centric AI also addresses data quality, privacy, and scalability.
- Edge AI refers to the use of AI techniques embedded in non-IT products, IoT endpoints, gateways and edge servers. It spans use cases for consumer, commercial, and industrial applications, such as autonomous vehicles, enhanced capabilities of medical diagnostics, and streaming video analytics.
- Intelligent applications utilize learned adaptation to respond autonomously to people and machines.
- Model operationalization (ModelOps) is primarily focused on the end-to-end governance and life cycle management of advanced analytics, AI, and decision models.
- Operational AI systems (OAISys) enable orchestration, automation, and scaling of production-ready and enterprise-grade AI, comprising ML, DNNs, and Generative AI.
- Prompt engineering is the discipline of providing inputs, in the form of text or images, to generative AI models to specify and confine the set of responses the model can produce.
- Smart robots are AI-powered, often mobile, machines designed to autonomously execute one or more physical tasks.

- Synthetic data is a class of data that is artificially generated rather than obtained from direct observations of the real world.

Critical technologies and concepts related to generative AI and its impact on various aspects of business are summarized in Table 8.1 (see Gartner, 2023).

These technologies and concepts collectively contribute to the advancements in generative AI and its impact on content discovery, creation, automation, and various business operations. They enable organizations to harness the power of AI for innovation and efficiency in a wide range of applications.

The expected impact of generative AI on businesses and their workforces is gaining momentum, generating:

1. **Business Disruption**: Generative AI has the potential to bring about significant disruption to various industries and organizations. This disruption can stem from the automation and augmentation capabilities of generative AI, which can transform traditional business processes, decision-making, and customer interactions.
2. **Workforce Changes**: Respondents anticipate meaningful changes to their workforces due to the adoption of generative AI. This can include both workforce cuts in certain areas where automation and AI-driven processes can replace human labor, as well as the need for large-scale reskilling efforts to equip employees with the skills necessary to work alongside and manage generative AI systems.
3. **Limited Impact on Other AI Technologies**: while generative AI adoption may lead to changes in how organizations approach AI, it does not necessarily translate into meaningful increases in the adoption of other AI technologies. This could be due to the specific use cases and industries where generative AI is being applied, or the readiness of organizations to invest in AI.

The adoption and impact of generative AI, as well as other AI technologies, can vary widely depending on the industry, organization size, and specific use cases. Some industries may see more rapid adoption of AI across the board, while others may focus primarily on generative AI for creative tasks or content generation.

Table 8.1 Artificial Intelligence taxonomy

Artificial General Intelligence (AGI)	AGI represents the hypothetical intelligence of a machine that can perform any intellectual task that a human can do. It is the goal of achieving human-like AI capabilities
AI Engineering	AI engineering is crucial for delivering AI solutions at an enterprise scale. It involves creating a coherent approach to developing, delivering, and operating AI-based systems within organizations
Autonomic Systems	Autonomic systems are self-managing physical or software systems that exhibit characteristics like autonomy, learning, and agency. They can perform specific tasks independently
Cloud AI Services	Cloud AI services provide tools, APIs, and middleware for building, training, deploying, and consuming machine learning models in the cloud. They facilitate AI model development and deployment
Composite AI	Composite AI involves combining different AI techniques to enhance learning efficiency and address a wider range of business problems more effectively. It leverages multiple AI approaches
Computer Vision	Computer vision encompasses technologies that capture, process and analyze real-world images and videos to extract meaningful information. It has applications in various domains, including image recognition
Data-Centric AI	Data-centric AI focuses on improving AI outcomes by enhancing training data quality, addressing data privacy concerns, and ensuring scalability
Edge AI	Edge AI involves embedding AI techniques in non-IT products, IoT devices, and edge servers. It enables real-time processing and applications at the edge, including autonomous vehicles and medical diagnostics
Intelligent Applications	Intelligent applications use learned adaptation to autonomously respond to both human users and other machines. They can provide intelligent and context-aware interactions
Model Operationalization (ModelOps):	ModelOps focuses on the end-to-end governance and life cycle management of advanced analytics, AI, and decision models, ensuring their effectiveness in production
Operational AI Systems (OAISys):	OAISys systems enable the orchestration, automation, and scaling of production-ready AI, including machine learning, deep neural networks (DNNs), and generative AI
Prompt Engineering	Prompt engineering is the discipline of providing specific inputs, often in the form of text or images, to generative AI models to guide and constrain the responses generated by the models

(continued)

Table 8.1 (continued)

Smart Robots	Smart robots are AI-powered machines designed to autonomously perform physical tasks. They are mobile and adaptable, capable of executing one or more physical tasks
Synthetic Data	Synthetic data is artificially generated data, not collected from direct observations of the real world. It is used for various purposes, including training and testing AI models while preserving data privacy

The introduction of gen AI into the business landscape is likely to be a complex and dynamic process, with both opportunities and challenges for organizations as they navigate the evolving AI landscape and its effects on their workforces and operations.

Generative AI has the potential to provide value across various areas and business functions:

1. Customer Operations: Generative AI can support interactions with customers in several ways. It can be used to develop chatbots or virtual assistants that can handle customer inquiries, provide personalized recommendations, and offer 24/7 customer support. These AI-powered systems can improve response times, enhance customer satisfaction, and reduce the workload on customer service teams.
2. Marketing and Sales: Generative AI can assist in generating creative content for marketing and sales purposes. It can automatically create personalized product descriptions, ad copy, and social media posts based on user preferences and target demographics. This technology can streamline content creation processes, improve marketing campaign effectiveness, and enhance customer engagement.
3. Software Engineering: Generative AI aids software engineers by automating certain tasks. For instance, it can generate computer code based on natural language prompts or automatically generate test cases for software testing. This can help accelerate software development, increase productivity, and reduce the likelihood of human errors.
4. R&D (Research and Development): Generative AI can contribute to various research and development activities. It can assist in

generating hypotheses, conducting simulations, and exploring large datasets to uncover patterns and insights.

While generative AI holds significant potential in these areas, its successful implementation requires careful consideration of ethical, legal, and privacy aspects, as well as ongoing monitoring and refinement to ensure optimal performance.

This chapter defines chatbots and, more generally, generative AI processes, as a prerequisite to the analysis of their main typologies and applications. Business models are built around market applications and are a precondition for business planning estimates. The economic appraisal represents the ending part of this value chain, extracting from the business plan its input parameters.

Chatbots are computer programs designed to interactively engage with users, replicating human-like conversational capabilities during service encounters.

The structure of the study is synthesized in Fig. 8.1.

In particular, the link between the market ecosystem, the business models, and the chatbot platform valuation is illustrated in Fig. 8.2.

The valuation is linked to the supply and value chain that is induced by the chatbot's use.

Many contents are readapted from Moro-Visconti (2022a), or, occasionally, Moro-Visconti (2022b), or Moro-Visconti (2021), extending digital intangible, startup, or business planning applications to specific AI valuation patterns. This chapter is an adaptation and update of Moro-Visconti (2023).

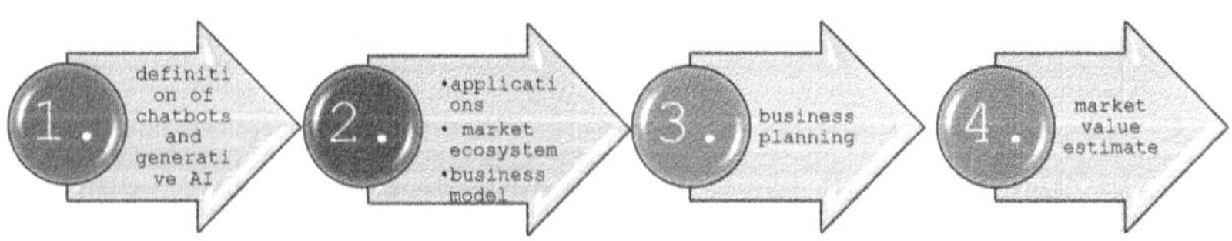

Fig. 8.1 Flowchart of the chapter

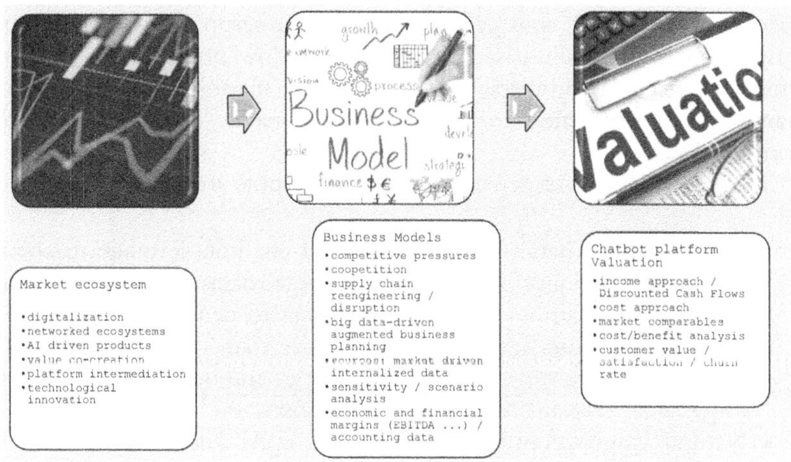

Fig. 8.2 From market ecosystem to business models and chatbot platform valuation

8.2 What are the Main Typologies of Chatbots? A Taxonomy

Chatbots can be categorized into two primary typologies: retrieval chatbots and generative chatbots, distinguished by distinct technical frameworks. Retrieval chatbots utilize predefined knowledge bases to provide responses, facilitating seamless interactions with minimal computational resource utilization. Furthermore, chatbots can be classified based on various factors such as their purpose, location, interface type, user quantity, access method, algorithm utilized, and functionality offered. This classification forms a comprehensive taxonomy that aids in comprehending the essence of chatbots, their creation methods, as well as their advantages and drawbacks. Generative AI involves training AI models on large datasets and using algorithms to learn patterns and generate new content that resembles the training data. Generative AI can be applied in various domains, including natural language processing, computer vision, and creative arts.

On the other hand, chatbots are based on computer programs designed to simulate human-like conversations and interact with end-users through text or speech. They utilize generative AI techniques to understand user input, process it, and generate appropriate responses. Chatbots can range from simple rule-based systems that follow predefined scripts to more advanced AI-powered models that use natural language understanding and generation to provide more dynamic and context-aware conversations.

The main features of generative AI and chatbots are:

- Learning from data: Generative AI and chatbots leverage machine learning techniques to learn from large datasets. They analyze patterns and relationships within the data to generate new content or understand user input. The models are trained on diverse examples to capture a wide range of possibilities and improve their ability to generate relevant and coherent responses.
- Natural language processing: Generative AI and chatbots utilize natural language processing (NLP) techniques to understand and generate human language. NLP enables the systems to process and interpret user input, extract relevant information, and generate appropriate responses that resemble a human conversation.
- Context awareness: Advanced chatbot models incorporate context awareness to provide more meaningful and relevant responses. They consider the conversation history, user preferences, and contextual cues to generate responses that align with the ongoing conversation and the user's needs.
- Real-time interaction: Chatbots aim to provide seamless and interactive conversations with users. They typically operate in real time, allowing users to engage in a back-and-forth conversation, ask questions, and receive immediate responses. Chatbots can be integrated into various platforms, such as websites, messaging apps, or voice assistants, to provide convenient and accessible interactions.
- Personalization and customization: Chatbots can be designed to offer personalized experiences based on user preferences, history, or specific requirements. They can adapt their responses and recommendations to cater to individual users' needs, enhancing the user experience. The business model of chatbots and generative AI can vary depending on the specific application and industry.

These are a few common business models associated with chatbots and generative AI:

- Service Providers: Some companies offer chatbots and generative AI solutions as a service automation tool (Corea et al., 2020). They develop and maintain the AI technology, provide customization options, and charge businesses a fee for using their chatbot or generative AI platform.
- Platform Providers: Companies may develop and provide platforms or frameworks that enable businesses to build and deploy their own chatbots or generative AI applications. These platforms may offer tools, APIs, and developer resources to support businesses in creating and managing their AI solutions. The revenue model can involve licensing fees, subscription plans, or revenue sharing based on platform usage.
- Integration and Customization: Some businesses specialize in integrating chatbots or generative AI capabilities into existing systems or workflows. They work with clients to understand their specific requirements, customize the AI solution to their needs, and provide ongoing support. Revenue is generated through professional services fees, customization charges, or maintenance contracts.
- Product Sales: In certain cases, companies develop and sell prebuilt chatbots or generative AI software products that can be deployed by businesses. These products may offer specific functionalities or cater to niche industries. Revenue is generated through product sales, licensing, or subscription fees.
- Resource Allocation: Businesses must allocate resources to develop or acquire chatbots and generative AI technology. This includes budgeting for hiring AI experts, investing in AI infrastructure, and potentially engaging third-party service providers or platform providers. The budgeting process should consider the costs associated with AI development, customization, integration, and ongoing maintenance.
- Training and Skill Development: Budgeting for training and skill development is essential to ensure that employees have the necessary knowledge and expertise to leverage chatbots and generative AI effectively. This includes providing training on AI technologies, NLP techniques, and chatbot management. Allocating funds for ongoing skill development helps businesses maximize the value and potential of AI implementations.

- Monitoring and Optimization: Businesses should allocate resources for monitoring and optimizing chatbot and generative AI performance. This includes analyzing user feedback, tracking key metrics, and continuously improving AI models and algorithms. Budgeting for ongoing monitoring, analytics tools, and AI optimization efforts can ensure that the AI solutions remain effective and aligned with business goals.
- Continuous learning and improvement: Generative AI models and chatbots can be designed to continuously learn and improve over time. They can be updated with new data, incorporate user feedback, and adapt to evolving user needs. This iterative learning process helps enhance the accuracy, relevance, and quality of generated content and responses.

While generative AI and chatbots offer potential for many applications, ethical considerations such as bias, privacy, and accountability should be considered.

There are many typologies of chatbots. These typologies are not mutually exclusive, and chatbot capabilities can overlap or evolve based on advancements in AI and NLP technologies. Additionally, the design and functionality of chatbots can vary depending on the specific industry, use case, and audience. Organizations can choose the chatbot typology that aligns with their objectives and user requirements.

8.3 Large Language and Multimodal Models

Large language models (LLMs), as shown in Stanford University (2023), have become one of the most prominent and influential areas within the field of Natural Language Processing (NLP). They have ushered in a new era of language understanding and generation, opening up a wide range of applications across various industries:

1. **Revolutionizing Language Understanding**: LLMs have revolutionized the way machines understand and generate human language. They are built on transformer architectures, which excel at capturing complex contextual relationships in text.
2. **Applications Across Industries**: LLMs power a diverse set of applications, including:

- **Machine Translation**: LLMs have significantly improved the quality of machine translation services like Google Translate.
- **Content Creation**: They are used for generating human-like text for content creation, marketing, and storytelling.
- **Virtual Assistants and Chatbots**: LLMs enhance the conversational abilities of virtual assistants and chatbots, making interactions more natural and helpful.
- **Information Retrieval**: LLMs enable better understanding of user queries and more accurate retrieval of relevant information from large datasets.

3. **Popularity of Transformer Architectures**: Transformer-related libraries and models had been gaining popularity in the NLP community even before the widespread attention garnered by LLMs like GPT-3. Transformers introduced a more effective way of modeling language by capturing long-range dependencies in text, which was a limitation in previous architectures.
4. **Public Awareness**: The introduction of models like GPT-3, ChatGPT, and others brought LLMs into the public consciousness. These models showcased the impressive capabilities of LLMs and their potential to transform various industries.
5. **Continued Research and Development**: The field of LLMs is evolving rapidly, with ongoing research and development efforts to create even larger, more capable models. Researchers are also focusing on addressing challenges such as bias and ethical concerns associated with these models.
6. **Accessibility**: LLMs are more accessible to developers and organizations through APIs and cloud services.

LLMs have made a deep impact on NLP. Their versatility and applicability across industries make them a driving force behind advancements in AI-driven language technologies. The popularity and growth of transformer-related libraries and models highlight the continuing importance of these architectures in NLP research and development.

Large language and multimodal models, often referred to as foundation models, have had a significant impact on economic, financial, and market valuation in several ways (Table 8.2):

The economic, financial, and market valuation impact of foundation models can vary depending on factors such as the quality of the

Table 8.2 Economic, financial, and market impact of Artificial Intelligence

Economic Impact	**Job Creation**: The development and deployment of these models have created jobs and economic opportunities in fields such as data science, machine learning research, natural language processing, and computer vision **AI as a Service**: Companies that offer AI-as-a-Service platforms, powered by these models, generate revenue **Increased Productivity**: Businesses can leverage foundation models to automate tasks, gain insights from data, and improve decision-making, which can lead to increased productivity and economic growth
Financial Impact	**Investment and Valuation**: Companies specializing in AI, particularly those with expertise in foundation models, have attracted significant investment and achieved high market valuations. Investors recognize the potential for these models to disrupt various industries **Revenue Generation**: Companies that use foundation models to develop AI-powered products and services, such as recommendation systems, content generation, and virtual assistants, can generate substantial revenue streams **Cost Reduction**: The use of foundation models can lead to cost savings by automating labor-intensive tasks and optimizing processes, which can positively impact a company's financial performance
Market Valuation Impact	**Market Disruption**: Companies that successfully leverage foundation models to innovate and disrupt traditional industries can experience rapid increases in market valuation. Examples include companies in e-commerce, content generation, and personalized marketing **Ecosystem Development**: The emergence of foundation models has led to the growth of an AI ecosystem, with companies building on top of these models to create new applications and services. This ecosystem development can increase the market value of companies within it **Mergers and Acquisitions**: Companies with expertise in foundation models are attractive acquisition targets for larger tech companies seeking to enhance their AI capabilities. Acquisitions can significantly impact market valuations

models, their application, regulatory considerations, and competition within the AI space. Additionally, there are ongoing discussions and debates surrounding ethical and societal implications of these models, which can influence their adoption and, in turn, their impact on various sectors of the economy.

Overall, foundation models have become a driving force in the AI landscape, with the potential to reshape industries, create economic opportunities, and impact the financial performance and market valuations of companies involved in their development and utilization.

8.4 Rule-Based Chatbots

Rule-Based Chatbots: Rule-based chatbots, also known as scripted chatbots, follow a decision tree or script to determine the appropriate response to user inputs. These chatbots are typically limited in their ability to understand complex queries or engage in dynamic conversations but can handle basic FAQs and provide predefined answers. The main features of rule-based chatbots are:

- Predefined Rules: Rule-based chatbots operate based on a set of predefined rules or decision trees. These rules are created and programmed by developers to guide the chatbot's responses to user inputs. The rules dictate the flow of conversation and the appropriate responses based on specific triggers or keywords.
- Limited Natural Language Processing (NLP): Rule-based chatbots typically have limited NLP capabilities compared to AI-powered chatbots. They often rely on keyword matching or simple pattern recognition to understand user inputs. These chatbots are designed to look for specific phrases or keywords within user messages and provide predefined responses based on those matches.
- FAQ Handling: Rule-based chatbots are commonly used for handling frequently asked questions (FAQs). They excel at providing predefined answers to commonly asked queries. The rules are created to cover a range of potential user questions, allowing the chatbot to quickly respond with relevant information.
- Clear and Predictable Responses: Rule-based chatbots provide responses that are predefined and predictable. Since the chatbot follows a set of rules, it offers consistent answers to user queries. The responses are typically concise, and direct, and lack the ability to engage in complex or dynamic conversations.
- Limited Context Awareness: Rule-based chatbots have limited context awareness capabilities. They may struggle to understand context beyond the specific rules programmed into them. If a user deviates from the expected flow or asks questions outside the predefined rules, the chatbot may provide unrelated or generic responses.
- Ease of Development and Maintenance: Rule-based chatbots are relatively straightforward to develop and maintain compared to more complex AI-powered chatbots. As the responses and decision trees

are predetermined, developers can easily update or modify the rules to address new user queries or refine the chatbot's performance.

- Lower Resource Requirements: Rule-based chatbots generally have lower resource requirements compared to AI-powered chatbots. They do not require extensive training on large datasets or complex machine learning algorithms. Rule-based chatbots can operate efficiently even on simpler systems or platforms.
- Limitations in Handling Ambiguity: Rule-based chatbots may struggle with ambiguous or contextually complex user inputs. Since they lack sophisticated natural language understanding, they can misinterpret user queries or fail to provide relevant responses when faced with ambiguity.

Rule-based chatbots are effective for handling specific use cases with well-defined scenarios, such as basic customer inquiries, information retrieval, or simple transactional interactions. However, they may not excel in complex or dynamic conversational scenarios that require advanced natural language processing or context understanding.

8.5 Artificial Intelligence-Powered Chatbots

AI-powered chatbots leverage natural language processing (NLP) and machine learning to understand and respond to user inputs. These chatbots can analyze user queries, extract intent, and generate more dynamic and context-aware responses. They can learn from user interactions and improve their performance over time.

These are the main features of AI-powered chatbots:

a) Natural Language Processing (NLP): AI-powered chatbots leverage advanced NLP techniques. They can analyze the meaning, intent, and context behind user messages, allowing for a more dynamic and flexible conversation.
b) Machine Learning and AI Algorithms: AI-powered chatbots employ machine learning algorithms and AI models to continuously learn and improve their performance. They are trained on large datasets to understand language patterns, recognize entities, and generate appropriate responses. With time and data, they can enhance their accuracy and relevance in understanding user queries.

c) Context Awareness: AI-powered chatbots excel at context awareness, allowing them to understand and remember the context of a conversation. They can maintain the context of previous interactions, including user preferences, history, or specific information mentioned earlier. This enables them to provide more personalized and contextually relevant responses.
d) Intent Recognition: AI-powered chatbots can recognize the intent behind user queries, even if they are expressed differently or contain variations. Through machine learning techniques, they can identify the purpose or goal of the user's message and generate appropriate responses based on that intent.
e) Dynamic Responses: AI-powered chatbots can generate dynamic and context-aware responses rather than relying solely on predefined answers. They can generate responses on the fly, considering the user's query, context, and intent. This allows for more natural and engaging conversations with users.
f) Learning and Adaptation: AI-powered chatbots can learn from user interactions and adapt their responses over time. They can improve their understanding, accuracy, and relevance by continuously analyzing user feedback and incorporating new data. This learning process helps them enhance their conversational capabilities and adapt to changing user needs.
g) Multilingual Support: AI-powered chatbots can often support multiple languages, allowing them to engage with users from different linguistic backgrounds. They can process and understand queries in different languages, enabling broader accessibility and user reach.
h) Integration with Backend Systems: AI-powered chatbots can integrate with backend systems, databases, or APIs to retrieve information, perform actions, or provide real-time updates. They can seamlessly connect with various systems to fulfill user requests, such as retrieving account information, making bookings, or initiating transactions.

AI-powered chatbots offer more advanced and intelligent conversational experiences compared to rule-based chatbots. Their sophisticated NLP capabilities, context awareness, and ability to learn and adapt make them well-suited for complex or dynamic conversational scenarios. They can provide personalized responses, handle ambiguous queries, and deliver more engaging interactions with users.

8.6 Virtual Assistant Chatbots

Virtual assistant chatbots aim to mimic human-like conversations and provide a range of services and functionalities. They often integrate with various systems, databases, or APIs to perform tasks such as booking appointments, providing personalized recommendations, answering complex queries, or initiating transactions. Virtual assistants offer a comprehensive and interactive user experience.

Virtual assistant chatbots combine the functionalities of AI-powered chatbots with additional features to provide comprehensive and versatile virtual assistant capabilities. These are the main features of virtual assistant chatbots:

a) Conversational Capabilities: Virtual assistant chatbots excel at natural language understanding and generation, enabling them to engage in human-like conversations with users. They can process complex queries, interpret context, and generate dynamic responses that go beyond simple predefined answers.
b) Multi-Tasking and Multimodal Support: Virtual assistant chatbots can handle multiple tasks and provide support across various domains. They can assist users with a wide range of requests, such as answering queries, providing recommendations, scheduling appointments, making reservations, or performing transactions. They can also support multiple communication channels, including text-based chat, voice interactions, or even visual interfaces.
c) Personalization and User Profiling: Virtual assistant chatbots can personalize the user experience by collecting and utilizing user information and preferences. They can remember user history, context, and preferences across interactions to deliver tailored recommendations, suggestions, or responses. User profiling allows virtual assistants to provide more relevant and personalized assistance.
d) Integration with Systems and Services: Virtual assistant chatbots can seamlessly integrate with various systems, databases, or APIs to retrieve information, perform actions, or connect users with relevant services. They can interact with backend systems, CRM platforms,

third-party APIs, or even IoT devices to provide real-time updates, access data, or facilitate transactions.

e) Context Switching and Task Management: Virtual assistants can handle context switching and manage multiple tasks within a single conversation. This allows users to address different needs or inquiries without having to start separate interactions.
f) Proactive Assistance: Virtual assistant chatbots can go beyond reactive responses by offering proactive assistance. They can anticipate user needs based on previous interactions, user preferences, or available data. Proactive assistance may involve offering relevant information, reminders, or suggestions without explicit user requests, enhancing the user experience, and providing proactive support.
g) Continuous Learning and Improvement: Virtual assistant chatbots continuously learn and improve their performance over time. They analyze user feedback, gather data, and incorporate new knowledge to enhance their understanding, accuracy, and responsiveness. This iterative learning process allows virtual assistants to adapt to user preferences and evolving needs.

Virtual assistant chatbots aim to provide comprehensive and personalized assistance across various domains and tasks. Their advanced conversational capabilities, integration with systems, and ability to personalize user experiences make them versatile tools for delivering efficient and user-friendly virtual assistant services.

8.7 Transactional Chatbots

Transactional chatbots focus on facilitating transactions or completing specific tasks within a conversation. They can handle tasks like making purchases, processing orders, or conducting financial transactions. These chatbots are often integrated with backend systems or e-commerce platforms to enable seamless transactional experiences.

These are the main features of transactional chatbots:

a) Transaction Handling: Transactional chatbots specialize in handling various types of transactions. They can process orders, make purchases, book appointments, initiate financial transactions, or perform other transactional activities within the conversation.

These chatbots are programmed to interact with backend systems, payment gateways, or APIs to complete the desired transactions.

b) Secure Payment Integration: Transactional chatbots integrate with secure payment gateways to enable secure and seamless payment processing. They provide users with payment options, verify payment details, and securely handle transactions within the conversation. This integration ensures a smooth and secure transactional experience for users.
c) Order Tracking and Updates: Transactional chatbots can provide real-time updates and status information for orders or transactions. They can retrieve order details, track shipments, or provide updates on the progress of the transaction. Users can inquire about order statuses or receive automated notifications through the chatbot interface.
d) Product Recommendations: Transactional chatbots can offer personalized product recommendations based on user preferences, purchase history, or contextual information. They can suggest related products, provide upselling or cross-selling opportunities, and help users make informed purchasing decisions within the conversation.
e) Inventory Management: Transactional chatbots can interact with backend inventory systems to check product availability, provide stock information, or inform users about out-of-stock items. They can update inventory levels in real time, ensuring accurate information is provided to users during the transaction process.
f) Order Customization: Transactional chatbots allow users to customize their orders or transactions based on their preferences. Users can specify customizations, special requests, or options within the conversation, and the chatbot can process the order accordingly. This feature enhances the user experience by allowing personalized transactions.
g) Return and Refund Handling: Transactional chatbots can assist users with return and refund processes. They can provide instructions, initiate return requests, or guide users through the necessary steps to obtain refunds or resolve issues related to transactions. This feature helps streamline the customer support process and improves user satisfaction.
h) Compliance and Security: Transactional chatbots prioritize compliance and security in handling sensitive transactional data. They

adhere to privacy regulations, utilize encryption, and ensure data protection throughout the transaction process. Compliance and security measures are implemented to instill user trust and protect sensitive information.

Transactional chatbots focus on streamlining and enhancing the transactional experience for users. Their features enable seamless transactions, personalized recommendations, and efficient order management. By integrating with backend systems and payment gateways, they simplify the transaction process and provide users with a convenient and user-friendly interface for their transactions.

8.8 Social Chatbots

Social chatbots are designed to engage users in social interactions, typically in messaging platforms or social media channels. They can handle casual conversations, provide entertainment, deliver news updates, or engage in small talk. Social chatbots are often employed for marketing, customer engagement, or brand promotion purposes. These are the main features of social chatbots:

a) Casual Conversations: Social chatbots are programmed to engage users in casual and informal conversations. They have a conversational style that resembles human-like interactions, including the use of emojis, casual language, or even humor. They are designed to create a friendly and approachable atmosphere for users.
b) Entertainment and Engagement: Social chatbots focus on providing entertainment value to users. They can offer quizzes, games, trivia, or interactive storytelling experiences. These chatbots are designed to keep users engaged, entertained, and coming back for more social interactions.
c) Content Delivery: Social chatbots can deliver content to users based on their preferences or interests. They can provide news updates, weather forecasts, event recommendations, or personalized content recommendations. The chatbot acts as a content curator, delivering relevant information to users in an interactive and conversational manner.

d) Social Media Integration: Social chatbots often integrate with social media platforms, such as Facebook Messenger, WhatsApp, or Twitter, to engage with users on their preferred channels. They leverage the existing social media infrastructure and user base to provide seamless social interactions and broaden their reach.
e) Small Talk and Chit-Chat: Social chatbots excel at engaging in small talk and chit-chat conversations. They can discuss topics like hobbies, movies, sports, current events, or general daily life. These chatbots are designed to simulate casual conversations and create a friendly and relatable experience for users.
f) Social Customer Support: Social chatbots can provide customer support services through social media channels. They can handle user inquiries, provide basic support, or guide users to relevant resources or human support agents when needed. Social chatbots streamline the customer support process and provide quick and responsive assistance.
g) Social Engagement and Brand Promotion: Social chatbots are often employed for brand promotion and engagement with users. They can showcase products, answer inquiries about services, or provide information about promotional offers. These chatbots aim to build brand awareness, engage with users, and create a positive brand experience.
h) Conversational Analytics: Social chatbots can collect conversational data and analyze user interactions. This data can provide insights into user preferences, interests, or sentiment, helping businesses understand their audience and optimize their social engagement strategies. Conversational analytics allow businesses to tailor their content, promotions, or experiences based on user feedback and behavior.

Social chatbots are designed to provide enjoyable and interactive social experiences for users. Their focus on entertainment, engagement, and personalized interactions allows them to create a unique social presence and build strong connections with users on social media platforms or messaging apps.

8.9 Hybrid Chatbots

Hybrid chatbots combine multiple chatbot technologies and capabilities to provide a more versatile and robust conversational experience. They may incorporate rule-based systems, AI-powered NLP, and integration with backend systems to handle a wide range of user queries and tasks. Hybrid chatbots aim to leverage the strengths of different approaches to deliver optimal performance. Here are the main features of hybrid chatbots:

a) Rule-Based and AI-Powered Components: Hybrid chatbots integrate both rule-based and AI powered components. They combine the structured and predictable nature of rule-based chatbots with the flexibility and intelligence of AI-powered chatbots. This allows them to handle a wide range of queries and provide dynamic responses.
b) Intent Recognition and NLP: Hybrid chatbots leverage natural language processing (NLP) and intent recognition techniques to understand user queries and extract meaning. They can analyze user inputs, recognize the intent behind the queries, and generate appropriate responses. NLP capabilities enable a more accurate understanding of user messages and enhance the conversational experience.
c) Context Awareness: Hybrid chatbots excel at context awareness, allowing them to understand and remember the context of ongoing conversations. They can retain information from previous interactions, such as user preferences, history, or specific details mentioned earlier. This enables them to provide personalized and contextually relevant responses.
d) Seamless Integration with Backend Systems: Hybrid chatbots can seamlessly integrate with backend systems, databases, or APIs to retrieve information, perform actions, or access real-time data. They can interact with various systems to provide users with relevant information, facilitate transactions, or retrieve personalized data.
e) Personalization and User Profiling. Hybrid chatbots can personalize the user experience by collecting and utilizing user information and preferences. They can remember user history, context, and preferences to deliver tailored recommendations, suggestions, or

responses. User profiling allows hybrid chatbots to provide more relevant and personalized assistance.

f) Learning and Adaptation: Hybrid chatbots can continuously learn and improve their performance over time. They can analyze user interactions, gather feedback, and incorporate new data to enhance their understanding, accuracy, and responsiveness. This learning process allows them to adapt to user preferences and evolving needs.
g) Dynamic Response Generation: Hybrid chatbots can generate dynamic and contextually relevant responses. They combine predefined rules with AI-powered algorithms to provide responses that align with the conversation flow, user intent, and context. This dynamic response generation allows for more engaging and natural conversations.
h) Scalability and Performance: Hybrid chatbots are designed to be scalable and capable of handling increased user demand. They can efficiently manage large volumes of conversations. This scalability ensures a smooth user experience even during peak usage periods.

Hybrid chatbots leverage the strengths of different chatbot technologies to deliver a versatile and robust conversational experience. They combine rule-based systems for structured responses with AI-powered capabilities for context awareness, intent recognition, and dynamic response generation. This combination allows hybrid chatbots to handle a wide range of user queries, provide personalized assistance, and deliver engaging conversations.

8.10 Business Models, Value Drivers, and Scalability

The business models of chatbots and generative AI can vary depending on the specific application and industry. These business models are causing a revolution across multiple industries. The utilization of large language model AI involves the use of generative pretrained transformers to generate responses that resemble human-like interactions in response to natural language queries, which are derived from a wide array of sources for training purposes. This approach is grounded on a sophisticated deep learning model known as the Generative Adversarial Network and adheres to a framework comprising of "corpus system+pre-training+fine-tuning".

The applications of these technologies are vast, ranging from facilitating customer engagement to improving healthcare services, thereby highlighting their potential to reshape the decision-making processes within businesses. Hence, these technological advancements present notable opportunities for organizations to enrich customer interactions, optimize operational procedures, and foster innovation across diverse industries. Here are some common business models and their impact on value drivers and scalability (Table 8.3).

The impact of these business models on the abovementioned value drivers and scalability depends on various factors such as market demand, competition, the quality of the chatbot or generative AI offering, and the ability to meet customer needs effectively. It is important for businesses to assess their value propositions, and market dynamics.

8.11 Economic Valuation Patterns

The influence of chatbots on economic assessment models, however, transcends the financial domain, as observed through their impact on service sectors like telecommunications, hospitality, insurance, banking, and retail. Companies in these sectors are utilizing chatbots to bolster profitability and achieve market share objectives. The economic significance of chatbots lies in their capacity to optimize operations, enhance customer engagements, and propel business expansion across a multitude of industries. The economic and financial valuation of a chatbot can be approached from various perspectives. Economic and financial valuation approaches may vary depending on the specific objectives, industry, and context of the chatbot implementation. A comprehensive evaluation considers a combination of these approaches to provide a holistic assessment of the economic and financial value derived from the chatbot investment.

Whereas it is difficult to use standard valuation approaches for the valuation of chatbots, it should not be forgotten that they can be appraised considering:

- Chatbot platforms (see https://www.cmswire.com/digital-experience/10-chatbot-providers-you-should-know-about/);
- Chatbot users.

Table 8.3 Business models, value drivers, and scalability

Model	*Value driver and scalability impact*
Service-based Model: In the service-based model, businesses develop and deploy chatbots or generative AI systems to provide customer support, assistance, or personalized recommendations as a service. Revenue is generated through subscription fees, licensing fees, or usage-based pricing. This model brings to:	Value Drivers: The service-based model can enhance customer satisfaction by providing efficient and round-the-clock support, personalized recommendations, and streamlined interactions. It can also reduce operational costs by automating repetitive tasks, freeing up human resources for more complex or high-value activities Scalability Impact: The service-based model allows businesses to scale their chatbot or generative AI services by serving a larger customer base without significant infrastructure investments. As demand increases, businesses can add more resources to handle the growing number of users and interactions
Virtual Assistant Model: Virtual assistant chatbots can be developed and marketed as stand-alone products or as part of a larger ecosystem. Businesses generate revenue by selling virtual assistants directly to consumers or by partnering with device manufacturers or platform providers to embed virtual assistants into their products. This model brings to:	Value Drivers: Virtual assistant chatbots offer personalized and comprehensive assistance across various domains. They enhance user productivity, convenience, and satisfaction by integrating with multiple systems, performing tasks, and providing relevant information. They also contribute to brand differentiation and customer loyalty Scalability Impact: The virtual assistant model can benefit from scalability through partnerships and integrations. By integrating virtual assistants into popular platforms or devices, businesses can reach a larger user base without the need for individual marketing or customer acquisition efforts. Scaling the virtual assistant offering involves expanding partnerships and integrations with compatible platforms and devices

(continued)

Table 8.3 (continued)

Model	*Value driver and scalability impact*
Data Monetization Model: Chatbots and generative AI systems generate valuable data through user interactions. Businesses can monetize this data by selling it to third parties, advertisers, or using it for targeted marketing and advertising campaigns. This model brings to:	Value Drivers: Data monetization allows businesses to generate additional revenue streams and maximize the value of the data collected through chatbot interactions. It enables better targeting of marketing efforts, more personalized customer experiences, and insights into customer behavior and preferences Scalability Impact: The scalability of the data monetization model depends on the size and quality of the user base, the volume and richness of the data collected, and the ability to attract data buyers or partners. As the user base grows, the data pool increases, potentially attracting more partners and increasing the revenue potential
Platform-as-a-Service (PaaS) Model: Some businesses provide chatbots or generative AI platforms as a service to other businesses. They offer a comprehensive platform that enables businesses to build, deploy, and manage their own chatbots or generative AI systems. Revenue is generated through subscription fees, licensing, or usage-based pricing. This model brings to:	Value Drivers: The PaaS model provides businesses with the tools, infrastructure, and support to develop and manage their own chatbots or generative AI systems. It reduces the time, cost, and complexity of building and maintaining the infrastructure from scratch. Businesses can focus on developing unique chatbot applications and tailor them to their specific needs Scalability Impact: The PaaS model allows businesses to scale their chatbot or generative AI deployments by onboarding more customers onto the platform. The platform provider can allocate additional resources to support the growing user base, ensuring scalability and performance as the demand increases

This distinction is crucial to understand the target of the valuation that concerns either the chatbot platforms, considered as a firm, or the users of the generative AI services.

Chatbots have gained significant popularity as a versatile tool for enhancing both external customer communication and internal workflows within organizations. While their initial adoption was primarily focused on customer service and support functions, businesses are now leveraging chatbots across various internal operations to improve efficiency and productivity. Internally, chatbots can be deployed to streamline processes, automate repetitive tasks, and facilitate seamless communication among employees (see Johannsen et al., 2021). This represents a strategic bridge between developers and users.

Some common approaches used to assess the economic and financial value of a chatbot are reported in the following subsections.

Fernandez (2019) describes the most widely used company valuation methods:

1. balance sheet-based methods;
2. income statement-based methods (including market comparables);
3. mixed methods;
4. cash flow discounting-based methods.

The conceptually correct methods are those based on cash flow discounting Singh, 2013).

The main valuation methods, already described in Chapter 2 (see also Damodaran, 2018; Fazzini, 2018; Koller & Goedhart, 2015), are recalled in Fig. 8.3.

The three main approaches described in the International Valuation Standard 210 concerning intangible assets are (see Moro-Visconti, 2022a):

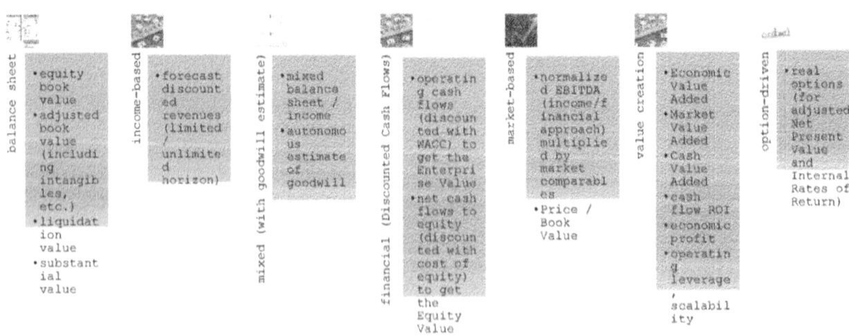

Fig. 8.3 Firm valuation approaches: A taxonomy

- The cost approach
- The income approach
- The market approach

Figure 8.4 synthetizes the main valuation approaches that often overlap: this is because the chatbot platform's value strongly depends on the perceived utility of its services from the perspective of its clients.

Some advantages of first movers like Open AI in the development of models like GPT (Generative Pre-trained Transformer) are the following:

1. High Fixed Costs as Barriers to Entry: Developing and training large AI models like GPT involves significant fixed costs, which can act as barriers to entry for potential competitors. These high costs can

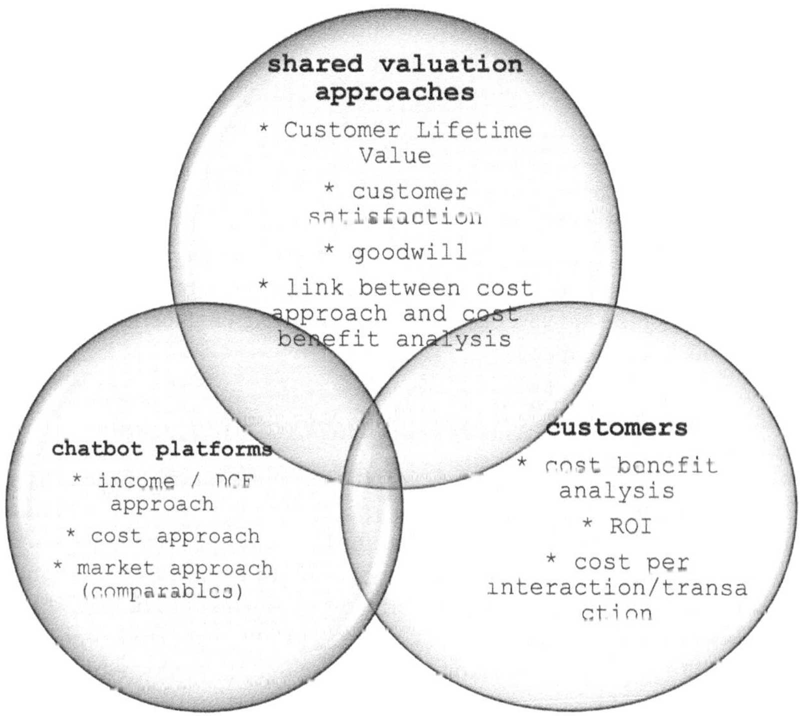

Fig. 8.4 Compared valuation approaches

deter other organizations from entering the market and competing directly with incumbents.

2. Locking in Corporate Customers: OpenAI's early presence in the market allows it to establish relationships with corporate customers who may prefer not to switch AI providers once they have integrated OpenAI's technology. Switching providers can be costly and may raise concerns about cybersecurity and data migration.
3. Data Fine-Tuning: Corporate clients may need to fine-tune AI models like GPT to suit their specific needs, and this often involves sharing internal company data with the AI provider. Many clients may prefer to do this process once and stick with a trusted provider to avoid the complexities and risks associated with changing providers.
4. Tacit Engineering Know-How: Developing and training large AI models requires deep engineering expertise, including the ability to recognize high-quality data, debug source code, and optimize the model's performance. This expertise is often built up over time and through experience, giving OpenAI an advantage as a pioneer in the field.

Being the first mover in the AI model development space, especially with large models like GPT, provides OpenAI with certain competitive advantages. These advantages include the ability to set high barriers to entry for potential competitors, establish long-term relationships with corporate clients, and leverage their accumulated engineering expertise in AI model development.

8.12 Valuation of Chatbot Platforms

Valuation of Chatbot Platforms entails the examination of various criteria to ascertain the optimal platform for specific requirements. A computational strategy has been recommended for forecasting chatbot acceptance based on factors like Intent, Conversation Flow, and Response Design, assisting in preliminary assessment prior to deployment. The assessment of chatbots commonly emphasizes efficacy, productivity, and user satisfaction, with a recent inclination towards evaluating productivity due to the emergence of task-oriented chatbots in corporate settings. Organizations can leverage these assessment techniques to improve their operational efficiency by opting for the most appropriate chatbot deployment solutions. Valuation approaches for chatbot platforms typically involve assessing various factors that contribute to the overall value of the platform. While specific methodologies may vary, here are some common valuation approaches used for chatbot platforms:

a) User base: The size and growth potential of the chatbot platform's user base are important. A larger user base implies a wider network and greater potential for network effects to occur.
b) Engagement and interaction: The level of engagement and interaction between users and the chatbot platform is evaluated. Platforms with high user engagement tend to generate more valuable data and insights, enhancing the network effects.
c) Data and intelligence: The quality and richness of the data collected by the chatbot platform, and the resulting intelligence and personalization capabilities are considered. The ability to leverage user data to continuously improve the platform's performance can contribute to its value.
d) Ecosystem and partnerships: The presence of a vibrant ecosystem around the chatbot platform, including partnerships with other businesses or developers, can enhance its network effects.
e) Competitive landscape: The competitive dynamics within the chatbot industry and the platform's positioning relative to competitors are considered. A chatbot platform with a strong network effect and a competitive advantage in attracting and retaining users may have a higher valuation.

By incorporating the network-based scalability approach, the valuation of a chatbot platform considers not only its current user base and financial metrics but also the potential for growth and the amplifying effects of network effects.

These approaches are not mutually exclusive, and a combination of methods may be used depending on the specific circumstances and availability of data. Valuation is a complex process, and it is recommended to consult with financial experts or professionals with experience in valuing technology companies for accurate assessments.

From the Cost Approach to Cost–Benefit Analysis

The cost approach is one of the three main approaches to valuation, alongside the market approach and the income approach. It estimates the value of an asset by considering the cost required to replace it with a similar asset of equal utility. The underlying concept is that a buyer would not pay more for an asset than the cost of acquiring a substitute asset that serves the same purpose. This approach can be used for the digital chatbot firm (how much does it cost to create a similar product from scratch?) but also for its customers who choose whether to buy or not the chatbot product by doing a cost–benefit analysis (is the cost of purchasing the service affordable and economically convenient, in terms of expected payoffs?).

Under the cost approach, the value of an asset is determined by calculating the cost to reproduce or replace it. The process involves several steps:

- Estimate the reproduction cost: This involves determining the current cost of constructing an identical asset with the same utility as the subject property, considering factors such as materials, labor, and overhead expenses.
- Account for depreciation: Various forms of depreciation need to be considered, including physical deterioration (wear and tear), functional obsolescence (changes in design or technology), and external obsolescence (external factors impacting value, such as changes in the neighborhood).
- Calculate the accrued depreciation: Accrued depreciation is the total depreciation incurred over the life of the asset up to the valuation date.
- Deduct the accrued depreciation from the reproduction cost: By subtracting the accrued depreciation from the reproduction cost, you arrive at the estimated value under the cost approach.

The cost approach is particularly useful when valuing new or specialized properties for which there is limited market data available, or when assessing properties with unique characteristics.

Cost–benefit analysis is essential in the economic and financial valuation of a chatbot. It helps assess the feasibility, profitability, and value of the chatbot project by comparing the costs involved with the expected benefits. Here's the impact of cost–benefit analysis on the economic and financial valuation approaches of a chatbot:

a) Financial Viability: Cost–benefit analysis helps determine the financial viability of implementing a chatbot. By quantifying the costs associated with development, implementation, maintenance, and infrastructure, businesses can assess whether the benefits derived from the chatbot outweigh the investment made. This analysis allows decision-makers to evaluate the financial feasibility of the project and make informed decisions about resource allocation.
b) Return on Investment (ROI): Cost–benefit analysis is a fundamental component of ROI calculation. It enables businesses to compare the total costs of the chatbot project with the expected financial benefits. By quantifying the potential cost savings, revenue generation, increased operational efficiency, and improved customer experience, cost–benefit analysis helps estimate the financial returns and calculate the ROI of the chatbot investment.
c) Risk Assessment: Cost–benefit analysis allows for a comprehensive evaluation of the potential risks and rewards associated with the chatbot project. By identifying and quantifying the costs and benefits, businesses can assess the level of risk involved and determine whether the potential benefits outweigh the associated risks. This assessment provides valuable insights for risk management and decision-making.
d) Decision-Making and Prioritization: Cost–benefit analysis provides decision-makers with quantifiable data to compare and prioritize different investment opportunities. It helps businesses evaluate the financial impact of investing in a chatbot relative to other initiatives or projects. By understanding the costs and benefits in monetary terms, decision-makers can make informed choices and allocate resources effectively.
e) Value Communication: Cost–benefit analysis facilitates effective communication of the value proposition of the chatbot project to stakeholders, including management, investors, and other key parties. By presenting the estimated financial benefits and cost savings, businesses can articulate the value and potential impact of the chatbot in a tangible and measurable way.
f) Iterative Improvement: Cost–benefit analysis is not a one-time exercise but an ongoing process. As the chatbot project evolves and

matures, businesses can reassess and update the analysis based on real-world data and feedback. This iterative approach helps refine financial projections, adjust cost estimates, and evaluate the actual benefits realized over time, leading to more accurate financial valuation and decision-making.

By conducting a comprehensive cost–benefit analysis, the economic and financial implications of implementing a chatbot are easier to understand. It provides valuable insights into the financial viability, risk assessment, ROI, and value communication of the chatbot project. Cost–benefit analysis helps ensure that the investment in a chatbot aligns with business objectives, maximizes financial returns, and drives sustainable growth.

Market Approach (Comparables)

The market approach is a widely recognized valuation methodology used in various valuation standards and practices, including the International Valuation Standards (IVS). The market approach determines the value of an asset by comparing it to similar assets that have recently been sold in the market. The underlying principle is that the market value of a property is influenced by the prices at which similar properties are bought and sold.

The market approach typically involves the following steps:

1. Identify comparable sales: Similar properties, known as comparables or "comps", are identified based on various factors such as location, size, condition, and other relevant characteristics. These properties should have recently sold in the market.
2. Analyze the comparables: The comparables are thoroughly examined and adjusted to make them as similar as possible to the subject property. Adjustments may be made for factors such as size differences, location variations, and differences in amenities or features.
3. Determine the market value: Once the comparables have been adjusted, a range of values is derived. This range is used to estimate the market value of the subject property based on the recent sales prices of the comparables.

The market approach is particularly useful when there is an active and well-functioning market with sufficient comparable sales data available. It provides insights into how buyers and sellers in the market perceive the value of similar assets.

Comparing the performance and financial impact of the chatbot with similar solutions in the market or industry can provide valuable insights. Benchmarking against industry standards or competitors can help understand the relative financial value and effectiveness of the chatbot8.4

Revenue Generation (Income Approach)

The income approach, also reported in the International Valuation Standard 210, typically involves the following steps:

a) Estimate the potential income: The first step is to determine the potential income that the asset can generate based on its existing or projected rental or income streams. This may involve analyzing historical financial data, market rents, lease agreements, or other relevant information.
b) Consider operating expenses: The next step is to account for operating expenses associated with the asset. These expenses may include property management fees, maintenance costs, insurance, property taxes, utilities, and other expenses necessary to maintain and operate the asset.
c) Determine the net operating income by subtracting the operating expenses from the potential income. This represents the income generated by the asset before considering financing costs or income taxes
d) Apply the capitalization rate or discount rate: To determine the value of the asset, the net operating income is divided by a capitalization rate or discounted using a discount rate. The capitalization rate or discount rate reflects the risk and return expectations of investors and is derived from market data, comparable sales, or other valuation techniques.
e) Calculate the value: The value of the asset is obtained by dividing the net operating income by the capitalization rate or discounting the net operating income using the discount rate. This provides an estimate of the present value of the income stream generated by the asset.

Table 8.4 Performance and financial impact of the chatbot

Performance and financial impact of the chatbot	Benchmarking: Comparing the performance of your chatbot with similar solutions in the market allows you to benchmark its effectiveness and identify areas for improvement. It is possible to evaluate parameters such as customer satisfaction, conversion rates, average order value, and cost savings to understand how your chatbot measures up against competiting platforms. This analysis helps you set realistic goals and objectives for your chatbot and strive for better financial outcomes
	Identifying Best Practices: By examining the performance of other chatbots in your industry, you can identify best practices that contribute to their economic and financial success. This analysis helps you understand what strategies and features are effective in generating revenue and improving customer experiences. You can then incorporate these insights into your own chatbot's design and implementation, potentially enhancing its market value
	Market Positioning: Comparing your chatbot's financial impact with similar solutions in the market helps you assess its market positioning. If your chatbot is surpassing competing platforms in terms of additional revenues, cost savings, or customer satisfaction, it can give a competitive edge. On the other hand, if the chatbot lags, it indicates areas that require attention and improvement to increase its market value

(continued)

Table 8.4 (continued)

	Investment Decisions: Comparing the financial performance of your chatbot with industry benchmarks can be useful for making investment decisions. It helps you evaluate the return on investment (ROI) of your chatbot implementation and determine whether additional investments are justified. If your chatbot demonstrates superior financial outcomes compared to similar solutions, it can justify allocating more resources to its development and maintenance
	Business Case Development: When presenting the economic and financial value of your chatbot to stakeholders or decision-makers, comparing it with industry competitors adds credibility and context. By showcasing how your chatbot outperforms or aligns with market standards, you can build a stronger business case for its implementation, expansion, or continued investment
	However, direct access to competitor data may not always be available. In such cases, industry reports, case studies, and market research can provide insights into the performance and financial impact of similar chatbot solutions

Some chatbots are designed to directly generate revenue through transactions, upselling, cross-selling, or providing value-added services. Evaluating the revenue generated by the chatbot, either directly or indirectly, helps assess its financial value and contribution to the business.

Chatbots are designed to directly generate revenue through transactions, upselling, cross-selling, or providing value-added services.

Chatbots can generate revenue directly through various means such as transactions, upselling, cross-selling, and providing value-added services. The impact of these revenue-generation activities on the economic and financial value of a chatbot can be significant. Here are some key points to consider (Table 8.5):

It is important to optimize the performance of the chatbot. Regular updates, personalized interactions, and integration with existing systems

Table 8.5 Impact of revenue-generation activities on the economic and financial value of a chatbot

Impact of revenue-generation activities on the economic and financial value of a chatbot	Increased Sales: Chatbots can actively engage with customers, understand their needs, and recommend relevant products or services. By providing personalized recommendations and offers, chatbots can drive sales and increase the average order value. The ability to guide customers through the sales process and answer their questions in real time can lead to higher conversion rates and revenue growth Cost Savings: Chatbots can automate routine tasks and handle a large volume of customer inquiries without requiring human intervention. By reducing the workload on human agents, chatbots help optimize resource allocation and cut operational costs. These cost savings contribute directly to the economic value of the chatbot implementation Enhanced Customer Lifetime Value: A chatbot that provides exceptional customer experiences and addresses customer needs effectively can improve customer loyalty and retention. Satisfied customers are more likely to make repeat purchases, leading to increased customer lifetime value (CLV). By extending the customer lifespan and fostering customer loyalty, chatbots contribute to long-term revenue growth Scalability and Efficiency: Chatbots can handle multiple conversations simultaneously, offering 24/7 support without any additional labor costs. They can handle high volumes of inquiries and provide instant responses, improving overall operational efficiency. This scalability allows businesses to accommodate increasing customer demand without proportional increases in staffing, positively impacting the financial value of the chatbot

(continued)

Table 8.5 (continued)

	Cross-selling and Upselling Opportunities: Chatbots can proactively suggest complementary products or services based on customer preferences (Chen et al., 2021) and behavior, leading to cross-selling and upselling opportunities. By leveraging customer data and providing targeted recommendations, chatbots can increase the average transaction value and drive additional revenue
	Competitive Advantage: Implementing a chatbot that excels in revenue generation and delivers superior customer experiences can differentiate a company from its competitors. A chatbot that drives sales, increases customer satisfaction, and enhances overall financial performance can give a business a competitive edge in the market

and processes can maximize the economic and financial value of the chatbot.

Return on Investment (ROI)

The return on investment (ROI) formula is:

$$\text{ROI} = \frac{(\text{Current Value Investment} - \text{Cost of Investment})}{\text{Cost of Investment}} \quad (8.1)$$

ROI analysis focuses on evaluating the financial returns generated by the chatbot in relation to the investment made. It considers the financial benefits, such as increased sales, reduced costs, or improved customer retention, and compares them to the total investment made in developing, implementing, and maintaining the chatbot. ROI analysis helps assess the profitability and financial impact of the chatbot project.

The impact of Return on Investment (ROI) using a chatbot is often significant for businesses. Here are some key aspects highlighting the ROI impact of implementing a chatbot:

a) Cost Savings: Chatbots can automate various tasks and processes that would otherwise require manual effort or human intervention. By handling routine inquiries, providing self-service options, and automating customer support, chatbots can significantly reduce operational costs. The cost savings arise from lower labor expenses, increased efficiency, and reduced handling time per customer interaction.
b) Increased Efficiency: Chatbots enable businesses to handle a higher volume of customer interactions simultaneously and provide real-time responses 24/7. This scalability and improved response time lead to increased efficiency in handling customer inquiries, resulting in faster resolution and reduced wait times. By handling inquiries more efficiently, businesses can serve more customers in less time, leading to higher productivity and improved ROI.
c) Improved Customer Experience: Chatbots enhance the customer experience by providing instant and personalized responses. They can offer immediate assistance, answer common queries, and guide customers through processes or transactions. Improved customer experience can lead to higher customer satisfaction, increased customer loyalty, and ultimately, greater customer lifetime value. Satisfied customers are more likely to make repeat purchases and recommend the business to others, positively impacting ROI.
d) Enhanced Lead Generation and Sales: Chatbots can act as virtual sales assistants, engaging with customers, understanding their needs, and offering product recommendations. By providing personalized suggestions, handling product inquiries, and guiding customers through the sales process, chatbots can improve lead generation and sales conversion rates. Increased sales and revenue directly contribute to improved ROI.
e) Reduction in Support Costs: Chatbots can reduce the load on human customer support agents by handling routine inquiries and providing initial support. This allows human agents to focus on more complex or critical issues, increasing their efficiency and reducing overall support costs. The cost savings from optimized resource allocation can positively impact ROI.
f) Scalability: Chatbots are highly scalable, and capable of handling many customer interactions simultaneously without significant additional costs. As businesses grow or experience increased customer demand, chatbots can easily scale to accommodate the increased

workload. The scalability of chatbots allows businesses to handle higher volumes of inquiries and transactions without proportional increases in resources, positively impacting ROI.

g) Data Collection and Insights: Chatbots gather valuable data on customer interactions, preferences, and behavior. By leveraging these insights, businesses can make informed decisions, refine marketing strategies, and enhance their products or services, leading to improved ROI.

The impact of ROI can vary based on the specific implementation, industry, and customer base. The extent of cost savings, efficiency gains, and revenue growth will depend on factors such as the complexity of the chatbot, integration with backend systems, quality of conversation design, and continuous improvement efforts.

Conducting a comprehensive ROI analysis specific to the business context is crucial to understanding the direct and indirect impacts of a chatbot on financial returns.

8.13 Customer Lifetime Value (CLV)

CLV estimates the total value a customer brings to a business over their entire relationship. CLV calculates the future cash inflows related to customers. Automated technologies like Chatbots play a significant role in enriching customer interactions and relationships with brands. Chatbots facilitate improved communication with brands, influencing long-term relationships and customer engagement. Furthermore, the attributes of Chatbots, including personalization, perceived control, and empathy, affect how customers perceive value creation or destruction, thereby influencing CLV by enhancing customer interactions and service experiences. Thus, effectively utilizing Chatbots can boost CLV by promoting customer loyalty, retention, and engagement, consequently leading to increased revenue and profits. Chatbots can impact CLV by improving customer experience, engagement, and loyalty. By analyzing how the chatbot enhances customer satisfaction, retention, and repeat purchases, businesses can estimate the impact on CLV and assess the long-term financial value of the chatbot. CVL influences the goodwill of both the chatbot platform and its clients.

CLV has a significant impact on the economic and financial evaluation of a chatbot. Here are some key aspects highlighting the impact of CLV on the evaluation (Table 8.6):

Cost per Interaction/Transaction

The evaluation of cost per interaction/transaction in chatbot assessment is a critical metric that can be influenced by a variety of factors. There are economic risks connected to chatbot failures and suggest a computational method for forecasting chatbot popularity. This method highlights the importance of assessing chatbots not only in terms of user satisfaction but also in terms of predicting their performance and potential economic impact per interaction/transaction. Businesses can evaluate the cost per interaction or transaction handled by the chatbot compared to alternative methods, such as human support or customer service. Chatbots that can efficiently handle a high volume of interactions at a lower cost per interaction can result in cost savings and improved operational efficiency. Calculating the cost per interaction helps assess the financial benefits and cost-effectiveness of the chatbot.

The Cost per Interaction/Transaction of a chatbot has a significant impact on the economic and financial value of the chatbot. Here are some key aspects highlighting its impact:

a) Cost Efficiency: A low Cost per Interaction/Transaction indicates that the chatbot is handling customer inquiries and transactions at a relatively lower cost compared to alternative methods, such as human support or customer service. This cost efficiency directly impacts the financial value of the chatbot by reducing operational expenses.
b) Scalability: Chatbots excel in scalability, meaning they can handle a large volume of interactions simultaneously without significant additional costs. A low Cost per Interaction/Transaction enables businesses to scale their customer support or service operations efficiently. As customer demand increases, the chatbot can handle more interactions without proportionately increasing resources, contributing to improved scalability and cost-effectiveness.
c) Resource Optimization: By automating routine inquiries and tasks, chatbots free up human resources, allowing them to focus on more complex or critical issues. This optimization of resources reduces the

Table 8.6 CLV's impact on the economic and financial evaluation of a chatbot

CLV's impact on the economic and financial evaluation of a chatbot	Revenue Generation: CLV represents the total value a customer brings to a business over their entire relationship. By improving CLV, a chatbot can positively impact revenue generation. Through personalized interactions, timely assistance, and tailored recommendations, chatbots can enhance customer satisfaction, engagement, and loyalty. Satisfied and loyal customers are more likely to make repeat purchases, spend more, and contribute higher revenue over time
	Customer Retention: Chatbots can play a vital role in customer retention by delivering consistent and personalized customer experiences. By addressing customer queries, resolving issues, and providing proactive support, chatbots contribute to improved customer satisfaction and loyalty. Higher customer retention rates lead to longer customer relationships and increased revenue opportunities, positively influencing economic and financial evaluation
	Upselling and Cross-Selling: Chatbots can analyze customer preferences, purchase history, and browsing behavior to identify upselling and cross-selling opportunities. By suggesting relevant products or services, chatbots can drive additional sales and increase the average order value. This, in turn, can contribute to higher CLV, as customers expand their purchases and explore additional offerings

(continued)

Table 8.6 (continued)

	Cost Savings: CLV impact goes beyond revenue generation. Chatbots can also contribute to cost savings by automating routine tasks, reducing the need for human intervention, and optimizing operational efficiency. By handling a significant portion of customer inquiries and support requests, chatbots free up resources, reduce support costs, and improve overall cost efficiency. These cost savings enhance the financial evaluation by improving profitability and return on investment
	Word-of-Mouth and Referrals: A positive customer experience delivered through chatbot interactions can lead to word-of-mouth referrals and recommendations. Satisfied customers are more likely to share their positive experiences with others, leading to increased customer acquisition through referrals. Chatbots that provide personalized and efficient support can generate positive word-of-mouth, expanding the customer base and increasing CLV

(continued)

Table 8.6 (continued)

	Personalization and Relationship Building: Chatbots enable personalized interactions by analyzing customer data and preferences. By delivering tailored recommendations, offers, and support, chatbots foster stronger customer relationships. Personalization contributes to a positive customer experience, strengthens brand loyalty, and increases the likelihood of customers staying with the business for an extended period, resulting in higher CLV
	Data-Driven Insights: Chatbots collect valuable data on customer interactions, preferences, and behavior. These insights can be analyzed to gain a deeper understanding of customer needs, preferences, and patterns. By leveraging this data, businesses can make data-driven decisions, refine their marketing strategies, and develop targeted campaigns, further enhancing CLV and overall financial evaluation Considering the impact of CLV in the economic and financial evaluation of a chatbot helps businesses assess the long-term value and return on investment of the chatbot project. By understanding the potential for increased revenue, customer retention, upselling, and cost savings, businesses can make informed decisions about chatbot implementation and measure the financial impact on their bottom line

need for additional support staff, leading to cost savings. The lower Cost per Interaction/Transaction demonstrates effective resource allocation and contributes to overall operational efficiency.

d) Increased Throughput: Chatbots can handle multiple interactions simultaneously, providing quick responses to customer inquiries. This increased throughput helps businesses handle a larger volume of interactions within a given timeframe. As the chatbot can handle more interactions, the overall cost per interaction decreases, increasing the efficiency and financial value of the chatbot.

e) Reduction in Support Costs: Chatbots can reduce support costs by automating repetitive tasks and providing self-service options. By deflecting common inquiries and empowering customers to find answers on their own, the chatbot reduces the need for human intervention and associated costs. A lower Cost per Interaction/Transaction signifies reduced support costs, positively impacting the economic and financial value of the chatbot.

f) Enhanced Customer Experience: Chatbots provide immediate responses and 24/7 availability, enabling customers to receive assistance at any time. This responsiveness and convenience contribute to an improved customer experience. A low Cost per Interaction/Transaction demonstrates that businesses can deliver efficient and cost-effective customer support, enhancing overall customer satisfaction and loyalty.

g) ROI and Financial Viability: The Cost per Interaction/Transaction directly influences the financial viability and return on investment (ROI) of the chatbot project. By reducing the cost per interaction, businesses can achieve a positive ROI more quickly. Lower costs and improved efficiency lead to higher financial returns and contribute to the overall economic value of the chatbot.

By optimizing the Cost per Interaction/Transaction, businesses can improve the cost-effectiveness, scalability, and efficiency of the chatbot. This, in turn, impacts the economic and financial value of the chatbot project by reducing operational expenses, increasing resource utilization, and enhancing customer satisfaction. Effective management and reduction of the cost per interaction significantly contribute to the success and value of the chatbot implementation.

8.14 Customer Satisfaction and Net Promoter Score (NPS)

Assessing customer satisfaction and NPS can provide insights into the impact of the chatbot on customer perception and loyalty. Higher customer satisfaction and positive NPS scores indicate that the chatbot is providing value to customers (Lo Presti et al., 2021), potentially leading to increased customer retention, word-of-mouth referrals, and positive financial outcomes. AI-powered systems scrutinize customer data, sentiments, and actions to furnish more precise marketing initiatives, individualized content, and enhanced customer service interactions. AI empowers organizations to automate operations, manage a substantial volume of inquiries competently, and make informed decisions driven by data that result in improved customer experiences and enduring allegiance.

Customer Satisfaction and Net Promoter Score (NPS) impact on the economic and financial value of a chatbot, as shown in Table 8.7.

The economic and financial impact of customer satisfaction and NPS on a chatbot is influenced by various factors such as the quality of the chatbot's design, functionality, accuracy, and the overall customer experience it provides. Continuous monitoring and improvement of the chatbot based on customer feedback and evolving customer needs are essential to maximize its economic and financial value.

8.15 Ethical Concerns

Some of the key ethical challenges associated with these models include:

1. **Bias and Fairness**: Generative AI models can inadvertently perpetuate and even amplify biases present in the data they are trained on. This can result in unfair or discriminatory outputs, particularly when it comes to issues related to race, gender, and other sensitive attributes.
2. **Misinformation and Manipulation**: These models can be used to generate highly convincing fake text. This poses significant risks for the spread of misinformation and disinformation.
3. **Privacy**: Generative AI models can be misused to generate fake content that invades individuals' privacy, such as generating fabricated text or emails that appear to come from someone else.
4. **Deepfakes**: While not exclusive to text-based models, deepfake technology often relies on similar AI principles. Deepfakes can be used to create realistic videos and audio recordings of individuals saying or doing things they never did, which can be damaging and deceptive.

Table 8.7 Customer satisfaction and net promoter score

Customer Satisfaction and Net Promoter Score	Customer Retention: High customer satisfaction and positive NPS scores indicate that customers are pleased with the chatbot's performance and the overall customer experience. Higher customer retention translates into increased revenue and reduced costs associated with acquiring new customers
	Word-of-Mouth Marketing: A high NPS indicates that customers are likely to recommend the chatbot to others. Positive word-of-mouth marketing generated through satisfied customers can lead to increased adoption of the chatbot, attracting new users without additional marketing expenses. This organic growth can result in a wider user base, expanded market reach, and increased revenue potential
	Cost Savings: An effective chatbot can significantly reduce operational costs by automating routine customer interactions and inquiries. When customers find the chatbot helpful and satisfying, they are more likely to utilize it for self-service rather than contacting customer support representatives. This reduces the workload on human agents, enabling them to focus on more complex and value-added tasks. The cost savings associated with decreased customer support interactions can positively impact the financial value of the chatbot implementation
	Upselling and Cross-selling Opportunities: A well-designed chatbot can be leveraged to identify customer needs and preferences through interactions. By analyzing customer data and behavior, the chatbot can provide personalized recommendations, product suggestions, and offers. Positive customer experiences with the chatbot increase the likelihood of customers accepting these recommendations and engaging in upselling and cross-selling opportunities, leading to increased sales and revenue
	Competitive Advantage: Customer satisfaction and positive NPS scores can give a company a competitive edge in the market. A chatbot that consistently delivers exceptional customer experiences sets a higher standard for customer service, which can differentiate the company from its competitors. This differentiation can attract new customers, retain existing ones, and improve the overall financial performance of the business

5. **Ownership and Attribution**: There are questions about who owns the content generated by these models and how attribution should work. For example, should the original data source or the model's creator be credited for generated content?
6. **Harmful Content**: The ability to generate content at scale means these models can be used to create harmful or offensive materials, such as hate speech, harassment, or propaganda.
7. **Security**: If these models fall into the wrong hands, they can be used for cyberattacks, social engineering, and other malicious activities.

Addressing these ethical problems includes improving the training data to mitigate biases, developing methods to detect generated content, and creating ethical guidelines for the use of these models. Governments and organizations are also exploring regulations and policies to govern the deployment of generative AI models and mitigate their ethical risks.

Ethical considerations in AI are a rapidly evolving field as technology continues to advance, and addressing these concerns is crucial for ensuring that AI benefits society while minimizing harm.

Growing concerns about privacy, data sovereignty, and the commodification of personal data for profit in AI applications can have significant impacts on economic, financial, and market valuation aspects:

1. **Economic Impact**:
   - **Regulatory Compliance Costs**: Addressing privacy concerns often requires significant investments in compliance with data protection regulations such as GDPR (General Data Protection Regulation) in Europe or CCPA (California Consumer Privacy Act) in the United States. Companies may need to allocate resources to update their data handling practices, which can increase operational costs.
   - **Data Monetization**: Concerns about commodification of personal data may impact business models that rely on data monetization. Companies may face pressure to reevaluate and potentially reduce their dependence on data-driven revenue streams, which can affect their economic performance.
2. **Financial Impact**:
   - **Legal Liabilities**: Failure to adequately address privacy concerns can result in legal liabilities, fines, and legal actions by individuals or regulatory bodies. These legal expenses can have a direct financial impact on organizations.
   - **Consumer Trust**: Privacy concerns can erode consumer trust. Loss of trust can lead to reduced customer retention, lower sales, and potentially higher customer acquisition costs, all of which affect a company's financial performance.
   - **Data Security Costs**: Organizations may need to invest in robust data security measures to protect personal data adequately. These investments can add to financial expenses.

3. **Market Valuation Impact**:
    - **Reputation**: Companies that are perceived as taking data privacy and security seriously may enjoy a more positive reputation among customers and investors. This can lead to higher market valuations.
    - **Investor Sentiment**: Investors may view companies with strong data privacy practices as less risky and more attractive investments. Conversely, those associated with data breaches or privacy scandals may face negative investor sentiment and a lower market valuation.
    - **Regulatory Risk**: Companies with significant exposure to regulatory risks related to data privacy may experience higher volatility in their stock prices and market valuation.
    - **Competitive Advantage**: Organizations that excel in data privacy and demonstrate commitment to protecting personal data may gain a competitive advantage in markets where data privacy is a critical concern.

Concerns about privacy, data sovereignty, and the commodification of personal data in AI applications can have multifaceted impacts on the economic, financial, and market valuation aspects of organizations.

Companies that proactively address these concerns, invest in data security, comply with regulations, and prioritize data ethics are more likely to maintain customer trust, attract investors, and enjoy a favorable market valuation. Conversely, those that neglect or mishandle data privacy may face legal liabilities, reputational damage, and financial setbacks.

8.16 Toxiticy in Natural Language Processing and Its Impact on Economic, Financial, and Market Valuation

A notable issue stems from the presence of harmful elements in NLP models, which have the potential to produce discriminatory or inappropriate language, thereby impeding their safe implementation. Despite the progress made in the realm of controllable text generation algorithms, there remains a risk that pretrained language models may devolve into producing toxic content, underscoring the necessity for improved methods of data curation during the training process to avert such occurrences. To sum up, while NLP contributes to the improvement of economic and financial analyses, the management of toxicity within language models is paramount for ensuring their ethical and efficient utilization within these sectors. The democratization of generative AI systems has lowered the technical barriers to entry, enabling startups and large companies alike to develop and deploy such technologies more easily. However, along with this accessibility comes a host of ethical considerations that must be carefully navigated by both developers and users of AI systems.

Addressing these ethical issues requires a multi-stakeholder approach involving collaboration between technologists, policymakers, ethicists, civil society organizations, and other relevant stakeholders. Regulatory frameworks, industry standards, ethical guidelines, and responsible AI practices can help guide the development, deployment, and use of generative AI systems in a manner that upholds ethical principles and protects societal values.

Fairness, bias, and ethics have indeed become prominent concerns as AI technologies, including generative models, have become more accessible and widespread:

1. **Fairness and Bias**: AI systems can inherit biases present in the data they are trained on. Biased AI can lead to unfair outcomes, perpetuate stereotypes, and discriminate against certain groups. Researchers and practitioners are now placing greater emphasis on developing methods to detect, mitigate, and prevent bias in AI systems.
2. **Ethical Considerations:** As AI systems become more powerful, they can have significant real-world impacts. Ethical considerations arise in areas such as privacy, surveillance, employment, and healthcare. There is a growing awareness that AI should be developed and deployed with careful ethical considerations, including transparency, accountability, and respect for human rights.
3. **Accessibility and Control**: The lowering of technical barriers means that more individuals and organizations can create and deploy AI systems. While this democratization of AI is a positive development, it also raises concerns about the responsible use of AI technology. Ensuring that individuals and organizations are educated about the ethical implications and best practices in AI is crucial.

4. **Regulation**: Governments and regulatory bodies are increasingly recognizing the need to address the ethical and fairness issues surrounding AI. There are ongoing discussions and efforts to establish regulations and guidelines for the development and deployment of AI systems, especially in critical domains like healthcare and finance.
5. **Public Awareness**: As you mentioned, the public is becoming more aware of AI and its implications. Public scrutiny and demand for transparency and accountability are driving companies and organizations to be more mindful of the ethical aspects of AI.
6. **Collaboration**: Collaboration among researchers, practitioners, policymakers, and ethicists is essential to address these issues effectively. Interdisciplinary efforts are underway to develop ethical AI guidelines, tools for bias detection and mitigation, and mechanisms for accountability.
7. **Responsible AI Development**: Many companies are now adopting principles of responsible AI development. This includes conducting ethics assessments, conducting regular audits, and actively seeking feedback from diverse stakeholders to ensure that AI systems are developed and deployed in ways that benefit society.

As AI technology becomes more accessible and pervasive, all stakeholders must work together to address the ethical challenges it presents. This includes not only addressing bias and fairness issues but also ensuring that AI benefits everyone and respects fundamental ethical principles.

Fairness, bias, and ethics have indeed become prominent concerns as AI technologies, including generative models, have become more accessible and widespread. What is the impact on AI's economic, financial, and market valuation?

The impact of fairness, bias, and ethics concerns in AI on the economic, financial, and market valuation aspects can be significant and multifaceted:

1. **Economic Impact**:

    - **Increased Costs**: Addressing fairness, bias, and ethics concerns often requires additional resources, including specialized personnel, tools, and processes. This can lead to increased development and operational costs for companies.

- **Market for Ethical AI**: Companies that can demonstrate ethical practices and fairness in their AI solutions may have a competitive advantage, attracting customers who prioritize ethical AI.
- **Reputation and Trust**: Companies that are perceived as responsible and ethical in their AI deployments are likely to build stronger brand reputations and trust among customers, partners, and investors.

2. **Financial Impact**:

- **Legal and Regulatory Compliance**: Failure to address fairness and bias issues can lead to legal liabilities and fines. Companies may incur financial penalties if their AI systems are found to discriminate or violate privacy laws.
- **Market Entry and Exit**: Companies that do not adequately address ethical concerns may face barriers to entering certain markets or industries where ethical considerations are paramount. Conversely, companies that prioritize ethics can enter markets where ethical AI is a requirement.
- **Investor Sentiment**: Ethical concerns in AI can affect investor sentiment. Investors may be more inclined to support companies that are proactive in addressing these issues and may divest from companies with reputations for unethical AI practices.

3. **Market Valuation Impact**:

- **Market Perception**: The market valuation of companies can be influenced by their perceived ethical practices in AI. Companies with a strong ethical track record may be valued more highly by investors who prioritize long-term sustainability and responsible AI practices.
- **Volatility**: Market valuation can be affected by public perception and media coverage of AI-related ethical controversies. Negative news or scandals related to biased or unfair AI systems can lead to stock price volatility and decreased market capitalization.
- **Long-Term Sustainability**: Companies that prioritize fairness and ethics in AI may be viewed as more sustainable in the long term, which can positively impact their market valuation.

Conversely, companies with reputations for unethical AI may face challenges in sustaining long-term growth.

The impact of fairness, bias, and ethics concerns in AI on economic, financial, and market valuation can vary widely depending on the industry, the specific AI applications involved, and how companies address these concerns. In general, though, there is a growing recognition that ethical considerations are not just a matter of compliance but can also have financial and market implications, making them an important aspect of AI strategy for businesses.

The AI, Algorithmic, and Automation Incidents and Controversies (AIAAIC) Repository is an independent, open, and public dataset of recent incidents and controversies driven by or relating to AI, algorithms, and automation.

The AI, Algorithmic, and Automation Incidents and Controversies (AIAAIC) Repository sounds like a valuable resource for tracking and studying incidents and controversies related to AI, algorithms, and automation. Such a repository can serve several important purposes:

1. **Transparency and Accountability**: By making incidents and controversies public and easily accessible, the repository promotes transparency in the field of AI and automation. This can hold organizations and developers accountable for the impacts of their technologies.
2. **Research and Analysis**: Researchers, policymakers, and ethicists can use the repository to study trends, patterns, and root causes of AI-related incidents and controversies. This can lead to a better understanding of the challenges and risks associated with these technologies.
3. **Learning and Best Practices**: The repository can be a valuable resource for learning from past mistakes and controversies. It can help organizations and developers identify best practices for ethical and responsible AI development and deployment.
4. **Public Awareness**: Making this information publicly available can raise awareness among the general public about the potential risks and ethical considerations associated with AI and automation.
5. **Policy and Regulation**: Policymakers and regulatory bodies can use the repository to inform the development of policies and regulations

related to AI, algorithms, and automation. It can provide real-world examples of the need for oversight and guidelines.

6. **Education**: The repository can be a useful educational tool for training AI practitioners, data scientists, and engineers on the ethical dimensions of their work. It can be used to illustrate the importance of considering the societal impact of AI technologies.

Overall, having an independent and public dataset like the AIAAIC Repository can contribute to a more responsible and accountable development and deployment of AI, algorithms, and automation. It allows stakeholders to learn from past incidents, take proactive measures to mitigate risks, and ensure that these technologies are used in ways that benefit society.

Toxicity in natural language processing (NLP) refers to the presence of harmful or offensive content in text data. This can include hate speech, harassment, misinformation, and other forms of harmful language. Toxicity in NLP can have various impacts on economic, financial, and market valuation aspects:

1. **Reputation and Branding**:
   - **Companies**: If a company's products or services rely on NLP, the presence of toxic content in their systems can harm their reputation. Negative media coverage or public perception of their platforms as fostering toxicity can lead to a loss of customers and investors.
   - **Online Platforms**: Social media and content-sharing platforms that struggle to effectively moderate toxic content may see their reputation suffer, impacting their ability to attract users and advertisers.
2. **Legal and Regulatory Risks**:
   - **Liability**: Companies that fail to adequately address toxicity in their NLP systems may face legal liabilities, including lawsuits or regulatory fines for hosting or disseminating harmful content.

3. **User Engagement and Trust**:
   - **User Engagement**: Toxic content can discourage users from engaging with online platforms, reducing user activity and diminishing the platform's attractiveness to advertisers.
   - **Trust**: A platform's inability to effectively moderate toxicity can erode user trust, affecting user retention and acquisition efforts.
4. **Monetization**:
   - **Advertiser Concerns**: Advertisers may be reluctant to place ads on platforms associated with toxic content, leading to reduced advertising revenue for those platforms.
5. **Investor Sentiment**:
   - **Investor Confidence**: Toxicity issues can raise concerns among investors about a company's ability to manage risks associated with its NLP systems, potentially affecting stock prices and market valuation.
6. **User Growth and Market Share**:
   - **User Acquisition**: High levels of toxicity can impede user acquisition efforts, particularly if potential users are deterred by harmful content on a platform.
   - **Market Competition**: Platforms that effectively address toxicity may gain a competitive edge in attracting users who prioritize safety and a positive user experience.
7. **Regulatory Scrutiny**:
   - **Regulatory Action**: Governments and regulatory bodies may impose stricter regulations on platforms and organizations to combat online toxicity. Compliance with such regulations may require significant investments in technology and personnel.
8. **Content Moderation Costs**:

- **Moderation Expenses**: Companies may need to invest in content moderation tools and teams to combat toxicity effectively. These expenses can impact profitability and financial performance.

Toxicity in NLP can have a range of economic and financial implications, affecting a company's reputation, legal standing, user engagement, monetization strategies, investor sentiment, and market valuation. Managing and mitigating toxicity in NLP systems is not only an ethical imperative but also a crucial business consideration in today's digital landscape. Companies that proactively address these issues are more likely to maintain investor and user trust and, in turn, preserve their economic and financial standing.

8.17 Factuality and Truthfulness

The factual accuracy and truthfulness of chatbots are fundamental factors influencing their economic appraisal. The integration of chatbots can have a notable impact on Business Process Outsourcing firms through process optimization and cost reduction. Furthermore, the perceived warmth and proficiency of chatbots have an effect on consumers' trust and their inclination to share personal details, thereby impacting their loyalty intentions. It is imperative to ensure that chatbots deliver precise and truthful data to establish trust with users, consequently enhancing the economic value for businesses that leverage these advancements. The development of AI systems for automated fact-checking and combating misinformation can have several impacts on economic, financial, and market valuation aspects of AI (Table 8.8):

AI systems designed for fact-checking and combating misinformation can have positive economic, financial, and market valuation impacts for AI companies. These impacts can manifest through increased market demand, revenue generation, investor confidence, litigation risk mitigation, enhanced reputation, competitive advantages, regulatory alignment, and improved user trust. As the fight against misinformation becomes increasingly important in the digital age, the value of AI technologies in this domain is likely to grow.

Even if fact-checking with natural language systems became popular, language models are usually trained on static snapshots of data without continual updates, and they may lack real-world fact-checkers.

Table 8.8 Factuality and truthfulness

Economic Impact	The increasing prevalence of misinformation in digital spaces has created a demand for AI-driven fact-checking solutions. Companies and organizations involved in the development and deployment of such technologies may see increased economic opportunities as they cater to this demand **Revenue Generation**: AI systems that excel in fact-checking and truthfulness assessment can be monetized through various channels, including licensing to media organizations, subscription-based services, or partnerships with online platforms. These revenue streams can positively impact the economic performance of AI companies
Financial Impact	**Investor Confidence**: Success in the field of fact-checking and misinformation detection can enhance investor confidence in AI companies. Demonstrating effective solutions in this area can attract investments and contribute to the financial growth of AI startups and established firms **Litigation Risk Mitigation**: AI systems that help identify and mitigate misinformation may reduce legal liabilities and potential lawsuits for companies associated with the dissemination of false information. This can result in cost savings and financial stability
Market Valuation Impact	**Reputation**: AI companies known for their contributions to fact-checking and truthfulness in NLP may enjoy a positive reputation. Positive public perception and a reputation for ethical AI practices can lead to higher market valuations **Competitive Advantage**: Organizations with advanced fact-checking AI systems may gain a competitive advantage in markets where misinformation is a prevalent concern. This can lead to a higher market share and, consequently, a stronger market valuation **Regulatory Compliance**: Developing AI systems that aid in fact-checking and truthfulness can align with evolving regulatory requirements related to misinformation and content moderation. Companies that are ahead of regulatory changes may be better positioned in terms of market valuation

These are important limitations of current natural language systems, especially in the context of fact-checking:

1. **Static Training Data**: Many language models are trained on static datasets that represent a snapshot in time. This means they may not be aware of real-time events, news, or changes in the world. As a result, they might not be able to provide up-to-date information or fact-check claims that are based on recent events or developments.
2. **Lack of Real-World Context**: Human fact-checkers can source information from various real-world contexts, including recent news articles, expert opinions, and historical knowledge. In contrast,

language models may lack this real-world context and may not be as effective in fact-checking claims that require such context.
3. **Continual Updates**: Human fact-checkers can continually update their knowledge and adapt to changing circumstances. Language models, on the other hand, typically require periodic retraining to incorporate new information. This means they may not be as agile in responding to rapidly evolving events or claims.

These limitations highlight the challenges in using language models for comprehensive fact-checking, especially when it comes to verifying claims in real time or in contexts that require a deep understanding of current events and evolving knowledge.

To address these limitations, there are ways to enhance natural language systems for fact-checking, including:

- **Real-time Data Integration**: Efforts are underway to integrate real-time data sources, such as news feeds and social media updates, into language models to provide more current information.
- **Contextual Understanding**: Researchers are working on improving language models' ability to understand and use context effectively, allowing them to better assess the veracity of claims in various contexts.
- **Continual Learning**: There is ongoing research into developing AI systems that can continually learn and adapt to new information without the need for frequent retraining, making them more agile in fact-checking.

While language models have made significant strides in natural language understanding, addressing these limitations is an active area of research and development to make them more effective tools for fact-checking and information verification.

8.18 Inaccuracy, Cybersecurity, and Intellectual Property Infringements

In the assessment of chatbots, concerns such as inaccuracies, vulnerabilities in cybersecurity, and violations of intellectual property rights are of considerable importance. The absence of standardized procedures and transparency in model publication often necessitates human judgments in current evaluation methods. Nevertheless, the potential of advanced chatbots may be underestimated by automatic evaluation metrics, leading to imprecise evaluations. It is imperative to ensure cybersecurity in chatbots to prevent unauthorized access and data breaches. The enhancement of security and protection of sensitive information transmitted through chatbot interfaces can be achieved by implementing measures such as encryption and authentication timeout. Overcoming these obstacles is crucial for enhancing the dependability, security, and ethical utilization of chatbots across various fields. The risks associated with generative AI adoption, including inaccuracy, cybersecurity, and intellectual property infringement, can have consequences on the economic, financial, and market valuation of AI-driven businesses and industries (Table 8.9):

The consequences of AI risks on economic, financial, and market valuation can vary depending on the severity and frequency of incidents, the industry in which AI is applied, and the specific risks involved. Companies that effectively manage and mitigate these risks through robust cybersecurity measures, accuracy improvements, and compliance with intellectual property laws are more likely to navigate the challenges and maintain or enhance their economic and financial positions.

While AI adoption offers significant opportunities, organizations must be aware of and proactively address the associated risks to minimize negative consequences on their economic, financial, and market valuations.

8.19 Conclusion

The assessment of chatbots and generative AI within business frameworks is of considerable interest and significance. The advent of generative AI models has transformed dialogues through the provision of human-like exchanges, presenting both challenges and prospects in the utilization of this technology across diverse sectors. These AI models present advanced responses that assist in compiling research, generating marketing content, and engaging with customers, enriching customer interactions and decreasing expenses. Despite apprehensions regarding the academic authenticity stemming from AI-generated materials, there exists a distinctive opening to enhance existing chatbots with sophisticated conversational functionalities for intelligent automation. The integration of chatbots in finance, online retail, tourism, and customer service centers demonstrates the potential for digital evolution and enhanced customer

Table 8.9 Inaccuracy, cybersecurity, and intellectual property infringements

Economic Consequences	**Costs of Inaccuracy**: Inaccurate AI-generated content or decisions can lead to economic losses. For example, in industries like healthcare or finance, inaccurate medical diagnoses or investment recommendations can result in financial harm to individuals or organizations **Resource Allocation**: Investing in AI adoption comes with significant costs, including research and development, infrastructure, and training. Misallocation of resources due to inaccurate AI models can have economic repercussions **Litigation and Regulatory Costs**: Intellectual property infringement and other legal issues related to AI can result in costly litigation and regulatory fines, impacting a company's bottom line
Financial Consequences	**Market Reputation**: High-profile incidents of AI inaccuracy or cybersecurity breaches can damage a company's reputation in the financial markets, leading to stock price declines and decreased investor confidence **Insurance Costs**: The risks associated with AI may lead to higher insurance costs for businesses, affecting their financial planning and profitability **Valuation Impact**: The financial performance and risks associated with AI adoption can directly impact the valuation of AI companies. Investors may adjust their valuation models based on the perceived risk factors
Market Valuation Consequences	**Volatility**: The uncertainty surrounding AI risks can lead to increased volatility in the stock prices of AI companies, making them more susceptible to market swings **Investor Sentiment**: Negative news or incidents related to AI can affect investor sentiment, leading to shifts in market valuation as investors react to perceived risks **M&A Activity**: Companies operating in the AI space may see changes in merger and acquisition activity. Concerns about the risks associated with AI adoption may impact deal terms and valuations in the M&A market

interactions. The valuation of chatbots and generative AI follow traditional standards, adapted to the specific business model, and consequent business planning that consider hype cycles (www.gartner.com). Digital firms represent, from this side, a useful template (Moro-Visconti, 2022b).

The valuation is double-sided as it considers both the chatbot platform and its users (clients).

The deployment of chatbots in public service delivery has indeed expanded in recent years, driven by the potential benefits they offer in terms of improving user experience and efficiency. However, their widespread adoption has also been accompanied by various challenges and controversies, as highlighted by Makasi et al. (2020). Addressing these challenges requires a comprehensive approach that considers technical, legal, ethical, and user-oriented perspectives.

The study by Fotheringham et al. (2022) highlights the rapid adoption of AI chatbots in customer service roles within firms, driven by advancements in conversational AI technology. Despite the growing prevalence of AI chatbots, the specific impact on shareholder wealth has not been extensively studied. However, recent findings suggest that investments in AI, including AI chatbots, may have a negative effect on firm value. B2B firms stand to gain more from implementing AI chatbot customer service compared to B2C firms. This observation implies that AI chatbots may offer unique benefits or opportunities for B2B firms, such as improved efficiency, scalability, or cost savings in serving their clients or customers.

The valuation of chatbots and generative AI follows traditional standards, but it also involves specific considerations adapted to the business model and planning:

1. **Double-Sided Valuation**:
    - Valuing chatbots and generative AI involves considering both the chatbot platform itself and its user base (clients). This dual perspective is essential because the value of chatbots often depends on their ability to serve and retain users effectively.
2. **Use of Digital Firms as Templates**:
    - Digital firms, which are often at the forefront of adopting advanced technologies like chatbots and generative AI, can serve as templates or examples for valuation. Their experiences can provide valuable insights into how to assess the value of these technologies in a business context.
3. **Chatbots in Public Services**:
    - Chatbots have been increasingly used in public service delivery, offering benefits such as improved user experiences and reduced waiting times. However, their deployment in this context has sometimes led to controversies, negative publicity, and legal challenges, indicating that the valuation must account for potential risks and challenges.

4. **Conversational AI**:
   - The advancement of conversational AI has led to the rapid adoption of AI chatbots in customer service roles across various industries.
5. **Shareholder Wealth Effects and Firm Value**:
   - While the impact of AI chatbots on shareholder wealth has not been thoroughly investigated, recent findings suggest that AI investments may have a negative effect on firm value. This could be due to the costs associated with implementing and maintaining AI technologies.
6. **B2B vs. B2C Firms**:
   - B2B (business-to-business) firms are highlighted as potentially benefiting more from implementing AI chatbot customer service compared to B2C (business-to-consumer) firms. The reasons for this difference in potential benefits would likely depend on the specific business models and industries involved.

Valuing chatbots and generative AI involves a complex assessment that considers not only the technical capabilities of these technologies but also their impact on user experiences, public perception, legal aspects, and their potential effects on shareholder wealth and firm value. Businesses need to carefully evaluate the costs and benefits, adapt their strategies, and consider industry-specific factors when incorporating chatbots and AI into their operations.

References

Chen, J.-S., Le, T.-T., & Florence, D. (2021). Usability and responsiveness of artificial intelligence chatbot on online customer experience in e-retailing. *International Journal of Retail & Distribution Management, 49*(11), 1512–1531.

Corea, C., Delfmann, P., & Nagel, S. (2020). Towards Intelligent Chatbots for Customer Care - Practice-Based Requirements for a Research Agenda, Proceedings of the 53rd Hawaii International Conference on System Sciences. https://app.amanote.com/v4.0.36/it/research/note-taking?resourceId=EI1i03MBKQvf0BhiZFNu

Damodaran, A. (2018). *The dark side of valuation*. Pearson FT Press PTG.

Fazzini, M. (2018). *Business valuation: Theory and practice*. Palgrave MacMillan.

Fernandez, P. (2019). *Valuation and common sense*. https://web.iese.edu/PabloFernandez/Book_VaCS/ContentsValuation.pdf

Fotheringham, D., & Wiles, M. A. (2022, March). The effect of implementing chatbot customer service on stock returns: An event study analysis. *Journal of the Academy of Marketing Science*.

Gartner. (2023, August 17). What's New in Artificial Intelligence from the 2023 Gartner Hype Cycle. https://www.gartner.com/en/articles/what-s-new-in-artificial-intelligence-from-the-2023-gartner-hype-cycle?_hsenc=p2ANqtz--amsgCXhwctyauNTofU9AgyDib3sN8S_RtfYA2VYnKhBD-HZq-b85sRmtHmnKqQOAFEI6m

Johannsen, F., Schaller, D., & Klus, M. F. (2021). Value propositions of chatbots to support innovation management processes. *Information Systems and e-Business Management, 19*, 205–246.

Koller, T., & Goedhart, M. (2015). *Valuation: Measuring and managing the value of companies*. McKinsey & Company.

Lo Presti, L., Maggiore, G., & Marino, V. (2021). The role of the chatbot on customer purchase intention: Towards digital relational sales. *Italian Journal of Marketing*, 165–188.

Makasi, T., Nili, A., Desouza, K., & Tate, M. (2020). Chatbot-mediated public service delivery: A public service value-based framework. *First Monday, 25*(12).

Moro-Visconti, R. (2021). *Startup valuation. From strategic business planning to digital networking*. Palgrave MacMillan.

Moro-Visconti, R. (2022a). *Augmented corporate valuation: From digital networking to ESG compliance*. Palgrave Macmillan.

Moro-Visconti R. (2022b). *The valuation of digital intangibles. Technology, marketing, and the metaverse*. Palgrave Macmillan.

Moro-Visconti R. (2023, May). Chatbots and generative artificial intelligence: From business planning to economic valuation. https://www.researchgate.net/publication/371110724_Chatbots_and_generative_artificial_intelligence_from_business_planning_to_economic_valuation

Stanford University. (2023). The Ai Index Report, Measuring trends in Artificial Intelligence.

CHAPTER 9

Sustainable Artificial Intelligence Issues: From ESG Valuation to Ethical Concerns

9.1 ESG Valuation

AI presents environmental, social, and economic sustainability challenges, necessitating a concerted effort involving diverse stakeholders. The mitigation of these challenges encompasses establishing ethical standards, the promotion of transparency, the investment in socially beneficial AI applications, and the consideration of the long-term societal and environmental repercussions of AI implementation. Achieving sustainable AI progress demands a careful equilibrium between technological advancement and responsible methodologies. This requires a shift in regulatory emphasis from reliability to sustainability, implementing transparency tools, and the integration of sustainability factors into legal frameworks. Through the alignment of initiatives among governmental bodies, businesses, scholars, and civil society, the cultivation of sustainable AI can be facilitated, thereby advancing ethical AI practices that serve the interests of both individuals and the environment, while also ensuring that governance structures remain resilient in the face of technological progress. AI presents a range of sustainability issues (Abdalmuttaleb et al., 2022) that span from ESG considerations (Burnaev et al., 2023; Gupta et al., 2021; Selim, 2020) to ethical concerns (Brusseau, 2023). These issues (see also specific websites such as https://www.sustainalytics.com/ or https://greenfutureproject.com/) include:

R. Moro-Visconti, *Artificial Intelligence Valuation*,
https://doi.org/10.1007/978-3-031-53622-9_9

- Environmental impact: AI training and deployment can consume significant amounts of energy, leading to greenhouse gas emissions. Additionally, the hardware used to run AI models can be a source of electronic waste.
- Social impact: AI has the potential to displace workers, exacerbate inequality, and lead to social unrest. Additionally, AI can be used to create harmful technologies, such as facial recognition systems that can be used for mass surveillance.
- Governance challenges: AI raises new questions about who is responsible for its development and use. Additionally, it is difficult to develop and enforce regulations for AI, given its rapid pace of development and complexity.

Addressing these issues requires collaboration among governments, businesses, researchers, and civil society. It involves:

- Developing and adhering to ethical standards: Ethical guidelines for AI should be developed and adopted by all stakeholders. These guidelines should address issues such as fairness, accountability, and transparency.
- Improving transparency: AI systems should be transparent and accountable. This means that developers and users of AI systems should be able to explain how the systems work and why they make the decisions they do.
- Investing in AI that benefits society: Governments and businesses should invest in AI research and development that is aligned with social and environmental goals. For example, AI can be used to develop new renewable energy technologies or to improve the efficiency of healthcare systems.
- Considering the long-term impact of AI on people, the planet, and governance structures: It is important to think about the long-term implications of AI before it is widely deployed. This includes considering how AI will impact jobs, inequality, and the environment.

Striking a balance between technological advancement and responsible, sustainable AI development is essential.

Here are some examples of how governments, businesses, researchers, and civil society can jointly address the sustainability issues of AI:

- Governments can design and enforce regulations that support responsible AI growth and application. For example, governments can require AI companies to disclose the environmental impact of their products and services.
- Businesses can invest in AI research and development that is aligned with social and environmental goals. For example, businesses can create AI systems that aid in reducing energy consumption or enhancing supply chain efficiency to improve the efficiency of supply chains.
- Researchers can develop new AI algorithms and techniques, striving to produce tools and methodologies for scrutinizing AI systems for equity and answerability. They can also develop tools for auditing AI systems for fairness and accountability.
- Civil society organizations can advocate for responsible AI development and application.

By working together, we can ensure that AI is developed and used in a way that benefits all of humanity and the planet.

Sustainability issues, ESG valuation, and ethical concerns are increasingly relevant in the context of AI applications. As AI technologies become more pervasive, their impact on society, the environment, and corporate governance is being closely scrutinized, as shown in Table 9.1

Ethical concerns are not just limited to the technology itself but extend to the broader societal impact of AI applications. Companies and organizations that prioritize ethical AI development and implementation are better positioned to gain public trust and avoid reputational and legal risks.

Various guidelines and frameworks, such as the OECD AI Principles and the IEEE Ethically Aligned Design, offer valuable guidance on incorporating ethics and sustainability considerations into AI applications. These principles advocate for responsible AI development, emphasizing the importance of transparency, accountability, fairness, and environmental sustainability.

Sustainability issues, ESG valuation, and ethical concerns are highly relevant in the field of AI. Companies and developers must integrate these considerations into their AI strategies to ensure that AI technologies are not only technically advanced but also socially responsible and environmentally sustainable.

Table 9.1 ESG and artificial intelligence

ESG Valuation in AI	a. Environmental Impact: AI infrastructure, including data centers and high-performance computing, consumes significant energy. Sustainable AI implementation involves reducing carbon emissions through energy-efficient hardware, data center design, and the use of renewable energy sources b. Social Impact: AI can have far-reaching social consequences, from job displacement to bias in algorithms. Companies developing AI systems must consider the social implications and take steps to mitigate negative effects. This includes ethical AI design, transparency, and fairness c. Governance: Governance in AI involves ensuring responsible development, deployment, and management of AI systems. Companies must have clear policies for handling AI ethics, accountability, and compliance with regulations like GDPR or HIPAA
Ethical Concerns in AI	a. Bias and Fairness: Bias in AI algorithms can lead to discriminatory outcomes, reinforcing existing inequalities. Ethical AI demands proactive efforts to identify and rectify biases in data and algorithms b. Privacy: AI often processes vast amounts of personal data. Ethical concerns center on data privacy, consent, and the responsible use of data. Companies must prioritize data protection and transparency in their AI applications c. Accountability and Transparency: Ethical AI systems should be transparent, with clear accountability for decisions made by AI algorithms. Explainability and auditing mechanisms are essential for building trust d. Job Displacement: The potential for AI to automate tasks and displace jobs raises ethical considerations related to workforce retraining, job displacement, and social support systems e. Autonomous Systems: AI-driven autonomous systems, such as self-driving cars and drones, raise ethical concerns about safety, accountability, and decision-making in critical situations

Some contents of this chapter are readapted mostly from Moro-Visconti (2022a), or, occasionally, Moro-Visconti (2022b), or Moro-Visconti (2021), extending digital intangible, startup, or business planning applications to specific AI valuation patterns.

Environmental Impact

AI has the capacity to make a substantial contribution to environmental sustainability through its support in various domains like climate change mitigation, agricultural enhancement, energy administration, wildlife preservation, and waste control. Nevertheless, the creation and utilization of AI systems also give rise to concerns regarding sustainability, owing to their extensive demands for computational resources, energy usage, and carbon emissions. The emphasis should be on the development of environmentally conscious and sustainable "Green AI" systems, with the objective of reducing greenhouse gas discharges, preserving natural resources, and enhancing overall societal sustainability. Sustainable AI, fueled by big data (Hassan et al., 2023) is essential to mitigate the environmental impact of the energy-intensive infrastructure that supports AI, including data centers and high-performance computing. Here are several observations for sustainability in AI infrastructure (Table 9.2):

Sustainable AI infrastructure not only reduces environmental impact but also often leads to cost savings over the long term through reduced energy consumption and operational efficiencies. By adopting these practices, organizations can minimize their carbon footprint while harnessing the power of AI for various applications.

The impact of AI on the carbon footprint can be both positive and negative, depending on how AI technologies are developed, deployed, and used:

Positive Impact:

1. **Energy Efficiency**: AI can be used to optimize energy consumption in various sectors, such as manufacturing, transportation, and buildings. Machine learning algorithms can analyze and adjust energy usage patterns in real time, leading to energy savings and reduced carbon emissions.
2. **Green Energy Integration**: AI can facilitate the integration of renewable energy sources like wind and solar into the power grid by predicting energy generation patterns, optimizing energy storage, and managing the grid more efficiently. This helps reduce reliance on fossil fuels.
3. **Climate Modeling**: AI-powered climate models can enhance our understanding of climate change, providing more accurate predictions and insights into mitigation strategies. This can inform policy decisions and actions to reduce carbon emissions.

Table 9.2 Artificial intelligence's environmental impact

Energy-Efficient Hardware	*Low-Power Processors*: Choose energy-efficient processors and GPUs for AI workloads. Many hardware manufacturers offer processors optimized for AI applications with improved performance per watt *Custom Hardware*: Develop or adopt custom AI-specific hardware, such as AI accelerators or TPUs (Tensor Processing Units), designed to perform AI tasks with high energy efficiency *Liquid Cooling*: Implement liquid cooling solutions to reduce the heat generated by high-performance computing hardware, which can lead to energy savings
Data Center Design	*Energy-Efficient Data Centers*: Design and construct data centers with energy-efficient cooling systems, power distribution, and lighting. Employ best practices in data center infrastructure management (DCIM) to optimize energy use *Data Center Location*: Choose locations that take advantage of natural cooling and renewable energy. Some companies build data centers near sources of renewable energy to reduce their carbon footprint *Modular Data Centers*: Select modular or containerized data centers, more energy-efficient and scalable than traditional data center designs AI for Data Center Optimization: Use AI algorithms to optimize data center operations, including workload management, cooling, and power distribution, to reduce energy consumption
Renewable Energy Sources	*Green Power Purchase Agreements (PPAs)*: Invest in PPAs with renewable energy providers to ensure a significant portion of data center's energy comes from clean sources *On-Site Solar and Wind*: put in place on-site solar panels or wind turbines to produce renewable energy directly at data center facilities *Energy Storage*: Implement energy storage solutions like batteries to store excess renewable energy during peak demand

(continued)

Table 9.2 (continued)

Energy-Efficient Software	*Optimized Algorithms*: Adopt AI algorithms that are computationally efficient and require less energy to run *AI Model Pruning*: Use model pruning and quantization techniques to reduce the computational resources needed for AI inference *Distributed Computing*: use distributed computing frameworks that optimize energy consumption across multiple servers or edge devices
Waste Heat Recovery	Explore options for repurposing the waste heat generated by data centers. For example, it can be used to heat nearby buildings or for industrial processes, improving overall energy efficiency
Monitoring and Reporting	Continuously monitor energy usage and carbon emissions related to AI infrastructure. Implement reporting mechanisms to track progress and identify areas for improvement
Regulatory Compliance	Stay informed about environmental regulations and industry standards related to energy efficiency and sustainability. Ensure compliance with applicable laws and standards
Green Computing Initiatives	Join or support industry initiatives and organizations focused on green computing and sustainability, which can provide guidance and resources for sustainable AI implementation

4. **Supply Chain Optimization**: AI can optimize supply chain logistics, reducing transportation-related emissions by optimizing routes, minimizing idle time, and improving inventory management.
5. **Precision Agriculture**: AI and data analytics can be used in precision agriculture to optimize resource usage, including water, fertilizers, and pesticides. This leads to reduced environmental impact and more sustainable farming practices.

Negative Impact:

1. **Data Center Energy Consumption**: The training of deep learning models, particularly large-scale models like GPT-3, requires significant computational power and energy. Data centers that support AI workloads can have a substantial carbon footprint if not powered by renewable energy sources.

2. **Electronic Waste**: The rapid advancement of AI technology can lead to a higher turnover of hardware and electronics, contributing to electronic waste. Proper disposal and recycling of AI-related hardware are essential to mitigate this impact.
3. **AI in Heavy Industries**: While AI can optimize energy usage in many sectors, it may increase energy consumption in heavy industries if not implemented carefully. For example, using AI to increase production efficiency in energy-intensive processes could lead to higher overall energy usage.
4. **Bias and Ethical Concerns**: Biased AI algorithms and unethical AI applications can exacerbate societal problems, leading to increased social and economic disparities that may indirectly contribute to environmental issues.

The impact of AI on the carbon footprint is complex and depends on how AI technologies are developed, implemented, and regulated. When used thoughtfully and strategically, AI has the potential to contribute positively to environmental sustainability by optimizing energy usage and enabling more efficient resource management. However, it is essential to address the potential negative impacts and work towards responsible.

AI development and deployment that considers environmental, ethical, and social considerations. This may include using renewable energy sources for AI workloads, minimizing electronic waste, and ensuring that AI applications align with sustainability goals.

IoT sources can help measuring the carbon footprint (see https://pub.nkumbauniversity.ac.ug/xmlui/bitstream/handle/123456789/975/The_internet_of_things_BY_Isaac_C_Zion_M_Israel_Y_K_and_Jireh_I.pdf?isAllowed=y&sequence=1).

Social Impact

The social impact of AI produces mixed results and outcomes. It is essential for firms and organizations to address social implications. The societal ramifications of AI are a complex issue that involves a variety of dimensions. AI technologies, which encompass generative models and algorithmic response suggestions, carry considerable social consequences. These consequences extend from alterations in communication patterns and interpersonal perceptions to possible biases, stereotypes, and representational damages. Additionally, the absence of standardized assessment approaches for analyzing these consequences presents a difficulty in comprehending and alleviating the societal effects of AI implementation. To tackle these challenges, sophisticated AI methodologies like Deep Graph Learning (DGL) may be used to address societal issues and encourage beneficial social applications. Here are some key aspects of the social impact of AI:

1. **Job Displacement and Workforce Transformation:**
    - **Impact**: AI utilization and automation may end up in job displacement in certain sectors, especially in routine and repetitive tasks.
    - **Mitigation**: It is advisable to engage in partnerships with academic establishments and governmental bodies to promote continuous learning opportunities.
2. **Algorithmic Bias and Fairness:**
    - **Impact**: AI systems can inherit biases from training data, leading to discriminatory outcomes, such as biased hiring or lending decisions.
    - **Mitigation**: Employ ethical AI design principles, including fairness and bias mitigation techniques, in the development of AI algorithms. Regularly audit and evaluate bias models. Promote diversity and inclusivity in AI development teams.
3. **Privacy Concerns:**
    - **Impact**: AI systems can collect, analyze, and store vast amounts of personal data, raising privacy concerns.
    - **Mitigation**: Implement strong data privacy and protection measures, comply with relevant data protection regulations (e.g., GDPR), and be transparent about data usage and storage practices.
4. **Economic Inequality:**
    - **Impact**: Unequal access to AI benefits may exacerbate economic disparities.
    - **Mitigation**: Consider the equitable distribution of AI benefits. Develop AI solutions that address societal challenges,

such as healthcare access or education, and ensure affordability and accessibility.

5. **Transparency and Accountability:**
   - **Impact**: AI decision-making processes can produce concerns.
   - **Mitigation**: Implement transparency mechanisms to make AI decisions more interpretable. Establish clear responsibility for AI systems.
6. **Ethical AI Design:**
   - **Impact**: They are essential to prevent harmful consequences.
   - **Mitigation**: Combine ethical frameworks, and review processes into AI development. Consider the broader societal implications of AI applications.
7. **Impact on Healthcare and Safety:**
   - **Impact**: AI systems in healthcare and autonomous vehicles, for example, have the potential to save lives but also raise safety and ethical concerns.
   - **Mitigation**: Rigorous testing, validation, and regulatory oversight are crucial to ensure the safety and reliability of AI applications in critical domains.
8. **Algorithmic Accountability:**
   - **Impact**: Responsibility can be diffuse.
   - **Mitigation**: Establish accountability mechanisms, liability frameworks, and codes of conduct for AI developers, operators, and users.
9. **Job Creation and New Opportunities:**
   - **Impact**: While AI may displace some jobs, it can also create new job opportunities in AI development, data analysis, and other related fields.
   - **Mitigation**: Encourage investment in AI research and development to stimulate job creation in AI-related sectors.
10. **Education and Digital Literacy:**
    - **Impact**: AI's ubiquity underscores the importance of digital literacy and education.

- **Mitigation**: Promote digital literacy and AI education at all levels, from K-12 to lifelong learning, to empower individuals to navigate the AI-driven world.

Companies and organizations that prioritize ethical AI design are better equipped to navigate the social impact of AI responsibly.

Governance Implications, Gender Diversity and Impact on Disabilities

Governance implications in AI are critical for AI systems. Gender diversity in AI governance has noteworthy implications. The dialogue surrounding disability diversity within organizational governance is progressing, emphasizing the importance of a broader ethical vantage point to propel institutional transformation. The global underrepresentation of women in governance positions underscores the significance of innovative methodologies to attract and retain female talent, recognizing their distinct leadership methodologies and viewpoints. Mitigating gender prejudices in AI and fostering diversity in governance represent critical strides towards cultivating inclusive environments that take into account the ramifications of disabilities and human rights. Companies must establish clear policies to address AI ethics, and compliance with all the relevant regulations (Table 9.3):

Effective AI governance is an ongoing process that adapts to evolving technologies, regulations, and ethical considerations. By prioritizing ethical AI principles, accountability, and regulatory compliance, organizations can build trust in AI systems and harness their benefits while minimizing risks and negative societal impacts.

The growing focus on AI governance by intergovernmental, national, and regional organizations has several economic, financial, and market impacts on the valuation of AI (Table 9.4):

The increasing focus on AI governance has multifaceted economic, financial, and market valuation impacts.

While regulatory compliance may entail costs, it can also provide legal certainty and build stakeholder confidence. AI companies that embrace ethical governance may benefit from improved investor sentiment and competitive advantages, potentially leading to higher market valuations. Additionally, governance efforts can stimulate innovation, industry growth, and industry standardization, further influencing market dynamics and valuations in the AI sector.

Table 9.3 Artificial intelligence's governance implications

Ethical AI Principles	Develop and adhere to a set of ethical AI principles that guide the design, development, and use of AI systems. These principles should encompass fairness, transparency, accountability, privacy, and societal benefit
AI Ethics Committees	Establish AI ethics committees or review boards that include experts from various disciplines, such as ethics, law, and AI research, to assess the ethical implications of AI projects and provide guidance
Accountability and Responsibility	Clearly define roles and responsibilities for AI systems within your organization. Assign accountability for AI system behavior and outcomes to specific individuals or teams
Regulatory Compliance	Ensure that AI systems comply with applicable regulations and standards, such as GDPR for data privacy or HIPAA for healthcare data. Regularly monitor and audit AI systems to maintain compliance
Data Governance	Implement robust data governance practices to manage data quality, security, and privacy. Clearly define data ownership and access controls
Transparency and Explainability	Make AI systems more transparent and explainable to users and stakeholders. Utilize techniques like explainable AI (XAI) to provide insight into AI decision-making processes
Biasand Fairness	Implement measures to detect and mitigate bias in AI algorithms. Regularly audit and evaluate models for fairness, especially in applications that impact individuals' lives, such as hiring or lending
Continuous Monitoring	Implement ongoing monitoring and auditing of AI systems to identify and address issues as they arise. Be prepared to adjust and improve system behavior
Data Security and Privacy	Prioritize data security and privacy by implementing robust encryption, access controls, and data anonymization techniques
Training and Awareness	Provide AI ethics and compliance training to employees and stakeholders to raise awareness and ensure adherence to AI governance policies
External Collaboration	Collaborate with external organizations, research institutions, and regulatory bodies to stay informed about evolving AI ethics and governance best practices

(continued)

Table 9.3 (continued)

Public Engagement	Engage with the public, customers, and users to gather feedback, address concerns, and build trust in AI systems. Transparency in AI usage is crucial for building public trust
Risk Assessment	Conduct risk assessments to identify potential ethical, legal, and societal risks associated with AI systems. Develop strategies to mitigate these risks
Impact Assessments	Assess the potential societal impact of AI projects, especially in areas like healthcare, education, and autonomous vehicles. Consider the broader implications of AI applications
Reporting Mechanisms	Establish mechanisms for reporting ethical concerns or issues related to AI system behavior. Ensure that employees feel comfortable raising ethical concerns
Documentation and Records	Maintain thorough documentation of AI development processes, decisions, and compliance efforts. This documentation can be valuable for auditing and accountability

Gender diversity, or the lack thereof, can have significant economic, financial, and market valuation implications for AI applications (Table 9.5):

Gender diversity can have a profound impact on the economic, financial, and market valuation aspects of AI. It can drive innovation, expand market opportunities, improve talent acquisition, mitigate risks, enhance investor confidence, strengthen reputation and brand, provide a competitive advantage, and contribute to the long-term sustainability of AI companies. Embracing gender diversity is not only a matter of ethics and fairness but also a strategic decision that can lead to improved economic and market performance in the AI sector.

AI has the potential to significantly impact the lives of individuals with disabilities by providing innovative solutions to alleviate their challenges and reduce the gap between disabled individuals and those without disabilities. The economic, financial, and market impacts of AI in this context are multifaceted:

1. **Accessibility and Inclusion**:

Table 9.4 Artificial intelligence's sustainability and valuation

Economic Impact	*Regulatory Compliance Costs*: Organizations operating in the AI space may incur costs associated with complying with AI governance regulations. These costs can include investments in ethical AI development, compliance audits, and reporting requirements *Legal and Regulatory Certainty*: Clear and robust AI governance frameworks can provide legal and regulatory certainty for businesses. This can reduce legal risks and uncertainties, leading to more stable economic conditions for AI-related companies *Stakeholder Confidence*: Ethical and responsible AI governance can build stakeholder confidence, including investors, customers, and partners. A more confident stakeholder base can lead to greater economic stability and investment in AI technologies
Financial Impact	*Market Entry and Exit*: AI governance regulations can affect market entry and exit strategies for AI companies. Companies that align with ethical and regulatory standards may find it easier to enter new markets or attract investors *Risk Mitigation*: Robust AI governance can help mitigate legal and reputational risks for AI businesses. Reduced risks can translate into better financial performance and a more positive outlook for investors

(continued)

Table 9.4 (continued)

Market Valuation Impact	*Investor Sentiment*: AI companies that demonstrate a commitment to ethical AI practices and compliance with governance standards may be viewed more favorably by investors. Positive investor sentiment can contribute to higher market valuations *Competitive Advantage*: Companies that proactively implement AI governance measures may gain a competitive advantage by differentiating themselves from competitors with weaker governance practices. This competitive edge can influence market valuations *Long-Term Sustainability*: AI companies that prioritize ethical and responsible AI governance are more likely to be viewed as sustainable and resilient in the long term. This perception can positively impact their market valuations
Innovation and Industry Growth	*Innovation Funding*: Governments and organizations supporting AI governance may allocate funding and resources to promote ethical AI innovation. This funding can stimulate research and development activities, potentially leading to technological breakthroughs and increased market valuations *Industry Standardization*: Governance efforts can lead to the standardization of ethical AI practices. Standardization can enhance interoperability and collaboration within the AI industry, potentially spurring growth, and market valuation

- **Economic Impact**: AI-driven accessibility solutions can enable individuals with disabilities to participate more fully in the workforce. When these individuals have better access to education and employment opportunities, it can lead to increased economic productivity and reduced reliance on government support programs.

Table 9.5 Economic, financial, and market impact of artificial intelligence's gender diversity

Economic Impact	*Diverse Perspectives*: Gender diversity brings diverse perspectives and ideas to AI development. This diversity of thought can lead to more innovative and inclusive AI solutions, potentially opening new markets and revenue streams *Market Expansion*: AI systems designed by diverse teams may better cater to a wider range of users, leading to expanded market opportunities. Products and services that consider the needs of diverse demographics can drive economic growth *Talent Pool*: A diverse workforce can attract talent from a broader pool of candidates, ensuring that organizations have access to the best talent available. This can improve the economic performance of AI companies
Financial Impact	*Risk Mitigation*: Gender diversity can mitigate the risk of gender-related legal issues, such as discrimination or harassment claims, which can result in financial liabilities and damage to a company's reputation *Investor Confidence*: Companies that prioritize gender diversity in their AI teams may be viewed more favorably by investors who appreciate a commitment to ethical and inclusive practices. This can positively affect financial investments and growth
Market Impact	*Reputation and Brand*: Companies with diverse AI teams often have stronger reputations and brands. A reputation for inclusivity and diversity can lead to higher customer trust and loyalty, potentially boosting market valuation *Competitive Advantage*: AI companies that leverage diverse perspectives in their product development may gain a competitive edge. They may be better positioned to address complex societal challenges and meet the needs of diverse user bases, influencing market share and valuation *Long-Term Sustainability*: Gender diversity can contribute to the long-term sustainability of AI companies. By fostering inclusive environments, organizations are more likely to attract and retain diverse talent, which can lead to greater innovation and value creation over time *Mitigating Bias*: Diverse teams are better equipped to identify and mitigate bias in AI systems. Reduced bias can lead to better user experiences and public trust, positively impacting market valuation

- **Financial Impact**: Accessibility enhancements can reduce the financial burden on individuals with disabilities. For example, AI-powered assistive technologies can lower the costs associated with specialized equipment and personal support services.
- **Market Valuation Impact**: Companies that develop and market AI-based accessibility solutions may benefit from a larger customer base. Inclusive products and services can attract

a broader range of users, potentially increasing market share and valuation.

2. **Healthcare and Rehabilitation**:
   - **Economic Impact**: AI-powered healthcare technologies can aid in the early detection and treatment of disabilities, potentially reducing long-term healthcare costs. Early intervention can also improve the quality of life for individuals with disabilities.
   - **Financial Impact**: AI-driven rehabilitation technologies can offer cost-effective alternatives to traditional physical therapy or rehabilitation programs. These solutions can lower healthcare expenses for both individuals and healthcare systems.
3. **Communication and Assistive Technologies**:
   - **Economic Impact**: AI-driven communication aids can enable individuals with disabilities to participate more actively in social and professional interactions. This can lead to improved social inclusion and employment opportunities.
   - **Financial Impact**: AI-powered assistive technologies, such as speech recognition and screen readers, can reduce the need for costly custom-built assistive devices, making accessibility more affordable for individuals with disabilities.
4. **Independent Living**:
   - **Economic Impact**: AI-enabled smart home technologies can enhance the independence of individuals with disabilities by automating tasks and helping with daily activities. This can reduce the need for live-in caregivers or institutional care, potentially lowering overall healthcare costs.
   - **Financial Impact**: The adoption of AI-driven independent living solutions can reduce the financial burden on individuals and their families. It can also free up resources for other uses, contributing to financial well-being.
5. **Inclusive Education**:
   - **Economic Impact**: AI-powered educational tools and personalized learning platforms can make education more accessible to students with disabilities. Improved educational outcomes

can lead to better employment prospects and economic self-sufficiency.
- **Market Valuation Impact**: Edtech companies that prioritize inclusive education solutions may gain a competitive advantage and attract investors who value ethical and socially responsible practices.

The impact of AI in alleviating disabilities is multifaceted and can have significant economic, financial, and market valuation implications. By reducing barriers, enhancing accessibility, and improving the quality of life for individuals with disabilities, AI can contribute to a more inclusive society, increase economic productivity, reduce healthcare costs, and create opportunities for those who may be the most vulnerable. It also opens up new markets for innovative AI-driven products and services that prioritize accessibility and inclusivity.

9.2 Ethical Concerns

Ethical considerations revolving around AI encompass a multitude of critical facets. Academic studies underscore the essential nature of tackling these concerns to guarantee the responsible advancement, deployment, and governance of AI technologies. Breaches in AI ethics can span from risks to data privacy to employment displacements, underscoring the imperative nature of integrating ethics into AI development. It so seems important to nurture an ethical ambiance in the progression of AI, with a focus on privacy, security, bias, fairness, trust, dependability, transparency, and human-AI interactions. Furthermore, the necessity for cooperation among various stakeholders in formulating and executing ethical protocols for AI systems is stressed, taking into account cultural, political, and economic frameworks. There is a pressing call to action in the establishment of primary legislation to tackle ethical concerns and privacy issues associated with advancements in AI. The six key principles for responsible AI—accountability, inclusiveness, reliability and safety, fairness, transparency, and privacy and security—are crucial in ensuring that AI systems are ethical, trustworthy, and beneficial to society, as shown in Table 9.6

Together, these principles form the foundation of responsible AI development and deployment. They guide developers and users alike in creating and using AI technologies that are ethical, beneficial, and

Table 9.6 Ethical concerns of artificial intelligence

Accountability	This principle emphasizes that there should always be a clear entity (individual, organization, or group) responsible for the outcomes of AI systems. Accountability in AI ensures that if something goes wrong, or if there are unintended consequences, there is a way to address these issues. It also involves adhering to legal and ethical standards, with mechanisms in place for redress and correction
Inclusiveness	AI should be developed with an inclusive approach, taking into consideration the diversity of users and their needs. This includes ensuring that AI systems do not perpetuate existing biases or inequalities and are accessible to people of different ages, genders, ethnicities, abilities, and other characteristics. Inclusiveness in AI design helps in creating systems that are fair and equitable to all sections of society
Reliability and Safety	AI systems should be reliable and safe, functioning as intended under various conditions and being resilient to manipulation and errors. This involves rigorous testing and validation of AI systems, ongoing monitoring, and ensuring they are secure against external threats and malfunctions
Fairness	Fairness in AI involves ensuring that the AI systems do not create or reinforce unfair bias against certain groups or individuals. This includes being aware of and actively mitigating biases in data, algorithms, and their interpretations. Fair AI systems treat all users equitably and make unbiased decisions
Transparency	This principle refers to the importance of making AI systems transparent and understandable to users. Transparency in AI involves clear communication about how AI systems work, the decisions they make, and the data they use. This transparency is critical for building trust and enabling users to understand and appropriately interact with AI systems
Privacy and Security	Ensuring the privacy and security of data used and generated by AI systems is crucial. This involves implementing strong data protection measures, respecting user consent, and ensuring data is used ethically and securely. Privacy and security in AI protect users from data breaches and misuse of their personal information

respectful of human rights and democratic values. As AI becomes more integrated into mainstream products and services, adhering to these principles becomes increasingly important to foster trust and acceptance among users and the broader society.

Several critical ethical concerns in AI may have a profound impact on its valuation assessment. Addressing these concerns is essential for responsible AI development and deployment:

a. **Bias and Fairness (as stated above):**

- Bias in AI algorithms can result from biased training data or flawed algorithmic design. It can lead to discrimination against certain groups, reinforcing societal inequalities.
- Ethical AI requires proactive efforts to identify and rectify biases. This includes carefully curating training data, using diverse datasets, and applying bias mitigation techniques.
- Regularly auditing AI systems for bias and conducting fairness assessments is essential to ensure equitable outcomes.

b. **Privacy:**

- AI often processes large volumes of personal data, raising concerns about privacy, consent, and responsible data use.
- Ethical AI demands robust data protection measures, including encryption, access controls, and data anonymization.
- Transparency about data usage and obtaining informed consent from individuals are crucial for maintaining trust.

c. **Accountability and Transparency:**

- Ethical AI systems should be transparent, and there should be clear accountability for AI-driven decisions.
- Explainability mechanisms, such as providing reasons for AI decisions, are essential for building trust and understanding.
- Auditing mechanisms and traceability help identify errors and hold AI developers and operators accountable for their systems' behavior.

d. **Job Displacement:**

- The potential for AI to automate tasks and displace jobs raises ethical concerns about economic inequality and workforce disruption.
- Ethical AI involves not only addressing job displacement but also proactively investing in workforce retraining and creating new job opportunities.
- Collaboration between governments, industries, and educational institutions is crucial to navigate the challenges of workforce transformation.

e. **Autonomous Systems:**

- AI-driven autonomous systems, such as self-driving cars and drones, introduce ethical considerations around safety, accountability, and decision-making in critical situations.
- Ethical AI in autonomous systems emphasizes safety standards, rigorous testing, and the ability to handle unexpected scenarios.
- Legal frameworks, liability, and regulations must be in place to ensure accountability for autonomous AI systems.

In addition to these concerns, ethical AI also involves broader principles, such as beneficence (AI systems should act in the best interests of humans), non-maleficence (AI systems should not harm), and fairness (AI systems should treat all individuals fairly).

Addressing these ethical concerns requires a multi-stakeholder approach involving governments, industries, researchers, and civil society. Ethical guidelines, codes of conduct, and best practices should be established and adhered to throughout the AI development lifecycle to ensure that AI technologies are designed and used for the benefit of humanity while minimizing harm and bias.

Incidents related to the ethical misuse of AI refer to cases where AI technologies are used in ways that raise ethical concerns or violate ethical principles. These incidents can encompass a wide range of issues, including:

1. Bias and Discrimination: AI systems can inadvertently perpetuate bias and discrimination when they are trained on biased data or when their algorithms are designed with inherent biases. This can lead to unfair treatment of certain groups of people.
2. Privacy Violations: AI can be used to collect and analyze vast amounts of personal data, raising concerns about privacy violations when this data is misused or mishandled.
3. Surveillance: The use of AI in surveillance systems can infringe on individuals' privacy rights, and the misuse of such systems can lead to unwarranted surveillance of citizens.
4. Deepfakes: AI-generated deepfake videos and content can be used to spread misinformation, impersonate individuals, or manipulate public opinion.

5. Job Displacement: The automation of jobs through AI and robotics can have ethical implications, such as job loss and economic inequality.
6. Autonomous Weapons: The development and deployment of lethal autonomous weapons systems (LAWS) raises ethical questions about the use of AI in warfare.
7. Misinformation and Manipulation: AI-powered algorithms can be used to spread false information and manipulate public discourse, which can have significant societal consequences.
8. Healthcare and Medical AI: Misuse of AI in healthcare can result in incorrect diagnoses, privacy breaches, and other ethical issues.
9. Criminal Justice: The use of AI in predictive policing and sentencing algorithms can lead to issues of fairness, bias, and discrimination in the criminal justice system.
10. Ethical Decision-Making: The design of AI systems that make ethical decisions or moral judgments raises questions about how these systems are programmed and the values they are built upon.

Efforts are being made to address these ethical concerns through the development of AI ethics guidelines, regulations, and responsible AI practices. Organizations and governments around the world are working to ensure that AI technologies are used in ways that respect ethical principles and human rights.

Automated fact-checking and decisions (see https://fastercapital.com/keyword/automated-decisions.html) using natural language processing (NLP) in AI is a complex task with its own set of challenges and limitations (Table 9.7):

Efforts are being made to address these challenges in automated fact-checking, including the development of more reliable and contextually aware models, as well as the improvement of training datasets. Additionally, the integration of real-time data sources and the use of techniques like claim context modeling are being explored to enhance the accuracy and timeliness of automated fact-checking systems. Despite the complexities involved, automated fact-checking remains an important area of research and development to combat misinformation and promote fact-based information in the digital age.

Fairness, bias, and ethics have become prominent concerns as AI technologies, including generative models, have become more accessible and widespread. Here are some key points to consider:

Table 9.7 Automated fact-checking using natural language processing

Data Availability and Quality	Developing effective automated fact-checking systems relies heavily on access to high-quality training data. If the datasets used for training these systems contain evidence that was not available at the time the claim was made, it can introduce inaccuracies and limit the system's ability to make accurate assessments
Temporal Misalignment	When evidence from fact-checking reports is used to validate claims made in the past, it can lead to temporal misalignment. In other words, the system may have access to information that was not available to the claimant at the time they made their statement, which can make it difficult to assess the accuracy of the claim as it was understood when it was made
Bias and Dependence on Fact-Checking Reports	Relying on fact-checking reports for training data can introduce bias, as these reports may have their subjective judgments. Additionally, if automated fact-checking heavily depends on such reports, it may not be truly independent and may merely reflect the biases or opinions of the fact-checkers
Real-time Fact-Checking Challenges	Truly real-time fact-checking, where claims are assessed as they are made, is challenging due to the need for immediate access to relevant and accurate information. The development of such systems often requires advanced techniques and access to real-time data sources
Contextual Understanding	NLP models need to understand the context of a claim, which can be a complex task. Claims are often made with implicit or unstated assumptions, and fact-checking systems must be able to identify and address these nuances

1. **Fairness and Bias**: With the increased use of AI in various applications, concerns about fairness and bias have grown. AI systems can inherit biases present in the data they are trained on. Biased AI can lead to unfair outcomes, perpetuate stereotypes, and discriminate against certain groups. Researchers and practitioners are now placing greater emphasis on developing methods to detect, mitigate, and prevent bias in AI systems.
2. **Ethical Considerations:** As AI systems become more powerful, they can have significant real-world impacts. Ethical considerations arise in areas such as privacy, surveillance, employment, and healthcare. There is a growing awareness that AI should be developed and deployed with careful ethical considerations, including transparency, accountability, and respect for human rights.
3. **Accessibility and Control**: The lowering of technical barriers means that more individuals and organizations can create and deploy AI systems. While this democratization of AI is a positive development, it also raises concerns about the responsible use of AI technology. Ensuring that individuals and organizations are educated about the ethical implications and best practices in AI is crucial.
4. **Regulation**: Governments and regulatory bodies are increasingly recognizing the need to address the ethical and fairness issues surrounding AI. There are ongoing discussions and efforts to establish regulations and guidelines for the development and deployment of AI systems, especially in critical domains like healthcare and finance.
5. **Public Awareness**: As you mentioned, the general public is becoming more aware of AI and its implications. Public scrutiny and demand for transparency and accountability are driving companies and organizations to be more mindful of the ethical aspects of AI.
6. **Collaboration**: Collaboration among researchers, practitioners, policymakers, and ethicists is essential to address these issues effectively. Interdisciplinary efforts are underway to develop ethical AI guidelines, tools for bias detection and mitigation, and mechanisms for accountability.
7. **Responsible AI Development**: Many companies are now adopting principles of responsible AI development. This includes conducting ethics assessments, conducting regular audits, and actively seeking

feedback from diverse stakeholders to ensure that AI systems are developed and deployed in ways that benefit society.

As AI technology becomes more accessible and pervasive, all stakeholders must work together to address the ethical challenges it presents. This includes not only addressing bias and fairness issues but also ensuring that AI benefits everyone and respects fundamental ethical principles.

The impact of fairness, bias, and ethics concerns in AI on the economic, financial, and market valuation aspects can be significant and multifaceted, as shown in Table 9.8.

The impact of fairness, bias, and ethics concerns in AI on economic, financial, and market valuation can vary widely depending on the industry, the specific AI applications involved, and how companies address these concerns. In general, though, there is a growing recognition that ethical considerations are not just a matter of compliance but can also have financial and market implications, making them an important aspect of AI strategy for businesses.

Artificial Intelligence, Algorithmic, and Automation Incidents and Controversies (AIAAIC) Repository

The Repository of Artificial Intelligence, Algorithmic, and Automation Incidents and Controversies (AIAAIC) has the potential to function as a valuable asset for documenting incidents and ethical dilemmas associated with AI applications, akin to the AI Incident Database (AIID) focusing on AI incidents. This repository could play a crucial role in pinpointing areas where AI is being unethically deployed, particularly in language and computer vision models, intelligent robots, and autonomous driving, thus shedding light on issues such as bias and safety concerns. Moreover, it could assist in comprehending the software engineering strategies employed by academic AI repositories, underscoring aspects like the incorporation of licenses and connections to other repositories as essential for distinguishing between popular and less popular academic AI repositories. Through the utilization of expert insights and input from the community, the AIAAIC Repository could offer a methodical classification system for examining the technical root causes contributing to failures and adversities in AI. The AIAAIC Repository is a valuable resource for tracking and studying incidents and controversies related

Table 9.8 Impact of fairness, bias, and ethics concerns

Economic Impact	*Increased Costs*: Addressing fairness, bias, and ethics concerns often requires additional resources, including specialized personnel, tools, and processes. This can lead to increased development and operational costs for companies *Market for Ethical AI*: There is a growing demand for AI systems that are developed with ethical considerations in mind. Companies that can demonstrate ethical practices and fairness in their AI solutions may have a competitive advantage, attracting customers who prioritize ethical AI *Reputation and Trust*: Companies that are perceived as responsible and ethical in their AI deployments are likely to build stronger brand reputations and trust among customers, partners, and investors
Financial Impact	*Legal and Regulatory Compliance*: Failure to address fairness and bias issues can lead to legal liabilities and fines. Companies may incur financial penalties if their AI systems are found to discriminate or violate privacy laws *Market Entry and Exit*: Companies that do not adequately address ethical concerns may face barriers to entering certain markets or industries where ethical considerations are paramount. Conversely, companies that prioritize ethics can gain entry into markets where ethical AI is a requirement *Investor Sentiment*: Ethical concerns in AI can affect investor sentiment. Investors may be more inclined to support companies that are proactive in addressing these issues and may divest from companies with reputations for unethical AI practices
Market Impact	*Market Perception*: The market valuation of companies can be influenced by their perceived ethical practices in AI. Companies with a strong ethical track record may be valued more highly by investors who prioritize long-term sustainability and responsible AI practices *Volatility*: Market valuation can be affected by public perception and media coverage of AI-related ethical controversies. Negative news or scandals related to biased or unfair AI systems can lead to stock price volatility and decreased market capitalization *Long-Term Sustainability*: Companies that prioritize fairness and ethics in AI may be viewed as more sustainable in the long term, which can positively impact their market valuation. Conversely, companies with reputations for unethical AI may face challenges in sustaining long-term growth

to AI, algorithms, and automation. Such a repository can serve several important purposes:

a. **Transparency and Accountability**: By making incidents and controversies public and easily accessible, the repository promotes transparency in the field of AI and automation. This can hold organizations and developers accountable for the impacts of their technologies.

b. **Research and Analysis**: Researchers, policymakers, and ethicists can use the repository to study trends, patterns, and root causes of AI-related incidents and controversies. This can lead to a better understanding of the challenges and risks associated with these technologies.
c. **Learning and Best Practices**: The repository can be a valuable resource for learning from past mistakes and controversies. It can help organizations and developers identify best practices for ethical and responsible AI development and deployment.
d. **Public Awareness**: Making this information publicly available can raise awareness among the general public about the potential risks and ethical considerations associated with AI and automation.
e. **Policy and Regulation**: Policymakers and regulatory bodies can use the repository to inform the development of policies and regulations related to AI, algorithms, and automation. It can provide real-world examples of the need for oversight and guidelines.
f. **Education**: The repository can be a useful educational tool for training AI practitioners, data scientists, and engineers on the ethical dimensions of their work. It can be used to illustrate the importance of considering the societal impact of AI technologies.

An independent and public dataset like the AIAAIC Repository can contribute to a more responsible and accountable development and deployment of AI, algorithms, and automation. It allows stakeholders to learn from past incidents, take proactive measures to mitigate risks, and ensure that these technologies are used in ways that benefit society.

Artificial Intelligence-Based Virtual Partners

Intelligent Personal Assistants (IPAs) or Virtual Collaborators (VCs) optimize daily activities by leveraging Natural Language Processing (NLP) and speech recognition technologies. VCs, positioned as coequals in the realm of digital cooperation, streamline collaborative efforts by incorporating AI into diverse functions and responsibilities. Furthermore, studies focusing on artificial partners illustrate their capacity to formulate coordination tactics akin to those observed in human-to-human scenarios. Breakthroughs such as a virtual artificial intelligence partner underscore the progressions in AI technology, empowering devices to aid in tasks, engage in communication, and even interact physically with users. These AI-powered virtual partners symbolize a transition towards more intricate and unified collaborations between humans and AI, thereby influencing the trajectory of work dynamics and interpersonal engagements. The topic of relationships with AI-based virtual partners is gaining more and more relevance. Social and romantic dynamics are undergoing significant changes due to the increasing availability of advanced technologies and AI-powered apps:

a. Growth of Virtual Relationships: many people are experimenting with AI virtual gender relationships. These interactions are fueled by the ability of AI to learn from data and respond to user needs, creating an illusion of real relationships.
b. Positive aspects: Some people can find comfort and satisfaction in these virtual relationships. They can offer an environment free of conflicts and problems typical of human relationships, allowing individuals to explore their emotional selves and develop self-confidence.
c. Risks and Concerns: However, there are also risks associated with this phenomenon. Social isolation, technology addiction, and loss of ability to manage real relationships with their challenges and ups and downs are some of the concerns raised by the growing adoption of AI relationships. Impact on society: The increase in virtual relationships could impact society on various levels. It could affect birth rates, people's mental health, and social dynamics in general. It is important to conduct further research to fully understand the impact of these dynamics.
d. Regulation and Ethics: As AI relationships increase, new ethical and regulatory questions may arise. For example, should there be guidelines on the use of AI in romantic contexts? How should personal data be protected in these interactions? Ultimately, relationships with AI-powered virtual partners represent a complex challenge for society, which must balance the benefits of technological innovation with concerns about social isolation and the balance between the virtual and real worlds. This is likely to be an increasingly relevant topic of discussion in the coming years, requiring further research and in-depth debate.

9.3 OECD Artificial Intelligence Principles

The OECD has developed a set of principles for AI that provide guidelines for the responsible development and use of AI technologies. These principles were adopted by OECD member countries in May 2019, and are intended to promote trustworthy AI systems that respect human rights, uphold democratic values, and contribute positively to society. The Framework developed by the OECD serves to categorize AI Systems, aiding policymakers in assessing the potential opportunities and risks linked with different AI systems, in alignment with the OECD Principles regarding Trustworthy AI. Governments' global recognition of the importance of AI is evident through formulating national AI strategies, with more than 60 countries already having such strategies in place. A comprehensive understanding of the AI workforce is paramount for countries aspiring to excel in AI advancement, as it facilitates talent development and ensures inclusivity in AI innovation. In light of the challenges presented by AI and emerging technologies, international collaboration is indispensable to establish credibility, exchange best practices, and guide policy formulation. The OECD's Recommendation on Artificial Intelligence, embraced by all member countries and numerous non-member countries, is designed to encourage responsible and reliable stewardship of AI. They consist of five key principles (Table 9.9):

In addition to these five principles, the OECD also provides specific recommendations and guidance for the implementation of these principles. The OECD AI Principles serve as a foundational framework for countries, organizations, and developers to shape AI policies, regulations, and practices in a way that aligns with ethical and responsible AI development and deployment.

Countries and stakeholders around the world have been adopting and adapting these principles to guide their own AI strategies and policies, contributing to a global effort to ensure that AI technologies are developed and used in a manner that serves the best interests of society while respecting ethical and human rights considerations.

Economics, Ethics, and Artificial Intelligence

The interconnection between Economics, Ethics, and AI is profound, given that the integration of AI raises ethical concerns that have significant impacts on society and the economy. The utilization of AI in various

Table 9.9 OECD artificial intelligence principles

Inclusive Growth	AI systems should benefit individuals, society, and the environment. They should be designed and used to enhance human well-being, promote fairness, and contribute to sustainable development
Human-Centered Values	AI should respect and uphold human rights and democratic values. This includes the principles of fairness, transparency, accountability, and non-discrimination
Transparency and Traceability	AI systems should be transparent and explainable. Individuals should understand the capabilities and limitations of AI systems and be able to trace the decision-making processes
Robustness, Security, and Safety	AI systems should be designed to be robust, secure, and safe throughout their lifecycle. Measures should be in place to prevent errors, biases, and other unintended consequences
Accountability	There should be mechanisms in place to ensure accountability for AI systems and their outcomes. This includes clarity regarding responsibilities, liability, and redress mechanisms in case of harm

sectors like autonomous driving and finance has led to enhanced efficiency; however, it has also introduced ethical risks, including privacy violations and discriminatory practices. Criticisms have been directed towards Big Tech companies for their promotion of AI ethics, labeling it as mere "ethics washing" that prioritizes economic gains over genuine ethical progress. Economics and ethics both offer important perspectives on our society, but they do so from two different viewpoints—the central focus of economics is how the price system in our economy values resources; the central focus of ethics is the moral evaluation of actions in our society (Korineck, 2019).

The intersection of economics, ethics, and AI is complex and controversial, due to contrasting aims that need to be reconciled and conducted to a common playground:

a. **Divergent Focuses of Economics and Ethics**: Economics primarily deals with the valuation and allocation of resources through the price system, while ethics is concerned with the moral evaluation of actions and decisions. These two fields offer different lenses through which to view societal issues.

b. **AI and the Convergence of Economic and Ethical Concerns**: The advent of AI has highlighted areas where economic value and ethical values may clash. This raises fundamental questions about the desirable direction of technological progress for society.
c. **Impact on Labor Markets**: One significant concern is how AI and automation affect labor markets. There's a risk that these technologies could exacerbate inequality, either by displacing human labor or by creating disparities in income and opportunity. Mitigating policies or steering technological development in a way that complements rather than replaces human labor could be crucial.
d. **AI Optimization and Ethical Externalities**: Another concern is that AI systems, in pursuit of narrow market-driven goals, may neglect broader ethical considerations. This can result in negative externalities like bias, discrimination, manipulation of human behavior ("hacking the human brain"), and a reduction in human autonomy.
e. **The Ultimate Ethical Question in AI Development**: The potential for creating AI systems that surpass human intelligence in a general sense poses a profound ethical dilemma. It raises questions about the future role of humanity and how to ensure that human interests and well being are preserved in the face of rapidly advancing technology.
f. **Navigating the Future with AI**: The challenge lies in finding a balance where AI can be used as a tool for enhancing human capabilities and addressing societal challenges without compromising ethical values or exacerbating social inequalities.

9.4 IEEE Ethically Aligned Design

The "Ethically Aligned Design for Artificial Intelligence" is a set of guidelines and recommendations developed by the Institute of Electrical and Electronics Engineers (IEEE). It aims to provide a framework for the ethical design and deployment of AI systems. While these guidelines primarily focus on ethical considerations, they can indirectly impact the valuation of AI-related companies in several ways (Table 9.10):

1. **Competitive Advantage:**

Table 9.10 Ethically aligned design for artificial intelligence

Ethical Reputation and Brand Value	Companies that adhere to ethical AI principles, such as those outlined by IEEE, can build a strong reputation for responsible AI development. A positive ethical reputation can enhance a company's brand value, potentially increasing its attractiveness to investors and customers
Risk Mitigation	Ethical AI practices, as recommended by IEEE, can help companies mitigate ethical and legal risks associated with AI. Lower risk profiles can be viewed favorably by investors and may positively impact a company's valuation
Market Adoption and Consumer Trust	Ethical AI practices can contribute to greater market adoption of AI products and services. Enhanced consumer trust in AI systems can lead to increased customer acquisition and retention, which can positively impact a company's financial performance and valuation
Regulatory Compliance	Adhering to ethical AI guidelines can help companies navigate and comply with evolving AI regulations and standards. Compliance with regulatory requirements can reduce legal and regulatory risks, which can influence a company's valuation
Long-Term Viability	Companies that prioritize ethical AI are more likely to be sustainable in the long term as they are less prone to ethical controversies and associated negative consequences. Long-term viability and stability can positively impact a company's valuation
Investor and Stakeholder Confidence	Companies that demonstrate a commitment to ethical AI practices may attract socially responsible investors and stakeholders. Positive investor sentiment can positively influence a company's stock price and valuation

(continued)

Table 9.10 (continued)

Competitive Advantage	Ethical AI practices can differentiate a company from competitors, potentially leading to a competitive advantage. A competitive edge can lead to increased market share and revenue, impacting valuation
Market Opportunities	Ethical AI principles can guide companies in identifying market opportunities and emerging trends aligned with responsible AI. Seizing these opportunities can lead to revenue growth, influencing valuation

- Ethical AI practices can differentiate a company from competitors, potentially leading to a competitive advantage.
- A competitive edge can lead to increased market share and revenue, impacting valuation.

2. **Market Opportunities:**

   - Ethical AI principles can guide companies in identifying market opportunities and emerging trends aligned with responsible AI.
   - Seizing these opportunities can lead to revenue growth, influencing valuation.

While adherence to ethical AI principles can positively affect a company's valuation, other financial, operational, and strategic factors also play a significant role. Ethical considerations are one aspect of a broader evaluation of a company's performance and potential. Nonetheless, the responsible and ethical development of AI is increasingly becoming a crucial factor for investors and stakeholders, and it can contribute to the long-term success and valuation of AI related companies.

9.5 Artificial Intelligence's Perception in Public Opinion and Social Media

The perception of public attitudes towards AI frameworks indicates that technology-oriented subreddits emphasize technical aspects, while non-tech subreddits voice apprehensions about job displacement. AI influences consumer behavior on social media, particularly in relation to micro and nano influencers, illustrating the significant influence of public opinion in enhancing marketing effectiveness and sales, particularly in the context of utilizing AI technologies. Public opinion plays a significant role in shaping the economic, financial, and market valuation of AI in various ways, including influencing its scalable use, addressing misconceptions and biases, and identifying threats and opportunities. Here's how public opinion can impact these aspects:

Impact on Scalable Use:

1. **Market Demand**: Positive public opinion regarding AI can stimulate market demand for AI products and services. When people trust and have confidence in AI technologies, they are more likely to adopt and use them, leading to increased economic opportunities for AI companies.
2. **Investor Sentiment**: Public sentiment can influence investor confidence in AI companies. Favorable public opinion can attract investments, facilitating the scaling of AI businesses.
3. **Regulation and Policy**: Public concerns and opinions can lead to the introduction of regulatory frameworks that either facilitate or restrict the use of AI. Regulatory clarity or barriers can impact the scalability of AI applications.

Addressing Misconceptions and Bias:

1. **Public Trust**: Public opinion affects trust in AI systems. If there are misconceptions or biases about AI technologies, it can erode public trust, leading to reluctance in adopting AI-driven solutions.
2. **Ethical Considerations:** Concerns raised by the public about AI bias, discrimination, and fairness can influence the development of ethical AI practices and guidelines. Addressing these concerns is essential to maintaining trust and market viability.

SWOT Analysis Concerning the AI's Perception of Public Opinion Shows the Following:

1. **Strengths**: Positive public opinion can amplify the strengths of AI, such as its potential to improve efficiency, decision-making, and innovation. This can enhance the economic and market value of AI.

2. **Weaknesses**: Negative public sentiment can highlight weaknesses in AI systems, such as their potential for bias, privacy violations, and job displacement. Addressing these weaknesses is crucial for sustained economic and market success.
3. **Opportunities**: Public interest in AI can create opportunities for AI education, training, and skill development. This can lead to a more skilled workforce, fostering AI innovation and growth.
4. **Threats**: Public concerns about job displacement, bias, and misuse of AI can pose threats to the AI industry. These concerns can lead to restrictive regulations and market resistance.

Public opinion plays a vital role in shaping the economic, financial, and market valuation of AI. Positive sentiment can drive demand, investor confidence, and innovation, while negative sentiment can lead to regulatory challenges and market resistance. Addressing misconceptions, bias, and ethical concerns is essential for building public trust and ensuring the long-term success of AI technologies. Public opinion also creates opportunities for AI education and workforce development, which can contribute to economic growth and market expansion.

There are several advantages and disadvantages of AI. Social media has a significant impact on the perception of AI potential and can influence the economic, financial, and market value of AI in several ways (Table 9.11):

Social media has the power to shape public perception, influence investor sentiment, educate the public, and impact advocacy efforts related to AI. These factors can, in turn, affect the economic, financial, and market value of AI.

9.6 Sustainable Development Goals

The SDGs are a set of 17 goals that support a more sustainable and equitable world. AI can be used to help achieve many of the SDGs, such as:

- Poverty reduction: AI can be used to develop new economic opportunities and create jobs.
- Education: AI can be used to personalize learning and make education more accessible.

Table 9.11 Social media and artificial intelligence

Shaping Public Perception	Positive Narratives: Positive stories and success stories related to AI on social media can create a sense of optimism and excitement about AI's potential. These narratives can generate enthusiasm among the public, investors, and businesses (Toniolo et al., 2020), positively impacting the market valuation of AI companies Negative Narratives: Conversely, negative narratives about AI, such as concerns about job displacement, bias, or misuse, can generate fear and skepticism. These narratives can lead to regulatory scrutiny and market resistance, potentially affecting the market valuation of AI companies
Influencing Investment and Funding	Investor Sentiment: Social media discussions and trends can influence investor sentiment. Positive sentiment can attract investments and lead to higher market capitalization for AI companies, while negative sentiment may deter investment Startup Success Stories: Social media platforms often feature success stories of AI startups that have disrupted industries or achieved significant milestones. These stories can inspire entrepreneurs and investors, leading to increased funding for AI ventures
Education and Awareness	AI Education: Social media platforms are used for sharing AI-related educational content. This educational outreach can increase awareness and understanding of AI technologies, potentially leading to more AI adoption and investment
Public Advocacy and Policy Influence	Advocacy Movements: Social media is a powerful platform for advocacy and awareness campaigns. Public support for ethical AI, responsible AI development, and fair AI policies can influence government regulations, which can impact the economic and financial aspects of AI

(continued)

Table 9.11 (continued)

Viral Trends and Challenges	AI Challenges: Viral trends or challenges related to AI (e.g., AI art generators, and chatbot interactions) can create public interest and curiosity. These trends can lead to increased user engagement and experimentation with AI applications
Feedback Loops	User Feedback: Social media provides a platform for users to share their experiences with AI technologies. Positive feedback can enhance AI developers' confidence and encourage further innovation, while negative feedback can drive improvements and refinement of AI systems

- Health: AI can be used to develop new medical treatments and improve healthcare delivery.
- Climate change: AI can be utilized for new renewable energy technologies and reduce carbon emissions.

The potential impact of AI on SDGs is widely acknowledged across different industries, particularly emphasizing societal progress, education, healthcare, and communication. While AI presents novel solutions for issues in agriculture, waste management, and intelligent water systems, it also brings forth potential risks that necessitate mitigation via ethical and responsible practices. The implementation of strategies involving AI has the capacity to facilitate the attainment of sustainable objectives in the long term, through the promotion of proactive technology adoption and the mitigation of adverse effects. The establishment of appropriate regulations is imperative to guarantee the responsible application of AI for sustainable development across all domains of SDGs. Some specific examples of how AI is being used to support the SDGs (Sætra, 2021) are recalled in Table 9.12

AI may substantially contribute alleviating poverty traps and advancing Sustainable Development Goals (SDGs):

a. **Ethical Considerations:** AI applications must be implemented respecting human rights and dignity. This includes avoiding bias in AI algorithms which can perpetuate or exacerbate

Table 9.12 Link between Sustainable Development Goals and Artificial Intelligence

SDG 1: No Poverty	AI is being used to develop new financial products and services that can help people escape poverty. For example, AI-powered microfinance platforms can provide small loans to entrepreneurs in developing countries
SDG 2: Zero Hunger	AI is being used to improve agricultural productivity and reduce food waste. For example, AI-powered drones can be used to monitor crops and identify pests and diseases
SDG 3: Good Health and Well-being	AI is being used to develop new medical treatments and improve healthcare delivery.
SDG 4: Quality Education	AI can personalize education, making it more accessible and effective, especially in underprivileged areas. Through adaptive learning platforms, AI can cater to individual student needs, help overcome language barriers, and provide high-quality educational resources where traditional schooling is lacking
SDG 5: Gender Equality	AI tools can help in identifying and addressing gender biases in various fields such as employment, education, and health services, thereby contributing to the empowerment of women and girls in impoverished communities
SDG 7: Affordable and Clean Energy	AI is being used to develop new renewable energy technologies and reduce carbon emissions. For example, AI-powered smart grids can help to distribute electricity more efficiently and reduce energy consumption

(continued)

Table 9.12 (continued)

SDG 8: Decent Work and Economic Growth	AI can create new job opportunities and improve productivity in various sectors. By automating routine tasks, it allows workers to focus on higher-value activities. However, it's crucial to manage the transition to an AI-driven economy carefully to avoid job displacement and ensure that workers are retrained for new roles
SDG 9: Industry, Innovation, and Infrastructure	AI-driven platforms can provide small businesses and farmers in impoverished areas with critical market information, helping them to get fair prices for their products and improve their livelihoods
SDG 11: Sustainable Cities and Communities	AI is being used to make cities more sustainable and livable. For example, AI-powered traffic management systems can help to reduce congestion and improve air quality
SDG 13: Climate Action	a. Climate Modeling and Prediction b. Renewable Energy Optimization c. Climate Monitoring d. Natural Disaster Prediction and Response e. Carbon Sequestration and Removal f. Climate Finance and Investment g. Climate Education and Awareness h. Policy Analysis and Decision-Making i. Supply Chain Sustainability
SDG 15: Life on Land	AI can improve sustainable natural resource management, forecasting environmental changes, and favuring less harmful agricultural practices. This is crucial as environmental degradation often disproportionately affects the poor
SDG 16: Peace, Justice, and Strong Institutions	AI can aid in improving transparency and accountability in governance. By analyzing large datasets, AI can help in detecting fraud and corruption, thereby improving the effectiveness of public resources and services

existing inequalities. Ethical AI requires transparency, accountability, and fairness in both development and deployment.

b. **Privacy Concerns**: As AI systems often rely on large datasets, including personal information, there is a substantial risk to individual privacy. It is essential to implement robust data protection and privacy measures to safeguard against unauthorized access and misuse of personal data.
c. **The Digital Divide**: The disparity in access to digital technologies and the internet between different regions and socioeconomic groups can lead to inequalities in the benefits gained from AI. Bridging this digital divide is crucial to ensure that AI technologies are accessible to those in poverty traps, especially in rural or underprivileged areas.
d. **AI Literacy and Capacity Building**: There's a need to improve AI literacy and skills among the global population, particularly in developing countries. Training and capacity-building initiatives can empower individuals to leverage AI for their development and well-being.
e. **Regulatory Frameworks**: Developing and implementing appropriate regulatory frameworks can guide the ethical use of AI, ensuring it aligns with the principles of sustainable development. This includes international cooperation to set global standards.
f. **Inclusive and Participatory Design**: AI solutions should be designed with the participation of those they aim to help. Inclusive design processes ensure that AI applications are tailored to the actual needs and conditions of target communities.
g. **Sustainability and Environmental Impact**: The environmental impact of developing and running AI systems, particularly the energy consumption of large data centers, must be considered. Sustainable practices in AI development and deployment are essential to align with environmental SDGs.
h. **Monitoring and Evaluation**: Continuous monitoring and evaluation are necessary to assess the impact of AI applications on poverty alleviation and sustainable development. This can help in fine-tuning strategies and ensuring that the intended benefits are being realized.

These challenges also concern international organizations. By collaboratively developing strategies that prioritize ethical, equitable, and sustainable AI deployment, the transformative potential of AI in advancing the SDGs and alleviating poverty traps can be fully realized.

9.7 Artificial Intelligence and Corporate Governance

AI plays a significant role in the realm of corporate governance, as different stakeholders advocate for a transition from AI ethics to AI policy. Private enterprises are increasingly being encouraged to take into account the societal repercussions and formulate strategies that are in line with environmental and social principles, mirroring a movement towards sustainable growth and ethical corporate conduct. The governance of AI entails an intricate interplay of various entities, such as private sector, governmental bodies, academic institutions, and international entities, all contributing to the dynamic normative framework of AI regulation. With AI's continuous impact on global spheres, the establishment of AI governance frameworks becomes imperative, with a combination of private arrangements and official regulations molding the regulatory landscape in which AI stakeholders function. AI can so significantly impact corporate governance in various aspects, as shown in Table 9.13.

AI also incorporates challenges and risks, including ethical considerations, bias in algorithms, and potential job displacement. Therefore, companies must implement AI responsibly and transparently, and corporate governance frameworks may need to adapt to address these new challenges and opportunities. Regulatory entities should develop guidelines and standards for the use of AI in corporate governance.

AI-driven corporate governance can impact different industries, organizations, and regions. Additionally, ethical considerations, data privacy concerns, and biases in AI systems can influence public perception and market reactions.

AI-driven corporate governance can generate economic value by improving efficiency, reducing risks, and enhancing decision-making. It can also impact financial performance and market dynamics, requiring companies and investors to adapt to the evolving landscape shaped by AI technologies. Responsible and transparent implementation of AI in corporate governance is essential to harness its benefits while mitigating potential risks.

Table 9.13 Artificial intelligence and corporate governance

Enhanced Decision-Making	AI analyzes big data, providing insights to support better informed decision-making. This can lead to better strategic planning and risk management
Improved Compliance	AI-powered tools can help organizations monitor and ensure compliance with various regulations, including financial reporting, data privacy, and environmental standards. AI can automate compliance checks and provide real-time alerts when violations are detected
Risk Assessment	AI can assist in identifying and mitigating risks by analyzing market trends, financial data, and external factors. This can help boards and management teams make more proactive decisions to protect the company's interests
Cybersecurity	AI can bolster cybersecurity efforts by detecting and responding to threats in real time. It can help protect sensitive corporate data and ensure the integrity of digital assets
Shareholder Engagement	AI-driven chatbots and virtual assistants can be used to engage with shareholders and answer their queries. This can improve transparency and communication between the company and its investors
Proxy Voting	AI can assist institutional investors and asset managers in analyzing proxy voting materials and making informed decisions regarding corporate governance matters, such as board elections and executive compensation
Board Diversity and Nomination	AI can aid in identifying qualified candidates for board positions, helping companies promote diversity and inclusion in corporate leadership
Fraud Detection	AI can detect financial fraud and unethical behavior within the organization by analyzing transaction data, employee behavior, and other relevant information
Stakeholder Sentiment Analysis:	AI can be used to analyze social media and news sentiment related to the company, helping boards and management gage public perception and sentiment regarding the organization
Predictive Analytics	AI can use historical data to make predictions about future corporate governance issues, enabling companies to take proactive measures to address potential challenges

More specifically, AI-driven corporate governance patterns have the potential to have a significant economic, financial, and market impact on value generation (Table 9.14):

Here are some specific examples of how AI-driven corporate governance patterns can impact value generation:

- AI can be used to identify and mitigate risks more effectively, which can lead to lower costs of capital and higher insurance premiums.
- AI can be used to improve the efficiency of board meetings and decision-making, which can lead to better strategic planning and execution.
- AI can be used to monitor and enforce compliance with corporate governance rules and regulations, which can reduce the risk of fines and penalties.
- AI can be used to enhance corporate transparency and accountability, which can improve investor confidence and boost stock prices.
- AI can foster innovative corporate governance models.

AI-driven corporate governance patterns have the potential to have a positive impact on value generation for companies of all sizes. Companies need to carefully consider their specific needs and goals when developing AI-driven corporate governance solutions.

It is still early days for AI-driven corporate governance, but the potential benefits are significant. As AI technology continues to develop and become more widely adopted, more innovative and transformative applications of AI in corporate governance will come out.

Table 9.14 Artificial intelligence driven corporate governance patterns

Economic Impact	AI can help companies to improve their efficiency and productivity, which can lead to lower costs and higher profits. AI can automate tasks, improve decisions, developing innovative products and services.
Financial impact	AI may help companies to improve their financial performance minimizing risk, reducing fraud, and automating routine compliance. This includes tailor made investment suggestions and algorithmic trading
Market impact	AI helps companies to improve their market value in several ways. AI is used to improve customer satisfaction. Additionally, AI can help companies improve their ESG performance, which can make them more attractive to investors and consumers

References

Abdalmuttaleb M. A. Musleh Al-Sartawi, Hussainey, K., Razzaque, A. (2022). The role of artificial intelligence in sustainable finance. *Journal of Sustainable Finance & Investment*, 04–07, https://doi.org/10.1080/20430795.2022.2057405.

Brusseau, J. (2023). AI human impact: Toward a model for ethical investing in AI-intensive companies. *Journal of Sustainable Finance & Investment, 13*(2), 1030–1057.

Burnaev, E., Mironov, E., Shpilman, A., Mironenko, M., & Katalevsky, D. (2023). Practical AI cases for solving ESG challenges. *Sustainability., 15*(17), 12731.

Gupta, A., Sharma, U., & Gupta, S. K. (2021). The role of ESG in sustainable development: An analysis through the lens of machine learning. *IEEE International Humanitarian Technology Conference (IHTC)* (pp. 1–5). United Kingdom.

Hassan, P., Passing, F., & Goméz, J. M. (2023). ESG fingerprint: How big data and artificial intelligence can support investors, companies, and stakeholders? In R. Schmidpeter & R. Altenburger, R. (Eds), *Responsible artificial intelligence. CSR, sustainability, ethics & governance*. Springer.

Korineck, A., (2019). Integrating ethical values and economic value to steer progress in artificial intelligence (NBER, Working Paper 26130).

Moro-Visconti, R. (2021). *Startup valuation. From strategic business planning to digital networking*. Palgrave Macmillan.

Moro-Visconti, R. (2022a). *The valuation of digital intangibles. Technology, marketing, and the metaverse,* Palgrave Macmillan.

Moro-Visconti, R. (2022b). *Augmented corporate valuation. From digital networking to ESG compliance*. Palgrave Macmillan.

Sætra, H. S. (2021). A framework for evaluating and disclosing the ESG-related impacts of AI with the SDGs. *Sustainability, 13*(15), 8503.

Selim. (2020). https://www.taylorfrancis.com/chapters/edit/10.4324/9780429351044-12/esg-ai-omar-selim

Toniolo, K., Masiero, E., Massaro, M., & Bagnoli, C. (2020). Sustainable business models and artificial intelligence: Opportunities and challenges. In F. Matos, V. Vairinhos, I. Salavisa, L. Edvinsson, & M. Massaro (Eds.), *Knowledge, people, and digital transformation. Contributions to management science*. Springer.

CHAPTER 10

Artificial Intelligence-Driven Industry Applications

10.1 A Taxonomy of the Main Artificial Intelligence Industry Applications

The capacity of AI to process extensive datasets, recognize patterns, and make forecasts has profoundly transformed operations within these sectors, enriching efficiency, decision-making, and customer interactions. In the realm of agriculture, for example, AI is revolutionizing methodologies through precision agriculture, predictive analytics, and optimization of supply chains, ultimately resulting in heightened productivity and sustainability. Furthermore, the influence of AI is projected to expand as technology progresses, presenting novel prospects for enterprises to innovate and enhance their strategies. With the continuous evolution of AI, its adaptability and prowess in data analysis are likely to persistently steer progress and efficiencies across a broad spectrum of industries, shaping the trajectory of business methodologies and customer engagements. AI's impact on economic, financial, and market valuation is significant, but it changes by sector and is influenced by factors such as technology, strategy, environment, and societal acceptance. An overview of how businesses are deploying AI in various ways and the AI capabilities that are commonly embedded in these businesses is the following:

R. Moro-Visconti, *Artificial Intelligence Valuation*,
https://doi.org/10.1007/978-3-031-53622-9_10

1. **AI Capabilities Incorporated in Businesses:**
   - **Robotic Process Automation (RPA)**: RPA is used for automating repetitive patterns, boosting operational efficiency.
   - **Computer Vision**: Computer vision is used for image and video analysis, object recognition, quality control in manufacturing.
   - **Natural Language Text Understanding**: NLP is employed to process and detect human language, enabling sentiment analysis, chatbots, and text-based data mining for insights.
   - **Virtual Agents**: Used for customer support, and aiding in various industries (Alsaleh et al., 2021).
2. **Commonly Adopted AI Use Cases:**
   - **Service Operations Optimization**: AI optimizes internal processes and workflows, leading to increased efficiency. This includes supply chain optimization, and demand forecasting.
   - **Creation of New AI-based Products**: These include smart devices, personalized recommendations, and innovative solutions.
   - **Customer Segmentation**: AI analyzes client data and segments customers according to their "spicy" differences.
   - **Customer Service Analytics**: AI-driven analytics help businesses to detect customer interactions, attitudes, and feedback. This information can be used to improve customer service and enhance customer satisfaction.
   - **New AI-based Enhancement of Products**: AI is integrated into existing products to boost their functionality and capabilities. AI-powered characteristics improve mobile phones, or software.

AI improves operational efficiency and incentivates new avenues for innovation and customer engagement.

AI applications impact on the economic, financial, and market value of traditional firms (Table 10.1):

The impact varies depending on the specific use case, industry, and how AI technologies are implemented. Successful AI adoption can lead to competitive advantages and improved financial performance for traditional firms. However, the exact magnitude of these impacts will be

Table 10.1 Artificial intelligence's industry applications

Healthcare	*Impact*: AI is used for disease diagnosis, drug discovery, and patient care optimization. It can improve patient outcomes, reduce healthcare costs, and enhance drug development *Economic Impact*: Traditional healthcare companies can benefit from AI by improving patient care and streamlining operations, potentially leading to increased revenues and decreased costs *Added Value*: AI can enhance diagnostic accuracy, improve treatment plans, and enable predictive analytics for early disease detection *EBITDA*: Higher EBITDA may result from cost savings and increased patient satisfaction
Finance	*Impact*: AI is employed in algorithmic trading, fraud detection, risk assessment, and customer service. It can increase trading efficiency, reduce fraud losses, and enhance customer experience *Economic Impact*: Traditional financial firms can gain a competitive edge by leveraging AI to make better investment decisions, manage risk, and improve customer service *Added Value*: AI can automate trading, provide real-time risk analysis, and offer personalized financial advice *EBITDA*: Improved decision-making can lead to higher profits, and AI-driven automation can reduce operational costs

(continued)

Table 10.1 (continued)

Retail	*Impact*: AI is used for demand forecasting, personalized marketing, and supply chain optimization. It can boost sales, reduce inventory costs, and improve customer satisfaction *Economic Impact*: Traditional retailers can leverage AI to optimize inventory management (Schrettenbrunnner, 2020), create targeted marketing campaigns, and enhance the customer shopping experience *Added Value*: AI can provide personalized product recommendations, optimize pricing strategies, and automate inventory replenishment *EBITDA*: Increased sales and reduced operational costs can positively impact EBITDA

Manufacturing (Li et al., 2018; Wan et al., 2021; Yang et al., 2021):	*Impact*: AI is employed for predictive maintenance, quality control, and process optimization. It can reduce downtime, improve product quality, and increase manufacturing efficiency *Economic Impact*: Traditional manufacturing companies can benefit from AI by minimizing equipment breakdowns, ensuring consistent product quality, and optimizing production processes *Added Value*: AI can predict equipment failures, identify defects in real-time, and optimize production schedules *EBITDA*: Reduced downtime and improved efficiency can lead to higher EBITDA
Transportation	*Impact*: AI can enhance safety, reduce transportation costs, and improve logistics *Economic Impact*: Traditional transportation companies can adopt AI to optimize routes, reduce fuel consumption, and enhance safety, leading to cost savings and improved services *Added Value*: AI can also enable predictive maintenance *EBITDA*: Reduced operational cost scan contribute to higher EBITDA

influenced by factors such as the scale of AI implementation, market dynamics, and the level of competition within each industry.

The incorporation of AI into sectors such as drug discovery, meteorology, materials science, and nuclear fusion investigation may result in substantial economic consequences by hastening technological advancements and enhancing productivity. AI, particularly deep learning, has exhibited notable advancements in drug discovery, improving the detection of novel drug targets and streamlining the process. The integration of AI across various scientific fields, including meteorology and materials science, has the potential to stimulate idea generation and scientific advancement, ultimately fostering economic growth through accelerated technological transformations and heightened investments in capital-intensive research and development. The integration of AI into various fields is shown in Table 10.2.

Some contents are readapted mostly from Moro-Visconti (2022a), or, occasionally, Moro-Visconti (2022b), or Moro-Visconti (2021), extending digital intangible, startup, or business planning applications to specific AI valuation patterns.

AI is already making research more productive.

1. **Drug Discovery**: AI significantly accelerates the process of drug discovery (see Sect. 10.2., below). It can analyze vast chemical libraries to predict how different compounds will behave and how likely they are to make an effective treatment. AI algorithms can also help in understanding disease mechanisms, which can lead to the discovery of new therapeutic targets.
2. **Weather Forecasting**: AI enhances the accuracy of weather predictions by processing massive amounts of data from satellites, sensors, and historical weather patterns. This leads to more accurate and localized weather forecasts, which is critical for agriculture, disaster management, and daily life.
3. **Materials Science**: In the search for new materials for batteries, solar panels, and other technologies, AI can predict the properties of materials before they are synthesized. This speeds up the discovery of new, more efficient materials, reducing the time and cost involved in traditional trial-and-error methods.
4. **Nuclear Fusion Research**: AI is playing a significant role in controlling nuclear fusion reactions, which require precise conditions and control. AI algorithms can predict and manage the complex plasma

Table 10.2 Artificial intelligence integration

Increased Efficiency and Productivity	This increased efficiency can result in higher productivity, which can impact the economic value of organizations and projects
Reduced Research and Development Costs	AI can reduce the time and resources required for research and development.
Competitive Advantage	Organizations that adopt AI gain a competitive advantage in their respective industries
Innovation and New Revenue Streams	AI-driven research can lead to the discovery of new products, services, or solutions that create additional revenue streams. For example, in drug discovery, AI can identify new drug candidates that can become blockbuster drugs, significantly impacting the valuation of pharmaceutical companies
Investment and Funding Opportunities	Organizations and research projects that successfully integrate AI may attract more investment and funding from venture capitalists, private equity firms, and government agencies. Increased financial support can contribute to higher valuations
Intellectual Property and Patents	AI-generated innovations may lead to the creation of valuable intellectual property and patents. These assets can be monetized through licensing agreements or sales, enhancing the economic value of the organizations holding them

(continued)

Table 10.2 (continued)

Data Monetization	AI relies on vast amounts of data. Organizations that generate, curate, and utilize data effectively can monetize their data assets, creating additional revenue sources and potentially increasing their valuation
Risk Mitigation	AI can help organizations better assess and mitigate risks. For instance, in nuclear fusion research, AI can optimize control systems to improve safety and reduce the likelihood of accidents, which can safeguard the economic value of the research

behaviors inside fusion reactors, potentially bringing us closer to achieving sustainable nuclear fusion.

5. **General Scientific Discovery**: As Demis Hassabis, co-founder of DeepMind, suggests, AI acts as a multiplier for human ingenuity. It can analyze vast amounts of data much faster than humans, uncovering new insights and patterns that might take humans much longer to find. This capability can lead to breakthroughs in a variety of fields, from cosmology to genetics.

AI's role is akin to that of the telescope in the realm of discovery—it extends the reach of human capability, allowing us to see further and understand more than we could unaided. The integration of AI into these research areas not only speeds up the pace of discovery but also opens new avenues for exploration that were previously inconceivable. As AI continues to evolve, its potential to facilitate breakthroughs in these and other fields will likely continue to grow.

10.2 The Impact of Artificial Intelligence in the BioTech and MedTech Business

AI substantially impacts biotechnological research's efficacy by enhancing analysis, reducing energy consumption, and improving experimental and analytical throughputs. AI models, such as those outlined in Efficient BioAI, can condense bioimaging AI models, thereby resulting in decreased energy expenditures and quicker inference durations without sacrificing precision. The fusion of AI with microfluidics within the realm of biotechnological research enables enhanced examination of vast datasets acquired from high-throughput microfluidics, ultimately refining experimental techniques and cutting down on expenses. Moreover, AI, particularly machine learning models, displays potential in drug exploration and creation, potentially heightening the efficiency and success rates of research and development protocols within these sectors. On the whole, the amalgamation of AI with numerous biotechnological applications like bioimaging, microfluidics, and drug exploration possesses the capacity to transform research procedures and results. AI has a notable impact on the economic, financial, and market value dimensions of the BioTech and MedTech industries. Incorporating AI into these fields is reconstructing strategies and business frameworks, as companies that invest in AI observe fluctuations in market value. While AI can enhance productivity and economic expansion, apprehensions regarding its influence on employment and income inequality endure, highlighting the need for public policies to alleviate adverse consequences. The rise of AI as a versatile technology comparable to past transformative innovations such as electricity and the digital computer implies a groundbreaking potential. The integration of AI into healthcare (Younis et al., 2024) is transforming the medical landscape and holds great potential to enhance medical practice, through.

1. **Data Processing and Diagnosis:** AI excels in processing large volumes of data rapidly. This capability can be harnessed to help physicians identify patterns and trends in medical data that might be challenging for humans to detect. For example, AI algorithms (see https://fastercapital.com/keyword/ai-algorithms.html) have shown high accuracy in diagnosing medical conditions from various types of imaging data such as medical images, retina scans, and dermatology images. This can aid in faster and more accurate diagnoses, leading to improved patient outcomes.
2. **Personalized Medicine:** AI has the potential to revolutionize personalized medicine (Tiwari et al., 2023). By analyzing a patient's unique genetic profile, medical history, and lifestyle factors, AI can assist physicians in creating tailored treatment plans. This personalized approach can optimize therapeutic interventions and improve clinical outcomes. Furthermore, AI can predict how a patient may

respond to specific treatments, anticipate potential side effects, and recommend the most suitable course of action.

3. **Preventive Care:** AI also plays a crucial role in preventive care. It can identify individuals at high risk of certain medical conditions by analyzing their health data. For instance, wearable devices powered by AI can continuously monitor vital signs and detect abnormalities. This early detection can enable timely interventions, helping both patients and healthcare providers address potential health issues before they become critical.

Understanding the capabilities and limitations of AI is essential for rapidly evolving technology. AI is a tool to augment the skills of healthcare professionals.

Traditionally, discovering new drugs has been a labor-intensive and time-consuming process, often described as finding a needle in a haystack. However, the use of AI in this context has transformed the process in several keyways:

a. **Speed and Efficiency:** AI models can rapidly sift through millions of candidate compounds. This capability significantly accelerates the initial stages of drug discovery, which traditionally involve a lot of trial and error.
b. **Training on Known Drugs:** The AI model can be trained on the chemical structures of thousands of known drugs and their effectiveness against various illnesses. This training enables the AI to understand and predict the effectiveness of new compounds.
c. **Identifying Links Between Chemical Structures and Effectiveness:** During its training, the AI model learns to correlate specific chemical structures with their success in combating diseases. This ability is crucial for predicting the potential effectiveness of new compounds.
d. **Shortlisting Potential Drugs:** The AI model generated a shortlist of promising compounds.
e. **Potential Against Antibiotic-Resistant Bacteria:** The notable aspect of these discoveries is their effectiveness against some of the most dangerous known antibiotic-resistant bacteria, addressing a critical need in modern medicine.

f. **Changing the Nature of Drug Discovery:** AI not only accelerates the drug discovery process but also changes the type of questions scientists ask in research. This implies a paradigm shift in how drug discovery is approached.

AI has had a significant impact on the development of new molecules and drugs (Hasselgren & Oprea, 2024) at various stages of the drug discovery and development process, from early research to FDA approval:

1. **Drug Discovery (Pre-clinical Phase):**
    - **Virtual Screening:** AI-powered algorithms analyze vast chemical databases, detecting compounds with the desired therapeutic effect.
    - **Drug Design:** AI-driven molecular modeling helps design novel drug candidates.
2. **Pre-clinical Testing (Phase 1):**
    - **Toxicology Prediction:** AI can predict potential toxicity and side effects of drug candidates. This helps in selecting safer candidates for further testing.
    - **Animal Testing Optimization:** AI optimizes pre-clinical animal testing protocols.
3. **Clinical Trials (Phases 2 and 3):**
    - **Patient Recruitment:** AI can analyze patient data to identify suitable candidates for clinical trials, potentially speeding up the recruitment process.
    - **Real-world Evidence:** AI can analyze real-world patient data to supplement clinical trial data, providing additional insights into drug efficacy and safety.
    - **Clinical Trial Optimization:** AI can help optimize the design of clinical trials, potentially reducing the time and cost required to reach meaningful conclusions.
4. **FDA Approval (Phase 4):**
    - **Post-marketing Surveillance:** AI can continuously monitor and analyze real-world data to detect safety issues and adverse events associated with approved drugs.

Value Creation and Cost Savings:

1. **Cost Savings:** AI can reduce the cost of drug discovery by identifying more promising drug candidates earlier in the process, optimizing research and development processes, and reducing the need for extensive experimental testing.
2. **Time Savings:** By accelerating the drug discovery and development process, AI can bring drugs to market faster, reducing the time it takes for patients to access new treatments.
3. **Increased Success Rates:** AI can help select the most promising drug candidates, reducing the number of failures in later phases of development, where costs are the highest.
4. **Personalized Medicine:** AI can enable the development of personalized treatments by analyzing genetic and clinical data, potentially increasing the effectiveness of drugs, and reducing adverse reactions.
5. **Drug Repurposing:** AI can identify existing drugs that may have new therapeutic applications, saving time and resources compared to developing entirely new molecules.

While AI has the potential to significantly impact drug development, there are challenges, including regulatory and ethical considerations, data quality, and the need for collaboration between AI experts and domain-specific scientists. Additionally, AI is not a panacea, and drug development will always involve rigorous testing, safety evaluations, and clinical trials to ensure patient safety and efficacy. Nonetheless, AI holds great promise for the MedTech and BioTech industry (Goyal et al., 2022; Guo et al., 2023) in accelerating drug discovery and development, reducing costs, and ultimately improving patient outcomes.

10.3 Artificial Intelligence, Transportation, and Self-Driving Cars

Incorporating AI into transportation management, planning, and control processes is crucial in optimizing traffic flow, reducing congestion, and improving public transport scheduling. The significant economic impact of AI in transportation is mainly attributed to the automation and productivity enhancements it brings. AI is significantly impacting the economy by automating processes and enhancing productivity. The utilization of AI technologies such as Convolutional Neural Networks (CNN) in computer vision systems is observed for monitoring and managing the behaviors of bus drivers, resulting in a notable decrease in undesirable actions like smoking or not wearing seat belts. AI and self-driving cars have the potential to significantly impact economic, financial, and market value creation in the transportation sector and beyond (Table 10.3):

The timing and extent of the economic, financial, and market value impacts may vary by region and depend on factors like regulatory approval and consumer acceptance.

Table 10.3 Artificial intelligence, transportation, and self-driving cars

Economic Impact	*Efficiency and Cost Reduction*: Self-driving cars have the potential to make transportation more efficient by reducing traffic congestion and optimizing routes. This can lead to cost savings for both individuals and businesses through reduced fuel consumption and less time spent in traffic *New Business Models*: The advent of autonomous vehicles could give rise to new business models, such as autonomous taxi services and delivery services. These innovations could create economic opportunities and new revenue streams *Job Creation*: While there may be concerns about job displacement in traditional driving roles, the development, deployment, and maintenance of autonomous vehicles create job opportunities in engineering, data analysis, cybersecurity, and vehicle maintenance
Financial Impact	*Investment and Funding*: The development of self-driving technology has attracted significant investment. This can lead to growth in the technology and automotive sectors *Insurance Industry*: The adoption of self-driving cars may disrupt the insurance industry. With fewer accidents caused by human error, the demand for traditional auto insurance could decrease, impacting the financial performance of insurance companies *Asset Utilization*: Companies that operate fleets of self-driving cars can potentially improve asset utilization rates
Market Value Creation	*Market Disruption*: The introduction of self-driving cars can disrupt traditional transportation markets. Companies that successfully develop autonomous vehicle technology create substantial market value *Technology Ecosystem*: The development of self-driving cars involves a complex ecosystem of technology providers, sensor manufacturers, software developers, and infrastructure companies. This creates opportunities for market value creation across various industries *Urban Planning and Real Estate*: Self-driving cars impact urban planning and real estate. Reduced parking requirements lead to the repurposing of parking spaces for other uses *Data and Connectivity*: Autonomous vehicles produce big data. Companies provide value-added services in data analytics, cybersecurity

Nonetheless, self-driving cars have the potential to reshape the transportation industry and create economic opportunities across a range of sectors.

10.4 Artificial Intelligence and FinTechs

AI facilitates FinTech companies in improving efficiency, decision-making, and customer satisfaction. Using AI, financial entities can enhance the precision of investment choices, enhance risk evaluation, identify fraudulent activities, and elevate customer service using AI-powered chatbots. Moreover, AI advancements such as artificial agents can aid in addressing challenges such as disseminating misinformation, which may impact algorithmic traders in financial sectors. In general, the influence of AI on FinTech organizations is significant, reshaping operational frameworks, offerings, and customer interactions within the financial domain. AI and fintech are transformative forces in the world today (Jakšič & Marinč, 2019). When combined, AI and fintech have the potential to revolutionize the financial services industry.

Here are some of the ways that AI is being used in fintech today:

- Fraud detection.
- Risk management: AI can be used to develop credit scoring models that are more accurate and inclusive than traditional models.
- Personalized financial advice: AI is being used to develop personalized financial advice tools that can help people make better financial decisions. For example, AI-powered chatbots can provide financial advice to customers based on their individual needs and circumstances.
- Automated trading: AI is used for automated trading systems on behalf of investors.
- Improved customer service.
- Identifying Market Inefficiencies: AI algorithms excel at detecting patterns in market data.
- Credit Scoring: AI models use big data to assess credit risk more accurately than traditional models.
- Bankruptcy Prediction: Machine learning algorithms can analyze financial data to predict the likelihood of bankruptcy, aiding in investment decisions and risk assessment.

AI is also being used to improve the overall efficiency and effectiveness of fintech operations. For example, AI is being used to automate back-office tasks, improve compliance processes, and develop new financial products and services.

The combination of AI and fintech (see also https://fastercapital.com/content/Future-of-fintech-startups.html) is creating new opportunities for both businesses and consumers. For businesses, AI-powered fintech solutions can help to reduce costs, improve efficiency, and increase sales. For consumers, AI-powered fintech solutions can provide more personalized and convenient financial services.

Here are some examples of how businesses and consumers are benefiting from AI-powered fintech solutions:

- Businesses: A small business uses an AI-powered fintech solution to automate its payroll processes. A large financial institution can use an AI-powered fintech solutions to improve fraud detection.
- Consumers: A consumer can use an AI-powered fintech solution to make mobile payments or transfer money.

AI Techniques in Financial Systems involve:

1. **Knowledge-Based Systems**: Use expert knowledge to make decisions.
2. **Machine Learning**: Algorithms learn from data to optimize forecasting. In finance, machine learning is used for predicting stock prices, identifying trends, and automating trading strategies.
3. **Natural Language Processing (NLP)**: NLP is used to analyze financial reports, news, and social media to gage market sentiment or to understand economic indicators that influence the markets.

AI has a significant impact on the FinTech (Financial Technology) industry, transforming various aspects of financial services and influencing economic, and market value (Table 10.4):

AI impacts the FinTech industry in many complementary ways:

1. **Transformative Impact**: AI has brought about significant transformations in the FinTech sector, influencing economic efficiency, financial performance, and market value.

Table 10.4 Artificial intelligence's valuation impact on FinTechs

Economic Impact	a. *Operational Efficiency*: AI automates manual and time-consuming tasks such as data entry, fraud detection, and customer service. This reduces operational costs and increases efficiency b. *Risk Management*: AI-based algorithms can analyze vast amounts of data in real-time to assess credit risk, detect fraudulent activities, and manage investment portfolios more effectively, reducing financial losses c. *Cost Reduction*: AI-powered chatbots and virtual assistants can handle customer inquiries and transactions 24/7, reducing the need for human customer support agents d. *Personalization*: AI enables FinTech companies to offer highly personalized financial services, such as personalized investment advice and tailored lending solutions
Financial Impact	a. *Revenue Generation*: AI can enhance customer acquisition and retention by offering personalized product recommendations and improved user experiences. This can lead to increased revenue streams b. *Risk Mitigation*: AI-driven fraud detection and risk assessment models help FinTech companies reduce financial losses due to fraudulent activities, loan defaults, or market volatility c. *Enhanced Decision-Making*: AI-powered analytics can provide insights into financial markets, customer behavior, and investment opportunities, enabling more informed and profitable decision-making d. *Cost Savings*: Automation of back-office functions and customer support through AI can lead to substantial cost savings, allowing FinTechs to allocate resources more efficiently e. *Product Innovation*: AI-driven algorithms can facilitate the creation of new financial products and services, potentially leading to additional revenue streams
Market Value Impact	a. *Competitive Advantage*: FinTech companies that leverage AI to offer innovative and efficient financial services can gain a competitive edge, attracting more customers and investors b. *Customer Loyalty*: Personalized and seamless AI-powered experiences can foster customer loyalty, leading to a stronger market position and higher market value c. *Investor Attraction*: FinTech firms incorporating AI often attract more investors due to their potential for growth and innovation. This can lead to higher market valuations d. *Data Monetization*: FinTechs accumulate vast amounts of financial data, which can be monetized by offering data analytics services to other businesses or by making data-driven investment decisions e. *Regulatory Compliance*: AI can assist in meeting regulatory requirements more efficiently, which can enhance trust among customers and investors

2. **Benefits of AI Integration**: FinTech companies that effectively integrate AI into their operations can realize several advantages, including:

    - **Cost Savings**
    - **Revenue Growth**
    - **Competitive Advantages**: AI produces a competitive edge.
    - **Enhanced Customer Loyalty**

3. **Data Privacy and Security**: While embracing AI, FinTech companies must prioritize data privacy and security to protect sensitive customer information. Robust cybersecurity measures are essential to maintain trust and comply with data protection regulations.
4. **Regulatory Compliance**: The regulatory landscape for FinTech is evolving, and companies must stay informed about changing requirements. Compliance with financial regulations is crucial to avoid legal issues and maintain credibility.

AI has the potential to revolutionize the FinTech industry, offering numerous benefits ranging from cost savings to enhanced customer experiences. However, companies must also remain vigilant in addressing data privacy, security, and regulatory concerns to ensure that they can harness the full potential of AI while managing associated risks.

Risk measurement is a key issue, especially when concerning AI applications in the FinTech industry. The Key AI Risk Indicators (KAIRI) framework, as shown by Guidici et al. (2024), assesses and ensures the trustworthiness of AI applications, particularly in financial services. Given the increasing adoption of advanced technologies in this industry, it is crucial to address concerns related to explain-ability, robustness, and fairness when implementing Machine Learning models for critical functions like credit scoring, anomaly detection, internal controls, and regulatory compliance. The KAIRI framework aligns with regulatory requirements and industry needs. It not only defines these essential principles but also proposes statistical metrics for each of them. This measurement and assessment approach can help organizations in the financial sector evaluate their AI systems effectively and take steps to manage and mitigate risks associated with AI deployment.

10.5 The Impact of Artificial Intelligence on Retail Businesses

AI is transforming the retail industry in terms of economics, finance, and the market. The utilization of AI improves customer satisfaction through virtual shopping assistants, personalized suggestions, and the streamlining of various processes such as inventory management and logistics. The significance of AI in the recovery phase post-COVID-19 is apparent, mainly through the implementation of advanced solutions like AI-powered devices that aid in upholding safety measures. Incorporating AI in the retail sector is restructuring operations, boosting competitiveness, and fostering economic advancement. AI is having an impact on retail businesses, including economic, financial, and market value (Table 10.5):

AI has a substantial impact on retail businesses, influencing their economic efficiency, financial performance, and market value. Retailers that exploit AI technologies gain a competitive advantage. However, the implementation of AI requires careful planning, data management. AI is reshaping the retail sector across a spectrum of economic, financial, and market facets. This assimilation of AI not only transforms retail functions but also fosters competitiveness and economic advancement, underscoring its significant influence on the industry's comprehensive restructuring and progression.

10.6 Artificial Intelligence and Manufacturing

The incorporation of AI within the realm of manufacturing yields substantial economic, financial, and market repercussions. AI is pivotal in augmenting productivity, diminishing errors, and reducing production expenses. Additionally, it enhances operational efficiency, bolsters quality assurance, and facilitates quicker entry of products into the market, thereby resulting in improved financial outcomes. Applying AI-powered predictive analysis diminishes operational downtimes, streamlines workflows, and furnishes crucial demand projections, thus positively influencing market competitiveness. Furthermore, deploying AI technologies in global supply chains elevates operational efficiency, curtails expenditures, and nurtures interactions among various network participants, consequently fostering economic growth. AI's involvement in the context

Table 10.5 Impact of artificial intelligence on retail businesses

Economic Impact	a. *Cost Reduction*: AI technologies such as machine learning and automation enable to streamline operational processes. This includes inventory management, supply chain optimization, and customer service. By reducing manual labor and improving efficiency, retailers can lower their operational costs b. *Personalized Marketing* (King, 2019): AI-driven algorithms analyze customer data to provide personalized product recommendations and targeted marketing campaigns. This personalization can increase customer engagement and drive higher sales c. *Inventory Management*: AI helps predict demand more accurately d. *Loss Prevention*: AI-powered surveillance systems detect theft and fraud in real-time e. *Customer Service*: Chatbots and virtual assistants powered by AI can handle routine customer inquiries and tasks, reducing the need for human customer service agents
Financial Impact	a. *Revenue Growth*: AI enables to improve customer targeting, optimize pricing strategies, and enhance the overall shopping experience b. *Profit Margins*: AI improves data-driven decisionst. This can result in improved profit margins c. *Fraud Detection*: AI helps in identifying fraudulent transactions d. *Credit Risk Assessment*: AI algorithms assess credit risk more accurately, helping retailers extend credit to customers with lower risk profiles and potentially increasing sales on credit
Market Value Impact	a. *Competitive Advantage*: Retailers that embrace AI can gain a competitive edge by offering superior customer experiences, optimized supply chains, and more efficient operations. This can lead to an increase in market share and valuation b. *Investor Confidence*: Companies that integrate AI into their retail operations attract more investors and enjoy a higher market valuation. AI is a driver of future growth and innovation c. *Customer Loyalty*: AI-driven personalization and recommendation fosters customer loyalty, which can positively impact market value d. *Data Assets*: Retailers collect vast amounts of data through AI applications. This data can have intrinsic value and can be monetized through data analytics or partnerships

of Industry 4.0 propels economic advancement by boosting productivity, engendering novel industries and employment opportunities, and facilitating the expansion of enterprises into uncharted markets. Nonetheless, apprehensions linger concerning AI's potential to exacerbate societal disparities, depress wages, and disrupt labor markets, underscoring the necessity for well-designed policies to mitigate adverse ramifications. AI has a significant impact on the manufacturing industry, transforming various aspects of operations and influencing economic, financial, and market value in the following ways (Table 10.6):

AI has a profound impact on the manufacturing industry, influencing economic efficiency, financial performance, and market value. Manufacturers that strategically implement AI technologies can improve their competitiveness, profitability, and market positioning. However, it's essential to invest in the right AI solutions, data management, and workforce training to fully realize these benefits.

10.7 Data Management, Processing, and Cloud Computing

AI significantly impacts data management, processing, and cloud computing. AI systems are employed to mimic professional decision-making processes using vast amounts of shared data, thereby enhancing data processing efficiency. Integrating AI into cloud data centers allows for intelligent automation operations management, improving algorithmic speed and data security. Within modern distributed computing systems such as Cloud Data Centers, AI-driven data-driven solutions in Resource Management Systems (RMS) enhance adaptability and efficiency, effectively tackling challenges in managing complex systems. A system for managing big data with AI in cloud computing improves the speed of data processing, classification, analysis, and management capabilities, facilitating swift data processing and efficient data organization. In general, AI transforms the handling, processing, and management of data in cloud environments, providing innovative solutions for efficient and secure operations. The integration of data management, processing, and cloud computing into AI has significant consequences on economic, financial, and market value creation. Here are some of the key impacts:

1. **Economic Growth and Efficiency**:
    - **Productivity Improvement**: AI-driven data management, with the scalability of cloud computing, boosts productivity. Automation leads to cost savings and increased efficiency.
    - **New Business Models**: AI and cloud computing enable the development of new business models. Companies can offer AI-powered services, such as subscription-based cloud services, creating new revenue streams.

Table 10.6 Artificial intelligence and manufacturing

Economic Impact	a. *Cost Reduction*: AI-powered automation and robotics can perform repetitive and labor-intensive tasks with high precision and efficiency. This reduces labor costs, minimizes errors, and enhances productivity b. *Predictive Maintenance*: AI-driven predictive maintenance systems can monitor the condition of machinery and equipment in real-time. This helps manufacturers detect potential issues early, preventing costly breakdowns and downtime c. *Supply Chain Optimization*: AI can optimize supply chain operations by predicting demand, improving inventory management, and optimizing logistics routes. This reduces excess inventory costs and transportation expenses d. *Quality Control*: AI-based computer vision systems can inspect products for defects more accurately than human operators, leading to reduced scrap and rework costs e. *Energy Efficiency*: AI algorithms can optimize energy consumption in manufacturing processes, resulting in reduced energy bills and a lower carbon footprint

(continued)

Table 10.6 (continued)

Financial Impact	a. *Revenue Growth*: AI can enhance product customization and quality, leading to higher customer satisfaction and increased sales. Additionally, AI-powered sales forecasting and pricing optimization can maximize revenue b. *Operational Efficiency*: By automating and streamlining processes, AI can improve operational efficiency, reducing production costs and increasing profit margins c. *Asset Utilization*: AI can optimize the use of manufacturing assets, such as machines and production lines, to ensure they are used to their full potential, thus improving return on investment d. *Risk Management*: AI can identify and mitigate risks in the manufacturing process, reducing potential financial losses due to disruptions or quality issues e. *R&D Acceleration*: AI can expedite research and development by simulating and testing product designs virtually, reducing the time and costs associated with physical prototyping
Market Value Impact	a. *Competitive Advantage*: Manufacturers that leverage AI technologies can gain a competitive edge by producing higher-quality products at lower costs and with shorter lead times. This can lead to increased market share and a stronger market position b. *Product Innovation*: AI can facilitate the development of innovative products and services, helping manufacturers differentiate themselves in the market and command higher prices c. *Customer Satisfaction*: Improved product quality and customization, enabled by AI, can enhance customer satisfaction and loyalty, potentially leading to higher market value through positive brand perception d. *Data Monetization*: Manufacturers can monetize the data generated by AI systems, selling insights or services to other businesses, or leveraging it for new revenue streams e. *Investor Confidence*: Companies that successfully integrate AI into their manufacturing processes often attract more investors and may experience a higher market valuation, as AI is associated with future growth potential and technological leadership

- **Job Creation**: While there are worries about job displacement, the AI and cloud computing sectors themselves create jobs.

2. **Financial Performance**:

- **Cost Reduction**: Cloud computing allows to scale up resources. This can lead to lower operational costs and improved profitability.
- **Revenue Growth**: AI-driven patterns enhance customer experiences. Personalized recommendations and targeted marketing, for example, can boost sales.
- **Risk Management**: AI can be used for risk assessment and fraud detection, helping financial institutions minimize losses and improve their overall financial performance.

3. **Market Value Creation**:

- **Competitive Advantage**: Companies that leverage AI and cloud computing gain a competitive advantage. This translates into higher market value.
- **Mergers and Acquisitions**: Companies with strong AI and cloud assets can command higher acquisition prices.
- **Startup Ecosystem**: AI and cloud computing can be combined, leading to a flourishing ecosystem of startups. These startups, often focused on AI-driven innovation, can reinvent traditional markets, and create opportunities for market value growth.

The mixed impact of AI, data management, processing, and cloud computing on various industries and regions is based on complementary aspects:

a. **Varied Consequences**: The impact of AI, data management, processing, and cloud computing can vary significantly depending on the industry and region.
b. **Benefits and Challenges**: These technologies offer substantial benefits, such as increased efficiency, data insights, and scalability. However, they also pose challenges, including data privacy concerns and ethical considerations related to AI, as well as the need for a skilled workforce proficient in AI and cloud technologies.

c. **Strategic Integration**: Successful integration of these technologies requires careful planning and investment.
d. **Transformative Forces**: AI, data management, and cloud computing drive economic growth, and create market value.

While AI, data management, and cloud computing offer significant opportunities for businesses and industries, they also necessitate thoughtful consideration of their implications and strategic planning to harness their full potential. These technologies are reshaping the business landscape and have the capacity to drive positive economic and financial outcomes when implemented effectively.

Edge computing (Sodhro et al., 2019) fosters AI adoption.

10.8 Education

AI is transforming education from an economic, financial, and market perspective. The economic implications of AI in the educational sector are considerable. Regarding finances, AI tools are known to improve teaching effectiveness, facilitate personalized learning experiences, and enhance assessment mechanisms, promoting a more inclusive and fair provision of high-quality education globally. From a market standpoint, incorporating AI technologies in education is associated with advancements in learning outcomes, tailored educational content, virtual learning environments, and innovative assessment procedures. The incorporation of AI-related education can have several impacts on economic, financial, and market valuation aspects (Table 10.7):

The inclusion of AI-related education can have far-reaching economic, financial, and market valuation implications. It can stimulate investments in AI education and technology.

As AI education continues to expand, it can exert a significant role in shaping the AI workforce.

10.9 The Metaverse

Using AI technologies such as large language models (LLMs) can enhance the quality of engagements with computational entities within virtual realms like the metaverse. These advanced AI models facilitate immersive and authentic encounters by effectively comprehending and responding to human interactions. Moreover, AI-driven avatars in the

Table 10.7 AI and education

Economic Impact	Skilled Workforce: Expanding AI education at all levels helps develop a more skilled and knowledgeable workforce. As AI technologies become increasingly important in various industries, having a workforce with AI expertise can lead to increased economic productivity and innovation Job Creation: A workforce educated in AI can lead to job creation in the AI sector itself, as well as in industries that leverage AI technologies. This can contribute to economic growth by expanding employment opportunities Global Competitiveness: Countries that prioritize AI education can enhance their global competitiveness in AI research, development, and applications. This can attract international investments and boost economic development
Financial Impact	Education Market: The inclusion of AI-related education in K-12 and postsecondary curricula can create new opportunities in the education market. Educational institutions and ed-tech companies that offer AI-related courses and resources may see increased revenue and financial growth Investment in AI Education: Governments, businesses, and philanthropic organizations may invest in AI education initiatives to promote digital literacy and AI skills. Such investments can have financial impacts on organizations and institutions involved in AI education

(continued)

Table 10.7 (continued)

Market Valuation Impact	Tech Industry Growth: AI-driven innovation and product development can attract investors and increase market capitalization Emerging Markets: Expanding AI education at the K-12 level can create a pipeline of talent in emerging markets. Companies may recognize these markets as sources of potential growth and market expansion, leading to higher valuations for businesses that invest in these regions AI Sector Growth: As AI education becomes more widespread, it can boost the AI sector. Increased demand for AI technologies and services can positively impact market valuations
Innovation and Entrepre-neurship	Startups: A well-educated workforce in AI leads to an increase in AI-focused startups that disrupt existing markets and contribute to innovation

metaverse can establish a feeling of social presence, thereby creating an illusion of interacting with independent entities, which fosters trust and active participation. Through the integration of AI, platforms within the metaverse can provide spatially enriched experiences, communal co-presence, and reliable interactions, ultimately transforming digital experiences and influencing the trajectory of user engagements within virtual environments. The impact of AI on the metaverse, a concept that envisions a three-dimensional, immersive internet experience akin to a globe-spanning video game, is multifaceted, covering economic, financial, and market value aspects:

a. **Enhanced User Experience and Interaction**: AI can significantly improve user experiences in the metaverse. This includes more realistic and responsive virtual environments, AI-driven non-player characters (NPCs) with advanced behaviors, and improved natural language processing for better interaction between users and AI entities. This leads to a more engaging and immersive experience, attracting a larger user base.
b. **Economic Opportunities**: The metaverse presents vast economic opportunities, especially in sectors like virtual real estate, digital commerce, and entertainment. AI can enhance these opportunities through personalized advertising, sophisticated market analysis, and the creation of unique, AI-generated virtual goods and experiences. This can lead to new revenue streams and business models that don't exist in the current internet framework.
c. **Financial Services and Transactions**: In the metaverse, financial transactions might take the form of cryptocurrencies or other digital currencies. AI can play a crucial role in securing these transactions, detecting fraud, and managing complex financial operations at scale. Moreover, AI can aid in the development of new financial products and services tailored for the virtual world.
d. **Market Value and Investment**: The integration of AI into the metaverse is likely to increase its overall market value, attracting investments from tech giants and venture capitalists. The unique combination of AI and virtual environments can lead to innovative products and services, potentially revolutionizing various industries and creating new markets.

e. **Data Analysis and Insights**: AI's ability to analyze vast amounts of data will be invaluable in understanding user behavior, preferences, and trends in the metaverse. This can inform business strategies, content creation, and marketing efforts, leading to more targeted and effective approaches.
f. **Challenges and Ethical Considerations**: While AI brings numerous advantages, it also presents challenges, particularly in areas like privacy, data security, and ethical use of AI. Ensuring responsible use of AI in the metaverse will be crucial to maintaining user trust and complying with legal and ethical standards.
g. **Job Creation and Transformation**: The AI-driven metaverse could create new jobs in AI development, virtual environment design, and digital asset creation. However, it might also transform or displace existing jobs, necessitating a focus on education and training for the skills needed in this new digital landscape.

AI's role in shaping the metaverse is significant, with the potential to transform economic models, create new market opportunities, and change the way financial and business operations are conducted in a virtual, immersive world. The intersection of AI and the metaverse presents a dynamic and rapidly evolving field with broad implications for society and the global economy.

References

Alsaleh, S., Tepljakov, A., Tamre, M., & Petlenkov, E. (2021). Towards artificial intelligence driven immersive environments in virtual reality for industrial applications. *2021 44th International Conference on Telecommunications and Signal Processing (TSP)* (pp. 340–345).

Giudici, P., Centurelli, M., & Turchetta, S. (2024). Artificial intelligence risk measurement. *Expert Systems with Applications, 235*, 121220.

Goyal, R., Khosla, C., Sood, M., Singh, K., Punam, K., & Goyal, K. (2022). A review on artificial intelligence driven biomedical engineering implants in healthcare. *2022 2nd International Conference on Advance Computing and Innovative Technologies in Engineering (ICACITE)* (pp. 1705–1708).

Guo, K., Wu, M., Soo, Z., Yang, Y., Zhang, Y., Zhang, Q., Lin, H., Grosser, M., Venter, D., Zhang, G., & Lu, J. (2023). Artificial intelligence-driven biomedical genomics. *Knowledge-Based Systems, 279*, https://doi.org/10.1016/j.knosys.2023.110937

Hasselgren, C., & Oprea, T. I. (2024). Artificial intelligence for drug discovery: Are we there yet? *Annual Review of Pharmacology and Toxicology, 64*, 527–550.

Jakšič, M., & Marinč, M. (2019). Relationship banking and information technology: The role of artificial intelligence and FinTech. *Risk Management, 21*, 1–18.

King, K. (2019). *Using artificial intelligence in marketing: How to harness AI and maintain the competitive edge*. Kogan Page Publishers.

Li, B., Chai, X., Hou, B., Zhang, L., Zhou, J., & Liu, Y. (2018). New generation artificial intelligence-driven intelligent manufacturing (NGAIIM). *2018 IEEE SmartWorld, Ubiquitous Intelligence & Computing, Advanced & Trusted Computing, Scalable Computing & Communications, Cloud & Big Data Computing, Internet of People and Smart City Innovation (SmartWorld/SCALCOM/UIC/ATC/CBDCom/IOP/SCI)* (pp. 1864–1869).

Moro-Visconti, R. (2021). *Startup valuation*. Palgrave Macmillan.

Moro-Visconti, R. (2022a). *The valuation of digital intangibles. Technology, marketing, and the metaverse*, Palgrave Macmillan.

Moro-Visconti, R. (2022b). *Augmented corporate valuation*. Palgrave Macmillan.

Schrettenbrunnner, M. B. (2020, June). Artificial-intelligence-driven management. *IEEE Engineering Management Review, 48*(2), 15–19, 1 Second quarter.

Sodhro, A. H., Pirbhulal, S., & de Albuquerque, V. H. C., (2019, July). Artificial intelligence-driven mechanism for edge computing-based industrial applications. *IEEE Transactions on Industrial Informatics, 15*(7), 4235–4243.

Tiwari, P. C., Pal, R., Chaudhary, M. J., & Nath, R. (2023). Artificial intelligence revolutionizing drug development: Exploring opportunities and challenges. *Drug Development Research, 84*(8), 1652–1663.

Yang, T., Yi, X., Lu, S., Johansson, K. H., & Chai, T. (2021). Intelligent manufacturing for the process industry driven by industrial artificial intelligence. *Engineering, 7*(9), 1224–1230.

Younis, H. A., Eisa, T. A. E., Nasser, M., Sahib, T. M., Noor, A. A., Alyasiri, O. M., & Younis, H. A. (2024). A systematic review and meta-analysis of artificial intelligence tools in medicine and healthcare: Applications, considerations, limitations, motivation and challenges. *Diagnostics, 14*(1), 109.

Wan, J., Li, X., Dai, N., Kusiak, A., Martínez-García, M., & Li, D. (2021, April). Artificial-intelligence-driven customized manufacturing factory: Key technologies, applications, and challenges. *Proceedings of the IEEE, 109*(4), 377–398.

CHAPTER 11

Artificial Intelligence Valuation: Empirical Cases and Templates

11.1 C3.AI

C3.AI, Inc., commonly known as C3 AI, is a listed AI software company. C3 AI has developed a business model that revolves around delivering AI solutions tailored for diverse sectors, encompassing education, healthcare, and bioeconomy. It was founded in 2009 and has since established itself as a leader in providing AI solutions for various industries:

Founding and Core Offerings

- **Founded in 2009:** The company was established by Thomas Siebel.
- **AI Software:** C3 AI specializes in proprietary, model-driven AI architecture that enhances data science and application development.
- **Machine Learning and Neural Networks:** Its software utilizes these technologies to address complex analytical challenges in diverse sectors including commerce, industry, and government.
- **Software Applications:** C3 AI's software finds applications in optimizing operations, reducing costs, improving employee safety, and detecting fraud.

R. Moro-Visconti, *Artificial Intelligence Valuation*,
https://doi.org/10.1007/978-3-031-53622-9_11

Services and Customer Base

- **Enterprise AI Applications:** C3 AI provides over 40 turnkey Enterprise AI applications catering to the critical needs of global enterprises across various sectors such as manufacturing, financial services, government, utilities, oil and gas, chemicals, agribusiness, defense, and intelligence.
- **Customer Base:** The company serves large energy, industrial, and government customers.
- **Strategic Partnerships:** It has formed strategic collaborations with notable companies like Baker Hughes, FIS, Raytheon, AWS, Intel, Google, and Microsoft.

Product Portfolio

- **C3 AI Platform:** This is an end-to-end platform for developing, deploying, and operating enterprise AI applications.
- **C3 AI Applications:** A portfolio of industry-specific SaaS (Software as a Service) enterprise AI applications designed to facilitate the digital transformation of organizations.
- **Global Operations:** C3.ai, Inc. operates not only in North America but also in Europe, the Middle East, Africa, the Asia Pacific, and other international regions.

Business Model and Solutions

- **Software as a Service Applications:** The company specializes in SaaS applications enabling rapid development, deployment, and operation of large-scale Enterprise AI applications across any infrastructure.
- **Divisions:** It offers solutions under three main divisions, with the C3 AI Suite being a comprehensive solution for enterprise AI needs.

C3 AI's focus on AI-driven solutions across various industries and its global reach makes it a significant player in the enterprise AI software landscape.

This business valuation report (with data and graphs extracted from Valutico.com—a leading valuation software powered with external databases sources and AI, as of December 1st, 2023) shows the following valuation procedures (mostly described in Chapter 2):

- DCF Entity Method
  - WACC
  - APV
  - FCFF
- DCF Equity Method
  - FCFE
- Income Approach
- Trading multiples
- Transaction
- DDM

These valuation approaches are described in Damodaran (1996), Damodaran (2018), Fazzini (2018), Fernandez (2001), Koller and Goedhart (2015). Singh (2013). Business planning is described in Moro-Visconti (2019).

Synthesis of the Valuation Methods

Figure 11.1 (sourced by valutico.com) provides an overview of valuation ranges and midpoints based on different valuation methods:

Business Plan

The Business plan, based on past public data and internal projections from valutico.com, is a prerequisite of the economic, financial, and market valuation (as shown in Chapter 2) since it contains an estimate of the future cash flows (for DCF analysis), average expected EBITDA (for market comparisons), etc.

Some contents are readapted mostly from Moro-Visconti (2022a), or, occasionally, Moro-Visconti (2022b), or Moro-Visconti (2021), extending digital intangible, startup, or business planning applications to specific AI valuation patterns.

The business plan (sourced by valutico.com) reflects the current best estimate for the future development of the company's most important financial figures and forms the basis for all further valuation analyses, as shown in Table 11.1.

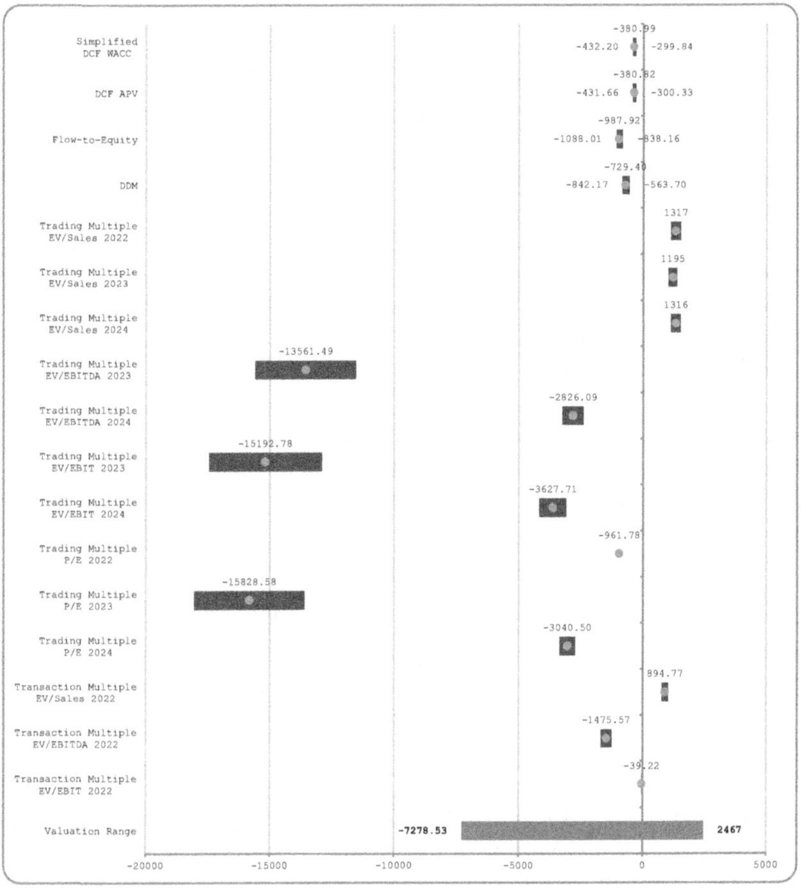

Fig. 11.1 Average valuation metrics

The estimated growth rates (once again, sourced by valutico.com) of the key income statement parameters and the economic margins are reported in Table 11.2.

Table 11.1 C3 AI - Business plan key figures

	2022	*2023*	*2024*	*2025*	*2026*	*2027*	*2028*	*2029*
Sales	252.8	266.8	307.5	368.1	452.1	601.8	859.0	1051.2
% growth	38.0	5.6	15.3	19.7	22.8	33.1	42.8	22.4
EBITDA	−191.6	−285.5	−76.6	−33.3	25.5	50.1	91.7	112.3
% margin	−75.8	−107.0	−24.9	−9.0	5.6	8.3	10.7	10.7
Depreciation & Amortization	4.5	5.0	10.4	4.6	5.6	7.5	10.7	13.1
% of Sales	1.8	1.9	3.4	1.2	1.2	1.2	1.2	1.2
EBIT	−196.1	−290.5	−87.0	−37.8	19.9	42.5	81.0	99.1
% margin	−77.6	−108.9	−28.3	−10.3	4.4	7.1	9.4	9.4
Net Income	−192.1	−268.8	−48.2	4.2	53.2	75.7	108.1	132.2
% margin	−76.0	−100.8	−15.7	1.1	11.8	12.6	12.6	12.6
Capex	3.8	70.5	36.4	27.7	40.2	50.0	62.0	44.8
% of Sales	1.5	26.4	11.8	7.5	8.9	8.3	7.2	4.3
Accounts Receivable	80.4	134.9	155.6	186.2	228.7	304.4	434.5	531.7
Days Sales Outstanding	116	185	185	185	185	185	185	185
Inventories	0.0	0.0	0.0	0.0	0.0	0.0	0.0	0.0
Days Sales of Inventory	0	0	0	0	0	0	0	0
Accounts Payable	54.2	24.6	17.1	17.9	19.0	24.6	34.2	41.8
Days Payable Outstanding	45	16	16	16	16	16	16	16
Cash & cash equivalents	992.2	812.4	936.5	1120.9	1376.6	1832.3	2615.7	3200.9
Debt	30.5	39.7	0.0	0.0	0.0	0.0	0.0	0.0

Table 11.2 Growth Rates and Economic Profitability Margins

Growth	*2022 (%)*	*2023 (%)*	*2024 (%)*	*2025 (%)*	...	*2029 (%)*	*TY (%)*
Sales growth	38.0	5.6	15.3	19.7		22.4	2.0
EBITDA growth		49.0	−73.2	−56.6		22.4	2.0
EBIT growth		48.1	−70.1	−56.5		22.4	2.0
Net income growth		40.0	−82.1	−108.7		22.4	2.0
Margins	*2022 (%)*	*2023 (%)*	*2024 (%)*	*2025 (%)*	...	*2029 (%)*	*TY (%)*
EBITDA margins	−75.8	−107.0	−24.9	−9.0		10.7	10.7
EBIT margins (return on sales)	−77.6	−108.9	−28.3	−10.3		9.4	9.4
Net income margins	−76.0	−100.8	−15.7	1.1		12.6	12.6
Profitability - Du Pont Analysis	*2022*	*2023*	*2024*	*2025*	...	*2029*	*TY*
Asset turnover (Sales/Assets)	5.81x	2.61x	2.40x	2.43x		3.38x	3.44x
x Profitability (Net income/Sales) (%)	−76.0	−100.8	−15.7	1.1		12.6	12.6
= Return on Assets (ROA) (%)	−441.3	−263.2	−37.6	2.8		42.5	43.2
x Leverage (Assets/Equity) (%)	4.4	11.0	14.5	17.1		30.7	30.7
= Return on Equity (ROE) (%)	−19.4	−28.9	−5.5	0.5		13.0	13.3
Profitability - ROCE	*2022*	*2023*	*2024*	*2025*	...	*2029*	*TY*
Fixed assets	43.5	102.2	128.1	151.2		311.2	311.9
Working capital	26.2	110.3	138.4	168.3		489.9	499.7
Capital employed	1062.0	1024.9	1203.0	1440.4		4002.0	4076.5
EBIT	−196.1	−290.5	−87.0	−37.8		99.1	101.1
- Tax	41.2	61.0	18.3	7.9		−20.8	−21.2
NOPAT	−154.9	−229.5	−68.7	−29.9		78.3	79.9
ROCE (NOPAT / Avg. Capital Employed) (%)		−22.0	−6.2	−2.3		2.1	2.0

Competitors

An analysis of the main competitors, again extracted from the valutico.com AI database, is reported in Table 11.3. It should be remembered, as anticipated in Chapter 2, that:

- EV/Sales compares the Enterprise Value of the firm (market value, including financial debt) to the sales;
- EV/EBITDA is the main parameter for comparability, as it shows the market value of competitors; it should be remembered that EV/EBITDA$_{\text{competitors - average}}$ * normalized EBITDA of the target firm = expected EV of the firm;
- EV/EBIT is complementary to the return on sales and EV/sales;
- The price-earnings ratio represents the market value of the listed company over its expected earnings (net profit);
- The price/book value reflects the market value of (listed) equity over its book (accounting) value.

WACC

The discount factors (sourced, once again from valutico.com) are mainly pre-ordinated at estimating the WACC to be used in the discount of expected Free cash Flows to the Firm (FCFF), to estimate the enterprise value, as shown in Chapter 2 (Fig. 11.2).

The main assumptions for the Simplified DCF WACC methodology are the following:

- WACC 12.6%
- G (long term growth rate) 2%
- CAPEX (Depreciation & amortization in terminal year) 105%

A sensitivity analysis (valutico.com) varies the weighted cost of capital and the perpetual growth rate to derive a valuation range, as shown in Table 11.4.

Table 11.3 Main Competitors

	Country	*EV/Sales*			*EV/EBITDA*			*EV/EBIT*			*P/E*			*P/Book Value*
		2022	*2023*	*2024*	*2022*	*2023*	*2024*	*2022*	*2023*	*2024*	*2022*	*2023*	*2024*	*2022*
Domo, Inc	US	1.60x	1.34x	1.30x			36.9x			93.9x				
Datadog, Inc	US	22.25x	17.71x	14.60x		74.6x	62.0x		81.9x	66.9x		71.4x	60.8x	36.6x
Jamf Holding Corp	US	4.74x	4.06x	3.54x		61.1x	44.0x		51.1x	33.5x		52.1x	36.1x	
JFrog Ltd	US	8.64x	7.00x	5.74x		49.9x	37.6x		72.6x	47.3x		58.5x	50.1x	8.4x
Alteryx, Inc	US	3.96x	3.54x	3.18x		24.4x	18.8x		32.8x	24.1x		40.1x	30.9x	
Momentive Global Inc	US	3.02x												
Sumo Logic, Inc	US	4.76x	3.83x											5.0x
Vertex, Inc	US	8.91x	7.77x	6.87x		45.1x	35.8x		53.4x	41.7x		72.1x	50.3x	
Appian Corporation	US	5.65x	4.89x	4.28x										23.3x
Disco Parent, Inc	US	7.58x												8.7x
Asana, Inc	US	11.97x	8.28x	7.01x										23.5x
Pegasystems Inc	US	3.61x	3.46x	3.21x		23.8x	15.9x		29.8x	17.1x		31.1x	19.8x	
Median		5.21x	4.48x	4.28x		47.5x	36.9x		52.3x	41.7x		55.3x	43.1x	16.0x
Software		2.75x	2.63x	2.50x	15.6x	14.7x	14.1x	18.5x	20.5x	17.9x	27.7x	30.0x	25.5x	3.7x
Discount/Premium to Median (%)		0	0	0	-	0	0	-	0	0	-	0	0	0
Applied metrics		5.21x	4.48x	4.28x		47.5x	36.9x		52.3x	41.7x		55.3x	43.1x	16.0x

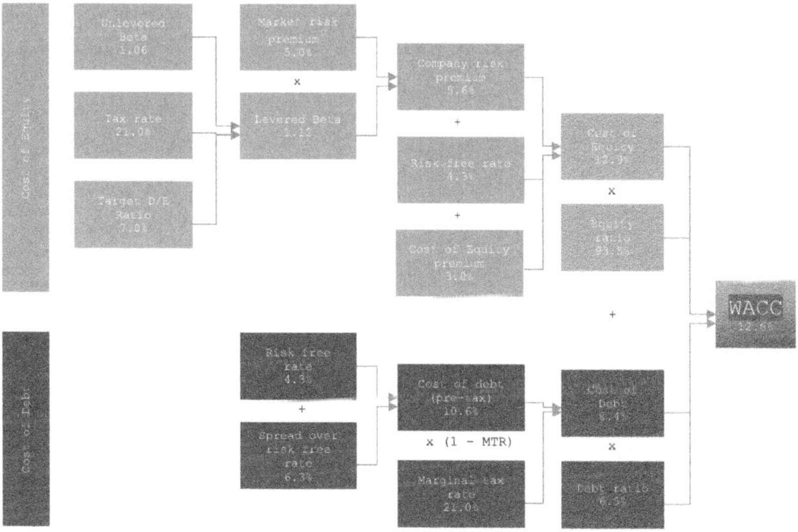

Fig. 11.2 WACC derivation

Enterprise and Equity Value

The calculation of the Enterprise Value (and the residual Equity Value, sourced by valutico.com) is reported in Table 11.5.

The WACC sensitivity (valutico.com) is important, as it describes the potential changes in valuation mostly induced by external factors (interest rates; country risk, etc.), and is sensitive to the perpetual growth rate (Table 11.6).

The DCF-APV methodology, described in Chapter 2, is conceptually like the DCF WACC method. However, in the APV method, the company is hypothetically rated as unleveraged and the value of the tax savings from the debt ("tax shield") is valued and added separately.

The model shown in Table 11.7 is based on valutico.com assumptions, and free cash flow calculations, eventually bringing to the enterprise and equity value.

The Simplified Flow to Equity approach (FCFE) is a discounted cash flow method in which the equity value is determined by discounting the cash flows to which the equity holders are entitled. It is conceptually like the Operating Discounted Cash Flow Analysis ('FCFF - DCF')

Table 11.4 Sensitivity Analysis

	2023	*2024*	*2025*	*2026*	*2027*	*2028*	*2029*	*TY*
Sales	266.8	307.5	368.1	452.1	601.8	859.0	1051.2	1072.2
EBIT	−290.5	−87.0	−37.8	19.9	42.5	81.0	99.1	101.1
- Tax	61.0	18.3	7.9	−4.2	−8.9	−17.0	−20.8	−21.2
NOPAT	−229.5	−68.7	−29.9	15.7	33.6	64.0	78.3	79.9
+ Depreciation & Amortization	5.0	10.4	4.6	5.6	7.5	10.7	13.1	13.4
- Capex	−70.5	−36.4	−27.7	−40.2	−50.0	−62.0	−44.8	−14.1
± Change in Net Working Capital	−84.1	−28.1	−29.9	−41.4	−70.1	−120.5	−89.6	−9.8
Free Cashflow to the Firm	−379.1	−122.8	−82.9	−60.2	−79.0	−107.8	−43.0	69.4
Time	0.5	1.5	2.5	3.5	4.5	5.5	6.5	
Discount Factor	0.94	0.84	0.74	0.66	0.59	0.52	0.46	
Discounted Free Cashflow	−357.3	−102.8	−61.6	−39.8	−46.3	−56.1	−19.9	302.8

Table 11.5 Enterprise Value and Equity Value

Present value of Discounted Free Cashflows	−683.7
Present value of Terminal Value (1.0% included)	302.8
Enterprise Value	−381.0
Net Debt	961.8
Equity Value	580.8

Table 11.6 WACC sensitivity

		Perpetual growth rate ('g')				
	(%)	0.0	1.0	2.0	3.0	4.0
Weighted Average Cost of Capital ('WACC')	10.6	−367.2	−331.7	−288.0	−232.9	−161.0
	11.6	−402.1	−374.5	−341.0	**−299.8**	−247.8
	12.6	−429.0	−407.1	−381.0	−349.5	−310.6
	13.6	−449.9	**−432.2**	−411.5	−386.8	−357.1
	14.6	−466.0	−451.6	−434.9	−415.3	−392.0

but provides the equity value instead of the enterprise value, as shown in Table 11.8, sourced by valutico.com.

Dividend Discount Model

The dividend discount model (also described in Chapter 2) is—like the flow to equity method—an approach in which the equity value is determined by discounting the projected dividends. It is therefore conceptually like the Discounted Cash Flows Analysis ('DCF'). The figures, sourced by valutico.com, are reported in Table 11.9.

Capitalized Earnings

The Capitalized Earnings Method is an income-based approach. It assumes that the current, normalized benefit stream (earnings or free cash flow) can be maintained in the future and capitalizes it using the capitalization rate (either WACC or Cost of Equity less perpetual growth rate).

This approach is theoretically equivalent to performing a discounted cash flow analysis with the assumption that forecast growth equals the perpetual growth rate and margins remain constant. The current benefit

Table 11.7 From Free cash flow calculations to enterprise and equity value

Assumptions								
								(%)
Cost of Equity ('CoE')								12.6
Long-term growth rate ('g')								2.0
Bankruptcy cost (as % of the EV)								0.0
Probability of bankruptcy								0.0
	2023	*2024*	*2025*	*2026*	*2027*	*2028*	*2029*	*TY*
Free Cashflow	−379.1	−122.8	−82.9	−60.2	−79.0	−107.8	−43.0	69.4
Time	0.5	1.5	2.5	3.5	4.5	5.5	6.5	
Discount Factor	0.94	0.84	0.74	0.66	0.59	0.52	0.46	
Discounted Free Cashflow	−357.3	−102.8	−61.6	−39.7	−46.3	−56.0	−19.8	301.4
								(%)
Present value of Discounted Free Cashflows					−683.4			178.9
Present value of Terminal Value (1.0% included)					301.4			−78.9
Unlevered Enterprise Value					−382.0			100.0
	2023	*2024*	*2025*	*2026*	*2027*	*2028*	*2029*	*TY*
Debt	39.7	0.0	0.0	0.0	0.0	0.0	0.0	0.0
Debt / EBITDA	−0.1	0.0	0.0	0.0	0.0	0.0	0.0	0.0
Interest rate (%)	10.6	10.6	10.6	10.6	10.6	10.6	10.6	
Interest expense	4.2	2.1	0.0	0.0	0.0	0.0	0.0	0.0

	2023	*2024*	*2025*	*2026*	*2027*	*2028*	*2029*	*TY*
Tax rate (%)	21.0	21.0	21.0	21.0	21.0	21.0	21.0	
Tax shield on interest	0.9	0.4	0.0	0.0	0.0	0.0	0.0	0.0
Time	0.5	1.5	2.5	3.5	4.5	5.5	6.5	
Discount Factor	0.94	0.84	0.74	0.66	0.59	0.52	0.46	
Discounted Tax shield	0.8	0.4	0.0	0.0	0.0	0.0	0.0	0.0
Present value of Projected Tax Shields					1.2			
Present value of Terminal Year Tax Shield					0.0			
Value of Tax shield					1.2			
Bankruptcy Cost					0.0			
Enterprise Value					−380.8			
Net Debt					961.8			
Equity Value					581.0			

		Perpetual growth rate ('g')				
	(%)	0.0	1.0	2.0	3.0	4.0
Unlevered Cost of Equity ('COE')	10.6	−367.1	−332.0	−288.6	−234.0	−162.8
	11.6	−401.8	−374.3	−341.2	**−300.3**	−248.8
	12.6	−428.5	−406.7	−380.8	−349.5	−311.0
	13.6	−449.2	**−431.7**	−411.1	−386.6	−357.1
	14.6	−465.2	−450.9	−434.3	−414.9	−391.8

Table 11.8 Free Cash Flow to Equity and Equity Value

Assumptions								
								(%)
Cost of Equity ('CoE')								12.9
Long-term growth rate ('g')								2.0
	2023	*2024*	*2025*	*2026*	*2027*	*2028*	*2029*	*TY*
Net Income	−268.8	−48.2	4.2	53.2	75.7	108.1	132.2	134.9
- Capex	70.5	36.4	27.7	40.2	50.0	62.0	44.8	14.1
+ Depreciation & Amortization	5.0	10.4	4.6	5.6	7.5	10.7	13.1	13.4
± Change in Net Working Capital	−84.1	−28.1	−29.9	−41.4	−70.1	−120.5	−89.6	−9.8
Sub-total	−149.7	−54.1	−53.0	−75.9	−112.6	−171.8	−121.3	−10.5
x (1 - 6.5% Debt ratio)	−139.9	−50.6	−49.5	−71.0	−105.3	−160.6	−113.4	−9.8
Free Cashflow to Equity (FCFE)	−408.8	−98.8	−45.3	−17.8	−29.6	−52.6	18.9	125.1
Time	0.5	1.5	2.5	3.5	4.5	5.5	6.5	6.5
Discount Factor	0.94	0.83	0.74	0.65	0.58	0.51	0.45	0.45
Discounted FCFE	−384.7	−82.4	−33.5	−11.6	−17.1	−27.0	8.6	521.6
Present value of discounted FCFEs					−547.7			
Present value of Terminal Value (1.0% included)					521.6			
Equity Value					−26.1			
Net Debt					961.8			
Enterprise Value					−987.9			

	Perpetual growth rate ('g')				
(%)	0.0	1.0	2.0	3.0	4.0

		Perpetual growth rate ('g')				
Cost of Equity ('COE')	10.9	−934.8	−875.6	−803.1	−712.3	−595.2
	11.9	−1008.8	−962.3	−906.5	**−838.2**	−752.5
	12.9	−1068.8	−1031.7	−987.9	−935.2	−870.7
	13.9	−1117.9	**−1088.0**	−1053.0	−1011.6	−961.9
	14.9	−1153.6	−1134.1	−1105.8	−1072.8	−1033.7

Table 11.9 Dividend Discount Model

Assumptions	(%)
Cost of Equity ('CoE')	12.9
Long-term growth rate ('g')	2.0
Payout rate	100.0

	2023	*2024*	*2025*	*2026*	*2027*	*2028*	*2029*	*TY*
Net Income	−268.8	−48.2	4.2	53.2	75.7	108.1	132.2	134.9
Dividend	−192.1	−268.8	−48.2	4.2	53.2	75.7	108.1	132.2
Time	0.5	1.5	2.5	3.5	4.5	5.5	6.5	
Discount Factor	0.94	0.83	0.74	0.65	0.58	0.51	0.45	
Discounted Dividend	−180.8	−224.1	−35.6	2.7	30.8	38.8	49.1	551.4
Present value of discounted dividends					−319.0			
Present value of Terminal Value (1.0% included)					551.4			
Equity Value					232.4			
Net Debt					961.8			
Enterprise Value					−729.4			

		Perpetual growth rate ('g')				
	(%)	0.0	1.0	2.0	3.0	4.0
Cost of Equity	10.9	−658.0	−595.4	−518.8	−422.8	−299.0
	11.9	−744.1	−695.0	−636.0	**−563.7**	−473.1
	12.9	−814.9	−775.7	−729.4	−673.7	−605.5
	13.9	−873.8	**−842.2**	−805.2	−761.5	−708.9
	14.9	−923.4	−897.5	−867.6	−832.6	−791.3

Table 11.10 Equity and Enterprise Value deriving from Capitalized Earnings

Net Income	−192.1
Adjustments	0.0
Normalized earnings	−192.1
Discount rate (CoE) (%)	12.9
- Growth rate (%)	2.0
Capitalization rate (%)	10.9
Equity Value	−1797.3
Net Debt	−961.8
Enterprise Value	−2759.1

		Perpetual growth rate (g)				
	(%)	0.0	1.0	2.0	3.0	4.0
Cost of Equity	10.9	−2723.8	−2921.2	−3163.0	−3465.9	−3856.7
	11.9	−2575.8	−2741.5	−2940.6	**−3184.6**	−3490.2
	12.9	−2450.7	−2591.9	−2759.1	−2960.0	−3206.1
	13.9	−2343.5	**−2465.5**	−2608.1	−2776.7	−2979.4
	14.9	−2250.8	−2357.4	−2480.4	−2624.2	−2794.3

stream can be normalized or adjusted to arrive at a sustainable benefit stream. Table 11.10 (valutico.com) shows the results.

Trading Multiples

The 'Comparable Company Analysis approach is a valuation method based on the idea that similar companies should also have similar valuations, as shown in Chapter 2. The value ratio relative to a company-specific ratio (sales, EBITDA, EBIT, net income, etc.) is similar within an industry and geographic region. Relative valuation models are an alternative to the absolute valuation model (e.g., DCF, also described in Chapter 2) that determines intrinsic enterprise value by discounting expected future cash flows.

The expected results for 2024 (accompanied by the historical performance and other projections consistent with the business plan, as calculated by valutico.com) are synthesized in the following figures, taken from valutico.com.

The discount on listed trading multiples is calculated following a qualitative assessment that is based on several weighted parameters. A simulation (extracted from valutico.com) is contained in Table 11.11.

Table 11.11 Discount on listed trading multiples

	Weights %	*100% weights*	*50% weights*	*0% weights*
General				
Company Size	35			
Positioning	2			
Market				
Market Size	3			
Market Growth	3			
Market Share	2			
Competition	5			
Exposure To Business Cycle	2			
Exposure To Political Legal Factors	1			
Management				
Management Quality	5			
Reliance On Key Persons	5			
Sales				
Reliance On Key Customers	5			
Reliance On Distribution Partners	2			
Customer Lock-In	2			
Purchasing				
Input Cost Risk	2			
Reliance On Key Suppliers	2			
Product				
Product Quality	3			
Innovativeness	3			
Intellectual Property Protection	3			
Risk Of Technological Disruption	2			
Financial				
Capital Intensity	2			
Leverage	10			
Foreign Exchange/Currency Risk	1			
Risk Factor		1	3	5
Cost of Equity Premium		0	5	10
Discount to Trading Multiples		0	−30	−60

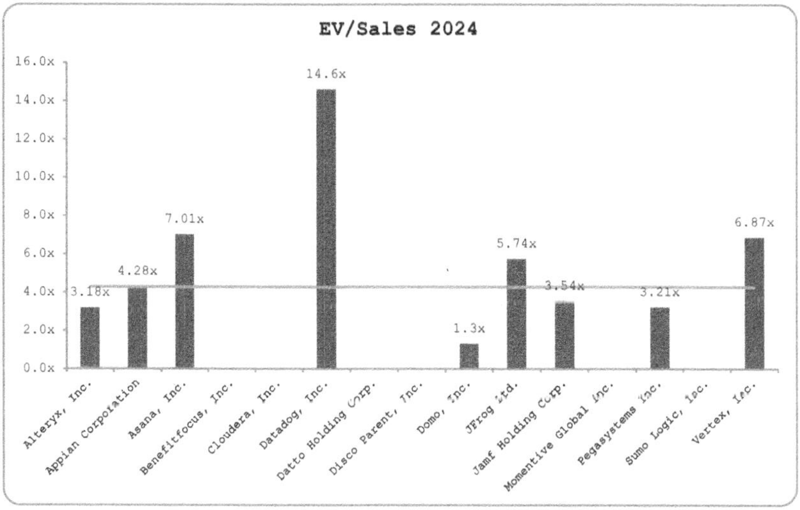

Fig. 11.3 EV/sales

The main market valuation ratios (from valutico.com) are reported in Figs. 11.3, 11.4, and 11.5.

Transaction Multiples

Transaction multiples valuation, introduced in Chapter 2, considers the sales of companies whose business model is like the one being valued. Transaction multiples are usually used for plausibility in conjunction with other valuation methods—such as e.g., DCF or trade multiples—used. Multiples may be affected by many factors, such as scarcity or attractiveness of a particular industry. In general, however, higher multiples can be seen in fast growing industries, as shown in Table 11.12.

The chart of the listed price of C3.AI versus the NASDAQ and the World Stock Index are reported in Fig. 11.6.

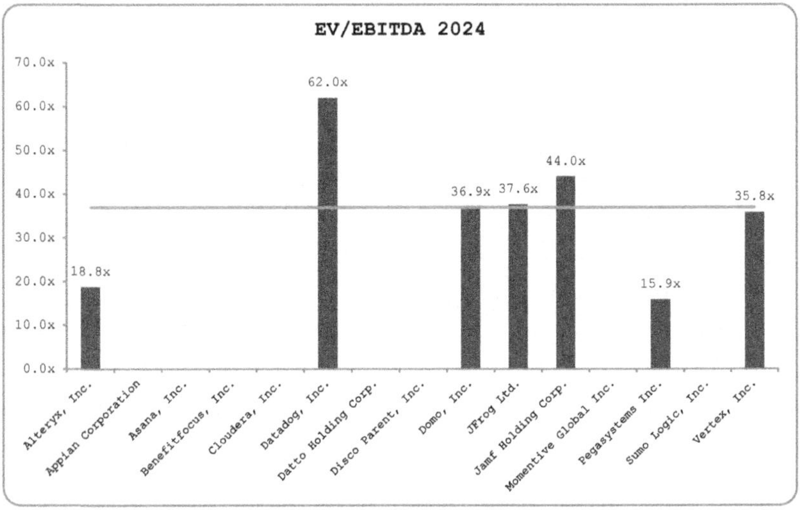

Fig. 11.4 EV/EBITDA

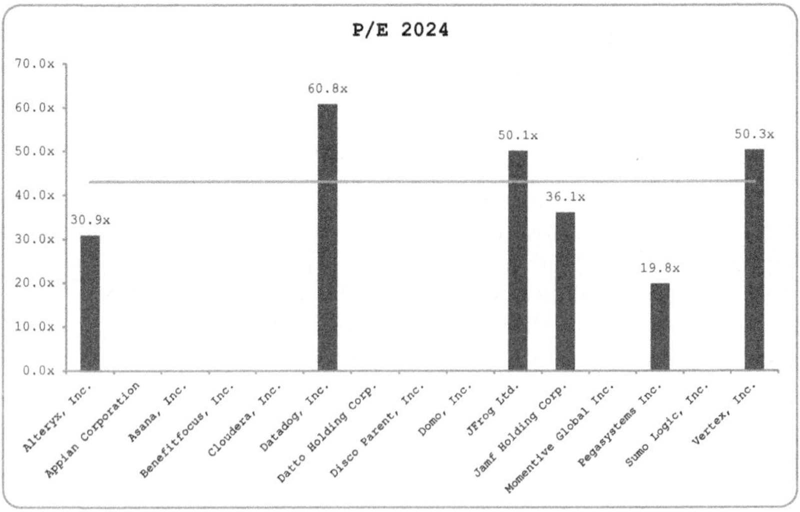

Fig. 11.5 Price Earnings

Table 11.12 Transaction Multiples based on Target Companies

	EV/Sales	*EV/EBITDA*	*EV/EBIT*	*P/E*
Median	3.5x	7.7x	0.2x	–
Software	2.3x	13.9x	16.7x	25.7x
Discount / Premium to Median (%)	0	1	0	–
Applied metrics	3.5x	7.7x	0.2x	0.0x

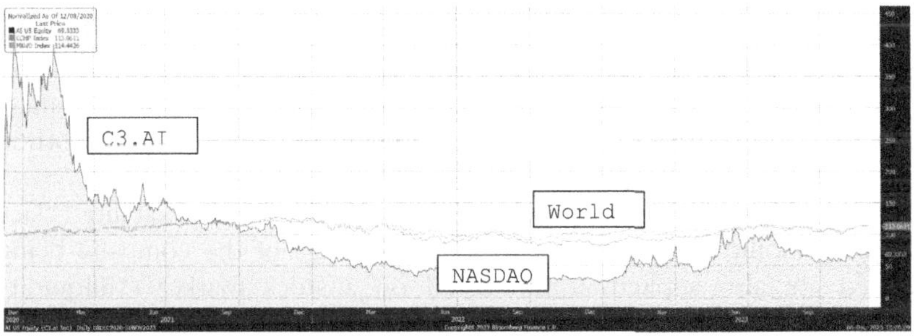

Fig. 11.6 C3.AI stock price versus the NASDAQ and the World Index

EBITDA-Driven Firm Valuation Benchmarking: Market Multiplier Discounts for Unlisted Comparables

EBITDA-driven firm valuation benchmarking for unlisted comparables involves adjusting the EBITDA multiples used to value these companies based on various factors that affect their marketability and risk profile. These adjustments are necessary because unlisted (private) firms typically trade at lower multiples compared to their listed counterparts due to factors like illiquidity and limited information availability. Managers' emphasis on EBITDA often results in an excessive allocation of resources towards capital and debt, consequently diminishing the firm's value in comparison to its industry counterparts. AI investments may yield contrasting outcomes despite the direct impact of EBITDA and individual investor trading on firm valuation. EBITDA-centric firm valuation benchmarking for private comparables engaging in AI entails evaluating the influence of AI investments on firm worth. Organizations that embrace AI technologies have exhibited resilience amid turbulent periods such as the COVID-19 crisis, as AI-related stocks have demonstrated expedited recovery compared to traditional stocks, underscoring AI's pivotal role as a catalyst for enduring operational efficiency. Integration of external data and advanced machine learning methodologies can enrich corporate valuation frameworks, wherein techniques like Gaussian Process Regression offer precise outcomes for establishing benchmarks for corporate value and evaluating default risk. Through the utilization of EBITDA and market multiplier concessions, unlisted enterprises investing in AI can effectively scrutinize their performance and competitive positioning within the marketplace.

In corporate valuations, based on empirical market multiples and comparable transactions, it is generally necessary to apply a size discount to the identified multiple, in consideration of the circumstances concerning the imperfect homogeneity of the sample considered, both in terms of size corporate and reference market.

In this context, discounts relating to the limited transferability ("lack of marketability discount") of the shareholdings of the company being valued are also applied, if not listed on a stock market ("illiquidity discount").

Illiquidity Discount for Lack of Marketability

The impact of illiquidity discount on the pricing of securities in private investments is substantial as it reflects the compensation sought by investors for the absence of immediate marketability and potential foregone trading opportunities. This discount's variation is contingent upon investors' perceived skill levels, where more proficient investors command higher discounts due to the increased opportunity costs associated with capital commitment. The duration of the trading restriction period is also a critical factor in determining the extent of the illiquidity discount, particularly in cases where the liquidity horizon is uncertain or undefined. Integrating illiquidity constraints into pricing models can lead to a notable reduction in non-marketability discounts, underscoring the significance of incorporating trading frequency and quantity limitations within theoretical frameworks. Ultimately, the illiquidity discounts can be considerable, sometimes reaching levels as high as 30%–50% in specific instances, thus accentuating the complex interplay among illiquidity, asset valuation, and market dynamics. Illiquidity can so pose a significant risk to investors. The discount for illiquidity is commonly presented as a percentage decrease in the assessment in comparison to a comparable, yet easily tradable, investment. For instance, if a publicly traded corporation within the same sector is appraised at a specific EBITDA multiple, the illiquidity discount would diminish the assessment of an unlisted corporation in the same sector by a specific percentage, frequently established utilizing market or sector information. The extent of the illiquidity discount might fluctuate based on factors such as the corporation's magnitude, sector, the investment's time frame, and the perceived risk linked with the absence of liquidity. Mitigation: Corporations can endeavor to alleviate the illiquidity discount by implementing measures that enhance their liquidity. This could encompass engaging in secondary market transactions, releasing preferred equity, or executing other tactics that render the corporation more attainable to investors.

If a publicly traded company in the same industry is valued at a certain EBITDA multiple, the illiquidity discount would reduce the valuation of an unlisted company.

a) Factors depend on company's size, industry, time horizon of the investment, etc.
b) **Mitigation:** Companies can mitigate the illiquidity discount pursuing secondary market transactions, issuing preferred equity, or engaging in other strategies accessible to investors

Investors often consider liquidity as a key factor when deciding the value of an asset, as shown by Damodaran (2005):

1. **Paying Higher Prices for More Liquid Assets**: Generally, investors pay a premium for more liquid assets. Liquidity concerns the ease with which an asset can be converted into cash without significantly affecting its market price.
2. **Premium for Liquid Assets**: The premium for liquidity varies and depends on factors, including market conditions, and investor demand. The premium for liquidity might be lower because the perceived risk is less. In a volatile market, the premium for liquidity increases.
3. **Estimating Discount for Illiquid Assets**: The discount for illiquid assets can be estimated by comparing them with similar, more liquid

assets. This discount often reflects the higher risks and costs associated with holding and eventually selling these assets. Illiquid assets, like certain real estate investments or private equity, might require a longer time to sell and could incur higher transaction costs, justifying a lower price.

4. **Continuum on Liquidity Concept**: Your suggestion to view liquidity as a continuum is insightful. It implies that all assets have some degree of liquidity, with the level varying across different assets. This approach recognizes the nuances in asset liquidity, moving away from a binary classification of 'liquid' vs. 'illiquid'.
5. **Transaction Costs and Illiquidity**: Transaction costs are indeed a significant factor in assessing the liquidity of an asset. Less liquid assets often have higher transaction costs, both in absolute terms and as a percentage of the asset value. These costs include fees, taxes, and the potential price concession an investor must make to sell the asset quickly.

The premium for liquid assets and the discount for illiquid ones depends on various factors, including market dynamics, asset characteristics, and the overall economic environment. The concept of a liquidity continuum offers a more flexible and realistic approach to understanding and pricing these differences.

The concept of an illiquidity discount in private investments revolves around several key ideas (Baz et al., 2021):

1. **Illiquidity Discount Definition**: This is the valuation discount applied by investors to account for the lack of immediate marketability of an investment. In private investments, this becomes particularly significant due to the extended periods during which investors might not be able to access their capital.
2. **Opportunity Cost Explanation**: investing in an illiquid asset, investors miss out on potential excess returns they could earn in more liquid markets.
3. **Relation to Trading Opportunities**: the illiquidity discount should correlate directly with the magnitude of expected trading opportunities. If an investor anticipates significant opportunities for excess returns in liquid markets, they would require a higher discount to justify locking up their capital in illiquid investments.

4. **Skill Level and Illiquidity Discount**: more skilled investors will demand higher illiquidity discounts. This stems from the belief that these investors are more capable of realizing excess returns in liquid markets, thereby increasing the opportunity cost of engaging in illiquid investments.
5. **Perception vs. Actual Skill**: the equilibrium illiquidity discount in private markets is influenced more by investors' perceived skill rather than their actual skill. This introduces a behavioral component to the valuation of private investments, where the discount reflects not just market and asset-specific factors but also the collective sentiment regarding investors' abilities to capitalize on other opportunities.
6. **Behavioral Implications**: there is a role of investor psychology in private market valuations. The perceived ability to generate excess returns in alternative investments can significantly affect how investors value liquidity and, consequently, how they price illiquid assets.

The concept presented by Baz et al., 2021 offers a nuanced view of the illiquidity discount, emphasizing the role of opportunity costs and investor psychology. This approach suggests that valuation in private markets is not only a function of traditional financial analysis but also of behavioral factors and market sentiment.

Small Size Impact

Small and medium-sized enterprises (SMEs) encounter obstacles in economic, financial, and market assessment owing to their dimensions, intricacy of financial information, and substantial labor expenditures. AI innovations can support SMEs in streamlining financial procedures, concentrating on tasks of higher value, and introducing digital conversions to enhance effectiveness and competitiveness. Notwithstanding the prospective advantages, family-owned enterprises, including SMEs, exhibit less enthusiasm towards AI technologies, potentially attributable to distinctive attributes and a predisposition to approach AI applications with skepticism. Smaller unlisted firms may indeed face unique challenges compared to larger ones. These challenges can include limited access to capital markets, resources, and economies of scale. Therefore, smaller firms might be considered riskier investments, which can result in a downward adjustment to their EBITDA multiple.

- **Calculation**: The adjustment for small size impact typically involves applying a lower EBITDA multiple to the smaller firm compared to a larger, more established company in the same industry. This reduction is based on the perceived additional risk associated with being a smaller player.
- **Factors**: The size impact adjustment can be influenced by factors such as the company's revenue, market share, competitive position, and growth prospects. Smaller companies with strong growth potential might receive a smaller adjustment than those with limited growth prospects.
- **Mitigation**: Smaller firms can work on strategies to demonstrate their growth potential, profitability, and ability to access capital to reduce the size impact discount. Building a compelling business case and demonstrating a clear path to scaling up can help mitigate this discount.

Smaller unlisted firms may face additional risks and challenges compared to larger ones, such as limited access to capital markets and resources. Adjust the EBITDA multiple downward for smaller companies.

The challenges faced by smaller unlisted firms impact on their EBITDA multiples:

1. **Challenges for Smaller Unlisted Firms**:
    - **Limited Access to Capital Markets**.
    - **Resource Constraints**: They may impact competitiveness and efficiency.
    - **Absence of Economies of Scale**: Smaller size means less ability to leverage economies of scale.
2. **Riskier Investments**:
    - Due to these challenges, smaller unlisted firms are often perceived as riskier investments compared to larger, established companies. This risk perception affects their valuation.
3. **Adjustment in EBITDA Multiple**:
    - **Calculation**: The EBITDA multiple is adjusted downward for smaller firms to reflect their higher risk profile. EBITDA (Earnings Before Interest, Taxes, Depreciation, and Amortization)

multiples are commonly used in business valuation. A lower multiple implies a lower valuation.

- **Factors Influencing the Adjustment**: The size impact adjustment considers the company's revenue, market share, competitive position, and growth prospects. Companies with better growth prospects and competitive positions might see a smaller adjustment.
- **Comparative Analysis**: Typically, the adjusted EBITDA multiple for a smaller firm is compared with that of larger firms in the same industry, acknowledging the additional risks and challenges inherent in smaller-scale operations.

4. **Mitigation Strategies**:

- **Demonstrating Growth Potential**: Smaller firms can focus on strategies that highlight their potential for growth and profitability. This might include innovative business models, niche market positioning, or unique product offerings.
- **Improving Access to Capital**: Developing relationships with investors, exploring alternative financing options, or strengthening financial management can enhance a small firm's access to capital.
- **Scaling Up Operations**: Demonstrating a clear plan for scaling up operations and improving market reach can help in reducing the size impact discount.

5. **Impact on Valuation**:

- The downward adjustment in the EBITDA multiple directly impacts the firm's valuation. A lower multiple results in a lower estimated enterprise value, reflecting the perceived higher risk and lower expected future earnings relative to larger companies.

The valuation of smaller unlisted firms needs to account for their unique challenges and risks. The downward adjustment of the EBITDA multiple is a method to quantify these risks in financial terms, which can be mitigated by strategies that demonstrate growth potential and scalability.

Information Asymmetries

Investment in AI has a significant impact on information asymmetries within financial decision-making procedures. AI has been suggested as a mechanism for addressing behavioral biases in financial planning, and companies that integrate AI technologies tend to disclose more valuable information, particularly concerning AI-related risks, which investors perceive positively. The utilization of AI to tackle information asymmetries can enhance the investment efficiency of firms, mitigate over-investments, and align with signaling and feedback theories that propose financial decisions convey valuable information to the public and guide managerial decisions based on external feedback. Information asymmetry is of great importance in the valuation of unlisted firms, impacting various aspects of their financial decisions and performance. Hence, when evaluating unlisted companies, it is crucial to comprehend and tackle information asymmetry to ensure accurate assessments of their value and potential risks:

a) Limited Public Financial Disclosures:
    a. Unlisted companies are not required to disclose their financial information to the same extent as publicly traded companies to investors.
b) Impact on Valuation:
    a. Information asymmetry arises when one counterpart in a transaction (e.g., the seller of an unlisted company) is more informed than the other. This can lead to uncertainty and perceived risk for investors, which may result in a discount to the EBITDA multiple.
    b. Discount Applied: Valuation professionals apply a discount to account for the lack of transparency and incomplete financial information.
c) Risk Mitigation:
    a. To reduce the discount applied to the EBITDA multiple, unlisted companies can take several actions:
    b. Improved Disclosure.
    c. Third-Party Valuation: to provide potential investors with a more objective view of the value and risk profile.

   d. Audited Financial Statements.
   e. Management Access: direct access to company management.

d) Due Diligence:

   a. Investors looking to invest in unlisted companies should conduct thorough due diligence.

Mitigation measures for addressing information asymmetries in unlisted equities encompass governance protocols, voluntary information disclosure, quality of financial disclosures, and collateral prerequisites. Augmenting the caliber of annual reports via voluntary disclosure leads to a noteworthy diminution in information asymmetry, whereas heightened collateral requirements might be enforced on smaller businesses owned by minorities and women to oversee riskier borrowers. Moreover, within the domain of public corporations, tactics such as screening, engagement with information mediators, and signaling mechanisms are deployed to tackle information asymmetries. Furthermore, within the sphere of investment entities, shareholders, and innovators, a variety of incentives including material rewards, reputation enhancements, control mechanisms, and stock options are employed to alleviate information asymmetry and mitigate investment hazards. These assorted strategies are designed to safeguard the welfare of stakeholders and enhance decision-making procedures within the financial sector. Information asymmetry is a challenge, and it can result in discounts applied to the EBITDA multiple. However, companies can improve transparency and mitigate discounts, while investors should try to make informed investment decisions.

ESG Metrics

Environmental, Social, and Governance (ESG) metrics may decrease some of the discounts associated with unlisted securities. ESG factors have become increasingly important for investors and can influence how they perceive and value a company. Here's how strong ESG practices can help mitigate various discounts for unlisted securities:

a) **Risk Mitigation**: Companies with strong ESG practices tend to be better at identifying and managing various risks, including ESG-related challenges.

b) **Attracting Responsible Investors**: Many investors are increasingly focused on ESG factors. Companies with strong ESG performance are more likely to attract responsible investors.
c) **Improved Reputation and Brand Value**: Companies with good ESG practices enjoy a stronger reputation and enhanced brand value. This can lead to better public image, bringing to higher sales and profitability.
d) **Reduced Legal and Regulatory Risks**.
e) **Access to Capital**: Companies that excel in ESG areas may find it easier to access capital, including debt and equity financing. This can reduce liquidity discounts.
f) **Long-Term Value Creation**: Strong ESG practices are often aligned with long-term value creation strategies.
g) **Stakeholder Engagement**.
h) **Sustainable Growth**: ESG considerations drive sustainable growth by identifying new market opportunities, reducing operational costs through efficiency improvements, and enhancing innovation.

The impact of ESG on discounts for unlisted securities can vary depending on the industry, region, and specific ESG factors involved. Additionally, investors may place different levels of importance on ESG criteria. Integrating ESG factors into a company's strategy can contribute to enhancing the attractiveness of unlisted securities to a broader range of investors.

While ESG metrics can soften some discounts, their impact may not fully eliminate the need for these adjustments, especially in cases where other significant risk factors are present in the valuation of unlisted comparables.

Beta Determinants

The stock market beta of a firm measures its sensitivity to overall market movements and is used in the estimate of the cost of equity. Whereas the beta only considers listed firms, it can indirectly be used as a proxy for non-quoted companies, as it affects their cost of equity calculation. The determination of a firm's stock market beta, which quantifies its responsiveness to overall market fluctuations and is essential for evaluating the equity cost, is subject to influence from various factors. Economic indicators such as the changing risk aversion surplus consumption ratio and the default premium have a notable effect on stock market betas within diverse investment portfolios. Furthermore, growth risk, which signifies the potential for fluctuations in firm sales that do not align with market patterns, is identified as a fundamental factor in elucidating the differences in market beta across different companies. By leveraging extended datasets for beta calculation and implementing adjustments, the accuracy of predicting future stock returns is improved, underscoring the critical nature of precise beta estimation in cost of capital computations. A beta greater than 1 indicates the stock is more volatile than the market, while a beta less than 1 suggests the stock is less volatile. A beta of 1 means the stock's returns move in line with the market. Several factors influence and determine the beta of a firm:

a) **Business Sector**: The industry or sector to which a company belongs can significantly impact its beta. Some sectors are inherently more cyclical and volatile than others. For example, technology and biotech companies tend to have higher betas.
b) **Company Size**.
c) **Financial Leverage**: Higher financial leverage can amplify the sensitivity of a company's stock price to market movements.
d) **Operational Leverage**: Companies with high operating leverage have a significant portion of their costs in fixed expenses. This can magnify the impact of changes in revenue on profitability.
e) **Economic Conditions**: The state of the economy and economic cycles can affect a firm's beta. During economic downturns, companies in cyclical industries (e.g., manufacturing, construction) may experience larger price swings, resulting in higher betas.
f) **Market Capitalization**.
g) **Geographic Exposure**.
h) **Product and Market Positioning**.
i) **Management and Strategy**.
j) **Beta Calculation Method**.
k) **Market Sentiment**.
l) **Dividend Policy**.

Beta is not a static measure, and it can change over time as a company's circumstances and market conditions evolve. It is a useful tool for investors to assess a stock's risk concerning the broader market, but it should be used in conjunction with other financial metrics and qualitative analysis when making investment decisions.

11.2 Unlisted Artificial Intelligence Firm: An Empirical Case

The second case is represented by an unlisted AI firm. What mainly matters is the adaptation to the evaluation models that typically concern a listed corporation, whose data (balance sheet, market value, etc.) are publicly available in real time. Valuation of an Unlisted AI Firm encompasses a variety of methodologies. One approach involves integrating market valuations of publicly traded companies to forecast default probabilities of private entities, underscoring the significance of market data in assessing credit risks in conjunction with accounting metrics. The Discounted Cash Flow (DCF) technique, when adjusted with external factors and data-driven linear methodologies, can yield impartial appraisals by aligning Free Cash Flows (FCFs) with Market Capitalization and enterprise value, underscoring the impact of FCFs on firm appraisal. Additionally, the utilization of Artificial Neural Networks (ANNs) in solving partial differential equations can assist in accurately valuing intricate financial options, showcasing the practical application of AI in financial analysis and appraisal. These varied approaches underscore the multifaceted aspect of valuing Unlisted AI Firms, amalgamating market perspectives, financial modeling strategies, and sophisticated AI techniques in a holistic valuation framework.

The "rough" idea is that unlisted firms should be comparable to quoted firms, with some adaptations that are described above (§ 11.2. and following sub-paragraphs).

The selected company (nicknamed ABC) has the following business model and purpose: it provides a tool designed to facilitate and streamline the user interface (UI) design process. It is particularly notable for its use of AI to assist in the creation of wireframes, mockups, and prototypes, allowing designers and developers to rapidly conceptualize and iterate on their ideas. Here are some key aspects:

a) **AI-Powered Design**: Company ABC leverages artificial intelligence to automate and simplify various aspects of the UI design process.

This includes generating design elements based on user inputs or even transforming hand-drawn sketches into digital formats.

b) **Rapid Prototyping**: The tool enables the quick creation of prototypes. This is crucial in the design process for testing and validating ideas before committing to full-scale development.
c) **Wireframe and Mockup Creation**: Company ABC aids in the creation of wireframes and mockups, fvwhich are essential for planning the layout and interaction flow of a UI. These features make it easier for designers to plan and communicate their ideas.
d) **User-Friendly Interface**: Designed to be accessible even to those without extensive design experience, Company ABC offers a user-friendly interface that simplifies the design process.
e) **Collaboration Features**: It often includes collaboration tools, allowing multiple team members to work on a project simultaneously, and providing a platform for sharing and feedback.
f) **Integration with Other Tools**: Company ABC may offer integrations with other design and development tools, enhancing its utility in a broader tech stack.

Company ABC is tailored for both experienced designers and non-designers, providing a platform where they can quickly turn ideas into tangible, testable design prototypes. This can be particularly beneficial in environments where speed and efficiency in design iteration are critical.

The graph below (sourced by valutico.com) provides an overview of valuation ranges and midpoints based on different valuation methods (Fig. 11.7):

A core part of the valuation is represented by the risk score that reflects the company-specific discount on trading multiples (see Holthausen & Zmijewski, 2012) of comparable listed companies. The theoretical basis for this is the empirical observation that two otherwise identical companies are valued differently if one of them is listed and the other is private. This is often explained by the difference in the liquidity or transferability of the units. In practice, the discount is usually assumed to be between 30 and 50%; In the following methodology, it is derived through a risk score.

Average data are here considered for simplicity, as the target of this example is just to show the valuation methodology. The multiple discount rates (sourced by valutico.com) are sensitive to several parameters, mostly

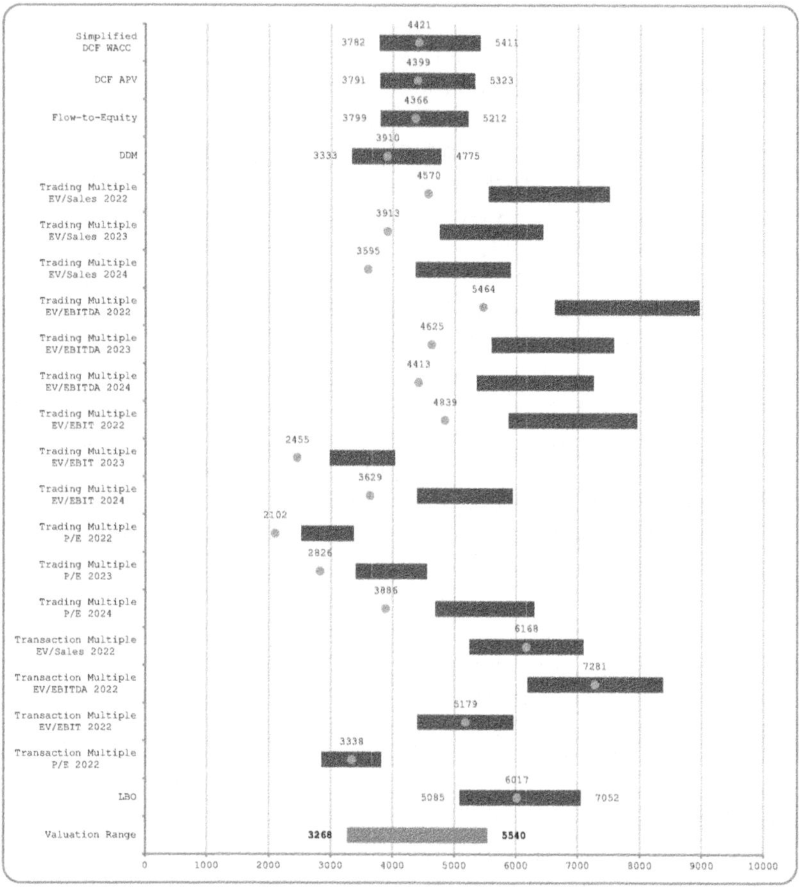

Fig. 11.7 Valuation ranges and midpoints based on different valuation methods

represented by the company size, as shown in Table 11.13 in the weighted score.

The business plan (sourced by valutico.com) is reported in Table 11.14.

The consequential steps to evaluate the WACC (sourced by valutico.com) are summarized in Fig. 11.8.

Table 11.13 Multiple Discount Rates

Name	Less Risk	Score					More Risk	Weight	Weighted Score
		1	2	3	4	5			
General									
Company size	Big		■				Small	35.0%	0.70
Positioning	Premium	■					Commodity	2.0%	0.02
Market									
Market Size	Big			■			Small	3.0%	0.09
Market Growth	High		■				Low	3.0%	0.06
Market Share	High					■	Small	2.0%	0.10
Competition	Low				■		High	5.0%	0.20
Exposure to the Business Cycle	Low	■					High	2.0%	0.02
Exposure to Political Legal Factors	Low	■					High	1.0%	0.01
Management									
Management Quality	High		■				Low	5.0%	0.10
Reliance on Key Persons	Low					■	High	5.0%	0.25
Sales									
Reliance on Key Customers	Low	■					High	5.0%	0.05
Reliance on Distribution Partners	Low					■	High	2.0%	0.10
Customer Lock-in	High		■				Low	2.0%	0.04
Purchasing									
Input-cost risk	Low				■		High	2.0%	0.08
Reliance on Key Suppliers	Low				■		High	2.0%	0.08
Product									
Product Quality	High				■		Low	3.0%	0.12
Innovativeness	Very Innovative					■	Not Innovative	3.0%	0.15
Intellectual Property Protection	High					■	Low	3.0%	0.15
Risk of Technological Disruption	Low		■				High	2.0%	0.04
Financial									
Capital Intensity	Low			■			High	2.0%	0.06
Leverage	Low	■					High	10.0%	0.10
Foreign exchange/currency risk	Low	■					High	1.0%	0.01

Simplified DCF WACC Methodology

The results (sourced by valutico.com) are reported in Table 11.15.

Simplified Flow to Equity Approach

The results (sourced by valutico.com) are reported in Table 11.16.

Table 11.14 Business Plan

	2022	*2023*	*2024*	*2025*	*2026*	*2027*	*2028*	*2029*
Sales	2400.0	2540.8	2791.4	3083.5	3396.4	3683.7	3885.9	4031.4
% growth	0.0	5.9	9.9	10.5	10.1	8.5	5.5	3.7
EBITDA	350.0	400.4	484.9	637.2	701.8	761.2	803.0	833.1
% margin	14.6	15.8	17.4	20.7	20.7	20.7	20.7	20.7
Depreciation & Amortization	112.5	226.8	122.4	184.8	203.5	220.7	232.8	241.5
% of Sales	4.7	8.9	4.4	6.0	6.0	6.0	6.0	6.0
EBIT	237.6	173.6	362.5	452.4	498.3	540.5	570.2	591.5
% margin	9.9	6.8	13.0	14.7	14.7	14.7	14.7	14.7
Net Income	47.6	140.2	284.8	369.6	407.1	441.5	465.7	483.2
% margin	2.0	5.5	10.2	12.0	12.0	12.0	12.0	12.0
Capex	33.7	71.8	81.1	88.1	96.0	93.6	103.3	180.4
% of Sales	1.4	2.8	2.9	2.9	2.8	2.5	2.7	4.5
Accounts Receivable	700.5	741.6	814.8	900.1	991.4	1075.2	1134.3	1176.7
Days Sales Outstanding	107	107	107	107	107	107	107	107
Inventories	0.0	0.0	0.0	0.0	0.0	0.0	0.0	0.0
Days Sales of Inventory	0	0	0	0	0	0	0	0
Accounts Payable	147.3	153.8	165.7	175.7	193.6	209.9	221.5	229.8
Days Payable Outstanding	26	26	26	26	26	26	26	26
Cash & cash equivalents	667.2	706.3	776.0	857.2	944.2	1024.1	1080.3	1120.7
Debt	805.1	921.0	1115.3	1465.5	1614.2	1750.7	1846.9	1916.0

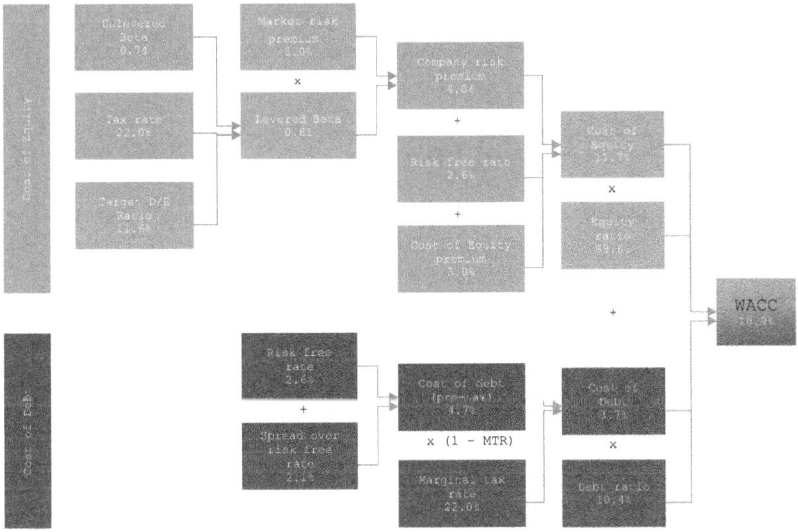

Fig. 11.8 WACC derivation

Dividend Discount Method

The results (sourced by valutico.com) are reported in Table 11.17.

Capitalized Earnings

The results (sourced by valutico.com) are reported in Table 11.18.

ESG Sensitivity

A core issue concerning ESG parameters relates to their sensitivity is assessing the cost of equity and the cost of debt, together with their weighted average (the WACC). A simulation, again extracted from valutico.com, shows the results reported below. It should be stressed that AI firms are typically software-based and consequently their emissions (that concern the environmental aspects) are negligible. Sensitivity analysis serves as a valuable tool for assessing the repercussions of uncertainties on investment ventures, particularly in a global setting where risks can substantially influence profitability. Furthermore, sensitivity pertains to a

Table 11.15 Simplified DCF WACC methodology

	2023	*2024*	*2025*	*2026*	*2027*	*2028*	*2029*	*TY*
Sales	2540.8	2791.4	3083.5	3396.4	3683.7	3885.9	4031.4	4112.1
EBIT	173.6	362.5	452.4	498.3	540.5	570.2	591.5	603.3
- Tax	−38.2	−79.8	−99.5	−109.6	−118.9	−125.4	−130.1	−132.7
NOPAT	135.4	282.8	352.9	388.7	421.6	444.7	461.4	470.6
+ Depreciation & Amortization	226.8	122.4	184.8	203.5	220.7	232.8	241.5	246.4
- Capex	−71.8	−81.1	−88.1	−96.0	−93.6	−103.3	−180.4	−258.7
± Change in Net Working Capital	−34.6	−61.2	−75.2	−73.5	−67.5	−47.5	−34.2	−18.9
Free Cashflow	255.8	262.8	374.4	422.7	481.2	526.7	488.3	439.3
Time	0.5	1.5	2.5	3.5	4.5	5.5	6.5	
Discount Factor	0.95	0.86	0.77	0.70	0.63	0.57	0.51	
Discounted Free Cashflow	242.9	225.1	289.0	294.3	302.1	298.2	249.3	2519.8
Present value of Discounted Free Cashflows					1900.9			
Present value of Terminal Value (1.0% included)					2519.8			
Enterprise Value					4420.7			
Net Debt					−137.9			
Equity Value					4282.8			

		Perpetual growth rate ('g')				
	(%)	0.0	1.0	2.0	3.0	4.0
Weighted Average Cost of Capital ('WACC')	8.9	4866.8	5225.8	5688.9	6309.0	7182.1
	9.9	4366.7	4636.7	4975.0	**5411.3**	5995.6
	10.9	3958.3	4166.1	4420.7	4739.6	5151.0
	11.9	3618.6	**3781.6**	3977.7	4217.8	4518.7
	12.9	3331.5	3461.5	3615.5	3800.5	4027.1

Table 11.16 Simplified Flow to Equity approach

Assumptions								
								(%)
Cost of Equity ('CoE')								11.7
Long-term growth rate ('g')								2.0
	2023	*2024*	*2025*	*2026*	*2027*	*2028*	*2029*	*TY*
Net Income	140.2	284.8	369.6	407.1	441.5	465.7	483.2	492.8
- Capex	71.8	81.1	88.1	96.0	93.6	103.3	180.4	258.7
+ Depreciation & Amortization	226.8	122.4	184.8	203.5	220.7	232.8	241.5	246.4
± Change in Net Working Capital	−34.6	−61.2	−75.2	−73.5	−67.5	−47.5	−34.2	−18.9
Sub-total	120.4	−19.9	21.5	34.0	59.7	82.0	27.0	−31.3
x (1—10.4% Debt ratio)	107.9	−17.9	19.2	30.4	53.5	73.5	24.2	−28.0
Free Cashflow to Equity (FCFE)	248.0	267.0	388.8	437.5	495.0	539.2	507.3	464.8
Time	0.5	1.5	2.5	3.5	4.5	5.5	6.5	6.5
Discount Factor	0.95	0.85	0.76	0.68	0.61	0.54	0.49	0.49
Discounted FCFE	234.7	226.2	294.8	297.0	300.8	293.4	247.1	2334.4
Present value of discounted FCFEs					1894.2			
Present value of Terminal Value (1.0% included)					2334.4			
Equity Value					4228.6			
Net Debt					137.9			
Enterprise Value					4366.5			

		Perpetual growth rate ('g')				
	(%)	0.0	1.0	2.0	3.0	4.0
Cost of Equity ('COE')	9.7	4785.7	5087.4	5467.6	5961.2	6628.0
	10.7	4338.2	4569.5	4854.0	5212.4	5677.7
	11.7	3967.4	4148.3	4366.5	4634.8	4972.8
	12.7	3655.2	3799.0	3969.7	4175.6	4428.9
	13.7	3388.8	3504.8	3640.6	3801.7	3996.1

heightened awareness of external information and changes, with a positive link identified between sensitivity and emotional intelligence among

Table 11.17 Simplified DDM approach

Assumptions								
								(%)
Cost of Equity ('CoE')								11.7
Long-term growth rate ('g')								2.0
Payout rate								100.0

	2023	*2024*	*2025*	*2026*	*2027*	*2028*	*2029*	*TY*
Net Income	140.2	284.8	369.6	407.1	441.5	465.7	483.2	492.8
Dividend	47.6	140.2	284.8	369.6	407.1	441.5	465.7	483.2
Time	0.5	1.5	2.5	3.5	4.5	5.5	6.5	
Discount Factor	0.95	0.85	0.76	0.68	0.61	0.54	0.49	
Discounted Dividend	45.0	118.7	216.0	250.9	247.4	240.2	226.9	2426.6
Present value of discounted dividends					1345.2			
Present value of Terminal Value (1.0% included)					2426.6			
Equity Value					3771.7			
Net Debt					137.9			
Enterprise Value					3909.6			

		Perpetual growth rate ('g')				
	(%)	0.0	1.0	2.0	3.0	4.0
Cost of Equity ('COE')	9.7	4316.4	4630.0	5025.2	5538.3	6231.4
	10.7	3866.1	4106.5	4402.2	**4774.7**	5258.4
	11.7	3494.8	3682.8	3909.6	4188.5	4539.9
	12.7	3183.9	**3333.4**	3510.8	3724.8	3988.0
	13.7	2919.9	3040.4	3181.6	3349.1	3551.2

Table 11.18 Capitalized earnings

Net Income	47.6
Adjustments	0.0
Normalized earnings	47.6
Discount rate (CoE) (%)	11.7
- Growth rate (%)	2.0
Capitalization rate (%)	9.7
Equity Value	500.0
Net Debt	137.9
Enterprise Value	637.9

		Perpetual growth rate ('g')				
	(%)	0.0	1.0	2.0	3.0	4.0
Cost of equity CoE	9.7	628.1	689.9	767.8	868.9	1005.5
	10.7	582.3	633.0	695.4	**773.9**	876.0
	11.7	544.3	586.7	637.9	700.8	780.1
	12.7	512.3	**548.4**	591.2	642.8	706.3
	13.7	485.0	516.0	552.4	595.6	647.7

individuals exhibiting elevated levels of mental well-being. Comprehending the diverse manifestations of context-sensitivity, whether indexical or parametric, proves crucial in understanding the interplay between compositionality and content within various semantic frameworks. Within life cycle assessment (LCA), the sensitivity of aggregation methods to weighting factors impacts the ultimate ranking of options, underscoring the significance of appropriate normalization techniques in integrating stakeholder preferences for precise decision-making in LCAs.

Some parameters may, however, be difficult to assess and may require specific databases (see, for instance, https://www.sustainalytics.com/).

Table 11.19. shows the main ESG results of an anonymous AI firm and their impact on the cost of capital (denominator of DCF).

The following factors have been identified as the main **strengths** in your ESG profile:

- (G) Materiality
- (G) Codes of Conduct
- (S) Lost-Time Injury Frequency Rate
- (S) Training & Development
- (S) Ratio Male & Female Compensation
- (G) Average Tenure: Management

Keep maintaining these factors!

The following factors have been identified as the main **weaknesses** in your ESG profile:

- (E) Climate Risk Management
- (S) Workforce Breakdown: Other Minorities (1/2)
- (S) Workforce Breakdown: Other Minorities (2/2)
- (S) Freedom of Association
- (S) Individual Performance Related Compensation
- (G) Tax Strategy

Table 11.19 ESG parameters and impact on the cost of capital

Question		Response
Environmental		
1	Scope 1 GHG Emissions	None
2	Scope 2 Indirect GHG Emissions Renewable Energy	None
3	Scope 3 GHG Emissions	None
4	Water Consumption	None
5	Waste Disposal	0.0
6	Environmental Reporting	25.0
7	Climate Risk Management	0.0
8	Climate-Related Targets	25.0
Social		
9	Workforce Breakdown: Gender (1/2)	100.0
10	Workforce Breakdown: Gender (2/2)	75.0
11	Workforce Breakdown: Other Minorities (1/2)	0.0
12	Workforce Breakdown: Other Minorities (2/2)	0.0
13	Freedom of Association	0.0
14	Human Rights Commitment	50.0
15	Turnover Rate	50.0
16	Lost-Time Injury Frequency Rate	100.0
17	Community Engagement and Philanthropy	50.0
18	Individual Performance Related Compensation	0.0
19	Training & Development	75.0
20	Ratio Male & Female Compensation	75.0
Governance		
21	Average Tenure: Management	50.0
22	Management Ownership	25.0
23	CEO to Median Salary	50.0
24	Materiality	100.0
25	Risk & Crisis Management	50.0
26	Tax Strategy	0.0
27	Customer Satisfaction Measurement	25.0
28	Information Security/Cybersecurity & System Availability	50.0
29	Codes Of Conduct	100.0

ESG Score	Environmental	Social	Governance
35.00	6.00	49.00	50.00

Cost of Equity	Cost of Debt
-0.05%	-0.12%

Cost of Equity

- Your ESG score results in a -0.05% **decrease** in the Cost of Equity compared to your industry peers.
- The Cost of Equity is a key component in the discount rate used in a discounted cash flow valuation.
- A decrease in the Cost of Equity will result in an **increase** in valuation.

Cost of Debt

- Your ESG score results in a -0.12% **decrease** in the Cost of Debt compared to your industry peers.
- The Cost of Debt is a key component for a valuation, a decrease in the Cost of Debt will result in an **increase** in valuation.

References

Baz, J., Sapra, S., Sracke, C., & Zhao, W. (2021, February). Valuing a lost opportunity: An alternative perspective on the illiquidity discount. *Journal of Portfolio Management, 47*(3), 112–121.

Damodaran, A. (1996). The stable growth DDM: Gordon Growth Model. http://people.stern.nyu.edu/adamodar/pdfiles/ddm.pdf

Damodaran A. (2005). Marketability and value: Measuring the illiquidity discount. http://people.stern.nyu.edu/adamodar/pdfiles/papers/liquidity.pdf

Damodaran, A. (2018). *The dark side of valuation*. Pearson FT Press PTG.

Fazzini, M. (2018). *Business valuation: Theory and practice*. Palgrave McMillan.

Fernandez, P. (2001). Valuation using multiples. How do analysts reach their conclusions? IESE Business School. https://www.researchgate.net/publication/4803035_Valuation_Using_Multiples_How_Do_Analysts_Reach_their_Conclusions

Koller, T., & Goedhart, M. (2015). *Valuation: Measuring and managing the value of companies*. McKinsey & Company.

Holthausen, R. W., Zmijewski, M. E. (2012, October 12). Valuation with market multiples: How to avoid pitfalls when identifying and using comparable companies. *Journal of Applied Corporate Finance, 24*(3), 26–38.

Moro Visconti, R. (2019). How to prepare a business plan with excel. https://ssrn.com/abstract=2039748

Moro-Visconti, R. (2021). *Startup valuation. From strategic business planning to digital networking*. Palgrave MacMillan.

Moro-Visconti, R. (2022a). *The valuation of digital intangibles. Technology, marketing, and the metaverse*. Palgrave MacMillan.

Moro-Visconti, R. (2022b). *Augmented corporate valuation. From digital networking to ESG compliance*. Palgrave MacMillan.

Singh, J. P. (2013). On the Intricacies of cash flow corporate valuation. *Advances in Management, 6*(3), 15–22.

valutico.com

Index

R. Moro-Visconti, *Artificial Intelligence Valuation*,
https://doi.org/10.1007/978-3-031-53622-9

C

K

L

M

N

SPRINGER NATURE

GPSR Compliance

The European Union's (EU) General Product Safety Regulation (GPSR) is a set of rules that requires consumer products to be safe and our obligations to ensure this.

If you have any concerns about our products, you can contact us on ProductSafety@springernature.com

In case Publisher is established outside the EU, the EU authorized representative is:

Springer Nature Customer Service Center GmbH
Europaplatz 3
69115 Heidelberg, Germany

The manufacturer's authorised representative in the EU is Springer Nature Customer Service Centre GmbH, Europaplatz 3, 69115 Heidelberg, Germany. If you have any concerns regarding our products, please contact ProductSafety@springernature.com

Printed and bound by CPI Group (UK) Ltd, Croydon, CR0 4YY

28/09/2026

02224060-0014